# Developing Essbase Applications

## Hybrid Techniques and Practices

# Developing Essbase Applications

*Hybrid Techniques and Practices*

Edited by
## Cameron Lackpour

With

John Booth • Tim German • William Hodges
Mike Nader • Martin Neuliep • Glenn Schwartzberg

CRC Press
Taylor & Francis Group
Boca Raton  London  New York

CRC Press is an imprint of the
Taylor & Francis Group, an **informa** business

AN AUERBACH BOOK

CRC Press
Taylor & Francis Group
6000 Broken Sound Parkway NW, Suite 300
Boca Raton, FL 33487-2742

First issued in paperback 2022

ISBN-13: 978-1-498-72328-2 (hbk)
ISBN-13: 978-1-03-234011-1 (pbk)
DOI: 10.1201/b18924

Publisher's Note

The publisher has gone to great lengths to ensure the quality of this reprint but points out that some imperfections in the original copies may be apparent.

**Library of Congress Cataloging-in-Publication Data**

Developing Essbase applications : hybrid techniques and practices / editor, Cameron Lackpour.
     pages cm
   Includes bibliographical references and index.
   ISBN 978-1-4987-2328-2
   1. Database design--Computer programs. 2. Finance--Computer programs. 3. Essbase (Computer file) 4. Application software--Development. I. Lackpour, Cameron.

   QA76.9.D26D495 2016
   005.74'3--dc23                                                                      2015015120

**Visit the Taylor & Francis Web site at**
**http://www.taylorandfrancis.com**

**and the CRC Press Web site at**
**http://www.crcpress.com**

# Contents

# Foreword

If you are actually reading the foreword and have not yet skipped to Chapter 1, I assume you are expecting to get some perspective about the book and not a blurb about the meaning of life. However, after reading the book and going through stories about Mike Nader's kids (cleverly disguised as an OBIEE and Essbase integration chapter), I figured that if he can do it, so can I. (If you are really here just to get an opinion about the book without much fluff, the book is great.) So here we go.

I have two memories of the first book, *Developing Essbase Applications: Advanced Techniques for Finance and IT Professionals*. The first is how I felt when Cameron asked me to write the foreword for it. At the time, I felt honored, but weird, to be asked. I had been the Essbase product manager for about 4 minutes (in dog years) and hadn't had the chance to do anything I would consider worthy, all the authors had been around Essbase longer than I had, and, while I would love to flatter myself, to be honest, Cameron didn't ask me to write it, he asked the Oracle Essbase product manager to do it.

Well, some things don't change.

The second memory is that when the book came out, I said in several private discussions that the Essbase team goal was to make sure the product evolved to the point that the team would need to write a new book every few years. I'm quite sure that at the time that the team didn't take my threats seriously (as we said, Essbase product manager for 4 minutes), but here we are—book 2. True, not everything in the book is about new features; many of the chapters cover important features and practices that didn't make it into the first book, but still, book 2. I win.

It is truly mind-boggling that in our dynamic industry, after almost 25 years of innovation, Essbase has always been there. Just in the last several years, we have seen major technology and market trends such as data warehousing, real-time, engineered systems, in-memory, mobile, big data, social, cloud, and many more. While some products have faded away, Essbase has always had its place in the mix. Although many times we heard that the next big thing is here and Essbase is obsolete, Essbase continued to prove that it can evolve, advance, and adapt while staying true to its core values. With all the new capabilities that came into Essbase in the last few years, our goal remained the same: Essbase will learn new skills and become better, faster, and stronger, but at the end of the day, Essbase will be the best at being Essbase.

This history and future are why we, at the Essbase team, are excited every time a new Essbase book is coming out. It is a great feeling to see the passion that people put into something that they are a part of. What makes Essbase truly amazing is the fact that it is not just a great product. It is a community with real passion for what it does. It is an ecosystem in which people, companies, and products come together to deliver the unique using a technology that continues to outperform in functionality and scale.

I enjoyed the first book because it was a collection of best practices, tips, tricks, and mini-guides. Listening to people talk about book 1, I noticed that, while everyone enjoyed it, everyone also had a suggestion for one more chapter. When the day came and the authors had made the decision to write a new book, I'm sure the real problem was which of the many suggested topics they would include. Reading the book, I was happy to find a wide representation of topics: brand new, forward-looking features like Hybrid Aggregation Mode; product offerings that are becoming popular such as Exalytics and OBIEE integration; topics relevant to many existing implementations; and even a representation of partner products. I hope you will find it as interesting and worthwhile as I have, and once you are done, I'm sure that, like me, you will be looking forward to book 3.

Thank you for being a part of the Oracle Essbase community.

**Gabby Rubin**
*Senior Director*
*Product Management*
*Oracle Business Analytics*

# Acknowledgments

This is the second time I have put pen to paper (really, I am writing this with my favorite fountain pen) to give thanks to the many people who contributed to this book, of which I have been proud and pleased to have been part.

### The Authors

In alphabetical order, I thank my fellow authors: John Booth, Tim German, William Hodges, Mike Nader, Martin Neuliep, and Glenn Schwartzberg. They are some of the most accomplished in our industry; it was a privilege and an honor to work with them.

Thank you all for your hard work, your willingness to share the experiences and knowledge of a professional lifetime, and your cheerfulness and good spirit in the face of a rigorous and difficult albeit ultimately satisfying process. The Essbase world is obliged to you, as am I.

### Our Editor

Thanks must also be given to our assiduous editor, Katy O'Grady of D&O Creative Group (www.docreative.com), who performed a miracle in corralling, revising, and improving the authors' work, including *yr. obt. svt.*, and making us better writers than we really are.

### My Coeditor in All but Name

Special notice must be made of Tim German. I drafted Tim early in the process as a sounding board—that role quickly grew into that of a coeditor. Every chapter you read, Tim read at least three times. The book reflects his unceasing efforts.

### Extra Special Help

Dan Pressman provided material help to the editing and reviewing process. Many of the authors received his "Did you think about this?" remarks; their chapters are the better for his input.

### Oracle

Gabby Rubin, Steve Liebermensch, and Matt Millela, as well as much of the Essbase development team, made this book possible through unprecedented access to Oracle resources; we literally could not have written this book without their support.

### Taylor & Francis

John Wyzalek pushed me to consider writing a follow-up volume, recommended Katy O'Grady as our editor, and has been our champion all along. There would be no book without him.

### A Personal Note

As editor-in-chief, I claim this space to thank my long-suffering family: my wife Hatsz, whose patience and forbearance were exceptional as I essentially disappeared for almost half a year during the writing and editing of this Magnificent Obsession; my parents, who supported me in yet another mad writing adventure; and my son, the Wee Laird Jamie, who kept on telling me to take naps when exhaustion overtook me.

**Cameron Lackpour**

# Introduction

I find it somewhat incredible to be writing an introduction to another book. After the moderately painful gestation of the last one (herding of cats, aka authors, coediting a book, packaging it for publication, and even selling the book), I believed at the time that one book was more than enough per career or even lifetime. The fact that you are holding another in the Developing Essbase Applications books belies that sentiment. How did a second book come about? *Developing Essbase Applications: Advanced Techniques for Finance and IT Professionals* covered what seemed like the gamut of Essbase development practices, from hardware to user and developer tools, with stops along the way for data management, database engines, and a variety of languages. What else could possibly be covered?

The spur for this book, *Developing Essbase Applications: Hybrid Techniques and Practices*, was the announcement of the Hybrid Essbase engine that bridges the gap between block storage option and aggregate storage option Essbase. Almost a decade has passed since aggregate storage option appeared as Essbase's second engine and changed the face of Essbase development; a third engine is just as revolutionary. Although Hybrid's announcement was the event that led us to think about another bout of book-writing madness, our discussions made clear that we had not exhausted Essbase as a subject for in-depth examination and exploration.

The aim and purpose of this book differ from the last, and consequently, the authors, for the most part, differ as well. This is not, in any way, a negative comment on the first group of contributors; we are exploring different areas of interest, and those dissimilar subjects dictate different contributors.

Some of this volume's chapters are in the same vein as the last: hardware, engines, and languages; others cover new ground with Oracle Business Intelligence Enterprise Edition (OBIEE), design philosophy, benchmarking concepts, and multiple client tools. As before, these subjects are covered from both technical and good practices perspectives. With this focus and philosophy, this book continues our tradition of defining, investigating, and explaining Essbase concepts like no other.

The custom of multiple voices, topics, and practices also continues. Think of this book, like the previous one, as the proceedings of the most cutting-edge and in-depth Essbase conference that could ever be. Just as the sessions at a conference vary in style and approach because of the difference in subject, presenter, and audience, you will find corresponding variations in the chapters.

Continuing the conference analogy, the single narrative that binds this book together is the subject of Essbase. Dip into individual chapters in *Developing Essbase Applications: Hybrid Techniques and Practices* as your job and interests dictate. However, I urge you to go beyond selective reading and read the entire book, even the subjects you think you know. I like to think that I am a fairly advanced Essbase developer, but I am not ashamed to share that editing the chapters during the writing process disabused me of that notion. The content between these covers contains amazing breadth and depth of Essbase knowledge; your reading of all of it will help make you the equal of seven talented Essbase professionals.

I hope that this book makes you love Essbase more and better.

### Downloading the Code

Our publisher has generously allowed us to share code samples at http://www.develop ingessbasebook.com.

### A Quick Note

The World Wide Web is a fluid ecosystem, and as time passes, links referenced in this text will become outdated. Use your favorite search engine and/or contact the author(s) regarding the resource in question.

### Contacting Us

You can contact the authors at various conferences, the Essbase message boards, our blogs, and at DevelopingEssbaseApplications@gmail.com.

**Cameron Lackpour**
*Yardley, Pennsylvania*

# Editor

**Cameron Lackpour** first worked with OLAP technology in the dinosaur days of mainframe multidimensional databases and saw the Essbase light in 1993. He has been in the consulting business since 1996, creating solutions for customers using Essbase, Planning, and anything else that ties to those two products. Cameron is active on OTN's and Network54's Essbase message boards, the ODTUG Hyperion Special Interest Group, the ODTUG EPM Community, the ODTUG board of directors, and his Essbase hackers blog—sharing knowledge makes his day interesting. An Oracle ACE since 2011 and an ACE director as of 2012, Cameron thought that writing yet another book would be "fun." He hopes you enjoy it.

# Contributors

**John Booth** is a managing director at Infratects, U.S. Division, and an Oracle Ace. He has more than 20 years of experience with information technology and is somewhat unusual by his focus on both Hyperion and BI Infrastructure and Hyperion Applications. He started his technical career as a support analyst for vinyl sign cutting systems in 1992 and moved through a variety of increasingly complex technical support and senior software development roles. Between 1998 and 2007, he spent his time in the corporate world at Capital One Financial, where, in the last several years, he managed the first five Capital One Hyperion Planning applications. John made the leap into consulting in 2008 and really embraced the Hyperion community online through the Oracle Technical Network forums and the Network54 Essbase forum. In 2009, he brought his blog Metavero.com online and has posted many technical articles, from making IE 8 work with earlier versions of Hyperion to focusing on the Amazon cloud. John is also actively involved in the Oracle Developer Tools Users Group (ODTUG) from the KSCOPE conference to Experts Panels. Contact him via e-mail: johnabooth@gmail.com, Twitter: @johnabooth, his blog: metavero.com, or LinkedIn: http://www.linkedin.com/in/johnabooth.

**Tim German** is an Oracle Ace and a director at Qubix, a boutique Oracle EPM consulting firm. He has been working with the EPM Suite for more than 15 years, with a particular focus on designing systems around Essbase and related tools. Tim blogs at CubeCoder.com, contributes regularly to OTN and Network54 Essbase forums, and is a frequent conference speaker. He can be reached on LinkedIn or via Twitter at @CubeCoderDotCom.

**William Hodges,** toward his tenth year of a stable career in academia specializing in decision support technologies, accepted an invitation to step into the trenches to participate directly in the implementation of the type of management-support applications he could only talk about in an academic environment. He has spent the last 15 years pursuing this line of work in various capacities, including as a certified Essbase boot camp instructor, an independent consultant, a coproprietor of a successful midsize consulting firm, and, more recently, on the consulting staff of The Hackett Group, one of today's largest international Oracle EPM implementers. This career evolution gives him a unique alternate perspective on the challenges and opportunities that EPM technologies offer to designers, implementers, and consumers of management and decision support.

**Mike Nader** is an Oracle Ace and has more than 18 years' experience working in the BI/EPM space. Mike has worked both in industry and directly for Hyperion Solutions and Oracle. He is a contributing and lead author on three books around EPM/BI technologies and has presented at more than 20 technical conferences over the years. Mike is the former Global Domain lead for BI and Analytics with Oracle. In addition, Mike was the former product manager for Essbase and Smart View at Hyperion Solutions and Oracle. He is currently a practice director for BI and Analytics for Huron Consulting.

**Martin Neuliep** has been designing and building multidimensional database systems since 1988, focusing on Essbase since 1994. He learned Essbase from its inventor, Bob Earle, and has worked on applications in a wide variety of areas ranging from healthcare utilization to international banking activity to fashion supply chain optimization, in addition to financial planning and analysis. He also focuses on related metadata and data integration solutions and specializes in system performance optimization. Besides crafting systems, Martin also concentrates on training. He was a coauthor of the original Essbase Bootcamp curriculum and has delivered courses worldwide. He founded General Analytics in 2001.

**Glenn Schwartzberg** has been an information technology professional for more than 30 years, falling in love with Essbase with version 3.1.1. He was honored to be named an Oracle ACE and, after that, an Oracle ACE director. He speaks at conferences all over the world, evangelizing Essbase and the other EPM products, not because he has to but because of his love of the products and of sharing information.

# 1

# ESSBASE ON EXALYTICS AND THE "SECRET SAUCE"

## JOHN BOOTH

### Contents

## 1.1  Introduction

Fast forward a few years from our first book, *Developing Essbase Applications*, and we are at it again with our second book. Little did I know when I started lurking on Network 54 years ago looking for Essbase secrets that I would become part of the rich community that cherishes the software. Exalytics was so new at the time I hadn't been able to touch it. Oracle product management made an X4-4 model available for my use while writing this chapter, and I also have had an X3-4 model at Huron. During

2013 and 2014, I worked on some of the largest North American Exalytics X3-4 and T5-8 deployments.

Essbase continues to evolve at a rapidly increasing pace owing to what I believe are three main factors:

- Exalytics: This is a well-known (to Oracle) hardware platform that facilitates efficient software customizations.
- PBCS: Oracle's Planning and Budgeting Cloud Services, like on-premise planning, uses Essbase at its heart.
- HyperRoll: In September 2009, Oracle acquired key technology, and portions have been integrated into the analytic engine powering features like Hybrid's rollup speed.

The first iterations of Exalytics really hosted BI Foundation Suite (TimesTen, Oracle Business Intelligence, and Oracle Essbase). Many other products now are certified to run on Exalytics, including Financial Management with the 11.1.2.4 release. This chapter focuses on Essbase on the Exalytics platform. If you are in the market for an Exalytics machine, you will likely have proof of value discussions. The goal of the Exalytics proof of value is to demonstrate one or more of the following: cost reduction, performance, and scalability versus your existing environment; usually, this is coupled with a software upgrade. Key processes typically are taken from your existing environment and replicated on an Exalytics environment to demonstrate the platform value. As the chapter progresses, I cover these points and summarize the case for Exalytics; if you wish to fast forward, see the last few pages of this chapter.

Today, Oracle has two main models of Exalytics: the X series, featuring top-of-the-line Intel processors, and the T series, featuring the Sparc T5 processor. Oracle Enterprise Linux is used as the operating system for the X series—the X4-4 has a memory bandwidth of 85 GB/second. Oracle Solaris runs the T series with a memory bandwidth of approximately 80 GB/second. Seagate's Nytro WarpDrive flash drives are currently used in both the X and T series, providing very-low-latency (84 microsecond write and 230 microsecond read), solid-state drives for the X4-4 and T5-8. Users can expect to experience between a two- and four-times speed increase on key input/output (I/O) bound activities when making use of flash versus the internal storage. The minimum amount of random access memory (RAM) in the Exalytics systems is 1 terabyte on the first generation X2-4, going all the way up to 4 terabytes on the latest T5-8.

## 1.2 The Hardware

Exalytics is an engineered system, a collection of hardware and software built to be compatible with each other and have optimum performance and capabilities that neither side can provide on its own. It is the chocolate and the peanut butter, or the grilled bread with your favorite cheese if you prefer savory. This section covers the hardware,

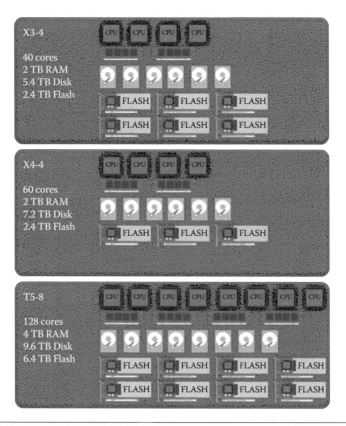

**Figure 1.1**   The hardware.

focusing on the processors and the storage options you receive out of the box. Figure 1.1 shows the X3-4, X4-4, and T5-8 model major hardware components. Note that the number of RAM chips is a much larger quantity than pictorially depicted—64 memory modules on the X series and 128 memory modules on the T5-8, each module 32 GB.

### 1.2.1 The Central Processing Unit

Oracle has selected the SPARC T5 processor and Intel's Xeon processors to be the brain of the current generation of Exalytics engineered systems. As of this writing, the major server architectures are Oracle SPARC, Intel Xeon, and IBM Power. Competition among the three companies has been fierce—all three server architectures have been doubling processing power every 2 to 3 years, using increasingly dense core counts, multiple threads per core, and greater memory bandwidth. The faster processors, which tend to have faster floating point performance, lend themselves to faster calculations for analytic engines like Essbase. Figure 1.2 and Table 1.1 show relative floating performance between a typical top-of-the-line server from a few years

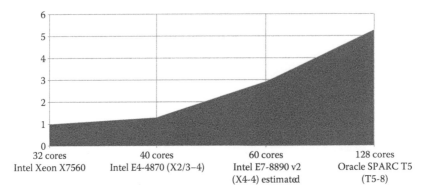

**Figure 1.2**    Relative floating point performance reference processor and Exalytics processors. Note: SPEC performance numbers have been normalized to show the relative floating point performance; the Intel E7-8890 processor is used to estimate the X4-4 performance.

**Table 1.1**    Floating Point Performance Data for Comparisons

| SYSTEM | SPECfp_RATE2006 |
| --- | --- |
| Sun Fire X4470 (Intel Xeon X7560 2.26 GHz) | 573 |
| Sun Fire X4470 M2 (Intel Xeon E7-4870 2.40 GHz) | 738 |
| IBM System x3950 X6 (Intel Xeon E7-8890 v2, 2.80 GHz) | 3340 |
| SPARC T5-8 | 3020 |

*Source:*    Data from www.spec.org as of December 4, 2014.

ago and the first four Exalytics systems. From this chart, we can see that the Exalytics T5-8 can provide almost 5 times the computing performance of the first generation Exalytics models, the X2-4 and X3-4.

I have found the performance information from www.spec.org, which you may use to calculate a per core performance, to be very useful to understand whether newer processors potentially provide lower performance than older models. This can be the case when taking a higher clock speed older processor and comparing performance with a more core-dense, lower-clock-speed processor. You may make use of this performance information when performing an infrastructure upgrade. If you are virtualizing, also consider the ratio of physical cores to virtual center processing units (VCPUs); I like to see a ratio of 1:2 or even pinned central processing units (CPUs) when supporting analytic and reporting engines like Essbase, Oracle Business Intelligence, and Financial Management.

*1.2.2 Included Storage Options*

The X3-4, X4-4, and T5-8 machines have internal disk, flash disk utilizing SAS/SATA2 flash controllers, and support for high-speed external storage via the Fiber

Channel and InfiniBand interfaces. Disk technologies have been changing at a rapid pace. Beginning with Open World 2012, we have seen a focus from Oracle on flash technologies; Oracle is one of six permanent governing board member companies of NVM Express, Inc. This organization oversees the NVM Express (NVMe) standard that established a common road map for manufacturers to create compatible storage systems based on low-latency PCI Express solid-state disks (SSDs). NVMe storage systems are important because of the high throughput that is required to keep the more powerful processors fully utilized. Expect future Exalytics flash drive controllers to be based on NVMe versus SAS/SATA2, having latencies at least 4 times better when they are adopted.

Figure 1.3 shows the relative performance of RAM, flash, and internal disks with the 11.1.2.501 Essbase release; one of the performance features in release 11.1.2.4 of Essbase on Exalytics increases the speed of internal physical disk and external file systems up to 400%. The charts in Figures 1.4 through 1.6 show that even a small amount of I/O wait translates to a huge performance gap on the 11.1.2.3.501 release. High-bandwidth, low-latency disks, such as a RAM drive, provide the most performance with earlier releases of Essbase. The amount of RAM in an Exalytics

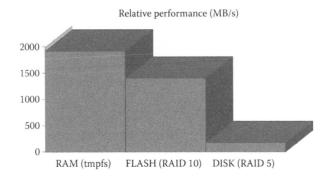

**Figure 1.3**   Relative performance of storage on an X4-4 with BSO Essbase 11.1.2.3.501.

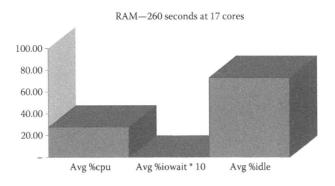

**Figure 1.4**   RAM performance on an X4-4 with BSO Essbase 11.1.2.3.501.

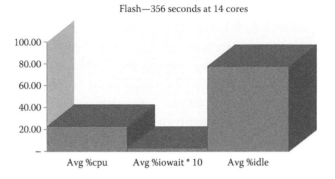

**Figure 1.5**   EXT4 RAID10 flash performance on an X4-4 with BSO Essbase 11.1.2.3.501.

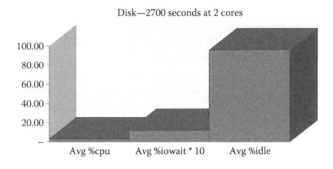

**Figure 1.6**   EXT4 RAID5 disk performance on an X4-4 with BSO Essbase 11.1.2.3.501.

machine does make something like a RAM drive for a cube feasible; special care should be taken on the backup and recovery procedures instituted, such as a more frequent backup schedule. I recommend that a RAM drive be used only in cases where extreme performance is needed, with flash preferred for very-high-performance needs. Performance on both flash and RAM is not impacted by fragmentation due to the lack of a mechanical drive head, which, on physical drives, must move larger distances per file for fragmented files. Exalytics features in the 11.1.2.4 release are intended to reduce Essbase page fragmentation on all file systems.

### 1.3 "Secret Sauce"

The "Secret Sauce" that Exalytics uses to make Essbase faster comes in three varieties: Exalytics First, Exalytics Restricted, and Exalytics Specific. Exalytics First will make its way into commodity Essbase in future releases. The Exalytics Restricted feature exists on both platforms; however, commodity is restricted in some manner; for example, FIXPARALLEL is restricted to eight threads on commodity while unrestricted on Exalytics. Exalytics Specific relies on the specifics of the Exalytics hardware, whether that is particular processors and their intrinsic capabilities, the amount of memory, or customized versions of the Linux and Solaris operating systems.

Disk latency is the non-Exalytics performance killer. Exalytics attacks this in two ways:

1. High performance and low latency disk
2. Secret sauce that incorporates nonblocking I/O and background writes

### 1.3.1 Exalytics First Software-Related Enhancements

Background writes and in-place block writes are two software-related enhancements we can likely look forward to commodity Essbase receiving at some future point. The background writes make use of nonblocking I/O—a method to send data to a device and not wait until it is completed to continue processing.

### 1.3.2 Exalytics Restricted Software-Related Enhancements

FIXPARALLEL allows the programmer to tell Essbase that logic may run in parallel on a set of sparse members and to assume that this logic has no cross-dependencies on the results. Commodity Essbase can make use of the feature with up to eight threads. Oracle recommends Exalytics systems not exceed 32 threads per calculation for FIXPARALLEL with low calculation concurrency and 16 threads with higher calculation concurrency. Attempting to use more than eight threads on commodity will result in eight threads being used.

### 1.3.3 Exalytics Specific Hardware-Related Enhancements

In software that supports multiple threads, such as Essbase, these threads must be managed carefully to avoid deadlock and contention and ensure the correctness of the solution. One of the new optimizations for Exalytics relies on hardware instructions to perform locking of the threads rather than performing this activity purely in software. This type of optimization, if not handled by the CPU with exact correctness, leads to unexpected behavior. Regression testing complex changes that require very-low-level programming (assembly) is one of the reasons the secret sauce only works and is only supported on the Exalytics platform: Oracle does not have the time or resources to test every Essbase-compatible CPU for compatibility with low-level instructions. Much more feasible is testing one specific CPU model every year and regression testing the prior Exalytics models.

### 1.4 Commodity Comparisons

Comparing Exalytics to commodity is difficult without going through a rigorous test—much more rigorous than the typical proof of value used to support a business case for Exalytics.

When comparing Exalytics to commodity hardware, processors, RAM, storage devices, and specialized algorithms make direct apples-to-apples comparison difficult because Exalytics brings so many different improvements and enhancements to the strike task of platform and comparison. In comparing Exalytics to commodity, one dimension to consider is the processors of the Exalytics machines versus commodity machines. The X4-4 machine uses a processor that Intel made especially for Oracle that features three processor speeds depending on system load. Lower individual CPU loads will allow the processor to run fastest, and highly loaded systems use a speed that allows all cores to operate within an appropriate temperature window for the processor. At the time of this writing, this processor is unique to the chip they made for Oracle among Intel's server processor line. The terabytes of RAM available on Exalytics systems enables performance in many ways: larger index and data caches and larger operating file system buffer that speeds lower-performance storage devices. The RAM also facilitates multiple virtualized machines supporting hardware consolidation. We should also consider the disk subsystems. Random access memory will be fastest, followed by solid-state technologies and then spinning disk technologies. From a software perspective, the enhanced multidimensional expression (MDX) query capabilities, the scalability of FIXPARALLEL, or the Exalytics Essbase 11.1.2.4 feature enabling faster performance on slower disk systems are some of the significant advantages from the secret sauce that no commodity server can offer.

Making this a bit more real, let's look at the improvements different parts of the system provide.

The scenario in Tables 1.2 and 1.3 presumes a top-of-the-line server, which is at a typical capital expenditure end-of-life between 3 and 5 years. The Intel X7560 was introduced in early 2010. Earlier, this chapter showed the X7560's performance

**Table 1.2** Exalytics Performance Drivers

| PERFORMANCE DRIVER | PERCENT INCREASE |
| --- | --- |
| Software: Essbase Exalytics "Secret Sauce" | 40% |
| Operating System: Windows vs. Linux | 20% |
| Storage: Essbase commodity vs. Essbase Exalytics on internal disks | 200% |
| Processor: 4 processor Intel Xeon X7560 vs. 4 processor Intel E4-8895 | 155% |

*Note:* 11.1.2.4 Exalytics contains specific enhancements that provide performance one would typically expect from an SSD using spinning disk, either internal or external.

**Table 1.3** Run Time Comparison

| SYSTEM | ESTIMATED RUN TIME |
| --- | --- |
| Windows System with SAN and Intel Xeon X7560 | 41.5 |
| Exalytics X4-4 on internal disks with Essbase 11.1.2.4 | 10 |
| Speed increase on Exalytics based on our hypothetical scenario; flash doubles the result and RAM is even faster. | 4.2 times |

relative to the X4-4 and T5-8 Exalytics processors. This information peels apart the layers of the performance onion and allows you to understand the directional impacts of the different performance factors. The interesting thing about software, and therefore the secret sauce, is that it can be improved over time, as Oracle has demonstrated. Since the first Exalytics release, Exalytics-specific software features have improved and the latest release of 11.1.2.4 has shown that the steady investment in software engineering is providing a large differentiator over commodity.

## 1.5 Architecture and Virtualization

You will set up your Exalytics architecture as physical machines or as virtualized servers. On the X series, the physical machine is referred to as bare metal, where the T series will always have a virtualization layer with a minimum of one logical domain (LDOM) and one zone (guest). A nonvirtualized architecture is more relevant for larger organizations that have thousands of users; multiple guest machines are more relevant for smaller organizations to support a common architecture across all environments. Virtualization on both the X series and T series is Oracle certified and supported. Both the X and T series make use of Oracle VM Server. The X series requires an external Oracle VM Manager, which must be installed to a Linux machine (external to your Exalytics hardware); I suggest a small VM for the Oracle VM Manager machine. The T series, which uses Solaris as its operating system, will always have at least one domain in the case where it is one large system. The X series is certified for up to four user domains and the T series is certified with two user domains. The T series domains can be further allocated to lightweight container operating systems (zones) as needed, up to the maximum of eight per domain on that platform, presenting much more flexibility for more complex architectures. The T series supports Infiniband when virtualized; however, as of January 2015, the X series does not support Infiniband when virtualized. Both systems are designed around nonuniform memory architecture (NUMA), which means that each processor has a block of memory that is closely coupled. Using the memory nearest is more efficient for processes running on that closely coupled processor. The implications of NUMA and the affinity of flash cards to certain processors (see Figure 1.7) led Oracle to certify certain virtualization configurations.

Oracle has a very specific set of supported T5-8 virtualized configurations, as Table 1.4 shows. Table 1.5 provides similar information for the X4-4 server, which complies with the maximum of 28 VCPUs per machine and 800 GB of RAM per machine. The latest releases of the Exalytics Patch Sets also provide support for Flash in a mirror configuration, leaving one flash without redundancy.

## 1.6 Sizing Exalytics for Your Deployment

This section presents a set of tools to assist in planning an Exalytics environment deployment. The full set of users for a given environment is usually assumed to have a

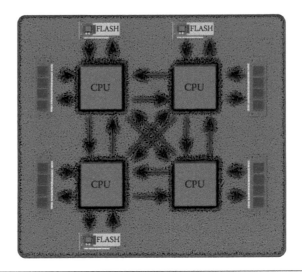

**Figure 1.7**    Illustration of memory and flash affinity to processors.

**Table 1.4**   T5-8 Configurations

| T5-8 CONFIGURATION | DOMAIN | PROCESSORS | RAM | HDD USABLE | FLASH USABLE |
|---|---|---|---|---|---|
| E1-1 | Domain 1 | 8 processors/128 cores | 4 TB | 7.6 TB RAID-Z | 5.2 TB RAID-Z |
| E2-1 | Domain 1 | 4 processors/64 cores | 2 TB | 3.3 TB RAID-Z | 2.2 TB RAID-Z |
|  | Domain 2 | 4 processors/64 cores | 2 TB | 3.3 TB RAID-Z | 2.2 TB RAID-Z |
| E2-2 | Domain 1 | 5 processors/80 cores | 2.5 TB | 3.3 TB RAID-Z | 2.9 TB RAID-Z |
|  | Domain 2 | 3 processors/48 cores | 1.5 TB | 3.3 TB RAID-Z | 1.5 TB RAID-Z |
| E2-3 | Domain 1 | 4 processors/64 cores | 2.5 TB | 3.3 TB RAID-Z | 2.9 TB RAID-Z |
|  | Domain 2 | 4 processors/64 cores | 1.5 TB | 3.3 TB RAID-Z | 1.5 TB RAID-Z |
| E2-4 | Domain 1 | 6 processors/96 cores | 3 TB | 3.3 TB RAID-Z | 2.9 TB RAID-Z |
|  | Domain 2 | 2 processors/32 cores | 1 TB | 3.3 TB RAID-Z | 1.5 TB RAID-Z |

**Table 1.5**   X4-4 Configurations

| X4-4 CONFIGURATION | DOMAIN | PROCESSORS | RAM | HDD USABLE | FLASH USABLE |
|---|---|---|---|---|---|
| No virtualization | N/A | 4 processors/60 cores | 2 TB | 1.1 TB RAID-1 / 3.6 TB RAID-5 | 1.2 TB RAID-10 or 1.8 TB RAID-5 |
| Two user domains | Dom0 | 1 processor/10 cores | 16 GB | 1.1 TB RAID-1 | None |
|  | DomU1 | 2 processors/20 cores | 800 GB | 1.8 TB RAID-5 | 800 GB (no RAID) |
|  | DomU2 | 2 processors/28 cores | 800 GB | 1.8 TB RAID-5 | 800 GB RAID-1 |
| Three user domains | Dom0 | 1 processor/10 cores | 16 GB | 1.1 TB RAID-1 | None |
|  | DomU1 | 1 processor/5 cores | 496 GB | 900 GB RAID-5 | None |
|  | DomU2 | 1 processor/15 cores | 512 GB | 900 TB RAID-5 | 800 GB (no RAID) |
|  | DomU3 | 2 processor/28 cores | 800 GB | 1.8 TB RAID-1 | 800 GB RAID-1 |
| Four | Dom0 | 1 processor/10 cores | 16 GB | 1.1 TB RAID-1 | None |
|  | DomU1 | 1 processor/5 cores | 496 GB | 900 GB RAID-5 | None |
|  | DomU2 | 1 processor/15 cores | 512 GB | 900 GB RAID-5 | 800 GB (no RAID) |
|  | DomU3 | 1 processor/15 cores | 512 GB | 900 GB RAID-5 | 800 GB RAID-1 |
|  | DomU4 | 1 processor/15 cores | 512 GB | 900 GB RAID-5 | None |

*Note:*   Oracle recommends Intel that hyper-threading be disabled when virtualization is used.

concurrency level; calendars, geography, and work schedules all allow you to assume the full user set will not be on the environment at the same time. For the purposes of the tools in this section, we use 30% concurrency as the assumption. The concurrent users by core is based on my experience and knowledge of the X4-4 and T5-8 machines; application complexities, user behaviors, and other factors can affect the maximum number of concurrent users. With a focus on the Essbase product, long-running parallel calculations that are used by a large percentage of the users can mean you need to lower the number of concurrent users. Conversely, single-threaded, very fast-running calculations translate to the capacity to support more users. Table 1.6 presents a basic sizing matrix, and Table 1.7 and Figure 1.8 present a sample environment usage.

One thing to consider about Exalytics is that the platform is made for speed and scale. To make a car analogy, not everyone needs a high-performance sports car or semitruck. While many companies using Essbase can do just fine with a nice family sedan, some may have very complicated models that require the utmost speed even with a smaller user base. In cases where a full Exalytics system is more power than

**Table 1.6**   Basic Sizing Matrix for Essbase, Oracle Business Intelligence Enterprise Edition, and Financial Management

| PRODUCT | ESSBASE | ORACLE BUSINESS INTELLIGENCE ENTERPRISE EDITION | FINANCIAL MANAGEMENT |
|---|---|---|---|
| Cores per product | 40 concurrent users per physical core | 475 concurrent users per physical core | 30 users per physical core |

**Table 1.7**   Sample Environment Usage

| ENVIRONMENT AT 30% USER CONCURRENCY RATIO | ESSBASE USERS | ORACLE BUSINESS INTELLIGENCE ENTERPRISE EDITION USERS | FINANCIAL MANAGEMENT USERS | SUPPORTING WEBLOGIC COMPONENTS WITH TWO VERTICAL CLUSTERS PER MACHINE |
|---|---|---|---|---|
| X4-4 Server 1 (PROD1) | 1 processor 2000 total users | 1 processor 7000 total users | 1 processor 1000 total users | 1 processor financial management Financial reporting FDM EE Foundation Oracle Business Intelligence Planning |
| X4-4 Server 2 (PROD2) | 1 processor passive | 1 processor 7000 total users | 1 processor 1000 total users | 1 processor financial management Financial reporting FDM EE Foundation Oracle Business Intelligence Planning |
| X4-4 DomU1 (QA at 28 VCPUs) | 8 VCPU 530 total users | 8 VCPU 3800 total users | 6 VCPU 300 total users | 6 VCPU |
| X4-4 DomU2 (DEV at 20 VCPUs) | 5 VCPU 330 total users | 5 VCPU 2400 total users | 5 VCPU 250 total users | 5 VCPU |

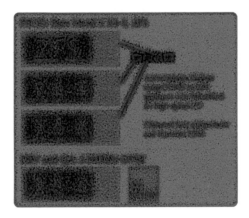

**Figure 1.8**   Sample environment usage illustration. Note: Network File System (NFS) is certified for 11.1.2.4 Essbase when using ZFS appliances.

needed, I suggest virtualizing Exalytics or reviewing Oracle's capacity on demand offering. For smaller use cases, use two physical Exalytics making use of Oracle VM to host three or more environments, such as DEV, QA, and PROD, on two physical Exalytics systems.

### 1.7 Tuning

When I think of tuning, I think of tweaking settings in the Essbase config file and modifying application and database settings (see the following list of operating system recommendations).

- vr.nr_hugepages (X series)/shmsys:shminfo_shmmax (T series)

    Memory page sizes are 4096 bytes on Linux and 8192 bytes on Solaris. Large/huge pages allow very large amounts of memory to be allocated with fewer number of pages. This is more efficient for programs like TimesTen when allocating/addressing large blocks of memory.

    These setting can very much restrict Essbase's ability to allocate memory. Because of this, it is usually recommended that Essbase and TimesTen never be installed in the same machine.

- Tmpfs

    tmpfs is a RAM drive; as you write to a tmpfs volume, it reduces the amount of memory available to the machine. For this reason, do not exceed 50% of available RAM in a given server and realize that restructuring operations can almost double index and page size at worst case. In short, be very careful to not exceed memory constraints and do treat the data with care from a backup perspective.

- vm.dirty_background_ratio = 10

    The percentage of system memory that can be in caches (unwritten to disk) before the system flush processes start.

- vm.dirty_ratio = 20

    The maximum percentage of system memory that can be in caches (unwritten to disk) before the system forces pauses to write caching and forces flushing to disk instead—if this ratio is reached, you will notice system pauses and very poor performance. Reaching this ratio would mean your disk systems are writing too slowly to keep up with the amount of data Essbase is generating.

    X series specific: these settings control the percentage and amount of memory Linux will use as file system cache for buffered I/O. Usually, these settings should not be changed. In cases where low bandwidth storage is used, it may make sense to modify these settings to allow more data to be stored in Linux cache. Modifying this value would cause an amount of risk to data in case of system failures.

Tuning, coupled with a good hardware platform and good application design, will provide the best performance—any one of the three areas can affect performance. From an aggregate storage option (ASO) perspective, some of the first things to look at are creating appropriate aggregate views, writing efficient MDX (or, where appropriate, the elimination of MDX in favor of stored hierarchy calculations), and considering use of the NONEMPTYMEMBER optimization directive to ensure that MDX does not do more work than necessary.

From a block storage option (BSO) perspective (this could go so far as to modify your Essbase outline order and further dense/sparse configurations), realize that dense/sparse configurations may have logic impacts, so full regression testing is very important on that type of change. If you also take tuning to mean modifying the number of threads in use, then we have to think about the use case and type of load we expect on the system. For instance, during your batch window, you may expect to have four to eight calculations running concurrently and no users on the system—and this assumes you have a batch window. In this case of our batch window with no users, we could run these calculations all with maximum threads. On a system with a very high number of users, you would look to have the majority of all calculations running with one thread, presuming they ran longer than 5 seconds and you had a very high concurrency. What you want to avoid is having a total number of calculation threads running that outnumbers the cores allocated to Essbase, so carefully consider the usage scenarios as you tune calculations in this manner. Before tweaking calculation settings, if possible, ensure your calculation is set up as a dense calculation, because that will be a much more efficient use of overall resources.

The lists in this section give general guidance on usage; do test everything in a non-production environment, and if you have never used these settings, test thoroughly.

Essbase server config recommendations:

- AGENTTHREADS 30

    Maximum number of threads allocated to the ESSBASE process. Set to 30; this setting works on the smallest and largest systems.

Agent threads handle logging in/out and starting/stopping an application, as well as other operations such as application copies.

- AGTSVRCONNECTIONS 10

  Controls the hand-off from ESSBASE to ESSSVR.

  Set this to 10; this setting works on the smallest and largest systems.

- CALCPARALLEL 1

  You may leave the CALCPARALLEL setting blank or set it to 1; never generically set to a higher level number for all applications and databases.

  CALCPARALLEL MYASO MYASODB 16

  For your aggregate storage applications, do set this. ASO aggregations will make use of the multiple threads.

- DLSINGLETHREADPERSTAGE FALSE

  DLTHREADSPREPARE 8

  DLTHREADSWRITE 8

  EXPORTTHREADS 40

  RESTRUCTURETHREADS 20

  These settings can be global or per application and/or database. If you are loading data quite frequently, consider the impact of these threads to the other operations on the specific Essbase server.

- MAXTOTALACTIVETRANSACTIONS

  Before 11.1.2.4: SERVERTHREADS/2

  The total number active threads for all thread-related, application-specific operations: calculations, data loads, queries, and other activities.

- MAXACTIVEUPDATETRANSACTIONS

  Before 11.1.2.4: MAXTOTALACTIVETRANSACTIONS/2

  Total number of active threads for operations that modify cube data.

  This setting becomes much more important on systems having few cubes and many concurrent transactions.

- ORACLEHARDWAREACCELERATION

  Exalytics: TRUE

  Commodity: not present; not licensed and does not work for non-Exalytics hardware.

  On Oracle Exalytics hardware, this enables all Exalytics acceleration optimizations including background writes, fix parallel optimizations, MDX optimizations, and in place block writes.

- SERVERTHREADS

  Set to 200 for T5-8, 120 for X4-4, and 100 for all other Exalytics and/or commodity servers.

  Thread pool that ESSVR uses to perform calculations, reports, client communications, and internal administration activities.

- WORKERTHREADS

    Workerthreads is a new setting that makes obsolete the MAXTOTAL ACTIVETRANSACTIONS and MAXACTIVEUPDATETRAN SACTIONS settings.

    WORKERTHREADS default to SERVERTHREADS/2.

Application/database settings and calculation commands/settings:

- ASO/BSO Retrieve Buffer Size

    Select 512k or 1024k; realize this is a per-user connection setting on individual cubes.

    The retrieve buffer and sort buffer can help user ad hoc queries and financial report performance.

- ASO/BSO Sort Buffer Size

    Select 512k or 1024k; realize this is a per-user connection setting on individual cubes.

    The retrieve buffer and sort buffer can help user ad hoc queries and financial report performance.

- BSO Commit Blocks

    For higher performance storage, start at 10,000 and test in 5000 block increments to 30,000. Between tests, stop and start your application and also consider using the Unix sync command to confirm that there are no outstanding I/O requests.

- BSO Data Cache

    On larger memory systems such as Exalytics, increasing this setting allows more blocks in memory at the same time; test for optimal settings. On non-Exalytics, start at 512 MB and on Exalytics, start at 4 GB.

    With a 4 GB data cache and a 256 KB block size:

    8192 = CALCLOCKBLOCKHIGH = data cache size in bytes/ (block size × 2)

    4096 = CALCLOCKBLOCKDEFAULT = data cache size in bytes/(block size × 4)

- BSO Index Cache

    It is recommended to make this equal to your page file size when memory permits. If you have quite a sparse cube, you may consciously decide to limit this at 4 GB or less.

- Calculation Setting CALCPARALLEL

    Affects individual calculation performance on BSO and cube aggregation performance on ASO when set in Essbase Config.

    Exalytics: recommended maximum of 32 threads.

    Commodity: recommended maximum of 16 threads.

Do not use very high settings without formal testing and/or load testing. The more concurrent users, the smaller the number of calculations that should have a CALCPARALLEL setting. All concurrent calculations should have fewer threads than the number of cores in your Essbase server.

- Calculation Setting CALCTASKDIMS

  On 11.1.2.2 and later, this is automatically set. At times, you may find that overriding the setting gives a more effective calculation for some cubes. On 11.1.2.4, you may make temporary use of the CALCDIAGNOSTICS setting to review calculations' parallel operations information.

- Control Flow Command FIXPARALLEL

  Oracle development recommends trying this in place of CALC PARALLEL.

- FIXPARALLEL can allow parallel operations on DATAEXPORT, DATACOPY, and other areas that CALCPARALLEL is not able to handle.

  Exalytics: recommended maximum of 32 threads.

  Commodity: limited to 8 threads.

  Read technical reference and database admin guide for specifics.

## 1.8 Testing

I used a test data set to arrive at the performance information presented thus far and draw conclusions based on those data. At KSCOPE 2013, Tim German, Cameron Lackpour, Dan Pressman, and I put together a presentation comparing Exalytics to commodity hardware; the large data set that was generated was the basis for my test cases. This is 13 GB of input data, which is just under 500,000 level 0 blocks and calculates to a total of 8,325,519 blocks.

I used two test applications to gather performance information. This information allows us to compare storage impacts on CPU usage and performance. Figure 1.9 and Table 1.8 present BSO outline statistics.

The aggregate storage outline used in my X4-4 testing was a copy of the BSO outline converted with the same data. I focus more on BSO because I believe that the significance of the speed increases is much more dramatic with that technology, which is very relevant to planning applications today and in the future. That said, the sheer

| Dimension | Type | Members in Dimension | Members Stored |
|---|---|---|---|
| Period | Dense | 19 | 13 |
| Account | Dense | 3219 | 2795 |
| Postcode | Sparse | 47865 | 47865 |
| Product | Sparse | 72214 | 72214 |
| Year | Sparse | 7 | 7 |
| Scenario | Sparse | 4 | 4 |
| Version | Sparse | 3 | 3 |

**Figure 1.9**  BSO outline statistics.

**Table 1.8** BSO Statistics

| BSO SETTINGS/STATISTIC (AGGREGATED CUBE) | VALUE |
| --- | --- |
| Index cache | 393,296 |
| Data cache | 8,192,000 |
| Number of existing blocks | 7,825,523 |
| Block size (B) | 290,680 |
| Existing level 0 blocks | 499,996 |
| Existing upper-level blocks | 7,325,527 |
| Block density (%) | 5.12 |

scale of Exalytics makes it very suitable for ASO purposes, in particular the ability to hold the entire .dat file in memory, which is especially important with unaggregated applications. Table 1.9 presents ASO statistics.

In one of my 2012 KSCOPE presentations, I suggested using a metric of 2500 IOPS per VCPU to make certain that your Essbase server can adequately ensure that the CPUs are fed enough data to keep them busy—based on my testing, this is still true for commodity Essbase. The typical way to identify a CPU starved for data is iowait, or how busy the disks are. Essbase has traditionally used blocking I/O, which makes it very difficult in many circumstances to identify the bottlenecks; for Essbase, the iowait values, even under bandwidth constrained configurations, do not represent a smoking gun. We can use the specifications of the flash drives on the Exalytics X4-4 to arrive at its maximum capability for IOPS of 240,000 at 8 KB transfer size. This is based on each flash card's operating specifications used in a RAID10 configuration.

Several years ago, I was working with a defense contractor out of Cedar Rapids, Iowa. We had just gone live with a Hyperion Planning application using a fully virtualized infrastructure. Our Essbase server had 16 VCPUs using a brand new EMC storage array and we were seeing variable calculation time ±25% and restructure times that were also inconsistent. We were lucky enough to have an enterprise SSD available for benchmarking on exactly the same server hardware and in our tests comparing the two systems, we

**Table 1.9** ASO Statistics

| ASO SETTINGS/STATISTIC (AGGREGATED CUBE) | VALUE |
| --- | --- |
| Current cache size limit (KB) | 524,288 |
| Buffer size (KB) | 1024 |
| Sort buffer size (KB) | 1024 |
| Number of input-level cells | 907,097,245 |
| Number of aggregate views | 25 |
| Number of aggregate cells | 1,041,520,619 |
| Input-level data size (KB) | 14,729,664 |
| Aggregate data size (KB) | 9,494,848 |

found that the SSD environment saw variability decreasing strike 100 times to fractions of a percentage coupled with faster calculation times. The information technology team at the client was not thrilled to have a single SSD standing up a corporate application versus the shiny new storage area network (SAN). The client had already tapped Oracle Consulting Services to perform application reviews of the financial management application and also had them work hand in hand with EMC. One of EMC's first responses was that we needed to drive more load with additional CPUs. We ran through various Oracle support processes where we showed that the CPUs on the virtual server were pinned. After 2 months, the client agreed to find a storage mechanism that could provide the throughput the directly attached SSD could. One take-away from this is as following: even the latest technologies that are expected to be high performance have a hard time competing with high-throughput, directly attached storage.

For directly attached, high-throughput storage, I believe the technique Oracle is using with multiple PCIe cards is one to follow if you were to "build your own" Exalytics. Today, we see that Essbase 11.1.2.4 on Exalytics is able to generate faster performance with what should be lower throughput storage—this is due mainly to the use of nonblocking IO and multiple write threads. We can look to IOMeter for how an application vendor may change their software to do something like this. IOMeter is a commonly used load generation tool for disk benchmarking. I have used it a few times but find that it is getting a bit long in the tooth. I prefer other tools at this time—on the Exalytics and Unix-based systems, a simple dd command is a quick and dirty way to arrive at effective throughput available. With enough write threads, you can keep the devices 100% busy; higher loads will maximize the queue depth of your storage devices and will also have a tendency to grow your operating system file cache up to its limit.

Running aggregations of our BSO test cube with 16 threads, a small allocation with a 16 thread Fix Parallel, followed by another 16 thread aggregation, gives a decently complex work load to arrive at relative performance numbers. The Unix command iostat may be used to capture CPU and disk statistics.

I used the test calculation below to arrive at the performance data. Originally, this was only an aggregation. Discussions with the Essbase development team regarding performance between commodity and Exalytics suggested that I modify the test to examine if the in-place block write feature really shines on subsequent operations once all page files exist from the first aggregation. It does, as the results illustrate. This consideration is especially important when comparing Exalytics to commodity with the 11.1.2.3.501 release, which does not have the background write Exalytics feature. The intent of the simple allocation in the middle is to replicate users locking/sending and/or running other business logic. In a more comprehensive test, we would have 5 to 10 separate business rules, a set of reports, calculation scripts, and data files. Design the test scenario to account for a typical usage scenario; the more users, the more complex these scenarios should be.

```
SET AGGMISSG ON;
SET UPDATECALC OFF;
SET CACHE ALL;
SET LOCKBLOCK HIGH;
SET CALCTASKDIMS 3;
SET CALCPARALLEL 16;

FIX(@RELATIVE("VERSION",0),@RELATIVE("Scenario",0),
@RELATIVE("Year",0),@RELATIVE("Account",0),@RELATIVE("Period",0))
AGG("PostCode","Product");
ENDFIX

SET CALCPARALLEL 1;
FIXPARALLEL(16,@Relative(PostCode,0))
FIX(FY12,Actual,Final,@RELATIVE("Account",0),@Relative(Product,0))
Jan = Jan * 1.10;
Feb = Feb * 1.23;
Mar = Mar * 1.5;
Apr = Apr * 1.6;
May = May * 1.7;
ENDFIX
ENDFIXPARALLEL

SET CALCPARALLEL 16;

FIX(@RELATIVE("VERSION",0),@RELATIVE("Scenario",0),
@RELATIVE("Year",0),@RELATIVE("Account",0),@RELATIVE("Period",0))

AGG("PostCode","Product");
ENDFIX
```

When testing ASO, I used a set of 1000 MDX queries spread evenly across 20 test users. These were run initially to gather query tracking data, which was used to generate aggregations, and then I ran the testing again. Before the aggregation, some queries took up to several minutes. The aggregation brought all queries down in the subsecond to second range. A purist approach to ASO design reduces the need for aggregations by leveraging the use of stored hierarchies (and alternate hierarchies) in place of MDX and dynamic hierarchies, even for complex calculation requirements. However, this can result in more complex cube designs. A simpler application that achieves excellent query performance through a handful of aggregate views may arguably be the pragmatic choice.

Using the identical hardware and flipping the acceleration flag for Exalytics, we can see the secret sauce in action as it relates to calculation throughput. The results in Figures 1.10 and 1.11 show that Exalytics is faster versus each storage mechanism and Exalytics flash beats out commodity RAM.

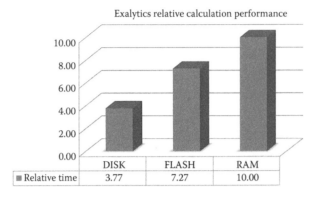

**Figure 1.10** Exalytics performance on an X4-4 with BSO Essbase 11.1.2.4.

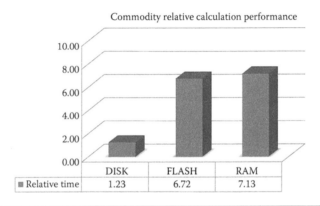

**Figure 1.11** Commodity performance on an X4-4 with BSO Essbase 11.1.2.4.

## 1.9 The Case for Exalytics

Exalytics has many factors that make it compelling, especially with the 11.1.2.4 release. In terms of raw speed, you can count on it being faster than any Windows, Linux, or Solaris server. The scale of the hardware allows for consolidation of many physical servers into fewer larger servers. The Exalytics secret sauce provides capabilities that are not available with other platforms.

### 1.9.1 Secret Sauce

Oracle has demonstrated a commitment to differentiate the Exalytics systems using specialized software that will maintain a speed advantage on like hardware and provide unique capabilities. The high thread count supported with the parallel Essbase operations allow many complicated use cases to be accelerated. The storage improvements for internal and SAN attached devices give higher performance for active/passive Essbase configurations. Once you are on an Exalytics platform, the software improvements allow for future speed increases.

*1.9.2 Performance and Scalability*

The high-performance Intel and SPARC processors, when coupled with Flash or Oracle ZFS appliances, provide unmatched performance, especially with the Exalytics-specific Essbase optimizations. The performance profiles of the X4-4 and T5-8 models lend themselves to supporting thousands and thousands of users while offering the flexibility to also have some highly intensive workloads for a smaller user population.

*1.9.3 Cost Reduction and Server Consolidation*

I view cost reduction and server consolidation as two sides of the same coin. Server consolidation is a means to cost reduction. There is a real opportunity to reduce physical server counts, which leads to a lower total cost of ownership. The X4-4 with its 60 cores and 2 terabytes of RAM or the T5-8 with its 128 cores and 4 terabytes of RAM, when coupled with the secret sauce, can easily do the work of 10 other large servers. Larger Essbase shops have between 20 and 80 servers among all environments; imagine reducing the server count by 50% while improving performance. At companies with financial management, the server consolidation topic becomes even more compelling with the 11.1.2.4 release. For smaller organizations, Oracle has an infrastructure as a service offering that can be a good choice for companies that do not require a full-capacity Exalytics system to meet their business goals; this offering allows the spread of Exalytics purchase price over time.

## 1.10  The Process of Attaining Exalytics Systems

Exalytics is an Oracle-engineered system of hardware and software made to work together. The Exalytics systems ship with only an operating system installed and no preconfigured software installations. While it would be nice if you could go to a web page, click a few buttons, put your purchase order number in, dial your information technology persons, and, at the end of next week, have your Exalytics system running in your server room, the process is a bit more complex and even includes a step in which the Exalytics machine acclimates to your data center. The Oracle application software is not installed because of export and tax reasons; all application software is installed after your Exalytics system is installed in your data center(s). Your data center team will need lead time (typically 6 to 8 weeks) and will need to ensure that the proper power and cooling capacity is available. Also consider what level of Unix skills your organization has—you may need to ensure that your support agreement with Oracle or your chosen partner is set up to cover any skill gap. Oracle Advanced Customer Support (ACS) has a defined process for basic configuration and racking the Exalytics systems and you may choose to have an Oracle partner do additional software installation or configuration in conjunction with or separate from ACS.

### 1.11 The Future

In June 2014, Intel communicated that a Xeon E5 chip (two-socket capable server processor) will be coming out with a field programmable gate array (FPGA). In a nutshell, FPGA allows for custom logic that can be reprogrammed to improve existing logic or perform new tasks. Shortly after that, in August, Oracle announced that the upcoming T/M7 processor (successors to the T5 and M6) will have "software in silicon." With Exalytics' trajectory of customizing the software to the hardware, we may be seeing an even greater view of this in the next few years, in which key Essbase logic is put directly on the processor. Oracle is cognizant of an upper cost limit that consumers are willing to pay, and I believe that the future Exalytics machines will have price points on the low end like the X4-4 and on the high end like the T5-8 machines.

### 1.12 Conclusion and Considerations

There really is nothing else like Exalytics, and the numbers tell the story of its unique blend of hardware and software that makes it the premier platform for Essbase.

When comparing commodity hardware to Exalytics, consider high-speed and low-latency storage while understanding that the secret sauce will only be on Exalytics.

Exalytics is a compelling solution for companies with multiple Hyperion products, when you have a need for extreme speed, or a drive to reduce server counts. Exalytics can be a game changer for organizations that are stuck with poorly performing virtual environments, allowing you to swap in a dedicated hardware platform. Test all configuration changes; strive to make regression testing and performance testing part of your Essbase vocabulary.

Calc on!

## Copyright Notice Information

## Acknowledgments

A big thank you and hug to my better half, Debra Bastian, for her support and patience while I geek out on technical activities or find unique ways to avoid house work.

Special thanks to the Oracle team for access and technical assistance with the Exalytics X4-4 and 11.1.2.4 Essbase: Steve Liebermensch, Barry Nuckolls, Kumar Ramaiyer, Gabby Rubin, and Karen Zubetz.

# 2

# Hybrid Essbase

## Evolution or Revolution?

### TIM GERMAN AND CAMERON LACKPOUR

**Contents**

## 2.1 Introduction

### 2.1.1 Why Are You Reading This Chapter?

The title of this book ought to give you a hint: *Developing Essbase Applications: Hybrid Techniques and Practices*. No, the book is not solely about Hybrid Essbase, but the introduction of the first new Essbase engine since Essbase 7.1 is simply the biggest thing to happen to Essbase in a long time. One could read that statement as hyperbole, but in fact, Hybrid is the biggest and best thing to happen to Essbase—better than Block Storage Option (BSO) and better than Aggregate Storage Option (ASO) because it is *both* engines all in one. In other words, it is a hybrid of both query processors keeping their best attributes and dropping the rest. The dichotomy between the two engines is finished and much of the bifurcated development approaches are as well.

One might argue that Hybrid Essbase is merely an evolution of the two existing engines. However, upon examination, we can see clearly that the combination of ASO and BSO is much more than the sum of the parts because Essbase is now a unified database capturing all of the power of ASO's scalability with BSO's accessibility and rich calculation language. Hybrid will bring new application types and new implementations of Essbase through a database design and implementation model that is accessible to all developers. Essbase excitement is back.

*2.1.1.1 Hybrid Is the Future*    Oracle is quite clear about this—Hybrid is the future of Essbase. You read that correctly: neither BSO nor ASO is where Oracle will spend the bulk of its development dollars. The promises are coming true that Gabby Rubin and Steve Liebermensch (Essbase product managers)* made about taking away the hard technical aspects of Essbase design and making room for implementers to focus on application design. Complicated design considerations (e.g., database size, aggregation time, hierarchy type limitations) are removed, allowing the focus of Essbase models to be on solving business problems.

So what about BSO and ASO: Are they going away? Will they be removed? Should anyone use anything but Hybrid? The answers are not exactly, no, and maybe. By that we mean that in the medium-term, Hybrid will become the default database and BSO and ASO will be outliers at either end of the bell curve. BSO may continue to be used for databases that absolutely require nothing but true BSO calculation flexibility and write-back functionality, and ASO will still be used for the biggest of Essbase databases. ASO Essbase also will likely remain part of Oracle Business Intelligence Extended Edition for the foreseeable future, although it, too, may end up being supplanted by Hybrid.

In the longer term, especially as the current limitations on Hybrid are lifted, we see Hybrid eliminating the BSO use case. In this chapter, we talk about the three

---

* Steve Liebermensch, director of Oracle Essbase Product Management; Gabby Rubin, senior director of Business Analysis Product Management.

(ASO, BSO, Hybrid) "engines" as if the latter two were truly distinct. In the current state of development, this is a reasonable perspective to adopt to make a design choice. However, as will be explained, Hybrid databases really are just BSO databases—with a very fast alternate query processing technique that permits dynamic sparse dimensions without the traditional performance penalties. Oracle's view, therefore, is that Hybrid will indeed replace BSO; in that future state, the only remaining choice is which sparse dimensions, hierarchies, or parts thereof the designer will select for dynamic versus stored aggregation. If these distinctions make little sense at this stage, we hope that all will become clear by the end of the chapter!

*2.1.1.2 The Current State of Hybrid*   The current state of Hybrid is that it is a 2.0 product. Many pieces and parts of Hybrid Essbase, both BSO and ASO in origin, simply do not execute in Hybrid mode. It can be a bit of an exercise in map reading and an act of frustration as one discovers that another feature is not supported yet in Hybrid.

Having said that, in fact Hybrid does work, it does return the right numbers every time, and the fact that it does all of this while seamlessly merging together two very different database engines is amazing. Make no mistake, Hybrid is a revolution in how we work with Essbase.

*2.1.1.2.1 A Revolution Is an Idea That Has Found Its Bayonets—Napoleon**   Hybrid is revolutionary because it removes the focus that Essbase implementers have had since the Essbase Year One—the "How Do I's": How do I design my database to aggregate quickly? How do I deal with multiple shared members in a hierarchy? How do I determine the best block size? How do I know what dimension is the best candidate for compression? How do I know that run-length encoding (RLE) or Bitmap or zlib is the best compression algorithm? How do I get my business users to own complex multidimensional expression (MDX) statements? These concerns and considerations are all about the *product* and have very little to do with the *database* that Essbase serves up to provide actionable *information*.

Essbase development has always contained a high degree of technical twirling of knobs and flipping of switches to achieve best performance. This necessary evil was born of a need to extract the most BSO performance possible in a computing world of 256 MB Essbase servers. The amount and level of technical knowledge increased and became more complex with the coming of ASO and its entirely different architecture. Good design practices are split across the engines and what is applicable to one engine is irrelevant for the other.

On the user side, Hyperion (now Oracle) realized that a common user experience had to be exactly the same regardless of database engine. From a user perspective, members, logical hierarchies, dimensions, navigation in client tools, the numbers themselves—all these elements of an BSO or ASO database are functionally identical.

---

* Columbia University School of International Affairs 1976.

In many respects, BSO and ASO design and implementation are identical: Dimensions, hierarchies, members, data, and developer and client tools are all the same. At the same time, many other database elements, from hierarchy types to calculation languages, are completely different and incompatible across the engines.

This development difference has held Essbase back and split the market. BSO's rich calculation language and functionality fail to scale to even moderately sized databases. ASO's powerful aggregation engine imposes restrictions on dimensions and its limited procedural calculation language can make allocations or calculations complex combinations of dimensionality, formulas, and data. Customers use both separately and jointly in BSO-to-ASO partitioned applications. There are many choices, but they are complicated.

In bringing together the two engines, and subsuming ASO underneath BSO's framework, Oracle has solved the functionality versus scaling question that currently drives Essbase engine selection. Hybrid will provide all components of the feature set that makes BSO so powerful and accessible while retaining all of the performance and scaling that ASO affords. And for trickle-fed or user-input applications, it will retain ASO's unique selling point: the instant reflection of changed or new input data in upper-level totals.

Thus, the true revolution of Essbase is of two parts: The first is that the hitherto separate and unequal engines are brought together as one; the second is that the effort to exploit Hybrid from a developer perspective is practically nil. A unified engine that does not require deep understanding of technical intricacies and nuances to develop efficient databases is simply a revolution in the way we developers approach Essbase. Where we once focused on the architectural design and the technical details behind that design, we can now simply focus on how the business needs to analyze data and let Essbase worry about the technical details.

*2.1.1.2.2 Technology Exploration and a Bit More*  Essbase 11.1.2.3.500 was released in May 2014; the 11.1.2.4 patch set followed in February 2015. BSO and ASO Essbase have many unique features and functions, and their complete merger will not occur in Hybrid's early days. Hybrid has, however, matured to the point that real applications, albeit somewhat limited, can now be created.

This chapter covers the current state of Hybrid functionality, with a focus on what can be done today and what can reasonably be expected in the future. Although some of the limitations in the tool can be frustrating, this is an artifact of its new nature, not a lack of investment or focus on Hybrid. Think of the current state of Hybrid as a bit beyond an exploration of technology and a manifestation of Oracle's product direction.

Although the tool has limitations, Oracle is rapidly addressing them. In some respects, writing this chapter on Hybrid Essbase in the early days of the tool is not ideal because the highlighted limitations will be addressed as the tool matures. Regardless, use this chapter as a guide to what Hybrid can do for you today.

*2.1.1.2.3 Hybrid Good Practices*  The best way to understand what Hybrid Essbase is and how to use it is through a good practices lens. This chapter approaches Hybrid from a descriptive and empirical perspective by examining documentation, reviewing known good practices for BSO and ASO, and then applying that background to Hybrid design.

The promise of Hybrid is that it is transparent not only to the user but also to the developer. The paucity of official documentation from Oracle on how to best design an application for efficiency and the incomplete database statistics have led us to derive the design and tuning sections of this chapter from observed performance with a variety of data sets and from educated guesses based on commonly known and understood BSO and ASO good practices.

Although enabling Hybrid is very simple, at least some understanding of how BSO and ASO work is essential to understand performance characteristics, good design practices, and database tuning.

*2.1.1.3 Who Are You?*   Before Hybrid, Essbase implementations and developers, by necessity, fell into two camps: BSO and ASO. Anecdotally at least, those who practice most in one technology tend to be deficient in the other; e.g., Planning implementers, because of Planning's focus on BSO databases, tend to create unsophisticated and simple ASO reporting cubes—it simply isn't what they mostly do for a living. The same holds true for ASO aficionados: The skills and design considerations that are required for large ASO applications are only somewhat applicable to BSO implementations. The authors of this chapter follow this split, as does the focus of their professional work: Cameron is a Planning geek and mostly works in BSO, while Tim is an Essbase geek and mostly works in ASO. Hybrid's unified engine will bridge that gap over time, but the split in skills and focus is still relevant today.

*2.1.1.3.1 BSO Power Geeks*   Given ASO's ability to scale to very large databases and sparkling performance, why would anyone still use BSO? Customers and especially ASO chauvinists have asked this question many times. On the face of it, many of the criticisms of BSO are difficult to argue: It does not scale well, large databases (by BSO standards) can take hours to aggregate, features like attributes simply do not perform when used with even moderately large dimensions, common usage in Planning implementations can be unacceptable unless the Focused Aggregation technique is used, and data explosion stemming from preaggregation of upper-level members results in very large data file sizes. This seems like a pretty damning list of limitations, but this is all offset by both history—BSO is the genesis of Essbase—and BSO's incredibly rich function set and accessible calculation language. When Hyperion created Planning, ASO was not available. ASO Planning has been available only in the past two releases of the tool and is limited in functionality although it can be very fast in specific use cases.

In short, BSO abides despite ASO's undeniable performance superiority. That superiority comes at the cost of design considerations used to get around limited potential database size and concomitant slow aggregation performance.

*2.1.1.3.2 ASO Speed Geeks* Any product criticism of ASO must acknowledge its ability scale and fast performance. Databases that are difficult to manage in BSO or are impossible because of size are easily handled in ASO. There has been a brisk consulting business for many years focused on converting BSO databases to ASO. As a real-world example, a 34 GB BSO database that took 5 hours to completely aggregate translated to a 1.2 GB ASO database that took 1 second to retrieve at a top-of-dimension level. Another is a 150 GB ASO cube that now behaves impeccably, replacing no less than 15 BSO cubes that, while logically a single application, had had to be split and then transparent-partitioned back together to obtain stability. ASO has raw power to spare.

At the same time, these conversions would have been much harder if the existing BSO databases had complex procedural calculations or many sophisticated member formulas. The common practice in those situations is a BSO database for complex calculations and allocations with a transparent partition to an ASO reporting cube. A partitioned solution, while powerful, is necessarily more complex than a single database because it encompasses two database engines, a partition definition, and increased cost in the form of dimensional maintenance rules that do not completely translate from one engine to the other. Furthermore, product limits on the size of transparent partition query grids place a hard stop on the scalability of this approach.

Another consideration is ASO's calculation language, MDX. Although powerful and flexible, it is a difficult skill to master for the finance department Essbase administrators who typically maintain Essbase applications. Some administrators certainly make the leap to MDX, but minor increases in calculation complexity can translate to involved MDX. The BSO calc script language looks and behaves much more like the familiar and widely understood Microsoft Excel formula language.

Simple ASO databases require little tuning or design optimizations—even inefficiently designed ASO applications can perform acceptably because of the power of the ASO aggregation engine. However, larger and more complex implementations typically require an understanding of the ASO kernel, dimension design that incorporates as many stored hierarchies as possible but requires workarounds to mirror in-built rich dimension types such as Account or Time, and a sophisticated understanding of database restructure event triggers.

And last, ASO imposes limitations that are simply not considered in BSO: stored versus dynamic hierarchies; limitations on shared members; and involved dimension building, data loading, and data management requirements. Although many of these differences are acceptable because of the performance improvement over BSO, the fact remains that ASO requires a higher knowledge level than BSO does.

*2.1.1.3.3 The Obvious Solution* Essbase practitioners have lived with this split between the tools because no other choice has existed and for years wondered why Hyperion and then Oracle resisted merging the two engines into one, using the best elements of each. Hybrid is that product. Hybrid is the best of BSO: flexible and powerful calc script language, unrestricted hierarchy functionality, and simple tuning considerations, combined with ASO's best feature: its powerful aggregation engine. Hybrid overcomes the product limitations in both engines by channeling ASO through a BSO lens. This is no product evolution but instead a true Essbase revolution. The Kings are dead, long live the King!

### 2.1.2 What This Chapter Does Not Cover

A chapter on Hybrid Essbase is not a chapter on all of the new features of 11.1.2.3.500 and 11.1.2.4 Essbase or Essbase and Exalytics. The many improvements in those releases include faster MDX functions, FIXPARALLEL, CALCPARALLEL with @XREF and @XWRITE, and advances in Exalytics. Read Chapter 1 by John Booth for information about Essbase's interaction and optimization with Exalytics. The authors (and you, the reader) are Essbase enthusiasts to the core and love every (just about) aspect of the tool, but to include these other areas would lose the focus of this chapter—and practically fill a book. We only examine Hybrid in Chapter 2.

### 2.1.3 What This Chapter Does Cover

If Hybrid is the focus of this chapter, what does it include? To understand and exploit Hybrid, Essbase practitioners must understand components of BSO and ASO, the best-guess architecture of Hybrid, design considerations, benchmarking, use cases, and the future of Hybrid. The reader can jump right to the benchmarking section to see Hybrid's performance, but a sequential read of this chapter provides insight into Hybrid internals, database configuration, design considerations, and use cases given the current state of Hybrid. One subject builds on the other and a complete understanding of the tool requires a full read of the chapter. Happy reading!

### 2.1.4 Our Opinion, Not Oracle's

One more note: When it comes to Hybrid futures or undocumented features, you are reading the best educated guess of the authors. We may, unfortunately, be proven wrong in the future as Oracle releases more details. This is not to say that our surmises are worthless, only that we are hedging our bets. We note in the text any speculative or semispeculative interpretations of the tool.

## 2.2 Just What Is Hybrid Essbase?

### 2.2.1 Licensing

Before we cover all of the really interesting bits about Hybrid, a note about actually using and owning Hybrid: Using ASO Essbase requires a license. Essbase is not crippleware as it was in the days of Hyperion—there is no software key or copy protection component that enforces feature availability. Hybrid Essbase is technically available to anyone who has a copy of Essbase 11.1.2.3.500 and above, but to legally use the product in a production environment, your friendly neighborhood Oracle sales representative or Oracle Licensing must be contacted. Planning 11.1.2.4 optionally uses Hybrid under the covers via its Autosave form property; using the Hybrid version of this feature may raise a licensing consideration for your firm.

### 2.2.2 The 30,000-Foot (9144-Meter) View of Hybrid Operations

Put simply, Hybrid is ASO viewed through a BSO lens. That means that a Hybrid database looks just like a BSO database with an ASO query engine working transparently under the BSO-like covers. Developers and users alike are unaware of the addition of ASO to BSO.

Given that the developer interface and configurable elements of a Hybrid database are BSO in nature, the familiar BSO components are all there: blocks, density and sparsity, a BSO outline file along with its properties, and BSO calculation functions. ASO controls are not available in Hybrid: Solve orders, compression dimensions, and hierarchy types, among other ASO properties, are not visible and not selectable.

Hybrid supports both aggregations and calculations. Hybrid ASO aggregations occur when the Hybrid Essbase config file switch is turned on and sparse dimension hierarchies are set to dynamic calc. Hybrid calculations can occur at any level and for any function; BSO calculations occur only when the Hybrid query processor does not support the function. Note that Hybrid ASO is the default engine with a failover to BSO only when necessary. A query causes Hybrid to examine the stored blocks required for consolidation, loads those needed blocks into the temporary tablespace as ASO input data, and uses ASO techniques to perform aggregation. If a query causes the Hybrid engine to fail (and at this stage of the tool, there are use cases that Hybrid cannot perform), the query will complete using the BSO query processor. This dual query processor can be seen with one or other of the following messages in the application log file:

```
Hybrid Aggregation Mode disabled
Hybrid Aggregation Mode enabled
```

Understanding which query processor is invoked, and when, and how that impacts a Hybrid database requires an understanding of the engine architecture.

### 2.2.3 A Brief Overview of Essbase

Given that most intermediate to advanced Essbase practitioners have at least a working knowledge of how the BSO and ASO engines work, the following BSO and ASO architecture overviews may seem redundant. We highlight them to illustrate how the disparate elements of the two engines are combined. Hybrid cannot exist without elements of both BSO and ASO. To not fully understand how Hybrid's components work is to not understand Hybrid.

*2.2.3.1 BSO*   A note about BSO architecture in Hybrid: Although the base of Hybrid is BSO, and data are persisted in BSO datastores, the role of BSO will be deprecated as increased calculation functionality is added to Hybrid. Until that replacement of BSO processing occurs within Hybrid, BSO concepts and precepts are important.

BSO-like concepts may never go away, no matter how sophisticated and full featured Hybrid becomes—Oracle has evidently decided that BSO is a more accessible database engine and has modeled Hybrid on it. Will Hybrid at some point look more like ASO? Will Hybrid lose all connections to either BSO or ASO? Hybrid is the beginning of a revolution in Essbase and the direction it takes in future is anyone's guess—even Oracle's.

*2.2.3.1.1 Original Storage Engine*   Essbase's origins start with BSO. A database comprising preaggregated sets of multidimensional arrays made sense in the context of memory and processor constraints of the 1990s. Relatively small amounts of RAM (a common Essbase server size in 1994 was 256 MB) and slow processor speeds (again, a 1994 server might have a single Pentium 90) meant that identifying locations for aggregation, calculating a subset of that aggregated data, and then writing it to disk were the only reasonable ways to store aggregated results larger than available memory.

That a block storage model made BSO Essbase disk bound rather than CPU or memory bound was an acceptable tradeoff to achieve fast query times.

*2.2.3.1.2 Data Architecture*

2.2.3.1.2.1 Blocks of Data   As noted, BSO Essbase stores on disk blocks of data. Blocks are multidimensional arrays of data; the dimensions that define an array are termed *dense dimensions*. Blocks are defined by the intersections of dimensions that do not occur within the block; these nonarray dimensions are described as sparse dimensions. Blocks are stored within paged data files called .PAG files after their extension. The pointer list of sparse intersections is stored in the .IND index files.

Both dimension types can store materialized aggregation values. Dense aggregations materialize upper-level cells within the block's multidimensional array. Sparse aggregations store upper-level intersections of data as additional blocks; those multidimensional sparse combinations may be conceptually thought of as a multidimensional array of blocks.

The essence of dense and sparse aggregations is that BSO Essbase trades off quick queries for aggregation time and expanded data storage to hold aggregated results. This phenomenon is often termed *data explosion*. Data explosion limits the practical scale of BSO databases long before that kernel's theoretical limits are reached.

Aggregations are not the only type of BSO calculation: Data values that are the result of simple to complex procedural calculations or outline-based member formulas are very common. When the results are precalculated and are stored in the block, they are not termed aggregations (although in fact there may be stored hierarchies) but instead are described as block calculations.

### Storage

BSO data storage is realized in the file system by three parts: data in the .PAG file, the index in the .IND file, and the metadata outline in the .OTL file. There is a 2 GB limit to the size of .PAG and .IND files; when BSO crosses that storage limit for either file type, multiple instances of each file type are automatically created.

### .PAG Files for Blocks

Blocks are stored in one or more .PAG, or page, files. .PAG files derive their name from the way data are paged in and out of memory on retrieval. The potential size of a BSO database might be many times the actual server memory. To save disk space, .PAG files are typically compressed via bitmap, RLE, or zlib compression algorithms. When a block is read into memory, it is expanded from its compressed state into a multidimensional array, ready for reading or writing.

### .IND Files for Index Pointer List

Data loads, calculations, and queries need a way to quickly find and read the required blocks for a query from disk and into memory. Rather than run through the entire set of blocks, from block 0 to block $n$, BSO instead consults a pointer list stored in .IND, or index, files. That pointer list finds the required blocks for reading into memory. On write to the page files, additional entries in the pointer list are created.

**Note:** Exalytics has a way to write data back to already existing blocks if a data value changes and recompression back to that physical drive block is possible through the Essbase.cfg setting INPLACEDATAWRITE.

### .OTL for Database Metadata

Last, hierarchies and member formulas are stored in the .OTL, or outline file. This outline file is nonpaged, i.e., reads, writes, and queries of the database outline require the entire outline file to be loaded into server memory. The outline defines calculation order via dimension type, order, density, and dynamic member calculations.

### Stored and Dynamic Upper Level

BSO calculations and storage thus far have focused on materialized calculations, but BSO has another calculation option: dynamic calculations.

Dynamic calculations can occur at any level of data—within the block's cells as dense dynamic calculations or across blocks as sparse dynamic calculations. Dense dynamic calculations are essentially free because the cost of fetching a block into memory from the physical disk for a query is far greater than any in-memory calculation.

For this reason, dynamic dense calculations, whether formula or unary aggregations, are commonly used because they reduce the size of blocks with little to no query cost.

Sparse dynamic calculations are also possible and have the same salutary effect on data scope. Sparse dynamic aggregations are performed at query time and do not need to be stored; sparse dynamic member formulas likewise do not need to be stored. One very important difference between dense and sparse dynamic calculations is that sparse calculations likely require reads of multiple blocks to perform the calculation, thus potentially making the query expensive in terms of time, disk operations, and CPU utilization. Dynamic sparse calculations are commonly used but their scope is limited to avoid these performance issues.

Attribute dimension calculations are dynamic sparse calculations and are consequently slow. Good BSO practice is to limit the use of attributes in queries because of this potentially poor performance.

## Calculating BSO

Excluding dynamic calculations, BSO databases are calculated through procedural calc scripts. Procedural calc scripts are the key to BSO's power and flexibility. Using the more than 50 calculation commands such as AGG, FIX...ENDFIX, and SET AGGMISSG; the almost 180 powerful calculation functions such as @CURRMBRRANGE, @MDALLOCATE, and @STDEVRANGE; and explicit member formulas, an Essbase calc script can perform complex and sophisticated data manipulation.

This melding of code and hierarchy was one of the keys to Essbase's early success in the 1990s. Many Structured Query Language (SQL)-based projects that foundered on complex data calculations were simply and quickly solved with the multidimensional nature of Essbase databases and calc scripts.

Calc scripts are procedural codes. As such, stored calculations and aggregations can occur in whatever order the code dictates irrespective of default calculation order. Dynamic dimension and member formula calculations can occur however the developer writes the calc script.

Calc scripts support writing dimension aggregations in an arbitrary order, but a more common approach is to use a variant of the default CALC ALL grammar in the form of AGG or CALC DIM along with dense dynamic calcs. When doing so, understanding the default stored and dynamic calculation order is important. Hybrid follows this calculation order when it performs its dynamic calculations, so despite the reduced importance of BSO overall, understanding BSO calculation order remains important.

**Stored.** Nonprocedural calculations are driven by dimension type, order, and storage type. The stored dimension calculation order is as follows:

1. Accounts
2. Time
3. Dense, in outline order

4. Sparse, in outline order

5. Two-pass calculations

**Dynamic.** Usually, some set of stored calculation occurs first via calc scripts. With those data as a base, query-driven dynamic calculations execute in the following order.

1. Sparse
   a.  If time is sparse, D-T-S
   b.  Otherwise, sparse dimensions in outline order
2. Accounts, if dense
3. Time, if dense
4. D-T-S
5. Dense
6. Two-pass calculations
7. Attributes

**Two-pass.** Two-pass calculations interact with both stored and dynamic calculations. Two-pass calculations force the recalculation of a value within the overall calculation order. If possible, two-pass calculations occur in the block, thus executing in a single pass through the data.

Dynamic dense calculations (i.e., calculations that reference only members of dense dimensions with no sparse member references) are computationally inexpensive because the block is loaded already for other queried dense members. No further I/O is required.

Sparse dynamic calculations that reference few blocks can perform quickly, but when many blocks must be loaded into memory for calculation, the fetching of blocks into memory from disk can be expensive. For this reason, common practice is to not implement large sparse dynamic calculations.

The rule about avoiding large sparse dynamic calculations has held since dynamic calculations were first introduced in Essbase 5. Essbase 6, however, introduced attribute calculations, which are effectively large sparse dynamic calculations with the attendant expected poor performance. Much amusement among already-cynical Essbase developers ensued.

The cynicism was not misplaced. The sparse dynamic nature of attribute calculations precludes the extensive use of BSO attribute calculations.

2.2.3.1.2.2 Member Values   Values can be loaded and written to upper-level member combinations. Stored upper-level members can be the targets of data loads, whether in dense or sparse dimensions.

2.2.3.1.2.3 Not an In-Memory Database   The large size of BSO databases, a product of the data explosion of stored aggregations, results in disk-persisted data. Queries and calculation processing queries subsets of stored data from disk, loads and expands the compressed data in RAM, and makes the data available for reporting or calculation purposes. Calculations write data back to .PAG files.

*2.2.3.1.3 Caches*   Caches are (or were) so important to BSO that the *Database Administrator's Guide* (DBAG) has a chapter devoted solely to describing and tuning them for optimal performance. The caches are used to locate and load blocks from disk, pull them into memory, and manipulate them during calculations and queries.

When memory was scarce, drive volumes were small, and processors were slow, much attention and effort were given to tuning caches to extract every possible advantage. All three constraints have largely been removed and Essbase has been rewritten to allow intrinsic operating system caching to take precedence, so the importance assigned to caches has diminished, although they are still part of the BSO tuning process.

Despite this change in behavior, the prominence of caches in the DBAG leads many Essbase developers to think that extensive time spent tuning caches is time well spent. Again, although we are not stating that caches are meaningless (the infamous and common "please increase CalcLockBlock setting and then retry" error message is almost always caused by an insufficiently large data cache), many have found that beyond the minimum, cache tuning is a thing of the past. Table 2.1 lists the cache types in BSO.

*2.2.3.1.4 BSO Today*   BSO continues to be widely used. It is the default engine in Planning through version 11.1.2.3.500, persists in many existing databases, and is still the choice for new databases when complex calculations are required. Legions of Essbase developers still view BSO as their primary development choice, only switching to ASO when a BSO database will not perform acceptably.

It is that potentially poor performance that is BSO's Achilles heel—databases that are a good fit for the tool otherwise are scuppered because BSO cannot scale adequately.

*2.2.3.2 ASO*   Despite the genius of the dense-sparse paradigm, developers continued to push the boundaries of what was practically possible within BSO's performance constraints. Hyperion's answer to the interrelated problems of data explosion, high

**Table 2.1**   Cache Types

| CACHE NAME | DESCRIPTION |
| --- | --- |
| Index | Pointer list from .IND file |
| Data | Expanded blocks |
| Data file | Direct I/O cache for expanded blocks |
| Calculator | Tracks blocks during calculation |
| Dynamic calculator | Buffer to store all of the blocks required for a dynamic calc member evaluation |

dimension counts, very sparse data sets, and million-member-dimensions was a completely new storage kernel optimized for a different type of application.

*2.2.3.2.1 Newest Engine until Hybrid, Starting in Essbase 7.1*    The ASO was released to much fanfare* in version 7.1. It promised to provide several significant improvements over BSO: smaller database sizes, support for much higher dimension counts, and so-called instant aggregation. The earliest ASO versions had painful functional limitations: All calculation had to be performed via member formulas, outline restructuring required all data to be reloaded, and users could not submit data via the Excel Add-In. Over time, however, these restrictions were removed, and more and more functionality made its way into the ASO kernel. Our (somewhat subjective) view is that around version 9.3, the key question for an Essbase designer changed from "Is it possible to build this in ASO?" to "Is there any reason not to build this in ASO?" ASO became the default kernel. The one situation in which this continued not to be the case was for Hyperion Planning applications. ASO Planning proper arrived in 11.1.2.3, although mapping to ASO reporting-only cubes was supported from 11.1.2.1. We understand from statements made by Oracle (subject to the usual "safe harbor" restrictions) that Hybrid will be integral to the future direction of Hyperion Planning.

*2.2.3.2.2 Data Architecture*
2.2.3.2.2.1 Data Storage and Tablespaces    ASO does not follow the dense-sparse paradigm and the associated division of data into .PAG (containing blocks—dense arrays) and .IND (containing, effectively, a list of populated sparse intersections) files. Instead, ASO data are stored in a single type of file, a .DAT. Within an ASO application's directory structure are a set of special directories known as tablespaces. The primary location for stored data is the "default" tablespace, with the "temp" tablespace used for operations that exceed available aggregate storage cache, such as aggregations, merges, or restructures, where a new .DAT file can be seen being created in much the same way that BSO Essbase creates .PAN and .INN files during a restructure. The "metadata" and "log" tablespaces are not used for data storage and, unlike the default and temp tablespaces, cannot be moved or resized.

The actual content of the .DAT file consists of a series of keys and associated values, the key representing the intersection from every dimension (except the compression dimension, if used) to which the data values relate. The format of the key is a bitmap, and for stored dimensions, both the level 0 member and ancestors are identified. At first sight, this might seem inefficient from a storage point of view (rather like adding all levels to a fact table, rather than using a star schema). However, the use of the bitmap makes the storage of the hierarchical path much more efficient than storing

---

* Not to mention years of patent-infringement dispute between Hyperion and HyperRoll, Inc., a company subsequently (2009) acquired in part by Oracle.

actual member names—or even surrogate keys—at each level. More important, this is the secret behind ASO's remarkable dynamic aggregation performance: The values that sum to a particular upper-level member can be extracted and accumulated very efficiently with a single pass through the data, rather than having to locate the data for each level 0 descendant separately (which, by comparison, is what BSO must do when retrieving a dynamic sparse upper-level member). Dan Pressman's chapter, "How ASO Works and How to Design for Performance," in the first volume of this book series provides a very detailed description of the content of the .DAT file and shows how this knowledge can inform ASO design practice.

2.2.3.2.2.2 Representation of Attributes (and Alternate Hierarchies)  Attribute dimensions are not represented directly in the bitmap keys, which means that large numbers of attributes can be added to an ASO cube without a storage or other performance penalty. Evidently (this has not been confirmed by Oracle but seems to fit in with empirical evidence), Essbase performs a transformation of the base dimension's bitmap to the attribute dimension's bitmap when a single attribute is queried against the root of the base dimension because these queries are extremely fast (this is the same technique used to represent alternate hierarchies in ASO). However, using multiple attributes on a dimension or querying an attribute against child members from the base dimension can result in much worse query performance, as ASO falls back to identifying, extracting, and summing level 0 members individually. This behavior is discussed in the *Database Administrator's Guide* under the heading "Design Considerations for Attribute Queries."

2.2.3.2.2.3 No Upper-Level Storage Available to Users  By default, the .DAT file contains only level 0 data, with all upper-level values calculated at retrieval as needed, and data may be input to ASO cubes only at level 0. This is in obvious contrast to BSO, where upper-level blocks can be created directly by data load or user input (Submit in Smart View terminology; Lock and Send in Excel Add-In terminology). Most BSO practitioners advise against loading to upper-levels directly, so this may not present too steep a learning curve to ASO converts, but upper-level loads are sometimes used in allocations, and we might expect to be able to store an intermediate value at upper-level temporarily during a calculation. The lack of upper-level stored values also makes it impossible for a parent in a stored hierarchy to contain a value that is not the sum of its level 0 ancestors. This can create problems when, for example, multiple input currencies cannot easily be prevented from summing to meaningless totals, rather than the #Missing value that could be returned in BSO, or for Planning (with a small or large p) applications, where we may want to permit an upper-level target that, temporarily at least, does not tally to the lower-level inputs.

The reason for the caveat "Available to Users" in the title of this section is explained in the Aggregation Scripts section below.

2.2.3.2.2.4 An In-Memory Database    The mechanism by which ASO answers queries is to compare a bitmap mask to each bitmap key in the stack that comprises the .DAT file. This potentially requires scanning the entire input-level data set. With BSO, in contrast, a search of the (typically) much smaller .IND index file returns the coordinates of just the requested data from the .PAG file. There is no need to scan the entire .PAG file when retrieving a single sparse intersection.

For this reason, being able to fit the entire .DAT file into server memory is a highly desirable design objective, RAM being much faster even than solid-state storage. This may sound like an unrealistic goal, but since ASO does not have to aggregate and store upper-level values, it usually produces a much smaller data file than the equivalent BSO cube does. This is not to say that very large (defined as hundreds of gigabytes) ASO cubes do not exist, but the authors have yet to encounter one that would not, alone at least, fit into the 1 TB of RAM available on the current generation of the Exalytics platform.

*2.2.3.2.3 Aggregation Scripts*    Having said that we should aim for a cube that fits into memory, we also recognize that this is sometimes not possible. Not every implementation can devote a server of Exalytics-like scale to a single Essbase application. In these circumstances, it is possible for specific upper-level slices to be calculated; these slices—defined as a combination of levels from all stored dimensions—are known as aggregate views. An aggregate view is, effectively, a subcube that looks just like the base cube shorn of one or more lower levels from one or more stored hierarchies. For example, an aggregate view might be created at the Quarter level in a time dimension. Queries that reference the Quarter level, rather than individual queries, can then be directed to the subcube (smaller and hence more easily retained in memory), rather than the full set of input-level data. Where aggregate views have been created, these data are also stored in the same .DAT file.

The slices represented by aggregate views are not selectable by the developer directly. An EAS wizard or MaxL process selects one or more (usually more) and either creates them directly, stores their definition in an aggregation script (a .csc extension file), or both. The definitions of the views are stored as an integer; although the method is undocumented, decoding these values is possible, and we have used this information to create arbitrary views. However, Oracle's view-selection algorithms are not publicly documented, and the interrelationships between multiple views are unknown. (It seems plausible that the selection of higher-level views changes depending on which lower-level views are chosen, for example.) Consequently, this should be considered an experimental technique to be used at your own risk.

Although the file extension .csc is shared with BSO calculation scripts, the purpose and creation of an aggregation script have very little in common. Absolutely no ability, for example, exists to consolidate only Quarter 1 (rather than creating a view at the Quarter level), or to calculate values using formulas that do not follow simple, additive outline consolidation.

*2.2.3.2.4 Procedural Calculations*   Like BSO, ASO permits members (in dynamic hierarchies) to be defined with formulas rather than being loaded directly with input data. The language used in ASO is an Essbase-specific flavor of the somewhat industry-standard MDX and not the BSO calculation language totally unique to Essbase.

Formula members in ASO have a couple of limitations, both of which stem from the fact that they are allowed only in dynamic hierarchies (meaning that they are equivalent to BSO dynamic calc members). First, MDX formulas can sometimes be slow; this is not so much of a problem with a stored formula member, where the value is being calculated once during a batch process, stored, and then retrieved many times, but that is not the ASO approach. Second, dynamic hierarchies are always calculated *after* stored hierarchies are consolidated. This makes certain types of rate calculation very difficult. For example, it is not possible to use a member formula to calculate a base currency value from two different local currency values and then roll the base currency results up a stored entity hierarchy. Instead, the local currency values are summed to a meaningless (e.g., GBP + EUR + INR) total, which the formula cannot convert to a base currency value. Inexperienced developers often assume that this can be resolved with ASO's solve order dimension and member properties, but despite the fact that solve order can be applied (confusingly and misleadingly) to stored hierarchy members, it makes absolutely no difference to actual calculation order.

As a consequence, in 11.1.2.0, ASO introduced procedural calculations. This allows developers to specify MDX member formulas, execute those formulas against either the whole cube or a subset, and then persist the results in the database by writing them back to a stored input-level member. Thus, returning to the above example, base currency values can be calculated for each of the GBP, EUR, and INR companies at level 0 in the entity dimension, the base currency results stored, and then finally rolled up at retrieve time like any other ASO input data. This is a useful feature but has seen relatively limited adoption in the Essbase world. There are several possible reasons for this. First, procedural calculations can be slow, especially when addressing a large set of potential result intersections, and limited guidance exists on optimizing them, compared to the vast amount of official documentation and tribal knowledge developed over two decades of BSO development. Second, MDX is not universally loved in the Essbase world. From one perspective, using an industry-accepted language like MDX with a multidimensional database is as logical a choice as using SQL with a relational database. Essbase developers who come from information technology departments quickly understand MDX and embrace its industry-standard nature. But despite that, there is clearly something many users and developers really, really like about the BSO calculation language. Essbase developers with their roots in finance typically find the switch harder to make. This highlights the current bifurcation in the Essbase development community, one that we hope Hybrid will erase in large part. Perhaps these users like the fact that BSO calculation language functions sometimes resemble Excel functions, rather than the programming language look of MDX. Perhaps they simply like the breadth of functions (especially financial and statistical) available out-of-the-box with BSO language that are not part of MDX. Or perhaps they dislike the fact that MDX's set-based operations are less easily followed than the top–down, macro-style (echoes of Excel again?) coding of a BSO calculation script.

In conclusion, the ASO experiment with industry-standard MDX has not been an unmitigated success, even if sometimes for reasons that may be more about acceptance than strict technical merit. The addition of procedural calculation to ASO, while an impressive and useful feature in the right circumstances, has done little if anything to improve matters. This is where Hybrid really comes in.

### 2.2.4 Hybrid Operations

Oracle product management and development have given presentations about Hybrid where they discussed at a very high level how Hybrid works, but they have not shared the internals of the product. This section is the authors' best guess as to how the tool works. Although we believe we have extrapolated correctly based on our understanding of BSO and ASO, it is certainly possible that we missed or misinterpreted a key concept. For that we are sorry, but until Oracle releases the inner details of Hybrid, this sort of educated guess approach is the best non-Oracle employees can do.

*2.2.4.1 ASO through a BSO Lens* The best way to understand Hybrid is to think of it as a way to use ASO through BSO constructs. Hybrid looks and acts like BSO but is ASO under the covers. Yes, BSO blocks still exist, but only to act as a persistent data store source for the temporary tablespace that the ASO query processor uses to return values or as a failover when Hybrid ASO cannot evaluate a query. Even level 0 queries use the Hybrid ASO engine for queries, although calc scripts and calculation functions that are not supported by Hybrid are still performed in BSO.

Determining what is BSO and what is ASO can be confusing. Hybrid uses a BSO .OTL file, calculation order follows BSO's stored and dynamic calculation order, BSO database statistics are displayed in database properties, and the BSO calc script language is used. However, under the covers, the ASO query processor loads blocks into the temporary tablespace, sets a solve order that mimics BSO calculation order, and dynamically writes MDX in to perform BSO calc script tasks. While Oracle is trying to shield us from thinking about the details of Hybrid architecture, the fact remains that the basic good design practices for BSO and ASO still hold sway. To effectively use Hybrid, one must understand both BSO and ASO.

*2.2.4.1.1 Calculation Engine* If a calculation is supported by Hybrid, regardless of dynamic or stored hierarchies, dynamic or stored intrablock calculations, or level of data, the Hybrid engine is invoked. If Hybrid's ASO query processor cannot process the query, the BSO query processor takes over.

There is very little or no performance or database improvement when addressing BSO stored data values—either the data are preaggregated or the calculations are fast, in-block calculations. Where Hybrid shines is dynamically aggregating sparse hierarchies that largely obviate the need for stored aggregations and their processing time penalty.

*2.2.4.1.2 Data Architecture*   At Hybrid's base are the familiar .PAG and .IND files that store and find data.

Why did Oracle use BSO and layer ASO on top instead of writing a pure ASO product that recognizes the BSO calc script language? It seems reasonable that if the effort to translate BSO to MDX is an accepted cost, surely wrapping that around an ASO data storage model would be simpler. The authors believe that Oracle did not do that for four reasons:

1. If BSO is the mimicked engine, BSO as the persisted data store makes sense.
2. Keeping BSO as the core allows the gradual introduction of BSO features in Hybrid ASO while defaulting to BSO when operations cannot execute in Hybrid ASO.
3. Generating a focused, temporary tablespace from limited block subselects can perform better than equivalent traditional ASO queries.
4. BSO is long in the tooth yet retains many adherents, so Hybrid is the path to migrate customers from BSO to a more modern and high-performing architecture.

Of course, the above reasoning is speculation, but as the chapter illustrates, these seem like reasonable educated guesses.

### 2.2.4.1.2.1 Storage

**.PAG, .IND, and Tablespaces**

BSO's data storage model is Hybrid's persisted data store; level 0 or higher persisted data are not stored in ASO's default tablespace but instead in the familiar .PAG and .IND files. When the Hybrid query engine is in use, the required BSO blocks are loaded into the ASO temporary tablespace. If the size of the tablespace exceeds the aggregate cache, the interim calculated results are written to the application's temporary tablespace file system folder.

**Hybrid ASO Engine Is Used for All Query Processing If Possible**

Sparse dynamic dimension hierarchies are the primary use case for Hybrid ASO query processing. However, thinking that only sparse upper-level data are processed in Hybrid ASO is a mistake—all querying, including level 0-only data and dense intrablock calculations, processes through the Hybrid ASO query engine. The role of Hybrid ASO applies even when sparse dimension hierarchies are stored because the act of switching the ASODYNAMICAGGINBSO config file setting to PARTIAL or FULL invokes the Hybrid query processor. BSO query processing occurs only if the query cannot be supported in Hybrid.

2.2.4.1.2.2 Tablespace Impact on Storage .PAG and .IND files remove the need for ASO's persisted default tablespace—BSO blocks are the persisted data store. The blocks-to-temporary-tablespace data architecture means that Hybrid ASO does not use the default tablespace. Data loads, whether from a spreadsheet or via a batch process, are written to BSO data structures.

Unlike traditional ASO, Hybrid ASO loses the tuning parameters that ASO uses to impact tablespace design and efficiency: hierarchy types, compression dimensions, and somewhat user-definable aggregate views. Instead, Hybrid controls (or eliminates, or makes redundant in at least one case—Hybrid supports multiple consolidation operators while apparently retaining the aggregation performance of an ASO stored hierarchy) these properties, with the theory being that Oracle's internal optimization algorithms perform better than humans do. Removing design and configuration complexity is one of the key goals of Hybrid, and removing this database design control is part of that philosophy.

*2.2.4.2 Tablespace Processing and the Aggregate Storage Cache* Although a conceptual overview of Hybrid ASO operations will aid in understanding Hybrid performance, note that the writing of this section occurred when Hybrid cache sizing was impossible. One day, perhaps, Oracle will allow Hybrid aggregate cache resizing. Until then, the tuning advice in this section is not applicable and is included in the hope that one day soon, it will be relevant.

Nevertheless, the following explanation of Hybrid ASO operations is pertinent when explaining Hybrid performance. This explanation also helps in recognizing the interaction of Hybrid, hard drive performance, and memory allocation, and thus optimizing hardware configuration. The authors also think that comprehending this at a theoretical level is geeky cool.

To understand how ASO within Hybrid works, an understanding of ASO's use of the temporary tablespace and the aggregate cache is instructive. On query, pure ASO reads data from the persisted default tablespace (default\ess00001.dat) and, if the query is sufficiently complex, writes interim results to the temporary tablespace before secondary processing and final presentation of calculated results. The temporary tablespace resides in the ASO aggregate cache if the cache is sufficiently large; if the space requirements exceed that of the cache, the excess temporary tablespace is written to the database temp file system folder (temp\ess00001.dat). Some examples of these complex queries are dynamic calculations, sorts, unions, or intersects of data. Simple queries that do not require interim data may not use a temporary tablespace. Multiple simultaneous simple queries consume the aggregate cache and can cause the same overflow to the file system temporary tablespace. On query completion, temporary tablespace, whether in the aggregate cache or in the file system, is released; temporary tablespace is not retained even for identical queries.

Modern hardware and operating systems obviate much of the potential performance impact of this spillover to the file system. The operating system uses its own caches when the aggregate cache cannot contain the temporary tablespace. Reads from the operating system cache do not invoke physical disk input/output; writes to the file system tablespace still incur a performance cost. Oracle has announced that, in the future, Exalytics will be able to resume processing before files are written to disk, thus removing even more of the operating system cache delay.

The above description of the internal processes of ASO and operating system interaction is transparent to Essbase developers and users alike. It is presented to better understand how to tune the aggregate cache for optimum performance.

Hybrid ASO, in contrast, only has a temporary tablespace, and thus, the Hybrid aggregate cache is always used for queries. Hybrid ASO requires data in the temporary tablespace before it can calculate results, unlike ASO, which may complete simple queries without recourse to the temporary tablespace. Queries cause Hybrid to read block-level data from .PAG files into the temporary tablespace where calculation operations occur. ASO does not have to go through the block-to-tablespace process because its persisted data reside in the default tablespace. When the Hybrid aggregate cache cannot contain all of the data read from BSO blocks for a given query, a temporary tablespace manifested in the temp file system folder is generated.

When a top-of-house query occurs, Hybrid does not create intermediate aggregated views in the temporary tablespace. Instead, it reads the required blocks and aggregates the result to the uppermost member combination. This is a relatively fast operation because it involves the same amount of I/O that ASO would perform reading from its persisted data store.

Top-of-house queries read all level 0 blocks into the temporary tablespace, aggregate on the fly, and write only a single data value to the temporary tablespace. In turn, the query processor must read that single value and present that to the user. The opposite end of the query spectrum is when a query reports all level 0 blocks. As with top-of-house queries, all blocks must be read, but the level 0 data also must be recreated in the temporary tablespace. All blocks are written to the temporary tablespace and then all of that temporary tablespace must be read and presented to the user. This level 0 read-all, write-all, present-all query is much more expensive than a top-of-house read-all and present-one value query.

*2.2.4.2.1 Tuning the Hybrid Aggregate Cache*    The Essbase 11.1.2.3.505 ReadMe file states that the Hybrid aggregate cache size cannot be changed from the 32 MB default. We do not know when or if Oracle will lift this restriction. The following section assumes that, at some point, Oracle will enable resizing the aggregate cache given the existence of MaxL Hybrid aggregate cache commands. For the releases available as of the publication of this book, consider the following cache tuning section as one that will be relevant when (we hope) Hybrid supports cache resizing.[*]

---

[*] Oddly, in 11.1.2.3.505, the aggregate cache can be resized, and querying the cache size shows that it has changed. Examining the actual memory consumed in the operating system shows that there is no actual change. After a restart, the queried cache value returns to 32 MB.

When server memory resources are constrained, the inability of OS caches to backfill the aggregate cache means that correctly sizing the Hybrid aggregate cache is important to performance. A query will read all required blocks from the disk into the temporary tablespace. If the aggregate cache is sufficiently large, that temporary tablespace is not written to the disk; if it is too small, it will be written to the temp file system folder.

Sizing the cache becomes more complex when simultaneous queries are considered. Will many of them be top-of-house queries that require all level 0 blocks to be read and loaded into the temporary tablespace? Or will a more likely scenario be queries that only require portions of the base data? The latter scenario is where Hybrid shines—subselects of required BSO blocks are Hybrid's secret query sauce. Populating the temporary tablespace based on query requirements produces fast performance, possibly faster than ASO queries based on observations of identical queries across equivalent ASO and Hybrid databases. Even when the query reads all base data, Hybrid and ASO are roughly equivalent in speed because the query process of persisted data to the temporary tablespace to user is identical for both engines although the technical details differ.

Simply sizing the aggregate cache to a multiple of the .PAG files is a fruitless task because it does not take into consideration the true number and nature of queries. Instead, as is common with tuning recommendations, set an estimated size, perform representative queries, and actively monitor the temp tablespace file system. If an ess00001.dat file appears in that folder, the aggregate cache can be increased by that size. Continuous monitoring of that file system folder will be a guide to correct sizing.

The forward-looking portion on aggregate cache sizing is now complete. The following information is true as of the writing of this book and will likely be so in future.

*2.2.4.2.2 More on Hybrid's Aggregate Cache and Temporary Tablespace*   In summary:

- As noted, if the temporary tablespace is contained within the aggregate cache, the temporary tablespace will not be written to the disk.
- Identical simultaneous queries do not share aggregate cache results; each query is independent of the other.
- Once a query is complete, its share of the aggregate cache is released for consumption by other queries—sizing need not be a consideration of all queries performed since the database start.
  - There seems to be a difference between the way the physical temporary tablespace file is managed between Windows and Unix operating systems.
    - The temporary tablespace file in Windows seems to show the high-water mark of tablespace size since application start.
    - Unix, in contrast, resizes the temporary tablespace file based on current demand. Identifying the largest temporary tablespace size requires constant file system monitoring.
- Although the default folder is part of the Hybrid database's file system, it is not currently used.

*2.2.4.2.3 Recommendations*

- Specify a server with a lot of free RAM to allow the operating system to handle cache overflows. This is especially important given the current inability to resize the aggregate cache beyond the default 32 MB.
- If the aggregate cache cannot be increased to accommodate all of the temporary tablespace, set the ASODYNAMICAGGINBSOFOLDERPATH to the fastest hard drive possible, preferably a RAM or Solid State Drive.
- If and when Oracle allows the Hybrid aggregate cache to be sized, define the aggregate cache size to contain all of the temporary tablespace.

*2.2.4.3 Materialized Aggregations and Stored Calculations in BSO*   In ASO, materialized aggregations are batch aggregations of selected upper-level views. These aggregate views are written as additions to the default tablespace. The persisted data store in Hybrid is BSO with its block structure, and the default tablespace is not used; therefore, there are no Hybrid ASO materialized aggregations. However, BSO aggregations and calculations are persisted to .PAG files.

As with ASO, Hybrid ASO member calculations are not persisted; all ASO calculations are dynamic in nature.

*2.2.4.4 Procedural Calculations*   Both BSO and ASO support procedural calculations. BSO calc scripts are a key part of that engine's continuing success. Aggregations, formulas, conditional logic, member text string manipulation—these are just a subset of calc script functionality. In contrast, ASO procedural calcs are significantly less powerful in intent and operation. They exist primarily as a means to perform simple allocations and level 0-only calculations. All other ASO calculations take place in the outline itself.

At the time of the writing of this chapter, calc scripts use the BSO engine only. There are no Hybrid ASO calc scripts.

Although BSO calc scripts are possible in Hybrid, ASO-like procedural calculations are not. For level 0-only calculations, BSO calc scripts take the place of the sometimes difficult and potentially poorly performing ASO procedural calculations.

Calculations that require allocation-like logic must be completed in the BSO mode of Hybrid. This scenario requires that upper-level members in Hybrid hierarchies be stored with the concomitant BSO aggregation time and increased .PAG file size. Overcoming the two hurdles of cross-dimensional indicators and Hybrid calc scripts are a key part of Hybrid's full parity with BSO. The authors do not have any insight into Oracle's direction or timing of these features, but their forthcoming inclusion seems both logical and a requirement for widespread adoption of Hybrid.

*2.2.4.5 Hybrid Is and Is Not an In-Memory Database*   Hybrid's BSO and ASO storage models mean that Hybrid is simultaneously a stored and in-memory database. BSO design must focus on the fastest way to load data into the Hybrid ASO tablespace instead of BSO query or aggregation performance if Hybrid functionality can perform the query. If the Hybrid ASO engine cannot support the query, BSO design must focus on the fastest possible BSO aggregations and calculations. ASO design is a different matter—there are no configurable ASO properties. Dimension types, hierarchies, and member formulas are only exposed as BSO objects; what the ASO portion of Hybrid does with them is out of the developer's control.

### 2.2.4.6 Outlines

*2.2.4.6.1 Hybrid Outline, Scaling, Dimension, and Hierarchy Types*   One of the more interesting design decisions on Oracle's part is to use the BSO outline structure instead of ASO's. Hybrid's ability to scale to larger databases than possible in BSO because of the ASO query engine suggests that ASO's paged outline format is a better fit than nonpaged BSO outline storage.

This, however, is negated by several design considerations driven by Hybrid's adoption of a BSO database point of view:

- Hybrid is primarily a replacement for BSO, although eventual replacement of ASO may occur. The outline structure and format must support BSO functions.
  - ASO outlines are a bitmap index interface; the bitmap defines aggregations and calculation order as defined by the outline interface.
  - BSO outlines are used both to define aggregation and calculation order and to define the structure of the .IND files. To support BSO, Hybrid must use a BSO outline.
  - The BSO model calculation order is determined by dimension density and sparsity, outline order, dynamic versus stored calculations, and TWOPASS tags.
- ASO's paged outline format has issues with outline fragmentation that require maintenance.

Despite its BSO format, the outline functions in two different manners, depending on query mode. In BSO, dimension types, dimension density and sparsity, outline order, dynamic or stored hierarchies and calculations, and TWOPASS member tags define calculation order. In Hybrid ASO, the outline maps bitmap key to member names on retrieval.

2.2.4.6.1.1 Scaling   The Hybrid ASO engine's dynamic aggregations means that as hierarchies grow in complexity and depth, the stored size of the database does not increase, one of the key features of ASO. ASO outlines have a theoretical limit of $2^{52}$ dimension level permutations with a real-world limit of approximately 10 to 50 million members. The BSO half of Hybrid dictates that the BSO $2^{128}$ sparse member limit and the $2^{52}$ cells per block limits are imposed. Given the new nature of Hybrid, the real-world limits of the engine are unknown although it seems reasonable that Hybrid will not scale to the same size as ASO.

2.2.4.6.1.2 *Hierarchy Types*    Hybrid supports all of BSO's dimension hierarchy types. Traditional ASO cannot do this and has multiple restrictions on storage type, operators, label-only members, and shared hierarchies. Hybrid, and thus Hybrid's ASO query processor, has none of those restrictions. Given the fast performance, the availability of all mathematical operators, and repeated shared member hierarchies that do not follow ASO's restrictive rules, we believe that Hybrid hierarchies work in some sort of improved Multiple Hierarchies Enabled manner.

### 2.3  Using Hybrid

Does the coming of Hybrid mean an additional outwardly similar but fundamentally different Essbase kernel with a new set of rules, features, and required knowledge as was true when ASO was introduced? It would be overstating the case to say that ASO's external differences from BSO—hierarchy types, MDX, MaxL procedural calc scripts, materialized aggregations, buffers, slices—were a mistake because those attributes are required to exploit the power of ASO. It is, however, reasonable to hold that the introduction of ASO required Essbase practitioners to essentially double their Essbase knowledge base. A common Essbase implementation design often contains BSO and ASO databases, with each engine used to its best purpose.

Hybrid does not incur that learning cost. Essbase practitioners who understand BSO have almost all the skills required to implement Hybrid (with the one unusual challenge of having to design around making upper-level sparse members dynamic).

If Hybrid is ASO applied to BSO, are ASO constructs and knowledge required or does Hybrid mean a yet another set of skills, properties, and administrative tasks?

### 2.3.1  *What Does It Look Like in EAS?*

This is the genius of Hybrid Essbase: it looks and behaves like BSO. Exploiting Hybrid requires only setting the Essbase.cfg Hybrid property ASODYNAMICAGGINBSO to PARTIAL or FULL and setting upper-level sparse members to dynamic calc. Do that to a database, and you have just converted a BSO database to Hybrid. There are no new skills or techniques beyond that for the Essbase developer.

This is not by coincidence. It is Oracle's approach to making Essbase development less of an emphasis on esoteric technical skills and more a question of problem analysis and application of high-performing applications. So what does a Hybrid database look like?

Just like a BSO database, but with dynamic upper sparse members.

Figure 2.1 shows a fully Hybridized Sample.Basic. The Dynamic Calc storage property is assigned to upper-level sparse dimension members in the Product and

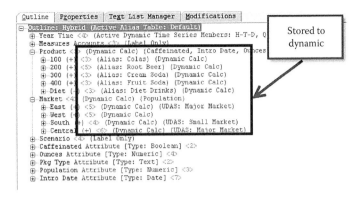

**Figure 2.1**   A fully hybridized Sample.Basic.

Market dimensions. That and the config file setting that enables Hybrid for this database are the sum total of database changes. This ease of conversion is keeping in spirit with Essbase's simplifying trend.

### 2.3.2 EAS Hasn't Caught Up to Hybrid Just Yet

As evinced by database statistics, Hybrid is a work in progress because only BSO database statistics are shown. Although these are valuable in understanding the state of the BSO portion of Hybrid, there is no information on the ASO tablespaces. Will Oracle add this in future releases or are these statistics difficult to quantify given that these are ephemeral in nature, changing with each query? Perhaps the best explanation is that the goal of Hybrid is to subsume complex architectural details: Hybrid Essbase manages the ASO portions of the database dynamically and automatically—there are no properties for the developer to tune.

Tuning and configuration still occur in the BSO half of Hybrid via dimension density, caches, and storage properties. The normal BSO statistics are available and, as far as the BSO portion of Hybrid goes, are correctly reflected in EAS (see Figure 2.2).

The standard BSO error message remains for dynamically calculated parents that have more than 100 children (see Figure 2.3). This was an important statistic in BSO, particularly in sparse dimensions. However, in Hybrid, this is an erroneous error message: Sparse dynamic aggregations are explicitly handled by ASO, as are dense dynamic aggregations above level 0.

### 2.3.3 Hybrid Calculation Functionality

Several of the most painful limitations in the original version 11.1.2.3.500 release of Hybrid have been lifted in version 11.1.2.4, but some remain. Table 2.2 provides an overview.

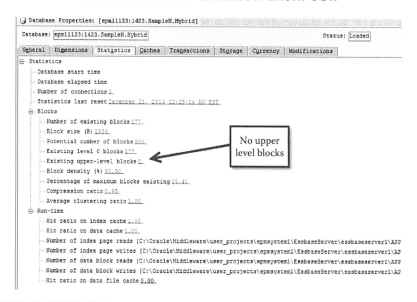

**Figure 2.2**    Database Statistics.

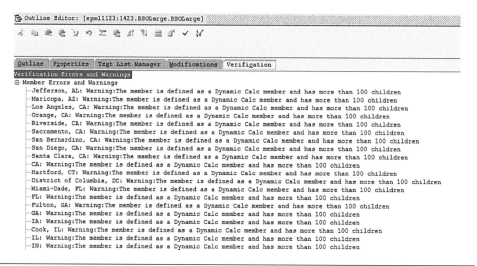

**Figure 2.3**    Dynamic calc warning.

### 2.3.3.1 What's Not in Hybrid

*2.3.3.1.1 Calc Scripts*    Calc scripts firing in Hybrid will be the final realization of Hybrid, the Essbase element that allows the complete replacement of BSO. As of the writing of this book, Hybrid-enabled calc scripts are not yet part of Essbase. This is a major product shortcoming, and the obvious next step in the product's evolution. Without it, Hybrid adoption will necessarily be impeded until this functionality arrives.

If we put on our we-do-not-work-at-Oracle speculative caps, this limitation is understandable in the face of the technical challenge. ASO procedural calculations

**Table 2.2**  Limitations in Hybrid 11.1.2.3.500

| Feature | 11.1.2.3.500 | 11.1.2.4 |
|---|---|---|
| Calc scripts | No | No |
| Cross-dimensional indicators | No | No |
| DATAEXPORT/report scripts/MDX queries | No/no/yes | No/no/yes |
| TOPDOWN | No | No |
| XOLAP | No | No |
| Attribute calculations | No | No, but attribute functions |
| Time balance | No | Yes |
| DTS | No | Yes |
| Supported member function count | 16 | Almost 130 |

are limited in comparison with BSO. If the upper levels of Hybrid are ASO, mimicking the rich BSO calculation functionality is not a trivial exercise. Furthermore, BSO calc scripts can access any level of preaggregated data. If these upper-level data are dynamically calculated based on query level 0 blocks, a Hybrid calc script that relies on upper-level data could cause either a very large temporary tablespace or a continuous cycle (and perhaps recycle) of level 0 blocks consumed and discarded to calculate upper-level values. Either approach is expensive and the tradeoffs involved are not trivial.

This is not to say that calc scripts are unavailable in Hybrid, only that the calc scripts execute in BSO only. Until Hybrid calc scripts are available, Hybrid databases that perform allocations or other upper-level-dependent calculations must take into consideration the balance between fast dynamic Hybrid calculations and the requirement for potentially slow BSO stored aggregations.

*2.3.3.1.2 Cross-Dimensional Indicators*  Cross-dims are the BSO notation used to define member tuples. A Sales, total Product, and total Market tuple is expressed as: `"Sales"->"Market"->"Product"`. The current lack of cross-dim support means that Hybrid calculations that require upper-level values must rely either on dynamic BSO aggregations or—and this is the more likely design given sparse dynamic BSO aggregation performance—on stored BSO hierarchies. The absence of cross-dim support at level 0 is less keenly felt because of Hybrid's impact on blocks: Block size can be increased to force in-memory BSO calculations and overall block count is vastly reduced because of Hybrid upper-level member intersection. A balanced design of stored and dynamic dimension hierarchies will be necessary until Hybrid supports cross-dims.

*2.3.3.1.3 DATAEXPORT/Report Scripts/MDX Queries*  Only MDX queries exploit the Hybrid engine. DATAEXPORT and Essbase Report Scripts only fire in BSO. Report scripts and DATAEXPORT calc script commands that access upper-level data force a failover to BSO. However, as with other BSO-only functions, so long as only stored data are used, DATAEXPORT and Report Scripts run just as quickly in Hybrid as they do in BSO.

*2.3.3.1.4 TOPDOWN* A top-down mode calculation is a formula evaluation that examines the blocks considered for calculation. Hybrid does not use blocks except at level 0, and then only as a persistent storage mechanism whose data are read into memory as queried, so the concept of a top-down calculation is irrelevant when the Hybrid ASO query engine is used.

*2.3.3.1.5 XOLAP* XOLAP, or extended online analytic processing, is a rarely used feature (in a combined 35+ years of Essbase practice, the authors have never seen or even heard of an XOLAP implementation, although they must surely exist). It combines an Essbase outline with 100% relationally stored fact data. XOLAP databases must follow many relational restrictions, such as avoiding ragged hierarchies, and do not support filters and user-defined level 0 members. XOLAP databases must be created through Essbase Studio.

Given that Hybrid scales up to near ASO data levels, the attraction of XOLAP is greatly diminished.

*2.3.3.1.6 Attributes* Attribute calculations via queries are not supported in either version of Hybrid. Given that attributes perform dynamic sparse aggregations, their absence is surprising.

However, 11.1.2.4 does support functions such as @ATTRIBUTE, @ATTRIBUTESVAL, @ISATTRIBUTE, and @ISMBRWITHATTR, among others. Progress is being made, and it is reasonable to expect that Attributes will be incorporated in a future release of the product.

In the interim, converting Attribute to base dimensions is a reasonable design compromise because the block count remains the same at level 0. In a BSO database, the subsequent data explosion would make this design approach untenable unless the database was very small. The dynamic upper-level nature of Hybrid obviates that concern because there are no additional upper-level blocks to create from the increased number of sparse intersections.

*2.3.3.2 Time Balance* This functionality is not available in the initial 11.1.2.3.500 release; any attempt to mimic Time Balance forces the BSO calculation engine. However, 11.1.2.4 fully supports it in all of its permutations: Time Balance Last, First, Average along with the skip missing and zero options (see Figure 2.4).

*2.3.3.3 Dynamic Time Series* Like Time Balance, Dynamic Time Series (DTS) is not supported in 11.1.2.3.500 but is in 11.1.2.4 (see Figure 2.5). Also of interest is that DTS is not supported in ASO, yet is in Hybrid.

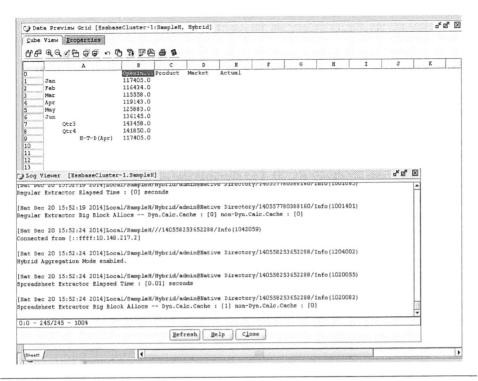

**Figure 2.4** Time balance.

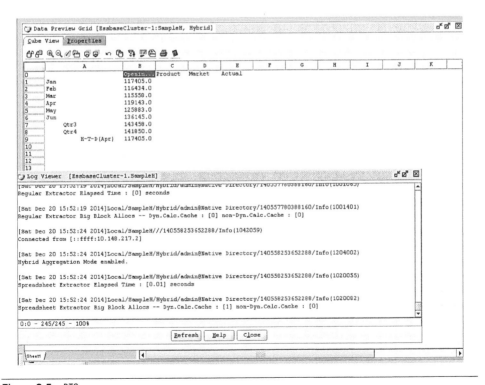

**Figure 2.5** DTS.

Several techniques in ASO provide DTS-like functionality, but they rely either on stored Time dimension hierarchies or MDX aggregations; both approaches require an additional Analytic or View dimension. The native inclusion of DTS in Hybrid is proof again that Oracle is not only dedicated to making ASO easier in its Hybrid guise but the company is also expanding the functionality of the ASO engine. Whether the classic ASO engine eventually incorporates Hybrid's innovations is an open question.

*2.3.3.4 Member Calculation Functions*    Listing the supported and unsupported functions is a job for the *Essbase Technical Reference* guide, but at a high level, the 11.1.2.4 release supports almost 130 functions, as listed in Table 2.3.

These functions only fire in Hybrid in member formulas. The Hybrid calc script limitation still applies.

The list for 11.1.2.3.500 is much simpler, as shown in Table 2.4.

*2.3.3.5 Formulas with Referenced Members*    If the formula references other members, the rules in Table 2.5 govern the use of the Hybrid processor.

*2.3.3.6 The State of Hybrid Calculations*    Calculations in Hybrid Essbase are still a work in progress, but one that is getting very close to the full BSO calculation set. The most glaring exceptions to that rule are calc scripts and cross-dimensional indicators. Developers can work around these limitations by either limiting procedural calc scripts to level 0 or utilizing stored hierarchies. Substituting stored base dimensions

**Table 2.3**   11.1.2.4 Functions

| SUPPORTED | CATEGORY | EXAMPLE FUNCTIONS |
|---|---|---|
| Yes | Aggregations | @SUM, @SUMRANGE |
| | Attributes/UDAs | @ATTRIBUTE, @UDA |
| | Dates | @DATEDIFF, @DATEROLL |
| | Strings | @EQUAL, @MBRCOMPARE |
| | Hierarchy selectors | @RELATIVE, @DESCENDANTS |
| | IS tests | @ISMBR, @ISISIBLING |
| | Range | @MINSRANGE, @MAXRANGE |
| | Calc mode | @CALCMODE |
| | Hierarchy movement | @NEXTS, @SHIFTMINUS |
| | Variance | @VAR, @VARPER |
| No | Allocations | @ALLOCATE |
| | Financial functions | @DISCOUNT, @IRR |
| | Multidimensional | @MDSHIFT, @MDALLOCATE |
| | Hierarchical values | @ANCESTVAL, @PARENTVAL |
| | Movement | @MOVAVG, @MOVSUMX |
| | Current member | @CURRMBR, @CURRMBRRANGE |
| | Extra-database reads/writes | @XREF, @XWRITE |
| | Blocks | @CREATEBLOCK |

**Table 2.4**    11.1.2.3.500 Functions

| SUPPORTED | FUNCTIONS |
|---|---|
| Yes | @CHILDREN |
| | @EXP |
| | @INT |
| | @ISMBR |
| | @MIN |
| | @MINSRANGE |
| | @MOD |
| | @MODE |
| | @NOTEQUAL |
| | @POWER |
| | @RANGE |
| | @REMAINDER |
| | @ROUND |
| | @VAR |
| | @VARIANCEP |
| | @VARPER |
| No | Everything else |

**Table 2.5**    Formulas with Referenced Numbers

| USE CASE | EXPLANATION |
|---|---|
| Sparse to sparse | Sparse dimension formula that references other sparse members |
| Dense to dense | Dense dimension formula that references other dense members |
| Sparse to dense/sparse | Sparse dimension formula that references member combinations from dense and sparse members; dense referenced members must be stored |

with dynamic Hybrid ASO aggregations in place of attribute dimensions is an acceptable design tradeoff because, unlike BSO, the performance impact is small.

### 2.3.4 Enabling Hybrid

Beyond defining sparse hierarchies as dynamic, the Essbase.cfg file must be modified to enable Hybrid. Although Hybrid ships with every copy of Essbase, only those customers with the correct ASO Essbase license are contractually able to use the functionality.

Enabling Hybrid is an Essbase.cfg setting. In contrast to most config file settings, enabling Hybrid at the application level requires only the ASODYNAMICAGGINBSO parameter and a restart of the application.

*2.3.4.1 Syntax in Essbase.cfg*    The config file setting ASODYNAMICAGGINBSO turns Hybrid on or off. The scope of that setting is definable at the server, application, and database level.

**Table 2.6**   Hybrid Enablement Values

| SETTING | BEHAVIOR |
|---------|----------|
| None | Turn Hybrid off. |
| Partial | Hybrid is enabled for simple aggregation operators: +, −, and ~. *, /, and % execute in BSO as do all member formulas. |
| Full | Turn on Hybrid for aggregations and formulas. |

The grammar is as follows:

```
ASODYNAMICAGGINBSO [appname [dbname]] NONE | PARTIAL | FULL
```

*2.3.4.1.1 NONE | PARTIAL | FULL*   Three Hybrid enablement values are possible at the server, application, and database level, as shown in Table 2.6.

*2.3.4.1.2 ASODYNAMICAGGINBSO NONE | PARTIAL | FULL*
**Example**

```
ASODYNAMICAGGINBSO NONE
```

**Notes**
If the optional application and database are not defined and a PARTIAL or FULL flag is used, all BSO databases will use Hybrid mode when possible. Unless you are an early Hybrid true believer, this is not an advisable configuration.

Using the NONE setting at the server level is good practice because Hybrid can then be turned on at the application and database level.

*2.3.4.1.3 ASODYNAMICAGGINBSO [appname] NONE | PARTIAL | FULL*
**Example**

```
ASODYNAMICAGGINBSO SampleH FULL
```

**Notes**
Unlike ASO, Hybrid shares BSO's support of multiple databases per application. For flexibility, turning on the Hybrid flag at the application level allows new databases to be created as Hybrid on the fly. Note that once this is enabled, all databases in that application are Hybrid.

*2.3.4.1.4 ASODYNAMICAGGINBSO [appname] [dbname] NONE | PARTIAL | FULL*
**Example**

```
ASODYNAMICAGGINBSO SampleH Basic FULL
```

**Notes**
A fully qualified setting sets an explicitly named database's Hybrid functionality.

*2.3.4.2 Recommended Settings*  Given the new status of Hybrid, a good practice is to turn Hybrid off for all applications and databases and then selectively enable it. The snippet from Essbase.cfg shown below, (a) turns off Hybrid at a server level, (b) enables it for the BSOHSamp application (and thus all databases in that application), (c) enables it for the SampleH.Basic (leaving any other databases under SampleH as BSO), and (d) enables it for the T3_Hybrd application.

```
ASODYNAMICAGGINBSO NONE
ASODYNAMICAGGINBSO BSOHSamp  FULL
ASODYNAMICAGGINBSO SampleH Basic  FULL
ASODYNAMICAGGINBSO T3_Hybrid  FULL
```

## 2.3.5  Tablespaces

Hybrid's ASO half creates the same tablespace folders in the file system as the traditional ASO engine: default, log, metadata, and temp. Hybrid has three differences from ASO's tablespace behavior: the ephemeral nature of the tablespace folders, observable tablespace usage, and tablespace location.

*2.3.5.1 Ephemeral Tablespaces*  In contrast to ASO file system tablespaces and folders that are defined at application creation and remain as file system objects regardless of application start status, Hybrid tablespaces are created when a database starts and destroyed on application stop.

### 2.3.5.1.1  Started

```
Directory of C:\Oracle\Middleware\user_projects\epmsystem1
\EssbaseServer\essbaseserver1\hybrid\SampleH

01/01/2015  12:00 AM    <DIR>          .
01/01/2015  12:00 AM    <DIR>          ..
01/01/2015  12:00 AM    <DIR>          default
01/01/2015  12:00 AM    <DIR>          log
01/01/2015  12:00 AM    <DIR>          metadata
01/01/2015  12:00 AM    <DIR>          temp
```

### 2.3.5.1.2  Stopped

```
Directory of C:\Oracle\Middleware\user_projects\epmsystem1
\EssbaseServer\essbaseserver1\hybrid

01/01/2015  12:01 AM    <DIR>          .
01/01/2015  12:01 AM    <DIR>          ..
```

The 11.1.2.4 release behaves as above, as did the 11.1.2.3.500 beta. The commercially shipped 11.1.2.3.500 persists the tablespace folders.

Despite the four tablespace file system folders, the default tablespace is not utilized although log, metadata, and temp are. The temporary tablespace's ess00001.dat file can be viewed only when particularly large database queries are executed and the aggregate storage cache is insufficient to contain the temporary tablespace. See Section 2.2.4.2 in this chapter for an overview of these operations.

### 2.3.6 Location of Tablespaces

The ASO MaxL command `alter tablespace` can change the location and size of each of the tablespace file objects.

In contrast, Hybrid uses the Essbase.cfg command `ASODYNAMICAGGINBSO FOLDERPATH`. The Essbase config file nature means that change cannot occur without bringing Essbase down and back up. The command can only move all tablespaces, not specific ones.

Despite this lower level of configurability, the tablespaces and the location of the BSO .PAG and .IND files can still be split across physical drives for optimal performance.

The default location for the tablespaces is the root Essbase applications folder:

```
ASODYNAMICAGGINBSOFOLDERPATH [appname] path-to-directory
```

Per the documentation, this setting can be made on an application or server basis. Good practice in the face of multiple Hybrid databases suggests that this setting should be made at the application level for best performance.

### 2.3.6.1 Fast Disk

The central role of the temporary tablespace and the limited 32 MB size (as of 11.1.2.3.505) of the aggregate cache means that cache overflow will be negatively impacted by slow disk operations. Obtain the fastest drive and point the tablespaces there. The best possible tablespace file performance will be when the physical drive is independent of all other Essbase processes (and not where the .PAG files for the same database reside) as both BSO and ASO operations will compete for disk throughput.

### 2.3.7 Aggregate Storage Cache and Its Role in Hybrid

As of 11.1.2.3.505, the aggregate storage cache cannot be resized from its 32 MB default. This section is provided in the hope that Hybrid will, in the future, support other aggregate cache settings.

The authors have observed that, while the .505 release will accept cache size changes and even report the new size, the actual amount of memory consumed by the database in the operating system on application restart remains the same.

In contrast to setting Hybrid's tablespace location via the Essbase.cfg file, defining and querying the aggregate storage cache are the same in Hybrid as they are in ASO: a MaxL statement.

After setting the cache size beyond the minimum default size of 32 MB, the application must be stopped and restarted to take effect.

*2.3.7.1 Setting the Cache*   Note that setting cache_size property must be in bytes.

```
alter application APP-NAME set cache_size ;
```

*2.3.7.2 Querying the Cache*   In contrast to the set cache_size command, get cache_size returns the cache size in megabytes.

```
query application APP-NAME get cache_size ;
```

*2.3.7.3 Setting and Querying in MaxL*   Figure 2.6 presents the MaxL statement for setting and querying the cache.

### 2.3.8 How Do We Know That Hybrid Worked or Didn't?

*2.3.8.1 Query Time*   The most obvious indicator of Hybrid engine utilization is the speed of dynamically calculated sparse dimensions. If it is very fast, Hybrid worked. If it is slow, a BSO dynamic sparse calculation occurred. It really is that simple to tell, except for the smallest of databases where dynamic BSO speed is fast. As always with Essbase, the log files tell the true story.

*2.3.8.2 Essbase Application Log File Review*   The application log file explicitly shows the success or failure of a given query evinced by either the message Hybrid Aggregation Mode enabled or Hybrid Aggregation Mode disabled for [operation] due to [reason].

*2.3.8.3 Sample Essbase Application Log Entries*   Happy Days:

```
[Sun Apr 13 13:36:14 2014]Local/SampleH/Basic/hypadmin@Native
Directory/12752/Info(1204002)
```

**Hybrid Aggregation Mode enabled.**

```
MAXL> alter application sampleh set cache_size 67108864 ;
    WARNING - 1270056 - Cache size setting changed to [64] MB. The change will not
take effect until application restart.
    OK/INFO - 1056013 - Application sampleh altered.

MAXL> query application sampleh get cache_size ;

  aso_cache_size_mega
+-------------------
                  64

  OK/INFO - 1241044 - Records returned: [1].

MAXL>
```

**Figure 2.6**   MaxL for setting and querying.

Sad Times:

```
[Sun Apr 13 13:37:12 2014]Local/SampleH/Basic /hypadmin@Native
Directory/2428/Info(1204002)
```

**Hybrid Aggregation Mode disabled** for [XREF test] due to [xref is
not supported yet].

### 2.4 Designing in Hybrid

What should be built in or converted to Hybrid, and how? Large BSO databases, with their attendant size and calculation costs, are obvious candidates; even small or moderately sized ones can benefit from Hybrid's dynamically aggregated nature and elimination of procedural aggregations. Before that conversion (or new development) can occur, calculation requirements within Hybrid's strictures and limitations must be first considered. Remember that Hybrid is still in an early-days state, and as such, some BSO calculation functionality is not yet available.

#### 2.4.1 Design Considerations

*2.4.1.1 No More AGGs/CALC DIMs*   At its heart, Hybrid is about replacing the stored aggregations of BSO with ASO's dynamic aggregations. With this in mind, AGGs and CALC DIMs in calc scripts should be the first target for conversion.

*2.4.1.2 Smaller Database Size*   Given the removal of all or most stored aggregations, Hybrid database size in .PAG and .IND files will be considerably smaller because BSO's data explosion of stored aggregated values is no longer valid. Smaller databases equal faster backup, faster moves, faster loads, and faster development times.

*2.4.1.3 Block Size Rules May No Longer Apply*   If the overall size of a database is vastly smaller, and BSO calculations occur only at level 0, BSO considerations about block size may no longer be as relevant as before. As an example, large blocks that perform acceptably at level 0, but because of size, are poorly designed for aggregation may now be acceptable because their stored aggregations have been eliminated. Indeed, work-arounds to current Hybrid limitations, like cross-dims to upper-level sparse dimension members, may perform efficiently in a formerly impossibly large block as dense BSO cross-dims.

Users must take care not to go too far in the large block direction, keeping in mind that blocks are the persisted storage of a Hybrid database. When queried, they are loaded into the Hybrid ASO tablespace and aggregated on the fly. As with BSO, block sizing must balance calculation needs and approaches with the speed at which

Essbase can load data off disk and into memory. In Hybrid, the analysis of performance to determine whether fewer larger blocks or more smaller blocks continues.

*2.4.1.4 Caches*   In a fully Hybrid design, the role of the traditional BSO caches also changes. Data caches need only be sized to support stored level 0 and fewer or no aggregated blocks. The index cache can also be considerably smaller because of the reduced number of blocks. Calculator and dynamic calculator caches follow the same reduction in scope logic.

See Section 2.2.4.2 in this chapter for an overview of the aggregate storage cache.

*2.4.1.5 Dimension Design*

*2.4.1.5.1 Interdimensional Irrelevancy Less Important*   Essbase databases have an upper practical limit that precedes the physical. Following the spirit of "If I can do it, I should," many Essbase databases are just…big. Big as in, "How many dimensions does this database have? How do they relate to one another? What is this data point, anyway? I am so confused." Yes, creating Essbase databases that contain unrelated data is one of the many bees buzzing in the authors' Essbase bonnet. BSO databases have largely been spared this mostly ASO affliction because BSO cannot scale well beyond 12 or so dimensions; avoiding interdimensional irrelevancy is a key design precept in BSO because of the impact of increased upper-level blocks that even nonrelated dimensions bring. This consideration becomes less important in Hybrid because stored upper-level data are optional, thus reducing or eliminating the aggregation time and database file size cost. Adding dimension combinations that do not have relevance to one another will now be technically possible; however, the authors of this chapter hope you will resist temptation because it is just bad design.

Getting rid of upper-level data explosion is key to Hybrid's power and, incidentally, is the reason those interdimensionally irrelevant dimensions are possible. For better or worse, Hybrid is still controlled by the BSO limits of $2^{128}$ sparse member combinations and $2^{52}$ cells per block. This means that Hybrid is still limited to smaller databases than ASO, so the good design practice of avoiding irrelevant dimension combinations, while lessened in emphasis, is still important.

*2.4.1.5.2 Attributes Can Become Stored Sparse Dimensions*   Hybrid does not currently support Attribute queries. BSO Attribute queries can perform poorly because of their dynamic sparse calculation. A Hybrid query that includes an Attribute dimension is doubly slow when pulling upper-level database because at least two sparse BSO dynamic aggregations will occur.

Converting an Attribute dimension to a base Hybrid dimension avoids dynamic BSO sparse calculations and Hybrid's fast ASO engine calculates aggregations on query. Attributes are now useful for reporting.

Although fact data must now contain the relationship attributes and other dimensions, the number of level 0 blocks is not increased. Maintaining an identical block count means that Hybrid aggregate performance is only slightly degraded by additional attribute-to-base dimensions.

*2.4.1.5.3 Mix and Match as Required*   Although the most dramatic use case for Hybrid in BSO is the complete elimination of stored sparse dimensions through ASO aggregations, Hybrid design can be more nuanced than that all-or-nothing approach. Enabling Hybrid in a BSO database does not mean that all sparse dimensions must be dynamically calculated. Traditional BSO stored hierarchies are still available either as fully stored dimensions or as dimensions with lower-level stored and upper-level dynamic hierarchies. This ability to accommodate a blend of dimension storage is important because Hybrid does not currently support critical functions like cross-dims, calc scripts, and other features and functions of BSO.

Two potential designs retain BSO functionality while taking advantage of Hybrid's fast dynamic aggregations: keeping some sparse dimensions stored and/or changing upper-level sparse hierarchies to dynamic. Both approaches could be combined in a single database to maximize the amount of Hybrid aggregation possible.

Changing one or more sparse dimensions to dynamic while retaining the stored hierarchy nature of the ones required for BSO calculations is akin to removing whole dimensions from a BSO database. Given this removal of a large number of upper-level blocks, the impact on BSO processing time and resources will likely be significant because so much less data will need to be processed.

Setting the top levels of some or all sparse dimensions to dynamic while retaining stored lower-level subtotals for BSO processing is analogous to removing layers of aggregation in a BSO database. The relatively small stored lower-level hierarchies are quickly aggregated, interrogated, and written back to Essbase.

Hybrid is a means to optimize BSO performance—how that is accomplished is dictated by the application's requirements and product functionality. Hybrid Essbase can mix and match the best of ASO and BSO in a single database.

*2.4.2 Benchmarking*

*2.4.2.1 Test Databases*   To see just how good a job Hybrid can really do, we created some large test outlines, data, and query sets. In fact, these databases were spun off from databases created to test ASO Planning performance, which meant cubes on a scale that would be a real stretch for regular BSO. That objective made them perfect for testing Hybrid.

We created six versions; the first three were "vanilla" BSO, Hybrid, and ASO cubes. Then we created a second set of cubes in which the (three) attribute dimensions were converted to be ordinary base dimensions. Why the second option is interesting is explained in more detail below, but the spoiler is that attribute-to-base conversion in Hybrid makes what would ordinarily be some very poorly performing queries (in either BSO or ASO) return much faster, while avoiding the data explosion penalty that would be paid attempting the same trick in BSO.

*2.4.2.2 Goals* Our benchmarking testing focused on three areas of performance. First is the time required to aggregate the database. This applies only to BSO, at least assuming that our Hybrid-ized BSO database has all noninput members (either dense or sparse) set to be dynamically calculated, in which case there are no upper-level blocks to create. Strictly speaking, Hybrid databases do not have to have every single-upper-level sparse member dynamic, in which case some aggregation might, in fact, be required. But we will ignore that possibility for these purposes and assume that the performance would fall between that of pure Hybrid and vanilla BSO. The second focus area was the amount of space required on the disk to store the databases. This applies to all three types; for Hybrid (again, with the caveat above), the size of the cube with just the input-level blocks size is the same as the total calculated cube. Third, and most interesting of all, we wanted to look at the query performance of the cubes. After all, even without Hybrid, we could set all the upper-level sparse members in a cube to be dynamically calculated, seeing the same benefits with respect to aggregation time and disk space consumption. However, anyone who has ever tried this with a realistically sized cube knows that upper-level query performance is correspondingly awful; presumably Essbase materializes in memory all the intervening blocks between the input data and the upper-level intersection queried.

*2.4.2.3 Dimension Counts* The actual dimension sizes of the test cubes are shown in Table 2.7. Where two figures are shown, these represent the actual versus stored member counts—the stored member count excluding any dynamically calculated member or any shared members, whether implied or explicit.

**Table 2.7**  Dimension Sizes of Test Cubes

| DIMENSION | BSO | ASO | HYBRID |
|---|---|---|---|
| HSP_Rates | 15 | N/A | 15/15 |
| Account | 3225/2800 | 3224/3192 | 3228/2800 |
| Period | 19/13 | 19/18 | 19/13 |
| Year | 7/7 | 7/6 | 7/7 |
| Scenario | 4/4 | 4/3 | 4/4 |
| Version | 3/3 | 3/2 | 3/3 |
| Currency | 3/3 | 3/2 | 3/3 |
| Product | 72,177/72,177 | 72,177/72,176 | 72,177/63,557 |
| PostCode | 45,468/45,468 | 45,468/45,467 | 45,468/43,589 |
| Analytic | N/A | 6/4 | N/A |
| Fx Rates | N/A | 14/13 | N/A |
| Product attribute 1 | 28 | 28 | 28 |
| PostCode attribute 1 | 1095 | 1095 | 1095 |
| PostCode attribute 2 | 31 | 31 | 31 |

A couple of dimensions in particular are worth calling out. First is the sizes of the Product and PostCode dimensions and the fact that these are the only sparse, aggregating dimensions. Second is the number of actual versus stored members for these two dimensions in the Hybrid cube. Note that the number of stored members is lower (by a few thousand) than the same dimensions in the regular BSO cube. This reflects that fact that the upper-level members have been set to be dynamically calculated.

### 2.4.2.4 Data Description

*2.4.2.4.1 Data Set*  To produce a sizeable volume of data for this application, we turned to Dan Pressman, who had written a sophisticated data generator to perform (originally) load testing on the Exalytics platform. Dan provided us with an input data set that would create blocks of 5% density and—more to the point—would create an awful lot of them. The data files, combined, were 16 GB in size when placed in an optimized, native export format and contained almost 1 billion input cells spread across approximately 80 million input rows.

For ASO, this is not a particularly large database—databases certainly exist in the wild with several billion input cells. For BSO, however, especially when combined with the large, deep, sparse dimensions—bringing with them the prospect of significant data explosion on aggregation—this is a monstrous size, probably to the point of being impractical without extremely powerful hardware. As will be seen, Hybrid appears to manage a cube containing this much input data quite comfortably. Our characterization is that Hybrid falls between the other two kernels, and that this is a moderate cube by its standards.

### 2.4.2.5 The Essence of BSO Data Explosion

*2.4.2.5.1 Aggregation Causes Upper-Level Members Combinations (Blocks) to Be Evaluated and Created*  For ASO, and for our Hybrid cube, there are no upper-level intersections to be preaggregated; they are all calculated as needed at query time. For BSO, this clearly is not the case. The genius of the dense-sparse paradigm of Bob Earle and Jim Dorrian is that the size of a multidimensional array to be calculated is not the size of all possible combinations, only the ones for which data actually exist. This is still, 20 years later, a very impressive invention, and in 1994, it doubtlessly made possible cubes that simply could not have existed without it on the type of hardware then available. However, developers and users are never satisfied, and—especially for operational reporting/business intelligence applications versus the old-school financial modeling that Essbase does so well—even the reduced size of the populated sparse array can become rather large.

In real cubes, the number of upper-level blocks is usually many times the number of input-level blocks. As the first sparse dimension is calculated, each input block results in the creation of blocks for however many ancestors it has in that sparse dimension. As the second sparse dimension is calculated, not only are the input blocks expanded in this fashion, but so are all the upper-level blocks created for the first sparse dimension. If more than two aggregating sparse dimensions are present, this process continues for each of them. In every case, the number of blocks is multiplied by some factor; the deeper the dimension (in terms of the number of members between the dimension root and the leaves), the larger the factor is. This is where the term *data explosion* comes from and is why ASO has historically been necessary to support requirements for cubes with, say, 10 or more aggregating sparse dimensions. Calculation log messages after a sparse aggregation show that aggregating the later dimensions typically takes much longer than aggregating the earlier dimensions; the earlier aggregations have fewer existing blocks and create fewer additional blocks as a result.

However, the number of input-level blocks does not change at all when a full database calculation is performed. Getting rid of the upper-level blocks, as Hybrid does, sidesteps the problem of data explosion. Of course, the question then becomes whether acceptable query performance can be maintained. The beauty of a fully stored, regular BSO cube is that every single existing value in the cube is simply sitting out in the .PAG file, waiting for users to come along and request it.

Careful readers might have spotted that the stored sizes of the sparse dimensions in our test cubes are not dramatically smaller in the Hybrid instance than the BSO one—several thousand members, yes, but out of several tens of thousands. Why does a relatively small number of upper-level (versus leaf) members account for such a huge volume of additional data? The answer is that the upper-level combinations are much more likely to be actually existing, i.e., populated. These are sparse dimensions; by convention, if not strictly by definition, they represent axes along which the vast majority of input-level combinations are not populated. Residents of any one of the 50,000 PostCodes are unlikely to have placed orders for more than a small percentage of all 70,000 available Products. However, at the other extreme—the very top of the trees—we are guaranteed that *any* input data whatsoever will result in a block for Product -> PostCode. At intermediate levels, the higher we go, the more likely we are to find populated blocks. This accounts for the impact that removing an apparently small number of upper-level members from consideration will have. The input-level grid is astronomical in scale but very sparsely populated. The upper-level grid is merely terrestrial but much more dense.

*2.4.2.6 How Big Is It in Essbase?*  Having discussed the theory at length, it is time to look at some empirical results. First, Figure 2.7 shows the time taken to load our input data set.

The BSO and Hybrid versions are in roughly the same ballpark. We were surprised to see that the BSO cubes with attributes converted to stored dimensions only took the same amount of time to load as the version with attributes, but on reflection, this does make sense. Since each base member is associated with one and only one member of each attribute dimension, converting attributes to regular dimensions does not actually increase the input-level block count at all. The ASO cube with stored "attributes" actually loaded more quickly than its sibling; we have no explanation for this—although again, the times are in roughly the same ballpark (within ~30 percent).

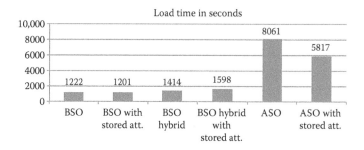

**Figure 2.7**   Comparing load time.

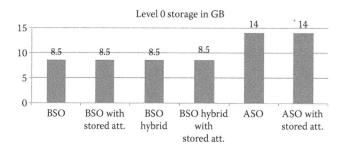

**Figure 2.8**   Comparing level 0 storage.

Next, Figure 2.8 shows the size of the input data.

As might be expected, given that the same number of blocks is being created, the BSO and Hybrid variants all consumed exactly the same amount of disk space. The ASO cubes again required a little more, and there was no variation between the two ASO versions.

*2.4.2.7 Converting Attributes to Base*   Before going on to the calculation and query performance testing results, a step back to discuss why we created the additional cube variants with pseudo-attribute stored dimensions. It is well known that attribute queries in BSO can have poor performance because they are effectively (and notoriously) dynamically calculated sparse dimensions. Attribute dimension queries in ASO follow complex rules too esoteric to fully describe here, but again, they have the potential for poor performance, especially when more than one attribute appears in a query. Hybrid does not currently support attribute queries (instead reverting to BSO mode) but apparently offers much better dynamic sparse performance; therefore, simply eliminating the attributes seemed an intriguing possibility.

*2.4.2.7.1 A Bad Idea in BSO*   In regular BSO, this approach doesn't work out so well, and we are reminded that data explosion is the primary reason for attribute dimensions to exist in the first place. Figure 2.9 shows the calculation time results for the BSO cubes with real and stored "attribute" dimensions.

There is no definite figure for the stored attribute variant because the test was abandoned at the point that the cube filled all of the available 1-TB disk storage (i.e., created 500

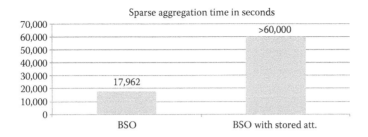

**Figure 2.9**  Sparse aggregation time.

.PAG files). In any case, 16 hours or more is unlikely to be a calculation window acceptable to users. Even the regular BSO aggregation is not especially speedy, taking around 5 hours. Not shown on this graph is that that aggregation created around 100 .PAG files (200 GB), hence the observation earlier that this is a large cube by BSO standards.

2.4.2.7.1.1 But What About Hybrid?   Hybrid, in contrast, handles this situation with no aggregation or disk space problems because there are no upper-level blocks to be created. The input-level block count (and storage requirement of approximately 8 GB) is, as with ASO, the final, total size of the database. However, there is presumably no completely free lunch, and at this point, we have to start looking at the query performance in more detail. We produced a number of test query sets, conforming to various general types, such as having sparse members in the grid, or in the point of view (POV), or having one or more attributes in the POV, etc. The individual queries themselves were randomized since hitting the same block over and over is (a) much less work for Essbase, because of caching, and (b) completely unrealistic with respect to real usage patterns. To gain some insight into whether Essbase or lower-level (i.e., storage or operating system) caching was having a significant effect, we ran each test set twice consecutively and compared the performance of the first and second passes.

The worst-case query for Hybrid (and ASO) is the top of both aggregating sparse dimensions, since every single input cell must be read and consolidated, on the fly. The results are remarkable (see Figure 2.10).

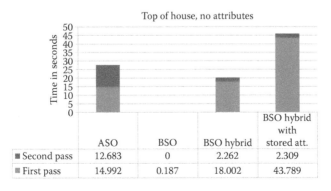

| | ASO | BSO | BSO hybrid | BSO hybrid with stored att. |
|---|---|---|---|---|
| ■ Second pass | 12.683 | 0 | 2.262 | 2.309 |
| ■ First pass | 14.992 | 0.187 | 18.002 | 43.789 |

**Figure 2.10**  Comparing query time for aggregating sparse dimensions.

Whether a retrieve time of 18 seconds (first pass; subsequent passes required close to two seconds) is acceptable is a valid question, but even with this extremely large database, Hybrid's performance was in the same general range as ASO. Hybrid with stored attributes did not perform quite as well, with an initial retrieve time of 44 seconds. Again, this fell to just 2 seconds on the subsequent pass.

The attribute query set results are also interesting. In this case, the times are the total execution time for a group of 25 queries. The 25 queries were generated randomly, but the same 25 are used in every case (see Figure 2.11).

With one attribute in the query POV, the Hybrid cube with real attributes performs much, much worse than any of the other options. This is not a particular surprise because Hybrid does not support attributes at present. The query is being processed as a regular BSO cube with fully dynamic sparse attribute dimensions. The result that really stands out, however, is the exceptional performance of the Hybrid cube with stored "attributes." In this case, the Hybrid cube performed many times faster than the ASO cube with regular attributes and almost as fast as the standard, calculated BSO cube with regular attributes.

As shown in Figure 2.12, the two-attribute case is more surprising: The Hybrid cube's disadvantage has all but disappeared. Our explanation for this effect is that BSO (remember, Hybrid is reverting to dynamic BSO for these queries) has to address

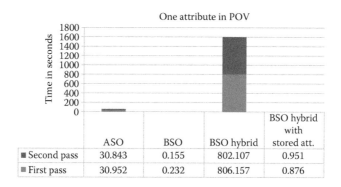

| | ASO | BSO | BSO hybrid | BSO hybrid with stored att. |
|---|---|---|---|---|
| ■ Second pass | 30.843 | 0.155 | 802.107 | 0.951 |
| ■ First pass | 30.952 | 0.232 | 806.157 | 0.876 |

**Figure 2.11**   Comparing query time with one attribute in POV.

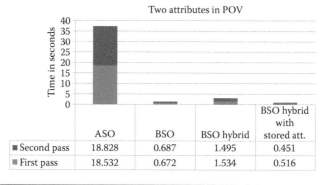

| | ASO | BSO | BSO hybrid | BSO hybrid with stored att. |
|---|---|---|---|---|
| ■ Second pass | 18.828 | 0.687 | 1.495 | 0.451 |
| ■ First pass | 18.532 | 0.672 | 1.534 | 0.516 |

**Figure 2.12**   Comparing query time with two attributes in POV.

and sum far fewer blocks when attributes from two different sparse dimensions are included in the query. Suppose that the average attribute member on the Product dimension filters down to 5% of Product leaves and, therefore, 5% of input-level blocks. Also suppose that the average attribute member on the PostCode dimension does the same thing. With no correlation between the distribution of input-level blocks on the Product and PostCode dimension, the total reduction in input-level blocks to be addressed would be 5% multiplied by 5%, or 0.25 percent of the total. This initially counterintuitive finding is a standard BSO effect, and it applies primarily when the two (or more) attributes are from different dimensions.

The ASO result in this case shows the well-known multiple attribute degradation; the Hybrid cube with stored "attributes" actually performs even better than regular BSO, which is encouraging.

*2.4.2.7.2 "Attributes" Are Now Useful for Reporting*  Taken together, a major benefit of Hybrid starts to become clear. First, even if we make all our attribute dimensions real, we have no increase in input-data size; because Hybrid does not store upper levels, this means no increase in database size, period—at least for a data set where attribute associations do not change over time. Second, Hybrid performs in the same ballpark or better than regular BSO on attribute queries (but—because it is hard to say this enough times—with absolutely no aggregation required). And third, we see that Hybrid generally performs as well as ASO, and in some cases better than ASO, with the single exception of very-high-level (e.g., dimension root) retrieves.

*2.4.2.8 Query Performance, or Why Those BSO Aggs Might Be Worthwhile*  We offer one final query testing result, and a little bit of respect for boring, circa-1994 Block Storage. In this test query set, no attributes are used, but members from both sparse dimensions appear in the query POV (see Figure 2.13).

This is yet another encouraging, ASO-beating result for Hybrid. No cheating is required via ASO's poor multiple attribute performance; Hybrid here performs better than ASO with the type of query that is usually the most common of all.

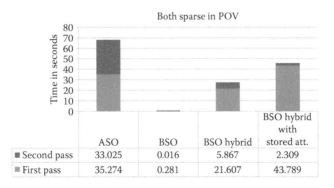

**Figure 2.13**  Comparing query results with both sparse dimensions in POV.

However, the BSO figures are truly remarkable, with the entire 25-query set retrieved in 0.281 seconds on the first pass and less than 2/100th of a second subsequently. Without taking anything away from the revolutionary potential of Hybrid, it's worth remembering that this is why we have historically accepted the pain of up-front aggregation time: Stored member queries are simple retrieval operations without any processing required beyond decompressing a single block.

### 2.5 Hybrid, the End of the Beginning

As noted in the beginning of this chapter, Hybrid is the future of Essbase. In two releases, Hybrid has gone from being little more than a rack and stack statement of technology direction with many restrictions on its use to an engine that has 80% of the functionality of BSO with all of the speed of ASO Essbase. It is the unification, finally, of the two Essbase engines. Who would refuse such a combination? You will develop in Hybrid because it is the union of the best of Essbase.

Developing an Essbase database will no longer include statements like the following:

- I can calculate everything in BSO, but how am I going to aggregate it?
- I can aggregate it with ease, but those complex allocations are impossible to figure out in ASO.
- I can calculate it in BSO, partition it to ASO, and report from there, but now I have to maintain and synchronize two databases and a partition definition. And I still need partial aggregations in the BSO source to perform allocations.

Instead, the design considerations will focus on the following:

- Can Hybrid do this natively?
- If not, what mix of stored and dynamic hierarchies can support the database requirements?

Note the brevity and simplicity of the second set of questions. Oracle is removing the complexity from Essbase. That is the promise of Hybrid, and that is why Hybrid is the future of Essbase. Hybrid allows you, the Essbase practitioner, to design solutions, not databases, while providing all of the functionality and power of today's BSO and ASO databases.

### 2.5.1 What's Coming to Hybrid?

Oracle is addressing Hybrid's limitations, but Hybrid has not yet reached BSO and ASO parity in some areas. Although the authors are not Essbase prophets, Hybrid must support some obvious functions for it to become the de facto Essbase engine. Table 2.8 lists these features.

**Table 2.8** Features Soon to Come in Hybrid

| ENGINE | FEATURE |
| --- | --- |
| BSO | DTS (in 11.1.2.4) |
| | Time balance (in 11.1.2.4) |
| | Cross-dimensional operators |
| | Hybrid calc scripts |
| | 100% of BSO calc functions |
| | Attributes |
| | TWOPASS and TOPDOWN calculations |
| | Report scripts |
| | Full partitioning support |
| | BSO to hybrid wizard |
| ASO | Solve order |
| | Paged outline file with the removal of BSO outline limits |
| | Materialized aggregations |
| | Configurable aggregate storage cache |
| | Full partitioning support |

### 2.5.2 What Will the Future Bring?

The case for Hybrid is compelling—all of the flexibility and power of BSO combined with the fast aggregation speed of ASO. Despite the promise, Hybrid still has elements that are incomplete and must be addressed before Hybrid becomes the default choice when creating a new Essbase database. The interim between the current unfinished state and the final nature of Hybrid will mean that Essbase practitioners will have to evaluate their application's suitability for Hybrid. As more features are added to Hybrid, this question will become one that is only rarely asked for the outlying BSO or ASO use cases.

Is Hybrid the ultimate expression of Essbase? Once complete, it is certainly the logical endpoint for the integration of BSO and ASO into one engine. What Essbase's product direction may be beyond Hybrid is unknown. What does seem likely, given the current level of investment, is that innovations in Essbase will continue.

Essbase is more than 20 years old, a mature software product by any measure. That it exists and is the subject of investment and improvements is testament to the uniquely powerful nature of the tool. Consultants, customers, and the authors of this book think Essbase is great. Hybrid is the proof that Oracle does as well. Essbase's best is yet to come.

## Acknowledgments

The catalyst for this book was the release of Hybrid Essbase. Steve Liebermensch and Gabby Rubin, the Oracle evangelists-in-chief of Essbase, believed in us and gave us unparalleled access and advice in the writing of this chapter. In addition, Kumar

Ramaiyer, head of Essbase development, and the hardworking developers of this book's subject—Essbase—made this chapter possible.

## Reference

Columbia University School of International Affairs. 1976. Napoleon Bonaparte. *Journal of International Affairs.* Book 27: 94.

# 3

# The Young Person's Guide to Essbase Cube Design

## Martin Neuliep

Contents

Perhaps you are a technology-savvy financial analyst, have just finished taking Essbase training, and are now facing building your first real Essbase application. You know how to build all the major components that make up an Essbase application, but how do you translate what your division controller is asking for into an actual Essbase design? How do you know you are headed in the right direction? Or perhaps you have one or two Essbase systems under your belt, but the experience of building them was not as straightforward as you thought it would be when you started, or the performance of the systems was disappointing when they were finished. Or perhaps you are an information technology (IT) professional who has worked with Essbase applications in your organization for some time, managing, administering, and maintaining them successfully, but now you are being asked to develop a new application based on relational databases that you know well. Where do you start? Will you be able to distinguish a good Essbase design from a bad one?

If any of these descriptions or questions resonates with you, you are the person this chapter is written for. It is assumed that you know what buttons to click and syntax to type to create Essbase application components such as outlines, rules files, calculation scripts, and so on. But just like Excel, Essbase is a blank slate. Sure, sample applications come with the product, but when you click OK in that Create Application dialog box for the first (or second, or third) time, nothing but an empty shell is staring you in the face, and it is totally up to you to create a useful design that will make implementation easy and performance good. You can learn the mechanics of how to build Essbase systems in lots of ways, but comparatively little has been written about what you should build. This chapter aims to provide you with the next level of information you need to succeed with Essbase after you've learned the basics of how it works.

With a good cube design in place, any difficulties you may encounter during implementation can usually be solved without too much pain. With bad cube design, solving problems after the fact is sometimes so difficult that it is easier to throw most of the system away and start over. Every one of the case studies in this chapter is based on actual Essbase cubes encountered in production at organizations whose names you would recognize. I hope they help you as you develop your Essbase design chops.

### 3.1 Is Essbase the Right Tool?

The first key to success with Essbase is to recognize whether it is the right tool to solve your problem. Essbase's multidimensional data model is not as general purpose as the relational model. It was designed to efficiently address a class of business problems, and it does that job very well indeed. Sometimes, with a little creativity, other problems can be cast in terms of a multidimensional model, and Essbase can be of value in unexpected places. Essbase Studio also provides a drill-through feature that lets you combine multidimensional analysis with relational queries, and this surprisingly infrequently used feature can be of enormous value. But you can definitely go too far and ask Essbase to do a job for which it simply is not suited. Here are some characteristics of Essbase that will help you decide on which technology to use.

### 3.1.1 Simple Size Limitations

Essbase was designed to allow fast access to summary information; it was never intended to be a transactional system. Because of this, it was not designed to handle the number of unique items you would see at a transactional level. So if you are the US Internal Revenue Service, you could not build an Essbase cube containing a Taxpayer dimension at the individual taxpayer level because Essbase (even using the Aggregate Storage Option [ASO]) has a limit on the total number of members in an outline in the tens of millions.

This is an area where the Essbase Studio drill-through capability can be very useful. Instead of building a Taxpayer dimension down to the individual level, you would stop at some higher summary level, say ZIP code. Since fewer than 50,000 ZIP codes are in use in the United States, you have no problem with Essbase limits. The drill-through feature lets users retrieve detail-level data that correspond to a particular cube cell. Drill-through is not a cure-all solution, however. For example, retrieving data for all the taxpayers in a ZIP code might return too much data, so you would need to configure drill-through to require additional dimensions to be part of the detail data query. But adding many dimensions to the drill-through query makes using the feature more difficult for users because they have to select lower-level members from more dimensions before drill-through is enabled. Drill-through also is not a workable solution if the lowest level of detail is needed within the cube itself, perhaps because you need to express calculations at that level. If this is the case, Essbase ceases to be a usable tool for your application.

Essbase does include an older feature called Hybrid Analysis that was intended to address dimension size limitations. (Do not confuse this older feature with the new Hybrid Essbase engine.) However, Hybrid Analysis imposes numerous restrictions on Essbase functionality and has never been a very popular solution.

### 3.1.2 Numeric Measures

Every cell in Essbase stores a number, even when you are using typed measures that look like they store text but do not—the predefined text values are simply mapped to numbers. If your application requires storing and manipulating large amounts of text, Essbase is not the tool to use.

### 3.1.3 Hierarchies

Essbase contains a multitude of features that assume your dimensions will be hierarchies and not just flat lists of values. Of course, a big flat list of members with a single parent is a very simple type of hierarchy, but if all the dimensions in your prospective cube have just one level of detail, you probably have a relational application, not a multidimensional one.

### 3.1.4 Nature of Calculations

Essbase was designed to handle certain families of calculations very well. They are easy to implement and run efficiently. Despite the differences between ASO and Block Storage Option (BSO), these calculations are most often found in financially oriented applications and include the following:

1. Consolidation: The simplest and most obvious calculation that Essbase does is driven by dimension hierarchies. Detail data roll up, most often by addition, to parent levels.
2. Simple formulas: These establish calculations among members of a dimension, often a (dense if BSO) dimension such as Accounts or Measures. Despite the fact that I call them simple formulas, they can do fairly complex work because of Essbase's rich set of numeric functions. Examples commonly include the results of driver-based forecast calculations.
3. Relationship-driven formulas: Technically, these are no different than any other formula, but I draw the distinction to emphasize Essbase's ability to base calculations on members relative to the cell being calculated or on attributes of members. For example, cost allocation formulas often reference a total cost by referring to an ancestor of the current member, say in an Organization dimension.

Recent enhancements to Essbase, in particular since version 11.1.2.3, have expanded the range of possible calculations that you can express in BSO in particular. For example, it is now possible to tackle a common financial calculation in BSO that previously (and still, if you are running a version of Essbase prior to 11.1.2.3) was not possible to express in a general-purpose way, namely, intercompany elimination. Intercompany elimination represents "backing out" data at a total level when the underlying data represent a transaction between two descendants of the total. For example, if Division A of a company sells its product to Division B of the same company rather than an external customer, that sale cannot be reported as part of the total sales for the company, even though it is reported for Division A. The sales from Division A to Division B need to be subtracted from the lowest common ancestor of Division A and Division B. Before version 11.1.2.3, about the only way to implement such a calculation in Essbase was to write a series of hard-coded formulas for all the possible intercompany activity. The resulting script is a maintenance headache because it will need to be changed whenever there is a related outline change. Calculation performance of such a script is usually not good, either. Version 11.1.2.3 contains numerous enhancements to functions that, in particular, enable you to determine the lowest common ancestor of two members. You can then use this dynamically determined member as the target of an assignment. An example of a formula attached to a member called Elim that takes advantage of these new features to create elimination values looks like this:

```
Elim(
  @Member(
    @Concatenate(
      @Name(
        @MemberAt(
          @Intersect(
            @Ancestors(@CurrMbr(Org)),
            @Ancestors(@Member(@SubString(@Name(@CurrMbr(Cust)),
              2)))
          ),
          1
        )
      ),
      "_E"
    )
  )
  =
  @Member(
    @Concatenate(
      @Name(
        @MemberAt(
          @Intersect(
            @Ancestors(@CurrMbr(Org)),
            @Ancestors(@Member(@SubString(@Name(@CurrMbr(Cust)),
              2)))
          ),
          1
        )
      ),
      "_E"
    )
  )
  -
  Input
  ;
)
```

(You can download calculation script and outline files for this example from the book's website.*) Some of the functions used in the above formula are new, and the formula also manipulates member names as strings, so the performance of such an approach is not yet well proven in a large number of real-world applications of varying scale.

Another design approach is to recognize that implementing the lowest common ancestor functionality in another tool such as a relational database is relatively

---

* http://developingessbasebook.com.

straightforward. Then, all that is required is to load intercompany data to the relational database, generate the required elimination data there, and load that generated data back to the Essbase cube. Depending on your cube design, the original intercompany data can be extracted from the cube or these can be obtained from other upstream data sources.

The question you will have to resolve is whether, for your particular application, the complex Essbase formula performs better or worse than the process of extracting, calculating in another tool, and reloading back to the Essbase cube.

### 3.1.5 Transactional versus Summary

Essbase is designed as an analytic system, not a transactional one. Its requirement that the outline be updated with appropriate metadata (with the restructuring that implies) before data with new members can be loaded imposes limits on the kinds of applications that can be built. Applications that require frequent metadata changes that must be immediately reflected to users will not work well with Essbase. Essbase has no built-in mechanism to write back to transactional level data outside of Essbase, only to the cube.

### 3.1.6 Nonfinancial Applications

Even though Essbase was designed with financial data in mind, don't think that you are limited to financial applications. Any application that fits with the other criteria in this section could well benefit from Essbase's capabilities. Organizations often miss out on all the benefits that multidimensional analysis can bring by limiting their applications to financial analysis only. Applications from customer satisfaction analysis to epidemiologic surveillance to petroleum storage tank utilization have been easily built and provided substantial benefits.

### 3.1.7 Custom Code

Essbase does provide several Application Programming Interfaces (APIs) that allow it to be customized and extended. In some cases, dealing successfully with some of the limitations presented here might be possible by writing customized processes that you integrate with Essbase. However, this approach will require a level of programming skill that is not always available in many organizations, increase the complexity of the implementation, and introduce possible dependencies on specific Essbase versions that may make migration to new versions in the future more difficult.

### 3.1.8 Case Study: Survey Analysis

Cycloanalysts, a nationwide retailer of bicycles, regularly sends satisfaction surveys to all its customers. The surveys ask for several types of demographic information from the customer, with about 50 questions about the customer's experience and satisfaction. The answers to all the questions, including the demographic information, are multiple-choice. The marketing department wants greater insight into their customers' responses and asked its IT department for some way to analyze the survey data. The key requirement was to be able to produce a crosstab report that showed all the answers to any question by all answers to any other question.

Having just completed their first Essbase implementation for Cycloanalysts' finance department, IT thought these requirements sounded like a match for Essbase. They built an ASO cube in which each question was represented by a separate dimension. Each dimension consisted of just two levels, one for the possible answers to the question and one for the total.

Results were mixed. On the one hand, getting basic results such as percentages of answers for each question was fast and easy, and generating the requested crosstab functionality was possible. On the other hand, Smart View's human factors were not ideal when connected to a cube with dozens of dimensions. The only drill-down performed was for just one level per dimension, so that aspect of Essbase was somewhat underutilized.

When Cycloanalysts' marketing department requested enhancements to calculate more advanced statistical analytics, they had to wait for the IT department to implement them in the cube. Marketing eventually concluded that Essbase was fine for basic results and crosstab reporting, but for more advanced functionality, they would investigate statistical packages and dedicated survey analysis software.

## 3.2 Dimension Content

Everything in Essbase revolves around dimensions, so it is critical to get the right dimensions with the right members established as your first design task. Everything else in the Essbase design and implementation process follows from this. Hierarchies are so common that recognizing them is usually not difficult. Building simple hierarchies is covered in every beginning Essbase training course, so there is no need to cover that here. But inexperienced Essbase designers often fail to correctly recognize the relationships between members so that dimensions can be designed in the most efficient way.

### 3.2.1 Member Relationships

When you begin to design your dimensions, you examine the members that your requirements dictate and you begin to look at the relationships between them to build hierarchies. Understanding one basic principle is critical: Many-to-one relationships are built within one dimension and many-to-many relationships are built using two dimensions. In the first case, the many members become children of the one member they are related to. In the second case, any member from the first set can be associated with any other member of a second set, which is to say that any possible combination of members from the two sets is an allowed relationship. This is the very definition of what the existence of two dimensions creates within an Essbase cube. But enough theorizing; seeing this idea in action is much easier.

### 3.2.2 Case Study: Level or Dimension?

Mick's Bag Company makes bags for the retail industry, including paper and plastic bags of all sizes at plants all around the country. They wanted to build a financial reporting cube and started by designing an Organization dimension. Mick's decided that the dimension needed three levels besides the total: Segment, Division, and Plant. These levels represent the levels of detail Mick's staff traditionally used to report on the business. Designing the Segment and Division levels was easy because they were well understood and everyone agreed on what they should be called. The problem arose when it came to the Plant level. The division under which to put a given plant was not clear. The problem was that a particular plant made bags for every division, so a plant's data couldn't all roll up to a particular division. So Mick's invented some artificial plant names, such as Plant1Division1, which represented the part of Plant 1's activity for Division 1. Now the new artificial names could be placed under the obvious division parent. But now there was another problem: There was no way to see the total activity for a whole plant. So another patch was applied to the design: Create alternate rollups of all the members for a given plant so the plant totals could be seen. The results are shown in Figure 3.1.

End users brought in to give early feedback about the design found the appearance of the dimension in Smart View confusing and asked if the system could be simpler. Mick's decided to call in some consulting help. The consultant gave the following feedback: Segment and Division were fine as levels in the Organization dimension because each division was associated with only one segment. But the relationship

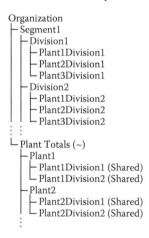

**Figure 3.1** Design using one dimension.

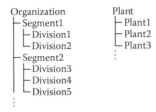

**Figure 3.2**   Design using two dimensions.

between plants and divisions was many-to-many and therefore plant and division should appear in separate dimensions. The consultant pointed out two things that should tip off Mick's Essbase team to consider splitting a proposed dimension into two: lots of member names that are composites of two other names, and lots of shared member rollups to get the subtotals required by users. Mick's decided to go with the two-dimension approach as shown in Figure 3.2.

### 3.2.3 Orthogonality

One of the most important characteristics of the dimensions you design is that they should all be orthogonal to each other. But what does this mean and why does it matter?

The simplest explanation of the concept of orthogonal dimensions is that dimensions must all be independent of one another. Your first reaction to this statement might be to say that Essbase dimensions are automatically independent, and, to some degree, you would be right. When browsing an Essbase cube with Smart View, you can certainly change the selected members of one dimension without having to change the members of another. So, to be more accurate, the meaning assigned to the members of each dimension should be independent of the meaning assigned to the members of the other dimensions. For example, if you have created a Product dimension in your Essbase cube, then everything semantically related to products should be contained in the Product dimension, or any of its associated attribute dimensions. You do not want any mention of products in any other dimension.

A somewhat ridiculous example may make the importance of this characteristic clearer. Consider the thermostat for your house's furnace and the thermostat in your kitchen's oven. You would normally assume that these two controls are completely independent of one another. If you turn up the heat in your house and the oven is on, you don't expect the temperature used to cook your dinner to change. But what if this was not true? What if the two thermostats had some kind of dependency or relationship? Now, if you raise the heat in the house, the oven temperature goes up...or perhaps down. This certainly makes it more challenging to avoid ruining dinner! Maybe a certain amount of fooling around with the two controls will allow you to figure out the relationship and you can run back and forth between them adjusting one and then the other so that you are comfortable and dinner is not burned or raw. But why would you want this? Of course, you would not.

Yet, surprisingly, finding Essbase cubes built with the data equivalent of this problem is not uncommon. Structures like that in Figure 3.3 are quite common.

In this case, there is also a Product dimension, but in the Account dimension, you see references to products. Why is this bad? One reason is that it is harder to browse the cube in an ad hoc way with Smart View. Let's say you were investigating the performance for product PROD1 and had arrived at a report that looks like Figure 3.4.

If you now want to look at PROD2, you cannot just change the product name in the point of view. You also have to change the sales account; otherwise, the sales data will disappear. You have to change the thermostats on both the oven and the furnace. As will be discussed later in this chapter, tracking all dimensions of a large cube simultaneously is already a pretty difficult cognitive task for users, so creating interdependencies between dimensions really is creating an unfair and unnecessary burden.

There is also a technical reason for avoiding interdependencies between members of different dimensions where possible. When you create these interdependences, you also simultaneously create cells in the cube space that have no logical meaning. The intersection of product PROD2 and account PROD3 Sales has no meaning and can never have a useful value, so why create a structure to hold such a value in the first place? These meaningless cells have the potential to slow cube performance, and they definitely make using the cube harder. We will see later in the chapter that it is desirable to design a cube so that all cells have potential meaning and this is a case where you should apply that principle.

Why do you so often see designs like this? In many cases, it is caused by old general ledger technology that allowed very limited dimensionality. Since many Essbase cubes are designed based on metadata that is sourced from general ledgers, Essbase cube designs often reflect the compromises made years ago when setting up the general ledger structures. If there was no easy way to represent the product sold as a separate item in the ledger, then the simplest thing was often to fold the product name into the chart of accounts, as you saw in the example above.

**Figure 3.3**   Product references in two dimensions.

|             | PROD1 | ACTUAL |     |     |
|-------------|-------|--------|-----|-----|
|             | Jan   | Feb    | Mar | Q1  |
| PROD1 Sales | –     | –      | –   | –   |
| Expenses    | –     | –      | –   | –   |
| Margin      | –     | –      | –   | –   |

**Figure 3.4**   Report investigating performance for PROD1.

| Month | Account | Value |
|-------|---------|-------|
| Jan | PROD1 Sales | 100 |
| Jan | PROD2 Sales | 200 |
| Jan | PROD3 Sales | 150 |
| Feb | PROD1 Sales | 110 |
| Feb | PROD2 Sales | 180 |
| Feb | PROD3 Sales | 170 |
| ⋮ | ⋮ | ⋮ |

| Month | Account | Product | Value |
|-------|---------|---------|-------|
| Jan | Sales | PROD1 | 100 |
| Jan | Sales | PROD2 | 200 |
| Jan | Sales | PROD3 | 150 |
| Feb | Sales | PROD1 | 110 |
| Feb | Sales | PROD2 | 180 |
| Feb | Sales | PROD3 | 170 |
| ⋮ | ⋮ | ⋮ | ⋮ |

**Figure 3.5** Mapping members into independent dimensions.

The solution to this problem is to design an effective data integration layer into your Essbase system that maps convoluted members like these into two or more separate members of independent dimensions, as in Figure 3.5.

Then you can get rid of the product-related children of Outside Sales in the Account dimension. In real life, of course, the data mapping will probably not be as easy as splitting the string with the account name. Rather, tables will need to be established to map individual account numbers into pairs of account numbers and product codes. This mapping will be required for both metadata and data. Use your favorite data integration tool, such as Oracle Data Integrator or Financial Data Quality Management Enterprise Edition, to split or remap the names as needed. The increase in development or run time will be well rewarded with increased usability and efficiency of the cube itself.

### 3.2.4 Case Study: Product or Entity?

This case study presents a more subtle example of the problem of independent dimensions. Spacely Space Sprockets makes numerous components for interplanetary spaceships. It has been in business for a long time and its product offerings are wide ranging. Spacely designed a basic finance cube and came up with, among others, the following two dimensions shown in Figure 3.6. The boxes represent levels of members in the dimension.

You probably have noticed two unusual things about these dimensions. First, the level called Division appears in both dimensions. Second, even though they are separate dimensions, they both are named something related to Organization. The first key to untangling the confusion is to observe that the Alternate Organization dimension's lowest level represents product lines. So despite its name, Alternate Organization actually represents a product view of Spacely. The cultural problem at Spacely is that, over

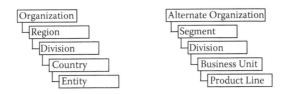

**Figure 3.6** Two dimensions from Spacely's finance cube.

time, they have given organization-sounding names like Business Unit and Division to what are essentially groupings of products.

This leads back to the first unusual thing about the dimensions. Again, over time at Spacely, the distinction between what was truly a grouping of organizational entities and what was a grouping of products became blurred, in no small part because of the nomenclature used. Nevertheless, having a Division view of data available was convenient, regardless of whether the discussion began from a product-related breakdown or an organization-related one. So Division was thought of in both contexts. When Spacely was run via a mass of spreadsheets, this was entirely possible; in the uncontrolled spreadsheet world, it is possible to make up any subtotal of anything and call it anything you like. It was even possible, by inventing sufficiently different member names, to replicate this structure in Essbase, even though it would look strange to an outsider.

The big problem arose when it came time to implement intercompany elimination calculations. Spacely required eliminations to be calculated for both of these dimensions. (Both the buyer and seller entity and product line were generally known for transactions within Spacely.) Instead of being a relatively straightforward exercise in dealing with each dimension's hierarchy separately, calculation of eliminations in the Organization dimension would have been very difficult. Because product-related breakdowns were intermixed with organizational ones, calculating the eliminations would have involved looking at the cross-product of both hierarchies.

Instead, the decision was made to remove the Division level from the Organization dimension. This left both dimensions as clean rollups of their respective lowest level members, with no semantic mixing between them. This made the elimination process much simpler, the cube smaller and more straightforward to navigate with Smart View, and with fewer intersections with no possible meaning. The only downside was that Spacely's analysts, who were used to the old hierarchies, had to adjust to the new, simplified approach.

### 3.3 How Many Cubes?

You now have a well-designed set of dimensions that will fulfill your users' requirements. A major part of the design task is now to decide how many cubes to construct out of the set of dimensions you have. Many people automatically assume the answer is one. But this decision is important and its outcome has a major impact on the usability and performance of the system. All too often, developers give little to no consideration to such a vital issue.

Let's look at the usability question first. In 1956, George A. Miller published a widely influential academic paper in psychology titled "The Magical Number Seven, Plus or Minus Two: Some Limits on our Capacity for Processing Information" (Miller 1956). To drastically oversimplify Miller's research, people seem to have the ability to remember roughly seven things at a time. (Miller's research is one reason telephone numbers in the United States are seven digits long.) Since the fundamental principle of a multidimensional cube requires us to remember something about each dimension simultaneously when interpreting the meaning of a given cell, you can see that a cube would be difficult to understand if it had more dimensions than you could effectively deal with simultaneously. Miller's paper points out that the magic number seven applies when remembering items from a single cognitive dimension, such as digits or letters. The magic number increases if the items are from more than one dimension, as they are, of course, in an Essbase cube, or if they can be "chunked" into related groups the way a Period and a Year dimension could be. Nevertheless, there is sound reason to believe that a cube with many more than seven dimensions or so is going to be hard for end users to interpret and thus use effectively. For that matter, it will also be harder for you as a developer if you have complex calculations to develop in such a cube.

For some people, the overwhelming temptation when building an Essbase system is to shovel everything possible into a single cube with the hope that all the users' requirements will be met somehow, somewhere in that seething mass of cells. The first mistake this approach makes is that it confuses Essbase with a data warehouse or mart. As shown in the previous section, Essbase is not intended to be a system that holds transaction-level information. Transaction-level data should live in your warehouse or mart; useful applications based on that data are built in Essbase. This implies that you know what the applications are beforehand and that you design your applications with specific uses in mind. Furthermore, the seeming simplicity of building any data you can find into one Essbase cube can often be an illusion. Numerous problems can flow from this decision. First, this approach is the pathway to performance problems. Even if Essbase advances such as ASO or Hybrid Essbase make such an approach technically possible, it is still not likely to be the fastest performing solution. And in 21 years of building Essbase solutions, I recall precisely zero instances of Essbase installations where the users or IT staff have said, "We wouldn't really mind if the system was slower." Second, as discussed above, the complexity of having to deal with everything simultaneously can greatly increase the cognitive burden on both users and developers. And third, that increased complexity often leads to subtle errors in calculations of rarely viewed portions of the cube that may not even be found until months or years have passed. Discovering such errors undermines user confidence in the system.

You need a much more intentional approach to cube design that avoids these problems as much as possible. An approach centered on business processes will accomplish this. Here is the approach at a very high level:

1. Understand and document all the users of the system by the processes they perform, including the dimensions required for each process.
2. Understand and document the calculation processes the system itself needs to perform, including the dimensions required.
3. Using a simple diagram process, design the smallest number of cubes that will meet the requirements but will not contain unneeded dimension combinations.

|          | One Big Cube   | Two Smaller Cubes |       |
|----------|----------------|-------------------|-------|
| Account  | 100 members    | 100               | 100   |
| Period   | 12 members     | 12                | 12    |
| Scenario | 3 members      | 3                 | 3     |
| Product  | 100 members    | 100               | 100   |
| Customer | 1000 members   |                   | 1000  |
| Plant    | 10 members     | 10                |       |
| Max Size | $3.6 \times 10^9$ | $0.0036 \times 10^9 + 0.36 \times 10^9 = 0.3636 \times 10^9$ | |

**Figure 3.7**   Cube design alternatives.

The fundamental idea of this design approach is simple: If no one (or no behind-the-scenes process) requires particular dimensions to be present simultaneously, then there is no reason to build a cube with all those dimensions present. This leads to a system with potentially more than one cube, but each one is smaller and less complex. And the sum of all the individual cubes is likely to be smaller than the one big cube, leading to performance benefits. For example, assume you know you have a set of data with the set of dimensions shown in Figure 3.7.

If you built a single cube with all these dimensions, the cube has a theoretical maximum of 3.6 billion cells. Then you discover that there is no process that needs the combination of Customer and Plant dimensions. You could build two cubes, one with all the dimensions except Customer and another with all dimensions except Plant. The maximum size of the first cube would be a thousandth of the one big cube and the maximum size of the second would be a tenth. Adding the two together still yields a system whose maximum size is barely more than a tenth of the one big cube. Of course, this is because when you combine dimensions in a single cube, you are multiplying sizes. Even if you had input data for this cube that were available by all six dimensions including both Customer and Plant, building the single cube might not be wise.

This example was intentionally simple to provide easy comparison between the sizes of different cube options. And this is a good time to point out that if these were the exact dimensions you had in real life, the one big cube might calculate so quickly that you would not bother to create the two smaller cubes because the savings in storage or time would be immaterial. But when dealing with large-scale Essbase implementations where the total number of dimensions may be much greater, the payback from a more efficient design can be much more significant. So let us look in more detail at how you might go through the design process.

### 3.3.1  First Step: Users and Processes

The process I am advocating is very much inspired by use case modeling. If you are experienced with this technique, you will find these steps familiar. This section provides only the briefest possible introduction to one or two use case modeling ideas, and

| Use Case | Dimensions |
|----------|------------|
| Finance Reports | Accounts, Periods, Scenario, Product, Customer |
| Manufacturing Reports | Accounts, Periods, Scenario, Product, Plant |
| Enter Monthly Sales Forecast | Accounts, Product |

**Figure 3.8**  Use cases and associated dimensions.

since the technique is so valuable, I recommend reading a good text on the subject. In the first step, you are identifying what in the use case world are called "actors." Actors represent roles that real people perform, so it is not important that you identify Chris Smith in particular, but rather that you identify the role of budget analyst, for example. In fact, Chris Smith may perform multiple roles, such as budget analyst and department administrator. It is important that you identify all the roles you expect for the system you are designing. Determining the roles is not important in determining the number of cubes per se, but knowing all the roles allows you to perform the next step.

Next, for each role, you identify all the ways in which that role interacts with the system, from a high-level business perspective. Each of these ways is a use case. Example use cases common in the Essbase world might be "Enter Monthly Forecast for Department," "Create Quarterly Reports," or "Investigate Request from Executive Management." Again, it is important to capture all the expected use cases for the system. Of course, when designing a system in its entirety, you need to determine many things about each use case (including identifying other necessary components beyond Essbase), but for the purposes of this chapter, the main thing to capture is a list of the dimensions needed to support the use case. For example, you might arrive at the list of use cases and associated dimensions shown in Figure 3.8.

### 3.3.2 Second Step: Calculation Processes

The second step is very much like the first except that, instead of focusing on real people and their roles as actors, you focus on the internal calculation processes. You identify all the major processes that are needed to transform system input into the necessary output demanded by the actors you identified in the first step. Examples of such processes could be "Allocate Fixed Costs to Products" or "Create Intercompany Elimination Data." Again, your goal is to identify all such processes along with the dimensionality needed for each, as in Figure 3.9.

| Calculation Process | Dimensions |
|---------------------|------------|
| Allocate Fixed Costs | Accounts, Periods, Product |

**Figure 3.9**  Calculation processes and associated dimensions.

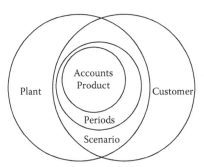

**Figure 3.10**  Graphical grouping of dimensions.

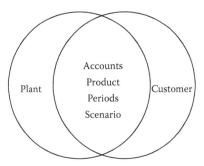

**Figure 3.11**  Minimum number of cubes without irrelevant dimension combinations.

### 3.3.3 Third Step: Cube Design Diagram

To design the cubes you need, you start by drawing a Venn diagram of the results from the first two steps. Draw circles for each process but show each dimension only once, overlapping the circles as needed. The diagram should look like Figure 3.10.

Then erase any circle that is completely contained within another circle. The remaining circles represent the minimum number of cubes needed to contain the dimension relationships you identified. You erased the completely contained circles because you need to build a cube for the outer circle anyway, and since the processes for the cube represented by the inner circle can be implemented with the larger cube, you do not need the smaller one. The resulting diagram looks like Figure 3.11.

### 3.3.4 Every Cell Means Something

The underlying goal of the previous process is to create cubes in which every cell has potential meaning. This does not mean that every cell will have a number in it, of course; sparse data are very much a fact of life. But at least you have built cubes in which there are no combinations of dimensions that will never be used and whose intersections are therefore meaningless. This is desirable because the big value of Essbase cubes is obtained when users are able to use Smart View to perform ad hoc queries to investigate business issues as they come up. (There are lots of tools, many of them simpler and cheaper than Essbase, that can crank out canned reports.) When users are interactively browsing through a cube, they become confused and lose context when the screen is filled with missing values because the cube was designed with a large percentage of intersections that have no meaning.

As a more advanced step, you can further refine the design process and get even closer to the goal of having every cell potentially mean something by recognizing that if a dimension appears in more than one cube, it need not contain exactly the same members in all of them. For example, you're likely to have an Account dimension in every cube but the specific accounts needed in one might not be the same as in another.

## 3.4  Designing for Change

When you first learn Essbase, you typically focus on how to build a cube that represents an organization at a point in time, for example, the products, accounts, customers, and so on that exist at the moment you build the cube. But in the real world, dimension members and their properties can be changing constantly. In the simplest case, new products, accounts, or customers appear and you need to add them to the cube. But the properties of existing members often change over time, and handling these changes in a way that meets users' needs can be challenging. That's what is covered in this section.

For the purposes of this discussion, the term *member properties* refers to anything about a particular member that is stored explicitly or implicitly in the outline. Probably the most important property of a member is where it appears in its dimension's hierarchy. Of course, other properties are also important: aliases, attribute associations, and a host of more system-related ones such as storage type, time balance, formula, solve order (in the case of ASO), etc. Different methods are required for handling property changes, depending on which properties are changing.

### 3.4.1  Changing or Unchanging?

When designing an Essbase system, you first design the dimensions for the requirements as you understand them to be when the system is to be launched. But you are not done with design at that point. For every dimension, you have to understand how the properties of the members of the dimension may change as the system operates over time. Some will never change: January will never move from its Qtr1 parent. On the other hand, the rollup structure of an Organization dimension might change frequently, at unpredictable times. The aliases for a set of products might change even more frequently. You should document every member property that you discover may change over the life of the system.

### 3.4.2  Restate or Preserve?

Next, you have to understand one very important characteristic for each of these changing properties: Is there a requirement to preserve the previous property for data already in the cube at the time of the property change? For example, if the Atlanta member is to move from the East region to the South region (i.e., its parent property is changing), is it important that Atlanta data continue to sum into East for data before the change and South for data after the change? Another way of asking this is: Does the cube have to continue reporting the East total as reported in the past, even if its children change in the future?

Unfortunately, if the answer to the previous question is yes, Essbase has no built-in features to automatically preserve historical results when dimension structures change (with one exception presented below). Fortunately, however, Essbase is used primarily as a management tool rather than a purely accounting tool. Management is usually concerned with reporting on the organization as it exists in the present and it often makes sense to compare historical data aggregated according to the current structure. So if you have an opportunity to influence the requirements, you'll have less work to do if restating history is acceptable.

But what do you do if your requirement is to preserve history as it was reported? The methods to deal with this requirement depend on which member property is changing. Let's first look at the most common case, in which a member's parent is changing. Three common ways of dealing with this requirement exist, each with their own advantages and disadvantages. First, you can design the system such that historical periods are never recalculated. Every calculation will need to be in a script that contains a Fix statement that excludes already calculated portions of the cube, such as historical periods, scenarios, or versions. From a structural standpoint, this is a simple solution: Move the member as required so that future calculations work as desired. But this method does have disadvantages. First, total members where one of the children has moved elsewhere no longer equal the sum of their remaining child members, which can result in reports that look misleading. Then, even worse, if source data for history should change and require restating, the hierarchy change will also become part of the restatement. The cube also becomes more difficult operationally. Your backup strategy must be to preserve the whole cube's data rather than just leaf-level cells. This strategy also does not work with ASO cubes because ASO computes parent-level values dynamically.

The second method for preserving history is to create new members. In the previous example, if Atlanta's parent is changing from East to South, do not actually change anything about the Atlanta member at all. Instead create a new member, say "Atlanta 2," as shown in Figure 3.12.

Then you will load all data after the change to "Atlanta 2" rather than Atlanta. This has the advantage that you can calculate any part of the cube at any time, which also works well with ASO. But, again, several disadvantages exist. First, users see two different names for Atlanta, which no choice of alias can completely disguise. If users want to see one member name for Atlanta across all time, there is no choice but to create yet another member, say "Atlanta Total," that is the sum of Atlanta and "Atlanta 2," as shown in Figure 3.13.

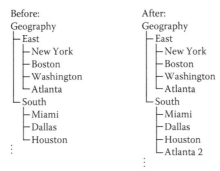

**Figure 3.12**  Preserving history by creating new member.

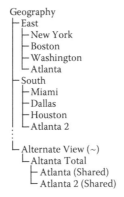

**Figure 3.13**  Additional complication when preserving history with new members.

As more and more changes occur over time, administering these alternate totals with their associated shared members becomes cumbersome.

The third method for preserving history is to say that cities and regions are completely independent of one another and therefore belong in different dimensions. You would slice the existing geography dimension in two, with everything from the cities down in one dimension and everything from regions and up in a second (see Figure 3.14).

Data must now be loaded to a combination of city (or whatever is the lowest level below city) and region. If a city moves from one region to another, this is simply a matter of loading its data to a new intersection whenever the change is effective. From an outline perspective, this is a simple solution. It can make the data integration task

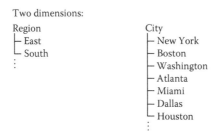

**Figure 3.14**  Creating two dimensions from one to preserve history.

more difficult, though. To use this approach, city and region must both be available in (or derivable from) the input data. The largest impact is on the user, who can no longer drill directly from a region to its cities when using a tool like Smart View. Instead, the user has to pivot another dimension into place and then drill down while taking care to suppress missing rows to avoid filling the report with unwanted cities.

As you can see, none of the three methods for preserving history when a member's parent changes is without some pretty severe drawbacks. You will have to pick the least painful one for your particular situation, or convince your organization that restating history is a good idea after all!

As you have just seen, preserving history when parents change is challenging. Essbase does provide the ability to preserve history when one particular kind of property changes. That property is attribute association. For example, you can declare that a member is associated with a particular attribute for January through June and a different attribute for July through December. In fact, you can make the association vary by combinations of members from more than one dimension. This Essbase feature is called "Varying Attributes" and can be employed manually with Essbase Administration Services or automated with Essbase Studio. (As of the writing of this chapter, conventional outline building rules files do not support Varying Attributes.) If you have not already learned about Varying Attributes, you can consult the Essbase Database Administrator's Guide and the Essbase Studio User's Guide.*

For one other property change, preserving history also is not too hard to deal with, and that property is formulas. If a formula needs to behave a certain way before a specific time and another way after, it is easy to modify the formula to check where in the cube it is executing and calculate appropriately. For any other member property, if you need to preserve history when that property changes, the only choice is the second method discussed for handling parent changes; namely, you have to create a second member with the changed property. For example, if you need a member's UDAs to change but preserve how they were set before some date, you really have no choice but to keep the old member unchanged and create a new member with the new UDAs, along with all the problems this method entails. Sorry.

For the sake of completeness, I will mention one additional way of keeping data available as it was reported historically when members or their properties change. You can simply make a copy of the cube before the change and then update the cube as desired. If users want to see historical values, they have to go back to the archived cube. If changes are infrequent enough, this method may be sufficient, but its disadvantages should be obvious: Reporting is not easy since users have to know which cube to access for reporting from a given era, and every time a new cube is created, more storage (and memory, if the cube is in its own application) is consumed.

---

* Database Administrators Guide: http://docs.oracle.com/cd/E57185_01/epm.1112/essbase_db/launch.html, and Essbase Studio User's Guide: http://docs.oracle.com/cd/E57185_01/epm.1112/essbase_studio_user /launch.html.

### 3.4.3 *Manual or Automated?*

Having now documented all the changing properties you will handle, and having decided whether history needs to be preserved when those changes are made, you now know what kind of outline changes will be required as the system operates. Your last decision is, how will those changes occur in operation? What is the source of information for each property that will change? Will an administrator be expected to make those changes or will you create an automated procedure to detect the property changes and create the required outline updates? In other words, what is your master data management strategy? Addressing all of the possible master data solutions available is beyond the scope of this chapter, but you should understand that this is a critical aspect of most Essbase applications; indeed, it is sometimes the most complex aspect.

## 3.5 Let Essbase Do the Iterating

One of the main reasons that Essbase is a practical tool for large-scale implementations is that, in many cases, it will repeat an instruction you give it many times across the cube space without you having to explicitly say so. This behavior is implicit in all the examples you see in beginning Essbase training, but it is worth examining a little more carefully. For example, if you write a formula in an Account dimension such as `Revenue = Units * Price;`, Essbase will automatically execute that formula for every other member combination in the cube, unless you specify not to. Similarly, if you use a security filter to grant write access to a particular set of Organization members, that write access will also apply to all other member combinations unless you specify otherwise. This behavior is the opposite of how spreadsheets generally operate, where you must explicitly put a formula into every cell where you want a calculated result. This behavior is essential in the large space of an Essbase cube. If you had to explicitly write or copy a formula to each calculated cell, you would never finish that task, for even a modest sized (by Essbase standards) cube.

Sometimes, manually repeating things in Essbase is appropriate. For example, when you are designing an Essbase cube, you virtually always have to represent time at least once and you then have the choice to keep time as a single dimension or split it into more than one dimension, say Year and Period as Hyperion Planning insists that you do in Figure 3.15.

The single-dimension design is sometimes preferable if you anticipate calculations that span years, such as rolling $n$-month averages, because the formulas are simpler to write. You do not have to write logic or use functions that switch to a different year member when shifting back from January or forward from December. But, as you can see, this design requires you to create repeated month and quarter members under each year. The two-dimension design in this case is a more natural fit for Essbase because it will create the multiple year–month combinations itself. End users also have

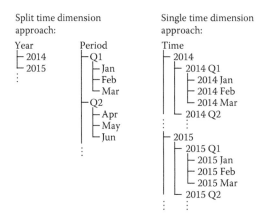

**Figure 3.15**  Time split into multiple dimensions versus one dimension.

more reporting flexibility with this approach, being able to put years on one report axis and months on another, which is not possible with the single time dimension design.

So Essbase is designed to automatically repeat. This means that under normal circumstances, the rules, filters, or other objects that you write are concise and explicitly reference only the things that are directly related to the business logic you are implementing. Sometimes, however, you may find yourself writing a calculation script and there seems to be no other way to get the job done than to write repeating sections of code over and over again, varying only slightly between repetitions. When this happens unexpectedly, it usually indicates a design flaw, often in the Essbase outline itself. The following case study illustrates how seemingly small errors in outline design can trigger difficulties down the line.

### 3.5.1 Case Study: Where Are the Accounts?

Watgo-Zupp Aircraft Manufacturers has built an Essbase application to help plan direct labor expense. One key part of the planning process starts by estimating headcount for all the various activities involved in producing airplanes. These headcounts are converted to hours at rates that are specific to each activity and hours are, in turn, converted to expense via another set of rates. Watgo-Zupp has built an Essbase cube to support this process, and updated results are expected from the cube for managerial review first thing each morning. Unfortunately, the cube calculation takes so long that there is barely enough time for it to complete between the time that user input is cut off the night before and the time the reports are required in the morning. Watgo-Zupp decided to bring in consulting help to determine why their cube's calculation performance was so poor.

The cube was examined, and at first glance, nothing appeared unusual about the cube, which contained the usual dimensions for such an application: Account, Time, Scenario, Department, and so forth. However, in addition to the Account dimension, there was a dimension labeled Measure (see Figure 3.16).

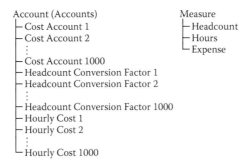

**Figure 3.16** Account and Measure dimensions.

When the poorly performing calculation script was examined, page after page of formulas that looked like this were found:

```
Fix(Hours)
    "Cost Account 1" = "Cost Account 1"->Headcount *
        "Headcount Conversion Factor 1";
    "Cost Account 2" = "Cost Account 2"->Headcount *
        "Headcount Conversion Factor 2";
    "Cost Account 3" = "Cost Account 3"->Headcount *
        "Headcount Conversion Factor 3";
...
```

And these were followed by many more pages that did the subsequent conversion to Expense:

```
Fix(Expense)
    "Cost Account 1" = "Cost Account 1"->Hours * "Hourly Cost 1";
    "Cost Account 2" = "Cost Account 2"->Hours * "Hourly Cost 2";
    "Cost Account 3" = "Cost Account 3"->Hours * "Hourly Cost 3";
...
```

This is a case where Essbase needed to do the iterating, not the calculation script author. But the author could perhaps be forgiven because underlying this suboptimal calculation script was a subtle flaw in outline design. The two sets of rates, the Headcount Conversion Factors and Hourly Costs, were placed in the wrong dimension. This was a natural enough mistake. Both these sets of rates seem as though they are accounts like any other, but in this case, they are not. If the original cube designer had been aware of the following principle, a much simpler calculation would have been apparent from the beginning.

When designing a cube, look for the dimension that represents the members among which most of the cube's calculations take place. Such a dimension will almost always be easily recognizable. Regardless of what you call it, this dimension should be the one tagged with the Accounts dimension type and (if BSO) should most likely have the Dense storage type.

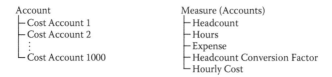

```
Account                          Measure (Accounts)
 ├─ Cost Account 1                ├─ Headcount
 ├─ Cost Account 2                ├─ Hours
 ⋮                               ├─ Expense
 └─ Cost Account 1000             ├─ Headcount Conversion Factor
                                  └─ Hourly Cost
```

**Figure 3.17**   Revised Account and Measure dimensions.

Watgo-Zupp's cube's primary job was to convert between Headcount, Hours, and Expense, involving two sets of rates. So Headcount Conversion Factor and Hourly Cost belong in the Measure dimension, not the Account dimension. The thousands of rate members collapse to two because they will be dimensioned by the cost accounts. The Measure dimension was the one truly acting as Accounts as far as Essbase is concerned and should have been tagged that way. The dimensions were revised (see Figure 3.17).

After making these changes, the calculation script was changed from thousands of lines to two:

```
Hours = Headcount * "Headcount Conversion Factor";
Expense = Hours * "Hourly Cost";
```

The changes did require some revision to the data load process because the two sets of rates were now being loaded to new member intersections. But after the changes were applied, the calculation time was reduced from eight hours to a few minutes.

### 3.6  Reusing Dimension Meanings

Many Essbase cubes that you see, especially when you first learn the product, contain one time related dimension (or possibly two, if split into Period and Year), one organization dimension, and so on. This seems natural. After all, the company using the cube is one organization, and how many kinds of time could there be? In fact, needing to build more than one dimension that seems to have the same meaning in a cube is quite common. The key word in the previous sentence is *seems*. The two dimensions that seem to be the same actually represent two different things in the real world. Because even experienced Essbase developers are sometimes confused by this idea the first time they encounter it, this section shows some common examples so you will be ready when you encounter this requirement.

#### 3.6.1  Case Study: Multiple Time Dimensions

Cogswell Cogs Company wants to build a sales analysis cube. Data extracted from Cogswell's sales management system are shown in Figure 3.18.

For every row, you can see that there are three dates: the date an order was entered, the date it shipped, and the date it was invoiced. So how do you design a time dimension

| Order Date | Ship Date | Invoice Date | Quantity | Item |
|---|---|---|---|---|
| 1/21/2015 | 1/22/2015 | 1/22/2015 | 17 | X42123 |
| 1/23/2015 | 1/30/2015 | 1/31/2015 | 8 | ABC456 |
| . | . | . | . | . |
| . | . | . | . | . |
| . | . | . | . | . |

**Figure 3.18**  Cogswell Cogs sales data extract.

for this? The answer, you may have guessed, is that you don't create one time dimension, you create three. (Assume that each dimension combines month and year.) This is perfectly fine because each time-related dimension records the month of a different event; each is completely independent from the other.

In the data warehousing world, if these data were represented in a star schema, chances are the fact table would be joined to a single time dimension table three times, making the names in the three time dimensions identical. But that approach does not work in Essbase, of course, because of the requirement to maintain unique names across all dimensions. Unless you are using Essbase's feature that enables duplicate member names (and most people find that feature makes Essbase more difficult to use), you will have to create unique member names in the three dimensions, as shown in Figure 3.19.

This works perfectly for the example data we saw, which was all completely additive. But issues arise when you have time balance accounts. The most obvious issue is that Essbase allows only one dimension to be tagged as Time. The time balance account will be summed across all the other dimensions, which is a problem when some of the others also represent time in some form. Your only choice is to skip Essbase's built-in time balance functionality and write custom formulas for such members. If your cube is ASO, the multidimensional expression (MDX) is not too difficult to write, using the MDX FirstChild or LastChild functions to calculate Time Balance First or Time Balance Last members, respectively. Until relatively recently, there were no equivalent functions available in BSO Essbase, making this type of calculation extremely challenging to write. However, version 11.1.2.3 of Essbase introduced two new functions, @RangeFirstVal and @RangeLastVal, which provide similar capability, and now you can implement custom time balance calculations. In general, the formula you write needs to check whether it is executing at a parent level in each of the cube's dimensions

**Figure 3.19**  Three time dimensions.

|          | P1 | P2 | P3 | Parent |
|----------|----|----|----|--------|
| Alt P1   | 1  | 2  | 3  | 3      |
| Alt P2   | 4  | 5  | 6  | 6      |
| Alt P3   | 7  | 8  |    | 8      |
| Alt Parent | 7 | 8 | 6  | 6 or 8? |

**Figure 3.20**  Difficulty with Skip Zero or Skip Missing.

and if so, return either the sum of the current member's children (if an additive dimension) or the appropriate time balance calculation (if one of the time dimensions).

One difficulty remains, though. As long as you are not using the Skip Zero or Skip Missing time balance functionality, the result that a custom time balance formula should return is well defined. This is not the case if you are using Skip Zero or Skip Missing. Figure 3.20 provides a small example to illustrate the problem.

Assume that the measure we are looking at should be treated as Time Balance Last, Skip Missing. Calculating the Parent values for the detail members of the alternate time dimension is easy, as is calculating the values for Alt Parent. But the detail value at the intersection of P3 and Alt P3 is missing. What should the result at the intersection of Parent and Alt Parent be? It is not clear whether the correct answer is 8 or 6. There really is not a correct answer, so it is best to avoid designing cubes with multiple time dimensions if you require time balance with skip functionality.

### 3.6.2 Case Study: From and to Organizations

Blinkenleitz Electronics makes a wide variety of electronic components and assemblies that they sell to other OEM electronic manufacturers. Because their products range from small basic components up to complex systems, very often, one department of Blinkenleitz will sell a basic part to another department to be used in building a more complex part. Because these intracompany sales account for a large proportion of sales for many departments, they must be understood in detail.

Blinkenleitz's IT group designs an Essbase financial reporting cube to support this analysis. It contains an Organization dimension that contains a hierarchy with department at the bottom, rolling up to the total company. Figure 3.21 shows the levels of this dimension.

The Organization dimension represents the entity that is selling a product. They also have a Customer dimension that represents the buyer. The Customer dimension contains a high-level list of Blinkenleitz's external customers but also needs to

**Figure 3.21**  Levels of Organization dimension.

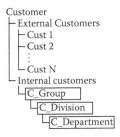

**Figure 3.22**  Customer dimension with internal and external customers.

represent the internal customers within the company. So the Customer dimension contains two branches and initially looks like Figure 3.22.

To satisfy Essbase's naming requirements, all the internal customer member names are the same as in the Organization dimension, except prefixed with "C_". Sales from one department to another are booked to an Internal Sales account and have a customer somewhere in the Internal Customers branch. Sales to other companies are booked to an External Sales account and the customer is in the External Customers branch.

In effect, the Organization dimension is duplicated inside the Customer dimension. After the system is in operation for a short time, it is observed that the Organization rollups are rarely used when looking at the buyer's (or customer's) point of view and are used only when analyzing from the seller's point of view. So as a performance improvement, the Blinkenleitz IT group removes some of the levels from the Internal Customers branch of the Customer dimension. The cube still meets all the analysis needs but calculates in less time.

### 3.6.3 Case Study: Medical Diagnoses

Lots o' Docs Medical Group wants to understand how their physicians compare with one another. They want to understand if one physician's outcomes and costs are different from another's for the same diagnosis. They build a cube prototype with the metrics that interest them. The prototype contains a Diagnosis dimension. The problem is that patients come to Lots o' Docs with more than one medical condition. The decision is made to add a Secondary Diagnosis dimension. The assumption is made that the first diagnosis listed in the patient's record is the primary diagnosis and the next one is secondary. This allows quite detailed analysis of combinations of diagnoses.

However, inspection of the detailed data used to feed the cube shows that an unexpected percentage of the records have more than two diagnoses. The number of diagnoses varies widely from patient to patient. Lots o' Docs decides to begin using the prototype cube but also decides that adding more diagnosis dimensions will make the cube increasingly hard to use. They decide to investigate other technologies besides OLAP to better handle the unpredictable number of diagnosis codes they encounter.

## 3.7 The Real Goal

The end of the chapter is here and we have covered a lot of ground. What should you understand about Essbase?

- Essbase is not a transactional database. Essbase is not a data warehouse. Essbase is an analytical application tool.
- Essbase manipulates numbers; that's it. But that's rather a lot.
- The more hierarchies that are part of your application, the better Essbase is suited to it.
- Essbase can do most financial calculations, some more easily than others. Do not be afraid to integrate other tools when Essbase is not a good fit.
- Lots of nonfinancial problems can be solved with Essbase's multidimensional data model.
- Many-to-many relationships mean multiple dimensions.
- One kind of thing in the real world lives in one dimension and no more.
- Essbase is used to build applications. Know your applications before you build them and build only what you need.
- Every cell in a cube should have potential meaning.
- Essbase really wants to restate calculations when dimensions change. You can get it to preserve history if you're willing to do a lot of work.
- If you find yourself repeating member names over and over in the outline or scripts or formulas, you might have made a design error.
- Hierarchies can appear multiple times in a cube, representing semantically different things. You will normally want to create unique names, however.

In fact, underlying most of the ideas in this chapter are just two fundamental aims: Make your cubes simple (both for you and your users) and make them perform fast. Simple is important because, as we saw earlier in the chapter, a multidimensional data structure is still a new concept to most users when they first encounter Essbase. Shock and awe are not your goals when launching a new Essbase system; user acceptance and productivity (dare I suggest delight?) are. No one cares that you wrote 50 pages of carefully crafted calculation script, or dozens of dazzlingly clever MDX formulas. Your organization mainly cares that your system gets the job done and is eagerly accepted by your users. User acceptance flows from how simple it is for new users to adapt to the system and simplicity stems from the principle of least astonishment. Whenever possible, the system should not surprise users with its behavior or results. This is key because the system you build is experienced for the first time all the time; all organizations experience turnover and new users are constantly coming to the system for the first time. If your system has a reputation for being hard to use, you will not build ongoing support for it, and, rather than growing and adapting to change, it will die. And that would be a shame because well-designed Essbase systems are a huge competitive advantage for those who employ them. Similarly, turnover is not limited to the user community. When you move on to another position, will the system you built be so complex that no one is able to make changes to it without breaking it? Ongoing support for the system has to come from the technical side of the house, too.

All the same arguments apply to the performance of your system. If your system is known to your IT group as a performance hog, you will not get their support, and again, your system will die when they find another technology to take its place. In my experience, simplicity and good performance are often linked. Come to think of it, perhaps there really is only one underlying idea in this chapter. I have seen as many (maybe more) Essbase systems perform poorly because they were too complicated as because they weren't sophisticated enough. Look for the simple solution and you will usually find the fast one at the same time. There usually are simple solutions to be found in Essbase, even to complex problems—it is an astoundingly powerful tool. If you refuse to be satisfied by bad Essbase implementations and search for the underlying ideas that lead to elegant solutions, you will stay on a path to constant growth, and so will your organization.

## Acknowledgments

I am grateful to Tim German, director, Qubix, and Ron Moore, solutions architect, TopDown Consulting, for their thoughtful suggestions, and to Katy O'Grady for helping the ideas shine through the words more brightly. I am especially grateful to Carol Blotter and Mitch Rubin for sharing their wisdom, experience, and guidance with a certain new consultant some time ago.

## Reference

Miller, G.A. 1956. The magical number seven, plus or minus two: Some limits on our capacity for processing information. *Psychological Review* 63:81–97. Available at http://psychclassics .yorku.ca/Miller/.

# 4

# ESSBASE PERFORMANCE AND LOAD TESTING

TIM GERMAN

Contents

## 4.1 Why Build Tests?

Most Essbase developers will, sooner or later, be placed in the uncomfortable position of being asked to vouch for the performance of a so-called system that exists only as a quick prototype—or perhaps even just as notes scrawled on a whiteboard. Alternatively, he or she may be asked to start writing and optimizing calculation scripts when the IT department announces that the anticipated data feeds are going to be delayed another couple of months. Or perhaps the business users want to add three more dimensions to an existing system averaging 500 concurrent users and would like some reassurance that retrieval times will not skyrocket when the changes are dropped into production.

One very common response to these types of situations is to make an intelligent guess, based on the limited available information, accumulated experience, and rules of thumb. In this chapter, I hope to point out some more methodical possibilities in three specific areas:

- Test data
- Test queries
- Automated load generation

On none of these topics do I have simple answers that are anywhere near as fast as the grizzled veteran's finger in the air. But spending time developing a more sophisticated approach will, at minimum, allow the developer to justify his or her hunch to the people writing the checks. And if the results are *not* as expected, some expensive and embarrassing mistakes might be prevented.

## 4.2 Test Data

### 4.2.1 Realistic Data Volume

For Block Storage Option (BSO) applications, the size of the input data set is a factor in both the number of input-level blocks and the number of blocks created by subsequent calculation operations. Writing compressed blocks to storage media (of whatever variety), reading them from storage, compressing, uncompressing, and processing are generally understood to be the major determinants of BSO performance; all things being equal, the fewer blocks, the better. For Aggregate Storage Option (ASO) applications, the size of the input data set is a factor in the number of rows in the bitmap "heap," which must be scanned (possibly in its entirety) when retrieving query results.

For both legacy engines—and, by association, for Hybrid Essbase—the need for a realistic volume of data to determine realistic performance is intuitively understood.

### 4.2.2 Realistic Data Distribution

Less well understood is the significance of the *content* of the input data set to accurate performance prediction or measurement. The way in which the data are distributed across the multidimensional space defined by the outline plays an important role for both BSO and ASO. Even the particular numeric values appearing in the data can have an impact (albeit a smaller one) since they affect compression. In this section, I will address BSO first.

*4.2.2.1 Demonstrating the Significance of Distribution in BSO*   Consider the two input data sets in Tables 4.1 and 4.2 prepared for the Sample.Basic application.

Both data sets contain the same number of rows (10); they have the same size. However, when loaded to an empty cube, data set A will create only one block

**Table 4.1**   Data Set A

| PRODUCT | MARKET | SCENARIO | YEAR | MEASURE | DATA |
|---------|--------|----------|------|---------|------|
| "100-10" | "New York" | "Actual" | "Jan" | "Sales" | 123.45 |
| "100-10" | "New York" | "Actual" | "Feb" | "Sales" | 123.45 |
| "100-10" | "New York" | "Actual" | "Mar" | "Sales" | 123.45 |
| "100-10" | "New York" | "Actual" | "Apr" | "Sales" | 123.45 |
| "100-10" | "New York" | "Actual" | "May" | "Sales" | 123.45 |
| "100-10" | "New York" | "Actual" | "Jun" | "Sales" | 123.45 |
| "100-10" | "New York" | "Actual" | "Jul" | "Sales" | 123.45 |
| "100-10" | "New York" | "Actual" | "Aug" | "Sales" | 123.45 |
| "100-10" | "New York" | "Actual" | "Sep" | "Sales" | 123.45 |
| "100-10" | "New York" | "Actual" | "Oct" | "Sales" | 123.45 |

**Table 4.2**   Data Set B

| PRODUCT | MARKET | SCENARIO | YEAR | MEASURE | DATA |
|---------|--------|----------|------|---------|------|
| "100-10" | "New York" | "Actual" | "Jan" | "Sales" | 123.45 |
| "100-20" | "California" | "Actual" | "Jan" | "Sales" | 123.45 |
| "200-10" | "Massachusetts" | "Actual" | "Jan" | "Sales" | 123.45 |
| "200-20" | "Oregon" | "Actual" | "Jan" | "Sales" | 123.45 |
| "200-30" | "Texas" | "Actual" | "Jan" | "Sales" | 123.45 |
| "300-10" | "Washington" | "Actual" | "Jan" | "Sales" | 123.45 |
| "300-20" | "Oklahoma" | "Actual" | "Jan" | "Sales" | 123.45 |
| "300-30" | "Illinois" | "Actual" | "Jan" | "Sales" | 123.45 |
| "400-10" | "Louisiana" | "Actual" | "Jan" | "Sales" | 123.45 |
| "400-20" | "Ohio" | "Actual" | "Jan" | "Sales" | 123.45 |

("100-10" -> "New York") while data set B will create 10. The differences do not stop there, as loading is only the first step for a typical BSO application. An aggregation of data set A produces blocks at the following sparse intersections:

"100-10" -> "New York" (the input block)
"100-10" -> "East"
"100-10" -> "Market"
"100" -> "New York"
"100" -> "East"
"100" -> "Market"
"Product" -> "New York"
"Product" -> "East"
"Product" -> "Market"

In other words, loading data set A to Sample.Basic and aggregating it will result in the creation of a total of nine blocks.

**Table 4.3**   Data Set C

| PRODUCT | MARKET | SCENARIO | YEAR | MEASURE | DATA |
|---------|--------|----------|------|---------|------|
| "200-10" | "New York" | "Actual" | "Jan" | "Sales" | 123.45 |
| "200-30" | "New York" | "Actual" | "Jan" | "Sales" | 123.45 |
| "200-40" | "New York" | "Actual" | "Jan" | "Sales" | 123.45 |
| "200-10" | "Massachusetts" | "Actual" | "Jan" | "Sales" | 123.45 |
| "200-30" | "Massachusetts" | "Actual" | "Jan" | "Sales" | 123.45 |
| "200-40" | "Massachusetts" | "Actual" | "Jan" | "Sales" | 123.45 |
| "200-10" | "Florida" | "Actual" | "Jan" | "Sales" | 123.45 |
| "200-30" | "Florida" | "Actual" | "Jan" | "Sales" | 123.45 |
| "200-40" | "Florida" | "Actual" | "Jan" | "Sales" | 123.45 |
| "200-10" | "Connecticut" | "Actual" | "Jan" | "Sales" | 123.45 |

Data set B produces dramatically different results. Running a sparse aggregation results in the creation of an additional 65 blocks, for a total of 75.* In summary, two input data sets of nominally identical size result in block counts differing by a factor of more than eight, proof—if any were required—that the size of test data is not alone a sufficient condition for realistic performance tests.

The obviously contrived example above took advantage of the BSO dense-sparse paradigm, loading all the cells in data set A (see Table 4.1) to a single block.

A more important point is that, even without dense dimension cheating—for example, even if each block contains only a single populated intersection—the distribution of input-level data can produce significantly different numbers of (to use a kernel-agnostic term) populated upper-level intersections.

*4.2.2.2 Sparse Distribution Effects*    The two data sets in Tables 4.3 and 4.4 repeat the exercise from Section 4.2.2.1, but this time, without populating more than one cell in any block.†

When data set C is loaded to Sample.Basic, 10 blocks are created. The same goes for data set D, which should not be a surprise because data set D is identical to data set B. Again, the aggregation of the database after loading data set D creates a total

---

* I will spare you the list. However, both data sets, along with all sample data and code discussed in this chapter, are available for download at www.developingessbasebook.com.

† Which cell (or cells) is populated has an impact on the size of upper-level blocks (or the size of the value portion of a specific row in the bitmap heap); if the only cell populated at level 0 is "Actual" -> "Jan" -> "Sales," then upper-level blocks will be no larger than input-level blocks. If a different single cell is populated in each input-level block, the upper-level blocks will be larger. I am going to assume this is a secondary-level effect, swamped by block count (or, incidentally, for ASO, bitmap heap size) in real-world data sets.

**Table 4.4**   Data Set D

| PRODUCT | MARKET | SCENARIO | YEAR | MEASURE | DATA |
|---------|--------|----------|------|---------|------|
| "100-10" | "New York" | "Actual" | "Jan" | "Sales" | 123.45 |
| "100-20" | "California" | "Actual" | "Jan" | "Sales" | 123.45 |
| "200-10" | "Massachusetts" | "Actual" | "Jan" | "Sales" | 123.45 |
| "200-20" | "Oregon" | "Actual" | "Jan" | "Sales" | 123.45 |
| "200-30" | "Texas" | "Actual" | "Jan" | "Sales" | 123.45 |
| "300-10" | "Washington" | "Actual" | "Jan" | "Sales" | 123.45 |
| "300-20" | "Oklahoma" | "Actual" | "Jan" | "Sales" | 123.45 |
| "300-30" | "Illinois" | "Actual" | "Jan" | "Sales" | 123.45 |
| "400-10" | "Louisiana" | "Actual" | "Jan" | "Sales" | 123.45 |
| "400-20" | "Ohio" | "Actual" | "Jan" | "Sales" | 123.45 |

of 75 blocks. The aggregation of the database after loading data set C creates only the following upper-level blocks:

"200-10" -> "East"
"200-30" -> "East"
"200-40" -> "East"
"200-10" -> "Market"
"200-30" -> "Market"
"200-40" -> "Market"
"200" -> "New York"
"200" -> "Massachusetts"
"200" -> "Florida"
"200" -> "Connecticut"
"200" -> "East"
"200" -> "Market"
"Product" -> "New York"
"Product" -> "Massachusetts"
"Product" -> "Florida"
"Product" -> "Connecticut"
"Product" -> "East"
"Product" -> "Market"

This adds 18 to the original 10 input-level blocks, for a total of 28. Therefore, to conclude, even without the reduction of blocks afforded by having multiple input values hit the same block, it is possible to create test data sets of identical input size, which produce databases that differ in calculated size by a factor of more than two.

*4.2.2.2.1 Distribution across Dimensions*   Evidently, the distribution of input-level data across dimensions is relevant to the creation of accurate test data. Eagle-eyed readers may have noticed the concentration of input data from data set C in non-diet Root Beer products and East region states. This resulted in the relatively small number of upper-level blocks compared with data set D, in which blocks were more widely distributed across both the Product and Market dimensions.

Investigating the distribution of data in some cubes would be interesting, but Essbase does not make this information available. Instead, the user must create a custom tool. The following Perl program consumes a level 0 columnar export and spits out the distribution of data across the level 0 members of each dimension.[*,†]

A quick note on Perl: I am neither attempting nor qualified to teach it. The scripts appearing in this chapter use Perl because it is good at processing text files (such as data exports) and it is available on every platform that will also run Essbase. Equivalent programs could very well be written in PowerShell, or awk/sed, or the language of your choice. The scripts in this chapter are all functional but should not necessarily be regarded as exemplars of Perl excellence.

**Perl Program: CountBlocks.pl**

```
#!/usr/bin/perl
# process columnar export file given in first parameter
# display number of blocks existing for sparse members
# found in column given by second parameter. column
# containing last sparse dimension must be given by
# third parameter (i.e. the count of sparse dimensions)

use warnings;
use strict;

use Text::ParseWords;

my %frequency;
my $prev_sparse = '';
my $sparse;
my @fields;

open lev0, $ARGV[0];

while (<lev0>) {
    if ($. > 1) { # skip export 'header' line
        @fields = parse_line(' ', 1, $_);
        $sparse = join(' ', @fields[0..$ARGV[2]-1]);
        if ($sparse ne $prev_sparse) {
            $frequency{$fields[$ARGV[1]-1]}++;
        }
        $prev_sparse = $sparse;
    }
}
```

---

[*] Perl implementations exist for many platforms (and certainly all on which Essbase can be run). See http://www.perl.org.

[†] A native export, the type more commonly used for backups, etc., will not work. Columnar exports contain one member from all but one header dimension on each row. ASO databases will not produce columnar exports, unfortunately.

```
foreach my $member (sort desc_frequency keys %frequency) {
    print $member, " ", $frequency{$member}, "\n";
}
sub desc_frequency {$frequency{$b} <=> $frequency{$a}}
```

Note that this simple program works only with a single export file; individual export files must be processed separately and the results summed.

The above program, CountBlocks.pl, can be used to analyze the Sample.Basic input data by loading the (default) calcdat.txt file and extracting a level 0 columnar export. The level 0 columnar export (named Lev0.txt in these examples) is processed with the following commands:

```
perl CountBlocks.pl Lev0.txt 1 2
perl CountBlocks.pl Lev0.txt 2 2
```

These two commands extract the distribution of level 0 blocks across the Product and Market dimensions, respectively. The second parameter indicates the column in which the relevant dimension appears; the third parameter indicates the number of sparse dimensions in the extract file.

The results are as shown in Tables 4.5 and 4.6.

Clearly, these are unlikely to be distributions derived from a random allocation (a statistics major can calculate the confidence interval!). On the other hand, Sample

**Table 4.5** Market Input Block Frequency Distribution in Default Sample.Basic Data

| MARKET | BLOCKS |
| --- | --- |
| Utah | 12 |
| California | 12 |
| Nevada | 11 |
| Oregon | 11 |
| Colorado | 11 |
| Washington | 10 |
| Illinois | 9 |
| Wisconsin | 9 |
| Florida | 9 |
| Missouri | 9 |
| Iowa | 9 |
| Ohio | 9 |
| New York | 8 |
| Oklahoma | 7 |
| Louisiana | 7 |
| New Hampshire | 7 |
| New Mexico | 7 |
| Texas | 7 |
| Connecticut | 7 |
| Massachusetts | 6 |

**Table 4.6**   Product Input Block Frequency
Distribution in Default Sample.Basic Data

| PRODUCT | BLOCKS |
| --- | --- |
| 300-10 | 20 |
| 100-10 | 20 |
| 200-10 | 20 |
| 200-20 | 17 |
| 400-10 | 16 |
| 100-20 | 16 |
| 300-30 | 16 |
| 400-20 | 12 |
| 400-30 | 12 |
| 200-30 | 9 |
| 100-30 | 8 |
| 300-20 | 8 |
| 200-40 | 3 |

.Basic is not a real-world data set. Repeating the above process for a much larger production database containing general ledger data produces more interesting results. In this case, with several hundred members in each dimension, I have shown the results as a graph (Figure 4.1). The $x$ axis (unlabeled) is the set of populated level 0 Entity dimension members, ordered by descending number of level 0 blocks. Visualizing the block distribution in this way makes immediately clear that the data are not distributed evenly. In this particular case, there is a very long tail of Entity members with a small number of blocks.

The distribution of data across cost centers is shown in Figure 4.2. The shape of the graph is similar to the Entity one.

*4.2.2.2.2 Clustering*   So far, I hope this chapter has demonstrated that a realistic data set requires both accurate volume and accurate distribution. Unfortunately, the characterization of distribution as frequency across each dimension is potentially inadequate. This is due to the fact that, for some pairs of dimensions, the data for a particular member in one dimension are more frequently associated with a particular

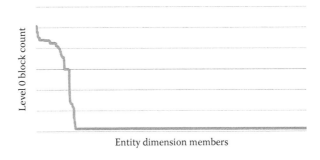

**Figure 4.1**   Entity distribution of a real-world GL cube.

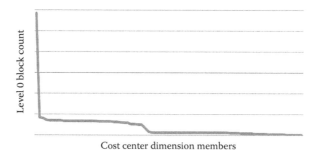

**Figure 4.2**   Cost center distribution of a real-world GL cube.

member or set of members in another dimension. Cola, for example, may be more frequently sold in East region states. A real-world example might be that most of the data for expense account "Computer Software Support Fees" appear against IT cost centers.

Consider the data sets in Tables 4.7 and 4.8. These two data sets have three properties that are interesting in combination. First, the volume of data is the same. Second, the distribution of data across the Product and Market dimensions is identical (and also even, in this particular case, although that isn't necessarily so in general), as shown in Tables 4.9 and 4.10

**Table 4.7**   Data Set E

| PRODUCT | MARKET | SCENARIO | YEAR | MEASURE | DATA |
|---------|--------|----------|------|---------|------|
| "100-10" | "New York" | "Actual" | "Jan" | "Sales" | 123.45 |
| "100-10" | "Connecticut" | "Actual" | "Jan" | "Sales" | 123.45 |
| "100-30" | "New York" | "Actual" | "Jan" | "Sales" | 123.45 |
| "100-30" | "Connecticut" | "Actual" | "Jan" | "Sales" | 123.45 |
| "200-10" | "California" | "Actual" | "Jan" | "Sales" | 123.45 |
| "200-10" | "Oregon" | "Actual" | "Jan" | "Sales" | 123.45 |
| "200-30" | "California" | "Actual" | "Jan" | "Sales" | 123.45 |
| "200-30" | "Oregon" | "Actual" | "Jan" | "Sales" | 123.45 |

**Table 4.8**   Data Set F

| PRODUCT | MARKET | SCENARIO | YEAR | MEASURE | DATA |
|---------|--------|----------|------|---------|------|
| "100-10" | "New York" | "Actual" | "Jan" | "Sales" | 123.45 |
| "100-10" | "California" | "Actual" | "Jan" | "Sales" | 123.45 |
| "100-30" | "Connecticut" | "Actual" | "Jan" | "Sales" | 123.45 |
| "100-30" | "Oregon" | "Actual" | "Jan" | "Sales" | 123.45 |
| "200-10" | "New York" | "Actual" | "Jan" | "Sales" | 123.45 |
| "200-10" | "California" | "Actual" | "Jan" | "Sales" | 123.45 |
| "200-30" | "Connecticut" | "Actual" | "Jan" | "Sales" | 123.45 |
| "200-30" | "Oregon" | "Actual" | "Jan" | "Sales" | 123.45 |

**Table 4.9** Product Distribution
in Data Sets E and F

| PRODUCT | CELLS |
|---------|-------|
| "100-10" | 2 |
| "100-30" | 2 |
| "200-10" | 2 |
| "200-30" | 2 |

**Table 4.10** Market Distribution
in Data Sets E and F

| MARKET | CELLS |
|--------|-------|
| "New York" | 2 |
| "Connecticut" | 2 |
| "California" | 2 |
| "Oregon" | 2 |

Third, while each data set produces the same number of input-level blocks (eight), data set E creates 23 upper-level blocks for a total of 31, while data set F creates 33 upper-level blocks for a total of 41.

This difference occurs because in data set E, the East region data (for New York and Connecticut markets) fall into "100" family Product members, while the West region data (for California and Oregon) fall into "200" family Product members. In data set F, on the other hand, both East and West regions' data are spread across "100" and "200" products. For the purposes of this chapter, this property of multidimensional data will be called "clustering."

*4.2.2.3 ASO Considerations* The above discussion relates primarily to BSO, but equivalent features exist in ASO applications. First, the ASO compression dimension functions similarly to a single dense dimension (Pressman 2012, 225–274). An example similar to the one in Section 4.2.2.1 can be created to take a 10-cell data set and produce either (a) a 10-row bitmap heap with just one member of the compression dimension populated in each or (b) a single-row bitmap heap with 10 members of the compression dimension populated.

Second, although in BSO, different distributions of a data set having the same basic size can result in a variable number of upper-level blocks, for ASO, the analogue is the size of upper-level aggregate views. If no aggregate views exist, then this is not a factor in database size. However, data distribution still has an impact upon query performance.

*4.2.3 Are Random Data Good Enough?*

Of course, some of my examples above were contrived to show the greatest possible difference. A more sophisticated and reasonable approach might be to generate random test data.

In fact, there is a quasi-official tool for doing this: ESSCMDQ. ESSCMDQ has been publicly available for some years, although it is not part of a default installation of the Essbase client. Originally, ESSCMDQ was written for use by internal Quality Assurance to perform testing, and in consequence, it exposes functions not present in the generally available ESSCMD. At the time of writing, its most common use is to perform ASO outline compaction, a feature inexplicably missing from MaxL (and the generally available ESSCMD). However, another little-known ESSCMDQ command is "FILLDB." No documentation is currently available for ESSCMDQ beyond a short PDF file describing the ASO outline compaction process, and Oracle provides no support for the utility.* However, the command continues to work through 11.1.2.3.500. Creating test data with ESSCMDQ can be very simple:

```
:::[0]->LOGIN "localhost" "admin" "password" "Sample" "Basic"
Login:

[Mon Jan 01 12:00:00 2014]Local////Info(1051034)
Logging in user [admin@Native Directory]

localhost:Sample:Basic:admin[1]->FILLDB
FillDb:

FillDb in progress (Hit <Esc> key to cancel).
FillDb completed
```

Running the above sequence of commands results in the Sample.Basic statistics shown below. In keeping with the "old school" vibe, I used ESSCMD's GETDBSTATS command—this is a subset of the output:

```
LOCALHOST:Sample:Basic:admin[1]->GETDBSTATS
GetDbStats:

-------Statistics of Sample:Basic -------

Actual Maximum Blocks                         : 475
Number of Non Missing Leaf Blocks             : 260
Number of Non Missing Non Leaf Blocks         : 0
Number of Total Blocks                        : 260
Average Block Density                         : 10.41667
Average Sparse Density                        : 54.73684
Block Compression Ratio                       : 0.159204
Average Clustering Ratio                      : 1
Average Fragmentation Quotient                : 0
```

In particular, note that 260 "leaf blocks" have been created. Since the leaf-level member counts of the two sparse dimensions Product and Market are 13 and 20, respectively, this represents 100% of potential leaf-level blocks. The average block

---

* An SR raised with Oracle Support confirmed this.

density is 10.42%—on closer examination, the first and then every subsequent 10th dense cell in each block has been populated.* These are evidently the defaults for FILLDB—create every single leaf-level block with (approximately) 10% density.

In summary, FILLDB created all possible input blocks, with each having both the same density and the exact same dense cells populated in each block. This may be a sufficient condition for testing performance in cubes with 100% dynamic dense calculations, but users would likely prefer test data that followed a more realistic distribution.

FILLDB also accepts three optional parameters:

- Maximum disk space consumption in MB
- The leaf-level block density (in place of the 10% default). Note that FILLDB never creates upper-level blocks, even when disk space consumption is specified to be higher than all leaf-level blocks
- The interval between created blocks, presumably according to default outline order of level 0 blocks (in place of the "0" default)†

Two final comments about FILLDB: First, it actually launches a server-side process, rather than generating and sending data from the client. Viewing sessions in Administration Services will show a "Fill Data Base" (sic) request running after FILLDB is launched, even if the ESSCMDQ client session is terminated. Second, it does not "play nice" with ASO databases.‡ The command runs for a minute or two but returns an error message and does not create any data.

At least one existing, publicly available, third-party test data application, the Cube Data utility by Jason Jones, implements a very similar technique. Cube Data randomly selects a member from each dimension for every input cell and accepts a "fill factor" parameter to determine the ratio of generated to potential intersections. Cube Data has a significant advantage in that it will also generate data for ASO cubes.

The criticisms of the random approach to test data generations that appear in this section are not directed at these utilities (nor their authors!). For many purposes, this method is entirely appropriate; highly accurate performance testing is generally not one of them.

I demonstrated above that that different distributions can produce radically different numbers of upper-level blocks, but that example was deliberately contrived and used the very small Sample.Basic database. It is instructive to repeat the process with

---

* Populating every *n*th cell results in a density that is approximately the reciprocal of *n*. In Sample.Basic (where a block contains 192 stored cells), populating the first then and every 10th cell results in 20 populated cells per block and a density of 20/192 = 10.42%. For more information with respect to the precise derivation of the block density statistic, see my blog post on the topic: http://www.cubecoder.com/reverse-engineering-block-density-statistics/.

† For more details, see the explanation of block numbering in the Database Administrator's Guide: https://docs.oracle.com/cd/E40248_01/epm.1112/essbase_db/dcacaord.html#dcacaord10635.

‡ Tested in version 11.1.2.3.500.

a real-world application (or any real-word BSO application of the reader's choice), comparing the following:

1. The actual number of upper-level blocks produced by aggregating the actual input-level blocks
2. The number of upper-level blocks created by generating the same number of input-level blocks with a random process (the FILLDB command)

For the purposes of the exercise, I selected a real-world cube having

- Approximately 60,000 input-level blocks
- Block density of 2.4%
- Approximately 1,000,000 potential level 0 blocks

I then ran FILLDB with the following parameters to generate an equally sized but randomly distributed equivalent data set.

1. Maximum disk space consumption of 999,999 MB. This value must be high enough to ensure that disk space does not terminate the data generation process before the required number of blocks has been created.
2. Block density of 1%. The density of the real-world cube can be disregarded; block density is irrelevant to the block count exercise, so this is simply an arbitrarily low value. The size of the .pag file may, of course, vary depending on the block density selected, but again, this is not relevant to a simple block count comparison.
3. The interval between created blocks set to 17. Ideally, FILLDB would accept an input parameter of number of blocks to create, but that is not how the utility was designed. So instead it is necessary to calculate—to the nearest integer—the potential number of level 0 blocks divided by the target number of blocks. The potential number of level 0 blocks is not the number of potential blocks visible in database properties; that is the potential number of blocks at all levels. I calculated the value as the product of the count of stored level 0 members from each sparse dimension (around 1,000,000 in this case). So the chosen interval is 1,000,000/60,000 = 17.

The requisite count of stored level 0 members from each sparse dimension is, incidentally, also not an available statistic in Administration Services or MaxL. It is not the number of stored members per dimension seen in EAS because that includes stored upper-level members. The correct value can be extracted most easily for each dimension with a multidimensional expression (MDX) query, such as the following example counting stored level 0 Product dimension members from Sample.Basic. The (undocumented) SHARED_FLAG property filters unwanted shared members, while the MEMBER_TYPE property excludes formula members:

```
WITH MEMBER [Measures].[ProductCount] AS
'Count(Filter(Filter([Product].Levels(0).Members, NOT [Product].
```

```
CurrentMember.SHARED_FLAG), [Product].CurrentMember.MEMBER_TYPE <>
2))'
SELECT {[Product]} ON AXIS(0),
       {[Measures].[ProductCount]} ON AXIS(1)
  FROM [Sample].[Basic];
```

An alternative option is to take a copy of the cube and delete all upper-level members from each sparse dimension; then the values in EAS will be correct. But the MDX solution is, let us hope, easier! The Applied OLAP Outline Extractor could also be used.

In any case, having decided on values for each parameter, the complete ESSCMDQ command sequence for this example is as follows:

```
LOGIN servername username password
SELECT appname dbname
FILLDB 999999 1 17
```

In this particular test (on a modestly specified development server), FILLDB created approximately 1500 blocks per minute, so be warned that this experiment may take some time with larger databases.

After the FILLDB process was run, the cube was calculated. The results of this example, at least, confirm the theory. Random data from FILLDB, having produced the same number of level 0 blocks as the real-world data, create more than twice the number of upper-level blocks.*

Returning to the original issue, it appears that the uneven distribution and clustering of real-world data render it more manageable for Essbase than random data. This should not be a surprise, as Essbase was always designed as a tool to deal with the real world. But it does have implications for the generation of test data, with is the subject of the next section.

### 4.2.4 A New Generator

Writing a completely generic data generator is beyond the scope of this chapter; however, the following shows the development of a very simple example using Structured Query Language (SQL) to generate data for Sample.Basic. For a realistic data generator, configuration is (as will be shown) nontrivial, to the point of requiring as much thought and effort as actually writing code. Garbage in, garbage out applies.

---

* Random data would actually produce slightly fewer level 0 blocks; given the way target data size is specified in FILLDB, one would have to be very lucky to hit precisely the same block count.

*4.2.4.1 Building and Populating Dimension Tables* The first step (required for pretty much any data generation scheme) is to create dimension tables. Each table will contain six fields:

1. Member Name: self-explanatory
2. Path: this is a fixed-length string field to be populated with the name of each ancestor of the member listed in the Member Name field. The field is fixed-width to make finding the ancestor at any particular level easy in code. This is not efficient from a storage point of view, but this is hardly a consideration in the Sample.Basic case. The first (level 1) ancestor name starts at position 1, the second at position 81, the third at position 161, and so on
3. Level: this contains the level number of the member. Level number can be ambiguous in ragged hierarchies; where this is the case, each member will be assigned the highest of the possible level numbers
4. Input: a 0 or 1 flag indicating whether data should be generated for the member. It will be 1 (i.e., true) only for unshared, nonformula, level 0 members
5. WeightFrom: this contains one part of the member weighting; its exact function is discussed in more detail below
6. WeightTo: this contains the second part of the member weighting

The table creation scripts for the tables are as follows, with each dimension being identical except for the table name.*

```
CREATE TABLE [Product] (
        [MemberName] [varchar](80) PRIMARY KEY,
        [Path] [char](800) NOT NULL,
        [Level] [int] NOT NULL,
        [Input] [int] NOT NULL,
        [WeightFrom] [int]  NULL,
        [WeightTo] [int]  NULL);
```

Note that these tables should be created and populated for each base (i.e., not attribute) dimension, leaving Weight NULL for the time being. The tables should be populated with unshared members only.† For Sample.Basic, doing this manually is easy; for larger, real-world databases, the Applied OLAP Outline Extractor would get most of the way there, with the construction of the Path requiring a little post-processing.‡ Various other options are possible (an API program, XML export with an XML parser, etc).

The Product table, for example, will look like Table 4.11. Note that ~ replaces multiple spaces in the Path field so that the records can be shown on one page.

---

* This is SQL Server syntax.
† Insert scripts to accomplish this (along with object creation scripts) for Sample.Basic are available at www.developingessbasebook.com.
‡ http://www.appliedolap.com/free-tools/outline-extractor.

**Table 4.11** Data Generator Product Table; WeightFrom and WeightTo Fields as Yet Unpopulated

| MEMBER NAME | PATH | LEVEL | INPUT | WeightFrom | WeightTo |
|---|---|---|---|---|---|
| 100 | Product | 1 | 0 | NULL | NULL |
| 100-10 | 100~Product | 0 | 1 | NULL | NULL |
| 100-20 | 100~Product | 0 | 1 | NULL | NULL |
| 100-30 | 100~Product | 0 | 1 | NULL | NULL |
| 200 | Product | 1 | 0 | NULL | NULL |
| 200-10 | 200~Product | 0 | 1 | NULL | NULL |
| 200-20 | 200~Product | 0 | 1 | NULL | NULL |
| 200-30 | 200~Product | 0 | 1 | NULL | NULL |
| 200-40 | 200~Product | 0 | 1 | NULL | NULL |
| 300 | Product | 1 | 0 | NULL | NULL |
| 300-10 | 300~Product | 0 | 1 | NULL | NULL |
| 300-20 | 300~Product | 0 | 1 | NULL | NULL |
| 300-30 | 300~Product | 0 | 1 | NULL | NULL |
| 400 | Product | 1 | 0 | NULL | NULL |
| 400-10 | 400~Product | 0 | 1 | NULL | NULL |
| 400-20 | 400~Product | 0 | 1 | NULL | NULL |
| 400-30 | 400~Product | 0 | 1 | NULL | NULL |
| Diet | Product | 1 | 0 | NULL | NULL |
| Product | | 2 | 0 | NULL | NULL |

Having created and populated tables for Year, Measures, Product, Market, and Scenario, the user should give thought to the population of the Weight column.

*4.2.4.2 Sparse Distribution and Clustering* The purpose of the WeightFrom and WeightTo fields is to distribute data according to real-world frequency (or a best estimate of real-world frequency if no real data are yet available). For example, if twice as much input data are expected for 100-10 as for 100-20, then the range of weighting for 100-10 should be twice as large as the weighting for 100-20. The WeightFrom and WeightTo values for 100-10 could be 1 and 20, respectively, while for 100-20, they could be 21 and 30, respectively (there must never be overlap or gaps in the weight distribution). Note that this is not quite as simple a question as "What are the relative (e.g.) sales for 100-10 vs. 100-20?" The question is, instead, "For how many Period/Scenario/Measures/Market combinations are 100-10 data expected relative to 100-20?"

A first step might be to apply weightings to each input-level member (only), assuming that the weightings will cover a range of 1 to 100. This could be scaled as appropriate for larger dimensions.

One data generation method would be to apply a weight value to each dimension, which, in conjunction with a random number function, will be used to create as many intersections as are required.* For, example, assume the WeightFrom and

---

* Technically pseudo-random, but you know what I mean.

WeightTo fields are assigned to the Scenario member Actual as 1 and 50, respectively. The WeightFrom and WeightTo fields are assigned to the Budget member as 51 and 100, respectively. For each piece of data to be generated, a random number between 1 and 100 is created. Values between 1 and 50 result in a piece of Actual data being generated. Values between 51 and 100 result in a piece of Budget data being generated. In the long run, 50% of data will be generated for Actual.

For example, Table 4.12 shows the Product table with a distribution applied to the WeightFrom and WeightTo fields.

Note that the input members only are given values that follow the outline order sequence, with no gaps. A similar distribution can then be applied to the Market dimension, as shown in Table 4.13.

At this point, a query can be written to generate sparse intersections according to these weightings.

**Sparse intersection generation:**

```
SELECT sm.MemberName AS Market,
       sp.MemberName AS Product
  FROM (SELECT CEILING(RAND()*100) AS MarketWeight,
               CEILING(RAND()*100) AS ProductWeight) AS sw
       INNER JOIN Market sm ON sw.MarketWeight
          BETWEEN sm.WeightFrom AND sm.WeightTo
       INNER JOIN Product sp ON sw.ProductWeight
          BETWEEN sp.WeightFrom AND sp.WeightTo;
```

**Table 4.12**  Data Generator Product Table, WeightFrom and WeightTo Populated

| MEMBER NAME | PATH | LEVEL | INPUT | WeightFrom | WeightTo |
|---|---|---|---|---|---|
| 100 | Product | 1 | 0 | NULL | NULL |
| 100-10 | 100~Product | 0 | 1 | 1 | 20 |
| 100-20 | 100~Product | 0 | 1 | 21 | 37 |
| 100-30 | 100~Product | 0 | 1 | 38 | 55 |
| 200 | Product | 1 | 0 | NULL | NULL |
| 200-10 | 200~Product | 0 | 1 | 56 | 65 |
| 200-20 | 200~Product | 0 | 1 | 66 | 72 |
| 200-30 | 200~Product | 0 | 1 | 73 | 76 |
| 200-40 | 200~Product | 0 | 1 | 77 | 80 |
| 300 | Product | 1 | 0 | NULL | NULL |
| 300-10 | 300~Product | 0 | 1 | 81 | 84 |
| 300-20 | 300~Product | 0 | 1 | 85 | 88 |
| 300-30 | 300~Product | 0 | 1 | 89 | 92 |
| 400 | Product | 1 | 0 | NULL | NULL |
| 400-10 | 400~Product | 0 | 1 | 93 | 96 |
| 400-20 | 400~Product | 0 | 1 | 97 | 98 |
| 400-30 | 400~Product | 0 | 1 | 99 | 100 |
| Diet | Product | 1 | 0 | NULL | NULL |
| Product | | 2 | 0 | NULL | NULL |

**Table 4.13**  Data Generator Market Table, WeightFrom and WeightTo Populated

| MEMBER NAME | PATH | LEVEL | INPUT | WeightFrom | WeightTo |
|---|---|---|---|---|---|
| New York | East~Market | 0 | 1 | 1 | 10 |
| Massachusetts | East~Market | 0 | 1 | 11 | 17 |
| Florida | East~Market | 0 | 1 | 18 | 22 |
| Connecticut | East~Market | 0 | 1 | 23 | 26 |
| New Hampshire | East~Market | 0 | 1 | 27 | 30 |
| East | Market | 1 | 0 | NULL | NULL |
| California | West~Market | 0 | 1 | 31 | 44 |
| Oregon | West~Market | 0 | 1 | 45 | 49 |
| Washington | West~Market | 0 | 1 | 50 | 53 |
| Utah | West~Market | 0 | 1 | 54 | 57 |
| Nevada | West~Market | 0 | 1 | 58 | 60 |
| West | Market | 1 | 0 | NULL | NULL |
| Texas | South~Market | 0 | 1 | 61 | 68 |
| Oklahoma | South~Market | 0 | 1 | 69 | 72 |
| Louisiana | South~Market | 0 | 1 | 73 | 76 |
| New Mexico | South~Market | 0 | 1 | 77 | 80 |
| South | Market | 1 | 0 | NULL | NULL |
| Illinois | Central~Market | 0 | 1 | 81 | 85 |
| Ohio | Central~Market | 0 | 1 | 86 | 90 |
| Wisconsin | Central~Market | 0 | 1 | 91 | 94 |
| Missouri | Central~Market | 0 | 1 | 95 | 96 |
| Iowa | Central~Market | 0 | 1 | 97 | 98 |
| Colorado | Central~Market | 0 | 1 | 99 | 100 |
| Central | Market | 1 | 0 | NULL | NULL |
| Market | | 2 | 0 | NULL | NULL |

Running this query 10 times produces the output shown in Table 4.14.

This is all very nice, and certainly better than random data. However, applying weights to each dimension provides no mechanism for reproducing the clustering effect between sparse dimensions discussed in Section 4.2.2.2.2.* Suppose that 50% of data relate to Colas products and 50% to Root Beer and, similarly, that 50% of data relate to East region markets and 50% to West. This is represented pictorially in Figure 4.3; the values in the grid show the proportion of data falling into each Market/Product combination.

However, suppose the objective is to produce data clustered such that 80% of the Colas data are in East markets and 80% of the Root Beer data are in West markets, as shown in Figure 4.4.

It is still the case that 50% of data are in East markets and 50% in Colas products, but no combination of weightings applied independently to Market and Product will produce this distribution. To achieve this type of distribution, the selection of a member in one sparse dimension must skew the selection of members in a different

---

* For ASO, all but the compression dimension should be regarded as "sparse."

**Table 4.14**  Sparse Intersection Generation

| MARKET | PRODUCT |
|---|---|
| Nevada | 100-10 |
| Texas | 100-20 |
| Connecticut | 100-20 |
| Massachusetts | 100-20 |
| Texas | 100-10 |
| New York | 200-30 |
| Connecticut | 200-10 |
| Utah | 100-10 |
| Louisiana | 300-10 |
| California | 300-20 |

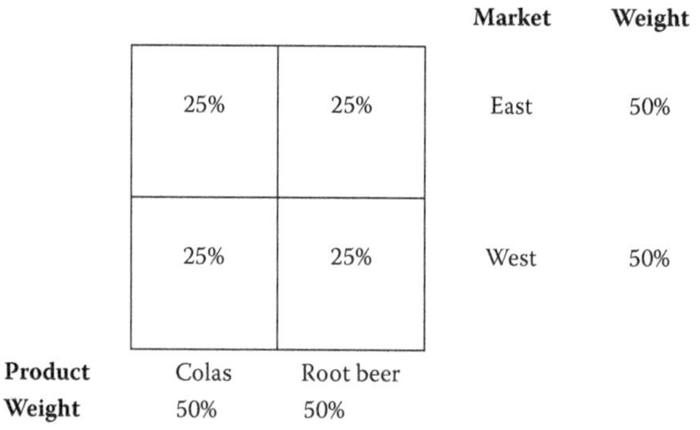

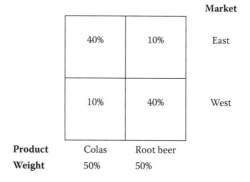

**Figure 4.3**  Per-dimension distribution results.

**Figure 4.4**  Clustered distribution.

dimension. One dimension must be regarded as a driver, with another dimension as a target. With real-world data, deciding which sparse dimension is the driver and which dimension(s) is (are) the target may have to be a judgment call.

An additional table is required to contain these data, mapping the members of the driver dimension to members of the target dimension(s) and assigning a distribution. Say that, for Sample.Basic, Market is the driver, with Product as the target. A suitable table can be created with the following structure:

```
CREATE TABLE [Cluster](
     [Market] [varchar](80),
     [Product][varchar](80),
     [WeightFrom] [int]  NULL,
     [WeightTo] [int]  NULL,
     CONSTRAINT Cluster_PK
        PRIMARY KEY ([Market], [Product]));
```

However, the configuration of this table is hard work if all possible level 0 combinations must be assigned a weight. Even Sample.Basic has 260 of them! Real-world databases will certainly have both larger sparse dimensions and a larger number of sparse dimensions (the technical concept of "sparse dimension" does not apply directly in ASO, but we can still identify dimensions that have the same sparse distributions). Potential sparse combinations will frequently run into millions, if not billions. The task of assigning weightings to each of the level 0 combinations is perilously close in magnitude to creating test data manually. At this point, the reason for including each member's ancestor path in the dimension tables (Section 4.2.4.1 above) may become apparent. Instead of assigning a weight to every sparse level 0 combination, the user can specify upper-level groupings, as in the example in Table 4.15.

Note that the 1–100 weights are repeated for each Market. The clustering can be defined at any level in each sparse dimension, but the entire dimension must be used at the same level each time.

A modified query can now be used in place of the sparse intersection generation query shown above. Most of the additional complexity in this query is due to recalculating the WeightFrom and WeightTo values of the Product table so that the range of

**Table 4.15**  Content of Cluster Table with Upper-Level Weights

| MARKET | PRODUCT | WeightFrom | WeightTo |
| --- | --- | --- | --- |
| Central | 100 | 1 | 10 |
| Central | 200 | 11 | 30 |
| Central | 300 | 31 | 60 |
| Central | 400 | 61 | 100 |
| East | 100 | 1 | 80 |
| East | 200 | 81 | 87 |
| East | 300 | 88 | 94 |
| East | 400 | 95 | 100 |
| South | 100 | 1 | 25 |
| South | 200 | 26 | 50 |
| South | 300 | 51 | 75 |
| South | 400 | 76 | 100 |
| West | 100 | 1 | 20 |
| West | 200 | 21 | 47 |
| West | 300 | 48 | 74 |
| West | 400 | 75 | 100 |

whatever subset (for example, just the 200 products) is chosen is shifted and expanded to cover the values 1 through 100.

Sparse intersection generation with clustering:

```
SELECT sm.MemberName AS Market,
       p1.MemberName AS Product
  FROM (SELECT CEILING(RAND()*100) AS MarketWeight,
               CEILING(RAND()*100) AS ClusterWeight,
               CEILING(RAND()*100) AS ProductWeight) AS sw
       INNER JOIN Market sm ON sw.MarketWeight
         BETWEEN sm.WeightFrom AND sm.WeightTo
       --Join Cluster table on level 1 of Market
       INNER JOIN Cluster c ON
         RTRIM(SUBSTRING(sm.Path, 1, 80)) = c.Market
           AND sw.ClusterWeight BETWEEN c.WeightFrom AND
c.WeightTo
       --Join Product table on level 1 of Product, recalculating the
       --Weights so that the Product subset specified is still 1-100
     INNER   JOIN(SELECT RTRIM(SUBSTRING(p2.Path, 1, 80)) AS Parent,
                         MIN(p2.WeightFrom) AS WeightFrom
                  FROM Product AS p2
                    GROUP BY RTRIM(SUBSTRING(p2.Path, 1, 80))) AS p2
         ON p2.Parent = c.Product
     INNER JOIN   (SELECT RTRIM(SUBSTRING(p3.Path, 1, 80)) AS Parent,
                         MAX(p3.WeightTo) AS WeightTo
                  FROM Product AS p3
                    GROUP BY RTRIM(SUBSTRING(p3.Path, 1, 80))) AS p3
         ON p3.Parent = c.Product
       INNER JOIN Product AS p1 ON sw.ProductWeight BETWEEN
         (p1.WeightFrom - p2.WeightFrom) *
         (100 / (p3.WeightTo - p2.WeightFrom + 1)) + 1 AND
         (p1.WeightTo - p2.WeightFrom + 1) *
         (100 / (p3.WeightTo - p2.WeightFrom + 1));
```

*4.2.4.3 Dense and Data Generation*   Generating dense intersections—where clustering is not an issue—is relatively straightforward. The query to do this is conceptually very similar to the original query used to generate sparse intersections, adding only the creation of a fact data value.

**Dense intersection generation:**

```
SELECT dm.MemberName AS Measures,
        ds.MemberName AS Scenario,
        dy.MemberName AS Year,
        RAND()*10000 AS data
  FROM (SELECT CEILING(RAND()*100) AS MeasuresWeight,
               CEILING(RAND()*100) AS ScenarioWeight,
                CEILING(RAND()*100) AS YearWeight) AS dw
```

```
INNER JOIN Measures dm ON dw.MeasuresWeight
    BETWEEN dm.WeightFrom AND dm.WeightTo
INNER JOIN Scenario ds ON dw.ScenarioWeight
    BETWEEN ds.WeightFrom AND ds.WeightTo
INNER JOIN Year dy ON dw.YearWeight
    BETWEEN dy.WeightFrom AND dy.WeightTo;
```

For ASO, a similar query can be used to select only from the single compression dimension.

*4.2.4.4 Putting It All Together*  The above sections have shown how to*

1. Set up dimension tables and assign weighted distributions.
2. Generate sparse member combinations according to either the per-dimension distribution or with a more sophisticated technique that can reflect the clustered nature of real-world Essbase data sets.
3. Generate dense members combinations along with an associated data value.

Fortunately, these tasks represent most of the effort involved in creating a data generator. However, it is necessary to incorporate these steps into a framework. The framework will call the sparse and dense generation processes iteratively, and ensure that

1. The output data set is captured for further use
2. A specified number of blocks are created
3. Each block is created with a specified density

Taking these in turn, the first step requires a simple table.

**Data output table:**
```
CREATE TABLE [data] (
    [Market] [VARCHAR](80),
    [Product] [VARCHAR](80),
    [Measures] [VARCHAR](80),
    [Scenario] [VARCHAR](80),
    [Year] [VARCHAR](80),
    CONSTRAINT data_PK
      PRIMARY KEY ([Market], [Product],
          [Measures], [Scenario], [Year]));
```

The second and third steps are accomplished with code that will call the sparse intersection query and, nested within that, call the dense intersection query. Creating a given number of blocks requires checking that each new sparse intersection returned

---

* As mentioned before, scripts required to both create and populate the tables discussed (along with query code) can be found at developingessbasebook.com. At this point, the reader can (with a suitable SQL Server instance) create the Sample.Basic data generator exactly as described in the text.

does not already exist in the output data. Likewise, creating a given number of cells requires checking that each new dense intersection returned does not already exist for the particular block.

To avoid repetition, the full code is not shown here.* The placeholder for the sparse selection query takes the place of a query identical to Sparse intersection generation with clustering in Section 4.2.4.2, except that the selected market and product are placed into the T-SQL variables @vcMarket and @vcProduct, respectively. The placeholder for the dense selection query takes the place of the data output table query above, except that the selected measure, scenario, year, and data value are placed into the T-SQL variables @vcMeasures, @vcScenario, @vcYear, and @decData, respectively.

```
DECLARE @intBlocks INT = 100;
DECLARE @intCellsPerBlock INT = 50;

DECLARE @vcMarket VARCHAR(80);
DECLARE @vcProduct VARCHAR(80);
DECLARE @vcMeasures VARCHAR(80);
DECLARE @vcScenario VARCHAR(80);
DECLARE @vcYear VARCHAR(80);
DECLARE @decData DECIMAL(10, 2);

DECLARE @intBlockCount INT = 0;
DECLARE @intCellCount INT = 0;

BEGIN
    TRUNCATE TABLE data;
    WHILE @intBlockCount < @intBlocks
    BEGIN


        -- Sparse Intersection Query Placeholder --

        --If there are no existing rows for this block
        IF (SELECT COUNT(*)
                FROM data d
            WHERE d.Market = @vcMarket
                    AND d.Product = @vcProduct) = 0
        BEGIN
            SET @intCellCount = 0;
            WHILE @intCellCount < @intCellsPerBlock
             BEGIN

                -- Dense Intersection Query Placeholder --

                 IF (SELECT COUNT(*)
                        FROM data d
```

---

* Again, it is available at developingessbasebook.com.

```
                WHERE d.Market = @vcMarket
                    AND d.Product = @vcProduct
                    AND d.Measures = @vcMeasures
                      AND d.Scenario = @vcScenario
                      AND d.Year = @vcYear) = 0
            BEGIN
              INSERT INTO data VALUES (@vcMarket,
                  @vcProduct, @vcMeasures,
                  @vcScenario, @vcYear, @decData);

              SET @intCellCount = @intCellCount + 1;
            END
        END
        SET @intBlockCount = @intBlockCount + 1;
      END
    END
END
```

Running this code populates the data table with data for 100 blocks, each having 50 non-Missing cells.

*4.2.4.5 Expanding the Approach*   This section has shown the design and construction of a working data generator for Sample.Basic. Sample.Basic is obviously a fairly simple database, so two additional considerations are significant for expanding these techniques to real databases.

First, many databases contain nonaggregating dimensions—scenario, version, year, and so on. A potential option in this situation is to omit these dimensions from the data generator altogether, generate the data for each nonaggregating slice separately, and then manually add those dimensions back in when loading data (via a load rule header or postprocessing of the data generator output).

Second, Sample.Basic has only two sparse dimensions. This means that the design of the Cluster table is straightforward, with one driver dimension and one target dimension. The table and queries could be modified to have a single driver dimension member associated with weightings for multiple target dimension combinations. Having multiple driver dimensions is also possible, which could be another approach to handling nonaggregating dimensions, especially where the distribution of data in one nonaggregating slice is expected to be very different from another, such as with actual versus budget data, for example.

### 4.2.5 Concluding Remarks on Data

This part of the chapter aimed to show that both the volume and distribution of data have significant performance implications.

No matter how sophisticated and carefully configured a data generator is developed, nothing beats real data. Even taking a single month of real data and duplicating them for additional periods are a reasonably good approach (although, since the same sparse input-level intersections will be populated in every period, this is likely to somewhat underestimate the number of upper-level blocks).

However, this is impossible in many situations, such as the early stages of a project, before data feeds have been developed, or, especially with Planning, in systems in which the primary source of data is user input. Random data are an option, of course, but be forewarned that it is likely to substantially overestimate the number of upper-level intersections compared with the same number of realistically distributed input-level cells.

## 4.3 Test Tasks

The most valuable performance tests are those showing expected performance under realistic conditions; in other words, how the system responds to a realistic number of users, performing a realistic set of tasks at a realistic rate against a realistic set of data. We have already dealt with the data set, and now, we will turn to creating a realistic set of tasks. Of course, filling in all of the components in that statement is a difficult task.

No single definition of *realistic* may actually exist; the usage patterns of a financial system at fiscal year-end may be very different from the patterns at fiscal month-end and again from the midmonth pattern.

### 4.3.1 Realistic Test Query Sets

Query response time is the most visible element of system performance for end users. Accurately estimating query performance for a new system or benchmarking it for an existing system requires a set of test queries that reflect real usage.

### 4.3.2 Frequency

For new systems, an estimate can be made of user concurrency (the number of users on the system at a given time) and the level of user activity (the rate at which each user will submit queries).

For existing systems, the application log may be parsed. A number of different statements appear in the log, depending on the extraction method used:

```
[Tue Dec 1 12:00:00 2014]Local/Sample/Basic/admin@Native
Directory/10320/Info(1001103)
Regular Extractor Elapsed Time for [Bottom.rep] : [0.01] seconds

[Tue Dec 1 12:00:00 2014]Local/Sample/Basic/admin@Native
Directory/6172/Info(1020055)
Spreadsheet Extractor Elapsed Time : [0] seconds
```

```
[Tue Dec 1 12:00:00 2014] Local/Sample/Basic/admin@Native
Directory/6172/Info(1260039)
MaxL DML Execution Elapsed Time : [0] seconds
```

### 4.3.3 Why Query Design Matters

*4.3.3.1 BSO*   For well-designed BSO applications, the performance of queries is driven primarily by the number of blocks touched (and how quickly they can be pulled into memory, should they not already be there). In general, BSO cubes do not encounter performance issues in response to queries; the performance hit is taken during the calculation phase.

*4.3.3.1.1 Block Count and Caching*   The number of blocks required to answer a particular query, assuming no dynamically calculated members, is the number of sparse intersections referenced in the query. However, significant differences in performance may occur even between queries requiring the same blocks. In particular, the blocks requested may already be cached, whether by the operating system in memory mapped file I/O or by Essbase—the data file cache, if Direct I/O is in use, or the data cache if not (the data cache contains uncompressed blocks). Reading blocks from physical storage is I/O intensive; placing them in the Essbase data cache involves uncompressing them, which is CPU intensive. Writing them back to storage involves recompressing them, although this will not be a factor during a time when the only cube activity is read-only (i.e., queries).

*4.3.3.1.2 Dynamic Calculation*   Queries that retrieve dynamically calculated members may require additional blocks to be pulled into memory beyond those explicitly referenced in the query if the dynamically calculated member formulas reference other sparse intersections. Dynamic calculation also requires the CPU to perform arithmetic, but the extra cost is primarily in any additional I/O.

*4.3.3.2 ASO*   With ASO, the factors that govern query performance are more complex. ASO queries can be either stored or dynamic. In the former, raw, aggregated data can be retrieved from stored hierarchy members and input-members from dynamic hierarchies. In the latter, the results of stored queries are used as the input for further calculation.

This section first discusses the factors controlling the performance of stored queries. These are generally very high performance, and the bulk of ASO performance variation for an unaggregated cube (since not all cubes require aggregations) is dependent on whether the portion of the ASO .dat file to be queried is in cache—either OS or Aggregate Storage cache—before the query. With ASO, it is highly recommended that this be true.

This is not intended to be a detailed discussion of all the variations impacting query performance. It is presented here merely to define the challenges that should be addressed when designing test queries.

*4.3.3.2.1 Levels*   Many, if not most, ASO cubes will contain aggregate views. An aggregate view is effectively a subcube. It contains the same data as the underlying cube, except that it is aggregated to a defined level in one or more stored dimensions. For example, an aggregate view on ASOsamp.Sample might contain data at level 0 in the Payment Type dimension but aggregated to level 1 in the Promotions and Age dimensions. This means that an individual aggregate view is always smaller (often by orders of magnitude) than the full input-level data set. In consequence, when Essbase receives a query that can be answered by an aggregate view, it is retrieved from a smaller data set. All things being equal with respect to the presence of data in the ASO cache or in memory-mapped file I/O, this is faster than retrieving the equivalent data from the input-level data set. Furthermore, the precalculation of totals in the aggregate view—such as Promotions in this hypothetical example—reduces the amount of math needing to be performed to return results. However, this effect is likely to be much less significant than the reduction in I/O.* Aggregate views only ever contain aggregations against stored hierarchies. ASO has no mechanism for the pre-calculation of upper-level members (or level-0 formula members) in dynamic hierarchies.

The net effect of the above is that queries against different combinations of levels in an ASO cube may have dramatically different performance and make similarly different I/O demands. A test query set against ASO should therefore be designed to hit a realistic distribution of level combinations. For example, if a cube contains data at a daily level of granularity but most reporting is done at a monthly level of granularity, the test query set should reflect this.

Ideally (but more difficult to achieve with programmatically generated queries), the test query set should reflect the combinations of levels most commonly queried. Consider the following four queries, split into sets A and B:

Set A:

```
SELECT {[Jan]} ON COLUMNS,
       {[Illinois]} ON ROWS
  FROM ASOsamp.Sample
WHERE ([Units]);

SELECT {[Qtr1]} ON COLUMNS,
       {[Mid West]} ON ROWS
  FROM ASOsamp.Sample
WHERE ([Units]);
```

Set B:

```
SELECT {[Qtr1]} ON COLUMNS,
       {[Illinois]} ON ROWS
  FROM ASOsamp.Sample
WHERE ([Units]);
```

---

* See "Pop's Rule" (Pressman 2012, 271).

```
SELECT {[Jan]} ON COLUMNS,
       {[Mid West]} ON ROWS
  FROM ASOsamp.Sample
WHERE ([Units]);
```

While both set A and set B hit level 0 and level 1 in the Time dimension ([Jan] and [Qtr1], respectively) and both hit level 3 and level 4 in the Geography dimension ([Illinois] and [Mid West], respectively), the individual queries do not address the same combinations of dimension levels. This means that each individual query may leverage a different aggregate view—or none. In consequence, different sets of queries may feature identical distributions of levels from each dimension yet have very different performance.

*4.3.3.2.2 Individual Stored Member Selections*    In the first volume of this book, Dan Pressman presented a list of rules that both explained the drivers of ASO performance and guided developers toward optimally designed solutions.[*] In particular, Dan's "Rule 3" stated, "All queries against the same aggregation level take the same time" (Pressman 2012, 236).

The fundamental insight behind Rule 3 was that, given a particular bitmap heap, there was no shortcut (such as an index) to the rows containing the data requested by a particular query. Every single row in the bitmap must be compared with the bitmap mask individually. It no longer appears that this is true.[†]

*4.3.3.2.3 MDX Formula Members and Dynamic Hierarchy Parents*    When Essbase processes a query containing a formula member, whether temporarily defined via the MDX WITH clause or permanently in the outline, it may need to break that query down into several queries against stored data.[‡,§] Anyone with more than passing experience of ASO development will have found that MDX formulas can have a major impact on query performance.

*4.3.4 Capturing Query Activity from an Existing Real System*

For existing systems, capturing real query activity is possible. Some caveats to this otherwise appealing approach are as follows: (a) Periodic usage patterns must be

---

[*] Dan Pressman's chapter remains the best available explanation of ASO internals. Refer to it to understand the concepts of a bitmap, stack, mask, etc.

[†] Oracle chooses to reveal very little information about ASO internals; my best guess is that each bitmap stack is sorted. If this is in fact the case, queries that select the same amount of data by filtering on the dimension that is the first column in the sort order should be faster than queries that filter on the last; further investigation is warranted.

[‡] For MDX WITH clause, see the Technical Reference: http://docs.oracle.com/cd/E40248_01/epm.1112 /essbase_tech_ref/mdx_with_spec.html.

[§] See my blog post on investigating how a single query breaks down into multiple "stored queries": http:// www.cubecoder.com/an-insight-into-aso-mdx-execution/.

considered when deciding on the time window to snapshot, and (b) it is less help-ful when trying to test the impact of a proposed change in structure, such as the addition of dimensions. This is because the queries as captured will reflect only the current structure of the cube and modification of the captured queries to mirror the new structure is very likely a nontrivial task. For testing, say, the impact of new hardware or a tuning tweak (with no associated cube changes), real activity is the gold standard.

*4.3.4.1 ASO "Query Tracking"*  Despite the name, ASO query tracking functionality does not expose any information to users. Query tracking data are stored in memory, persisting only for as long as the application is running. The sole function of the fea-ture (if enabled) is to optimize aggregate view selection. Fortunately, there are some other options.

*4.3.4.2 Query Logging*  Essbase provides some query-logging capabilities as a native feature.* There is considerable flexibility in the configuration of query logging, but for the purposes of this chapter, I focus on the use of query logging to reconstruct in full the queries executed against a database.

Enabling query tracking for a database requires creating a file dbname.cfg in the database folder (ARBORPATH/app/appname/dbname). For example, to record each query against Sample.Basic in its entirety, create the following Basic.cfg file in the ARBORPATH/app/Sample/Basic directory:

```
QUERYLOG [Year]
QUERYLOG [Measures]
QUERYLOG [Product]
QUERYLOG [Market]
QUERYLOG [Scenario]
QUERYLOG LOGPATH /home/essbase/app/Sample/Basic/
QUERYLOG LOGFORMAT CLUSTER
QUERYLOG LOGFILESIZE 1024
QUERYLOG TOTALLOGFILESIZE 1024
QUERYLOG ON
```

An application restart is required to pick up the new query log configuration. The LOGFORMAT setting is particularly noteworthy. This controls whether queries are logged in "TUPLE" or "CLUSTER" format. The cluster format is more compact but contains exactly the same information as the tuple format.

The Technical Reference states that query logging "tracks all queries performed against the database regardless of whether the query originated from Smart View

---

* For full details, see the Technical Reference: https://docs.oracle.com/cd/E40248_01/epm.1112/essbase _tech_ref/qlovervw.html.

or other grid clients, an MDX query, or Report Writer."* Despite that claim, MDX queries executed directly from MaxL or Smart View (via the "Execute MDX" option) are not recorded.†

*4.3.4.3 TRACE_MDX* As noted above, normal query logging will not record MDX queries. Fortunately, there is an undocumented Essbase.cfg file setting that does enable the recording of MDX queries: TRACE_MDX. The output of normal query logging and TRACE_MDX can be combined to capture (almost) all activity.

As of November 2014, the syntax for this setting is not described in the Technical Reference. This is somewhat surprising since the functionality has been available since version 11.1.2.2. In any case, a brief guide to the syntax is available in support document ID 1543793.1. To track MDX queries on a particular database, include the following line in Essbase.cfg:

```
TRACE_MDX appname dbname 2
```

*dbname* and *appname* are optional; excluding them results in the logging of queries against all databases in the application or all applications, respectively. The function of the value 2 is not explained.‡ TRACE_MDX logs MDX queries issued from (for example) MaxL and Smart View.

Unlike query logging, TRACE_MDX provides no user control over the location of the log files, which are written to a file named mdxtrace.log in directory ARBORPATH/app/*appname*/*dbname*. The output appears as follows:

```
============================================================
Following MDX query executed at Tue Nov 25 22:32:22 2014
============================================================
select {[Jan],[Feb]} on columns,
{[Sales], [COGS]} on rows
from Sample.Basic
=== MDX Query Elapsed Time : [0.010] seconds ==============
```

This format is clearly much more user-friendly than query logging output from the perspective of generating a sequence of MDX queries!

TRACE_MDX also logs metadata queries produced by the Member Selection dialog in Smart View. This might be desirable because, to the limited extent that

---

* See my blog post on investigating how a single query breaks down into multiple "stored queries": http://www.cubecoder.com/an-insight-into-aso-mdx-execution/.

† Tested in 11.1.2.3.504, and possibly the case in earlier versions. Oracle Support accepted that MDX queries were not logged and raised a documentation bug (meaning that the Technical Reference may be corrected in a future revision to remove the phrase "an MDX query").

‡ The following blog entry from Cameron Lackpour contains more detail about this and other TRACE_MDX quirks: http://camerons-blog-for-essbase-hackers.blogspot.com/2013/04/going-under-covers-with-tracemdx.html.

metadata queries load the server, they do represent real activity; unfortunately, as of 11.1.2.3.504, the member selection queries are not logged as valid MDX queries. Specifically, there is no FROM clause or indication of which cube the MDX was executed against. For example:

```
============================================================
Following MDX query executed at Tue Nov 25 22:32:50 2014
============================================================
SELECT {Hierarchize( HEAD( DESCENDANTS([Market],[Market].
LEVELS(0)),5001 ),POST )} PROPERTIES [MEMBER_ALIAS],[MEMBER_UNIQUE_
NAME],[SHARED_FLAG] ON COLUMNS
=== MDX Query Elapsed Time : [0.070] seconds ==============
```

The following Perl script will extract the valid MDX queries (in other words, those that contain a FROM clause) from the log file given in the first parameter and place them into a file given by the second parameter.

**Perl script ProcessMDXTraceLog.pl:**
```perl
#!/usr/bin/perl
# process mdx trace log file given in first parameter,
# extracting all mdx queries to flat file given by
# second parameter (one line per MDX query with a
# semicolon terminator)
# exclude queries that don't contain a FROM clause
# depends on fact that if FROM is part of member or
# dimension name that it will be contained in [ ]

use warnings;
use strict;

my $counter = 0;
my $without_sqr = "";
my $from_found = 0;
my $query_line = 0;
my @query = ();

open MTL, $ARGV[0];      # open mdx trace log
open OUT, '>', $ARGV[1]; # open output file

while (<MTL>) {
    chomp;
    if ($_ =~ /^===/) # check whether first three characters
    {                 # of line are ===
        $counter ++;
    }
    elsif (($counter + 1)%3 == 0)
    # retrieve queries from between every 2nd and
    # 3rd lines starting with ===
```

```
        {
            # test for from keyword anywhere except inside
            # square brackets
            ($without_sqr = $_) =~ s/\[([^\]]*)\]//g;
            $from_found += ($without_sqr =~ /from/i);

            $query_line++;          # count number of lines in
            if ($query_line == 1) # query (to avoid leading
            {                       # space in first line)
                push(@query, $_);
            }
            elsif ($_ ne "") # ignore blank lines
            {
                push(@query, " ".$_);
            }
        }
    elsif (($counter) % 3 == 0)  # after third line beginning
    {                            # with === print query (with
            if ($from_found != 0) {    #  trailing ';') unless not
                print OUT @query, ";\n"; # valid (no FROM clause)
            }
            $from_found = 0; # reset variable for next query
            $query_line = 0;
            @query = ();
    }
}

close (MTL);
close (OUT);
```

An MDX trace log file can be processed by running the command:

```
perl ProcessMDXTraceLog.pl MDXTrace.log Output.mdx
```

Using a short example file generated from the Sample.Basic database, the script produces these results:

```
select {[Jan],[Feb]} on columns, {[Sales], [COGS]} on rows from
Sample.Basic;
select {[Jun]} on columns, {[Sales]} on rows from Sample.Basic;
```

### 4.3.5 *Generating Test Queries: Follow the Data*

Generating test queries using a similar technique to the data generation in Section 4.2 of this chapter is appealing (perhaps with enhancements to account for the fact that data are created at level 0, whereas queries are often at upper levels). However, this approach has a significant problem that I have encountered in real benchmarking exercises: Essbase data are very sparse. More than 10% of potential intersections existing is unusual, and less than 1% of potential intersections existing is very common. Taking Sample.Basic as an example, the input-level grid contains 260 potential blocks. This is the product of the stored level 0 members of the Market and Product dimensions (20 and 13 members, respectively). If even 10% of these blocks are populated randomly with an equal probability distribution, only 26 of 260 blocks contain data. Nine out of 10 randomly generated queries against a single block will return no data. In BSO, this means that queries will not hit .pag files at all (after consulting the index and finding no block), which does not reflect the performance of real-world query activity (the typical user wants to query intersections that contain data). ASO is somewhat different, in that queries must address the .dat file to determine whether data exist, without the benefit of an index file to give the game away. However, and without going in to excessive detail on ASO internals, there is reason to believe that some sort of shortcut may be available within ASO.

Use of an unequally weighted distribution improves the odds of having queries find data, but it makes much more sense to tie the data- and query-generation processes together. This ensures that the majority of queries do, in fact, return data—as they do under real user load.

### 4.3.6 *Writing a Custom Tool (or Leveraging a Data Generation Technique)*

For data generation, we have ESSCMDQ, not to mention third-party utilities. For query generation, there are no generally available tools from any vendor.*

Consequently, the only available option is to create a custom tool. The remainder of this section will outline the custom development of a first pass at a query generator while trying to avoid the issues discussed in Section 4.3.5. This will leverage the work done in Section 4.2 of this chapter, where the Sample.Basic data generator was presented. Fortunately, much of the setup and configuration work for a query generation tool is the same as for data generation (dimension tables, etc.). As mentioned above, the key advantage to this approach is that queries can be written with reference to the output data table, consistently retrieving populated intersections.

### 4.3.6.1 *Query Generation: Query Requirements* Before moving on to the configuration and code, a description of the objective is in order. The (admittedly simple) query generator will meet the following criteria.

1. Two, and only two, dimensions will appear in each query grid.
2. One member from each additional dimension will appear in the point of view (POV).

---

* Scapa apparently marketed a Hyperion load/stress testing suite during the 2000s, which may have had a query component, but it appears to have been discontinued.

3. Both grid and POV members will be chosen at varying levels according to a weighted distribution.
4. Only POV combinations that actually contain data will be permitted.
5. Once the grid selections have been made, POV selections will be made to ensure that data are returned.
6. The size of the grid will vary, with the maximum number of members from the grid dimensions being a limit specified in the configuration table. The minimum number of members from a grid dimension will be the minimum number of populated members for the particular POV selected.
7. The output will be in the form of MDX statements.

Criteria 1 above is somewhat artificial and limiting; however, adding grid dimensions typically places more stress on the presentation layer and not on the underlying Essbase engine itself. Although testing this aspect of the system is important, this need not be accomplished using the massive variety of queries generated in the technique to be presented. Instead, this could be done by many concurrent queries (not all being different) from a large number of users. The stress comes from the design of a few large, complex query grids (which users will be happy to provide) and not from the variety of POVs from which those grids are applied.

In summary, I will continue to describe a technique designed to stress the Essbase engine itself.

*4.3.6.2 Query Generation Overview: The Four Steps*   Query generation will now proceed in the following logical steps. I say logical steps because, in some cases, the same query step actually performs more than one logical step.

1. Select the two dimensions to use in a two-dimensional query grid.
2. Select a level from each grid dimension.
3. Select a grid size (i.e., the number of members to select) for each grid dimension.
4. Select one level from each remaining dimension (which will be POV dimensions).
5. Select one member from each POV dimension ensuring that the selected tuple actually contains data.
6. Select members from the chosen grid dimensions/levels, ensuring that the combinations contain data given the POV selections already made.
7. Combine all these components into a valid MDX.

*4.3.6.3 Grid Dimension and Level Selection*   The first step is selecting two dimensions, choosing a level from each of them, and specifying the size (i.e., member count) of that axis on the grid.

*4.3.6.3.1 Additional Configuration*   Meeting the above criteria requires some additional tables and setup. A table is needed to keep track of the levels in each dimension and to specify weights for each in both the POV and grid. The table is structured as follows.

```
CREATE TABLE [QueryLevels] (
     [Dimension] [VARCHAR](80),
     [Level] [INT],
     [GridMaxSize] [INT],
     [GridWeightFrom] [INT],
     [GridWeightTo] [INT],
     [POVWeightFrom] [INT],
     [POVWeightTo] [INT]
     CONSTRAINT QueryLevels_PK
          PRIMARY KEY ([Dimension], [Level]));
```

Note that the GridWeightFrom and GridWeightTo values must cover the range 1–100 for all dimensions together, whereas the POVWeightFrom and POVWeightTo values cover the range 1–100 within each dimension. This is because the grid weighting determines which dimensions appear in the grid; the POV weight only determines which level from the remaining (POV) dimensions will be used after the grid dimensions have been selected.

Notice two features of the data in Table 4.16: First, the values ensure that Measures and Year are the most commonly selected grid dimensions. This is a common, realistic query pattern. Second, level 1 in the scenario dimension is never selected. This is appropriate in the case of nonconsolidating dimensions.

*4.3.6.3.2 Selections* Two grid dimensions, associated levels and sizes, can be selected using the following procedural code (with the results placed into the set of declared variables).

**Table 4.16**  Query Levels Table Sample Data

| DIMENSION | LEVEL | GridMaxSize | GridWeightFrom | GridWeightTo | POVWeightFrom | POVWeightTo |
|---|---|---|---|---|---|---|
| Measures | 0 | 5 | 1 | 20 | 1 | 25 |
| Measures | 1 | 2 | 21 | 25 | 26 | 50 |
| Measures | 2 | 1 | 26 | 30 | 51 | 75 |
| Measures | 3 | 1 | 31 | 35 | 76 | 100 |
| Year | 0 | 1 | 36 | 65 | 1 | 50 |
| Year | 1 | 1 | 66 | 70 | 51 | 100 |
| Market | 0 | 5 | 71 | 75 | 1 | 34 |
| Market | 1 | 4 | 76 | 78 | 35 | 67 |
| Market | 2 | 1 | 79 | 80 | 68 | 100 |
| Product | 0 | 5 | 81 | 85 | 1 | 34 |
| Product | 1 | 4 | 86 | 88 | 35 | 67 |
| Product | 2 | 1 | 89 | 90 | 68 | 100 |
| Scenario | 0 | 1 | 90 | 100 | 1 | 100 |
| Scenario | 1 | 1 | 0 | 0 | 0 | 0 |

```
--Select populated grid dimensions
DECLARE @vcGrid1      VARCHAR(80);
DECLARE @intLevel1    INT;
DECLARE @intSize1     INT;
DECLARE @vcGrid2      VARCHAR(80) = '';
DECLARE @intLevel2    INT;
DECLARE @intSize2     INT;

BEGIN
      --Select first grid dimension
      SELECT @vcGrid1 = [Dimension],
             @intLevel1 = [Level],
             @intSize1 = [GridMaxSize]
        FROM [QueryLevels],
             (SELECT CEILING(RAND()*100) AS GridWeight) AS gw
      WHERE gw.GridWeight BETWEEN [GridWeightFrom] AND
[GridWeightTo];
      --Select second grid dimension, checking
      --that it differs from the first
      WHILE @vcGrid2 = '' OR @vcGrid2 = @vcGrid1
      BEGIN
            SELECT @vcGrid2 = [Dimension],
                   @intLevel2 = [Level],
                   @intSize2 = [GridMaxSize]
              FROM [QueryLevels],
                   (SELECT CEILING(RAND()*100) AS GridWeight) AS gw
            WHERE gw.GridWeight BETWEEN [GridWeightFrom]
    AND [GridWeightTo];
      END
END
```

*4.3.6.4 POV Generation*  Once the grid dimensions have been selected, a level and member must be chosen from each POV dimension.

*4.3.6.4.1 Dimensions and Levels*  Having selected the grid dimensions, the POV dimensions are simply the set of all remaining dimensions in the QueryLevels table. A level from each of those dimensions can be chosen with the following code (assuming @vcGrid1 and @vcGrid2 variable to be already populated).

```
DECLARE @vcPOV1          VARCHAR(80);
DECLARE @intPOVLevel1    INT;
DECLARE @vcPOV2          VARCHAR(80);
DECLARE @intPOVLevel2    INT;
DECLARE @vcPOV3          VARCHAR(80);
DECLARE @intPOVLevel3    INT;
```

```
BEGIN

    SELECT TOP 1
            @vcPOV1 = [Dimension],
            @intPOVLevel1 = [Level]
      FROM [QueryLevels],
            (SELECT CEILING(RAND()*100) AS Weight) AS w
     WHERE w.Weight BETWEEN [POVWeightFrom] AND [POVWeightTo]
            AND [Dimension] NOT IN (@vcGrid1, @vcGrid2);

    SELECT TOP 1
            @vcPOV2 = [Dimension],
            @intPOVLevel2 = [Level]
      FROM [QueryLevels],
            (SELECT CEILING(RAND()*100) AS Weight) AS w
     WHERE w.Weight BETWEEN [POVWeightFrom] AND [POVWeightTo]
            AND [Dimension] NOT IN (@vcGrid1, @vcGrid2,
                                    @vcPOV1);

    SELECT @vcPOV3 = [Dimension],
            @intPOVLevel3 = [Level]
      FROM [QueryLevels],
            (SELECT CEILING(RAND()*100) AS Weight) AS w
     WHERE w.Weight BETWEEN [POVWeightFrom] AND [POVWeightTo]
            AND [Dimension] NOT IN (@vcGrid1, @vcGrid2,
                                    @vcPOV1, @vcPOV2);
END
```

*4.3.6.5 Selecting POV Members*   At this point, the grid dimensions and POV dimensions have all been chosen and placed into variables (along with associated level). The next step is to select POV members. This query selects a POV combination that actually exists in the data. The majority of the complexity arises from logic to handle the fact that the POV dimensions may comprise any three of the five dimensions in Sample. Basic; the SUBSTRING functions are used to retrieve the upper-level member associated with an input-level member found in the data when the selected POV level is not zero. Finally, the POV members are placed into the @vcPOV$n$Member variables.

This code is given in Appendix A (the query is quite long).

*4.3.6.6 Grid Member Selection*   It may seem odd that the process jumps from POV back to grid, but this is because grid member selections can only be chosen once POV members have been selected, to ensure that data exist for them.

The queries are again complicated by the requirement to handle whichever dimensions have been chosen and map from the level 0 data to (potentially) upper-level grid members. Furthermore, because the grid contains multiple members from each of the dimensions, tables will be used to contain the result:

```
CREATE TABLE Grid1(
      Member VARCHAR(80) PRIMARY KEY);

CREATE TABLE Grid2(
      Member VARCHAR(80) PRIMARY KEY);
```

The code itself is given in Appendix B, as the queries span multiple pages.

*4.3.6.7 Assembling the Queries*  At this point—finally—all the components for a valid MDX query have been obtained. The query POV members are stored in the variables:

- @vcPOV1Member
- @vcPOV2Member
- @vcPOV3Member

And the grid members are stored in the tables:

- Grid1
- Grid2

The very last step is to pivot the list of values in each grid table to a list of values and build up the MDX as a string. The approach shown here using XML PATH for performing the pivot is definitely dialect specific to T-SQL. In other dialects, at worst, a programmatic cursor-based approach could be used.

```
SELECT 'SELECT {' +
      SUBSTRING(
      (SELECT ',' + '[' + g1.Member + ']'
        FROM Grid1 g1
         FOR XML PATH('')),2,100) +
           '} ON AXIS(0), {' +
      SUBSTRING(
      (SELECT ',' + '[' + g2.Member + ']'
        FROM Grid2 g2
         FOR XML PATH('')),2,100) +
           '} ON AXIS(1) FROM Sample.Basic WHERE ([' +
           @vcPOV1Member + '], [' +
      @vcPOV2Member + '], [' +
           @vcPOV3Member + ']);'
```

*4.3.6.8 We Have Output*  Finally, some MDX queries! A handful of sample runs of the above code produced the following queries:

```
SELECT {[East],[South],[West]} ON AXIS(0),
      {[Aug],[Feb],[Jan],[Mar],[Oct]} ON AXIS(1)
```

```
   FROM Sample.Basic
WHERE ([Measures], [100], [Budget]);


SELECT { [Additions],[COGS],[Ending Inventory],[Marketing],[Sales]}
ON AXIS(0),
       {[California],[Louisiana],[New Mexico],[Oregon],[Texas]} ON
AXIS(1)
   FROM Sample.Basic
WHERE ([400], [Actual], [Qtr3]);


SELECT {[Measures]} ON AXIS(0),
       {[Apr],[Mar],[Nov],[Oct],[Sep]} ON AXIS(1)
   FROM Sample.Basic
WHERE ([Oklahoma], [200], [Budget]);
```

These queries demonstrate all the desired qualities, hitting populated (by the data generator described above) data intersections, at multiple levels, across different dimensions. The number of queries that can be generated is effectively unlimited.

*4.3.6.9 Putting It All Together*   Generating more queries is a matter simply of executing the code above multiple times.* The set of queries produced by this approach can be executed by MaxL, ESSCMD, a VBA program in Excel, or the Java API (potentially in combination with an automated test tool, as will be discussed in Section 4.4). This may involve writing the MDX out to a spreadsheet, or a text file, or one text file per query. Because this part of the process is so dependent on the testing approach to be adopted, it is left to the reader.

*4.3.6.10 Expanding the Approach*   This sample query generator is intended to show the design considerations that relate to such a tool, not to provide a fully featured, generic piece of software. Inspecting the code makes clear that this particular example works only for Sample.Basic. Several other valuable features are beyond the scope of a single chapter, and therefore are missing:

1. Multiple grid dimensions: Real queries sometimes have more than two dimensions in the grid. Allowing the number of grid dimensions to vary complicates the code further; in fact, any realistic fully generic generator is likely to involve dynamically generated SQL.
2. The above code does not generate queries against alternate hierarchies or attribute dimensions.
3. Perhaps most important, the above example does not generate queries against noninput formula members, such as the Variance member in the Scenario

---

* A fully working stored procedure to do this is available at www.developingesssbasebook.com.

dimension. Working out which formula members will actually be populated based on a given input data set is easy when the formula members are, for example, YTD, or Variance, but potentially much more difficult with complex formulas.

### 4.3.7 Developing Realistic Test Calculation Sets

Developing a realistic test calculation set for either ASO or BSO is much more difficult than generating a query test set. Most calculations are likely to fall into one of a handful of categories—aggregation, allocation, or currency conversion, for example—but beyond that, the details are very specific to the application. Calculations also are typically part of a larger process, following some change in the data or metadata (an FX rate change, new input data, or a restructure). No one runs the same calculations twice on unchanged data, at least not intentionally. This is completely different from the query case.

There are no easy answers to this, probably, except to point out that the range of calculations on a system is generally much, much smaller than the range of queries. Creating a tokenized template script and then generating more scripts by replacing parameters is often possible (for example, in the case of a focused aggregation type calculation script). This type of task is beyond the scope of this chapter.

### 4.3.8 Capturing Calculation Activity on Existing Systems

TRACE_MDX and query logging together provide reasonable facilities for capturing query activity. Again, capturing calculation activity is much more difficult.

Application logs capture a variable level detail, according to the use of the SET MSG calculation command.* However, even with the highest logging level, reconstructing, for example, the members referenced by calculation script (if driven by prompts, or substitution variables) may be impossible. Specifically, long lists of members to be calculated, or members on which the calculation is fixed, are truncated in the log file.

Calc scripts that have been run are identified:

```
[2014-01-01T12:00:00.00-05:00] [Sample] [NOTIFICATION:16] [REQ-163]
[] [ecid: 1399992024787,0] [tid: 13881] Received Command
[Calculate] from user [admin@Native Directory] using [CALCNAME.csc]
```

Therefore, parsing the application log could at least provide data about which scripts are run and with what frequency.

---

* For more details, see the SET MSG command documentation: https://docs.oracle.com/cd/E40248_01/epm.1112/essbase_tech_ref/set_msg.html.

*4.3.9 Why the Design of Test Calculations Matters*

Despite the difficulty of both capturing and generating calculations by anything other than a manual process, the realism of test calculations is obviously important. For Planning-style applications or reporting applications fed with very frequent data updates, the speed of calculations can be critical to the end-user experience (as opposed to batch process calculations performed during system downtime).

For ASO, procedural calculations can vary from lightning fast to never completing, depending on the design of the calculation and the size of the grid addressed. Memory and temp table space consumption are equally variable. For BSO, the number of blocks touched is the key factor. When using intelligent calculation on BSO, test calculations may need to be modified so that realistically sized slices of the cube are touched (or the calculation scripts modified to disable intelligent calculation altogether, and fix on appropriately sized cube regions).

## 4.4 Running Tests and Capturing Results

*4.4.1 JMeter as an Essbase Tool*

The field of load testing and of automated testing in general is the subject of hundreds of books, and any number of tools could potentially be pressed into service to run tests against Essbase. This chapter presents as an example Apache JMeter (jmeter.apache.org).

Although widely used for testing web applications, JMeter is also particularly suitable in this context for several reasons. First, it is open source, meaning that it is downloadable free of charge. Providing examples that depend on a commercially licensed testing package would not be very helpful. Second, JMeter provides a relatively simply mechanism to integrate tests built using the Java programming language. This is useful with Essbase since the Java API exposes almost every available function, from simple MDX queries through to calculation, outline modifications, and so on.

This is not to say that JMeter is the best cost-is-no-object tool, or even the best free tool in every circumstance. Some alternatives are mentioned briefly in Section 4.4.8. The remainder of this section describes how to set up JMeter, how to use it to generate query and calculation load (that is, to submit query and calculation requests with a user-controllable level of concurrency), and how to extract the output of those tests for subsequent analysis.

*4.4.2 Getting Started with JMeter, and Available Resources*

*4.4.2.1 JMeter Resources*   JMeter is a complex and capable piece of software, and the use cases in this chapter hardly scratch its surface. Very few books are available on JMeter, perhaps because the online documentation and tutorials (again, see jmeter.

apache.org) are well written. The documentation and tutorials are also included as part of the installation package, with the user manual being accessible from the Help option.

That said, little step-by-step help is available for creating custom Java Sampler tasks (see Section 4.4.4), especially from the perspective of those who are only occasional Java developers or unfamiliar with the JMeter architecture.

*4.4.2.2 Installation* For the purposes of this chapter, I will assume a Windows client and JMeter 2.12. JMeter requires Java version 1.6 at a minimum, but this should be a nonissue for an Essbase client machine. Full prerequisites are given at http://jmeter .apache.org/usermanual/get-started.html.

The first step in using JMeter is to download the application ("binaries") and its source code. A .zip (or .tgz) file for each is available at https://jmeter.apache.org /download_jmeter.cgi.

Extract the source and application .zip files into a single suitable directory, such as C:\JMeter. Any duplicate file conflicts when unzipping the second can be safely ignored. This will create a subdirectory named apache-jmeter-2.12; all file paths given subsequently in this chapter will, except where a drive letter is specified, be relative to this location. No further installation steps should be necessary; JMeter can now be run by double-clicking \bin\jmeter.bat. This JMeter console appear as shown in Figure 4.5.

*4.4.2.3 Fundamental JMeter Components* JMeter tests are constructed by assembling and configuring various prebuilt components. The most important components for our purposes are samplers, listeners, logic controllers, timers, configuration elements, thread groups, and test plans.

**Figure 4.5** JMeter console on initial startup.

*4.4.2.3.1 Sampler* A sampler is the component that actually performs the work of the test.* Out-of-the-box samplers are provided to, among many other things, perform HTTP requests, call operating system processes, or run Java programs. For example, it would be possible to use JMeter to test Essbase using these first two options, submitting queries via Essbase web services and running MaxL with a CMD/shell script. However, the Java Request sampler permits complete integration with all the functions of the Essbase Java API; for that reason, this is the approach presented here. Each unit of work performed by a sampler is a Sample, i.e., a single test, such as an Essbase query.

*4.4.2.3.2 Listener* A listener handles the results of work done by samplers and presents or records those results for user analysis.† The content and format of the results recorded depend on the listener type and configuration. For example, a listener can produce a graph showing Sample time over the course of a test run. Alternatively, a listener can log Sample details to a file including many parameters, such as the result grid of a query, the duration, etc.

*4.4.2.3.3 Logic Controller* A logic controller manages the execution of samplers.‡ For example, a Loop controller can be used to execute a set of sampler tasks a specified number of times. This is obviously a useful function in the context of load testing.

*4.4.2.3.4 Timer* A timer creates a delay before the execution of a Sample.§ Depending on the timer type, this delay may be constant, random, or varying around a constant with Gaussian distribution. Without the use of a timer, a sampler inside a Loop will fire one task immediately when the preceding task completes. This may or may not be desirable, depending on what exactly is being tested.

*4.4.2.3.5 Configuration Element* A configuration element contains a default or user-defined variable that can be referenced by samplers or other components.¶ For example, a Counter configuration element can be defined that tracks and gives access to the number of iterations made by a Loop logic controller.

*4.4.2.3.6 Thread Group* A thread group functions as a container for other components, allowing multiple instances of those same components to be created and executed concurrently.** For example, suppose that a sampler runs a calculation against an Essbase cube and is placed inside a Loop controller so that five calculations are

---

* See http://jmeter.apache.org/usermanual/component_reference.html#samplers.
† See http://jmeter.apache.org/usermanual/component_reference.html#listeners.
‡ See http://jmeter.apache.org/usermanual/component_reference.html#logic_controllers.
§ See http://jmeter.apache.org/usermanual/component_reference.html#timers.
¶ See http://jmeter.apache.org/usermanual/component_reference.html#config_elements.
**See http://jmeter.apache.org/usermanual/component_reference.html#Thread_Group.

executed in series. To simulate 10 users performing the same action, the Loop controller (and sampler) would be placed inside a thread group configured to create two threads.

*4.4.2.3.7 Test Plan*  A test plan is the set of actions for JMeter to take when instructed to run by the user.* It is composed of the elements discussed above. A test plan can be saved to a file and subsequently recalled.

### 4.4.3 A Simple Plan

As a quick introduction to JMeter, the following steps describe the development of a test plan against the Sample.Basic database.

The scenario to be simulated is that of a (highly simplified!) Planning application. Three concurrent users will (a) load a small volume of data to their respective Markets (i.e., US states), (b) calculate these data, and (c) submit an MDX query to view updated Market totals.

The reader may be keen to try using queries or data generated in the earlier parts of this chapter; initially, however, this section describes JMeter usage more generically. Each of these actions will, for the purposes of this example, be accomplished with MaxL running on Windows (more advanced techniques are shown later). Therefore, a little MaxL script setup is required. For each individual user, three MaxL scripts are required: User*N*_Load.msh, User*N*_Calc.msh, and User*N*_Query.msh, where *N* is either 1, 2, or 3. For this example, assume that users 1, 2, and 3 are from New York, California, and Massachusetts, respectively. In sets 2 and 3, references to New York must be replaced with California and Massachusetts. Username, password, and server names must (of course) also be replaced.

Script: UserN_Load.msh

```
login username password on servername;
import database Sample.Basic data from data_string '"Sales" "100-
10" "New York" "Jan" "Actual" 123' on error abort;
logout;
exit;
```

Script: UserN_Calc.msh

```
login username password on servername;
execute calculation 'SET UPDATECALC OFF; FIX("New York") CALC DIM
("Measures", "Year", "Product", "Scenario"); ENDFIX' on Sample.
Basic;
logout;
exit;
```

---

* See http://jmeter.apache.org/usermanual/component_reference.html#Test_Plan.

Script: UserN_Query.msh

```
login username password on servername;
select {[New York]} on columns, {[Sales]} on rows from Sample.
Basic;
logout;
exit;
```

Once all nine scripts have been created, save them into C:\JMeterExamples or equivalent. If a different path is used, be careful to replace all references to this location in the following description.

Next, launch JMeter. The default console will appear (see Figure 4.5), and JMeter will open with an empty test plan, imaginatively titled "Test Plan." Rename it to "Sample Basic Planning Simulation" by editing the value in the Name box. Then select File | Save, which pops up a standard dialog. Navigate to C:\JMeterExamples, and click the Save button (see Figure 4.6).

Step 2 is to add a thread group to the test plan. Right-click on the test plan in the tree view pane (the Erlenmeyer flask icon) and select Add | Threads | Thread Group, as shown in Figure 4.7.

The thread group is added as a child of the test plan in the tree view pane (the thread group icon is a spool of cotton). "Thread Group" appears in the pane on the right. The defaults may be accepted, except that Number of Threads (users) must be set to 3 and Ramp-Up Period (in seconds) must be set to 0 (see Figure 4.8). Number

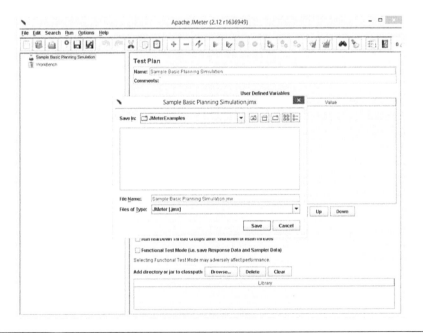

**Figure 4.6**  Saving a new test plan.

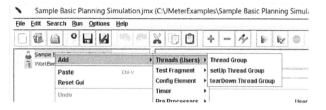

**Figure 4.7**    Adding a thread group.

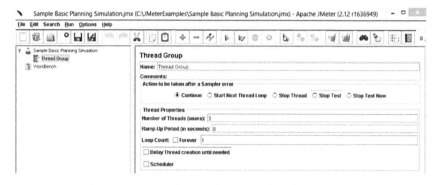

**Figure 4.8**    Specifying the number of threads.

of Threads is self-explanatory; Ramp-Up Period is the total time over which threads will be created (the setting of 0 results in all threads executing simultaneously. A setting of 30 would result in each of three threads being created at 10-second intervals).

Having created a thread group, the threads need to be given some work to do. Work is done by samplers, in this case, an OS Process Sampler. To create a sampler, right-click on the thread group and select Add | Samplers | OS Process Sampler (see Figure 4.9).

A sampler will appear in the tree view, as a child of the thread group, as shown in Figure 4.10. The icon for a sampler (in keeping with the laboratory glassware theme) is a pipette. In the Command textbox, enter "startMaxl.cmd" (or "startMaxl.sh" on Unix/Linux) with the full path to startMaxl. On my test system, this full path is C:\Oracle\Middleware\EPMSystem11R1\Products\Essbase\EssbaseClient\bin\startMaxl.cmd. In the Working Directory textbox, enter "C:\JMeterExamples" (or a chosen alternate).

Edit the name of the sampler to be "Load Data."

Finally, a command parameter must be added, to pass in one of the MaxL scripts (see Figure 4.11). This step is slightly more complex because each of the three threads should execute a different script. To achieve this, a JMeter function will be used as part of the script specification. Functions are easily identified because they begin with a dollar sign ($) and are enclosed in braces. In this case, the requisite function is ${__threadNum}. Note that there are two underscores between the opening brace and "threadNum." ${__threadNum} returns—not surprisingly—the number of the thread being executed.

Click Add in the Command parameters frame, and enter the following:

```
User${__threadNum}_Load.msh
```

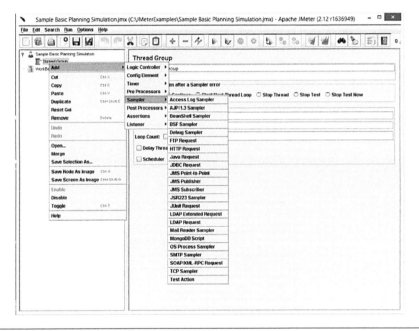

**Figure 4.9**  Adding a sampler.

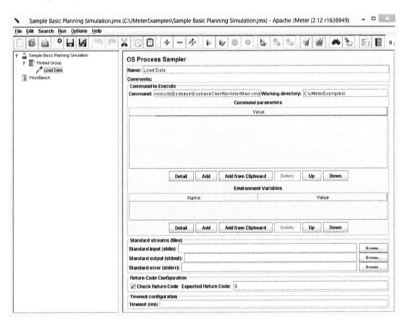

**Figure 4.10**  A new OS process sampler.

The thread group creates three threads when the test plan is executed. The value returned by the function will be 1 in the context of the first thread, 2 in the second, and 3 in the third. In the MaxL parameter, this value is substituted in place of the JMeter function. Consequently, the first thread will execute the script User1_Load.msh; the second thread, User2_Load.msh; and so on.

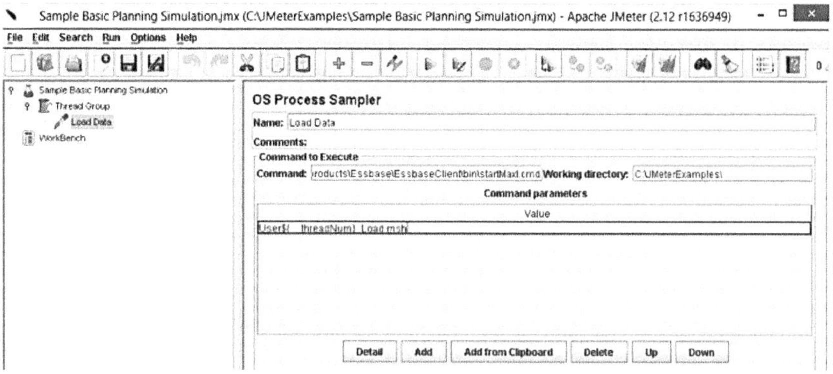

Figure 4.11    Adding a command parameter.

Repeat this process to add additional OS Process samplers for the calculation and query MaxL scripts, naming them "Calculate Data" and "Query Data," respectively. At this point, the entire test plan is complete, as shown in Figure 4.12. Click the Disk icon or File | Save to save the test plan.

At this point, nothing remains but to execute the plan. Click the green Play button or select Run | Start. The experience may initially be underwhelming since (aside from the Play button becoming temporarily grayed out and the Stop button becoming ungrayed) very little visual feedback occurs. A check of the Sample application log, however, indicates that the test is indeed running:

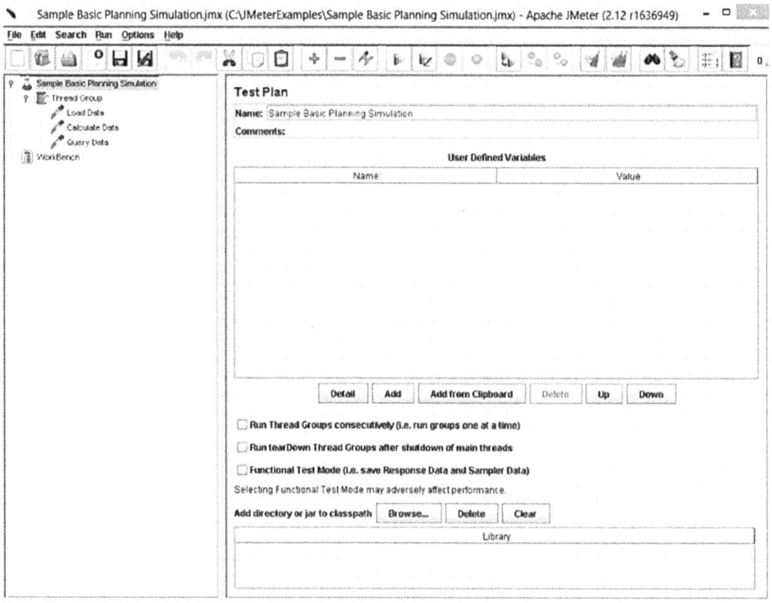

Figure 4.12    A finished test plan.

```
Received Command [Dataload] from user [admin@Native Directory]
Data Load Elapsed Time : [0.23] seconds
Received Command [Dataload] from user [admin@Native Directory]
Data Load Elapsed Time : [0.1] seconds
Received Command [Dataload] from user [admin@Native Directory]
Data Load Elapsed Time : [0.17] seconds
Received Command [Calculate] from user [admin@Native Directory]
Total Calc Elapsed Time : [0.01] seconds
Received Command [Calculate] from user [admin@Native Directory]
Total Calc Elapsed Time : [0.01] seconds
Received Command [MdxReport] from user [admin@Native Directory]
MaxL DML Execution Elapsed Time : [0] seconds
Received Command [Calculate] from user [admin@Native Directory]
Total Calc Elapsed Time : [0] seconds
Received Command [MdxReport] from user [admin@Native Directory]
MaxL DML Execution Elapsed Time : [0] seconds
Received Command [MdxReport] from user [admin@Native Directory]
MaxL DML Execution Elapsed Time : [0] seconds
```

In this case, the time taken to initialize each thread practically swamps the time taken to execute it; i.e., each data load completes in sequence, and all the data loads have completed before the first calculation begins. In this particular example, only by the bolded calculation and MDX query have two threads begun crossing over. This is an artifact of the trivial (in terms of execution time) test cases and limited concurrency, not indicative of a general problem. Creating longer running tasks against larger databases to prove that threads do, in fact, execute concurrently is easy.

### 4.4.4 Java API Integration

Running a MaxL script is a useful way to launch a test, but it does not always give the most fine-grained control possible, especially in terms of flow control. For example, feeding a sequence of queries to Essbase from a file, such as might be produced by a query generation tool, is difficult.

As mentioned above, JMeter provides a Java Request sampler permitting the execution of arbitrary Java code. A Java Request sampler can be added in the same way as the OS Process sampler in the example above (see Figure 4.13).

After adding the sampler, notice that the Classname drop-down box contains two options, JavaTest and SleepTest. These two classes do not perform any useful work for Essbase testing purposes. Instead, the user will need to write and compile a Java class using the Essbase Java API.

The following example shows how to create a class that will read an MDX query from a text file and execute it against a database. Step 1 is to come up with some Java code. Explaining how to use Java in general, or the Java API in particular, is far beyond the scope of this chapter (not to mention my area of expertise—I'm grateful to John A. Booth for the original code, developed in the course of performing Exalytics

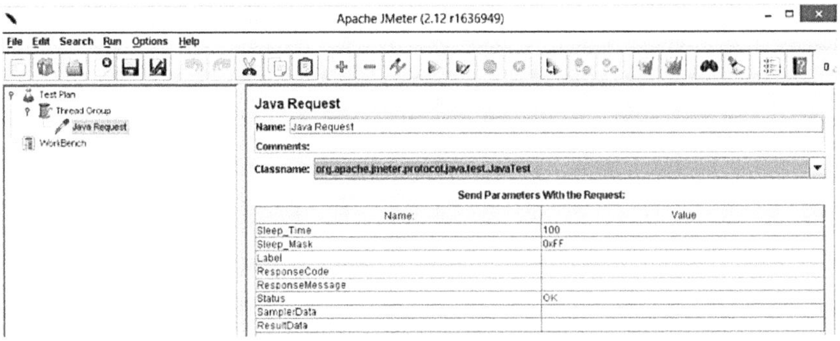

**Figure 4.13** Java Request sampler.

benchmarking). Consequently, I will offer little description of the code itself beyond the comments; the main objective of the exercise is to show the minimum necessary steps to integrate custom code into JMeter tests. The full source file, MdxTest.java, is available at www.developingessbasebook.com.

Create a new subdirectory named MdxTest under C:\JMeter\apache-jmeter-2.12\ src\protocol\java\org\apache\jmeter\protocol\java. This requires the JMeter source to have been downloaded and installed as prescribed in Section 4.4.2.2. The source code of the custom Java class, in a file named MdxTest.java, should be placed in this location.*

Several points should be highlighted with respect to the source code because they apply to any custom Java class created for integration with a Java Sampler.

First, the custom subclass extends the AbstractJavaSamplerClient class.†

```
import org.apache.jmeter.protocol.java.sampler.
AbstractJavaSamplerClient;
...
public class MdxTest extends AbstractJavaSamplerClient
implements Serializable
```

The subclass must define the *runTest* method. This is the method that actually performs whatever test task is required.

JMeter also uses the getDefaultParameters method so that when the custom sampler is displayed in the GUI, custom properties and settings can be displayed and modified:

```
public Arguments getDefaultParameters()
{
  Arguments params = new Arguments();
    params.addArgument("App","Sample");
    params.addArgument("DB","Basic");
  return params;
}
```

---

* The full source for MDXTest.java is available at developingessbasebook.com. The code is too long for inclusion here, and in any case, rekeying code listings from a book went out of style in the 1980s.

† See http://jmeter.apache.org/api/org/apache/jmeter/protocol/java/sampler/JavaSamplerClient.html.

Finally, the runTest method accepts a JavaSamplerContext object. This gives access to thread information and task-specific arguments, including these parameters.

*4.4.4.1 Compiling a Custom Java Sampler Using the Java API*   The process to add a custom Java Sampler task (having written the code) is as follows.

1. Copy the code (i.e., the .java file) to a new directory under C:\JMeter\apache-jmeter-2.12\src\protocol\java\org\apache\jmeter\protocol\java\. In this case, the new directory is called mdxtest, and the code file itself is MdxTest.java.
2. Open a command prompt and navigate to that location. Compile the Java code (referencing the location of the Essbase Java API dependency, which may vary depending on environment):
```
javac -cp "C:\Oracle\Middleware\EPMSystem11R1\common\EssbaseJava
API\11.1.2.0\lib\*;C:\JMeter\apache-jmeter-2.12\lib\ext\*;C:\
JMeter\apache-jmeter-2.12\lib\*;" MdxTest.java
```
3. This creates a file named MdxTest.class, in the same location. Run the following statement to package the class into an archive:
```
jar cvf C:\JMeter\apache-jmeter-2.12\lib\ext\MdxTest.jar MdxTest.
class
```
This drops the .jar file into lib\ext.
4. Modify user.properties in JMeter/bin, with the following line:
```
plugin _ dependency _ paths=C:/Oracle/Middleware/
EPMSystem11R1/common/EssbaseJavaAPI/11.1.2.0/lib;
```

In Java Sampler requests, "MdxTest" now appears as a third option in the Classname dropdown. The set of parameters is specific to the sampler, containing properties such as Essbase Server, APS Provider, etc., as shown in Figure 4.14.

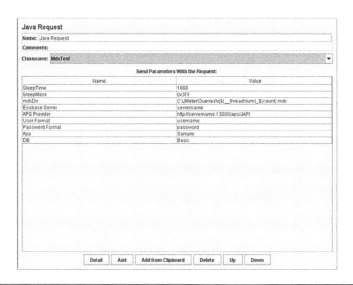

**Figure 4.14**   MdxTest sampler properties viewed in JMeter.

*4.4.5  Running MDX with JMeter*

Actually using the MdxTest sampler requires a little explanation. First, a review of the parameters:

- SleepTime controls the time between successive queries and is specified in milliseconds.
- SleepMask permits a degree of variability in the SleepTime. The SleepTime and SleepMask parameters function in the MdxTest sampler in exactly the same way as they do in the example JavaTest sampler (the JMeter documentation provides a full explanation of their interaction).*
- mdxDir specifies the location of a set of files, each containing one MDX query. These might have been manually defined or created with output from the query generator tool described earlier. For example, the default value is C:\JMeter\Queries\q${__threadNum}_${count}.mdx. In the example given below, the ${count} variable is associated with a Loop controller, while ${__threadNum} is native to a group of threads. Supposing that there are three threads, each set to loop three times, the first thread will look in C:\JMeter\Queries for q1_1.mdx, q1_2.mdx, and q1_3.mdx. The second thread will look for q2_1.mdx, and so on.
- Essbase Server is the target Essbase server for the MDX query.
- APS Provider specifies the location of provider services, for example, http://servername:13080/aps/JAPI.
- User Format contains the user name. As with the mdxDir property, this can take advantage of variables so that, for example, each thread uses its own user (e.g., test${__threadNum} means that the first thread will use a username of test1, the second a username of test2, and so on).
- Password Format contains the password. This can either be entered directly as a literal or, again, with the use of variables. If special testing users are created there is little reason for them not to share the same password.
- App is the name of the Essbase application under test, e.g., Sample.
- DB is the name of the Essbase database under test, e.g., Basic.

*4.4.6  Putting It All Together*

To test the use of the custom sampler, create a new test plan and save it as JavaMDXTest. Nine queries are required by this example; any valid MDX query against Sample. Basic is acceptable; these must be saved into separate files and placed in subdirectory C:\JMeter\Queries. The names of the MDX files must be named q$x$_$y$.mdx, where both $x$ and $y$ run values 1 through 3 (for a total of nine combinations). Having set

---

* See https://jmeter.apache.org/api/org/apache/jmeter/protocol/java/test/JavaTest.html.

up the queries, add a thread group and configure with three threads, as shown in Figure 4.15.

Add a Loop controller to the thread group. The Loop controller must have a loop count of 3, as shown in Figure 4.16.

Add a Counter configuration element to the Loop controller, configured to count from 1 to 3, with a reference name of "count." Check the "Track counter independently for each user" option (see Figure 4.17).

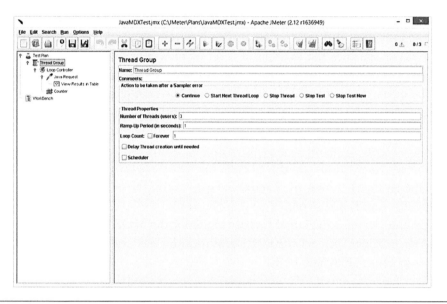

**Figure 4.15**   JavaMDXTest Thread Group setup.

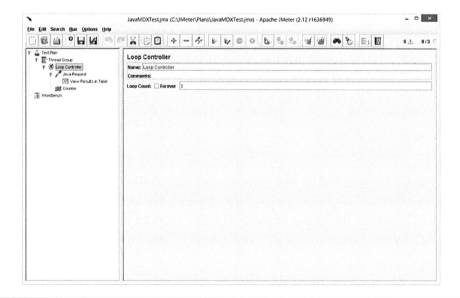

**Figure 4.16**   JavaMDXTest Loop controller setup.

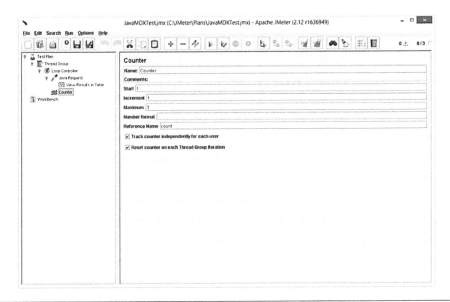

**Figure 4.17**   JavaMDXTest Counter setup.

Add a Java Request sampler to the Loop controller. Select the MdxTest classname. Specify the following settings:

- SleepTime: 1000
- SleepMask: 0
- mdxDir: C:\JMeter\Queries\q$\{__threadNum\}_$\{count\}.mdx

In the Essbase Server, APS Provider, User Format, Password Format, App, and DB properties, enter values appropriate to the Essbase and APS environment (and for Sample.Basic, assuming the queries are also designed for Sample.Basic), as shown in Figure 4.18.

At this point, the test plan can be saved and then run. Looking at Sample.log demonstrates that queries are, in fact, being executed (the following messages appear nine times):

```
[Sat Dec 27 12:00:00 2014]Local/Sample/Basic/user1@Native
Directory/6172/Info(1013091)
Received Command [MdxReport] from user [user1@Native Directory]

[Sat Dec 27 12:00:00 2014]Local/Sample/Basic/user1@Native
Directory/6172/Info(1260039)
MaxL DML Execution Elapsed Time : [0] seconds
```

*4.4.7 JMeter Output*

Relying on Essbase logs to capture test output is not particularly convenient, especially as the reader develops more advanced tests (perhaps querying multiple applications, hence writing to more than one Essbase log file).

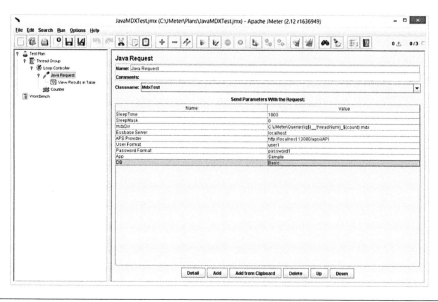

**Figure 4.18**　Java Request setup.

The elapsed time of each Sample can instead be captured by adding a View Results in Table listener. The listener will display the results in the JMeter GUI but can also write output to a file for offline analysis, in this case, C:\JMeter\Results\output.log (see Figure 4.19).

After running the test, the results are captured in the table view, along with the time taken (in milliseconds) for each Sample (see Figure 4.20).

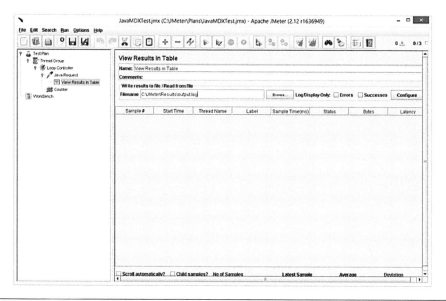

**Figure 4.19**　Listener setup.

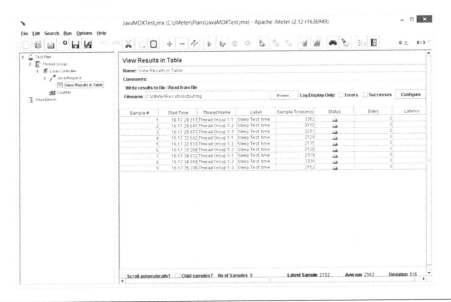

**Figure 4.20** Listener results.

### 4.4.8 Other (Non-JMeter or Non-Open Source) Tools

Simple tests can, of course, be scripted directly in MaxL, especially if no requirements exist for concurrent tests. Using a combination of another scripting language (CMD, shell scripts, Perl, etc.) and MaxL is also possible, although this is unlikely to allow quite the level of coordination and synchronization of an actual test tool without a lot of effort to duplicate functionality already available elsewhere.

Other third-party test tools, such as LoadRunner, can certainly be used with Essbase. Wikipedia provides a partial list of such tools (including JMeter) at https://en.wikipedia.org/wiki/Load_testing#Load_testing_tools.

### 4.4.9 Hardware Activity Monitoring

As shown in Section 4.4.7, JMeter can capture the duration of the Java API operations (such as MDX queries); as an option, custom Sampler components can write actual results, such as query output. Unfortunately, however, JMeter does not, out of the box, provide monitoring of system resources—CPU, IO, memory, etc. Various custom sampler/listener components have been written, which, in conjunction with server-side daemons, capture server performance parameters while tests are running. However, these are not part of the official JMeter distribution.

As an alternative, standard hardware monitoring tools can be used, but they provide no synchronization between the monitoring tool and the load generation tool, and the results from each must be aligned manually (or via script) after the fact. The topic of monitoring hardware performance on an Essbase server is discussed by John A. Booth in his chapter on infrastructure in the first volume of this book (Booth 2012, 1–22). In particular, Table 1.15 provides a helpful list of hardware monitoring tools for a variety of different platforms, and that chapter's Section 1.5 as a whole contains guidelines for monitoring resource usage.

### 4.4.10  Stress Tests and Their Function

This final section provides a note on "stress testing." A stress test involves applying a higher—sometimes by orders of magnitude—load to a system than is expected in normal use. For Essbase systems, this can provide valuable information beyond the satisfaction of intellectual curiosity. First, the performance of a system as load increases typically degrades discontinuously as resource (CPU, RAM, I/O) limits are exceeded. Stress testing can reveal the point at which these limits will be reached and, therefore, the safety margin between current or expected usage and unacceptable performance. Second, stress testing can indicate inefficiencies in resource allocation. For example, stress test scenarios might consistently show that CPU limits are reached before RAM is fully utilized. Although stress tests and typical load tests are quantitatively different, the methods for performing them against Essbase databases are qualitatively similar.

### 4.5  Conclusion

The practical examples in this chapter have used small databases and simple tests. However, my aim is that the general principles described are understood to have very broad applicability, and the techniques can be scaled up and applied to real-world problems. Benchmarking and formalized, controlled load testing of Essbase are quite uncommon, and the whole area of Essbase performance is often described as "more art than science." I don't dispute that experience, judgment, and rules of thumb have a role to play in design and tuning. But careful design coupled with automation makes it possible to build repeatable, measurable, and shareable tests, which helps add a quantitative aspect that can often be lacking, quickly capturing the impact of changes across multiple performance metrics (including those that affect users most directly). I hope that this chapter makes a case for both the possibility and desirability of moving in that direction.

## Copyright Information

## Acknowledgments

I thank the following: Dan Pressman, nTuple, for his technical review, comments and discussion; Cameron Lackpour, CL Solve, for his helpful comments on the draft;

Jason Jones, Key Performance Ideas, for his review and advice with respect to Java and JMeter; Zaf Kamar, Linium, for his valuable insight on data distribution and cube size estimation; and my wife, Monica McLaughlin.

# Appendix A

```
DECLARE @vcPOV1Member VARCHAR(80);
DECLARE @vcPOV2Member VARCHAR(80);
DECLARE @vcPOV3Member VARCHAR(80);

SELECT @vcPOV1Member = d.POV1,
       @vcPOV2Member = d.POV2,
       @vcPOV3Member = d.POV3
  FROM (SELECT TOP 1
               CASE @vcPOV1
                   WHEN 'Measures' THEN
                   CASE @intPOVLevel1
                       WHEN 0 THEN m.[MemberName]
                       ELSE RTRIM(SUBSTRING(m.Path,
                               (80*(@intPOVLevel1-1))+1, 80))
                   END
                   WHEN 'Year' THEN
                   CASE @intPOVLevel1
                       WHEN 0 THEN y.[MemberName]
                       ELSE RTRIM(SUBSTRING(y.Path,
                               (80*(@intPOVLevel1-1))+1, 80))
                   END
                   WHEN 'Scenario' THEN
                   CASE @intPOVLevel1
                       WHEN 0 THEN s.[MemberName]
                       ELSE RTRIM(SUBSTRING(s.Path,
                               (80*(@intPOVLevel1-1))+1, 80))
                   END
                   WHEN 'Market' THEN
                   CASE @intPOVLevel1
                       WHEN 0 THEN mk.[MemberName]
                       ELSE RTRIM(SUBSTRING(mk.Path,
                               (80*(@intPOVLevel1-1))+1, 80))
                   END
                   WHEN 'Product' THEN
                   CASE @intPOVLevel1
                       WHEN 0 THEN p.[MemberName]
                       ELSE RTRIM(SUBSTRING(p.Path,
                               (80*(@intPOVLevel1-1))+1, 80))
                   END
               END AS POV1,
               CASE @vcPOV2
                   WHEN 'Measures' THEN
```

```
        CASE @intPOVLevel2
           WHEN 0 THEN m.[MemberName]
           ELSE RTRIM(SUBSTRING(m.Path,
                     (80*(@intPOVLevel2-1))+1, 80))
        END
        WHEN 'Year' THEN
        CASE @intPOVLevel2
           WHEN 0 THEN y.[MemberName]
           ELSE RTRIM(SUBSTRING(y.Path,
                     (80*(@intPOVLevel2-1))+1, 80))
        END
        WHEN 'Scenario' THEN
        CASE @intPOVLevel2
           WHEN 0 THEN s.[MemberName]
           ELSE RTRIM(SUBSTRING(s.Path,
                     (80*(@intPOVLevel2-1))+1, 80))
        END
        WHEN 'Market' THEN
        CASE @intPOVLevel2
           WHEN 0 THEN mk.[MemberName]
           ELSE RTRIM(SUBSTRING(mk.Path,
                     (80*(@intPOVLevel2-1))+1, 80))
        END
        WHEN 'Product' THEN
        CASE @intPOVLevel2
           WHEN 0 THEN p.[MemberName]
           ELSE RTRIM(SUBSTRING(p.Path,
                     (80*(@intPOVLevel2-1))+1, 80))
        END
   END AS POV2,
   CASE @vcPOV3
        WHEN 'Measures' THEN
        CASE @intPOVLevel3
           WHEN 0 THEN m.[MemberName]
           ELSE RTRIM(SUBSTRING(m.Path,
                     (80*(@intPOVLevel3-1))+1, 80))
        END
        WHEN 'Year' THEN
        CASE @intPOVLevel3
           WHEN 0 THEN y.[MemberName]
           ELSE RTRIM(SUBSTRING(y.Path,
                     (80*(@intPOVLevel3-1))+1, 80))
     END
      WHEN 'Scenario' THEN
      CASE @intPOVLevel3
           WHEN 0 THEN s.[MemberName]
           ELSE RTRIM(SUBSTRING(s.Path,
                     (80*(@intPOVLevel3-1))+1, 80))
        END
      WHEN 'Market' THEN
```

```
                      CASE @intPOVLevel3
                         WHEN 0 THEN mk.[MemberName]
                         ELSE RTRIM(SUBSTRING(mk.Path,
                                   (80*(@intPOVLevel3-1))+1, 80))
                      END
                      WHEN 'Product' THEN
                      CASE @intPOVLevel3
                         WHEN 0 THEN p.[MemberName]
                         ELSE RTRIM(SUBSTRING(p.Path,
                                   (80*(@intPOVLevel3-1))+1, 80))
                      END
                   END AS POV3
         FROM [Data] d
               INNER JOIN [Measures] m ON d.[Measures] =
m.[MemberName]
               INNER JOIN [Year] y ON d.[Year] = y.[MemberName]
               INNER JOIN [Scenario] s ON d.[Scenario] =
s.[MemberName]
               INNER JOIN [Market] mk ON d.[Market] =
mk.[MemberName]
               INNER JOIN [Product] p ON d.[Product] =
p.[MemberName]
         ORDER BY NEWID()) d;
```

## Appendix B

```
TRUNCATE TABLE Grid1;
TRUNCATE TABLE Grid2;

INSERT INTO Grid1
SELECT TOP (@intGridSize1) g1.Member
FROM (SELECT DISTINCT(CASE @vcGrid1
                  WHEN 'Measures' THEN
                      CASE @intGridLevel1
                          WHEN 0 THEN m.[MemberName]
                          ELSE RTRIM(SUBSTRING(m.Path,
                                   (80*(@intGridLevel1-1))+1, 80))
                   END
                  WHEN 'Year' THEN
                      CASE @intGridLevel1
                          WHEN 0 THEN y.[MemberName]
                          ELSE RTRIM(SUBSTRING(y.Path,
                                   (80*(@intGridLevel1-1))+1, 80))
                   END
                  WHEN 'Scenario' THEN
                      CASE @intGridLevel1
                          WHEN 0 THEN s.[MemberName]
                          ELSE RTRIM(SUBSTRING(s.Path,
                                   (80*(@intGridLevel1-1))+1, 80))
                   END
```

```
              WHEN 'Market' THEN
                    CASE @intGridLevel1
                          WHEN 0 THEN mk.[MemberName]
                          ELSE RTRIM(SUBSTRING(mk.Path,
                                (80*(@intGridLevel1-1))+1, 80))
                    END
              WHEN 'Product' THEN
                    CASE @intGridLevel1
                          WHEN 0 THEN p.[MemberName]
                          ELSE RTRIM(SUBSTRING(p.Path,
                                (80*(@intGridLevel1-1))+1, 80))
                    END
              END) AS Member
        FROM [Data] d
              INNER JOIN [Measures] m
                    ON d.[Measures] = m.[MemberName]
              INNER JOIN [Year] y
                    ON d.[Year] = y.[MemberName]
              INNER JOIN [Scenario] s
                    ON d.[Scenario] = s.[MemberName]
              INNER JOIN [Market] mk
                    ON d.[Market] = mk.[MemberName]
              INNER JOIN [Product] p
                    ON d.[Product] = p.[MemberName]
        WHERE @vcPOV1Member =
              CASE WHEN @vcPOV1 = 'Measures' THEN
                    CASE @intPOVLevel1
                          WHEN 0 THEN d.[Measures]
                          ELSE RTRIM(SUBSTRING(m.Path,
                                (80*(@intPOVLevel1-1))+1, 80))
                    END
              WHEN @vcPOV1 = 'Year' THEN
                    CASE @intPOVLevel1
                          WHEN 0 THEN d.[Year]
                          ELSE RTRIM(SUBSTRING(y.Path,
                                (80*(@intPOVLevel1-1))+1, 80))
                    END
              WHEN @vcPOV1 = 'Scenario' THEN
                    CASE @intPOVLevel1
                          WHEN 0 THEN d.[Scenario]
                          ELSE RTRIM(SUBSTRING(s.Path,
                                (80*(@intPOVLevel1-1))+1, 80))
                    END
              WHEN @vcPOV1 = 'Market' THEN
                    CASE @intPOVLevel1
                          WHEN 0 THEN d.[Market]
                          ELSE RTRIM(SUBSTRING(mk.Path,
                                (80*(@intPOVLevel1-1))+1, 80))
                    END
```

```
WHEN @vcPOV1 = 'Product' THEN
        CASE @intPOVLevel1
                WHEN 0 THEN d.[Product]
                ELSE RTRIM(SUBSTRING(p.Path,
                    (80*(@intPOVLevel1-1))+1, 80))
    END
    END
AND @vcPOV2Member =
CASE WHEN @vcPOV2 = 'Measures' THEN
        CASE @intPOVLevel2
                WHEN 0 THEN d.[Measures]
                ELSE RTRIM(SUBSTRING(m.Path,
                    (80*(@intPOVLevel2-1))+1, 80))
    END
WHEN @vcPOV2 = 'Year' THEN
        CASE @intPOVLevel2
                WHEN 0 THEN d.[Year]
                ELSE RTRIM(SUBSTRING(y.Path,
                    (80*(@intPOVLevel2-1))+1, 80))
    END
WHEN @vcPOV2 = 'Scenario' THEN
        CASE @intPOVLevel2
                WHEN 0 THEN d.[Scenario]
                ELSE RTRIM(SUBSTRING(s.Path,
                    (80*(@intPOVLevel2-1))+1, 80))
    END
WHEN @vcPOV2 = 'Market' THEN
        CASE @intPOVLevel2
                WHEN 0 THEN d.[Market]
                ELSE RTRIM(SUBSTRING(mk.Path,
                    (80*(@intPOVLevel2-1))+1, 80))
    END
WHEN @vcPOV2 = 'Product' THEN
        CASE @intPOVLevel2
                WHEN 0 THEN d.[Product]
                ELSE RTRIM(SUBSTRING(p.Path,
                    (80*(@intPOVLevel2-1))+1, 80))
    END
    END
AND @vcPOV3Member =
CASE WHEN @vcPOV3 = 'Measures' THEN
        CASE @intPOVLevel3
                WHEN 0 THEN d.[Measures]
                ELSE RTRIM(SUBSTRING(m.Path,
                    (80*(@intPOVLevel3-1))+1, 80))
    END
WHEN @vcPOV3 = 'Year' THEN
        CASE @intPOVLevel3
                WHEN 0 THEN d.[Year]
                ELSE RTRIM(SUBSTRING(y.Path,
```

```
                                        (80*(@intPOVLevel3-1))+1, 80))
                        END
            WHEN @vcPOV3 = 'Scenario' THEN
                CASE @intPOVLevel3
                        WHEN 0 THEN d.[Scenario]
                        ELSE RTRIM(SUBSTRING(s.Path,
                                (80*(@intPOVLevel3-1))+1, 80))
                END
            WHEN @vcPOV3 = 'Market' THEN
                CASE @intPOVLevel3
                        WHEN 0 THEN d.[Market]
                        ELSE RTRIM(SUBSTRING(mk.Path,
                                (80*(@intPOVLevel3-1))+1, 80))
                END
            WHEN @vcPOV3 = 'Product' THEN
                CASE @intPOVLevel3
                        WHEN 0 THEN d.[Product]
                        ELSE RTRIM(SUBSTRING(p.Path,
                                (80*(@intPOVLevel3-1))+1, 80))
                END
            END) g1
ORDER BY NEWID();

INSERT INTO Grid2
SELECT TOP (@intGridSize2) g2.Member
FROM (SELECT DISTINCT(CASE @vcGrid2
            WHEN 'Measures' THEN
                CASE @intGridLevel2
                        WHEN 0 THEN m.[MemberName]
                        ELSE RTRIM(SUBSTRING(m.Path,
                                (80*(@intGridLevel2-1))+1, 80))
                END
            WHEN 'Year' THEN
                CASE @intGridLevel2
                        WHEN 0 THEN y.[MemberName]
                        ELSE RTRIM(SUBSTRING(y.Path,
                                (80*(@intGridLevel2-1))+1, 80))
                END
            WHEN 'Scenario' THEN
                CASE @intGridLevel2
                        WHEN 0 THEN s.[MemberName]
                        ELSE RTRIM(SUBSTRING(s.Path,
                                (80*(@intGridLevel2-1))+1, 80))
                END
            WHEN 'Market' THEN
                CASE @intGridLevel2
                        WHEN 0 THEN mk.[MemberName]
                        ELSE RTRIM(SUBSTRING(mk.Path,
                                (80*(@intGridLevel2-1))+1, 80))
                END
```

```
       WHEN 'Product' THEN
           CASE @intGridLevel2
               WHEN 0 THEN p.[MemberName]
               ELSE RTRIM(SUBSTRING(p.Path,
                   (80*(@intGridLevel2-1))+1, 80))
       END
   END) AS Member
FROM [Data] d
   INNER JOIN [Measures] m
       ON d.[Measures] = m.[MemberName]
   INNER JOIN [Year] y
       ON d.[Year] = y.[MemberName]
   INNER JOIN [Scenario] s
       ON d.[Scenario] = s.[MemberName]
   INNER JOIN [Market] mk
       ON d.[Market] = mk.[MemberName]
   INNER JOIN [Product] p
       ON d.[Product] = p.[MemberName]
   INNER JOIN [Grid1] g1
       ON g1.Member =
       CASE WHEN @vcGrid1 = 'Measures' THEN
           CASE @intGridLevel1
               WHEN 0 THEN d.[Measures]
               ELSE RTRIM(SUBSTRING(m.Path,
                   (80*(@intGridLevel1-1))+1, 80))
           END
       WHEN @vcGrid1 = 'Year' THEN
           CASE @intGridLevel1
               WHEN 0 THEN d.[Year]
               ELSE RTRIM(SUBSTRING(y.Path,
                   (80*(@intGridLevel1-1))+1, 80))
           END
       WHEN @vcGrid1 = 'Scenario' THEN
           CASE @intGridLevel1
               WHEN 0 THEN d.[Scenario]
               ELSE RTRIM(SUBSTRING(s.Path,
                   (80*(@intGridLevel1-1))+1, 80))
           END
       WHEN @vcGrid1 = 'Market' THEN
           CASE @intGridLevel1
               WHEN 0 THEN d.[Market]
               ELSE RTRIM(SUBSTRING(mk.Path,
                   (80*(@intGridLevel1-1))+1, 80))
           END
       WHEN @vcGrid1 = 'Product' THEN
           CASE @intGridLevel1
               WHEN 0 THEN d.[Product]
               ELSE RTRIM(SUBSTRING(p.Path,
                   (80*(@intGridLevel1-1))+1, 80))
           END
```

```
                END
       WHERE @vcPOV1Member =
           CASE WHEN @vcPOV1 = 'Measures' THEN
               CASE @intPOVLevel1
                   WHEN 0 THEN d.[Measures]
                   ELSE RTRIM(SUBSTRING(m.Path,
                       (80*(@intPOVLevel1-1))+1, 80))
               END
           WHEN @vcPOV1 = 'Year' THEN
               CASE @intPOVLevel1
                   WHEN 0 THEN d.[Year]
                   ELSE RTRIM(SUBSTRING(y.Path,
                       (80*(@intPOVLevel1-1))+1, 80))
               END
           WHEN @vcPOV1 = 'Scenario' THEN
               CASE @intPOVLevel1
                   WHEN 0 THEN d.[Scenario]
                   ELSE RTRIM(SUBSTRING(s.Path,
                       (80*(@intPOVLevel1-1))+1, 80))
               END
           WHEN @vcPOV1 = 'Market' THEN
               CASE @intPOVLevel1
                   WHEN 0 THEN d.[Market]
                   ELSE RTRIM(SUBSTRING(mk.Path,
                       (80*(@intPOVLevel1-1))+1, 80))
               END
           WHEN @vcPOV1 = 'Product' THEN
               CASE @intPOVLevel1
                   WHEN 0 THEN d.[Product]
                   ELSE RTRIM(SUBSTRING(p.Path,
                       (80*(@intPOVLevel1-1))+1, 80))
               END
           END
       AND @vcPOV2Member =
           CASE WHEN @vcPOV2 = 'Measures' THEN
               CASE @intPOVLevel2
                   WHEN 0 THEN d.[Measures]
                   ELSE RTRIM(SUBSTRING(m.Path,
                       (80*(@intPOVLevel2-1))+1, 80))
               END
           WHEN @vcPOV2 = 'Year' THEN
               CASE @intPOVLevel2
                   WHEN 0 THEN d.[Year]
                   ELSE RTRIM(SUBSTRING(y.Path,
                       (80*(@intPOVLevel2-1))+1, 80))
               END
           WHEN @vcPOV2 = 'Scenario' THEN
               CASE @intPOVLevel2
                   WHEN 0 THEN d.[Scenario]
```

```
                        ELSE RTRIM(SUBSTRING(s.Path,
                                (80*(@intPOVLevel2-1))+1, 80))
                    END
                WHEN @vcPOV2 = 'Market' THEN
                    CASE @intPOVLevel2
                        WHEN 0 THEN d.[Market]
                        ELSE RTRIM(SUBSTRING(mk.Path,
                                (80*(@intPOVLevel2-1))+1, 80))
                    END
                WHEN @vcPOV2 = 'Product' THEN
                    CASE @intPOVLevel2
                        WHEN 0 THEN d.[Product]
                        ELSE RTRIM(SUBSTRING(p.Path,
                                (80*(@intPOVLevel2-1))+1, 80))
                    END
                END
            AND @vcPOV3Member =
                CASE WHEN @vcPOV3 = 'Measures' THEN
                    CASE @intPOVLevel3
                        WHEN 0 THEN d.[Measures]
                        ELSE RTRIM(SUBSTRING(m.Path,
                                (80*(@intPOVLevel3-1))+1, 80))
                    END
                WHEN @vcPOV3 = 'Year' THEN
                    CASE @intPOVLevel3
                        WHEN 0 THEN d.[Year]
                        ELSE RTRIM(SUBSTRING(y.Path,
                                (80*(@intPOVLevel3-1))+1, 80))
                    END
                WHEN @vcPOV3 = 'Scenario' THEN
                    CASE @intPOVLevel3
                        WHEN 0 THEN d.[Scenario]
                        ELSE RTRIM(SUBSTRING(s.Path,
                                (80*(@intPOVLevel3-1))+1, 80))
                    END
                WHEN @vcPOV3 = 'Market' THEN
                    CASE @intPOVLevel3
                        WHEN 0 THEN d.[Market]
                        ELSE RTRIM(SUBSTRING(mk.Path,
                                (80*(@intPOVLevel3-1))+1, 80))
                    END
                WHEN @vcPOV3 = 'Product' THEN
                    CASE @intPOVLevel3
                        WHEN 0 THEN d.[Product]
                        ELSE RTRIM(SUBSTRING(p.Path,
                                (80*(@intPOVLevel3-1))+1, 80))
                    END
                END) g2
ORDER BY NEWID();
```

# References

Booth, J.A. 2012. Building the foundation: Essbase infrastructure. In *Developing Essbase Applications: Advanced Techniques for Finance and IT Professionals*, ed. C. Lackpour. Boca Raton, FL: CRC Press

Pressman, D.A. 2012. How ASO works and how to design for performance. In *Developing Essbase Applications: Advanced Techniques for Finance and IT Professionals*, ed. C. Lackpour. Boca Raton, FL: CRC Press.

# 5

# UTILIZING STRUCTURED QUERY LANGUAGE TO ENHANCE YOUR ESSBASE EXPERIENCE

## GLENN SCHWARTZBERG

Contents

The ability to use Structured Query Language (SQL) with Essbase has been available since the early years; however, since most administrators were end users and not part of the information technology (IT) group, SQL was not widely used. As IT has gotten more involved with building cubes, Essbase has increasingly interfaced with other applications. The features and functionality of Essbase itself have expanded, and thus, the need for administrators and developers to have an understanding of SQL has increased. This chapter presents some of the basics of SQL and then expands to Essbase-specific use cases including dimension building and loading data (load rules) and exporting data back to relational targets. Reading the chapter also will make you a better developer with Essbase Studio, allowing you to customize data load SQL and drill-through reports SQL, making it more efficient, and helping you understand user-defined tables and filtering conditions in Essbase Studio. We will not go into Essbase Studio in great detail, as that is beyond the scope of this chapter.

This chapter is not intended to make you an SQL expert but to give you enough information to get you started…and make you somewhat dangerous. A few short years ago, I was on a project with a friend and colleague of mine, to whom I affectionately refer as "MMIP" (My Man in Philadelphia). The project required extracting data from Hyperion Financial Management (HFM) utilizing a product called Extended Analytics (EA). EA wrote the HFM metadata and data to relational tables. MMIP's assignment was to write the extracts and put together the process for loading the metadata and data into an Essbase cube. He was quite honest at the start of the project: He told me that the extent of his SQL knowledge was the ability to write "SELECT * FROM table/view." I worked with MMIP to help him through his assignment, and by the end of the project, he was proficient in simple SQL and, since then, has surpassed me in SQL abilities. The goal of this chapter is to get you comfortable using SQL to empower you in your Essbase endeavors.

## 5.1 Getting Started

Using SQL with Essbase applications requires setting up a few things first. We will assume that an Essbase instance has already been installed and set up. In addition to the standard setup, an instance of a relational database (RDB) and a user account to access it are also needed. Any of a number of Open Database Connectivity (ODBC) compliant databases would work. For this chapter, I used SQL Server 2008. If another RDB will be used, the SQL syntax may be slightly different. The user account will need to be a native account, since connecting to SQL from Essbase is not allowed using external authentication. That user account also should have enough access to create tables, views, and stored procedures; write to tables; and execute stored procedures and triggers. Depending on what functionality is utilized in an actual production application, an account with lesser access rights may be used; for example, the account may only need "select" table access for loading data.

An SQL development tool is needed as well. SQL Server ships with SQL Server Management Studio, Oracle uses SQL Server Developer or Toad, and other tools are also available. Install one of these tools on the client.

Next, you will need to set up ODBC connections on the Essbase server to connect to the newly created database. The process for setting up and enabling ODBC connections is different depending on the RDB and the operating system on which Essbase is installed. Please refer to the Essbase SQL Interface guide for the steps to set ODBC connections for your environment.

Last, for the examples in this chapter, I created a database called TBC_Sample and utilized the tables and data that are shipped with Essbase Studio. The Data Definition Language (DDL) and SQL for loading this database are provided in the \Oracle\ Middleware\EPMSystem11R1\products\Essbase\EssbaseStudio\Server\sqlscripts directory. I used the tbc_create_sqlsrv.sql and tbc_sampledata.sql files to load the database. If SQL Server is being used, just open these files in SQL Server Management Studio, select the TBC_Sample database you created, and execute the files. While the DDL will build almost instantaneously, the data loading can take a few minutes, so don't panic if it does not come back right away. If a different RDB management system (RDBMS) will be used, read the readme file that is in the sqlscripts directory. Some things might need to be done differently to get the DDL and data to load properly. If the database has loaded in SQL Server correctly, it should look something like Figure 5.1.

Another database can be used, such as the Adventure Works DB that ships with SQL Server, but you will have to modify my examples to make it work.

### 5.2 Putting Together an SQL Statement: The Very Basics

This section will describe the very basics of SQL. If you are experienced with SQL, you may want to skip this section, or you can read through it quickly and laugh at my feeble attempts to enlighten and inform. Even if you are an experienced user, you might find a few tidbits be that useful, so skip the section at your own risk. Just as in designing an Essbase cube or writing a calc script, SQL has multiple ways of doing the same thing. What I present may not be the way you have seen something written, but most times, methods are interchangeable.

**Figure 5.1**    Database loaded in SQL Server.

In basic terms, an SQL statement has the following format:

```
SELECT something
FROM somewhere
optionally
WHERE some condition occurs
GROUP BY columns when summing numeric data
ORDER BY columns to sort
```

### 5.2.1 SELECT Statement

The statement SELECT * FROM Product would return all rows and columns from the product table because the * is a wildcard meaning all columns. Since the statement includes no filtering, we would get all rows. This simple statement is very powerful but can get us into trouble. It is much better to explicitly write out the columns we need for a few reasons:

1. We don't get extra data that are unneeded and unnecessary. In large tables, this could speed up retrievals as the bits and bytes don't get passed across the network. Also, if these columns have differing data values, and we are grouping data, the data will not group properly.
2. If a database administrator (DBA) adds new columns into a table, we won't automatically get the new columns. If we did get them, it could cause an error in existing processes, perhaps shifting the columns in a load rule or adding additional columns.
3. Specifying the columns allows us to know at a glance what is being returned.

### 5.2.2 Column Aliases

Building on this simplicity, we will, at times, want to change the name of a column when it is returned. For example, instead of SKU, maybe we want to call the column

"Level0,product" and call SKU_Alias "Alias0,Product." To do this, add an "AS" keyword with the new column aliases. This is one place where technique differs. I prefer including the AS keyword, but it is optional. You would get the same results if it were excluded. I use the AS for readability. In my example, do not get confused by the column name being SKU_Alias and the concept of adding an alias to a column. It is unfortunate that the designer of the table called the column SKU_Alias.

```
SELECT
      SKU AS "Level0,Product"
      ,SKU_ALIAS AS "Alias0,Product"
FROM PRODUCT
```

Why would we do this? Changing the column alias has many uses. First, it can make the alias easier to read. Second, if you are using a column more than once, it makes the name unique. And finally, as in Figure 5.2, it could now be used as a column header in a dimension build rule without having to explicitly put it in the rule. Alas, if only the last statement was true. In Rules Files, we will see later that the alias can be used with data load rules but not with dimension build rules.

### 5.2.3 Table Aliases

Quickly moving on and building on our simple SQL, there are times when we want to give the table or view name itself an alias. When we talk about joins later, this may make more sense. Adding the table alias is easily done in a similar manner to the column alias. Just put what you want to call the table after the table name. Let's call the

| LEVEL0,PRODUCT | ALIAS0,PRODUCT |
| --- | --- |
| 100-10 | Cola |
| 100-20 | Diet Cola |
| 100-30 | Caffeine Free Cola |
| 200-10 | Old Fashioned |
| 200-20 | Diet Root Beer |
| 200-30 | Sasparilla |
| 200-40 | Birch Beer |
| 300-10 | Dark Cream |
| 300-20 | Vanilla Cream |
| 300-30 | Diet Cream |
| 400-10 | Grape |
| 400-20 | Orange |
| 400-30 | Strawberry |
| 100-20 | Diet Cola |
| 200-20 | Diet Root Beer |
| 300-30 | Diet Cream |

**Figure 5.2**  Column aliases.

Product table "prod." When using a table alias, we now need to also prefix the column names with that alias in the format of prefix.column name.

```
SELECT
      Prod.SKU
      ,prod.FAMILYID
FROM Product AS prod
```

We will discuss later the use of aliases on column names and when using SUBSELECT clauses (yes, I know I have not talked about them yet, but I will).

### 5.2.4 WHERE Clauses

So far, so fun. Let's get a little more complicated and add a WHERE clause. A WHERE clause can be used as a filtering mechanism in your SQL statement. This filter can be based on column values, data values, or matching columns between tables. For our simple product query, we will filter based on the package type being a can. To do this, we add the WHERE statement and the column for comparison, the comparison operator, and the value being compared to. In this case, since the comparison is a literal, it is enclosed in quotes. The comparison operator can be a number of different things, including =, <, >, != (or <> for not equal), IS NULL, IS NOT NULL, IN, or LIKE. IN and LIKE are interesting. IN specifies a list of items, so we could say PKGTYP IN ('Bottle','Can') and get both values. LIKE is a more generic comparison. We can get substrings of items easily using wildcards. Suppose we want to get any product where the SKU_ALIAS starts with the word *Diet*. I could specify SKU_ALIAS LIKE 'Diet%.' Note the quotes around the literal and the %, which is a wild card specification for the LIKE clause. Results are shown in Figure 5.3.

| SELECT prod.SKU ,prod.SKU_ALIAS FROM PRODUCT prod WHERE prod.PKGTYPE = 'Can' | | SELECT prod.SKU ,prod.SKU_ALIAS FROM PRODUCT prod WHERE prod.SKU_ALIAS LIKE 'Diet' | |
|---|---|---|---|
| SKU | SKU_ALIAS | SKU | SKU_ALIAS |
| 100-10 | Cola | 100-20 | Diet Cola |
| 100-20 | Diet Cola | 200-20 | Diet Root Beer |
| 300-30 | Diet Cream | 300-30 | Diet Cream |

**Figure 5.3**  WHERE clause filter results.

## 5.2.5 *DISTINCT and GROUP BY*

Next, in our SQL, we might want to get a list of values or get rid of duplicates. This is where we can apply one of two keywords DISTINCT or GROUP BY. In the next example, the two keywords are interchangable, but in cases where we will be doing an aggregation (sum, count, min, max), GROUP BY is the required verb. For this example, we are switching to the ProductDim table (Figure 5.4).

Notice the SKU and SKU_Alias are repeated for the diet drinks. There are 16 rows in this table, but we just want a list of the individual products. If we use a standard SELECT, we will get all 16 rows. Using DISTINCT or GROUP BY just gives us the 13 unique rows (see Figure 5.5).

Had we added FAMILY to the query, we would have generated all 16 rows because the FAMILY would have made each row unique (see Table 5.1). This is a reason to be wary of including columns that are not necessary in your SQL. It can cause extra rows to be returned because the rows are no longer unique. We will discuss the topic of uniqueness when we get to aggregations. I will also show later how DISTINCT can be effective in subselect statements.

```
SELECT DISTINCT
      FAMILY
      ,SKU
      ,SKU_ALIAS
FROM TBC_Sample.dbo.PRODUCTDIM
```

| FAMILY | FAMILY_ALIAS | CONSOLIDATION | SKU | SKU_ALIAS |
|--------|--------------|---------------|--------|-------------------|
| 100 | Colas | + | 100-10 | Cola |
| 100 | Colas | + | 100-20 | Diet Cola |
| 100 | Colas | + | 100-30 | Caffeine Free Cola |
| 200 | Root Beer | + | 200-10 | Old Fashioned |
| 200 | Root Beer | + | 200-20 | Diet Root Beer |
| 200 | Root Beer | + | 200-30 | Sasparilla |
| 200 | Root Beer | + | 200-40 | Birch Beer |
| 300 | Cream Soda | + | 300-10 | Dark Cream |
| 300 | Cream Soda | + | 300-20 | Vanilla Cream |
| 300 | Cream Soda | + | 300-30 | Diet Cream |
| 400 | Fruit Soda | + | 400-10 | Grape |
| 400 | Fruit Soda | + | 400-20 | Orange |
| 400 | Fruit Soda | + | 400-30 | Strawberry |
| Diet | Diet Drinks | + | 100-20 | Diet Cola |
| Diet | Diet Drinks | + | 200-20 | Diet Root Beer |
| Diet | Diet Drinks | + | 300-30 | Diet Cream |

**Figure 5.4**  ProductDim table.

| SELECT DISTINCT SKU ,SKU_ALIAS FROM TBC_Sample. dbo.PRODUCTDIM | SELECT SKU ,SKU_ALIAS FROM TBC_Sample.dbo. PRODUCTDIM Group by SKU ,SKU_ALIAS |
|---|---|

| SKU | SKU_ALIAS | SKU | SKU_ALIAS |
|---|---|---|---|
| 100-10 | Cola | 100-10 | Cola |
| 100-20 | Diet Cola | 100-20 | Diet Cola |
| 100-30 | Caffeine Free Cola | 100-30 | Caffeine Free Cola |
| 200-10 | Old Fashioned | 200-10 | Old Fashioned |
| 200-20 | Diet Root Beer | 200-20 | Diet Root Beer |
| 200-30 | Sasparilla | 200-30 | Sasparilla |
| 200-40 | Birch Beer | 200-40 | Birch Beer |
| 300-10 | Dark Cream | 300-10 | Dark Cream |
| 300-20 | Vanilla Cream | 300-20 | Vanilla Cream |
| 300-30 | Diet Cream | 300-30 | Diet Cream |
| 400-10 | Grape | 400-10 | Grape |
| 400-20 | Orange | 400-20 | Orange |
| 400-30 | Strawberry | 400-30 | Strawberry |

**Figure 5.5**   DISTINCT or GROUP BY filter results.

**Table 5.1**   DISTINCT or GROUP BY Filter Results with FAMILY

| FAMILY | SKU | SKU_ALIAS |
|---|---|---|
| 100 | 100-10 | Cola |
| 100 | 100-20 | Diet Cola |
| 100 | 100-30 | Caffeine Free Cola |
| 200 | 200-10 | Old Fashioned |
| 200 | 200-20 | Diet Root Beer |
| 200 | 200-30 | Sasparilla |
| 200 | 200-40 | Birch Beer |
| 300 | 300-10 | Dark Cream |
| 300 | 300-20 | Vanilla Cream |
| 300 | 300-30 | Diet Cream |
| 400 | 400-10 | Grape |
| 400 | 400-20 | Orange |
| 400 | 400-30 | Strawberry |
| Diet | 100-20 | Diet Cola |
| Diet | 200-20 | Diet Root Beer |
| Diet | 300-30 | Diet Cream |

In the examples above, the table name TBC_Sample.DBO.PRODUCTIM is fully qualified. The first part, TBC_SAMPLE, is the database name. DBO (Database owner) is who owns the database, and PRODUCTDIM is the actual table. In production systems, we might be referencing different databases or a database could have tables with different owners. In some situations, we would need to have the fully qualified name to reference the table we are using. This does not apply in our sample situation. Also, I have been cavalier with the use of case. In SQL Server, unless turned on, databases are not case sensitive. In other RDBMSs, case can matter. In databases where case sensitivity is turned on, you have to be careful when doing comparisons in your WHERE clause. If case sensitivity is turned on, had we said WHERE PKGTYP = 'can' we would get zero rows returned since 'Can' <> 'can.' As a general rule, try to use the case of tables and columns as created in the database. It will save you problems.

### 5.2.6 ORDER BY

To finish off our discussion of the very basics of SQL, we will talk about the ORDER BY clause, which is used for sorting the results in the columns. ORDER BY is the last verb used in the select statement, and we specify the columns to sort either by column name or by column number (columns start at 1). By default, the sort is ascending, but we can add ASC for ascending or DESC for descending at the end of our ORDER BY list. We can order by multiple columns and it will order by the first column then the second and so on. The two returned sets of data in Figure 5.6 are in the exact

```
SELECT DISTINCT                        SELECT DISTINCT
    FAMILY                                 FAMILY
    ,SKU                                   ,SKU
    ,SKU_ALIAS                             ,SKU_ALIAS
FROM TBC_Sample.dbo.PRODUCTDIM         FROM TBC_Sample.dbo.PRODUCTDIM
ORDER BY SKU_ALIAS                     ORDER BY 3 DESC
```

| FAMILY | SKU | SKU_ALIAS | FAMILY | SKU | SKU_ALIAS |
|---|---|---|---|---|---|
| 200 | 200-40 | Birch Beer | 300 | 300-20 | Vanilla Cream |
| 100 | 100-30 | Caffeine Free Cola | 400 | 400-30 | Strawberry |
| 100 | 100-10 | Cola | 200 | 200-30 | Sasparilla |
| 300 | 300-10 | Dark Cream | 400 | 400-20 | Orange |
| 100 | 100-20 | Diet Cola | 200 | 200-10 | Old Fashioned |
| Diet | 100-20 | Diet Cola | 400 | 400-10 | Grape |
| 300 | 300-30 | Diet Cream | 200 | 200-20 | Diet Root Beer |
| Diet | 300-30 | Diet Cream | Diet | 200-20 | Diet Root Beer |
| 200 | 200-20 | Diet Root Beer | 300 | 300-30 | Diet Cream |
| Diet | 200-20 | Diet Root Beer | Diet | 300-30 | Diet Cream |
| 400 | 400-10 | Grape | 100 | 100-20 | Diet Cola |
| 200 | 200-10 | Old Fashioned | Diet | 100-20 | Diet Cola |
| 400 | 400-20 | Orange | 300 | 300-10 | Dark Cream |
| 200 | 200-30 | Sasparilla | 100 | 100-10 | Cola |
| 400 | 400-30 | Strawberry | 100 | 100-30 | Caffeine Free Cola |
| 300 | 300-20 | Vanilla Cream | 200 | 200-40 | Birch Beer |

**Figure 5.6**   ORDER BY filter results.

opposite order from each other because of the sorting of the Alias column. In cases where multiple rows have the same sort value, we cannot predict the order for the same value; adding additional columns to sort on could resolve the ordering issue.

*5.2.6.1 An Important ORDER BY Caveat*   In Section 5.2, I indicated that the use of the ORDER BY clause is optional: If we do not care what order your rows are reported back, do not use it. However, quite often, beginning SQL developers will write a SELECT without an ORDER BY clause, thinking, "That is the order I wanted, so why bother writing an ORDER BY clause?" Big mistake. The SQL definition explicitly states that there is no guarantee of any particular order unless an ORDER BY clause is used. As you grow more experienced with SQL, you will hear about the SQL Optimizer. This critical part of every SQL implementation figures out the fastest way to answer your query. Often, either changes in how the optimizer works or (more likely) the amount and frequency of repeats in your data will change how it works. Your code could be great one day and just plain wrong on another.

Having said that, I will not clutter up the examples here by adding ORDER BY clauses when the point I am trying to make is independent of the row report order. You should not be so cavalier in your SQL work.

*5.2.7 Format Your SQL to Make It Readable and Editable*

Now is a good time to talk about code formatting. Properly formatted code is much easier to read, and formatting makes it easier to edit your code. I typically use a few simple rules when putting code together. The SQL statement below shows my preferred method of formatting a statement:

```
SELECT
       T1.COLUMN1
       ,t1.COLUMN2
FROM TABLE t1
WHERE
       Condition1 = something
       And condition2 <> something
GROUP BY
       T1.COLUMN1
       ,T1.COLUMN2
ORDER BY 1,2
```

What are my rules?

1. The keywords SELECT, FROM WHERE, GROUP BY, and ORDER BY are all capitalized to be easy to find.
2. The column names are indented so I can easily find the next keyword.
3. I use the same case for the column names as they exist in the database.

4. The second column name row has a comma preceding it. The statement could have been written with the coma following column1, but putting it at the front of the column2 name more easily allows columns to be commented out without having to remember to remove the extra commas.
5. When putting in math statements or conditional statements, have them indented and on separate lines to make them easier to read and change.
6. Use table aliases whenever possible to shorten long table names.

As a side note, comments can be done in two ways. To comment out a single line, multiple dashes can be used; I like three: ---. To comment out multiple lines, we can use /* */.

There you have it, the very basics of a simple SQL statement. Of course, rarely will we have the luxury of such simple statements. In the next section, we will get a little more complicated and see how we can use multiple tables together.

## 5.3 Putting Together an SQL Statement: Altering Columns

Bringing back the columns as they exist in the database is easy, as we have seen, but many times, we need to alter the columns to make them work in the Essbase environment. Often, we need to concatenate columns together, split them, or make a choice on a column value. Luckily for us, SQL has a lot of built-in functionality to allow us to do these things.

### 5.3.1 Concatenating Columns

First of all, since you are likely an Excel formula whiz, note that the SQL concatenation operator is "+" symbol and not the "&" operator. You may have also noticed in my examples that strings in SQL get surrounded by single quotes, not double quotes as in Excel. I guarantee that this will frustrate you often. But there will come a day when you go to write a formula in an Excel spreadsheet and you use the + sign or the single quotes. On that day, you will know that you are well on your way to mastering SQL.

As experienced Essbase developers, we can guess that a good example of the need to concatenate columns is in building our product dimension. The users want to have the product number appended to the end of the product alias and have it separated by a dash (see Table 5.2).

```
SELECT
      SKU
      ,SKU_ALIAS + '-' + SKU as ALIAS
FROM PRODUCT
```

That was easy, but what if we want to concatenate the Alias with the number of ounces? In this case, SKU_ALIAS has a data type of Varchar and OUNCES has a data type of integer. What will happen? The suspense is killing me! We run the following query:

**Table 5.2**  Concatenating Columns

| SKU | ALIAS |
| --- | --- |
| 100-10 | Cola-100-10 |
| 100-20 | Diet Cola-100-20 |
| 100-30 | Caffeine Free Cola-100-30 |
| 200-10 | Old Fashioned-200-10 |
| 200-20 | Diet Root Beer-200-20 |
| 200-30 | Sasparilla-200-30 |
| 200-40 | Birch Beer-200-40 |
| 300-10 | Dark Cream-300-10 |
| 300-20 | Vanilla Cream-300-20 |
| 300-30 | Diet Cream-300-30 |
| 400-10 | Grape-400-10 |
| 400-20 | Orange-400-20 |
| 400-30 | Strawberry-400-30 |

```
SELECT
      SKU
      ,SKU_ALIAS + ' - ' + SKU as ALIAS
      ,SKU_ALIAS + '-' + OUNCES as ALIAS_OUNCES
FROM PRODUCT
```

Alas, what we get back is an error message:

```
Conversion failed when converting the varchar value 'Cola-' to data
type int.
```

But wait. Why did it try to convert the text 'Cola-' to an integer? Even a newbie SQL programmer like me knows that it should have left 'Cola-' as text and converted ounces to text. Well, the computer is not as smart as we are and does not know what we are trying to do. The syntax parser can only follow simple, unambiguous rules.

What the parser thought is, "Oh, they might have a text string like '4.5' that I could convert to a number, which I could have added to the integer ounces to get a number." At least, that is what the programmer who taught it the rules thought would be what you wanted most often. There is no way it can convert 'Cola-' to an integer, so it broke.

To do this concatenation, we need to do a data type conversion. Each column has a specified data type. To take a slight side trip, Table 5.3 presents common data types and their meanings.

Different RDBs will have different and additional data types. For our purposes, the most common type of conversion is converting numeric values to Varchar (or Varchar2 for Oracle). Of course, simple conversion functions are available, and we will use a very common function named CAST. This allows you to convert data from one data type to another as long as the conversion is meaningful. For example, if we tried to convert "aaa" to a number, it would fail as that does not make sense to convert. But if

**Table 5.3**  Common Data Types and Their Meanings

| DATA TYPE | DESCRIPTION |
|---|---|
| Char(n) | Fixed width string up to 8000 characters |
| Varchar() | Variable length string up to 8000 characters |
| Varchar2() Oracle | Used in Oracle instead of Varchar. Stores strings up to 4000 characters |
| Tinyint | Whole number between 0 and 255 |
| Smallint | Whole number between −32,768 and 32,768 |
| Decimal (*p*,*s*) or Numeric (*p*,*s*) | A decimal number. $p$ = total digits stored and $s$ = number of positions to the right of the decimal point |
| Money | Monetary data from −922,337,203,685,477.5808 to 922,337,203,685,477.5807 |
| Float() | Floating precision number data from −1.79E + 308 to 1.79E + 308 |
| Datetime | From January 1, 1753, to December 31, 9999 |
| Date | The date only portion of datetime |
| Time | The time only portion of datetime |

**Table 5.4**  Data Type Conversion

| SKU | ALIAS | ALIAS_OUNCES |
|---|---|---|
| 100-10 | Cola-100-10 | Cola-12 |
| 100-20 | Diet Cola-100-20 | Diet Cola-12 |
| 100-30 | Caffeine Free Cola-100-30 | Caffeine Free Cola-16 |
| 200-10 | Old Fashioned-200-10 | Old Fashioned-12 |
| 200-20 | Diet Root Beer-200-20 | Diet Root Beer-16 |
| 200-30 | Sasparilla-200-30 | Sasparilla-12 |
| 200-40 | Birch Beer-200-40 | Birch Beer-16 |
| 300-10 | Dark Cream-300-10 | Dark Cream-20 |
| 300-20 | Vanilla Cream-300-20 | Vanilla Cream-20 |
| 300-30 | Diet Cream-300-30 | Diet Cream-12 |
| 400-10 | Grape-400-10 | Grape-32 |
| 400-20 | Orange-400-20 | Orange-32 |
| 400-30 | Strawberry-400-30 | Strawberry-32 |

we tried to convert the text string of "12345" to a number, it could convert. The syntax for CAST is

```
CAST(Column AS data type).
```

So to fix our earlier SQL, we need to change the numeric ounces to a Varchar since the alias is a Varchar. We need to make the Varchar big enough to hold the value; in this case, 10 is bigger than the longest string. We added extra so it would never fail to convert. See results in Table 5.4.

```
SELECT
      SKU
      ,SKU_ALIAS + ' - ' + SKU as ALIAS
```

```
        ,SKU_ALIAS + '-' + CAST(OUNCES AS VARCHAR(10)) as
ALIAS_OUNCES
FROM PRODUCT
```

### 5.3.2 Replacing Parts of a String

We all know that Essbase has limitations on member names, such as characters that are not allowed or the length of the names. Were we to have an alias that started with a period or a parenthesis, Essbase would complain (loudly). If only a few of these issues are present, we can correct them in the SQL. SQL Server has a REPLACE command, and other RDBMSs have similar commands, although they may be named differently. The syntax of the command is REPLACE (Column, Old Value, New Value). As an example, suppose the users wanted the format of the SKU in the PRODUCT table to be xxx.xx instead of xxx-xx. We would alter the query from the last example to

```
SELECT
        REPLACE(SKU,'-','.') as SKU
        ,SKU_ALIAS + ' - ' + SKU as ALIAS
        ,SKU_ALIAS + '-' + CAST(OUNCES AS VARCHAR(10)) as
ALIAS_OUNCES
FROM PRODUCT
```

As the user requested, the first column now has the dash replaced with a period (see Table 5.5). The good thing about this command is it will replace the character no matter where it is found in the string. The bad thing about this command is it will replace all occurrences of the value to be replaced. If we changed the command to replace 0 instead of dash,

```
REPLACE(SKU,'0','.') as SKU
```

the first SKU would look like 1..-1, even if we only wanted the first or last 0 replaced.

**Table 5.5**   REPLACE Results

| SKU | ALIAS | ALIAS_OUNCES |
|---|---|---|
| 100.10 | Cola-100-10 | Cola-12 |
| 100.20 | Diet Cola-100-20 | Diet Cola-12 |
| 100.30 | Caffeine Free Cola-100-30 | Caffeine Free Cola-16 |
| 200.10 | Old Fashioned-200-10 | Old Fashioned-12 |
| 200.20 | Diet Root Beer-200-20 | Diet Root Beer-16 |
| 200.30 | Sasparilla-200-30 | Sasparilla-12 |
| 200.40 | Birch Beer-200-40 | Birch Beer-16 |
| 300.10 | Dark Cream-300-10 | Dark Cream-20 |
| 300.20 | Vanilla Cream-300-20 | Vanilla Cream-20 |
| 300.30 | Diet Cream-300-30 | Diet Cream-12 |
| 400.10 | Grape-400-10 | Grape-32 |
| 400.20 | Orange-400-20 | Orange-32 |
| 400.30 | Strawberry-400-30 | Strawberry-32 |

This REPLACE command is good if we have one or two values to correct and the command can be nested, but if there are a lot of values, then we should use other methods. Perhaps utilizing different functions like the combination of SUBSTRING, RIGHT, LEFT, and LEN could give us what we want. This REPLACE method works well if there are just a few changes and they are very static; however, if we need to replace many different values, then creating a table with the conversion 'from' and conversion 'to' values and using an OUTER JOIN (described later) would be a better solution.

### 5.3.3 Using CASE Statements

At times, we will need to have a value set based on multiple possible values, the result of a mathematical expression, or based on multiple conditions. One of the easiest ways to do this is with a CASE statement. There are multiple forms of the CASE statement. The two I use most often are a simple case and a searched case. In a simple case statement, the format is as follows:

```
CASE column
WHEN some literal or value THEN
     Literal or mathematical expression
WHEN some other literal or value THEN
     Different literal or expression
ELSE (This is an optional fall through default)
     Literal or expression
END
```

This is good for when distinct values are used to create a value based on other values. In my example, I know all of the values for the column OUNCES, and based on the value, I want to return a different literal. The ELSE statement is an optional fall-through for any items I might have missed or where new values were not accounted for. Table 5.6 shows the results.

**Table 5.6** Simple CASE Statement Results

| SKU | SKU_ALIAS | OUNCES | SIZE |
|---|---|---|---|
| 100-10 | Cola | 12 | Small |
| 100-20 | Diet Cola | 12 | Small |
| 100-30 | Caffeine Free Cola | 16 | Medium |
| 200-10 | Old Fashioned | 12 | Small |
| 200-20 | Diet Root Beer | 16 | Medium |
| 200-30 | Sasparilla | 12 | Small |
| 200-40 | Birch Beer | 16 | Medium |
| 300-10 | Dark Cream | 20 | Large |
| 300-20 | Vanilla Cream | 20 | Large |
| 300-30 | Diet Cream | 12 | Small |
| 400-10 | Grape | 32 | Extra Large |
| 400-20 | Orange | 32 | Extra Large |
| 400-30 | Strawberry | 32 | Extra Large |

```
SELECT
        SKU
        ,SKU_ALIAS
        ,OUNCES
        ,CASE OUNCES
        WHEN 12 THEN
              'Small'
        WHEN 16 THEN
              'Medium'
        WHEN 20 THEN
              'Large'
        ELSE
              'Extra Large'
        END as Size
FROM PRODUCT
```

I believe the searched CASE expression is more flexible and more powerful, so it is the syntax I use more often. The format for this type of CASE statement is as follows:

```
CASE
WHEN Boolean expression THEN
      Some literal or calculated expression
WHEN (additional statements)…
ELSE
      Default literal or expression
END
```

By "Boolean expression" in the statement, I mean anything that will return a true or false. An Expression Column Name < 50 or ColumnA = ColumnB would both meet this criterion. I think this is more powerful because you don't have to specify explicit values, but rather ranges. The multiple WHEN statements don't even have to reference the same columns. Results are shown in Table 5.7.

**Table 5.7**   Searched CASE Statement Results

| SKU | SKU_ALIAS | OUNCES | PKGTYPE | SIZE |
| --- | --- | --- | --- | --- |
| 100-10 | Cola | 12 | Can | Small |
| 100-20 | Diet Cola | 12 | Can | Small |
| 100-30 | Caffeine Free Cola | 16 | Bottle | Medium |
| 200-10 | Old Fashioned | 12 | Bottle | Small |
| 200-20 | Diet Root Beer | 16 | Bottle | Medium |
| 200-30 | Sasparilla | 12 | Bottle | Small |
| 200-40 | Birch Beer | 16 | Bottle | Medium |
| 300-10 | Dark Cream | 20 | Bottle | Large |
| 300-20 | Vanilla Cream | 20 | Bottle | Large |
| 300-30 | Diet Cream | 12 | Can | Small |
| 400-10 | Grape | 32 | Bottle | Extra Large |
| 400-20 | Orange | 32 | Bottle | Extra Large |
| 400-30 | Strawberry | 32 | Bottle | Extra Large |

**Table 5.8**   Nested CASE Statement Results

| SKU | SKU_ALIAS | OUNCES | PKGTYPE | SIZE |
|-----|-----------|--------|---------|------|
| 100-10 | Cola | 12 | Can | Small |
| 100-20 | Diet Cola | 12 | Can | Small |
| 100-30 | Caffeine Free Cola | 16 | Bottle | Medium |
| 200-10 | Old Fashioned | 12 | Bottle | Small |
| 200-20 | Diet Root Beer | 16 | Bottle | Medium |
| 200-30 | Sasparilla | 12 | Bottle | Small |
| 200-40 | Birch Beer | 16 | Bottle | Medium |
| 300-10 | Dark Cream | 20 | Bottle | Large |
| 300-20 | Vanilla Cream | 20 | Bottle | Large |
| 300-30 | Diet Cream | 12 | Can | Small |
| 400-10 | Grape | 32 | Bottle | Extra Large |
| 400-20 | Orange | 32 | Bottle | Extra Large |
| 400-30 | Strawberry | 32 | Bottle | Extra Large |

```
SELECT
      SKU
      ,SKU_ALIAS
      ,OUNCES
      ,PKGTYPE
      ,CASE WHEN OUNCES <= 12 THEN
          'Small'
      WHEN OUNCES <= 16 THEN
          'Medium'
      WHEN OUNCES <= 20 THEN
          'Large'
      ELSE
          'Extra Large'
      END as Size
FROM PRODUCT
```

CASE statements can be nested for more advanced conversions. Although I could do this using compound expressions in the statement, nesting the statements requires less code and is easier to understand. My example is pretty simple: When the package type is a can, then the material is aluminum. When it is a bottle, if it is 16 ounces or less, then it is glass; otherwise, it is plastic. See the results in Table 5.8.

```
SELECT
      SKU
      ,SKU_ALIAS
      ,OUNCES
      ,Case PKGTYPE
          WHEN 'Can' Then
                'Aluminum'
          ELSE
```

```
    CASE WHEN OUNCES <= 16 THEN
            'Glass'
        ELSE
            'Plastic'
        END
    END as Container
FROM PRODUCT
```

These complex case statements have limits. In SQL Server, we can nest case statements only 10 levels deep. As this section shows, CASE statements can be very powerful as a data conversion tool.

### 5.4  Putting Together an SQL Statement: JOINS

When the data you want to produce are spread across multiple tables, we use a join to combine them. There are four types of joins used in SQL. The first and most common is an INNER JOIN (also just represented by JOIN). In this type of join, tables are combined based on one or more matching columns. In a LEFT OUTER JOIN, all of the rows are returned from the first table listed and matching information is included from the second table based on the columns being joined. The third join, as you might guess, is a RIGHT OUTER JOIN, in which all rows from the second table are returned and matching information from the first table is included when the columns being joined match. Last, we have a FULL OUTER JOIN, in which all the data from both tables are returned, regardless of matching columns in the join. On the three outer joins, if you specify a column where the join condition does not match, a null is returned from that column. Most of the time, inner joins are used, but sometimes, I will use an outer join when I have matching columns. For an example, let's go back to our product SQL. If we select all columns and do not restrict the rows with a WHERE clause, we will get everything from the table. We will see the FAMILYID is a code and not the name of the family (see Table 5.9).

```
SELECT
    prod.*
FROM PRODUCT prod
```

If I look at the FAMILY table (see Table 5.10), I can see the same FAMILYID there.

```
SELECT *
FROM FAMILY
```

### 5.4.1  INNER Joins

To get the Family and Family Alias, I have to join the PRODUCT and FAMILY tables together. We can do this by adding the JOIN clause after the FROM table. We then add the condition that we are joining on using the ON clause. Notice that I did

**Table 5.9**  Sample PRODUCT Table

| PRODUCTID | FAMILYID | SKU | SKU_ALIAS | CAFFEINATED | OUNCES | PKGTYPE | INTRODATE |
|---|---|---|---|---|---|---|---|
| 1 | 1 | 100-10 | Cola | TRUE | 12 | Can | 1996-03-25 00:00:00.000 |
| 2 | 1 | 100-20 | Diet Cola | TRUE | 12 | Can | 1996-04-01 00:00:00.000 |
| 3 | 1 | 100-30 | Caffeine Free Cola | FALSE | 16 | Bottle | 1996-04-01 00:00:00.000 |
| 4 | 2 | 200-10 | Old Fashioned | TRUE | 12 | Bottle | 1995-09-27 00:00:00.000 |
| 5 | 2 | 200-20 | Diet Root Beer | TRUE | 16 | Bottle | 1996-07-26 00:00:00.000 |
| 6 | 2 | 200-30 | Sasparilla | FALSE | 12 | Bottle | 1996-12-10 00:00:00.000 |
| 7 | 2 | 200-40 | Birch Beer | FALSE | 16 | Bottle | 1996-12-10 00:00:00.000 |
| 8 | 3 | 300-10 | Dark Cream | TRUE | 20 | Bottle | 1996-06-26 00:00:00.000 |
| 9 | 3 | 300-20 | Vanilla Cream | TRUE | 20 | Bottle | 1996-06-26 00:00:00.000 |
| 10 | 3 | 300-30 | Diet Cream | TRUE | 12 | Can | 1996-06-26 00:00:00.000 |
| 11 | 4 | 400-10 | Grape | FALSE | 32 | Bottle | 1996-10-01 00:00:00.000 |
| 12 | 4 | 400-20 | Orange | FALSE | 32 | Bottle | 1996-10-01 00:00:00.000 |
| 13 | 4 | 400-30 | Strawberry | FALSE | 32 | Bottle | 1996-10-01 00:00:00.000 |

**Table 5.10**   Sample FAMILY Table

| FAMILYID | FAMILY | FAMILY_ALIAS | INTRODATE |
|----------|--------|--------------|-----------|
| 1 | 100 | Colas | 1996-03-25 00:00:00.000 |
| 2 | 200 | Root Beer | 1995-09-27 00:00:00.000 |
| 3 | 300 | Cream Soda | 1996-06-26 00:00:00.000 |
| 4 | 400 | Fruit Soda | 1996-10-01 00:00:00.000 |

not say INNER Join, because the default is an inner join. Also, see that we are returning columns from both tables. We have prefixed the columns with the alias for which table the column is coming from. (See Table 5.11 for results.) If we did not prefix the columns, we would get a message that the column name is ambiguous because the FAMILY column exists in both tables and the SQL parser does not know which table to display the column from.

```
SELECT
      fam.FAMILY
      ,fam.FAMILY_ALIAS
      ,prod.SKU
      ,prod.SKU_ALIAS
FROM PRODUCT prod
JOIN FAMILY fam
      ON fam.FAMILYID = prod.FAMILYID
ORDER BY
      fam.FAMILY
      ,prod.SKU
```

Notice how the ON clause works as a filter on the combined table, similar to how WHERE clauses filtered data.

**Table 5.11**   JOIN Results

| FAMILY | FAMILY_ALIAS | SKU | SKU_ALIAS |
|--------|--------------|-----|-----------|
| 100 | Colas | 100-10 | Cola |
| 100 | Colas | 100-20 | Diet Cola |
| 100 | Colas | 100-30 | Caffeine Free Cola |
| 200 | Root Beer | 200-10 | Old Fashioned |
| 200 | Root Beer | 200-20 | Diet Root Beer |
| 200 | Root Beer | 200-30 | Sasparilla |
| 200 | Root Beer | 200-40 | Birch Beer |
| 300 | Cream Soda | 300-10 | Dark Cream |
| 300 | Cream Soda | 300-20 | Vanilla Cream |
| 300 | Cream Soda | 300-30 | Diet Cream |
| 400 | Fruit Soda | 400-10 | Grape |
| 400 | Fruit Soda | 400-20 | Orange |
| 400 | Fruit Soda | 400-30 | Strawberry |

*5.4.2 OUTER Joins*

We take a similar example and use the PRODUCTDIM table, which has 16 rows, and join on the FAMILY column.

```
SELECT
      fam.FAMILY
      ,fam.FAMILY_ALIAS
      ,prod.SKU
      ,prod.SKU_ALIAS
FROM PRODUCTDIM prod
JOIN FAMILY fam
      ON fam.FAMILY = prod.FAMILY
```

We see in Table 5.12 that we only return 13 rows. What is missing are the rows with "Diet" as the Family. The FAMILY table does not have Diet as a value. If I change the query to LEFT OUTER JOIN (by the way, LEFT JOIN also works because OUTER is implied), I get all the rows from the PRODUCTDIM table (see Figure 5.7).

```
SELECT
      fam.FAMILY
      ,fam.FAMILY_ALIAS
      ,prod.SKU
      ,prod.SKU_ALIAS
FROM PRODUCTDIM prod
LEFT OUTER JOIN FAMILY fam
      ON fam.FAMILY = prod.FAMILY
```

**Table 5.12**   JOIN Results Error Illustration

| FAMILY | FAMILY_ALIAS | SKU | SKU_ALIAS |
|--------|--------------|--------|-------------------|
| 100 | Colas | 100-10 | Cola |
| 100 | Colas | 100-20 | Diet Cola |
| 100 | Colas | 100-30 | Caffeine Free Cola |
| 200 | Root Beer | 200-10 | Old Fashioned |
| 200 | Root Beer | 200-20 | Diet Root Beer |
| 200 | Root Beer | 200-30 | Sasparilla |
| 200 | Root Beer | 200-40 | Birch Beer |
| 300 | Cream Soda | 300-10 | Dark Cream |
| 300 | Cream Soda | 300-20 | Vanilla Cream |
| 300 | Cream Soda | 300-30 | Diet Cream |
| 400 | Fruit Soda | 400-10 | Grape |
| 400 | Fruit Soda | 400-20 | Orange |
| 400 | Fruit Soda | 400-30 | Strawberry |

| FAMILY | FAMILY_ALIAS | SKU | SKU_ALIAS |
|--------|--------------|-----|-----------|
| 100 | Colas | 100-10 | Cola |
| 100 | Colas | 100-20 | Diet Cola |
| 100 | Colas | 100-30 | Caffeine Free Cola |
| 200 | Root Beer | 200-10 | Old Fashioned |
| 200 | Root Beer | 200-20 | Diet Root Beer |
| 200 | Root Beer | 200-30 | Sasparilla |
| 200 | Root Beer | 200-40 | Birch Beer |
| 300 | Cream Soda | 300-10 | Dark Cream |
| 300 | Cream Soda | 300-20 | Vanilla Cream |
| 300 | Cream Soda | 300-30 | Diet Cream |
| 400 | Fruit Soda | 400-10 | Grape |
| 400 | Fruit Soda | 400-20 | Orange |
| 400 | Fruit Soda | 400-30 | Strawberry |
| NULL | NULL | 100-20 | Diet Cola |
| NULL | NULL | 200-20 | Diet Root Beer |
| NULL | NULL | 300-30 | Diet Cream |

**Figure 5.7** OUTER JOIN results.

NULL was returned for the first two columns in rows 14–16 because they don't exist in the FAMILY table. We could get the value for the FAMILY column if we changed the SQL statement to return data from the PRODUCTDIM table instead of the FAMILY table. In real-world situations, we probably would not want a null value returned. SQL has functions to turn null values into something else. In SQL Server, it is the ISNULL function; in Oracle, it is the NLV function. They both work the same way. The syntax is ISNULL (column name, replacement value). If the replacement value is a string, then it has to be enclosed in quotes. In our case, we want to replace the null FAMILY with "Unknown" and the Alias with "Unknown Family" (see results in Table 5.13).

```
SELECT
      ISNULL(fam.FAMILY,'Unknown') AS FAMILY
      ,ISNULL(fam.FAMILY_ALIAS,'Unknown Family') AS Alias
      ,prod.SKU
      ,prod.SKU_ALIAS
FROM PRODUCTDIM prod
LEFT JOIN FAMILY fam
      ON fam.FAMILY = prod.FAMILY
```

*5.4.2.1 NULL Values*  Why would we want to replace NULL values with a value? In the example above, we would most likely be building a dimension from these data. In the real world, someone might have added products without updating the Essbase hierarchy. We don't want the data load to reject because we are missing products, so we can convert the null values to a place holder family where the members would be added. Another issue with NULL is how it performs with math. Like #Missing in

**Table 5.13** Replacing NULL Values

| FAMILY | FAMILY_ALIAS | SKU | SKU_ALIAS |
|--------|--------------|------|-----------|
| 100 | Colas | 100-10 | Cola |
| 100 | Colas | 100-20 | Diet Cola |
| 100 | Colas | 100-30 | Caffeine Free Cola |
| 200 | Root Beer | 200-10 | Old Fashioned |
| 200 | Root Beer | 200-20 | Diet Root Beer |
| 200 | Root Beer | 200-30 | Sasparilla |
| 200 | Root Beer | 200-40 | Birch Beer |
| 300 | Cream Soda | 300-10 | Dark Cream |
| 300 | Cream Soda | 300-20 | Vanilla Cream |
| 300 | Cream Soda | 300-30 | Diet Cream |
| 400 | Fruit Soda | 400-10 | Grape |
| 400 | Fruit Soda | 400-20 | Orange |
| 400 | Fruit Soda | 400-30 | Strawberry |
| Unknown | Unknown Family | 100-20 | Diet Cola |
| Unknown | Unknown Family | 200-20 | Diet Root Beer |
| Unknown | Unknown Family | 300-30 | Diet Cream |

Essbase, NULL in math statements return NULL. Adding, subtracting, multiplying, or dividing by NULL always returns NULL. The code below and Table 5.14 show this clearly and show how we can convert the NULL to 0 in most cases to get the desired result. The exception to this, of course, is division by 0. In that case, I had to add another function, NULLIF, to turn the 0 back to a NULL.

```
SELECT
      1 + NULL as adding
      ,1 * NULL as multiplying
      ,1 - NULL as subtracting
      ,1 / NULL as division
      ,1 + ISNULL(NULL ,0)
      ,1 * ISNULL(NULL ,0)
      ,1 - ISNULL(NULL,0)
      ,ISNULL (1/NULLIF (ISNULL(NULL,0),0),0)
```

It is very important to get this right, especially when doing aggregations of calculations (which we do later in this chapter), or we could get incorrect results. In the preceding example, we don't specify a FROM clause or table name. We don't need this because we are not specifying any real column names, only text.

**Table 5.14** Replacing NULL with Numeric Values

| ADDING | MULTIPLYING | SUBTRACTING | DIVISION | (NO COLUMN NAME) | (NO COLUMN NAME) | (NO COLUMN NAME) | (NO COLUMN NAME) |
|--------|-------------|-------------|----------|------------------|------------------|------------------|------------------|
| NULL | NULL | NULL | NULL | 1 | 0 | 1 | 0 |

*5.4.3 OUTER JOINS Continued*

Back to our regularly scheduled section: Our example of an OUTER JOIN replaced a null with a text string, a literal. In some cases, we would want a column value to be used. In our example, the FAMILY was correct in the PRODUCTDIM table even though it was missing from the FAMILY table. By simply referencing the FAMILY in the PRODUCT table, we can get the values to show as we want them (see Table 5.15).

```
SELECT
        ISNULL(fam.FAMILY,prod.FAMILY) as FAMILY
        ,ISNULL(fam.FAMILY_ALIAS,prod.FAMILY) as Alias
        ,prod.SKU
        ,prod.SKU_ALIAS
FROM PRODUCTDIM prod
LEFT JOIN FAMILY fam
        ON prod.FAMILY = fam.FAMILY
```

One of my most frequent uses of a left outer join is build dimension SQL. Quite often, I will be able to get the hierarchy information but am missing important information for specific members. This information could include formulas, consolidation operators, solve order, and other properties. Typically, this information is very static and does not change once set. This makes our work easy: We can create a properties table to hold this information. We could create the table for a specific dimension, but I prefer to make it a bit more generic, so I have one table for all my special needs.

**Table 5.15**  OUTER JOIN Results with Corrected Values

| FAMILY | ALIAS | SKU | SKU_ALIAS |
|--------|-------|-----|-----------|
| 100 | Colas | 100-10 | Cola |
| 100 | Colas | 100-20 | Diet Cola |
| 100 | Colas | 100-30 | Caffeine Free Cola |
| 200 | Root Beer | 200-10 | Old Fashioned |
| 200 | Root Beer | 200-20 | Diet Root Beer |
| 200 | Root Beer | 200-30 | Sasparilla |
| 200 | Root Beer | 200-40 | Birch Beer |
| 300 | Cream Soda | 300-10 | Dark Cream |
| 300 | Cream Soda | 300-20 | Vanilla Cream |
| 300 | Cream Soda | 300-30 | Diet Cream |
| 400 | Fruit Soda | 400-10 | Grape |
| 400 | Fruit Soda | 400-20 | Orange |
| 400 | Fruit Soda | 400-30 | Strawberry |
| Diet | Diet | 100-20 | Diet Cola |
| Diet | Diet | 200-20 | Diet Root Beer |
| Diet | Diet | 300-30 | Diet Cream |

In our same tables, we have the Measures table that has a number of special columns, but they are specific for block storage option (BSO) cubes. Let's extend that to include aggregate storage option (ASO) properties. First, we will create a table to hold the properties:

```
CREATE TABLE [dbo].[ASO_PROPERTIES](
       [Dimension] [varchar](80) NOT NULL,
       [Member_Name] [varchar](80) NOT NULL,
       [ASO_Consolidation] [varchar](50) NULL,
       [ASO_Solve_Order] [smallint] NULL,
       [ASO_Formula] [varchar](4000) NULL,
       [ASO_Storage] [varchar](50) NULL
)
```

With this table, we can define a dimension and member to join on, as well as its ASO properties. I add a member for Profit percent from the measures dimension and a Var member for the Scenario dimension.

```
INSERT INTO ASO_PROPERTIES VALUES
('MEASURES','Profit %','~',5,'[PROFIT]/[SALES]/100',NULL)
INSERT INTO ASO_PROPERTIES VALUES
('SCENARIO','VAR','~',5,'[ACTUAL]-[Budget]',NULL)
```

Let's create a join to get our ASO properties for the MEASURES dimension. We have to include both the join condition and what dimension we want the join on.

```
SELECT
       m.PARENT
       ,m.CHILD
       ,ASO.ASO_Formula
FROM MEASURES m
LEFT JOIN ASO_PROPERTIES aso
       ON m.CHILD = aso.Member_Name
       AND aso.Dimension = 'Measures'
```

In our query results (Table 5.16), we see the formula being populated. Remember, MEASURES is a recursive hierarchy, but for our query (joining on the member name), it does not matter whether it is recursive or not. We might need special code if there are shared hierarchies.

### 5.4.4 Older JOIN Syntax

There is also an older syntax that bypasses the JOIN clause but has the same effect as an INNER JOIN. In this case, the tables are listed one after the other separated by commas, and the join condition is part of the WHERE clause. The results are the same, but I find the JOIN clause easier to read.

**Table 5.16**   LEFT OUTER JOIN Results

| PARENT | CHILD | ASO_FORMULA |
|---|---|---|
| Measures | Profit | NULL |
| Profit | Margin | NULL |
| Margin | Sales | NULL |
| Margin | COGS | NULL |
| Profit | Total Expenses | NULL |
| Total Expenses | Marketing | NULL |
| Total Expenses | Payroll | NULL |
| Total Expenses | Misc | NULL |
| Measures | Inventory | NULL |
| Inventory | Opening Inventory | NULL |
| Inventory | Additions | NULL |
| Inventory | Ending Inventory | NULL |
| Measures | Ratios | NULL |
| Ratios | Margin % | NULL |
| Ratios | Profit % | [PROFIT]/[SALES]/100 |
| Ratios | Profit per Ounce | NULL |

```
SELECT
        fam.FAMILY
        ,fam.FAMILY_ALIAS
        ,prod.SKU
        ,prod.SKU_ALIAS
FROM PRODUCT prod
        ,FAMILY fam
WHERE
        fam.FAMILYID = prod.FAMILYID
ORDER BY
        fam.FAMILY
        ,prod.SKU
```

Be very careful to include all of the necessary join conditions between tables. If you were to remove the join condition from the previous example, you would get what is called a Cartesian product, which is the joining of every row in the first table to every row in the second table. In the example above, the PRODUCT table has 13 rows in it and the FAMILY table has 4 rows. Our example query had valid join conditions for every row in the tables and returned 13 rows. If this became a Cartesian product join, we would have gotten 52 rows back (13 × 4). These sample tables are small; were they tables with thousands or millions of rows, the amount of data trying to be returned would be astronomical and could likely consume more space than is allowed on your system.

In fact, if you have been paying attention, you already learned about Cartesian joins. We described them above when we discussed FULL OUTER JOIN.

Using the first syntax shown, we are less likely to get a Cartesian product because the ON condition must be supplied (unless we explicitly include the keyword FULL), but it is still possible because we might need to join on multiple columns for the join to be correct or the join could be to the wrong tables. The moral of the story? We must be very careful to make sure our joins are correct or we will get more than we expect and can consume mass amount of system resources doing bad things.

This older syntax is seen less and less often. We have not mentioned how to indicate LEFT or RIGHT or even OUTER as join types. Just to make sure you recognize them, this is how you would do it using Oracle's SQL:

```
Inner Join:         fam.FAMILYID = prod.FAMILYID
Left Outer Join:    (+) fam.FAMILYID = prod.FAMILYID
Right Outer Join:   fam.FAMILYID = prod.FAMILYID (+)
```

IBM's SQL would be:

```
Inner Join:         fam.FAMILYID = prod.FAMILYID
Left Outer Join:    fam.FAMILYID *= prod.FAMILYID
Right Outer Join:   fam.FAMILYID =* prod.FAMILYID
```

Just look it up if you ever see something that looks like these older syntaxes.

### 5.5  Putting Together an SQL Statement: Aggregation Functions

Based on what we have learned so far, we can only return the rows that we have in our tables and not reduce the number of rows. This means if I have a daily SALES table, which I do, and I want to get a monthly total, I would have to manually add up all the individual rows to get that total. That would be unreasonable—I could have millions of rows and want a single grand total. Of course, we don't need to do that manual work because SQL includes a number of aggregation functions. Table 5.17 lists standard functions.

Depending on the flavor of SQL, additional functions could be available. For example, SQL Server has Standard deviation (STDEV) and variance (VAR) related functions. The simplest format for the statement is as follows:

```
SELECT
      Aggregate Function (Column)
FROM TABLE
```

**Table 5.17**  SQL Standard Functions

| FUNCTION | SQL SERVER SYNTAX | DESCRIPTION |
|---|---|---|
| AVERAGE | AVG | Averages the group of numbers; has optional arguments |
| MINIMUM | MIN | Returns the minimum value |
| MAXIMUM | MAX | Returns the maximum value |
| COUNT | COUNT | Returns the number of items in a group |
| SUM | SUM | Totals the group of items |

Using this basic format, to get the above functions from our SALES table, we could use the SQL:

```
SELECT
        AVG(AMOUNT) as Average
        ,MIN(AMOUNT) as Minimum
        ,MAX(AMOUNT) as Maximum
        ,COUNT(*) as "Count"
        ,SUM(AMOUNT) as "Sum"
FROM SALES sls
JOIN MEASURES acct
        ON sls.MEASURESID = acct.MEASURESID
WHERE acct.CHILD = 'Sales'
```

Table 5.18 shows the results.

The query was based on all rows of data for the Sales account, for all products, for all markets, for all time periods, but what if I want more granular results? If I add other columns to the query that are the basis of the summation, I have to use the following syntax:

```
SELECT
        ,Column(s)
        Aggregate Function(Column)
FROM TABLE
GROUP BY non-aggregating columns
```

Let's change our last query so it gives us these metrics for each child account. It is an easy change: We just have to add the column to the SELECT clause, remove our WHERE clause, and add a GROUP BY clause. Results are in Table 5.19.

**Table 5.18**   SQL SALES Table Results

| AVERAGE | MINIMUM | MAXIMUM | COUNT | SUM |
|---|---|---|---|---|
| 81.5698777403038 | 0.2 | 1130 | 9488 | 773,935.000000003 |

**Table 5.19**   SQL Granular SALES Table Results

| ACCT | AVERAGE | MINIMUM | MAXIMUM | COUNT | SUM |
|---|---|---|---|---|---|
| Additions | 86.9019895287956 | 0 | 1094.4 | 9550 | 829,913.999999998 |
| COGS | 36.0289700713601 | 0.1 | 450 | 9389 | 338,276 |
| Marketing | 13.5404140835186 | 0.04 | 145.08 | 8549 | 115,757 |
| Misc | 0.438908145580589 | 0.01 | 1 | 2308 | 1013 |
| Opening Inventory | 289.620646766169 | 1.9 | 2520 | 804 | 232,855 |
| Payroll | 9.25272667180789 | 0.1 | 51.41 | 9077 | 83,987.0000000002 |
| Sales | 81.5698777403038 | 0.2 | 1130 | 9488 | 773,935.000000003 |

```
SELECT
      acct.CHILD as Acct
      ,AVG(AMOUNT) as Average
      ,MIN(AMOUNT) as Minimum
      ,MAX(AMOUNT) as Maximum
      ,COUNT(*) as "Count"
      ,SUM(AMOUNT) as "Sum"
FROM SALES sls
JOIN MEASURES acct
      ON sls.MEASURESID = acct.MEASURESID
GROUP BY acct.CHILD
```

With aggregation functions, remember that anything you want in the output that is not an aggregation function must be a part of the GROUP BY statement or you will get errors. You will also get an error if the column in the GROUP BY has an Alias. Had I copied the acct.CHILD row from the SELECT statement to the GROUP BY, I would have had to remove the "As Acct" for the statement to work. Having the nonaggregating columns in the GROUP BY is another reason to not have extra columns in your query.

Suppose I want to get the sales account by period/year. But I also want to see the transaction date.

```
SELECT
      acct.CHILD
      ,MONTH(sls.TRANSDATE) as Period
      ,YEAR(sls.TRANSDATE) as YR
      ,sls.TRANSDATE
      ,AVG(AMOUNT) as Average
      ,MIN(AMOUNT) as Minimum
      ,MAX(AMOUNT) as Maximum
      ,COUNT(*) as "Count"
      ,SUM(AMOUNT) as "Sum"
FROM SALES sls
JOIN MEASURES acct
      ON sls.MEASURESID = acct.MEASURESID
WHERE acct.CHILD = 'Sales'
GROUP BY acct.CHILD
      ,MONTH(sls.TRANSDATE)
      ,YEAR(sls.TRANSDATE)
      ,sls.TRANSDATE
```

This query returns 336 rows, but notice I get multiple rows for each period/year combination, as shown in Table 5.20.

We can see that we got too granular with these data. We have one entry for each day, and it looks like sales are always posted with a time of 00:00:00.000. If the system reported time in more detail, we would have seen many more rows than 336!

If we modify the query to remove the sls.TRANSDATE from the select and group by, we now get 12 rows of data (Table 5.21) that truly reflect the values for the Period/Year.

**Table 5.20**   Issues with Aggregating

| CHILD | PERIOD | YR | TRANSDATE | AVERAGE | MINIMUM | MAXIMUM | COUNT | SUM |
|-------|--------|----|-----------|---------|---------|---------|-------|-----|
| Sales | 1 | 2000 | 2000-01-01 00:00:00.000 | 88.6079310344827 | 1.9 | 640 | 29 | 2569.63 |
| Sales | 1 | 2000 | 2000-01-02 00:00:00.000 | 52.7813793103448 | 1.1 | 130 | 29 | 1530.66 |
| Sales | 1 | 2000 | 2000-01-03 00:00:00.000 | 71.6419230769231 | 3 | 224.64 | 26 | 1862.69 |
| Sales | 1 | 2000 | 2000-01-04 00:00:00.000 | 88.7470967741935 | 0.45 | 464.1 | 31 | 2751.16 |
| Sales | 1 | 2000 | 2000-01-05 00:00:00.000 | 67.3792307692308 | 3.25 | 469.3 | 26 | 1751.86 |
| Sales | 1 | 2000 | 2000-01-06 00:00:00.000 | 51.9666666666667 | 1.2 | 288.3 | 21 | 1091.3 |
| Sales | 1 | 2000 | 2000-01-07 00:00:00.000 | 140.717741935484 | 0.9 | 840 | 31 | 4362.25 |
| Sales | 1 | 2000 | 2000-01-08 00:00:00.000 | 107.342954545455 | 0.9 | 560 | 44 | 4723.09 |
| Sales | 1 | 2000 | 2000-01-09 00:00:00.000 | 111.576923076923 | 0.43 | 644.1 | 26 | 2901 |
| Sales | 1 | 2000 | 2000-01-10 00:00:00.000 | 77.11625 | 1.6 | 405.84 | 24 | 1850.79 |

**Table 5.21**   Corrected Aggregated Results

| CHILD | PERIOD | YR | AVERAGE | MINIMUM | MAXIMUM | COUNT | SUM |
|-------|--------|----|---------|---------|---------|-------|-----|
| Sales | 6 | 2000 | 88.8732026143791 | 0.2 | 739.2 | 765 | 67,988 |
| Sales | 4 | 2000 | 79.68375 | 0.4 | 690 | 800 | 63,747 |
| Sales | 11 | 2000 | 77.8620253164557 | 0.3 | 623 | 790 | 61,511 |
| Sales | 3 | 2000 | 77.5316770186336 | 0.41 | 675 | 805 | 62,413.0000000001 |
| Sales | 1 | 2000 | 76.4636591478697 | 0.4 | 840 | 798 | 61,018 |
| Sales | 10 | 2000 | 77.4224999999999 | 0.4 | 770 | 800 | 61,938 |
| Sales | 8 | 2000 | 88.0554854981084 | 0.4 | 1130 | 793 | 69,828 |
| Sales | 12 | 2000 | 81.2177215189874 | 0.4 | 699 | 790 | 64,162 |
| Sales | 5 | 2000 | 81.378277153558 | 0.4 | 902.4 | 801 | 65,184 |
| Sales | 9 | 2000 | 81.8301404853129 | 0.4 | 715.4 | 783 | 64,073 |
| Sales | 7 | 2000 | 88.0553459119497 | 0.4 | 866.4 | 795 | 70,004 |
| Sales | 2 | 2000 | 80.8190104166667 | 0.3 | 800 | 768 | 62,069 |

## 5.6  Putting Together an SQL Statement: Subquery

Have you heard of a turducken? It is a chicken inside of a duck inside of a turkey. Just like the turducken, a subquery (also called a subselect) is a query (SQL statement) inside of another SQL statement. You might ask, "Why the heck would I want to do that?" The answer is because subqueries are very powerful to give the results you want and need, and in some cases, no other way exists to easily get those results. Subqueries can be in the SELECT, the FROM, or the WHERE clauses of an SQL statement. Like other elements of SQL, they are very powerful but can cause serious trouble if used incorrectly.

*5.6.1  Subquery in a SELECT Clause*

Let's look at the subquery in a SELECT statement first. Our PRODUCT table contains the SKU and the FAMILYID with which the SKU is associated. Suppose I want to find out how many siblings a SKU has. Since the FAMILYID is the parent of SKU, counting the number of rows that have the FAMILYID tells us the sibling count. This sounds very easy, but it could be very difficult if we did not have the subquery. Counting the number of FAMILYIDs for an SKU would always result in a value of 1 because an SKU has only one parent. Trying to do a self-join would not easily give us the results we want. A subquery in the SELECT could be our rescuer. If we can count the number of occurrences of a FAMILYID for each SKU, we can come up with the number of siblings each SKU has. When used in a select, the subquery must return a single value. If it tries to return multiple values, we will get an error. This is why aggregation functions are frequently used in subqueries. When used in the select portion of a query, the subquery is enclosed in parentheses () and should have a join condition to relate it to the main query (see results in Table 5.22).

```
SELECT
      prod.SKU
      ,FAMILYID
      ,(SELECT COUNT(*)- 1 FROM PRODUCT sq
      WHERE sq.FAMILYID = prod.FAMILYID
      ) as siblings
FROM PRODUCT prod
```

As you can see (and count), from our subquery, we now know how many siblings each SKU has. In the subquery, I subtracted 1 from the count because the subquery counts all occurrences of the FAMILYID. Had I wanted to, I could have modified

**Table 5.22**    Results for Subquery in a SELECT Clause

| SKU | FAMILYID | SIBLINGS |
| --- | --- | --- |
| 100-10 | 1 | 2 |
| 100-20 | 1 | 2 |
| 100-30 | 1 | 2 |
| 200-10 | 2 | 3 |
| 200-20 | 2 | 3 |
| 200-30 | 2 | 3 |
| 200-40 | 2 | 3 |
| 300-10 | 3 | 2 |
| 300-20 | 3 | 2 |
| 300-30 | 3 | 2 |
| 400-10 | 4 | 2 |
| 400-20 | 4 | 2 |
| 400-30 | 4 | 2 |

**Table 5.23**   Results for Two Subqueries in a SELECT Clause

| SCENARIO | STATE | SKU | PERIOD | YR | AMT | TOT_AMT | PCT_OF_TOTAL |
|---|---|---|---|---|---|---|---|
| Actual | California | 100-10 | 1 | 2000 | 678 | 395,454 | 0.00171448512342776 |
| Actual | Colorado | 100-10 | 1 | 2000 | 190 | 395,454 | 0.000480460432818988 |
| Actual | Connecticut | 100-10 | 1 | 2000 | 310 | 395,454 | 0.00078390912723098 |
| Actual | Florida | 100-10 | 1 | 2000 | 210 | 395,454 | 0.000531035215220987 |
| Actual | Illinois | 100-10 | 1 | 2000 | 345 | 395,454 | 0.000872414996434478 |
| Actual | Iowa | 100-10 | 1 | 2000 | 62 | 395,454 | 0.000156781825446196 |
| Actual | Louisiana | 100-10 | 1 | 2000 | 85 | 395,454 | 0.000214942825208495 |
| Actual | Massachusetts | 100-10 | 1 | 2000 | 494 | 395,454 | 0.00124919712532937 |
| Actual | Missouri | 100-10 | 1 | 2000 | 190 | 395,454 | 0.000480460432818988 |
| Actual | Nevada | 100-10 | 1 | 2000 | 76 | 395,454 | 0.000192184173127595 |

the subquery to exclude that member we were on. To do that, I would replace the subquery with

```
(SELECT COUNT(*) FROM PRODUCT sq WHERE sq.FAMILYID = prod.FAMILYID
and sq.SKU <> prod.SKU )as siblings
```

To provide a more realistic and complete example using the SALES table and aspects we have not yet discussed, I want to get the ratio sales amount for each product, location to all locations, and all products for each month. To do this, I need a subquery to get the total. In the example, SUM is used because I want the total for the period and the SALES table is by day. I am converting the day into a period and year using SQL functions. The example uses two subqueries. The first subquery shows the total amount and the second shows the same amount but used in the mathematical equation. The results in Table 5.23 show only the first 10 of 2112 rows, just to illustrate what the results will look like.

```
SELECT
        scn.SCENARIO
        ,m.STATE
        ,p.SKU
        ,Month(s.TRANSDATE) as period
        ,YEAR(s.TRANSDATE) as yr
        ,sum(s.AMOUNT) as amt
        ,(SELECT sum(sq.AMOUNT) from SALES sq
            WHERE MONTH(sq.TRANSDATE) = Month(s.TRANSDATE) and
YEAR(sq.TRANSDATE) = YEAR(s.TRANSDATE)
        ) as Tot_amt
        ,sum(s.AMOUNT) / (SELECT sum(sq.AMOUNT) from SALES sq
            WHERE MONTH(sq.TRANSDATE) = Month(s.TRANSDATE) and
            YEAR(sq.TRANSDATE) = YEAR(s.TRANSDATE)
        ) as Pct_of_Total
FROM SALES s
JOIN PRODUCT p
        ON p.PRODUCTID = s.PRODUCTID
JOIN MARKET m
        ON m.STATEID = s.STATEID
```

```
JOIN SCENARIO scn
       ON s.SCENARIOID = scn.SCENARIOID
JOIN MEASURES acct
       on Acct.MEASURESID = s.MEASURESID
WHERE scn.SCENARIO = 'Actual'
       AND acct.CHILD = 'Sales'
GROUP BY
       scn.SCENARIO
       ,m.STATE
       ,p.SKU
       ,Month(s.TRANSDATE)
       ,YEAR(s.TRANSDATE)
ORDER by 3,4,5,2
```

### 5.6.2 Subquery in a WHERE Clause

Sometimes, a join will give you a wrong answer. Suppose you have a dimension table that contains alternate rollups, similar to our PRODUCTDIM table, which has a rollup of diet drinks. If we join that back to the PRODUCT table based on SKU, it looks like:

```
SELECT prod.SKU
       ,Prod.SKU_ALIAS
       ,prod.FAMILYID
FROM PRODUCT prod
JOIN PRODUCTDIM pd
ON prod.SKU = pd.SKU
```

Figure 5.8 shows the results.

| SKU | SKU_ALIAS | FAMILYID |
|-----|-----------|----------|
| 100-10 | Cola | 1 |
| 100-20 | Diet Cola | 1 |
| 100-20 | Diet Cola | 1 |
| 100-30 | Caffeine Free Cola | 1 |
| 200-10 | Old Fashioned | 2 |
| 200-20 | Diet Root Beer | 2 |
| 200-20 | Diet Root Beer | 2 |
| 200-30 | Sasparilla | 2 |
| 200-40 | Birch Beer | 2 |
| 300-10 | Dark Cream | 3 |
| 300-20 | Vanilla Cream | 3 |
| 300-30 | Diet Cream | 3 |
| 300-30 | Diet Cream | 3 |
| 400-10 | Grape | 4 |
| 400-20 | Orange | 4 |
| 400-30 | Strawberry | 4 |

**Figure 5.8**  Results for subqueries in a WHERE clause.

**Table 5.24**   Corrected Results for Subqueries in a WHERE Clause

| SKU | SKU_ALIAS | FAMILYID |
|------|-------------------|------|
| 100-10 | Cola | 1 |
| 100-20 | Diet Cola | 1 |
| 100-30 | Caffeine Free Cola | 1 |
| 200-10 | Old Fashioned | 2 |
| 200-20 | Diet Root Beer | 2 |
| 200-30 | Sasparilla | 2 |
| 200-40 | Birch Beer | 2 |
| 300-10 | Dark Cream | 3 |
| 300-20 | Vanilla Cream | 3 |
| 300-30 | Diet Cream | 3 |
| 400-10 | Grape | 4 |
| 400-20 | Orange | 4 |
| 400-30 | Strawberry | 4 |

Notice how the diet drinks are repeated. If I were joining this to sales data and trying to get a total for sales, I would be double counting the diet drinks, giving me inflated actual sales. Rather than do that, as I've sworn off diet drinks (well, as you can see, I still drink them, but only under their original numeric family name—I can't tell the difference unless I look at the label on the can), I can use a subquery to find the SKUs that are in the PRODUCTDIM table (see Table 5.24 for results). Again, just like the subquery in a SELECT, the subquery is wrapped in parentheses ():

```
SELECT prod.SKU
      ,Prod.SKU_ALIAS
      ,prod.FAMILYID
From PRODUCT prod
WHERE prod.SKU in (SELECT DISTINCT SKU from PRODUCTDIM)
```

This is invaluable when we want to ensure that the data coming from one table are included in the second table without actually getting data or columns from the second table. In my query, I used DISTINCT in the subquery. Although this is not necessary (the query just looks to see if the value is in the subquery; it does not care how many times it occurs), I think it is more efficient. If I am doing a subquery on a 10-million-row table, I might get back a thousand rows instead of the million. It must be more efficient for the query to look at those thousand rows rather than the millions. In this subquery, we can see that only one column is being returned. Like the subquery in the select clause, only a single column is allowed.

### 5.6.3 Subquery in a FROM Clause

Subqueries in FROM clauses are the most complicated. This type of query returns a full result set into a temporary system table that can then be used in a JOIN

**Table 5.25** Results for Subquery in a FROM Clause

| SCENARIO | STATE | SKU | PERIOD | YR | CURRENT_ MTH_AMT | PRIOR_ MTH_AMT | CURRENT – PRIOR |
|----------|-------|-----|--------|-----|-----------------|----------------|-----------------|
| Actual | California | 100-10 | 1 | 2000 | 7458 | 16,482 | −9024 |
| Actual | Colorado | 100-10 | 1 | 2000 | 2090 | 1764 | 326 |
| Actual | Connecticut | 100-10 | 1 | 2000 | 3410 | 12,356 | −8946 |
| Actual | Florida | 100-10 | 1 | 2000 | 2310 | 10,312 | −8002 |
| Actual | Illinois | 100-10 | 1 | 2000 | 3795 | 4665 | −870 |
| Actual | Iowa | 100-10 | 1 | 2000 | 682 | 1512 | −830 |
| Actual | Louisiana | 100-10 | 1 | 2000 | 935 | 1123 | −188 |
| Actual | Massachusetts | 100-10 | 1 | 2000 | 5434 | 24,032 | −18,598 |
| Actual | Missouri | 100-10 | 1 | 2000 | 2090 | 5796 | −3706 |
| Actual | Nevada | 100-10 | 1 | 2000 | 836 | 2631 | −1795 |

condition with other tables (or other subqueries) to get a result set. Because of this, this type of subquery can be inefficient because no indexes are created to be used in JOIN conditions. I suggest that you attempt to use other methods before employing this method. Unlike subqueries in SELECT or WHERE clauses, this subquery can have multiple columns and multiple rows returned. Like the other subqueries, it is wrapped in parentheses () and must include an alias. Depending on the RDBMS (Oracle, for example), the AS keyword for the alias must sometimes be omitted.

It is amazing to me the parallels that exist. As I was writing this chapter, I ran into a real-world situation where I needed to use subqueries in a FROM clause. In my case, I had a table that had YTD balances and I needed to load monthly activity into my cube. That meant I had to take the current period (whatever it was) and subtract from it the previous period value. To complicate matters, it was possible that there might not be a value from the last period. I tried various solutions, but the best I came up with utilized two subqueries in my FROM clause, one for the current period and one for the previous period. The example shown here is not the actual query I used, but mimics it. It is fairly complicated. The query uses ISNULL to ensure I get a member or value and it has a subquery in the WHERE clause to get the previous period and proper year. The period and year are concatenated together so I return a single value from that subquery. It has a FULL OUTER JOIN so I don't miss any data and uses a SUM function to get period totals. I have truncated the result set (Table 5.25) to show only the first 10 rows.

```
SELECT
        ISNULL(scn.SCENARIO,sqf.SCENARIO) AS Scenario
        ,ISNULL(m.STATE,sqf.STATE) as "State"
        ,ISNULL(p.SKU,sqf.SKU) as SKU
        ,ISNULL(MONTH(s.TRANSDATE),sqf.period) as period
        ,ISNULL(YEAR(s.TRANSDATE),sqf.yr) as yr
        ,ISNULL(SUM(s.amount),0) as Current_mth_amt
        ,ISNULL(SUM(sqf.amt),0) as Prior_mth_amt
```

```
        ,ISNULL(sum(s.AMOUNT),0) - ISNULL(sum(sqf.amt),0) as "Current
- Prior"
FROM SALES s
JOIN PRODUCT p
        ON p.PRODUCTID = s.PRODUCTID
JOIN MARKET m
        ON m.STATEID = s.STATEID
JOIN SCENARIO scn
        ON s.SCENARIOID = scn.SCENARIOID
JOIN MEASURES acct
on Acct.MEASURESID = s.MEASURESID
FULL OUTER JOIN
/**** Prior period Amt SUB-query *****/
(SELECT
        scn.SCENARIO
        ,m.STATE
        ,p.SKU
        ,s.MEASURESID
        ,s.PRODUCTID
        ,s.SCENARIOID
        ,s.STATEID
        ,Month(s.TRANSDATE) as period
        ,YEAR(s.TRANSDATE) as yr
        ,sum(s.AMOUNT) as amt
FROM SALES s
JOIN PRODUCT p
        ON p.PRODUCTID = s.PRODUCTID
JOIN MARKET m
        ON m.STATEID = s.STATEID
JOIN SCENARIO scn
        ON s.SCENARIOID = scn.SCENARIOID
JOIN MEASURES acct
on Acct.MEASURESID = s.MEASURESID
WHERE Month((s.TRANSDATE))+'-'+ YEAR((s.TRANSDATE)) in
        /**** Where Clause Sub Query ****/
        (SELECT (month(DATEADD(MONTH,-1,sq.TRANSDATE)))+'-'+
(YEAR(DATEADD(MONTH,-1,sq.TRANSDATE))) from SALES sq
        WHERE (month(DATEADD(MONTH,-1,sq.TRANSDATE))) = Month(s.
TRANSDATE) and (YEAR(DATEADD(MONTH,-1,sq.TRANSDATE))) = YEAR(s.
TRANSDATE) )
/**** END of WHERE Clause sub-query ****/
GROUP BY
        scn.SCENARIO
        ,m.STATE
        ,p.SKU
        ,s.MEASURESID
        ,s.PRODUCTID
        ,s.SCENARIOID
        ,s.STATEID
```

```
      ,Month(s.TRANSDATE)
      ,YEAR(s.TRANSDATE)
      ) sqf
/**** End of Prior period Amt SUB-query *****/
ON sqf.MEASURESID =s.MEASURESID
and sqf.PRODUCTID = s.PRODUCTID
and sqf.SCENARIOID = s.SCENARIOID
and sqf.STATEID = s.STATEID
WHERE scn.SCENARIO = 'Actual'
      AND acct.CHILD = 'Sales'
GROUP BY
      ISNULL(scn.SCENARIO,sqf.SCENARIO)
      ,ISNULL(m.STATE,sqf.STATE)
      ,ISNULL(p.SKU,sqf.SKU)
      ,ISNULL(MONTH(s.TRANSDATE),sqf.period)
      ,ISNULL(YEAR(s.TRANSDATE),sqf.yr)
ORDER by 3,4,5,2
```

## 5.7  Putting Together an SQL Statement: UNIONS

As we wrap up our discussion on putting together an SQL statement, I would be remiss if we did not talk about UNIONS. I am not asking you to join the AFL-CIO or Teamsters, but rather to consider how to bring back two sets of rows glued together as one. Suppose we have two tables, "Current_Year_Sales" and "Historical_Sales" and I need to bring the same columns back from each table. I could write two queries and get two sets of rows and deal with them individually. But I am lazy and want to deal only with a single set of data.

Notice I am not suggesting we bring back one set of rows with two columns, one for current and one for historical. (Besides, we are join experts now and already know how to do that.)

What I do suggest is writing the first query, removing the ORDER BY clause, adding the keyword UNION (or UNION ALL), and then adding the second query. Last, you can add back in the ORDER BY at the end that will sort the complete set of returned data.

```
SELECT
      Columns
FROM TABLE
UNION
SELECT
      COLUMNS
FROM TABLE
ORDER BY XXX
```

As long as the number of columns, the order of the columns, and the data types of the columns in the two queries are the same, we will get the complete set of data from both tables. Notice that it is only the types of columns that have to match—names do not have to match. I could leave the field named Current_Year_Sales with that name and Historical_Sales as Historical_Sales as long as they are both the same data type. The difference between the UNION and UNION ALL is the UNION will remove any row that is a duplicate while UNION ALL will return those duplicate rows. I use a UNION a lot. Typically, in source systems metadata tables, there are no placeholders for "No" members. In our sample Product table, we might have data that do not relate to particular products and we need a "No product" member added to the hierarchy.

```
SELECT
        '1' as sort_order
        ,fam.FAMILY
        ,fam.FAMILY_ALIAS
        ,prod.SKU
        ,prod.SKU_ALIAS
FROM PRODUCT prod
JOIN FAMILY fam
ON prod.FAMILYID = fam.FAMILYID
UNION
SELECT
        '2'
        ,NULL
        ,NULL
        ,'No Product'
        ,NULL
Order by 1,2,3
```

I now have my No Product included (see Figure 5.9). I used NULL to fill in for values I did not need and added a literal so I could get the members in the order I want.

| SORT_ORDER | FAMILY | FAMILY_ALIAS | SKU | SKU_ALIAS |
|---|---|---|---|---|
| 1 | 100 | Colas | 100-10 | Cola |
| 1 | 100 | Colas | 100-20 | Diet Cola |
| 1 | 100 | Colas | 100-30 | Caffeine Free Cola |
| 1 | 200 | Root Beer | 200-10 | Old Fashioned |
| 1 | 200 | Root Beer | 200-20 | Diet Root Beer |
| 1 | 200 | Root Beer | 200-30 | Sasparilla |
| 1 | 200 | Root Beer | 200-40 | Birch Beer |
| 1 | 300 | Cream Soda | 300-10 | Dark Cream |
| 1 | 300 | Cream Soda | 300-20 | Vanilla Cream |
| 1 | 300 | Cream Soda | 300-30 | Diet Cream |
| 1 | 400 | Fruit Soda | 400-10 | Grape |
| 1 | 400 | Fruit Soda | 400-20 | Orange |
| 1 | 400 | Fruit Soda | 400-30 | Strawberry |
| 2 | NULL | NULL | No Product | NULL |

**Figure 5.9**  Using a UNION in SQL.

## 5.8  Putting Together an SQL Statement: Views versus Tables

In this chapter, I have referred mostly to tables, but I have used the nomenclature table/view on a few occasions. Are they interchangeable? Why would I prefer to use one over the other? First, here are some similarities between tables and views.

1. When writing an SQL statement to retrieve data, there is no difference in the statement when selecting from a table or a view. As with Essbase ASO and BSO cubes, you do not know whether you are retrieving data from a table or a view.
2. Both tables and views have columns and data types for each column.
3. Security can be assigned to either tables or views.
4. A user can perform joins between tables and views.

Of course, tables and views are not the same thing. Here are some differences.

1. A table is a single source of data, while a view can join multiple tables together.
2. Views can be optimized by the DBA to ensure best performance, while joins written on the fly might not perform as well
3. Views will shield us from table changes. If table changes, the view may not or can mask the changes (this saves us especially if we use SELECT *).
4. Large table joins can use what are called materialized views that actually create tables that are updated automatically with changes.
5. Tables can be updated, while a view, if it joins multiple tables together, cannot be used in updates.
6. Views return a result that can be the join from multiple tables, which can make it easier to do some aggregation functions.

From a query perspective, there is no difference in using a table or view, but there are advantages to using views, so I prefer to use them whenever I can. The standard DDL for creating a view is

```
Create View View_name
(View column name(s))
AS
SELECT …
FROM …
```

A client site typically will have standards for how tables and views are named. In many cases, I've seen views prefixed or suffixed with V or VW (e.g., V_ or _VW). View names have to be unique from table names, so a view on my Product table might be PRODUCT_V. The view column names can be different from the column names in the tables. I recently had an instance in which a colleague wanted to use the Planning Outline load utility and needed specific column headers for each column. Using the View names, she was able to format the names to match what the utility needed. Finally, the SQL can be almost any SQL SELECT statement that returns rows of data. The SELECT can include most functions we have already discussed. When using a UNION in the DDL for a view, the number of columns in each SELECT has to match. If we need to change a view, the syntax differs between SQL versions. SQL Server uses an ALTER command, while ORACLE employs the SYNTAX CREATE OR REPLACE. Using one of the SQL statements we tested before, to create a view out of it, we would use the following:

```
CREATE VIEW PRODUCT_V
("FAMILY","FAMILY_ALIAS","SKU","SKU_ALIAS")
AS
SELECT
      ISNULL(fam.FAMILY,prod.FAMILY) as FAMILY
      ,ISNULL(fam.FAMILY_ALIAS,prod.FAMILY) as Alias
      ,prod.SKU
      ,prod.SKU_ALIAS
FROM PRODUCTDIM prod
LEFT JOIN FAMILY fam
      ON prod.FAMILY = fam.FAMILY
```

When executed, the return shows:

```
Command(s) completed successfully.
```

When I issue an SQL Command:

```
SELECT *
FROM PRODUCT_V
```

I get the rows as expected, as shown in Table 5.36.

**Table 5.26**   SELECT from a View

| FAMILY | FAMILY_ALIAS | SKU | SKU_ALIAS |
|--------|--------------|--------|-------------------|
| 100 | Colas | 100-10 | Cola |
| 100 | Colas | 100-20 | Diet Cola |
| 100 | Colas | 100-30 | Caffeine Free Cola |
| 200 | Root Beer | 200-10 | Old Fashioned |
| 200 | Root Beer | 200-20 | Diet Root Beer |
| 200 | Root Beer | 200-30 | Sasparilla |
| 200 | Root Beer | 200-40 | Birch Beer |
| 300 | Cream Soda | 300-10 | Dark Cream |
| 300 | Cream Soda | 300-20 | Vanilla Cream |
| 300 | Cream Soda | 300-30 | Diet Cream |
| 400 | Fruit Soda | 400-10 | Grape |
| 400 | Fruit Soda | 400-20 | Orange |
| 400 | Fruit Soda | 400-30 | Strawberry |
| Diet | Diet | 100-20 | Diet Cola |
| Diet | Diet | 200-20 | Diet Root Beer |
| Diet | Diet | 300-30 | Diet Cream |

## 5.9 Putting Together an SQL Statement: Summary

Although we have covered the basics of SQL, remember that books upon books have been written about the topic. My ramblings are enough to get you started, but Google is your friend if you are trying to do something that I didn't discuss. For example, if you want to do a recursive QUERY, SQL Server and Oracle offer Common Table Expressions for doing the recursion, while other databases require you to create unioned queries.

## 5.10 Essbase SQL Setup Information

When using SQL with Essbase, you should be aware of a few minor things. First, a few settings should be in the Essbase.cfg file to control interactions with SQL. The first setting is:

```
SQLFETCHERRORPOPUP TRUE
```

This setting controls whether an error is generated when retrieving data during an SQL dimension or data load. The command enables the IFERROR MaxL error handling and, if loads are being performed from EAS, turns on popup messages. This is important: We can get a false sense of a load completing successfully when it did not.

The second setting deals with the DATAEXORT command when writing to a relational DB. By default, rows are inserted one at a time, which means if we have millions of rows, each is done as a single insert. This can be slow. If the ODBC driver and DB support batch insert, then we can turn on the ability to use it with the configuration file settings:

```
DATAEXPORTENABLEBATCHINSERT TRUE
And
DEXPSQLROWSIZE [appname [dbname]] n
```

Using these settings, you can specify if batch insert is allowed and how many rows are grouped together before a write to the database occurs. This can speed up the rate of insert significantly. However, many of the ODBC drivers do not support batch insert. When they do, we have to create an essSQL.cfg file in the proper path to turn on the feature. For information about the essSQL.cfg file, refer to the Essbase SQL interface guide.

Next, although not a configuration file setting, we need to be aware that Essbase does not support all data types. When a data type is used that Essbase does not like, the process will not produce blanks in rows and/or columns of load rules. In many cases, it is best to cast the metadata columns as Varchar (Varchar2 for Oracle) and as float for numeric data.

```
CAST(OUNCES AS VARCHAR(10))
```

## 5.11  Rules Files Using SQL

### 5.11.1  Rules File SQL Basics

The most common use of SQL in Essbase is when SQL is used in rules files. SQL is commonly used for both building dimensions and loading data. Because of the inherent flexibility with case statements, null replacements, sorting, and joining, managing our data with SQL is much easier than using load rule functionality to do the management. (Our editor, Cameron Lackpour, loves that I agree with him on this because we battle about load rules all the time.)

To use SQL in load rules, first we have to create a load rule. Once open, go to the File menu and select Open SQL (see Figure 5.10).

When the dialog box opens (see Figure 5.11), click OK.

The SQL Dialog has two major sections, one for connecting and one for the actual SQL (see Figure 5.12). In the connection area, we are presented with multiple ways to connect.

1. An ODBC connection
2. A substitution variable that defines an ODBC connection
3. An Oracle-specific OCI connection
4. A manual free-form connection

**Figure 5.10**   File menu, Open SQL.

**Figure 5.11**   SELECT Database dialog box.

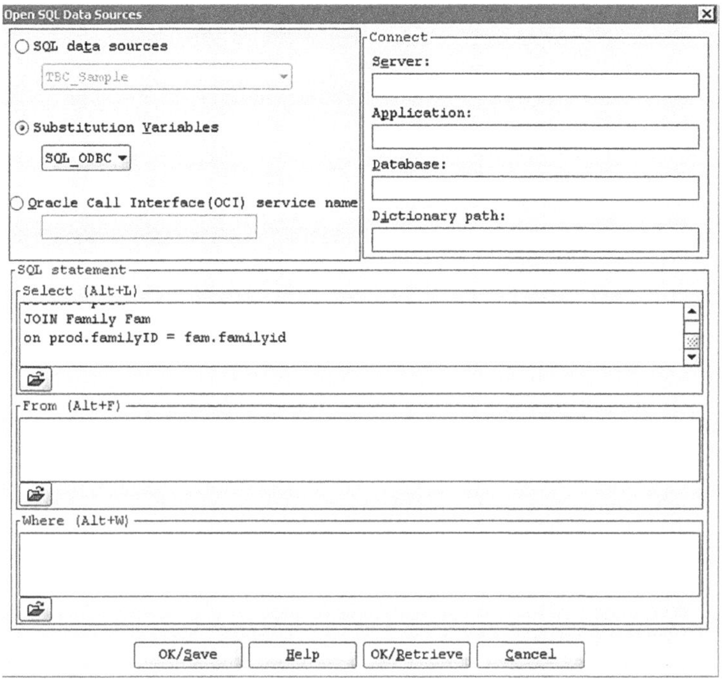

**Figure 5.12**   SQL dialog.

When using the ODBC or substitution variable connection, the ODBC driver already has to have been configured on the Essbase server. The substitution variable connection gives us versatility when migrating between systems. In our development system, we could have an ODBC connection called "testdb," and in production, the ODBC could be called "proddb." On each Essbase system, I can have a variable that points to the ODBC connection name, so when I migrate between systems, it connects to the correct connection without having to edit the load rule.

For the OCI connection to work, the Oracle client has to be installed on the Essbase server box. Connecting with the OCI connection allows for faster retrievals than using a standard ODBC connection and allows for more Oracle-specific SQL syntax than the ODBC connection allows.

The fourth section in the connection area is simply labeled "Connect" and allows for manually creating the connection to a relational DB (see Figure 5.13). Here, we specify the server information for connecting.

The manual method is how Essbase Studio creates a connection. I prefer to use one of the other methods for doing my connections because I know they are properly defined, and I have to have more knowledge to connect using the manual method.

However you make the connection, you will now have to enter your SQL in the "SQL Statement" section of the dialog (Figure 5.14), which has three parts, SELECT, FROM, and WHERE.

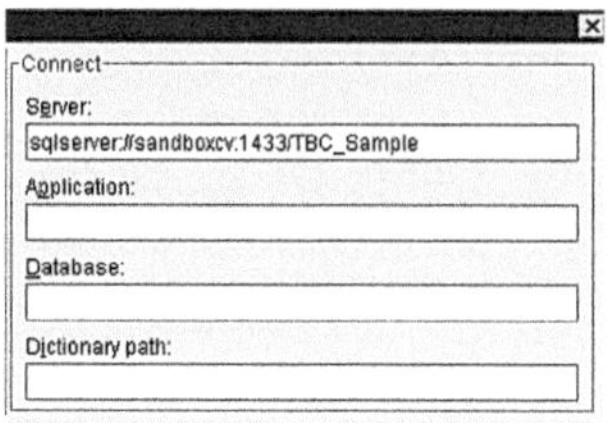

**Figure 5.13** Manually created connections.

**Figure 5.14** Parts of the SQL Statement.

By default, Oracle throws an * into the select area. Clicking on the "open folder" buttons (boxed in Figure 5.14) helps you actually see your SQL better and lets you see an expanded view of the SQL, as shown in Figure 5.15.

The most important thing to know when using these three boxes is that Essbase automatically inserts the word SELECT, FROM, and WHERE into the respective

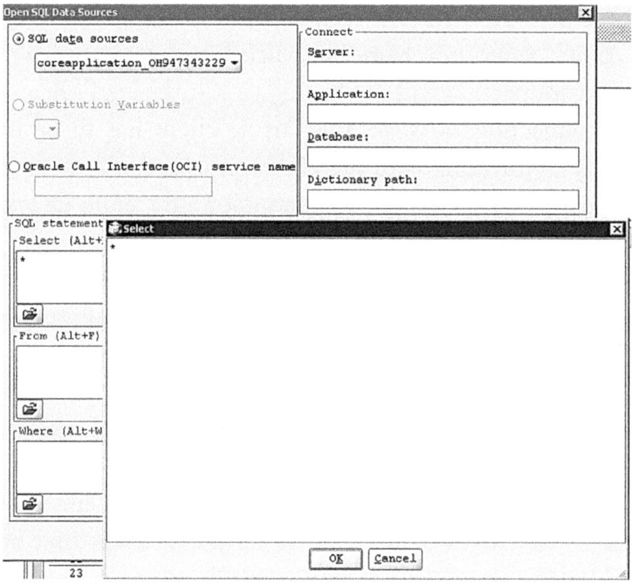

**Figure 5.15** Opened Select area.

boxes. If we have an SQL statement that we have already worked out and tested directly against our SQL engine before putting it into our load rule, such as

```
SELECT
*
FROM PRODUCT
ORDER BY 1,2,3
```

and we want to use it in the Essbase SQL interface, do the following in each area:

SELECT—Do nothing. Essbase already put the * there.
FROM—Type "Product" (without the double quotes).
WHERE—See below.

We do not need a WHERE clause, so leaving it blank would seem appropriate. But how are we going to do the ORDER BY? We know that ORDER BY follows WHERE, so maybe that is the best place. But when you try to simply type "ORDER BY 1,3" in the WHERE section, you will get an error message. That is because Essbase assembled the whole thing to look like

```
SELECT *
      FROM Product
      WHERE ORDER BY 1, 2, 3
```

We can fix this problem by tricking Essbase :

```
WHERE - 1=1 ORDER BY 1, 2, 3
```

That works, because now Essbase assembles the whole thing as:

```
SELECT *
      FROM Product
      WHERE 1=1 ORDER BY 1, 2, 3
```

That is not quite identical to the original, but the results will certainly be the same!

Frankly, I find using all three boxes cumbersome, especially if I have queries with UNIONS, complex queries, or if I have already developed the statement and tested it elsewhere. (As you might guess, that is my suggestion on anything beyond the simplest SQL statement.) I often forget to remove the SELECT, FROM, or WHERE keywords and thus get syntax errors when I try to retrieve data. Although not documented anywhere, except in presentations I have done, the much simpler approach is to just include the entire SQL in the SELECT area (see Figure 5.16). We do still need to remember to remove the first SELECT keyword but do not have to worry about the FROM or WHERE sections. A word of warning: If you type anything into the FROM or WHERE areas, including a space, you will get a syntax error because Essbase will try to add those clauses to your query.

**Figure 5.16** SQL in Select area.

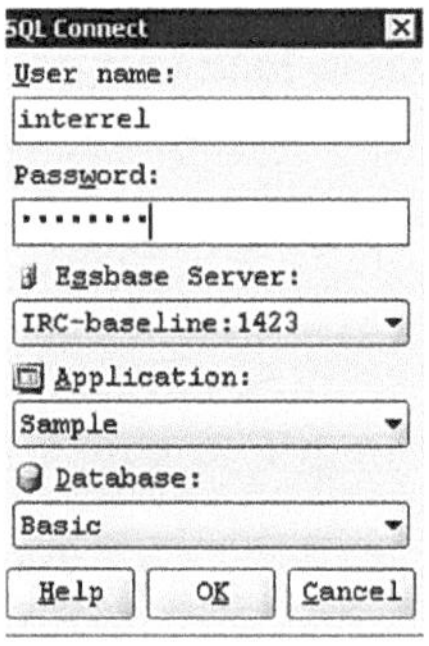

**Figure 5.17** Enter ID and password for SQL Connect.

Once we have the query inserted as we like it, we can see a sample of the data by clicking the OK/Retrieve button. Doing so will bring you to a screen allowing you to input an ID and password (Figure 5.17).

Once you are done and have clicked the OK button, sample data are brought into the rules file, as shown in Figure 5.18.

The column names from the SQL are used as the names of the columns in the rules file. One of the shortcuts I take is to name the columns using the AS aliases to name data load SQL to be the dimension or column names. It saves me the time required to have to name the columns in the load rule itself. This trick only works for data loads, not, unfortunately, for dimension build files.

### 5.11.2 Variables in Rules Files

As mentioned earlier, we can use variables to define the ODBC source for a load rule, and we can use substitution variables as aliases and in the WHERE clause of an SQL

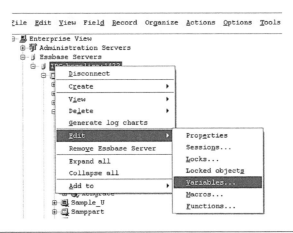

```
Data Prep Editor [Untitled1]
Ω  A  Σ  Σ  ⊒  ⏹  ⏹  ⏹  ⏹  ⏹  ⏹  ⏹  ⏹  ⏹  ⏹  ⏹
Encoding:Unknown
1    1    1    100-10  Cola       TRUE   12    Can     1996-03-25 00:00:00.000
2    2    1    100-20  Diet Cola        TRUE  12    Can     1996-04-01 00:00:00.000
3    3    1    100-30  Caffeine Free Cola    FALSE  16    Bottle  1996-04-01 00:00:00.000
4    4    2    200-10  Old Fashioned  TRUE   12    Bottle  1995-09-27 00:00:00.000
5    5    2    200-20  Diet Root Beer  TRUE   16    Bottle  1996-07-26 00:00:00.000
6    6    2    200-30  Sasparilla       FALSE  12    Bottle  1996-12-10 00:00:00.000
7    7    2    200-40  Birch Beer      FALSE  16    Bottle  1996-12-10 00:00:00.000
8    8    3    300-10  Dark Cream      TRUE   20    Bottle  1996-06-26 00:00:00.000
```

| | PRODUCTID | FAMILYID | SKU | SKU_ALIAS | CAFFEI... | OUNCES | PKGTYPE | INTRODATE |
|---|---|---|---|---|---|---|---|---|
| 1 | 1 | 1 | 100-10 | Cola | TRUE | 12 | Can | 1996-0... |
| 2 | 2 | 1 | 100-20 | Diet Cola | TRUE | 12 | Can | 1996-0... |
| 3 | 3 | 1 | 100-30 | Caffei... | FALSE | 16 | Bottle | 1996-0... |
| 4 | 4 | 2 | 200-10 | Old Fa... | TRUE | 12 | Bottle | 1995-0... |
| 5 | 5 | 2 | 200-20 | Diet R... | TRUE | 16 | Bottle | 1996-0... |
| 6 | 6 | 2 | 200-30 | Saspar... | FALSE | 12 | Bottle | 1996-1... |
| 7 | 7 | 2 | 200-40 | Birch ... | FALSE | 16 | Bottle | 1996-1... |
| 8 | 8 | 3 | 300-10 | Dark C... | TRUE | 20 | Bottle | 1996-0... |
| 9 | 9 | 3 | 300-20 | Vanill... | TRUE | 20 | Bottle | 1996-0... |
| 10 | 10 | 3 | 300-30 | Diet C... | TRUE | 12 | Can | 1996-0... |
| 11 | 11 | 4 | 400-10 | Grape | FALSE | 32 | Bottle | 1996-1... |
| 12 | 12 | 4 | 400-20 | Orange | FALSE | 32 | Bottle | 1996-1... |
| 13 | 13 | 4 | 400-30 | Strawb... | FALSE | 32 | Bottle | 1996-1... |

**Figure 5.18**  Sample data in the rules file.

statement. We can also use them as column global headers and field names in a rules file, but this chapter does not address those items.

Of course, to use variables in load rules, you first have to create the variable. EAS and MaxL have multiple ways to do this. In EAS, right click on the server and select Edit -> Variables (see Figure 5.19).

For our use, we will create a global variable named CurrMth and give it the value of Jan (see Figure 5.20).

In our rules file, we create the SQL as normal but utilize the CurrMth variable (Figure 5.21).

We notice a few things about this, as illustrated in Figure 5.22.

1. As typical, the substitution variable is prefixed with an "&."
2. We have single quotes around the variable names in the SQL. At least in the version of EAS I am working in, if I put single quotes around the variable

**Figure 5.19**  Creating a variable in EAS, step 1.

| Application | Database | Variable | | Value |
|---|---|---|---|---|
| (all apps) | (all dbs) | CurrMth | Jan | |

**Figure 5.20**   Creating a variable in EAS, step 2.

```
Select
        scn.SCENARIO
        ,m.STATE
        ,p.SKU
        ,'&Currmth' as period
        ,YEAR(s.TRANSDATE) as yr
        ,sum(s.AMOUNT) as 'Sales'
FROM SALES s
JOIN PRODUCT p
        ON p.PRODUCTID = s.PRODUCTID
JOIN MARKET m
        ON m.STATEID = s.STATEID
JOIN SCENARIO scn
        ON s.SCENARIOID = scn.SCENARIOID
JOIN MEASURES acct
on Acct.MEASURESID = s.MEASURESID
WHERE scn.SCENARIO = 'Actual'
        AND acct.CHILD = 'Sales'
        AND SUBSTRING(Convert( varchar(10),TRANSDATE ,13),4,3) = '&Currmth'
GROUP BY
        scn.SCENARIO
        ,m.STATE
        ,p.SKU
        ,YEAR(s.TRANSDATE)
ORDER by 1,2,3,4,5
```

**Figure 5.21**   Using the variable in SQL.

```
1       Actual  California       100-10  Jan     2000    678.0
2       Actual  California       100-20  Jan     2000    118.0
3       Actual  California       100-30  Jan     2000    144.99999999999997
4       Actual  California       200-10  Jan     2000    250.0
5       Actual  California       200-20  Jan     2000    546.0
6       Actual  California       200-30  Jan     2000    456.0
7       Actual  California       300-10  Jan     2000    452.0
8       Actual  California       300-20  Jan     2000    189.99999999999997
9       Actual  California       300-30  Jan     2000    234.0
```

| | SCENARIO | STATE | SKU | period | yr | Sales |
|---|---|---|---|---|---|---|
| 1 | Actual | Califo... | 100-10 | Jan | 2000 | 678.0 |
| 2 | Actual | Califo... | 100-20 | Jan | 2000 | 118.0 |
| 3 | Actual | Califo... | 100-30 | Jan | 2000 | 144.99... |
| 4 | Actual | Califo... | 200-10 | Jan | 2000 | 250.0 |
| 5 | Actual | Califo... | 200-20 | Jan | 2000 | 546.0 |
| 6 | Actual | Califo... | 200-30 | Jan | 2000 | 456.0 |
| 7 | Actual | Califo... | 300-10 | Jan | 2000 | 452.0 |
| 8 | Actual | Califo... | 300-20 | Jan | 2000 | 189.99... |
| 9 | Actual | Califo... | 300-30 | Jan | 2000 | 234.0 |
| 10 | Actual | Califo... | 400-10 | Jan | 2000 | 219.0 |
| 11 | Actual | Califo... | 400-20 | Jan | 2000 | 134.0 |
| 12 | Actual | Califo... | 400-30 | Jan | 2000 | 180.0 |
| | Actual | Colorado | 100-10 | Jan | 2000 | 100.0 |

**Figure 5.22**   Results of using variables in load rules.

names, EAS strips them off. Since the substitution variable is a literal in the rules file, we have to add them back in for the SQL to work properly.

3. We are using the substitution variable in both the SELECT list and in the WHERE clause.

4. In SQL Server, there is not an easy way to get the literal 'JAN' from a datetime column, so we use SUBSTRING and convert to get just a part of the formatted date and compare it to our variable.

5. For ease of loading, we have given an alias of "Sales" to the amount column. This allows us to get it as the column header in the rules file.

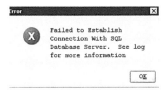

**Figure 5.23**    Essbase SQL error message.

*5.11.3  Dealing with SQL Errors in Essbase*

How does one figure out what the problem is when the SQL does not work properly? We will get a fairly innocuous error message that looks something like Figure 5.23.

The message gives us a hint: We need to look in the application log. There, we will see something like

```
[Tue Dec 16 01:14:05 2014]Local/Sample/Basic/admin@Native
Directory/1032/Info(1021006)
SELECT Statement [SELECT scn.SCENARIO
      ,m.STATE
      ,p.SKU
      ,&'Currmth' as period
      ,YEAR(s.TRANSDATE) as yr
      ,sum(s.AMOUNT) as amt
FROM SALES s
JOIN PRODUCT p
      ON p.PRODUCTID = s.PRODUCTID
JOIN MARKET m
      ON m.STATEID = s.STATEID
JOIN SCENARIO scn
      ON s.SCENARIOID = scn.SCENARIOID
JOIN MEASURES acct
on Acct.MEASURESID = s.MEASURESID
WHERE scn.SCENARIO = 'Actual'
      AND acct.CHILD = 'Sales'
      AND SUBSTRING(Convert( varchar(10),TRANSDATE ,13),4,3) =
'Jan'

GROUP BY
      scn.SCENARIO
      ,m.STATE
      ,p.SKU
      ,Month(s.TRANSDATE)
      ,YEAR(s.TRANSDATE)
ORDER by 3,4,5,2
] is generated
[Tue Dec 16 01:14:06 2014]Local/Sample/Basic/admin@Native
Directory/1032/Info(1021013)
ODBC Layer Error: [S1000] ==> [[NQODBC] [SQL_STATE: S1000]
[nQSError: 10058] A general error has occurred.
```

```
[nQSError: 12002] Socket communication error at call=Connect:
(Number=0) Call=NQRpc: An unknown socket communications error has
occurred.
[nQSError: 12010] Communication error connecting to remote end
point: address = IRC-baseline; port = 9706.
[nQSError: 12008] Unable to connect to port 9706 on machine
IRC-baseline.]
```

We actually have two errors here, one that is easy to see and another that is a bit more obtuse. The first error is that I misplaced the single quote so the substitution variable did not properly expand. This is represented by

```
,&'Currmth' as period
```

The second problem is that we could not connect properly to the database. This puzzled me until I realized I had forgotten to select the proper ODBC connection and it defaulted to the first ODBC connection in the drop-down list, which was not the correct database. The tables we were looking for don't exist in that database. Sometimes, the messages are easier to interpret, like when I enter a wrong password and get the error:

```
ODBC Layer Error: [37000] ==> [[Microsoft][ODBC SQL Server Driver]
[SQL Server]Cannot open database "TBC_Sample" requested by the
login. The login failed.]
```

Although the messages are often cryptic, one nice thing is that we can copy and paste the SQL from the log into an SQL development tool and get better reasons for the errors if they are syntax related or related to the way Essbase filled in our substitution variables and assembled our statement.

### 5.11.4 Calculation Formulas in SQL

The discussion on dimension building would not be complete without information regarding the idiosyncrasies of utilizing formulas from SQL. First, in the earlier discussion on LEFT OUTER JOINS, I showed a table I built for storing ASO properties with a column for a formula (see Table 5.16). I made that column a very large Varchar (4000). Too often, I've seen clients not anticipate having a large formula and undersizing that column in the table. When they encounter having to add a very large formula, they have to go through an exercise of redefining the table. In development, that is not bad, but in production, it could have greater impact as DBAs are reluctant to make on-the-fly changes to production tables.

Second, I love nicely formatted code, whether SQL or calc Script code. Formatting makes it easier to follow and understand. If we look at the formula for the Measures dimension member Opening Inventory, the formula looks like the following:

```
IF(NOT @ISMBR(Jan)) "Opening Inventory"=@PRIOR("Ending Inventory");
ENDIF; "Ending Inventory" = "Opening Inventory"+Additions-Sales;
```

This code is all on a single line within the column. All of the formatting has been removed (the line breaks, carriage returns, and tabs). It is not very pretty, but this is how the formula needs to be stored in the SQL table. When the formula is loaded into Essbase, it is not, unfortunately, in the pretty, easily readable format that we like to see.

Last, if we actually try to load the formula for Opening Inventory (above) into Essbase, we will have an unpleasant surprise. Upon validation, we will get an error that the member Opening is unknown. Looking at the statement, we see "Opening Inventory" enclosed in quotes, but in our Essbase cube, the quotes were stripped off. The quotes were stripped off in the load rule because load rules think that double quotes are defining fields and automatically remove them. To have the quotes appear properly in our formula, we have to add an escape character to each double quote. The escape character for load rules is the backslash "\" character. We can accomplish this two ways. First, when we put the code into the SQL table, we could manually go through the code and insert the backslashes and hope we don't miss any. The second approach is to insert them programmatically in our SQL by creating a view that does the conversion. Using our Opening Inventory example, we can use a simple replace function to include our backslashes:

```
SELECT
      CHILD
      ,Formula
      ,REPLACE(FORMULA,'"' ,'\"')as Corrected_Formula
FROM MEASURES
WHERE CHILD = 'Opening Inventory'
```

Table 5.27 displays the results.

**Table 5.27**   Results of REPLACE Function in Formulas

| CHILD | FORMULA | CORRECTED_FORMULA |
|---|---|---|
| Opening Inventory | `IF(NOT @ISMBR(Jan)) "Opening Inventory"=@PRIOR("Ending Inventory");ENDIF;"Ending Inventory"="Opening Inventory"+Additions-Sales;` | `IF(NOT @ISMBR(Jan)) \"Opening Inventory\"=@PRIOR(\"Ending Inventory\");ENDIF;\"Ending Inventory\"=\"Opening Inventory\"+Additions-Sales;` |

**Figure 5.24** Loading interactively from EAS.

I find it interesting that the sample tables do not load correctly, but as we can see, it is an easy fix to get them to load properly into Essbase.

*5.11.5 Rules File Automation*

Once we have the rules file written and saved, we need to be able to use it either interactively or in automated processing. I don't know about you, but I don't want to be up at 3:00 a.m. to load data.

When loading interactively from EAS (see Figure 5.24), the process for SQL-based rules files is very similar to that for flat file loads. From the database, we right click and select Load Data, which is no different from what we normally do. Then instead of selecting "Data File," we drop down the list—trust me, it is a list even though it does not look like one—and select "SQL." Then we enter the user ID and password for the SQL and click OK, just like normal. The Load rule will then run normally.

Since we do not want to be up to do this at 3:00 a.m., we want to automate the process and we need to write a MaxL command. Again, the import commands used are similar to those for flat files, with a little additional functionality for ASO cubes. The MaxL command uses a connection string instead of a file path for pulling in the data. The format is as follows:

```
IMPORT Database APP.DB DIMENSIONS(or DATA) CONNECT AS 'SQL User ID'
IDENTIFIED BY 'SQL Password' …….
```

For our Opening Inventory sample, the code would look something like

```
IMPORT Database 'Sample'.'Basic' DIMENSIONS
CONNECT AS 'interrel' IDENTIFIED BY 'training'
USING SERVER RULES_FILE 'SQL_Prod'
Preserve all data
ON error write to 'c:\datafiles\sql_prod.err';
```

When I ran this MaxL statement, I got the following log entries showing that it ran properly:

```
[Sun Dec 21 12:29:27 2014]Local/Sample/Basic/admin@Native
Directory/11052/Info(1013091)
Received Command [BuildDimFile] from user [admin@Native Directory]
[Sun Dec 21 12:29:27 2014]Local/Sample/Basic/admin@Native
Directory/11052/Info(1090047)
```

```
Building Dimensions, Available Memory: 31088512 Kilobytes
[Sun Dec 21 12:29:27 2014]Local/Sample/Basic/admin@Native
Directory/11052/Info(1021004)
Connection String is generated
[Sun Dec 21 12:29:27 2014]Local/Sample/Basic/admin@Native
Directory/11052/Info(1021041)
Connection String is [DSN=TBC_Sample;UID=...;PWD=...;]
[Sun Dec 21 12:29:27 2014]Local/Sample/Basic/admin@Native
Directory/11052/Info(1021006)
SELECT Statement [SELECT prod.SKU
,prod.SKU_ALIAS
,Fam.Family
FROM
Product prod
JOIN Family Fam
on prod.familyID = fam.familyid
] is generated
[Sun Dec 21 12:29:27 2014]Local/Sample/Basic/admin@Native
Directory/11052/Info(1021043)
Connection has been established
[Sun Dec 21 12:29:27 2014]Local/Sample/Basic/admin@Native
Directory/11052/Info(1021044)
Starting to execute query
[Sun Dec 21 12:29:27 2014]Local/Sample/Basic/admin@Native
Directory/11052/Info(1021045)
Finished executing query, and started to fetch records
[Sun Dec 21 12:29:27 2014]Local/Sample/Basic/admin@Native
Directory/11052/Info(1021000)
Connection With SQL Database Server is Established
[Sun Dec 21 12:29:27 2014]Local/Sample/Basic/admin@Native
Directory/11052/Info(1021047)
Finished fetching data
[Sun Dec 21 12:29:27 2014]Local/Sample/Basic/admin@Native
Directory/11052/Info(1021002)
SQL Connection is Freed
```

Loading a data file is the same as loading a dimension file; of course, we have to change "Dimensions" to "Data" in the import statement.

As I alluded to earlier, additional functionality is available if we are loading an ASO database. We have a special version of the IMPORT statement that allows us to load up to eight data load rules at once. The data rules files must all be SQL-based load rules and must use the same user ID and password. According to the Essbase technical reference, the syntax of the command is as follows:

```
IMPORT Database ASOsamp.Sample DATA
Connect as USERID identified by 'password'
USING MULTIPLE rules_file 'rule1','rule2'
TO load_buffer_block starting with buffer_id 100
ON error write to "error.txt";
```

When you use this syntax, MaxL will automatically generate all of the buffers it needs, and when the process is done, it will merge the buffers and commit them. As mentioned earlier, if the same ODBC connection is used for this operation, the connection must be configured for parallel SQL connections.

### 5.11.6 MaxL Encryption

I know what you are thinking: This is great, but I'll never get it past the auditors to have the user ID and password in the MaxL file. This is where encryption is our friend. Luckily for us, Oracle has built into MaxL the option to encrypt IDs and passwords in our MaxL files. Although this is not an SQL-specific topic, it does impact our SQL-based imports.

This topic is covered in the Tech reference; search for "Encrypt." First, we navigate to where the StartMaxL command is located. The easiest way I have found to do this if the EAS thick client was installed on your systems is to navigate through the start menu on the Essbase server. Select ORACLE EPM SYSTEM => Essbase => Essbase Client => MaxL Client. Right click on MaxL Client and select Open file location (see Figure 5.25).

If we don't have that location, we can open Windows Explorer and search for the StartMaxL command file. Once we have the location open—for me, it was D:\Oracle\ Middleware\EPMSystem11R1\products\Essbase\EssbaseClient\bin—we copy the location from the Explorer window by clicking on the path and pressing Ctrl-C to copy it.

Open a command window (go to the Start menu and in the search box, type "Cmd" without the quotes, and hit "Enter," then a command box should open).

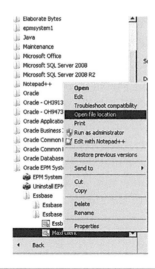

**Figure 5.25**   Navigate to StartMaxL command.

Next to the > sign, type in the drive letter that has the Oracle install (in my case it is "D"). Then hit enter. Type in the letters CD and a space, then go to the top left corner of the box and right click. Select Edit => Paste. The path for the StartMaxL script should now be shown in the command window (see Figure 5.26).

Hit Enter and the path should appear before the > symbol (see Figure 5.27).

This has gotten us to the correct location for MaxL. Now, we need to get the public/private key configuration for our implementation. We type in StartMaxL –gk and hit enter. It is important to note that the –gk is case sensitive even on Windows servers; typing –GK will give us an error.

If we are successful, we will see the screen in Figure 5.28.

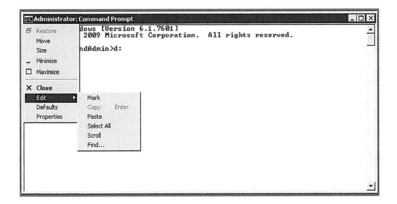

**Figure 5.26**    Finding the path for the StartMaxL command.

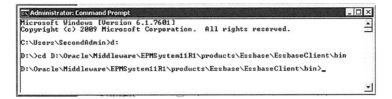

**Figure 5.27**    Path for the StartMaxL command.

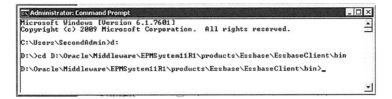

**Figure 5.28**    Public/private key configuration.

This is our public key, private key set for encrypting/decrypting our MaxL files. We can then use the public key for encrypting our MaxL files. The syntax to encrypt is

```
StartMaxL -E maxl_file_path public_key
```

For my file, it looks like:

```
Startmaxl -E d:\automation\import_dims.mxl 12095,1111027079
```

After hitting enter, we note it completed successfully, as in Figure 5.29.

If we navigate to the folder that has the MaxL command, it now has both the original file, "Import_Dims.mxl," and a new file, "Import_Dims.mxls." The "S" on the end most likely means secured or something similar. Opening up the preencrypted file, the syntax shows the IDs and passwords:

```
SPOOL on to 'd:\Temp\Import_Dims.log';
LOGIN 'admin' 'password' on 'localhost';
IMPORT DATABASE 'Sample'.'Basic' DIMENSIONS
CONNECT as 'interrel' identified by 'training'
USING server rules_file 'SQL_Prod' PRESERVE all data
ON ERROR write to 'c:\Temp\sql_prod.err';
SPOOL OFF;
EXIT;
```

In the encrypted file, we can see that the ID and passwords are now encrypted.

```
spool on to 'd:\Temp\Import_Dims.log';
login $key 8724569601925769524051564183907643051380 $key 7844142570
9832128870818140867026572583001177840730 on 'localhost';
Import database 'Sample'.'Basic' DIMENSIONS CONNECT as $key 2217914
90180752625015315143110149305264000959522810 identified by $key 2413
8984909257695240925769524082646835900247197790
USING server rules_file 'SQL_Prod' PRESERVE all data
ON ERROR write to 'c:\Temp\sql_prod.err';
SPOOL OFF;
EXIT;
```

```
Administrator: Command Prompt                                    _ □ ×
D:\Oracle\Middleware\EPMSystem11R1\products\Essbase\EssbaseClient\bin>Startmaxl
-E d:\automation\import_dims.mxl 12095,1111027079

 Essbase MaxL Shell 64-bit - Release 11.1.2 (ESB11.1.2.3.000B4412)
 Copyright (c) 2000, 2013, Oracle and/or its affiliates.
 All rights reserved.

  MaxL Shell completed

D:\Oracle\Middleware\EPMSystem11R1\products\Essbase\EssbaseClient\bin>_
```

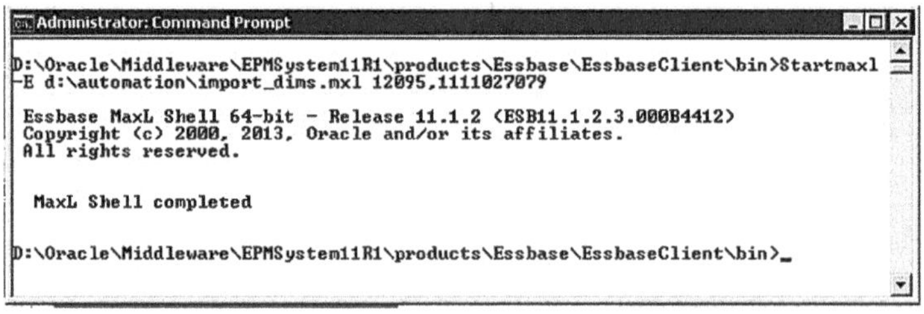

**Figure 5.29** Successful encryption.

Here are a few things to be aware of.

1. Both the Login and Import Connect statements have been encrypted.
2. We could copy the Login statement to other MaxL files and not have to individually encrypt them.
3. If the SQL ID and password are the same for other connections, we can also copy them.
4. We can migrate the encrypted IDs and passwords to other systems if the ID and passwords are the same on the different systems. If they are not, we will have to redo the encryption.
5. The original unencrypted files are not removed, and that has to be done manually. If not removed, it defeats the purpose of encrypting. Some clients I have store these preencrypted files in a secure location in case of later issues (such as forgetting the passwords needed for new MaxL scripts).

To run our encrypted MaxL, we have to tell MaxL how to decrypt by adding some parameters to the MaxL. The syntax is

```
STARTMAXL -D secured MaxL file path and name private key
```

My example would be the following:

```
startmaxl.bat -D Import_Dims.mxls 249012575,1111027079
```

When I run this against my newly encrypted MaxL file, the output looks like the following:

```
MAXL> login $key 87245696019257695240515641839076430513805 $key 7844
14257098321288708181408670265725830011778407305 on 'localhost';
OK/INFO - 1051034 - Logging in user [admin@Native Directory].
OK/INFO - 1241001 - Logged in to Essbase.
MAXL> Import database 'Sample'.'Basic' DIMENSIONS CONNECT as $key
22179149018075262501531514311014930526400959522810 identified by
$key 24138984909257695240925769524082646835900247197790
 2> USING server rules_file 'SQL_Prod' PRESERVE all data
 3> ON ERROR write to 'c:\Temp\sql_prod.err';
OK/INFO - 1053012 - Object [Basic] is locked by user [admin@Native
Directory].
 OK/INFO - 1021004 - Connection String is generated.
 OK/INFO - 1021041 - Connection String is
[DSN=TBC_Sample;UID=...;PWD=...;].
 OK/INFO - 1021006 - SELECT Statement [SELECT prod.SKU
,prod.SKU_ALIAS
,Fam.Family
FROM
Product prod
JOIN Family Fam
```

```
on prod.familyID = fam.familyid
] is generated.
 OK/INFO - 1021043 - Connection has been established.
 OK/INFO - 1021044 - Starting to execute query.
 OK/INFO - 1021045 - Finished executing query, and started to fetch
records.
 OK/INFO - 1021000 - Connection With SQL Database Server is
Established.
 OK/INFO - 1021047 - Finished fetching data.
 OK/INFO - 1021002 - SQL Connection is Freed.
```

The statement ran and even the output is encrypted like it should be; otherwise, someone could simply look in the log files for the passwords. Those Essbase developers think of everything.

### 5.12 Exporting Essbase Data to Relational Sources

Users often want to take the data in Essbase and port them to another system. Perhaps we want to get the budget information into our GL system or forecasted sales into an ERP system. This could also help us ensure that all of the data were loaded properly as an audit. We could export summary-level data from Essbase and compare them to the source system to make sure values match. How about exporting data from one cube to be used in another cube with different dimensionality? We can easily accomplish all of these exports from a BSO cube utilizing the Dataexport calc script command. This command allows us to fix on a subset of data and export them to either flat files or relational systems. The command is pretty simple but has a number of Set parameters to allow us to modify the behavior. The Dataexport command has three variations: flat file extract, BINFILE extract, and relational extract. Flat file and relational are self-explanatory; however, BINFILE is not. BINFILE exports in the format of the .pag file for quick backup and recovery. The syntax for the exports is as follows:

```
DATAEXPORT "File" "delimiter" "fileName" "missingChar"
DATAEXPORT "Binfile" "fileName"
DATAEXPORT "DSN" "dsnName" "tableName" "userName" "password";
```

The unfortunate part of the relational export is that we have to include the ID and password in the calc script and these items are not encrypted. We could slightly hide them using substitution variables, but that does not accomplish much. For relational, DSN is hard coded, the DSNName is the ODBC connection name on the Essbase server being used, and the tablename, of course, is the name of the relational table that will hold the data. The table has to be predefined; Dataexport will not create a table. You should be aware of two slight functional differences between an export to a flat file and a relational file:

1. FIXPARALLEL can be used in exporting to a flat file; it cannot be used for relational extracts
2. Dataexport will replace a flat file, but it will append to relational tables.

Using Set commands, we can change how the Dataexport functions. For example, we can control whether dynamically calculated members are included in the export. The set commands and options are as follows:

```
SET DATAEXPORTOPTIONS {
DataExportLevel ALL | LEVEL0 | INPUT;
DataExportDynamicCalc ON | OFF;
DataExportDecimal n;
DataExportPrecision n;
DataExportColFormat ON | OFF;
DataExportColHeader dimensionName;
DataExportDimHeader ON | OFF;
DataExportRelationalFile ON | OFF;
DataExportOverwriteFile ON | OFF;
DataExportDryRun ON | OFF;
};
```

When we use the Dataexport command, sparse members and all but one dense dimension are used as row members and are exported in basic outline order; you can't control the order of row members. You can somewhat control the column members. Column members are always a dense dimension. By default, Essbase will pick a dense dimension to be the columns. You can force a dense dimension to be the columns using the following:

```
DataExportColHeader dimensionName;
```

We want the columns to be from a dense dimension with a static group of members. If the number of members changes, the number of columns in the relational table would need to be changed for the extract to work properly. Many times, a "Periods" dimension works well because it typically just has the periods of the year and that does not change over time. Another method that seems to work well when we want all of the dimensions to be row members is to add a one-member, dense dimension to the cube, such as a dimension named "Data." Since it is a one-member dimension, it does not increase the size of the database nor affect calculation speed. By specifying that dimension as our column header, we are assured of nonchanging data. This method works well if we design the cube this way to begin with. If we try to retrofit this, any data loads and reports would have to change to add the new dimension.

As mentioned above, the order of the row members is based on the order of the dimensions in the database. If the order is changed in the outline, the order of the columns in the export is changed as well.

When using the setting

```
DataExportRelationalFile ON;
```

other settings like DIMHEADER and DIMCOLHEADER are turned off. And when using this setting with a file, the "Missing_Char" parameter is ignored. (Missing Char is only used in flat file extracts when we want to replace #missing with some other character like a 0 or dash.)

So how can we use this command? For an example, we want to export budget data from Sample.Basic into an RDB. We need to determine what level of data we want, if we want calculated members to be included, and what our columns should be. In our case, we just want level 0 data, no formulas because exporting dynamically calculated members is much slower, and we want the periods to be our column headers.

My preferred method for exporting data to relational tables is to first export a sample of the data to a flat file and then use the flat file to understand the column order in the table. I will also sometimes create the relational table by importing the flat file using relational tools. For our example, I can use the following script:

```
SET AGGMISSG ON ;
SET UPDATECALC OFF;
SET DATAEXPORTOPTIONS {
DataExportLevel LEVEL0 ;
DataExportDynamicCalc OFF;
DataExportColFormat ON ;
DataExportDIMHEADER ON ;
DataExportColHeader "Year";
DataExportOverwriteFile ON ;
DataExportDryRun OFF;
};
FIX((@relative("Year",0),@Relative("Measures",0),
@relative("Product",0),@Relative("Market",0),"Budget"))
     DATAEXPORT "File" "|" "d:\sample_data\Budget.txt" "-";
ENDFIX
```

to export to a flat file. Notice, I have COLFORMAT and DIMHEADERS turned on and I do not have the RELATIONALFILE option. What I get as results is something like:

```
"Product"|"Market"|"Measures"|"Scenario"|"Year"
"Jan"|"Feb"|"Mar"|"Apr"|"May"|"Jun"|"Jul"|"Aug"|"Sep"|"Oct"|"Nov"|"
Dec"
"100-10"|"New York"|"Sales"|"Bud
get"|640|610|640|670|710|840|860|860|750|540|560|620
"100-10"|"New York"|"COGS"|"Bud
get"|260|240|250|270|280|340|340|340|300|210|220|250
"100-10"|"New York"|"Marketing"|"Bud
get"|80|80|80|80|90|110|110|110|90|70|70|80
```

If I edit the file and combine the first and second lines, I have a complete header for understanding the columns and order. From this, we can create the DDL to create a budget cube. In SQL Server, the syntax would be as follows:

```
CREATE TABLE [dbo].[Budget](
        [Product] [varchar](80) NOT NULL,
        [Market] [varchar](80) NOT NULL,
        [Measures] [varchar](80) NOT NULL,
        [Scenario] [varchar](80) NOT NULL,
        [Jan] [float] NULL,
        [Feb] [float] NULL,
        [Mar] [float] NULL,
        [Apr] [float] NULL,
        [May] [float] NULL,
        [Jun] [float] NULL,
        [Jul] [float] NULL,
        [Aug] [float] NULL,
        [Sep] [float] NULL,
        [Oct] [float] NULL,
        [Nov] [float] NULL,
        [Dec] [float] NULL
)
```

I actually cheated and imported the flat file using SQL Server's import wizard. Other DBs have similar tools. Once the table was created, I modified the calc script to export to the relational table by using the calc script. The columns for the member names are all defined as Varchar(80). Since the maximum length for a member name in Essbase is currently 80 characters, we might truncate the names if we make it smaller. Essbase stores its numbers as floating point so it makes sense to store it relationally the same way.

```
SET AGGMISSG ON ;
SET UPDATECALC OFF;
SET DATAEXPORTOPTIONS {
DataExportLevel LEVEL0 ;
DataExportDynamicCalc OFF;
DataExportColHeader "Year";
DataExportRelationalFile ON;
DataExportOverwriteFile ON ;
DataExportDryRun OFF;
};
FIX((@relative("Year",0),@Relative("Measures",0),
@relative("Product",0),@Relative("Market",0),"Budget"))
     DATAEXPORT "DSN" "TBC_Sample" "BUDGET" "interrel" "training";
ENDFIX
```

After running the calc script, we can query the table with the SQL:

```
SELECT *
FROM BUDGET
```

**Table 5.28**  Export to a Relational Table

| PRODUCT | MARKET | MEASURES | SCENARIO | JAN | FEB | MAR | APR | MAY | JUN | JUL | AUG | SEP | OCT | NOV | DEC |
|---------|--------|----------|----------|-----|-----|-----|-----|-----|-----|-----|-----|-----|-----|-----|-----|
| 100-10 | New York | Sales | Budget | 640 | 610 | 640 | 670 | 710 | 840 | 860 | 860 | 750 | 540 | 560 | 620 |
| 100-10 | New York | COGS | Budget | 260 | 240 | 250 | 270 | 280 | 340 | 340 | 340 | 300 | 210 | 220 | 250 |
| 100-10 | New York | Marketing | Budget | 80 | 80 | 80 | 80 | 90 | 110 | 110 | 110 | 90 | 70 | 70 | 80 |

The first rows returned look correct and match when verified from a Smart View retrieval (see Table 5.28).

When running the SQL,

```
SELECT COUNT(*)
FROM BUDGET
```

we find that I have 1234 rows in the table. If we rerun the calc script and then rerun the previous SQL to count the rows, we find we now have 2468 rows of data. We expected this because, as stated earlier, relational data exports append data to the table and don't replace it. How can we deal with this? This is a wonderful segue to our next topic, triggers and stored procedures.

### 5.12.1  Triggers and Stored Procedures

Triggers are objects that execute based on specific events, just like Essbase triggers. Triggers can fire based on inserts, deletes or updates to tables, and (depending the RDBMS) on specific values like an amount being negative or a specific literal.

Stored procedures are a way to execute a series of SQL statements together. These would be analogous to a calc script in Essbase. In an Essbase script, I can do one calculation followed by another calculation. In a stored procedure, I could copy data into a table then do calculations on that table, then do calculations on the results, move the data to a summary table, and so on.

Triggers and stored procedures can be very helpful to us when we are using the DATAEXPORT command. As I mentioned earlier, when writing to a relational table, the DATAEXPORT command does not remove existing rows in the table but appends to them. This can be very problematic if we are loading a full set of data and want a summary. We would be replicating the rows, and if we were to try to get a summation of amounts, we would be overcounting them. Utilizing triggers, with or without stored procedures, we can easily delete the rows from the table before reloading it. And while I say "delete," in most cases, we want to truncate a table and not delete the rows from it. What is the difference? In most systems, a delete will log all of the rows being deleted so it can roll back the transaction if it fails. A truncate deletes without logging; therefore, truncates are much quicker, especially on large tables.

This section demonstrates a very simple trigger. It will truncate the BUDGET table we created earlier based on a change to a new table we add named Essbase _Trigger_Table. We will write out a single row to this Essbase_Trigger_table to force the BUDGET table truncation before us writing to the table. We are writing only a single row because we only want the trigger to fire once. We could be more elaborate and have the trigger investigate the scenario name and/or values in the trigger_flag we send to run complete stored procedures or more elaborate trigger steps.

To get this to work, we first need to modify the Sample.Basic outline. We add a measure named "Trigger_flag" in the section called Ratios (see Figure 5.30).

Next, we need a table to hold the trigger values and for the Trigger to operate against. We can copy the DDL for the Budget table, name it ESSBASE_Trigger_Table, and create it. (Again, I cheated a little. SQL has a command to get the top number of rows just by adding TOP X into the query.) I also can insert these values into a table based on another table using an INSERT INTO command. The INSERT will copy the data types and the column names and order. Using the following SQL:

```
SELECT TOP 0 *
INTO ESSBASE_Trigger_Table
FROM BUDGET
```

I was able to create the table quickly (this may not work the same way for Oracle or other DBs). We can run this only once because once the table is created, this syntax will give us errors. We would have to issue a DROP TABLE statement before this SQL, or, once the table is created, if we wanted to insert rows into it, we could change the syntax to

```
INSERT into Essbase_Trigger_Table
SELECT * form Budget
```

or the SQL for whatever the statement should insert. We can even add or subtract columns by not using * and selecting column names. In Oracle, this is even simpler:

```
"CREATE TABLE AS"
CREATE TABLE schema.newtable AS SELECT * FROM schema.oldtable;
```

So far, we have created a placeholder for the trigger in our Essbase database and created a relational table to hold the trigger information. Next, we will modify the Dataexport calc script we created earlier. We need to populate a single block with a value for the Trigger_flag member. We can do this by assigning a constant to a sparse intersection. Why sparse? Remember, a dense calculation will not create a block but

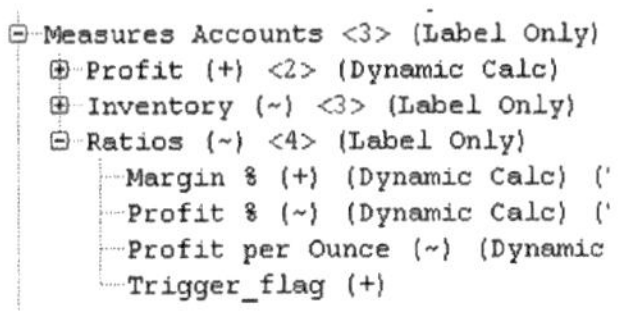

```
⊟ Measures Accounts <3> (Label Only)
   ⊞ Profit (+) <2> (Dynamic Calc)
   ⊞ Inventory (~) <3> (Label Only)
   ⊟ Ratios (~) <4> (Label Only)
      ┌─Margin % (+) (Dynamic Calc) ('
      ├─Profit % (~) (Dynamic Calc) ('
      ├─Profit per Ounce (~) (Dynamic
      └─Trigger_flag (+)
```

**Figure 5.30**   Adding Trigger_flag.

only insert values to an already created block. Once the intersection is created, we then export it to the Relational table using its own DATAEXPORT statement. Then the script will export the BUDGET information like it did before. The entire script is shown here, even though if we run it, we still won't be clearing out the data yet. For testing, I recommend commenting out the last section and testing that the trigger file is properly written to before running the entire script.

```
SET AGGMISSG ON ;
SET UPDATECALC OFF;
SET DATAEXPORTOPTIONS {
DataExportLevel LEVEL0 ;
DataExportDynamicCalc OFF;
DataExportColFormat ON ;
DataExportDIMHEADER ON ;
DataExportColHeader "Year";
DataExportRelationalFile ON;
DataExportOverwriteFile ON ;
DataExportDryRun OFF;
};
/* set the trigger to 1 for a single sparse intersection */
FIX("Trigger_flag",@relative("Year",0),"New York","Budget")
     /* populate the intersection with a 1 */
"100-10" (
     "100-10"= 1;
     )
     /*export the trigger value to the trigger table */
     DATAEXPORT "DSN" "TBC_Sample" "Essbase_trigger_table"
"interrel" "training";
ENDFIX
/* Export the budget information */
FIX((@relative("Year",0),@Relative("Measures",0),
@relative("Product",0),@Relative("Market",0),"Budget"))
     DATAEXPORT "DSN" "TBC_Sample" "BUDGET" "interrel" "training";
ENDFIX
```

Now that these pieces are in place, we need to create the trigger. This example in SQL Server shows the most basic trigger possible. It will always truncate (clear out) the BUDGET table. As mentioned earlier, we could do a lot more: We could capture the value of the Trigger_Flag and scenario and clear out different tables, or we could write to an audit log about what values were passed. For Planning, we could pass the points of view into the table and maybe use them for doing something special with the data being loaded. The possible iterations are only limited to your imagination and willingness to push the limits of your SQL knowledge to try different things. (Remember, Google is your friend here.) The syntax for the sample SQL trigger is as follows:

```
USE TBC_Sample
GO
Create TRIGGER Essbase_Updates ON dbo.Essbase_trigger_table
     FOR Insert
AS
Truncate table budget;
GO
```

We can then run the calc script we created (and remembered to save) earlier. Before running the calc, I tested the table to see how many rows it contained. Hint, I used the SQL:

```
SELECT COUNT(*) from BUDGET
```

I found that I had 3705 rows in my BUDGET table. Apparently, I had run the script a few times in testing it. Once I had this baseline, I ran the full calc script with the trigger in place. Running the count SQL again, I was confused that I came up with 1235 rows. In my earlier exercises, I had 1234 rows. I forgot that I added an intersection in BUDGET for my FLAG. If we query the BUDGET table for the Trigger_Flag measure using the SQL:

```
SELECT *
from BUDGET
WHERE Measures = 'Trigger_Flag'
```

we get one row returned that looks like Table 5.29.

If we wanted to, we could make another trigger to delete that row for the data after the table is loaded. In my testing, I ended up creating about 10 rows in the Essbase_Trigger_Table table. This would keep growing forever. This might be acceptable if we would not be running the process much. I like to clean things up, so I added a line into the trigger to truncate the table entries in the Essbase_Trigger_Table when I was done:

```
Alter TRIGGER Essbase_Updates ON dbo.Essbase_trigger_table
     FOR Insert
AS
Truncate table budget;
Truncate table Essbase_trigger_table
GO
```

**Table 5.29**  Result From a Trigger_Flag Measure

| PRODUCT | MARKET | MEASURES | SCENARIO | JAN | FEB | MAR | APR | MAY | JUN | JUL | AUG | SEP | OCT | NOV | DEC |
|---------|--------|----------|----------|-----|-----|-----|-----|-----|-----|-----|-----|-----|-----|-----|-----|
| 100-10 | New York | Trigger_flag | Budget | 1 | 1 | 1 | 1 | 1 | 1 | 1 | 1 | 1 | 1 | 1 | 1 |

A useful approach could be creating an audit table into which we insert the trigger value with an extra column for a datetime stamp. This would tell us when the process was run. This would be particularly helpful if I was passing different scenarios and flag values to the trigger file. As an exercise, try creating a table with an extra column for an audit_date and insert the row before truncating the table.

I use an audit table all the time to keep track of what steps were run in a stored procedure. If there is an error, I can log that and trigger an e-mail that there was a problem.

### 5.13 Conclusion

This chapter discusses a lot of basic SQL syntax and explores some of the ways we can utilize that SQL in rules files and calc scripts. This is just the beginning; you can do so much with SQL in your Essbase or Planning implementation. You can access blogs on hacking the Planning tables so you can see what is in them. Custom Defined Functions allow you to query SQL tables and bring back a value or member name to your calc script, and Essbase Studio can make your relational data easier to deal with. The topics described here, with the possible exceptions of Triggers and Stored Procedures, are the foundation of a good Essbase Studio developer. Understanding how the tables relate and how to create views and joins allows us to create our own custom SQL in studio on both data loading and drill-through reports, giving us more efficient SQL than is generated from Essbase Studio. Knowing and under-standing how the SQL works are what can make us stronger and better Essbase developers.

## Acknowledgments

I thank my technical editor, Dan Pressman, president of nTuple Solutions, for keeping me honest in my work. I also thank my boss, Edward Roske, chief executive officer of interRel Consulting, who allowed me to write a chapter for a competing book. As he says, it is all about sharing knowledge. Finally, I thank Cameron Lackpour, my friend and fellow Essbase nerd, for allowing me to have sleepless nights and angst by asking me to write a chapter in the book.

# 6

# COPERNICUS WAS RIGHT

## Integrating Oracle Business Intelligence and Essbase

### MIKE NADER

## Contents

Siblings fight. While I cannot speak for females, I can say that male siblings born 18 months apart go out of their way to cause chaos for each other.

It is not uncommon, for example, for a 14-year-old brother to lie in wait and shoot his 16-year-old sibling in the back with a paperclip launched from a rubber band. The 14-year-old (of course) states that this was all a school project measuring the concepts of velocity and the nature of impact—in short, physics. To make the experiment more effectual, he waits until his brother has gotten out of the shower and is wearing nothing more than a towel.

The 16-year-old, conversely (after rising from a convulsive fit that rivals European footballers), often attempts to replicate the experiment using a book (or whatever blunt object is in reach). This scene is disturbing on many levels, not the least of which is that the towel generally remains on the floor as the scene plays out.

Siblings fight. As a parent, a caretaker if you will, we try to assign reason to these actions. It is possible there is a genetic predisposition—like Bears and Packers fans.* The longer I live around siblings, the more I think their quarrels stem from a desire to make themselves unique. They are always together, often at the same birthday parties, competing for the same friends or just competing for attention in general. They simply want to find a level of confidence in who they are and what they do well. They have to come to a realization that they are not the center of the universe, just part of it. The challenge is to do this with a level of maturity and not to resort to makeshift sling shots or trebuchets (the latter is a long but funny story).

If you think about the siblings in the Oracle Business Intelligence (BI) Foundation, the situation is not radically different. Oracle Business Intelligence Enterprise Edition (OBIEE) and Essbase each have unique qualities. Together, they make a pretty strong family. Growing up, in a manner of speaking, in the Essbase community, I am as guilty as anyone for looking at Essbase and thinking it can do pretty much anything. I have friends that are excellent OBIEE consultants and feel the same way about OBIEE. We put our favorites at the center of the known universe. This is a key problem with integrating the two technologies.

From the Essbase perspective, we often look at OBIEE and start a wish list. We wish, for instance, that after almost 10 years of owning an "integrated" BI stack that Oracle actually integrated it. We wish that write-back from OBIEE was as simple as it was in Analyzer (dating myself here) 15 years ago. We wish that asymmetrical models and columns were simple to work with. However, the interesting thing is, for everything we wish, there is a viable counter argument (or more important priority) in the rest of the BI world.

In the 16th century, the mathematician Nicolaus Copernicus dared theorize that it was the Sun, not the Earth, that was the center of our solar system. The idea, while not popular at the time, was transformational. Over the last few years, as a recovering Essbase addict, I have come to feel that there is beauty in coming to the realization that you (or your technology in this case) are not the center of the known universe. Essbase is spectacular at aggregating quantitative data. It suffers spectacularly with detailed and qualitative analysis. The beauty comes from looking past the perceived cosmos and realizing there is neat stuff out there you might never have considered.

The marriage of Essbase and OBIEE provides unique opportunities for real detailed analysis (operational or otherwise) side by side with your aggregate data. It makes

---

* For those readers not familiar with the American football reference, simply insert Manchester United and Liverpool for the team names. I had thought of using a political reference, but that would make this chapter altogether too serious.

leveraging something like Web Analysis for reporting akin to using leeches to cure a cold (keeping with the 16th century analogy). In short, Copernicus was right, about children and technology.

## 6.1 Why This Exists

This chapter is intended, primarily, for Essbase consultants who are starting to work with OBIEE. That is not to say it is not useful for the OBIEE consultant who is starting to work with Essbase. Some of the procedures illustrated in this chapter, while fundamental to the long-time OBIEE consultant, are less so to their Essbase siblings. This chapter assumes the reader has very good familiarity with Essbase and at least a fundamental understanding of OBIEE modeling and reporting techniques.

When thinking about Essbase and OBIEE integration techniques, I tend to segregate the world into two areas. In the first are fundamental design and modeling considerations that need to be performed on the Essbase and OBIEE side. And in the second are integration tips and tricks that let us transform simple analysis on the Essbase model into analytic application. Of the two, the latter is more interesting, but both are necessary.*

## 6.2 Fundamental Design Techniques

Before we get to the fun stuff, we need to first focus on the fundamentals. OBIEE does not query Essbase like Web Analysis, or like Financial Reporting, or like Smart View. OBIEE queries Essbase like a BI tool (not dissimilar from tools like Tableau). As Essbase consultants (where OBIEE is concerned), we should start thinking about each dimension as a table and each generation in our model as a column. That is how OBIEE sees an Essbase cube.

To take advantage of the capabilities that OBIEE provides, we as Essbase developers need to make fundamental design choices when building our models. In addition, there are tricks that we can do in the RPD layer of OBIEE that make the user experience (and building our analytic applications) better.

### 6.2.1 Why Symmetry Matters

We in the Essbase community have trained ourselves over the years that asymmetrical hierarchies are natural. Take a standard product hierarchy, for example. Our users tell us that their hierarchies look nice and symmetrical, with each subgroup rolling neatly into another (see Figure 6.1).

---

* All of the examples in this chapter are created using the sample Essbase applications (Sample Basic, ASOSamp Basic) and the TBC relational data set. The latter data set is part of the Essbase Studio samples that are laid down as part of the Essbase Studio installation.

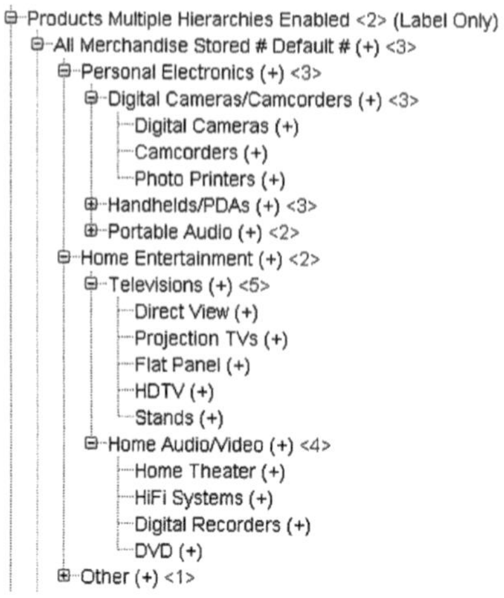

```
Products Multiple Hierarchies Enabled <2> (Label Only)
  All Merchandise Stored # Default # (+) <3>
    Personal Electronics (+) <3>
      Digital Cameras/Camcorders (+) <3>
        Digital Cameras (+)
        Camcorders (+)
        Photo Printers (+)
      Handhelds/PDAs (+) <3>
      Portable Audio (+) <2>
    Home Entertainment (+) <2>
      Televisions (+) <5>
        Direct View (+)
        Projection TVs (+)
        Flat Panel (+)
        HDTV (+)
        Stands (+)
      Home Audio/Video (+) <4>
        Home Theater (+)
        HiFi Systems (+)
        Digital Recorders (+)
        DVD (+)
    Other (+) <1>
```

**Figure 6.1**    Symmetrical dimension.

When you build your Essbase model based on data provided, you often end up with a very different picture. This picture, more frequently, is what the client wants to report against.

Figure 6.2 shows how our customers are used to seeing the structure in Smart View. The problem from an OBIEE point of view, of course, is that OBIEE looks at the world differently. Symmetry matters to OBIEE. Starting your reporting journey with asymmetry makes things more complicated. That is not to imply that you cannot report effectively when leveraging asymmetry; you can. There is just more to consider.

One feature that provides great reporting flexibility in OBIEE is also one that we do not often consider with Essbase: the ability to select specific portions of the dimensionality based on similar characteristics. In Essbase, we often use user-defined attributes (UDAs) or Attribute dimensions to make these selections. These techniques are not without overhead. UDAs are often difficult to manage outside of a Data Relationship Management or Enterprise Performance Management Architect deployment, and attributes have a performance overhead.

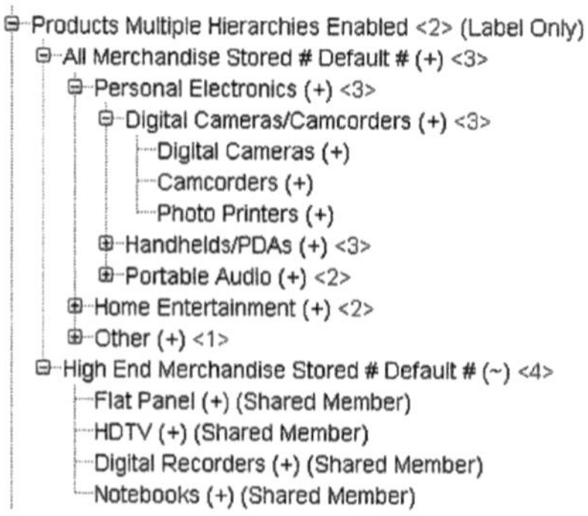

```
Products Multiple Hierarchies Enabled <2> (Label Only)
  All Merchandise Stored # Default # (+) <3>
    Personal Electronics (+) <3>
      Digital Cameras/Camcorders (+) <3>
        Digital Cameras (+)
        Camcorders (+)
        Photo Printers (+)
      Handhelds/PDAs (+) <3>
      Portable Audio (+) <2>
    Home Entertainment (+) <2>
    Other (+) <1>
  High End Merchandise Stored # Default # (~) <4>
    Flat Panel (+) (Shared Member)
    HDTV (+) (Shared Member)
    Digital Recorders (+) (Shared Member)
    Notebooks (+) (Shared Member)
```

**Figure 6.2**    Asymmetrical dimension.

| ALL_PRODUCTS | PRODUCT_CATGORIES | PRODUCT_DEPARTMENTS | PRODUCT_LINES | PRODUCT_SKU | PRODUCT_SKU_SECONDARY |
|---|---|---|---|---|---|
| 1 Products | All Merchandise | Personal Electronics | Digital Cameras/Camcorders | Digital Cameras | (null) |
| 2 Products | All Merchandise | Personal Electronics | Digital Cameras/Camcorders | Camcorders | (null) |
| 3 Products | All Merchandise | Personal Electronics | Digital Cameras/Camcorders | Photo Printers | (null) |
| 4 Products | All Merchandise | Personal Electronics | Handhelds/PDAs | Handhelds | (null) |
| 5 Products | All Merchandise | Personal Electronics | Handhelds/PDAs | Memory | (null) |
| 6 Products | All Merchandise | Personal Electronics | Handhelds/PDAs | Other Accessories | (null) |
| 7 Products | All Merchandise | Personal Electronics | Portable Audio | Boomboxes | (null) |
| 8 Products | All Merchandise | Personal Electronics | Portable Audio | Radios | (null) |
| 9 Products | All Merchandise | Home Entertainment | Televisions | Direct View | (null) |
| 10 Products | All Merchandise | Home Entertainment | Televisions | Projection TVs | (null) |
| 11 Products | All Merchandise | Home Entertainment | Televisions | Flat Panel | (null) |
| 12 Products | All Merchandise | Home Entertainment | Televisions | HDTV | (null) |
| 13 Products | All Merchandise | Home Entertainment | Televisions | Stands | (null) |
| 14 Products | All Merchandise | Home Entertainment | Home Audio/Video | Home Theater | (null) |
| 15 Products | All Merchandise | Home Entertainment | Home Audio/Video | HiFi Systems | (null) |
| 16 Products | All Merchandise | Home Entertainment | Home Audio/Video | Digital Recorders | (null) |
| 17 Products | All Merchandise | Home Entertainment | Home Audio/Video | DVD | (null) |
| 18 Products | All Merchandise | Other | Computers and Peripherals | Systems | Desktops |
| 19 Products | All Merchandise | Other | Computers and Peripherals | Systems | Notebooks |
| 20 Products | All Merchandise | Other | Computers and Peripherals | Displays | (null) |
| 21 Products | All Merchandise | Other | Computers and Peripherals | CD/DVD drives | (null) |
| 22 Products | High End Merchandise | Flat Panel | (null) | (null) | (null) |
| 23 Products | High End Merchandise | HDTV | (null) | (null) | (null) |
| 24 Products | High End Merchandise | Digital Recorders | (null) | (null) | (null) |
| 25 Products | High End Merchandise | Notebooks | (null) | (null) | (null) |
| 26 Products | Mike's Products | xx | xxx | My Sku | (null) |

**Figure 6.3**   OBIEE Perception.

OBIEE, being built from a relational perspective, looks similar to the image in Figure 6.3.

This presents two challenges:

1. Because OBIEE thinks about dimensionality from a relational perspective, it reads the Essbase model top-down (or generation based, in Essbase parlance) only.
2. OBIEE does not look for or query individual members from Essbase, unless used directly in a filter or formula. Instead, OBIEE queries Essbase using column names, as if it were querying a relational structure.

When OBIEE reads the Essbase metadata, it derives the "column" names based on the generation designation, such as "Gen3,All Merchandise" as in Figure 6.4.

The generation-based names, of course, are not intuitive to the user community. As such, we need to provide proper names so users understand what they are querying when using the tool. You can provide logical names for OBIEE by either naming the generation in Essbase (Figure 6.5) or renaming the columns in the OBIEE business layer (Figure 6.6).

**Figure 6.4**   Column names based on generation designation.

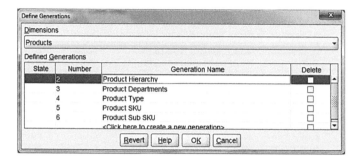

**Figure 6.5**   Naming the generations in Essbase.

**Figure 6.6**   Renaming columns in the OBIEE BMM layer.

The obstacle to working easily with asymmetric hierarchies is that it is difficult to name a portion of the dimension to denote what a user sees on a report. Take our dimension example. If we assume that the names should be All Merchandise -> Product Departments -> Product Categories -> Product Types -> Product SKU, then a user would expect to see only Product Categories when using that column on a report, as in Figure 6.7.

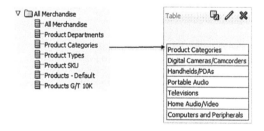

**Figure 6.7**   Using one dimension in a report.

| Product Category | Product Type |
|---|---|
| Personal Electronics | Digital Cameras/Camcorders |
| | Handhelds/PDAs |
| | Portable Audio |
| Home Entertainment | Televisions |
| | Home Audio/Video |
| Other | Computers and Peripherals |
| Flat Panel | |
| HDTV | |
| Digital Recorders | |
| Notebooks | |

**Figure 6.8** Results from asymmetrical hierarchy.

Instead, based on the asymmetric hierarchy, they get a mix of Categories and Types. With an asymmetric hierarchy, we get a mixture of Categories and Types. In this example (Figure 6.8), "Notebooks" is a Type, not a Category.

Users can choose to build an analysis with the hierarchical columns. Using these columns, however, has limitations from a reporting and export perspective. Hierarchical columns

- Cannot be used in page section of reports
- Restrict the import of OBIEE objects leveraging Smart View
- Can cause performance issues (because of the verbose multidimension expression [MDX] generation)

Other restrictions also cause challenges. Instead of going directly to the portion of the hierarchy they want to see, users must now navigate the tree to find the Essbase members they are interested in seeing. Furthermore, OBIEE does not provide the same kind of member selector used in Smart View or Financial Reports. As such, creating dynamic member selections is difficult without leveraging Selection Steps or custom coding. The use of the hierarchical column, while valid, is not a panacea for dealing with asymmetrical hierarchies in Essbase.

Changing the hierarchy type for the specific dimension to value in the physical layer of the RPD can provide search capabilities similar to Smart View or Financial Reports. However, value-based hierarchies have other limitations. For example, the columns representing most Essbase generations are removed. When drilling using the flat columns, OBIEE queries each generation dynamically as a user drills down.

Wherever possible, using symmetrical dimensions in your Essbase model is to your advantage.* The user community, of course, needs to get used to navigating through these levels to see their data. In those situations where you cannot negotiate symmetry into the design, you have to rely on other techniques to provide nomenclature and logical navigation.

---

* Although we are not discussing the concept of conformed and federated relational and Essbase dimensionality in this chapter, it is important to note that the use of asymmetrical dimensionality eliminates the ability to leverage conformed drilling from Essbase summary into relational detail.

*6.2.2 Leveraging Attributes to Provide Symmetry*

The hierarchical column, as previously mentioned, provides a means to navigate through the dimension in a logical fashion. It does not, however, allow for direct selection of a specific level inside of Essbase. From the Essbase design perspective, the easiest way to allow OBIEE to handle the direct query on an Essbase level in an asymmetric hierarchy is through the use of Essbase Attribute dimensions. There also is a way to do this directly in the OBIEE business layer, which is discussed later in this chapter.

By adding an attribute to each member at a given level, you can use the attribute columns brought into OBIEE to select those members in that specific hierarchy depth (for example, for all departments within an organization), as in Figure 6.9.

Essbase attributes within OBIEE queries only pull the summed value of those members assigned with that attribute. To enable the attribute drill capability, you simply add a drill path to the attribute column. This allows OBIEE to move from the attribute total to the specific attribute members (see Figure 6.10).

Although leveraging an Essbase UDA for this type of query is also possible, the UDA columns exposed in OBIEE are Boolean in nature. They return either a 1 or 0 to denote whether a member has the specific UDA. To leverage these for specific level selection, you have to create a custom column formula or apply secondary filtering on a report (see Figure 6.11). Both of these solutions limit the ad hoc capability of the solution.

```
⊟ Products Stored # Default # <3> (Product Series)
   ⊟ 10001 (+) <2> (Alias: BizTech) (UDAS: Partition Area)
      ⊟ 1001 (+) <4> (Alias: Communication) (UDAS: Major Product)
         ─ 8 (+) (Alias: V5x Flip Phone) (Product Series: Product SKUs)
         ─ 17 (+) (Alias: CompCell RX3) (Product Series: Product SKUs)
         ─ 9 (+) (Alias: Touch-Screen T5) (Product Series: Product SKUs)
         ─ 10 (+) (Alias: KeyMax S-Phone) (Product Series: Product SKUs)
      ⊟ 1002 (+) <2> (Alias: Electronics)
         ⊟ 104 (+) <2> (Alias: Accessories)
            ─ 1 (+) (Alias: MP3 Speakers System) (Product Series: Product SKUs)
            ─ 20 (+) (Alias: Bluetooth Adaptor) (Product Series: Product SKUs)
         ⊞ 103 (+) <2> (Alias: Audio)
```

**Figure 6.9**   Selecting levels with attributes.

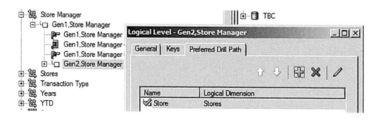

**Figure 6.10**   Added drill path.

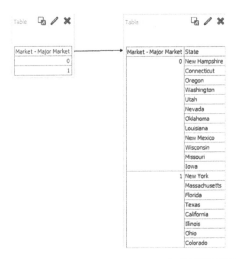

**Figure 6.11**    Leveraging UDAs in OBIEE reports.

### 6.2.3 *Naming in the RPD or the Essbase Outline*

One of the key benefits of symmetry is consistent naming. But where should that naming take place? It is possible, as previously discussed, within either the Essbase outline or the RPD. Of the two techniques, I prefer to rename in the OBIEE business layer. Simply put, it provides better overall control of the Essbase/OBIEE metadata for two primary reasons:

1. You can build multiple business models from a single cube import. Doing this lets you modify both the dimensionality and the naming of each respective business model, independent of one another. Note: A specific example of where this technique provides value is discussed later in this chapter.
2. When leveraging an aggregate storage option (ASO) model, you can name each hierarchy of a "Multiple Hierarchies Enabled" dimension independently.

To effectively discuss these points, you need to understand how OBIEE reads block storage option (BSO) and ASO models.

#### 6.2.3.1 *Working with ASO versus BSO Models in the RPD*    In general, there is little difference in working with an ASO versus a BSO model in the RPD. However, when using an ASO model in the RPD, a couple of unique capabilities exist for both naming and dimension display.

When an ASO application is brought into the RPD, it is inspected to determine specific dimension types. By default, all "Multiple Hierarchies Enabled" dimensions are split into multiple dimensions, with each hierarchy represented as an individual dimension in the business and presentation layers.

Figure 6.12 shows the Products dimension from the ASO Sample application in the Physical, Business, and Presentation layers, respectively.

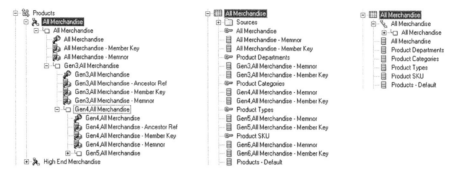

**Figure 6.12** Products dimension in Physical, Business Model and Mapping (BMM), and Presentation layers.

This split has two distinct advantages. Each portion of the dimension can be named independently. This allows a dimension that is otherwise asymmetrical across the hierarchies (but symmetrical within) to be represented properly. For example, Figure 6.13 shows the Product hierarchy in the ASO Sample application.

The dimension cannot be named easily for user consumption in OBIEE. However, since "All Merchandise" and "High End Merchandise" represent independent hierarchies, they can be split and named in the RPD (see Figure 6.14).

Moreover, because these are now independent dimensions, the hierarchical columns for each are filtered representations of the dimensions. Using the "High End

**Figure 6.13** Product hierarchy in the ASO sample application.

**Figure 6.14** One dimension split into independent hierarchies.

Merchandise" hierarchy on an analysis filters out the "All Merchandise" members. The converse is true for "All Merchandise" (see Figure 6.15).

Even though the "Multiple Hierarchies Enabled" dimension is split, it does not have to appear that way to the end-user community. As the dimensions are related, regrouping these dimensions using a Presentation Table is logical. Once regrouped, the hierarchies appear again as portions of a single dimension. However, they retain the independent naming and hierarchy columns (see Figure 6.16).

To create a Presentation Table and regroup, perform the following steps:

1. Right-click on the subject area in the Presentation layer and select New -> Presentation Table (Figure 6.17). On the General Tab, name the Presentation Table and select the Child Presentation Tables tab.
2. Click the green plus to add a child table.
3. In the table list, select the desired child tables and click Select.
4. Click OK, save, and deploy the RPD.

When working with a split "Multiple Hierarchies Enabled" dimension, there is a query limitation. You cannot use a member from both independent hierarchies on the grid simultaneously. Doing so will result in an analysis error as shown in Figure 6.18.

| Pivot Table | |
|---|---|
| | Price Paid |
| High End Merchandise | |
| ▽ High End Merchandise | 9,836,522.08 |
| Flat Panel | 1,557,881.89 |
| HDTV | 5,703,763.20 |
| Digital Recorders | 865,334.49 |
| Notebooks | 1,709,542.50 |

| Pivot Table | |
|---|---|
| | Price Paid |
| All Merchandise | |
| ▽ All Merchandise | 37,765,664.76 |
| ▷ Personal Electronics | 17,762,745.07 |
| ▷ Home Entertainment | 15,613,373.19 |
| ▽ Other | 4,389,546.50 |
| ▷ Computers and Peripherals | 4,389,546.50 |

**Figure 6.15** Prefiltered hierarchical columns.

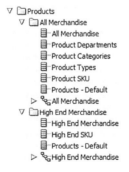

**Figure 6.16** Regrouping using a Presentation Table.

**Figure 6.17** Creating a Presentation Table.

**Figure 6.18**   Error due to query limitation with a dimension split across hierarchies.

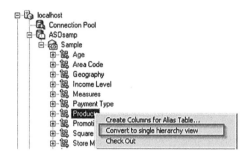

**Figure 6.19**   Convert back to unified view.

Having a "Multiple Hierarchies Enabled" dimension split is the default behavior when working with an ASO model in the RPD. You can override this behavior in the Physical layer of the RPD and set the dimension back to a unified view (Figure 6.19). Doing so will negate the ability to name and navigate each hierarchy separately. It will, however, allow for members from both hierarchies to exist on the same report.

**Note:** If you want to maintain the split hierarchy but still query across both on a single report, you can create analysis using the alias table column for that dimension. The alias table column(s) spans all hierarchies and does not return an error.

When working with an ASO model, the dimension tagged as Accounts is "dynamic." Dynamic dimensions do not have the same behavior as other dimensions. It may be possible to remove the Accounts designation and tag the dimension as "Multiple Hierarchies Enabled" to allow the various hierarchies in the accounts dimension to be split out into independent dimensions (i.e., balance sheet, income statement, cash flow, etc.). As Multiple Hierarchy dimensions in Essbase require the first-generation member to be stored, you may need to add a dummy member and mark it as stored. This member can be removed from OBIEE in the presentation layer.

*6.2.4  Why You Should Flatten Accounts and When You Should Not*

For most Essbase models, the Accounts dimension is often the hardest in which to achieve symmetry. Depending on the nature of the model, the dimension could be more than 10 generations deep. The problem is further exacerbated when you have to report across multiple account hierarchies, such as a Balance Sheet hierarchy and an Income Statement hierarchy (Figure 6.20).

```
⊟ Outline: FinStmt (Active Alias Table: Default)
   ⊟ Account Accounts <8> (Never Share)
      ⊞ Drivers and Assumptions (~) <4> (Label Only) (UDAS: Saved Assumption, Flow)
      ⊞ Income Statement (~) <1> (Dynamic Calc) (UDAS: Revenue, Flow)
      ⊞ Balance Sheet (~) <2> (Dynamic Calc) (TB Last) (UDAS: Asset)
      ⊞ Balance Sheet Change (~) <2> (Dynamic Calc) (UDAS: Revenue, Flow)
      ⊞ Cash Flow (~) <2> (Label Only) (UDAS: Revenue, Flow)
      ⊞ Other FinStat Metrics (~) <4> (Label Only) (UDAS: Saved Assumption, Flow)
      ⊞ Balance Sheet Input Method (~) <3> (Label Only) (UDAS: Saved Assumption, Flow)
      ⊞ Measures and Ratios (~) <12> (Label Only) (UDAS: Saved Assumption, Flow)
```

**Figure 6.20** Multiple account hierarchies in Essbase.

In an ideal situation, when having to do detailed financial reporting, you should consider using either Financial Reporting or Smart View. You can do financial reports in OBIEE against Essbase; however, generation naming aside, the asymmetrical nature of many financial reports makes them prohibitive to do. It is not the subject of the report that causes problems, but the layout, nature, and style of reports and the need to cherry-pick members from a ragged hierarchy to fit that tabular layout that creates complexity.

Later sections of this chapter focus on the use of the Evaluate function for a series of tricks with Essbase. The creation of asymmetrical columns, for example, is one of them.

The generation naming issue aside, when you leave the Essbase accounts hierarchical within OBIEE, you limit the overall capability of your analysis. When accounts are left as hierarchical, OBIEE creates a dummy fact that you must use to pull numeric data onto the report (Figure 6.21).

You can remove that dummy fact and assign another dimension as accounts, such as scenario. Depending on the nature of your analysis, making this change may make sense. The next section of this chapter deals specifically with this technique and the reasons for implementing it.

Not only do I generally recommend flattening accounts, but also I recommend taking a key performance indicator approach to reporting. Instead of assuming that all accounts (measures) in an Essbase model are of equal importance, work with your end users to determine which metrics are required for your dashboards. In a recent deployment of OBIEE on Hyperion Planning, I worked with a client to determine 100 required metrics across 40 reports and 10 dashboards. The Accounts dimension was flattened in the RPD, the required accounts were added as physical cube columns, and then they were logically grouped in the presentation layer using presentation folders (Figure 6.22).

**Figure 6.21** Dummy fact in OBIEE.

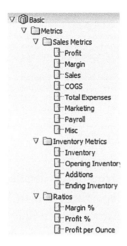

**Figure 6.22**   Logical grouping of accounts in the presentation layer.

*6.2.4.1 Building Physical Cube Columns*   When importing an Essbase model into the RPD, you have the option of converting the Measures dimension to a flattened group of cube columns (Figure 6.23). Although this saves the process of defining the required columns for analysis, it can also create many more columns than required. Further, depending on the number of accounts in the Essbase model, it can over-burden the user interface. It is not uncommon, for example, for a single Essbase model to have thousands of accounts.

There is an option to manually add columns to the RPD rather than importing them from Essbase. Although manually creating cube columns takes longer, it is a more controlled deployment process. Instead of adding the cube columns in bulk, only those required for the initial analysis are created. As the BI deployment grows and

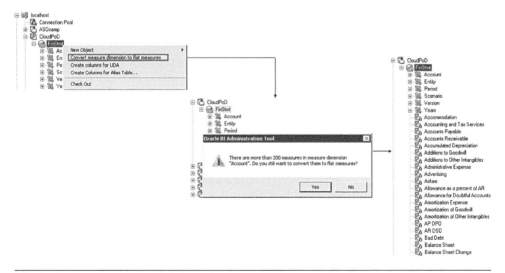

**Figure 6.23**   Converting to flattened columns.

analytics are required, additional cube columns can be added to the RPD and exposed to the user community.

To manually create cube columns:

1. After importing the cube into the physical layer of the RPD, expand the physical cube table and delete the dummy measure column (Figure 6.24).
2. Right-click on the physical cube table and select New Object -> Physical Cube Column (Figure 6.25).
3. On the Physical Cube definition dialog, provide the required information and click OK. As shown in Figure 6.26, the "External Name" must match the Essbase member name, Essbase type is always set to double, and aggregation is always set to External Aggregation.

**Figure 6.24**   Manually create cube columns, step 1.

**Figure 6.25**   Manually create cube columns, step 2.

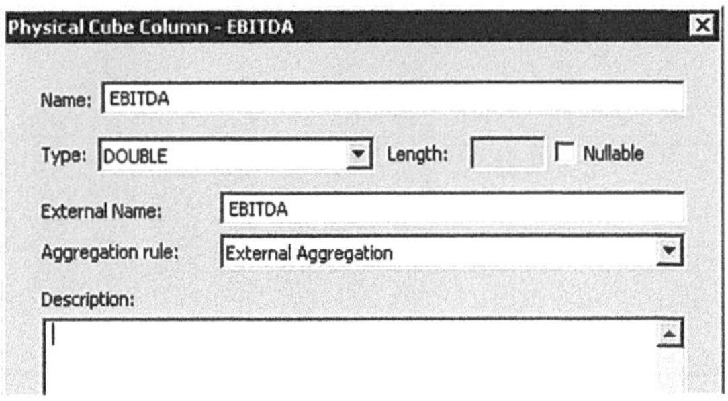

**Figure 6.26**   Manually create cube columns, step 3.

4. Repeat steps 1–3 for all required Essbase metrics.
5. Once placed in the Business and Presentation layers, the Accounts hierarchy no longer shows and the defined columns are represented as the Facts.

A further advantage of flattening the Accounts dimension is to provide direct access to the most commonly used metrics. OBIEE is designed assuming that a relational fact table is the source of the data. These tables break the metrics across columns. When this is shown in a standard OBIEE subject area, they show as single, accessible metrics (Figure 6.27).

Moreover, having the Essbase accounts broken into individual metrics columns allows for more dynamic analysis. For example, assume you want to create a line-bar chart showing how Original Price trends against Price Paid for a specific set of Product SKUs (see Figure 6.28).

If you have the Essbase accounts hierarchical, leaving only the single dummy fact (or leveraging a secondary dimension as facts), you cannot readily perform this analysis. To create the line-bar combination, you need two separate accounts. If the Essbase accounts are left in a hierarchy, they are not individually exposed and you cannot build the analysis.

**Figure 6.27**  Accounts dimension as single, accessible metrics.

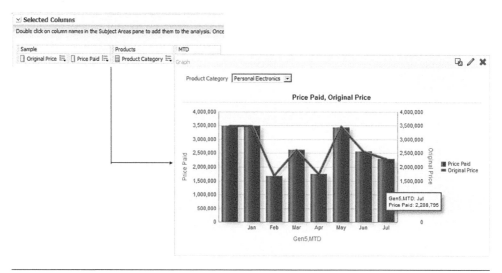

**Figure 6.28**  Line-bar chart example using individual metrics.

**Note:** It is possible to break out the accounts leveraging the Evaluate function. This technique is discussed later in this chapter.

Depending on the nature of the deployment, and specific analysis, there may be instances when you want to leave the accounts hierarchical. You might want to create a true income statement in OBIEE, for example. It is possible within the RPD to import a cube a second time and leave the accounts as hierarchical for the purposes of this analysis. It is important to realize that these cubes are seen as independent in the RPD. Any dimensional or calculation modeling would have to be done in both versions of the business model.

To create a second instance of the Essbase model in the RPD:

1. Import the initial version of desired cube using the metadata import capabilities in the RPD.
2. Before flattening the accounts, right-click and select Duplicate. A second instance of the cube displays in the RPD.
3. Flatten the accounts as desired in one instance, and leave the other as hierarchical (Figure 6.29).

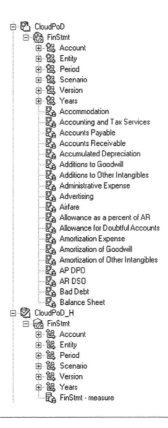

**Figure 6.29** Flattened accounts.

*6.2.5 Views on the Data*

One of the things that Essbase does exceedingly well is calculate hierarchical data. Over the years, we have come to rely on this capability for period-to-date and other calculation views (such as scaled versions). There are multiple schools of thought when working with period-to-date and other calculation views.

When working with period-to-date analysis, for example, Essbase deployments in BSO can use the built-in Dynamic Time Series (DTS). OBIEE, unfortunately, cannot take direct advantage of the DTS capabilities within Essbase. As such, when trying to create period-to-date and other view-based calculations, there are a few options, two of which are shown in Figures 6.30 and 6.31.

**Note:** You can also create calculated columns in the RPD for time balance. However, building directly in Essbase often provides greater reporting flexibility. A specific example leveraging the alternate hierarchy technique is discussed later in this chapter.

Of the two options pictured below, the latter best fits the majority of use cases. Although at times you will not be able to alter the underlying data structures, I am a firm believer that, where possible, calculation should be pushed to the data source layer.

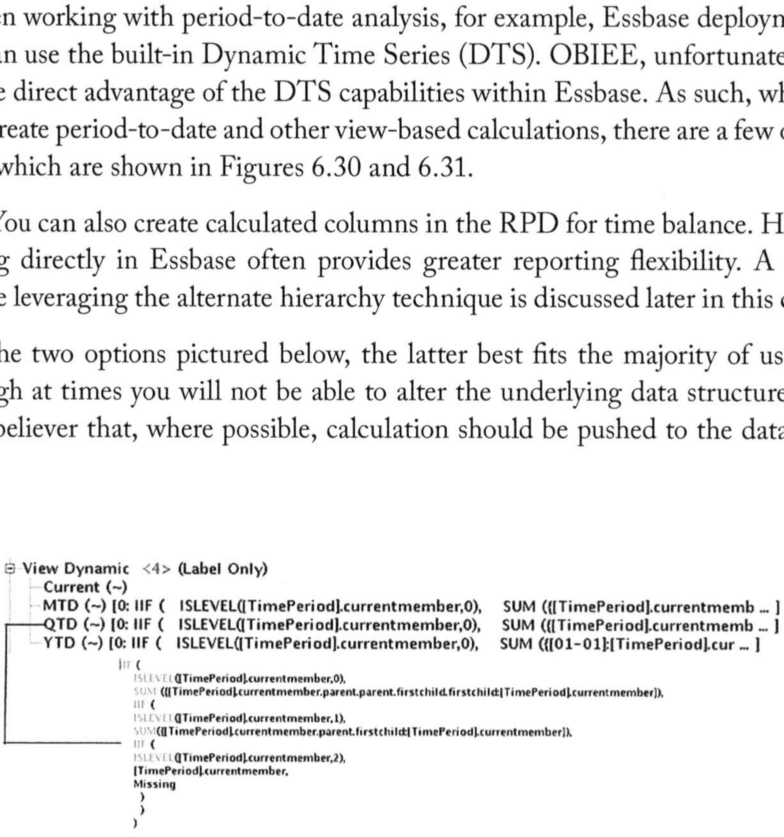

**Figure 6.30**  Example of an Essbase view dimension.

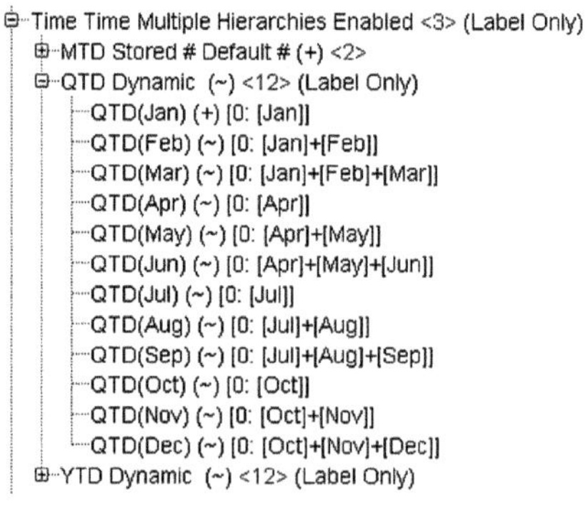

**Figure 6.31**  Example of an alternate hierarchy within the time dimension in the Essbase model.

| | | Price Paid | | | | | | | | | |
|---|---|---|---|---|---|---|---|---|---|---|---|
| | High End SKU | CT | MA | ME | NJ | NY | RI | DC | DE | FL | GA |
| QTD(Mar) | Flat Panel | 18,892.50 | 21,155.75 | 14,850.00 | 37,042.50 | 140,746.38 | 5,995.00 | 3,162.50 | 2,805.00 | 15,537.50 | 32,725.00 |
| | HDTV | 82,117.50 | 179,962.50 | 87,262.50 | 143,812.50 | 388,916.25 | 11,625.00 | 28,387.50 | | 61,672.50 | 163,020.00 |
| | Digital Recorders | 9,212.00 | 23,572.50 | 14,051.80 | 12,943.70 | 69,256.95 | 4,615.80 | 7,180.60 | 2,013.90 | 10,790.50 | 29,354.33 |
| | Notebooks | 21,525.00 | 58,950.00 | 29,595.00 | 48,174.00 | 100,746.00 | 4,830.00 | 7,935.00 | 1,560.00 | 11,280.00 | 62,815.50 |

**Figure 6.32** Drilling down to underlying detail.

The question then remains as to which method (view dimension or alternate hierarchy) I would recommend. Quite frankly, that varies based on the reporting tool and analysis.

A view dimension allows you to quickly apply calculations to an entire grid or subgrid of data, but often, these types of views are used in asymmetrical analysis (as was the case in the previous image). If this is the required analysis, using a view dimension is possible in OBIEE, although not necessarily recommended. If I am dealing specifically with OBIEE on Essbase, then my preference is to leverage an alternate hierarchy. I recommend this for one primary reason: the ability to drill from the alternate totals to the underlying detail (see Figure 6.32).

Although this might seem trivial on the surface, the fact that the hierarchy exists under the DTS member provides greater capability and simpler maintenance in OBIEE.

## 6.3 Creating Analytic Applications

The most interesting value proposition of OBIEE on top of Essbase is not how it handles Essbase queries or visualization. If Essbase is your only data source, any number of tools (by Oracle and other vendors) provide greater direct capability—Smart View, Financial Reports, Tableau, or Dodeca, to name just a few. OBIEE is a good, not great, ad hoc tool. The real value of OBIEE on Essbase is its ability to link data across the enterprise and provide a more holistic view of an organization's data. With OBIEE, you have the ability, for instance, to report on aggregate data from Essbase and see the support detail (relational or otherwise) on the same dashboard. Moreover, you have the ability to link the analysis and let the users navigate from aggregate to detailed values using a custom analytic workflow.

### 6.3.1 Evaluate Is Your Friend

The biggest complaint when working with OBIEE on Essbase is the fact that OBIEE (or rather, the logical Structured Query Language [SQL] it generates) does not seem to understand Essbase and how to effectively query the model. Limitations like a lack of symmetrical columns, inability to read the model from the bottom up, and inability to take advantage of DTS and Time-Balance capabilities make it frustrating at times to report against Essbase models.

With all of that said, the advantages that OBIEE provides for general reporting, inclusive of Essbase and other sources, far outweigh the limitations. The really neat thing about OBIEE is that it is customizable (not dissimilar from Essbase). To extend OBIEE, you simply need to find the proper work-around. When reporting against Essbase, Evaluate is your friend.

This section may seem a little out of place, but the topics that follow refer back frequently to Evaluate usage. Longtime OBIEE practitioners are, no doubt, familiar with the Evaluate function. As an Essbase consultant moving into the OBIEE space, leveraging Evaluate is going to be critical. Evaluate lets you pass a function from OBIEE to the underlying database. This works with either a relational source or an Essbase model. Many of the limitations of OBIEE against Essbase are a result of the logical SQL generation, so the Evaluate function lets you bypass SQL and pass an MDX statement (or substatement) to the Essbase model. If you cannot generate an asymmetric column or find level 0 descendants with OBIEE natively, you can do it with Evaluate.

The first challenge with the Evaluate function is understanding the syntax. Evaluate syntax, at first glance, is confusing:

```
EVALUATE('db_function(%1...%N)' [AS datatype] [, column1, columnN])
```

The Evaluate function ships the desired database function "db_function" to the underlying database and works on optional columns "Column1" and so forth. The database function (in our case, MDX) needs parameters on which to act. As such, you can use the %1, %2, and so forth to designate dimension/member parameters. Personally, I have had two complaints in leveraging the Evaluate function for Essbase:

1. The theoretically "optional" columns need to be represented.
2. The %1, etc., syntax does not always make sense with MDX.

On the second point, I simply want more control (at least visually) as to the exact members from the Essbase model I am passing into the Evaluate function. I luckily stumbled into a trick to make it easier. Like all good solutions, this one came from researching mistakes and solutions other consultants had made. For this syntax trick, I have to give credit to the folks at PWG Consulting.* Instead of leveraging the standard Evaluate syntax, you can effectively ignore the %1 parameter. Further, depending on the MDX you write, the "Column1" parameter need only be a valid column in the Essbase model, but it will never be used. For example, assume you want to grab all of the level 0 descendants of the asymmetrical Product dimension. You can use an evaluate function that looks like this:

---

* For the complete entry that inspired the Evaluate syntax, please see this site: http://everythingoracle
  .com/obieeteval.htm.

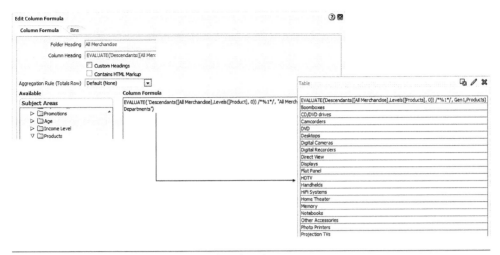

**Figure 6.33**   Results of Evaluate function in a column formula.

```
EVALUATE( 'Descendants([Products],Levels([Products], 0)) /*%1*/',
"All Merchandise"."Gen3,All Merchandise")
```

This sample breaks down as follows:

- '{[Product].levels(0).Members}—Uses standard MDX syntax to take the level 0 members of the Product dimension
- /*%1*/—Comments out the %n syntax. It has to be present for the Evaluate function to work, but we do not need it
- "All Merchandise"."Gen3,All Merchandise"—A valid column from the Product dimension. This example uses the generation 3 column. Any column, except the alias columns, can be used

The example in Figure 6.33 is done by leveraging a column formula. Although useful, this would have to be done on every analysis. More useful is building a column to do this in the RPD—and you can. That example is presented later in this chapter. Also, with the way this formula is written, we run the risk of pulling shared members into the report and duplicating data. It would be more useful if the input of the evaluate function can be a variable—and it can be. That example is also shown later in this chapter.

*6.3.2 Scaling the Essbase Hierarchy for Metadata Queries*

By leveraging the Evaluate function, you have the ability to issue MDX directly against the Essbase model. The requests, in general, are metadata queries; therefore, they are extremely fast. Instead of placing these queries in a single analysis document, you can create these columns directly in the RPD layer and expose them as custom columns for the user community.

These queries can be as simple as a method for selecting a subportion of the hierarchy (such as level 0 member) or they can be persisted metadata sets. For instance, you might want to create a dynamic set of call products that have more than $10,000 in sales in a given month.

To create a metadata column:

1. Open the RPD and expand the Business model for the Essbase cube (Figure 6.34).
2. Right-click on the desired dimension table and select New Object -> Logical Column (Figure 6.35).
3. On the General tab, name the column and select the Column Source tab.
4. At the bottom of the dialog, select the radio button for "Derived from existing column using expression" and click the function button (see Figure 6.36).
5. In the Expression Build window, enter the Evaluate function. To generate a list of members with units sold greater than 1000:
   ```
   EVALUATE( 'Filter(Descendants([Products],Levels([Products],
   0)),[Units]>1000) /*%1*/',  "ASOsamp"."All
   Merchandise"."Gen3,All Merchandise" )
   ```

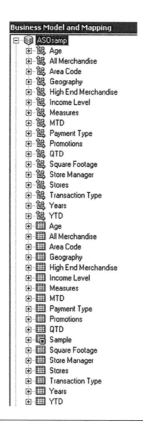

**Figure 6.34** Expand the BMM model.

**Figure 6.35** Create a logical column.

**Figure 6.36** Open the formula editor.

To generate a list of level zero members:
```
EVALUATE( 'Descendants([Products],Levels([Products], 0))
/*%1*/',  "ASOsamp"."All Merchandise"."Gen3,All Merchandise" )
```

6. Click OK and select the Levels tab.
7. A level designation is required to allow the new column to show facts when on an analysis. With a level designation, the column displays an error when you try to use it and a numeric fact on an analysis. Select ANY level; it does not need to be a specific level (see Figure 6.37).
8. Click OK to finish the column creation.
9. Drag the column to the dimensions folder in the Presentation layer.
10. Save and deploy the RPD.
11. Use the column on an analysis (see Figure 6.38).

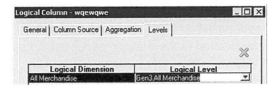

**Figure 6.37** Assign a logical level.

| Products G/T 10K | Sample - measure<br>Price Paid |
|---|---|
| Boomboxes | 1,708,629.22 |
| Camcorders | 2,731,930.88 |
| DVD | 2,158,379.03 |
| Desktops | 2,680,004.00 |
| Digital Cameras | 1,336,237.00 |
| Digital Recorders | 865,334.49 |
| HDTV | 5,703,763.20 |
| Home Theater | 1,488,503.75 |
| Memory | 2,588,663.25 |
| Notebooks | 1,709,542.50 |
| Other Accessories | 6,433,281.34 |
| Photo Printers | 1,317,036.70 |
| Radios | 1,646,966.68 |
| Stands | 1,843,224.83 |

**Figure 6.38** Using a metadata column.

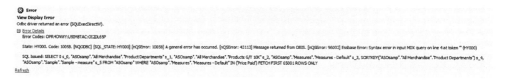

**Figure 6.39**   Error from using custom column with standard dimension column.

The "Products G/T 10K" row in Figure 6.38 is a persisted dynamic metadata set. It could have easily been a column that selected a specific level or another subportion of the hierarchy. A limitation affects the use of custom metadata columns: They cannot be used on an analysis with another column from the same dimension. The custom metadata columns are specific MDX queries and OBIEE cannot join them to the standard model and represent them in respect to the delivered columns. Trying to use the custom columns with a standard dimension column results in an error (Figure 6.39).

### 6.3.3  Mimicking Drill-Through Reports with the Action Framework

Evaluate is simply a building block, and with the foundation of Evaluate out of the way, we can move on to the really cool techniques. With the growth of data over the years, Essbase has been taxed more and more, both with handling detail within the cube and with linking to detail in underlying structured models.

In a more classical Essbase implementation, you might solve the link to detailed data by leveraging Essbase Studio or direct MaxL to embed drill-through reports into the model. Drill-through reports are, in general, a good solution. They travel with the specific dimensional intersection of the Essbase model and can pass that context from a single data value to the underlying relational system and execute an SQL query to bring back the detail.

Unfortunately, drill-through reports have a few significant limitations:

1. The data brought back from the drill-through process are dead. It is simply a data dump with no ability to pivot the results (short of building a pivot table in Excel).
2. They do not function in Financial Reports or OBIEE.

You can use Essbase Studio to build a drill-through that will take you from Smart View to OBIEE, but that means your analysis has to start outside of OBIEE. What if you want to contain your analysis within OBIEE? Although not exactly the same as a drill-through report, you can use the OBIEE Action Framework to mimic drill-through capabilities from Essbase to the relational model.

In its simplest form, the OBIEE Action Framework can be used to create a link from an existing report and based intersections to a detail report. The most basic form of this is done with the OBIEE GO URL. The GO URL is a method used to call a specific target analysis in OBIEE and pass a series of parameters from the source analysis. The parameters of the GO URL are well documented; this example focuses on leveraging the GO URL with Essbase.

The GO URL is shown on a report when it is opened in OBIEE. The address bar of your browser will show the server name and the action to navigate "GO" to the specified analysis (Figure 6.40).

If the target analysis in question is relational detail, we can set an Essbase source report to both navigate to the target report and pass context. Take the source report in Figure 6.41 as an example.

If we want to link this report to a report containing the underlying relational detail, we can start with the GO URL:

```
http://mp1epm01.huronconsultinggroup.com:19000/analytics/saw.dll?Por
talGo&Action=prompt&path=%2Fshared%2FBook%2FRelational%20Detail
```

The base GO URL contains a single parameter, the Portal Path:

```
%2Fshared%2FBook%2FRelational%20Detail
```

This path is simply the location of the target report. In our example, however, we want more than the location. We also want to pass a parameter. To do this, we need to alter the report to accept the desired dimension as prompted (such as Product) and the GO URL and add additional parameters. Instead of the base URL, we can expand it to include dimensions:

**Figure 6.40**   GO URL.

| Product SKU | State | Sales | | | | | | | | | | | |
|---|---|---|---|---|---|---|---|---|---|---|---|---|---|
| | | Jan | Feb | Mar | Apr | May | Jun | Jul | Aug | Sep | Oct | Nov | Dec |
| | New Hampshire | $278.00 | $283.00 | $301.00 | $311.00 | $333.00 | $372.00 | $400.00 | $376.00 | $313.00 | $290.00 | $298.00 | $294.00 |
| | New York | $1,168.00 | $1,225.00 | $1,198.00 | $1,276.00 | $1,299.00 | $1,565.00 | $1,458.00 | $1,453.00 | $1,357.00 | $1,415.00 | $1,298.00 | $1,356.00 |
| | Massachusetts | $835.00 | $810.00 | $817.00 | $844.00 | $849.00 | $947.00 | $956.00 | $955.00 | $886.00 | $796.00 | $817.00 | $816.00 |
| | Florida | $410.00 | $406.00 | $424.00 | $489.00 | $508.00 | $560.00 | $622.00 | $563.00 | $479.00 | $423.00 | $442.00 | $541.00 |
| | Connecticut | $310.00 | $325.00 | $309.00 | $292.00 | $275.00 | $232.00 | $225.00 | $225.00 | $258.00 | $313.00 | $325.00 | $289.00 |
| | Texas | $822.00 | $844.00 | $840.00 | $804.00 | $862.00 | $857.00 | $897.00 | $929.00 | $828.00 | $792.00 | $771.00 | $792.00 |
| | California | $1,397.00 | $1,356.00 | $1,405.00 | $1,459.00 | $1,546.00 | $1,676.00 | $1,733.00 | $1,695.00 | $1,535.00 | $1,367.00 | $1,308.00 | $1,494.00 |
| | Oregon | $580.00 | $544.00 | $524.00 | $472.00 | $465.00 | $427.00 | $389.00 | $397.00 | $472.00 | $493.00 | $491.00 | $414.00 |
| | Washington | $430.00 | $472.00 | $489.00 | $499.00 | $506.00 | $567.00 | $623.00 | $597.00 | $466.00 | $448.00 | $432.00 | $482.00 |
| | Utah | $604.00 | $591.00 | $594.00 | $576.00 | $531.00 | $508.00 | $497.00 | $448.00 | $478.00 | $509.00 | $539.00 | $483.00 |
| | Nevada | $181.00 | $180.00 | $181.00 | $183.00 | $192.00 | $195.00 | $200.00 | $219.00 | $206.00 | $188.00 | $181.00 | $200.00 |
| | Oklahoma | $380.00 | $386.00 | $391.00 | $448.00 | $443.00 | $441.00 | $487.00 | $487.00 | $442.00 | $489.00 | $533.00 | $587.00 |
| | Louisiana | $346.00 | $364.00 | $353.00 | $357.00 | $383.00 | $379.00 | $356.00 | $377.00 | $394.00 | $381.00 | $340.00 | $336.00 |
| | New Mexico | $284.00 | $284.00 | $300.00 | $323.00 | $344.00 | $375.00 | $418.00 | $364.00 | $308.00 | $279.00 | $307.00 | $327.00 |
| | Illinois | $579.00 | $608.00 | $634.00 | $757.00 | $777.00 | $823.00 | $943.00 | $843.00 | $685.00 | $665.00 | $690.00 | $846.00 |
| | Ohio | $430.00 | $397.00 | $380.00 | $361.00 | $354.00 | $318.00 | $290.00 | $282.00 | $358.00 | $352.00 | $377.00 | $340.00 |
| | Wisconsin | $490.00 | $518.00 | $535.00 | $549.00 | $555.00 | $609.00 | $657.00 | $688.00 | $571.00 | $558.00 | $525.00 | $590.00 |
| | Missouri | $360.00 | $358.00 | $352.00 | $345.00 | $321.00 | $311.00 | $301.00 | $270.00 | $286.00 | $319.00 | $334.00 | $292.00 |
| | Iowa | $161.00 | $162.00 | $162.00 | $157.00 | $169.00 | $180.00 | $190.00 | $185.00 | $155.00 | $143.00 | $126.00 | $134.00 |
| | Colorado | $643.00 | $665.00 | $640.00 | $646.00 | $702.00 | $767.00 | $767.00 | $744.00 | $679.00 | $657.00 | $580.00 | $611.00 |

**Figure 6.41**   Sample Essbase source report.

```
http://mp1epm01.huronconsultinggroup.com:19000/analytics/saw.dll?
PortalGo&Action=Navigate&path=%2Fshared%2FBook%2FRelational%20
Detail&P0=1&P1=eq&P2=%22A_N_PRODUCT%22.%22SKU%22&P3=%22100-20%22
```

In this new example, the parameters break down as follows:

- `path=%2Fshared%2FBook%2FRelational Detail`—Path to the target analysis
- `P0=1`—Represents the number of dimensions being passed, in this case 1
- `P1=eq`—States that the URL is looking for exact (equal) filtering
- `P2%22A_N_PRODUCT%22.%22SKU%22`—Denotes the column being filtered
- `P3=%22100-20%22`—Denotes the value the URL should filter on

Executing this URL displays the report in Figure 6.42.

To make the URL dynamic from the source report, we have to add it an Action Link in the source report. To do this, we need only edit the source report and the action of the fact column.

To create a URL Action Link on an Essbase Analysis:

1. Edit the source report and click the criteria tab.
2. Edit the metric column property and select the Interaction tab (Figure 6.43).
3. Change the Primary Interaction (under Value) to Action Links and click the green plus to add an Action Link.
4. Name the Action Link and set it to "Navigate to a Web Page" (Figure 6.44).
5. In the Create New Action dialog, paste the target report URL (Figure 6.45).
6. Click Define Parameters (Figure 6.46). The parameters dialog effectively converts the GO URL into a series of variables. You can hide these or let them display so that a user can alter the value before execution.
7. Scroll down to the Val1 Prompt and click the down arrow next to the value (for example "Cola") and select Column Value (Figure 6.47).
8. Use the drop-down to select the Product SKU column.
9. Select to hide all of the parameters and click OK three times to save the Action Link.
10. Save the report, open the report and test the link (Figure 6.48).

**Relational Detail**

| STATE | TRANSDATE | SKU | MARKETING | COGS | SALES | Fiscal Period |
|-------|-----------|-----|-----------|------|-------|---------------|
| Illinois | 1/11/2000 12:00:00 AM | 100-10 | 12.80 | 48.00 | 115.20 | Jan |
| | 1/13/2000 12:00:00 AM | 100-10 | 47.00 | 144.00 | 345.00 | Jan |
| | 1/18/2000 12:00:00 AM | 100-10 | 26.80 | 100.50 | 241.20 | Jan |
| | 1/28/2000 12:00:00 AM | 100-10 | 0.40 | 1.50 | 3.60 | Jan |

**Figure 6.42** Sample report from GO URL.

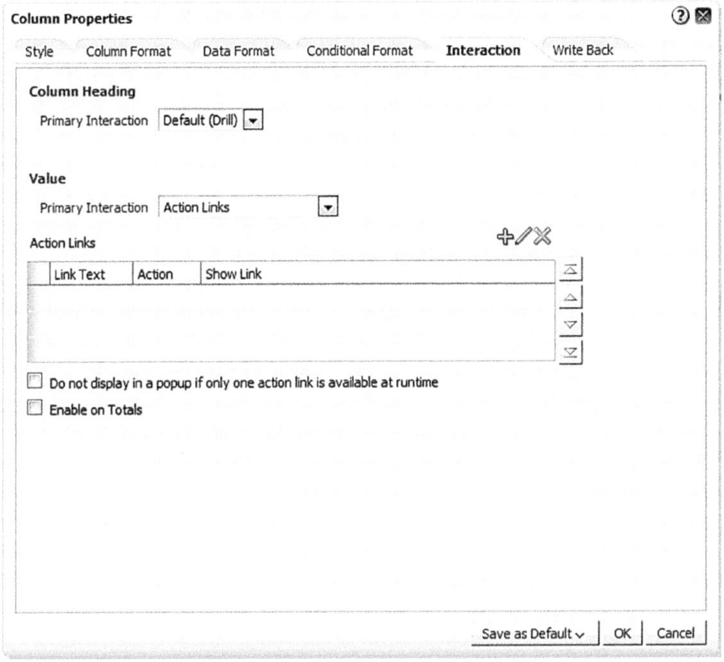

**Figure 6.43** Selecting column interactions.

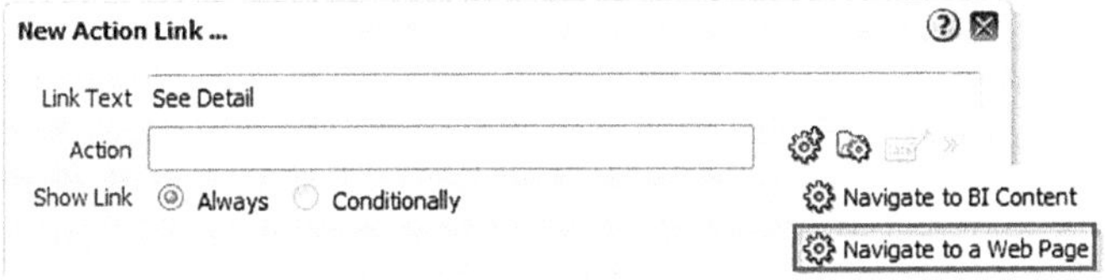

**Figure 6.44** Create a URL Action Link.

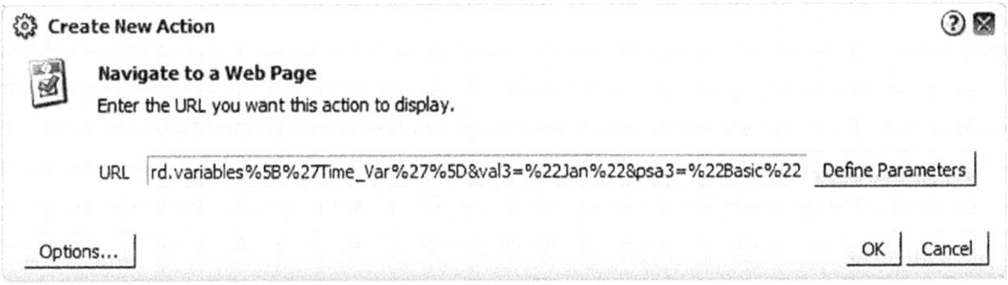

**Figure 6.45** Defining URL parameters.

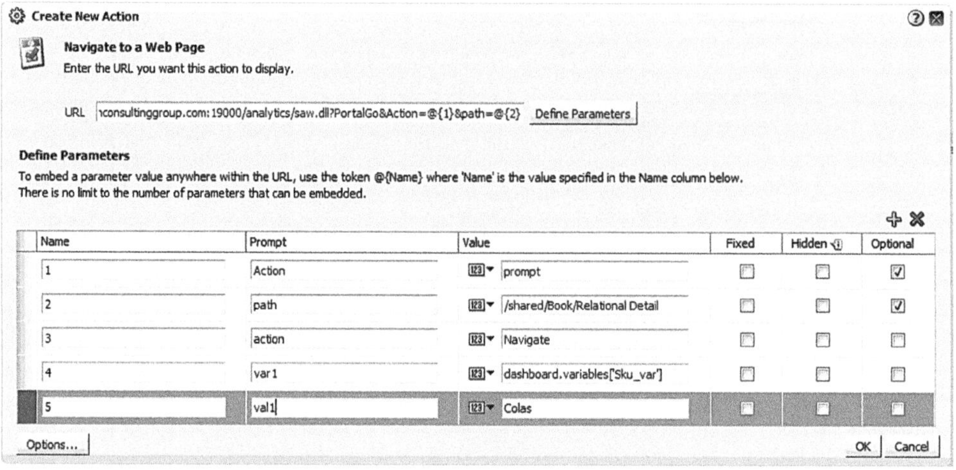

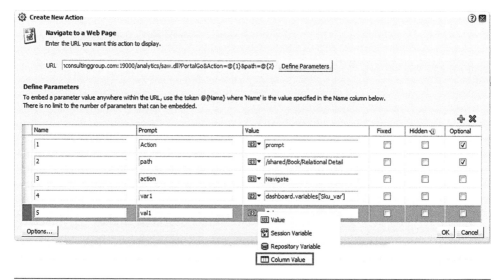

**Figure 6.46**  Create parameter variables.

**Figure 6.47**  Edit a variable reference column value.

By changing the link parameter to a column value, it picks up the value dynamically from the source report and filters the relational target.

Although this technique is neat, it is not without drawbacks:

- The source report, as it stands, passes only level 0 values. What if you want to take an upper-level product and pass all SKUs underneath?
- What if you want to pass multiple base- or upper-level members or the entire intersection? The GO URL in its current form allows for only six dimensions to be passed.

Other limitations also exist, but they can be overcome.

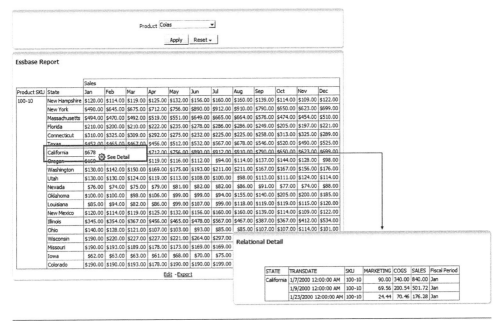

**Figure 6.48**   Test the Action Link.

### 6.3.4 Leveraging Driving Documents and Variables to Link Aggregate and Detail Analysis

To really make the analysis dynamic, the preceding example needs to be expanded in three ways:

1. Convert the source and target reports to dashboards.
2. Create a series of presentation variables.
3. Build driving documents to filter the target analysis.

By putting these three techniques in place, the simple use of source and target reports can evolve into a guided analytic application.

Before moving into the specifics on these techniques, a brief discussion on federation is called for. One of the most powerful capabilities OBIEE provides is federation. OBIEE can, in a single subject area, query across both Essbase and detailed source systems. When you have a model that leverages both symmetrical Essbase hierarchies and conformed dimensionality between Essbase and the underlying system, you can create a model in OBIEE that allows a user to simply drill down on a dimension and move from Essbase to relational. This paradigm of analysis is both elegant and extremely powerful. Having said that, two practical limitations affect the use of federation:

1. Often, Essbase models are asymmetrical, and the client requirements do not allow that to be changed. If the model is asymmetrical, then vertical federation with Essbase does not work.
2. Vertical federation also assumes that you have similar dimensionality requirements in the Essbase and detailed systems. For example, if the Essbase model

has 10 dimensions, that detailed analysis is valid based on those 10 dimensions. In the case, however, where the requirement is to bring additional dimensionality into play (and provide ad hoc capabilities on those dimensions) when moving from the Essbase source to the detail, simple vertical federation is not possible.

This chapter does not specifically discuss federation because this topic and the steps for integrating OBIEE and Essbase in this fashion are well documented (both by Oracle and the partner community).

*6.3.4.1 Why Dashboards Matter*   Two reasons support moving basic reports (in this case) to dashboards. The first is performance. When leveraging page drop-downs on reports, OBIEE acts very differently from how it does with dashboard prompts. When the prompt (page filter) is on the report, OBIEE pulls back all required data for all pages and shows the user only the required data based on the filter. When using a dashboard prompt, the data set is filtered before sending the request to Essbase. As such, OBIEE only brings back that page. The latter scenario results, of course, in better performance.

Second, and more important, is functionality. By using dashboard prompts on our source reports, we can effectively control OBIEE Presentation variables. This concept is key to making the source-to-target reporting scenario more functional.

Continuing with our previous example, we first need to determine which dimensions members we pass from Essbase to the relational target. For the sake of this example, assume we are passing SKU, Market, and Time period. Step 1 is to create a dashboard prompt and define all three as Presentation variables (see Figure 6.49). The single dashboard prompt is used on both the source and target dashboards. Even though the prompt is created off of the Essbase subject area, it can be used to filter both the Essbase and relational reports. If the strings/codes match from Essbase to relational, then filtering is automatic. If they do not match, we can translate them using the driving documents (discussed later in this chapter).

It is important to note that variable names in OBIEE are case sensitive. Note that in this example, we are using initial capitalization. Once all of the variables are defined in a single dashboard prompt object, the source and target reports are placed (by the user) to appear on dashboards as opposed to being stand-alone reports. Next, the Essbase source report needs to be modified to respond to the dashboard prompts containing the Presentation variables. In Figure 6.50, we are only filtering the Essbase report by SKU. This does not limit us from filtering the target report effectively.

Once the initial filtering is in place, the Action Link can be updated to feed a dashboard instead of feeding a stand-alone report. Unlike getting the stand-alone analysis URL, for a dashboard, you select the properties drop-down in the upper-right of the dashboard and select "Create Prompted Link." After selecting this option, the browser address bar displays the prompted URL link. To use this in the Action Link process, it simply needs to be copied. See Figure 6.51.

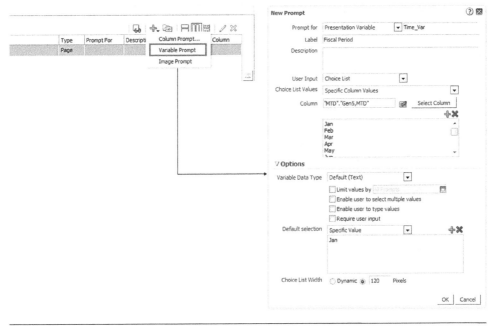

**Figure 6.49** Creating a dashboard prompt.

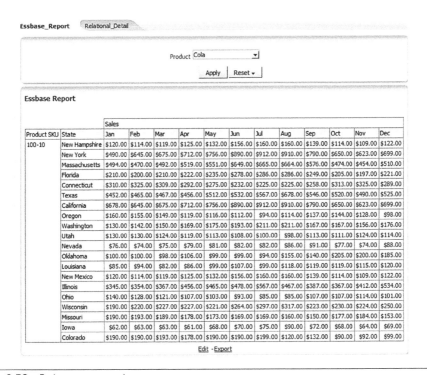

**Figure 6.50** Essbase source report.

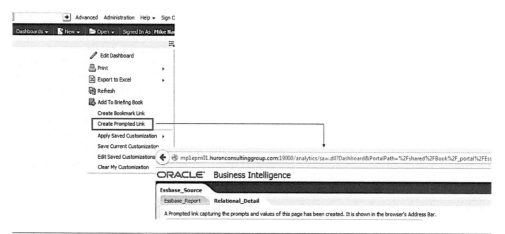

**Figure 6.51** Creating a prompted link.

Instead of editing existing Action Links, I prefer to delete existing ones and rebuild. Using the same process discussed earlier in this chapter, the Action Link from the Essbase source report needs to be rebuilt. The difference this time is that the URL points to a target dashboard, not a specific report. The primary difference in this URL, as compared with the previous, is that the parameters now reflect the dashboard prompts (Figure 6.52).

Similar to the previous process, the required, specific prompt values need to be changed to match the columns on the Essbase reports. For example, the dashboard prompt for Market value is changed to the "Market.State" column (see Figure 6.53).

One additional recommended step in this process is to quote any string sent from Essbase to the relational detail. If there are spaces or special characters in the Essbase member name being passed in the Action Link process, the filter fails on the target

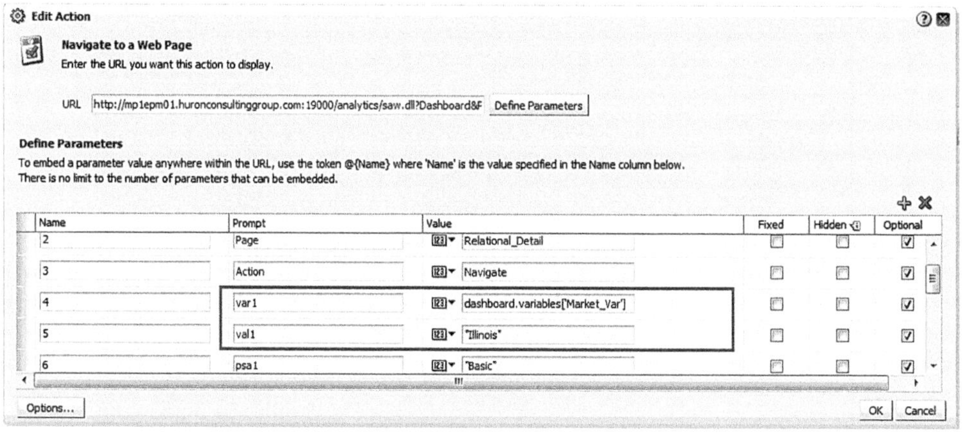

**Figure 6.52** Rebuilding an Action Link.

**Figure 6.53**  Set prompt value to match column value.

side. To add a quote to each string, you simply create an additional parameter in the "Create New Action" dialog and define it as a quote. Then you place this new variable on either side of those variables being passed to the relational detail report. For instance, in the current example, variable 13 is defined as single double-quote (") and then placed on either side of the variables representing Market, Time, and SKU (see Figure 6.54).

Testing the updated Action Link shows that the cell context from the data grid passes from the Essbase analysis to the dashboard prompt in the relational analysis (see Figure 6.55).

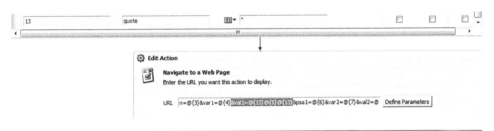

**Figure 6.54**  Adding parameter to quote a string.

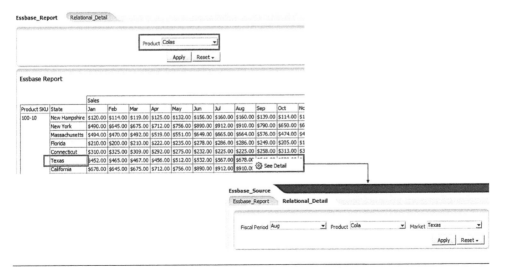

**Figure 6.55**  Parameters passing from the Essbase source to detail target report.

*6.3.4.2 Driving Documents and General Functions*   We are getting closer to completing the loop between Essbase and the underlying detail; however, a couple of underlying issues still exist:

1. How do we handle a situation when we want to pass the descendants (or a portion of the Essbase tree) to the supporting detail report?
2. How do we handle a situation in which the names on the Essbase dashboard do not match the relational detail dashboard?

Up to this point, our example has not updated the supporting detail report to respond to the dashboard prompts. In the case of Market, it would work just fine, but the Essbase product descriptions are not in the detail report. Furthermore, the Essbase fiscal periods do not match the date-time stamp shown in the supporting detail report. To resolve both of these issues, the example needs to be expanded, leveraging OBIEE driving documents and basic OBIEE functions.

Inspecting the Essbase model and passing levels or subportions of the hierarchy can easily be accomplished with a driving document. This document can then complete the loop and feed the target detail report. A driving document, simply put, is a set of members that is then used to filter another analysis, such as a set of product codes. Filtering based on the results of another analysis is one of the standard options for filtering in OBIEE.

In our example, we are following a process to ultimately filter the target analysis (it is a little like the game Mousetrap):

1. The Action Link takes the detail from the Essbase cell on the source report and feeds the dashboard prompt on the target dashboard.
2. The target dashboard prompt updates a presentation variable.
3. The updated presentation variable feeds a driving document.
4. The driving document filters the target analysis.

Aside from executing the Action Link, all of this is hidden from the end user. Our example already includes the first two steps in this process. To complete the final steps, we need to look back to the Evaluate function.

To create a driving document:

1. Create a new analysis off of the Essbase subject area.
2. On the new analysis, drag the "Product–Default" column onto the Selected Columns area.
3. Alter the column formula for "Product–Default" as follows:
   ```
   EVALUATE( 'Descendants([@{Sku_Var}],Levels([Product], 0))
   /*%1*/', "Product"."Product SKU").
   ```
   This returns the level 0 members from the Product dimension based on the name of the product in the Sku_Var variable. See Figure 6.56. The variable reference must match the name of the variable (including the case) that was

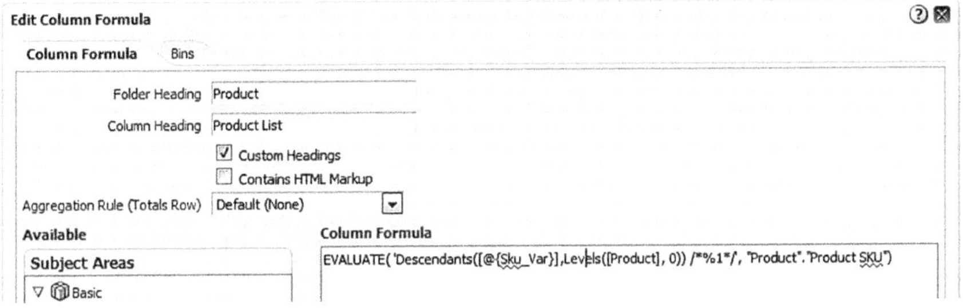


**Figure 6.56** Setting up the driving document formula.

set up on the dashboard prompt. At this point, whatever value ends in the dashboard prompt on the supporting detail report is passed into the function. If that is a level 0 member, then it returns just that member. If it is an upper-level member, then the level 0 descendants of that member are returned. Note that the @{} syntax is required for using variables in OBIEE.

Save the document and add it to a new section on the target dashboard. This section is only used for testing purposes and can be removed (or hidden) when complete. To test, change the Product drop-down on the dashboard prompt and click Apply. Note that Figure 6.57 shows the list of all Product

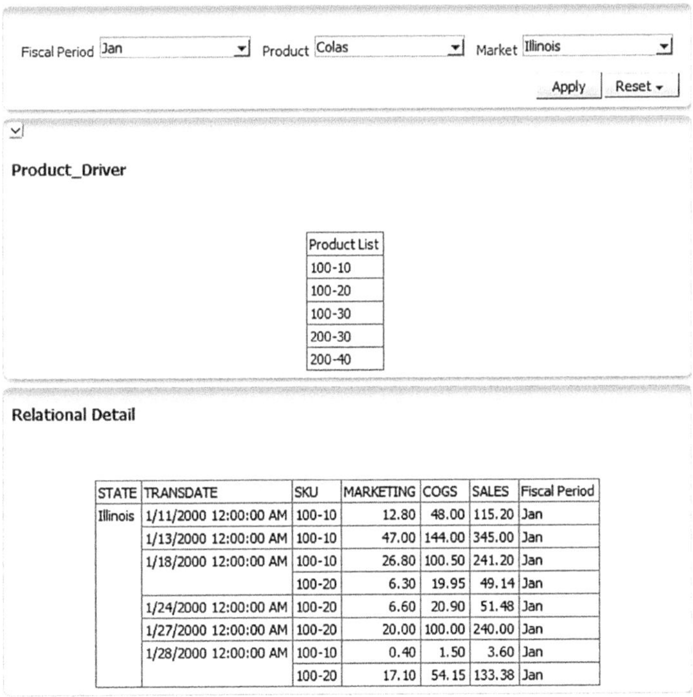


| Product List |
|---|
| 100-10 |
| 100-20 |
| 100-30 |
| 200-30 |
| 200-40 |

| STATE | TRANSDATE | SKU | MARKETING | COGS | SALES | Fiscal Period |
|---|---|---|---|---|---|---|
| Illinois | 1/11/2000 12:00:00 AM | 100-10 | 12.80 | 48.00 | 115.20 | Jan |
| | 1/13/2000 12:00:00 AM | 100-10 | 47.00 | 144.00 | 345.00 | Jan |
| | 1/18/2000 12:00:00 AM | 100-10 | 26.80 | 100.50 | 241.20 | Jan |
| | | 100-20 | 6.30 | 19.95 | 49.14 | Jan |
| | 1/24/2000 12:00:00 AM | 100-20 | 6.60 | 20.90 | 51.48 | Jan |
| | 1/27/2000 12:00:00 AM | 100-20 | 20.00 | 100.00 | 240.00 | Jan |
| | 1/28/2000 12:00:00 AM | 100-10 | 0.40 | 1.50 | 3.60 | Jan |
| | | 100-20 | 17.10 | 54.15 | 133.38 | Jan |

**Figure 6.57** Testing the driving document.

SKUs residing under the Colas member (both diet and regular). The driving document automatically updates based on the dashboard prompt.

4. Edit the Relational Detail report and add a filter on the SKU column to make it "based on the results of another analysis." Browse to and select the Product driving document (see Figure 6.58).

5. Save the analysis, return to the dashboard, and test the dashboard prompt again to verify that changing the prompt ultimately drives the filtering in the target analysis (see Figure 6.59).

The Product driving document does not need to remain on the final dashboard. Because the Relational detail report is filtered by the document, OBIEE executes the driver automatically when executing the query for running that analysis. The Product driving document requires the Sku_Var presentation variable; therefore, it will always evaluate the current value on the dashboard prompt. The exception to this is editing the target report. When in edit mode, OBIEE does not evaluate the dashboard prompt, so the presentation variable is null. As such, when editing the target report and viewing the Results tab, it returns an error (see Figure 6.60).

This example also shows how the dashboard can be prompted using the Essbase aliases while returning the underlying member names.

Earlier, we discussed using shared members under the DTS parent to allow for drill capabilities. If we leverage the DESCENDANTS MDX functionality referenced in

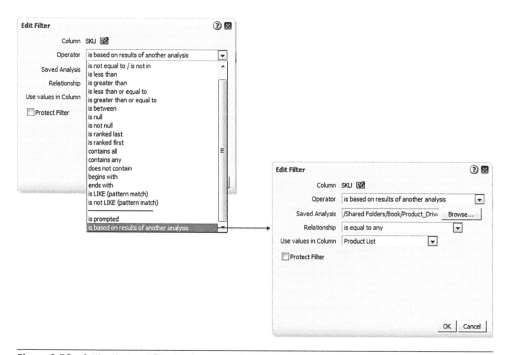

**Figure 6.58**  Setting the target filter to reference the driving document.

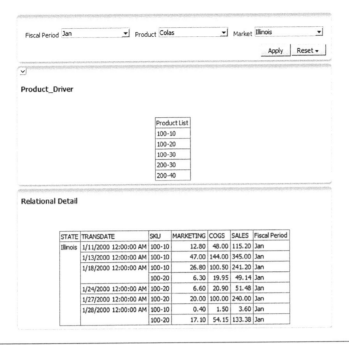

**Figure 6.59**   Final driving document test.

**Figure 6.60**   Error in edit mode.

this chapter, we can return the shared members under parent. This is particularly useful when trying to pass alternate member parents into a driving document. For example, if you pass YTD(Mar) into the driving document, the way the code is written, it returns Jan through Mar into the driving document.

Now that we have one driving document passing the level 0 descendants of the selected Essbase member (inclusive of the member itself), we need to create a final filter using standard OBIEE functions. For readers familiar with OBIEE, this is standard functionality; those of us who have spent years working with Essbase need to realize that OBIEE has a series of calculation functions similar to those found in Essbase. In respect to string and date functions, OBIEE has similar capabilities to standard SQL. In our example, the Essbase time members are three-character months. The relational equivalent members are date-time stamps. Filtering the latter using the former is simply a matter of leveraging the presentation variable and some of these native OBIEE functions.

To add filtering using OBIEE functions:

1. Edit the Relational Detail report. On the Criteria tab, add a filter for the TRANSDATE column.
2. On the New Filter dialog, select the option to "Convert filter to SQL" and click OK (Figure 6.61).
3. In the Advanced SQL Filter dialog, enter a statement similar to the following: `LEFT(MONTHNAME("A_N_SALESFACT"."TRANSDATE"),3)='@{Time_Var}'`. This formula extracts the month name from the date-time column, substrings it to the left three characters, and compares it with the value of the Time_Var presentation variable. The presentation variable is set by our dashboard prompt. The single quotes (') are required around the Time_Var variable as it is returning a string from Essbase.
4. Save the analysis and test the prompt filter against it (Figure 6.62).

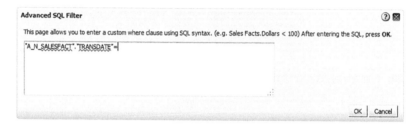

**Figure 6.61** Setting up the filter.

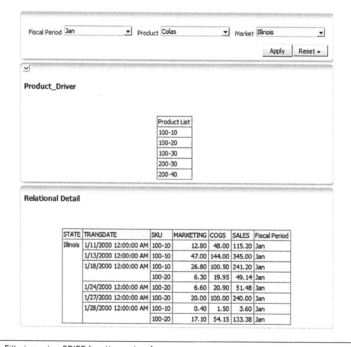

**Figure 6.62** Filtering using OBIEE functions, step 4.

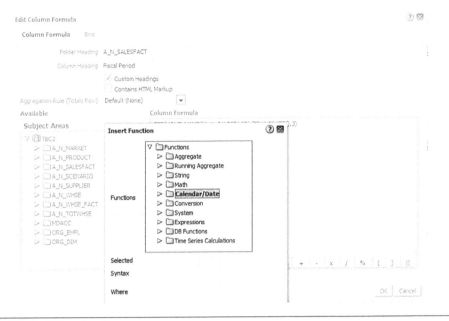

**Figure 6.63**  Adding a function.

If you do not know the syntax or specific function required for an SQL-based filter, the easiest thing to do is to drag the required column onto the report for a second time and edit the column formula (see Figure 6.63). The formula editor is similar to the Essbase member formula editor and provides function templates and links to documentation.

*6.3.4.3 Summarizing the Analytic Application*  The latter portion of this chapter has gone through a series of techniques within OBIEE to expand analytic capabilities. With all of that, keeping sight of the goal is important. We are able to create an analytic application that starts with aggregate data in Essbase and finishes with direct analysis of the supporting detail.

- Action Links allow us to pass full dimensional context from a report (originating from Essbase) to the underlying detail. This is similar to an Essbase drill-through report. The important difference is that the detail data are not simply a dead data dump in Excel. OBIEE allows extended analysis.
- The use of the Evaluate function lets us scale the Essbase model and return desired metadata in either an RPD column or on a specific analysis.
- A driving document provides a way to capture lists of members (similar to an array) and filter other queries.
- OBIEE functions perform all required conversions between Essbase and the underlying source system.

## 6.4 There Are Universes with Two Suns

Realistically speaking, we are only scratching the surface in this chapter. The goal of this chapter was to provide some depth beyond the fundamentals of importing Essbase into the RPD. It is not meant to be the definitive list of capabilities. Oracle has published a modeling guide for Essbase; hundreds of bloggers have posts discussing these and other issues and creative solutions for integrating the technologies. The future of this integration will be borne out by applying each technology in its ideal position for our end users. There is no doubt that the combination of the two technologies, Essbase and OBIEE, solves complex business problems.

The theories that Copernicus put forward eventually led to the discovery of binary solar systems (solar systems having two suns) more than 200 years after his death. Nature has already figured out how to integrate two stars. The solution is simple: Put the paperclip down and look at the universe around you.

## Acknowledgments

For my boys, you make me want to keep learning; for DJ for putting up with it all; for my occasional reader for always inspiring me with your faith; for Dave Collins for teaching me the ropes so many years ago.

# 7

# MANAGING SPREADSHEETS (AND ESSBASE) THROUGH DODECA

## CAMERON LACKPOUR

Contents

## 7.1 Why Is a Non-Oracle Product in an Oracle Essbase Book?

If you are not familiar with the software tool Dodeca, it is in fact not authored, managed, or distributed by Oracle but instead is the product of the software company Applied OLAP. Although some might argue that a third-party product has no place in a book about Oracle Essbase, Dodeca's heavy Essbase orientation, unique development environment, and faithfulness to Essbase's origins as a reporting tool for power users qualify it, in my mind at least, for inclusion in this book.

Dodeca inspires fanatical geek enthusiasm and advocacy just as Essbase does. Where it differs from other current end-user products is in the way developers evangelize Dodeca at a grassroots level. For those Essbase practitioners who were present at Essbase's year zero, the fervor and enthusiasm Dodeca inspires feel the same. Great products inspire passion.

Essbase and Dodeca are closely related in their philosophy of user analysis and control of data. One is like the other; a book about Essbase that does not include Dodeca is a book that is diminished.

Dodeca is not as widely known as Essbase; this chapter will attempt to rectify that and make you as much a fan of the tool as I am. To that end, this chapter defines and describes Dodeca, provides a high-level overview of Dodeca's technical architecture, and reviews administering Dodeca. It takes a tour through Dodeca's client, documents development terminology, and provides step-by-step solutions to common Essbase use cases. With all of this, I hope to convince you that you, too, should be using Dodeca to interact with Essbase.

I love Dodeca for its power, ease of development, and just general coolness. I think Dodeca is such a well thought-out tool that to not use it is to not exploit all of Essbase's power. I hope that after reading this chapter, you will think the same.

## 7.2 Just What Exactly Is Dodeca?

Although describing a product by what it is not can be dangerous, an examination of Oracle's Essbase client tools provides a basis for comparison. Oracle currently has three major Essbase reporting products: Oracle Hyperion Financial Reports (Financial Reports), Oracle Smart View for Office (Smart View), and Oracle Business Intelligence Enterprise Edition (OBIEE). Given that they all work with Essbase, there is surprisingly little overlap in functionality. This uniqueness stems from the products' intended use, audience, and data sources other than Essbase. Although all of these tools access Essbase data, how they address Essbase differs and those differences define them.

### 7.2.1 Financial Reports

Financial Reports is Oracle's tool for highly formatted reports whose data sources are Hyperion Financial Management (HFM), Planning, and Essbase. Browser access,

HTML or PDF display, single report, briefing books, batch e-mail distributions—these properties are the hallmarks of a centrally managed, standard reporting tool.

Financial Reports provides a structured approach to data. Its limited ad hoc nature and data exploration features mean that while it can consume Essbase data, it is not optimized for Essbase but instead is a general multidimensional reporting tool.

Financial Reports is for users who receive Essbase data, not those who need to analyze Essbase data.

### 7.2.2 Smart View

Smart View is a hybrid tool. Like Financial Reports and OBIEE, it can access many data sources, one of which is Essbase. Where Smart View differs from those tools' structured reporting focus is its customizable ad hoc nature.

Smart View is primarily a tool for power users who need the freedom that a Microsoft Excel add-in provides. That user class happily embraces the complexity of Smart View and Excel because the whole of Essbase and Excel is greater than the sum of its parts.

However, the extensively customizable nature of the tool is a double-edged sword. Functionality and features that work very well in ad hoc analysis become difficult to control when those workbooks are distributed or used for standard reporting. This is not a fault of Smart View but more of a problem with the innately open nature of Excel.

Excel is a general-purpose data tool that presents numbers and text in a spreadsheet interface. Those data are manipulated through Excel data controls and its powerful formula language. Users can do virtually anything with Excel—they can use it as a financial data spreadsheet, a database, a statistical calculator, a desktop business intelligence program, a graphing tool—anything.

Essbase got its start with the classic Essbase add-in for Excel, and power users continue to embrace the Excel/Essbase paradigm because it so powerful. Smart View hews to the Essbase tradition of empowering ad hoc user analysis. This flexibility makes Excel an incredibly popular package but also makes it very difficult to deliver ordered and defined Essbase content because that structure is antithetical to the nature of Excel.

### 7.2.3 OBIEE

OBIEE is by far the most comprehensive of the three Oracle Essbase client products. It can access far more than just Essbase and, through data federation, can present those data through dashboards, standard reporting, ad hoc queries, and mobile. It is a framework for understanding, defining, and managing data.

This wide breadth and depth of functionality make OBIEE a compelling, enterprise-level business intelligence (BI) solution. At the same time, these powerful features preclude quick or simple implementations. OBIEE is a tool for the large enterprise that needs to provide comprehensive data in a structured manner.

For the enterprise looking for a comprehensive BI solution, OBIEE has few peers. As an Essbase tool, OBIEE uses Essbase, but it is not of Essbase.

### 7.2.4 Dodeca

Where, then, does that leave Dodeca? From an Essbase perspective, Dodeca occupies a unique niche of exposing the combined power of Essbase and spreadsheets in a managed and controlled way; Dodeca is a spreadsheet management tool. This chapter illustrates that Dodeca does not compete with Oracle's Essbase clients but complements them through its unique attributes, features, and functionality.

The heart of Dodeca is Essbase data in spreadsheets, just as with Smart View. Spreadsheets are the businessperson's sketchbook and power users love the functionality and ease of development that spreadsheets provide.

#### 7.2.4.1 Power without Control
At the same time, those in information technology (IT) departments, who often become responsible for distributing and maintaining spreadsheet systems, hate spreadsheets. Why?

- Establishing control over an intrinsically open tool is very hard to do.
- Ensuring that the spreadsheets are correct is difficult. Quality control within a spreadsheet is difficult because they are, by design, open to manipulation.
- There is no native process to manage spreadsheets. Again, spreadsheets are an end-user open tool.
- Backup and version control of a spreadsheet that is distributed by e-mail or shared drive locations is impossible once recipients begin local modifications.
- Standardization of spreadsheets is difficult, if not impossible, without a managed solution.

In short, the open nature of spreadsheets is both the blessing and the curse of spreadsheets and Essbase.

#### 7.2.4.2 Managed Spreadsheets
This is where Dodeca really shines, as it leverages all of the power, flexibility, and interaction with Essbase that spreadsheets provide, while at the same time imposing control over those spreadsheets. Dodeca uses spreadsheets to distribute and interact with Essbase in a centrally managed way. This server-based approach means that every Dodeca report is displayed consistently, both in spreadsheet layout and content. This managed nature also means that making a mistake is almost impossible for users through inadvertent or purposeful changes to a standard spreadsheet.

Dodeca spreadsheets are stored and distributed from a central server. The spreadsheets are developed either in Excel or Dodeca and are stored in a relational metadata repository. This relational nature means that backups and migrations across server environments are managed processes. Centrally storing templates also means that developers can check spreadsheets in and out of the repository to collaborate in building spreadsheets. This is different from a shared drive in that no local saves or e-mails of files are possible, thus eliminating version mismatches. No local saves means that the correct version of the spreadsheet template is distributed to both developers and users.

Excel is a wide-open tool with many tabs, ribbons, and controls. This interface makes sense within the context of general spreadsheets but can become distracting and irrelevant when used for structured Essbase interaction. Developers of Smart View-based reporting systems spend a lot of time and effort in locking down Excel's interface. By default, Dodeca exposes only the required interface to support Essbase functionality. Developers can expand the user interface as required.

Errors are easy to introduce in spreadsheets because business users are not developers and do not bring the programmer's mindset of auditability and code review. As an example, during the writing of this book, a spreadsheet error that overstated a software company's equity value resulted in a $100 million loss for shareholders.* The base numbers were correct, but a formula logic error resulted in double counting of data. Although common, formula logic errors are not the only spreadsheet error. Other common mistakes include incorrect source data values and uncontrolled data entry errors such as overtyping a formula cell with a data value. Good programming practice is to perform formal code analysis, manage updates through change control procedures, and on change, do unit and regression testing. Spreadsheets rarely, if ever, receive this level of scrutiny.

Although creating erroneous spreadsheets in Dodeca is possible, the risk of this is significantly lowered because spreadsheet templates are created and modified only by qualified users, base data from Essbase are retrieved and sent to and from reports in a controlled manner, centrally managed spreadsheets are readily audited and tested, and sheet protection is a standard property of all Dodeca spreadsheets. IT department objections around the open nature of spreadsheets—including control, quality, version control, backup, and standardization—are addressed by Dodeca's managed spreadsheets.

### 7.2.4.3 Dodeca Advantages

*7.2.4.3.1 Administrative Productivity* The advantages of managed spreadsheets in Dodeca are clear, but what about administrative productivity? How does Dodeca compare with other tools?

Despite strenuous efforts by IT departments, IT environments are complex and fragile, making Enterprise Performance Management (EPM) system management

---

* Link to this document: http://ww2.cfo.com/spreadsheets/2014/10/spreadsheet-error-costs-tibco-share holders-100m/.

difficult. In the case of Microsoft Office, the general nature of Excel counts against it as a tool for automated Essbase reporting. Excel crashes can cause changes that are difficult to respond to because of the divide between Essbase add-ins and Excel architecture, and corporations do not necessarily enforce common versions of Office across the enterprise.

Regarding Office versions, I have personally witnessed (and suffered) clients that had Excel 2007, 2010, and 2013 simultaneously approved as corporate standards right alongside multiple versions of Internet Explorer. Which ones work with the current release of Smart View? Excel differs across versions; how does an add-in interact with those different versions? 32 or 64 bit? Cloud or on premises? Web browsers are no better—what release of Workspace works with IE8? IE11? When will the latest release of Internet Explorer be supported? EPM administrators are small fish in a large IT pond and are generally not able to control the corporate IT environment. They expend much work and effort trying to lock down what is fundamentally not a uniform environment.

The Dodeca client sits outside the Microsoft software suite (although it is uses Microsoft's .NET architecture under the covers). Version issues simply do not exist because the correct version of the client is automatically updated when the Dodeca server is upgraded.

*7.2.4.3.2 Built-In Essbase Functionality* Although Financial Reports (FR) and OBIEE present Essbase data, they do so within the context of web-based reporting and analysis. As noted before, they do not offer the power, accessibility, and business domain understanding of spreadsheets.

Excel add-ins such as Smart View have those desirable spreadsheet characteristics, but that comes at the development cost of coding Essbase functionality such as automated connections, retrieves, sends, etc., alongside the administrative cost of trying to manage those Essbase-enabled spreadsheets.

Dodeca understands and is optimized for Essbase. Connections, dimension controls, managed spreadsheets, retrieves, sends, and calculations are all part of the developer's framework and require no coding. Dodeca consumes Excel spreadsheets. Spreadsheet functionality such as formatting, graphing, and formulas (Dodeca supports all Excel formula functions) is retained. When additional functionality is required, Workbook Scripts, a built-in automation feature, provides a way to intelligently and quickly extend spreadsheets.

*7.2.4.3.3 Easy and Quick Implementations* A typical Dodeca installation is as a component of an already existing EPM environment. The server is installed as an application deployed with the existing web application server.

System implementations are similarly lightweight. Proof-of-concept engagements vary from 1 to 2 weeks, and full implementations are typically performed by the customer. The high level of developer productivity, coupled with a small training curve, means that customer developers perform system development and management; Dodeca consultants are rarely required beyond the first implementation.

*7.2.4.4 Why Dodeca?* Although other Essbase client tools are very powerful, their focus in data, usage, and distribution differ from Dodeca.

As previously noted, Dodeca occupies a unique position within the world of Essbase tools in three important ways:

- It quickly and powerfully exposes Essbase data through spreadsheets and its application framework.
- It controls those spreadsheets.
- It is easily administered within a corporate IT environment.

Dodeca's functional power and flexibility, coupled with its ease of development and management, result in a product that users, developers, and administrators love. Where other tools have developers and users, Dodeca has evangelists. There really is nothing else like it.

### 7.3 Dodeca Architecture

Dodeca's architecture is multitiered, as shown in Figure 7.1. At the very bottom level sits data and metadata in Essbase and Structured Query Language (SQL) data sources. Where and how those Essbase and relational data are sourced are irrelevant to the Dodeca client because the Dodeca and Dodeca Essbase application servers abstract that connectivity. Dodeca users, administrators, and developers need only concern themselves with the Dodeca client.

#### 7.3.1 Client

The Dodeca client is a Windows-only .NET application written in C#. It uses Microsoft's ClickOnce deployment method to allow installation irrespective of a client machine's Windows administrator access.

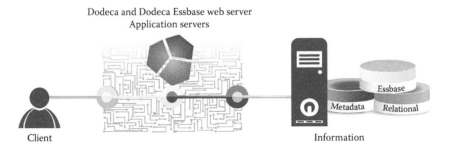

**Figure 7.1** Dodeca architecture.

ClickOnce's web-based technology distributes Dodeca client binaries to user machines. ClickOnce technology solves the IT asset management problems of application version updates, installation impact on the target client machine, and the requirement of Windows administrator access to perform installs. Dodeca is installed via a web browser as part of ClickOnce. Of the typical Big 3 browsers (Internet Explorer, Firefox, and Chrome), Microsoft's own Internet Explorer is the browser of choice because of its native integration with ClickOnce. Firefox users can download and install the Microsoft .NET Framework Assistant add-on to enable ClickOnce.

The ClickOnce software platform is highly secure in that client software installs and runs within its own security sandbox and cannot execute privileged operating system actions unless the code is trusted. Dodeca is created as a trusted application by its vendor, Applied OLAP.

Dodeca can also be deployed by copying a directory of files to the client machine. This is called XCopy deployment. Dodeca also works on Mac OS inside the open source Wineskin wrapper.

### 7.3.2 Server Architecture

Both the Dodeca and Dodeca Essbase servers are Java-based web services running within the context of a Java application server such as WebSphere, Tomcat, or WebLogic. The Dodeca Essbase server exclusively handles Essbase connectivity and processes, while the Dodeca server is used for relational access to Dodeca metadata and access to external relational stores (see Figure 7.2).

The web application architecture means that the Dodeca servers are operating system or Java application server agnostic.

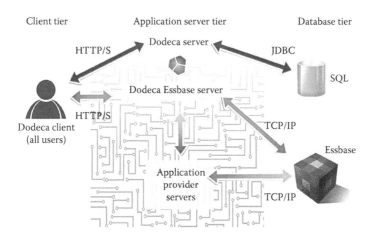

**Figure 7.2** Dodeca server architecture.

The Dodeca web server communicates with relational sources via Java Database Connectivity (JDBC). Oracle, SQL Server, IBM DB2, and MySQL are the most common databases, but any JDBC-compliant database can be used.

### 7.3.3 Tenant and Application Codes

Dodeca uses two different kinds of codes, tenant and application, to separate metadata constructs.

Dodeca metadata is demarcated within the Dodeca metadata schema by unique tenant codes. Multiple applications can exist within a tenant code to allow the sharing of Views, SQL and Essbase connections, Toolbars, Selectors, and other Dodeca objects. Tenant codes are absolute dividers, and objects in one tenant code cannot be shared with another. Within a given application tenant, application codes are used to define different classes of users such as administrators and input users.

### 7.3.4 Backup and Migration

The relational metadata layer is archived via normal database backup processes. However, this relational repository when used for migration will move the entire relational store, including all applications. It will also migrate all server metadata, such as server names, ports, etc., resulting in scenarios like development server names and ports within a production environment.

A better approach is to use the Dodeca client's metadata export feature, which writes discrete application components to compressed XML files. These files can also be exported directly to a local drive and then migrated. The standard metadata import/export is performed interactively in the Dodeca client. To enable automated backup and migration, the Dodeca Backup Utility offers the same functionality in the form of a command line tool.

### 7.3.5 Dodeca Smart Client

The Dodeca client is driven by application metadata stored in the relational store. When a user makes a request, the Dodeca application server receives the request, instantiates a query against the relational metadata store, and fetches Essbase data via the Dodeca Essbase server and, if required, additional relational data before serving up the result in an XML stream to the Dodeca client, which displays the result.

### 7.3.6 User Provisioning

User provisioning similar to Oracle's EPM products is possible in Dodeca through Dodeca authentication services based on Essbase, Windows, or Active Directory

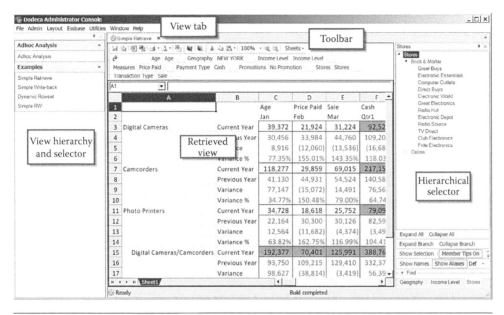

**Figure 7.3** Sample Dodeca administrator interface.

credentials. A lightweight way of separating administrators from users is to use application-level password protection.

## 7.4 Dodeca Administration

Documenting all of the features of Dodeca's administrative functions, even at a high level, is beyond the scope of this chapter. To learn more about Dodeca administration, see the *Dodeca Administrator's Guide.**

### 7.4.1 A Tour through the Dodeca Client

The Dodeca client exposes administrator functionality, logically enough, only to the administrator; the end user interface shows only those elements relevant to data interaction (see Figure 7.3).

The Dodeca client presents applications to the user. Figure 7.3 represents the Essbase application covered later in this chapter. Note the View Selector on the left, the View tab containing the open View, the Toolbar, and the Essbase Dimension Selector on the right.

---

* Link to this document (requires login): http://appliedolap.com/resources/downloads/dodeca-technical -docs/dodeca-admin-guide.

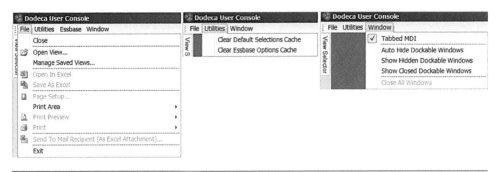

**Figure 7.4**   Dodeca user menus.

*7.4.1.1 Menus*   A note about the sections below that deal with menus and toolbars: Menus differ by user type in an application; toolbars can vary by View.

This ability to customize the interface means that the following descriptions of menu and toolbar objects are typical of most applications but are not mandatory.

*7.4.1.2 Dodeca User Menus*   Although menus in Dodeca are user-type aware, the menus shown in Figure 7.4 are typically displayed for both users and administrators. Menus are completely customizable for all user classes.

*7.4.1.2.1 File, Utilities, and Windows*   The File menu controls opening and closing Views, as well as exporting them to Excel and the file system, printing, and e-mailing Views.

Dodeca caches the latest dimension selections and Essbase options as default values for later use. Although these cached settings are for user convenience and faster response time, in some instances, a user may want to reset those values to the defaults. The Utilities menu can be used to clear either or both of the available caches.

Dodeca can have many Views open at the same time and pin, auto hide, or close dockable windows. Each of these objects can be manipulated separately (such as closing a specific View) or managed centrally via the Window menu.

*7.4.1.3 Dodeca Administrator Menus*   In addition to the File and Window menus that Dodeca administrators share with users, they also have two unique menus: Admin and Layout, as well as an expanded Utilities menu (see Figure 7.5).

The Admin menu contains the primary developer functions—everything from basic View, connection, and Dimension Selector objects to Workbook scripts and supporting Wizards. Administrators can also access utilities like a metadata search function and import/export functionality through the Admin menu.

The Layout menu allows the administrator to save the current client state to a file or binary artifact, which can later be loaded to restore the interface, including Views, Selector choices, and other application options.

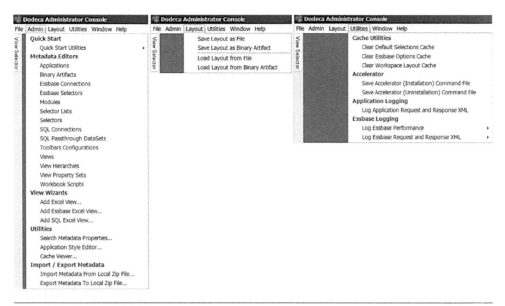

**Figure 7.5** Dodeca administrator menus.

Although the administrator Utilities menu shares its name with the user version, the administrator view of this menu also contains additional cache clearing, installation commands, and logging options.

*7.4.1.4 Toolbars* Toolbars are defined at the Application level and then applied to individual Views. Toolbar functionality typically follows View type.

Dodeca comes with 20 preassembled toolbars that can be customized. New toolbars can be created based on application requirements. Shown in Figures 7.6 through 7.9 are four sample toolbars in the Essbase, SQL, and PDF categories.

**Figure 7.6** Essbase View Standard All.

**Figure 7.7** Essbase View Standard All Excel Add-in.

**Figure 7.8** SQL View Standard.

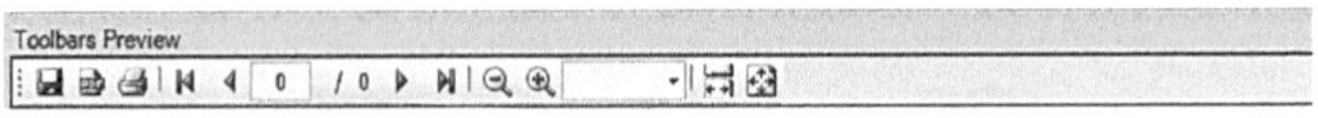

**Figure 7.9** PDF View Standard.

*7.4.1.5 View Template Designer* Although Excel can be used to create and maintain worksheet templates, the Dodeca client contains an integrated View Template Designer that is optimized for creating Dodeca-centric spreadsheets. These templates also can be exported as Excel files.

## 7.5 Developing in Dodeca

Developers who are familiar with Smart View's Visual Basic for Applications (VBA) functions and its procedural code approach may find Dodeca's nonprocedural environment unusual and even frustrating because it does not conform to typical development methods. Often, the reaction is to try to find a way to write procedural code in Dodeca. Although a rich, event-driven programming language called Workbook Scripts does exist, much of the extensibility in Dodeca is a combination of native spreadsheet behavior and Dodeca object property sheets. In contrast to Excel and its general-purpose nature, Dodeca's architecture team examined typical and not-so-typical spreadsheet/Essbase application requirements and then created Essbase-centric objects and properties. Even when writing event-driven Workbook Scripts, which do have a procedural nature, the actual amount of programming is very small.

The key to exploiting Dodeca's functionality is to understand the object model, object properties, and Workbook Scripts and spreadsheet functionality. With Dodeca, developers do not write code; they combine prebuilt elements of Dodeca functionality with spreadsheets. This approach to application development is highlighted in Section 7.6 of this chapter. Connections, dimensional controls, retrieve and send ranges, Toolbars, report selection, SQL connectivity, text commentary, and other features are all intrinsic Dodeca functionality. Developing this application framework in VBA is not a trivial task; for example, tying Essbase events to Excel is impossible except in a very limited way. Dodeca's focus on Essbase-aware objects and event models coupled with spreadsheet functionality results in a highly productive development environment.

### 7.5.1 *Terminology*

Application
   A Dodeca Application is a logical collection of Views, Binary Artifacts, Menus, Toolbars, Selectors, and Workbook Script objects along with configuration settings that define the organization and user interface for those objects.
View
   Users interact with Views, the spreadsheet presentation interface. Users navigate to Views via the View Selector, choose dimension metadata with

Selector Lists, drive functionality with Toolbars, interact with Essbase/ SQL data within a spreadsheet Binary Artifact, and consume custom View functionality through optional Workbook Scripts. Views are the core of Dodeca applications.

Binary Artifacts

Spreadsheet templates, whether created in Excel or via Dodeca's View Template Designer, are stored in an object known as a binary artifact. Spreadsheet templates can be versioned.

View Property Sets

View metadata settings, or properties, drive View functionality. Many properties can retain their default settings; customization occurs through property modifications.

View Hierarchies

Application View Selectors are populated and organized by View Hierarchies. A View Hierarchy is a categorized list of Views that may be accessed by a group of users.

Selectors

Selectors are abstracted links to dimensions that may be sourced from Essbase, relational data sources, or even delimited text lists. Through these Selectors, members are defined for use in spreadsheets, Essbase report scripts, multi-dimensional expression queries, Essbase calc scripts, and SQL queries. User selections are used to create tokens, which are substitutable dimension string replacements driven by user selections.

Selector Lists

Selectors are abstractions to dimensions; Selector Lists are those dimensions manifested into controls that users can use to control View content. The controls can be a treeview, listbox, or combobox. Depending on the Selector List properties, single or multiple member selections may be possible as can the level of dimensional hierarchy displayed for selection.

Toolbars

Toolbar Configurations are more than just toolbars and their buttons. They also drive menus, both in the menu bar and context menus shown in spreadsheets.

Workbook Scripts

Workbook Scripts provide event-driven extensibility. The word *Scripts* is something of a misnomer as there is little to no actual code written within a Workbook Script. Think of them as actions that react to Essbase and user events that are fully aware of spreadsheet content and function.

Workbook Scripts can be triggered by more than 100 events, many of which are Essbase-centric, such as *ActiveSheetChanged*, *AfterRangeRetrieve*, *BeforeRangeRetrieve*, *SelectorSelectionChanged*, and many more. Events are tied to procedures, which are collections of actions that occur in response

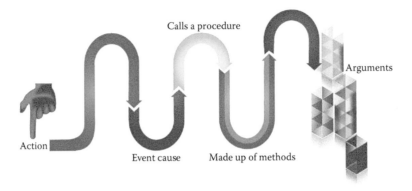

Calls a procedure

Arguments

Action

Event cause      Made up of methods

**Figure 7.10**  Workbook Script hierarchy.

to a user-triggered event. Individual actions within a procedure are considered methods; each method supports multiple arguments. Figure 7.10 illustrates the Workbook Script hierarchy. For more information, see the Dodeca Workbook Scripting Reference.*

Essbase Connections

Essbase connections define server name, application, database, web services endpoint, and other connection related properties.

SQL Passthrough DataSets

Relational data stores are accessed through SQL Passthrough DataSets that contain SQL connections, queries, and results in the form of virtual DataTables.

Modules

Extensions beyond core Dodeca functionality can be written in VB.NET or C#.

### 7.5.2 What Is a View?

Dodeca Applications are, at their core, collections of Views. Understanding how to develop in Dodeca requires understanding View concepts, properties, and the interaction of Views with other Dodeca objects.

*7.5.2.1 A Basic Definition*  A View is a Dodeca object that allows users to interact with data. Views use Dodeca objects like Essbase and SQL connections, Dimension Selectors, Selector Lists, and usually an Excel template Binary Artifact to present data to and receive input from the user. All of these objects are stored centrally and retrieved as necessary from Dodeca's relational metadata service.

---

* Link to this document (requires login): http://appliedolap.com/resources/downloads/dodeca-technical
 -docs/workbook-script-reference-guide.

The most common View type in Dodeca is based on an Essbase-aware spreadsheet, but Views can also be the following:

- Spreadsheets
  - Ad hoc Essbase
  - Essbase Report Scripts
  - SQL
  - Static Excel spreadsheets
- Other data sources
  - PDFs
  - Microsoft SQL Server Reporting Services
  - Web browsers

As noted, Essbase Excel spreadsheets and SQL Excel spreadsheets are the most common View type; they will be the focus of the development use cases.

### 7.5.3 Conclusion

With this overview of Dodeca architecture, terminology, and development concepts, the balance of this chapter will illustrate the power and functionality of Dodeca by presenting use cases that highlight how to build a variety of Views.

## 7.6 Dodeca Use Cases

A step-by-step description of how to build a View and its supporting objects is the best way to communicate the power, flexibility, and speed that Dodeca offers developers. These View use cases also highlight the advanced functionality that Dodeca brings to Essbase and SQL data sources. Much of the functionality on display is either impossible or extremely difficult to do in other tools or is severely reduced.

The use cases are as follows:

- Simple Retrieve with write-back to Essbase
- Dynamic Rowset
- SQL Products by City
- SQL drill-through from Dynamic Rowset to Products by City
- Text commentary

Each View builds on the last to show a progression of increased functionality. This requires at least a cursory understanding of each of the preceding use cases.

### 7.6.1 About the Database

ASOsamp.Sample is a variant of the sample aggregate storage option (ASO) Essbase database that comes with each copy of Essbase. The examples in the following section are based on that database with the exception of the lowest level of Geography and Stores, which had their level 0 members removed to illustrate drill-though from Essbase to relational data.

### 7.6.2 Simple Retrieve View

*7.6.2.1 Logic* The simplest of Views is a static Essbase Excel spreadsheet. "Static" is something of a misnomer as the data are based on dimension selections. Subsequent Views will be more dynamic in nature. This View and all subsequent Views present the nested Product and Years dimensions as rows and the Time dimension as columns.

*7.6.2.2 The Excel Template* Excel workbooks relationally stored as internal Binary Artifacts are the scaffolding for the most common functionality, Essbase Excel Views. To build this simple Essbase example, we must first have a core template in the form of an Excel file. The heart of a spreadsheet View is, unsurprisingly, the spreadsheet. To understand how View properties and other Dodeca objects interact with spreadsheets, it is first important to have a basic understanding of Essbase Excel spreadsheets.

**Note:** The Excel template below was created within Dodeca using the Dodeca Template Designer. Although workbooks can be edited directly in Excel and imported into Dodeca, it is usually easier to do all editing within Dodeca itself.

*7.6.2.2.1 Defining a Retrieve Range* Retrieving Essbase data in Dodeca is no different from in Excel via an Essbase add-in. Data intersections must be fully defined for each dimension. Essbase's Query by Example (QBE) technique allows dimensional metadata to be wrapped around a core retrieve range without requiring a full dimensional specification at each cell. Instead, QBE uses the concept of rows, columns, and point of view (POV) areas to define data cell dimensional intersections.

*7.6.2.2.2 The Role of Tokenization* Although Essbase Excel Views can use hardcoded dimension values, which would be static worksheets filled with live Essbase data, a far more common approach is to make some or all of the dimensions driven from Dimension Selectors.

Dodeca automatically creates Dimension Selectors when an Essbase connection is defined. This act also creates default Tokens, or replaceable strings. The default Token naming convention is [T.*dimensionname*]; an example is [T.Income Level], which corresponds to the dimension *Income Level*. Note that the square bracket delimiters allow dimension and Token values containing spaces. Those tokens are used in lieu of dimension member names and are replaced on retrieval. The use cases in this chapter illustrate the use of Tokens.

*7.6.2.2.3 Converting Areas to Ranges* Once the View developer has designed a query in accordance with Essbase QBE retrieval requirements, the developer must choose to either retrieve the entire sheet or define the retrieve range. Typically, ranges are

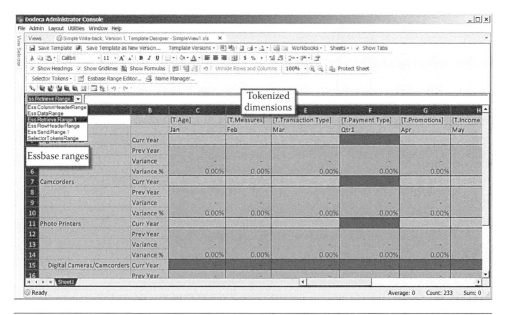

**Figure 7.11**  Template with Ess.Retrieve.Range.1 range selected.

used to interact with Essbase. The retrieve range is used by Dodeca to determine what and where to retrieve data using a naming convention of Ess.Retrieve.Range.x where x can be the numbers 1, 2, 3, etc. This numbering convention allows multiple named retrieve (and other) ranges per View.

Figure 7.11 shows an Essbase Excel template with the Ess.Retrieve.Range.1 range selected—this is where Essbase data will be retrieved.

The range drop-down menu lists both the required Essbase retrieve range, Ess. Retrieve.Range.1, and optional ranges exploited in later use cases. The Dynamic Rowset example illustrates the optional range usage.

*7.6.2.2.4 Required Template Components*  In the example shown in Table 7.1 and Figure 7.12, the following areas are present:

1. Row headers that define the Age and Year dimensions
2. A tokenized Page or POV that contains Products, Measures, Transaction Types, Promotions, Income Level, Stores, and Geography

**Table 7.1**  Simple Retrieve Ranges

| RANGE NUMBER | RANGE NAME | ADDRESS |
| --- | --- | --- |
| 1 | Ess.RowHeaderRange | Sheet1!$A$3:$B$18 |
| 2 | Ess.PageHeaderRange | Sheet1!$C$1:$J$1 |
| 3 | Ess.ColumnHeaderRange, SelectorTokensRange | Sheet1!$C$2:$S$2 |
| 4 | Ess.DataRange | Sheet1!$C$3:$S$18 |
| 5 | Ess.Retrieve.Range.1 | Sheet1!$A$1:$S$18 |

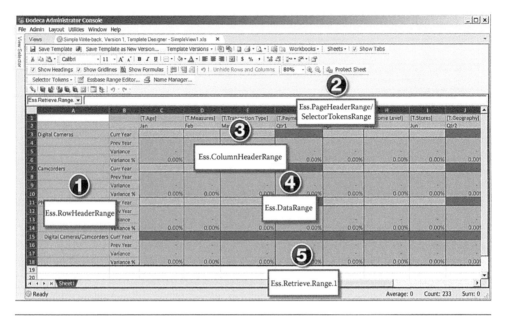

**Figure 7.12** Sample template showing ranges.

3. Column headers that specify the Time dimension selections
4. A core data range that mixes Essbase data with Excel formulas
5. The retrieve range Ess.Retrieve.Range.1

Note that ranges 1 through 4 are optionally created by Dodeca on retrieval.

*7.6.2.3 The View Wizard*   Although a developer can create a View and link all of the appropriate metadata to it through the Views metadata editor, an easier and faster approach for creating a View and linking the required pieces of metadata is to use one of the available View Wizards. The View Wizards gather and set a few of the common and all of the required properties for a View in a step-driven process and create all of the new objects required by the View. Once the View has been created by the appropriate Wizard, the full set of View properties is available for adjustment in the Views metadata editor. For the purposes of this chapter, the Views metadata editor will be used to illustrate advanced functionality not exposed by the wizard.

*7.6.2.3.1 View Information*   The View Information panel displays the View Name, ID, Type, and Description. These properties are typically set during View creation, but the Name and Description can be updated from the Views metadata editor. The View ID can be set explicitly or automatically created by the View Wizard. The View Description is optional.

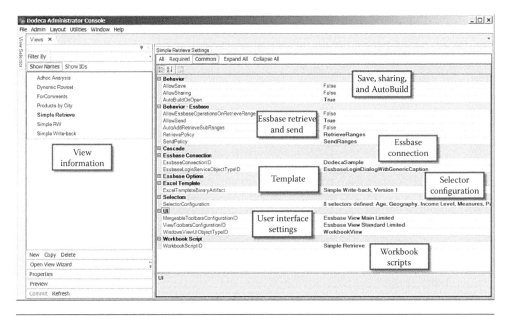

**Figure 7.13**  Sample View settings.

*7.6.2.4 View Settings*   View settings are displayed and set via the Views metadata editor. The View properties are organized according to functional groupings, e.g., Behavior, Selectors, and Workbook Script (see Figure 7.13.)

With these settings and a valid spreadsheet template, the View is ready to run.

*7.6.2.5 Retrieval*   The View settings displayed in the Views metadata editor define the retrieval View shown in Figure 7.14. The spreadsheet template, Essbase connection, Dimension Selectors, Toolbars, and sheet retrieve ranges are all on display. From a read-only perspective, this View is complete.

*7.6.2.6 Conclusion*   Creating a Simple Retrieve View is easy. A spreadsheet template with named Dodeca ranges and tokenized dimensions is the core object. This spreadsheet can be an empty retrieve range or, as in the case of this sample View, it can incorporate defined retrieve ranges, tokenized dimensions, and Excel formulas.

*7.6.3 Simple Write-Back View*

*7.6.3.1 Sending Data to Essbase*   What the Simple Retrieve View does not support is interactive responses to input and sending data back to. To do that, this View must

- Allow data input for the Current Year member but forbid it for other members of the Year dimension.
- Calculate Variance and Variance % from Current Year and Previous Year dynamically via a spreadsheet formula.

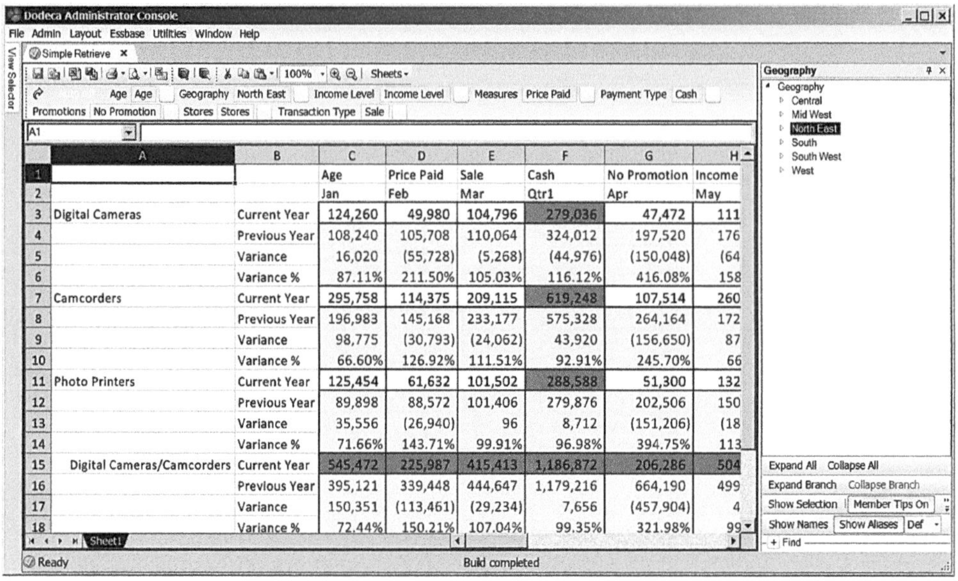

**Figure 7.14**  Simple Retrieve View.

- Dynamically calculate upper-level Time dimension members.
- Restrict sends to level 0 only (upper-level sends will not be rejected by Essbase but are meaningless in an ASO database).

These write-back requirements highlight one of Dodeca's key features: melding Essbase and spreadsheet functionality in a powerful and controlled fashion.

*7.6.3.1.1 Protecting the Sheet*   As shown in Figure 7.15, preventing the user from entering data in retrieve or formula cells is as easy as

1. Locking the relevant cells.
2. Protecting the sheet.

This protection is separate from Essbase filter security and can overload security definitions if desired.

**Note:** The name of the template is SimpleView1.xls although the View name is Simple Retrieve. Dodeca can label template Binary Artifacts and use them in multiple Views.

*7.6.3.1.2 Calculating Variances and Totals*   On-sheet dynamic calculations are performed by simple cell formulas. These values are also calculated in the Year and Time dimensions in the sample database. Although these variance members are also in the Essbase database, the database values are not overridden because they are database calculated values; remember that ASO calculated values are read-only. Also, these members could be removed from the database and still calculated in the spreadsheet.

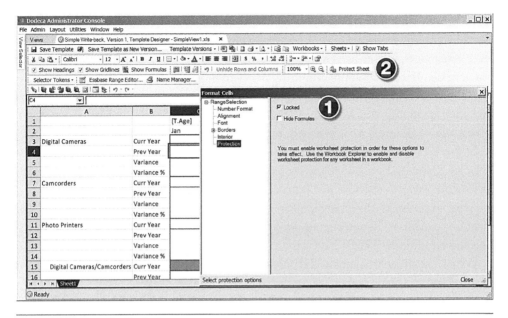

**Figure 7.15** Protecting the sheet.

| | A | B | C | D | E | F |
|---|---|---|---|---|---|---|
| 1 | | | [T.Age] | [T.Measures] | [T.Transaction Type] | [T.Payment Type] |
| 2 | | | Jan | Feb | Mar | Qtr1 |
| 3 | Digital Cameras | Curr Year | | | | =SUM(C3:E3) |
| 4 | | Prev Year | | | | |
| 5 | | Variance | =C3-C4 | =D3-D4 | =E3-E4 | =F3-F4 |
| 6 | | Variance % | =IF(C3=0,0,C4/C3) | =IF(D3=0,0,D4/D3) | =IF(E3=0,0,E4/E3) | =IF(F3=0,0,F4/F3) |
| 7 | Camcorders | Curr Year | | | | =SUM(C7:E7) |
| 8 | | Prev Year | | | | |
| 9 | | Variance | =C7-C8 | =D7-D8 | =E7-E8 | =F7-F8 |
| 10 | | Variance % | =IF(C7=0,0,C8/C7) | =IF(D7=0,0,D8/D7) | =IF(E7=0,0,E8/E7) | =IF(F7=0,0,F8/F7) |
| 11 | Photo Printers | Curr Year | | | | =SUM(C11:E11) |
| 12 | | Prev Year | | | | |
| 13 | | Variance | =C11-C12 | =D11-D12 | =E11-E12 | =F11-F12 |
| 14 | | Variance % | =IF(C11=0,0,C12/C11) | =IF(D11=0,0,D12/D11) | =IF(E11=0,0,E12/E11) | =IF(F11=0,0,F12/F11) |
| 15 | Digital Cameras/Camcorders | Curr Year | =SUM(C3,C7,C11) | =SUM(D3,D7,D11) | =SUM(E3,E7,E11) | =SUM(F3,F7,F11) |
| 16 | | Prev Year | =SUM(C4,C8,C12) | =SUM(D4,D8,D12) | =SUM(E4,E8,E12) | =SUM(F4,F8,F12) |
| 17 | | Variance | =C15-C16 | =D15-D16 | =E15-E16 | =F15-F16 |
| 18 | | Variance % | =IF(C15=0,0,C16/C15) | =IF(D15=0,0,D16/D15) | =IF(E15=0,0,E16/E15) | =IF(F15=0,0,F16/F15) |
| 19 | | | | | | |

**Figure 7.16** Sheet illustrating formulas.

Indeed, removing entire classes of calculated members in Essbase databases is possible so long as the results are queried through Dodeca Views, thus potentially improving Essbase performance. The sheet in Figure 7.16 illustrates formulas; cell formulas used by Dodeca are Excel-compliant.

*7.6.3.1.3 Restricting Sends to Level 0 Only*   ASO Essbase only allows sends to level 0. This is not completely accurate as upper-level member combinations can receive sends without error, but these data sends are ignored, however, as ASO does not store upper-level data points. If this sample database was a block storage option database, it would be possible, although not advisable, to send data to upper-level member combinations.

To prevent this ASO Essbase View from sending data to upper-level members, a simple approach might be to disable dimensional member selections for anything but level 0 members. Upper-level members would be viewable in Dimension Selectors, but not actually usable. Disabling anything other than level 0 for the Geography dimension can be accomplished by creating a copy of the Geography_Default Selector List and then changing the MaxLevelSelectable property from the default value of –1, which allows all levels to be selected, to 0 (see Figure 7.17).

In the View properties, the SelectorConfiguration can now be changed so that the Selector List used by the Geography Selector is the newly created "Geography_Tree_Lev0Only" Selector List, as in Figure 7.18.

After committing the change, when the Simple Retrieve View is opened, the Build button is disabled whenever an upper-level Geography member like NEW YORK is selected (see Figure 7.19).

When the level 0 member NEW YORK–NY is selected, the Build button is enabled and the Geography Selector is filled (see Figure 7.20).

This same restriction to level 0 would need to be applied to all Dimension Selector Lists to enable restricted sends to an ASO database.

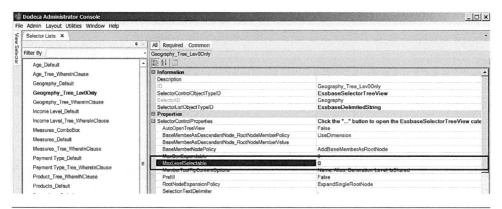

**Figure 7.17** Changing the MaxLevelSelectable property.

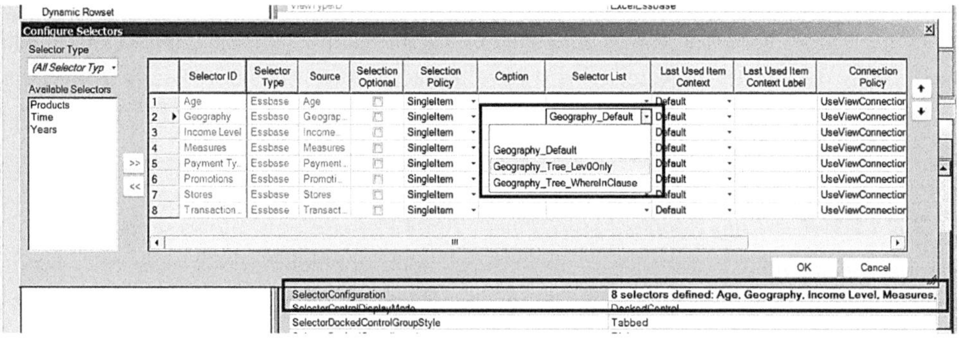

**Figure 7.18** Changing the SelectorConfiguration.

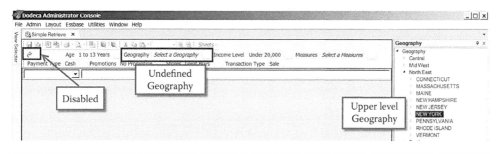

**Figure 7.19**   Build disabled for upper-level member.

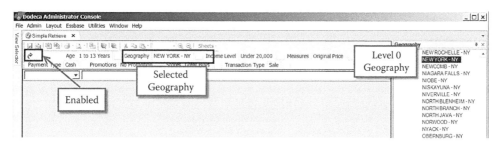

**Figure 7.20**   Build enabled for level 0 member.

A downside to this approach, and a not inconsiderable one, is that reporting at above level 0 is impossible. Moreover, each Dimension Selector List needs to be modified and substituted into the View. A more sophisticated way to manage retrievals at any level and sends only at level 0 for all dimensions is to test for level 0 via a Workbook Script.

*7.6.3.1.4 Using a Workbook Script to Control Essbase Sends*   Remember that Workbook Scripts are programmatic extensions to Dodeca functionality, tied to worksheet and Essbase-centric events driven by user actions. A Workbook Script can read the level value of a POV dimension selection and then appropriately show or hide the Essbase Send toolbar button. Removing the MaxLevelSelectable Selector List restriction and adding such a Workbook Script allows retrievals at any level but sends at level 0 only.

7.6.3.1.4.1  Logic   The following steps enable read/write functionality at level 0 only:

1. Although this step is not strictly necessary, for debugging purposes, show the workbook.
2. Turn on the Essbase toolbar Send button to ensure its visibility.
3. Test to make sure that all selectable dimensions (Product, Year, and Time are excluded as they are in the rows and columns) are at level 0.
4. If the test fails, hide the Send button, then exit the Workbook Script.
5. If the test succeeds, leave the Send button visible.

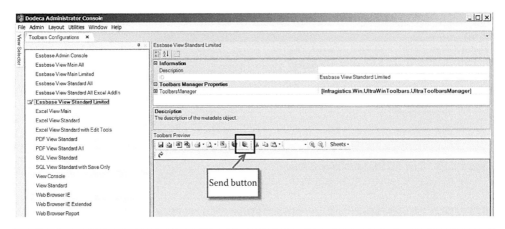

**Figure 7.21** Essbase Toolbar Send button.

| On Event... | Activ | Run Procedure | | Comment |
|---|---|---|---|---|
| AfterBuild | ☑ | OnAfterBuild | · | Execute after the worksheet build |
| AfterWorkbookOpen | ☑ | 1-OnAfterWorkbookOpen | · | Execute on initial workbook open |

**Figure 7.22** Workbook Script events.

7.6.3.1.4.2 Toolbar  This View uses the predefined Toolbar, Essbase View Standard Limited. By default, the Essbase Toolbar Send button (Figure 7.21) is enabled.

7.6.3.1.4.3 Events  The On Event... column is sorted in alphabetical order (see Figure 7.22). The actual execution order of these events is AfterWorkbookOpen and then AfterBuild, which makes sense when considering how a View executes: A build of a View cannot occur until the workbook has been opened. Good practice is to number the associated procedures to show execution order.

7.6.3.1.4.4 Procedures
A. OnAfterWorkbookOpen procedure

As noted previously, the SetCover method (see Figure 7.23) sets the Cover property to FALSE to ensure that the workbook is visible during development for debugging purposes. It should be removed when the View is put into production.

B. OnAfterBuild procedure

OnAfterBuild has two methods: SetTool and ExecuteProcedure.

a. SetTool method

SetTool uses the ToolKey and Visible arguments to show the EssbaseSend button in the toolbar, as shown in Figure 7.24.

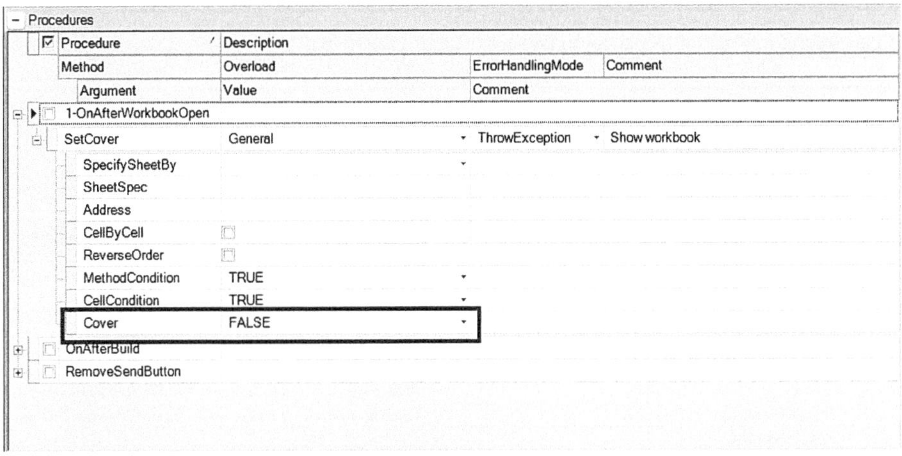

**Figure 7.23** SetCover method for OnAfterWorkbookOpen procedure.

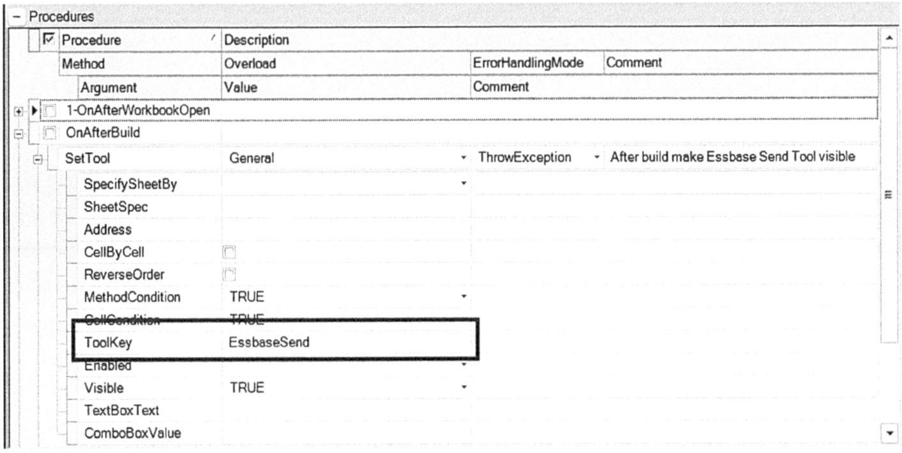

**Figure 7.24** SetTool method for OnAfterBuild procedure.

b. ExecuteProcedure method

ExecuteProcedure uses the Address, CellByCell, and CellCondition arguments to test the level of each selection in the SelectorTokensRange (Figure 7.25).

In this case, the ExecuteProcedure method is running within the context of the OnAfterBuild procedure.

When the MethodCondition argument is set to TRUE and the CellByCell argument is checked, a cell-by-cell evaluation of each cell in the range specified by the Address is performed using the CellCondition (see Figure 7.26).

| | C | D | E | F | G | H | I | J |
|---|---|---|---|---|---|---|---|---|
| [T.Age] | | [T.Measures] | [T.Transaction Type] | [T.Payment Type] | [T.Promotions] | [T.Income Level] | [T.Stores] | [T.Geography] |
| Jan | Feb | Mar | Qtr1 | Apr | May | Jun | Qtr2 | Jul |

**Figure 7.25**  SelectorsTokensRange.

```
- Procedures
   ☑ Procedure              ' Description
      Method                  Overload                    ErrorHandlingMode   Comment
         Argument             Value                       Comment
   ⊞ ☐ 1-OnAfterWorkbookOpen
   ⊟ ☐ OnAfterBuild
      ⊞ ▶ SetTool             General              ▾      ThrowException  ▾  After build make Essbase Send Tool visible on t
      ⊟ ▶ ExecuteProcedure    General              ▾      ThrowException  ▾  If all selectors are Not level 0 members, call Re
           SpecifySheetBy                           ▾
           SheetSpec
           Address            SelectorTokensRange
           CellByCell         ☑
           ReverseOrder       ☐
           MethodCondition    TRUE                  ▾
           CellCondition      =IF(@MbrLevel("@ValueText()")>0,T  ▾
           Procedure          RemoveSendButton
   ⊞ ☐ RemoveSendButton
```

**Figure 7.26**  Cell-by-cell evaluation using CellCondition.

Dodeca functions, which can be used for most argument values, are used to provide information not available via Excel worksheet functions. They are identified by a leading @ symbol. Dodeca has more than 130 functions; custom functions can be created as required. The CellCondition argument uses a formula to test the POV dimension members using a combination of spreadsheet formula syntax, =IF(*test, true, false*), and Dodeca functions, (@MbrLevel, @ValueText). By using the argument editor, the user can interrogate the @MbrLevel and @ValueText functions.

@MbrLevel is used to determine the dimensional level of the member name as each cell in the SelectorTokensRange is evaluated. This function requires a member name in the form of a text string (see Figure 7.27). The @ValueText function turns the contents of a worksheet cell into a text string (see Figure 7.28).

```
CellCondition Value Editor                                        ⊠
Font  Courier New              ▾ 12 ▾ A˙ A˙
 fx | Functions  MemberLevel, @MbrLevel(<MemberName>, [<AliasTable>], [<Connectio  ▾
Function name: MemberLevel                                        ▲
Usage: @MbrLevel(<MemberName>, [<AliasTable>], [<ConnectionID>], [<DefaultValue>])
Description: Returns the Essbase Level of the specified member.
Parameters:
   MemberName: The member specified can be an alias or a member name.
   AliasTable: Optional (default is the view's AliasTable);  The alias table to use.
   ConnectionID: Optional (defaults to view's connection);  The ID of the Essbase
                                                                 ▼
=IF(@MbrLevel("@ValueText()")>0,True,False)


☑ Trim trailing linefeeds                          OK        Cancel
```

**Figure 7.27**  Text string member name.

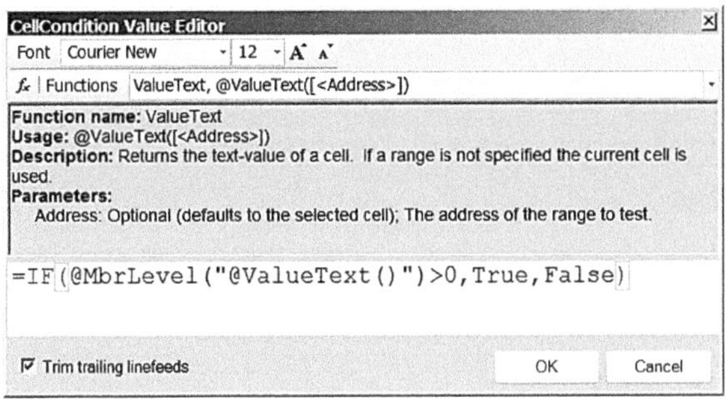

**Figure 7.28**  @ValueText function.

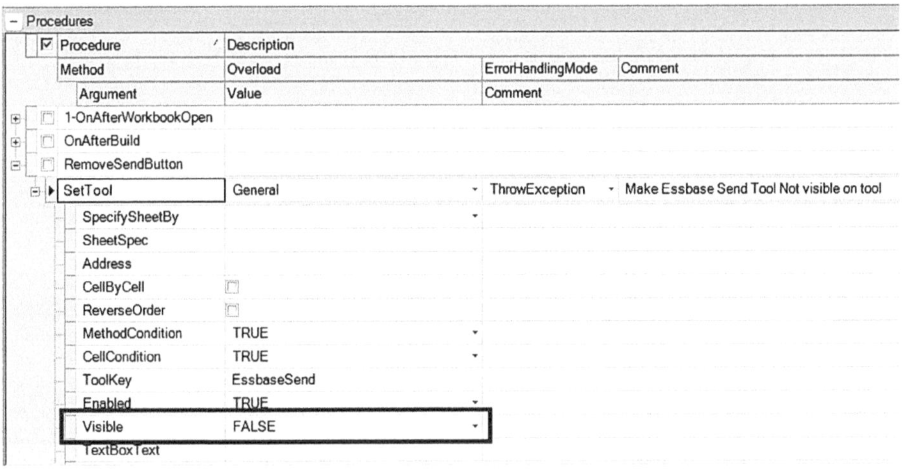

**Figure 7.29**  SetTool method.

The IF statement test is functionally identical to the Excel IF formula syntax. Dodeca functions are resolved before the formula logic so that the above formula is resolved as the Excel formula IF(1>0, TRUE, FALSE). If the member level is greater than 0, the CellCondition argument is FALSE and the cell-by-cell testing continues until the SelectorsTokenRange is exhausted. If it evaluates to TRUE, execution passes to the Procedure argument and RemoveSendButton is executed.

The RemoveSendButton procedure only fires in response to the TRUE Cell Condition result in the OnAfterBuild.ExecuteProcedure method.

In the SetTool method, the ToolKey argument is the key to the send button on the View's toolbar. When the Visible argument is set to FALSE, the send button is hidden and data above level 0 cannot be sent to Essbase (see Figure 7.29).

*7.6.3.2 Retrieval* The Workbook Script approach allows retrieves at any level of dimensionality across all dimensions. The example in Figure 7.30 shows Geography at level 0 but Payment Type at an upper level. This causes the Send button to be hidden so that the View is read-only.

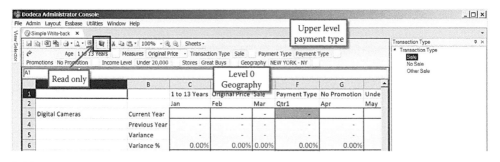

**Figure 7.30**  Retrieval with mixed level types.

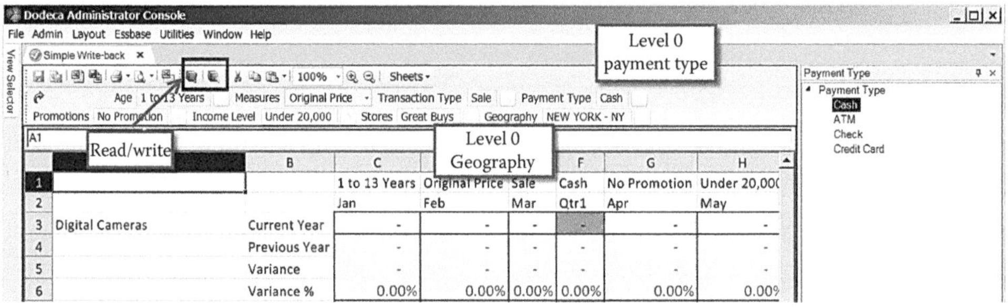

**Figure 7.31**  Retrieval with level 0 only.

When Payment Type is set to a level 0 member, Cash, the Send button is shown and read/write operations are possible (see Figure 7.31).

*7.6.3.3 Conclusion*  Workbook Scripts significantly increase View customization possibilities and, in combination with spreadsheet functionality like cell locking and sheet protection, create feature-rich, controlled interfaces for Essbase. Workbook Scripts that call dimensional query functions allow Dodeca to seamlessly manipulate the View's user interface and overall functionality. Workbook Scripts will be central to all subsequent View use cases.

### 7.6.4 Dynamic Rowset View

Spreadsheets, range definitions, tokenized dimension labels, and Essbase properties combine to create a simple yet powerful environment for creating read and write Views. This approach satisfies many Essbase reporting and data submission requirements, is easy and fast to implement, and requires little to no Workbook Scripting.

While this often suffices for many Essbase needs, it necessarily means that spreadsheet rows and columns are static and, although data can change in response to user actions, the metadata that defines the View itself cannot. A more flexible approach is to use Essbase Dimension Selectors and Workbook Scripts to programmatically change sheet metadata in the form of members, ranges, and formulas. This approach is commonly called Dynamic Rowsets.

*7.6.4.1 Logic* Using a combination of ranges, cell formulas, Essbase report scripts, and Workbook Scripts, the Dynamic Rowset View will

- Set up the View for retrieval.
- Expand/contract the rows to show level 0 Product members based on an upper-level Product dimension member.
- Insert cell formatting and formulas for dynamic rows.
- Create a dynamic subtotal at the bottom of the sheet reflecting dynamically generated level 0 data.
- Ensure that sends are only possible at level 0 of all dimensions.

*7.6.4.2 Before and After* In contrast to the Simple View's static template and results, the Dynamic Rowset's template (Figure 7.32) and results (Figure 7.33) differ greatly.

*7.6.4.2.1 Template* Hidden rows, columns, ranges, and cell content that are valued and visible in the template are manipulated, copied, and hidden in the final retrieve result.

*7.6.4.2.2 Result* Based on the selection of the Product member Digital Cameras/ Camcorders, the level 0 descendants Digital Cameras, Camcorders, and Photo Printers have been written to the sheet with corresponding data, formulas, and formatting. The Digital Cameras/Camcorders' Current Year row is not valued from Essbase but instead has a SUMIF formula-driven total that reflects retrieved and input values.

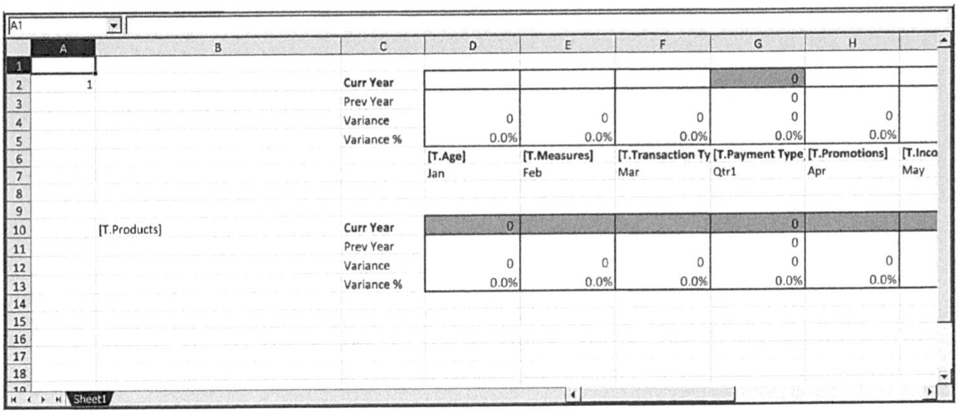

**Figure 7.32** Dynamic Rowset template.

| | A | B | C | D | E | F | G | H | I | J | K | L |
|---|---|---|---|---|---|---|---|---|---|---|---|---|
| 1 | | | 26 to 30 Years | Price Paid | No Sale | Cash | No Promotion | 30,000-49,999 | Electronic World | NEW YORK - NY | | |
| 2 | | | Jan | Feb | Mar | Qtr1 | Apr | May | Jun | Qtr2 | Jul | Aug |
| 3 | Digital Cameras | Current Year | - | - | - | | - | - | - | | - | - |
| 4 | | Previous Year | 1,380 | - | - | 1,380 | - | - | - | | - | - |
| 5 | | Variance | (1,380) | - | - | (1,380) | - | - | - | | - | - |
| 6 | | Variance % | 0.00% | 0.00% | 0.00% | 0.00% | 0.00% | 0.00% | 0.00% | 0.00% | 0.00% | 0.00 |
| 7 | Camcorders | Current Year | - | - | - | | - | - | - | | - | - |
| 8 | | Previous Year | - | - | - | | - | - | - | | - | - |
| 9 | | Variance | - | - | - | | - | - | - | | - | - |
| 10 | | Variance % | 0.00% | 0.00% | 0.00% | 0.00% | 0.00% | 0.00% | 0.00% | 0.00% | 0.00% | 0.00 |
| 11 | Photo Printers | Current Year | - | - | - | | - | - | - | | - | - |
| 12 | | Previous Year | - | - | - | | - | - | - | | - | - |
| 13 | | Variance | - | - | - | | - | - | - | | - | - |
| 14 | | Variance % | 0.00% | 0.00% | 0.00% | 0.00% | 0.00% | 0.00% | 0.00% | 0.00% | 0.00% | 0.00 |
| 15 | Digital Cameras/Camcorders | Current Year | - | - | - | | - | - | - | | - | - |
| 16 | | Previous Year | 1,380 | - | - | 1,380 | - | - | - | | - | - |
| 17 | | Variance | (1,380) | - | - | (1,380) | - | - | - | | - | - |
| 18 | | Variance % | 0.00% | 0.00% | 0.00% | 0.00% | 0.00% | 0.00% | 0.00% | 0.00% | 0.00% | 0.00 |
| 19 | | | | | | | | | | | | |
| 20 | | | | | | | | | | | | |

**Figure 7.33**   Selection outcomes in Dynamic Rowset.

*7.6.4.3 Dynamically Creating Rows, Columns, and Ranges*   Dodeca combines native spreadsheet functionality and Workbook Scripts to manipulate worksheet content and data in response to user actions. In the case of a Dynamic Rowset View, a Workbook Script can write and interrogate sheet content. Often, this information is written to cells in one step and then subsequently used either by another Workbook Script step or in cell formulas, as this use case shows. In either instance, this content is hidden from the user after processing.

*7.6.4.3.1 Hidden Rows and Columns*   Hidden template rows, columns, and ranges store results and act as a cell formatting and formula source. On retrieval, these objects are hidden from the user. To prevent users from confusion on seeing missing rows and column headers, the RowAndColumnHeadersVisibility View property is often set to FALSE.

*7.6.4.3.2 The Role of Ranges*   In contrast to the Simple Retrieve View example, where the retrieve and send ranges overlapped, the Dynamic Rowset View uses five ranges to resize the retrieve and send ranges based on dimension selections, identify where to insert and how to size retrieve and send ranges, define the formatting and formulas of inserted content, and define POV headers (see Table 7.2).

**Table 7.2**   Dynamic Rowset View Ranges

| RANGE NAME | RANGE ADDRESS | PURPOSE |
|---|---|---|
| Ess.Retrieve.Range.1 | Sheet1!$B$6:$T$13 | Dynamic retrieve range |
| Ess.Send.Range.1 | Sheet1!$B$6:$T$9 | Dynamic send range |
| SelectorTokensRange | Sheet1!$D$6:$K$6 | POV range |
| Insert.Marker | Sheet1!$A$8 | Insert anchor |
| Row.Template | Sheet1!$A$2:$T$5 | Copied formatting |

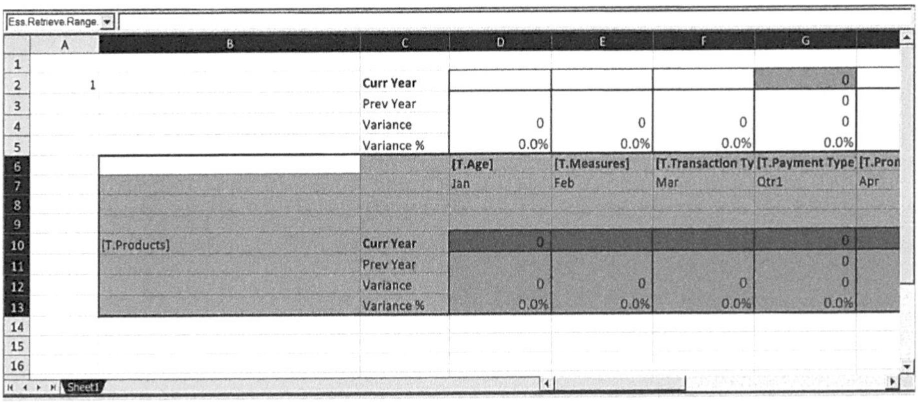

**Figure 7.34** Ess.Retrieve.Range.1.

7.6.4.3.2.1 Ess.Retrieve.Range.1 The initial Ess.Retrieve.Range.1 defines the retrieve range for a single, tokenized Product (see Figure 7.34). This range will be expanded based on the number of level 0 Products. The tokenized Product in cell B10 receives the user-selected member used to determine those level 0 descendants.

7.6.4.3.2.2 Ess.Send.Range.1 Note the difference in location and size of the send versus the retrieve range (see Figure 7.35). The send range is a subset and does not contain member metadata. This range will be expanded based on the number of level 0 Products; it will not expand to include the selected upper-level Product.

7.6.4.3.2.3 SelectorTokensRange As in the Simple Retrieve View, this range contains POV dimension values that will be interrogated to determine their level; if all POV members are not at level 0, the Send toolbar button is hidden (see Figure 7.36).

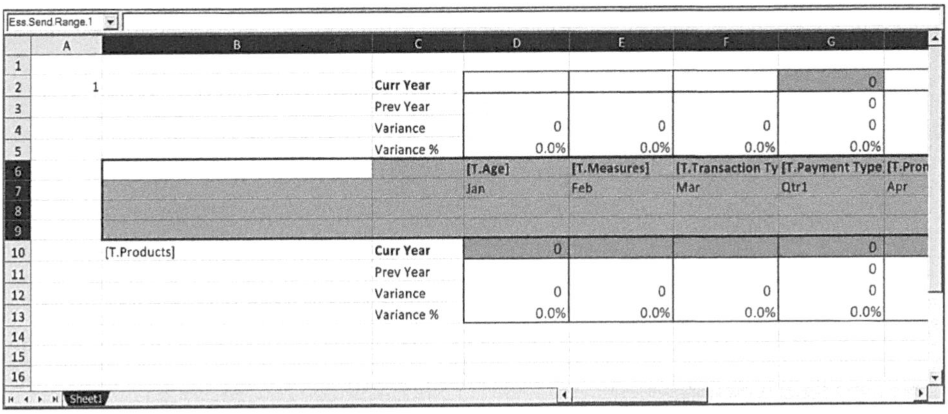

**Figure 7.35** Ess.Send.Range.1.

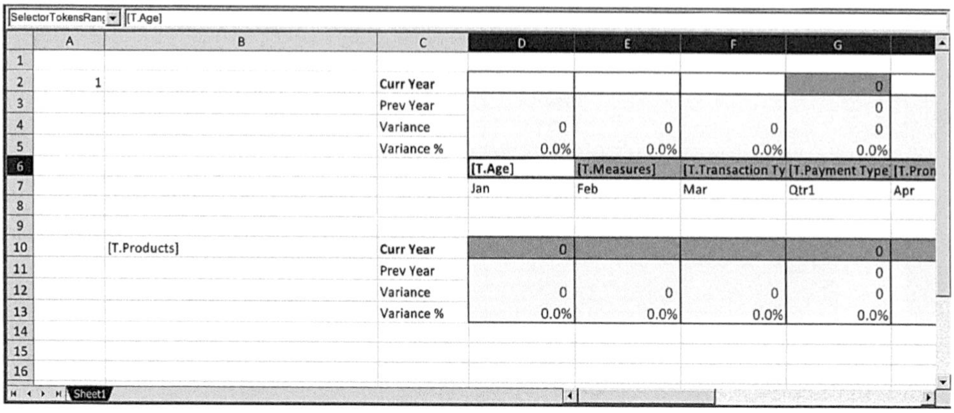

**Figure 7.36**   SelectorTokensRange.

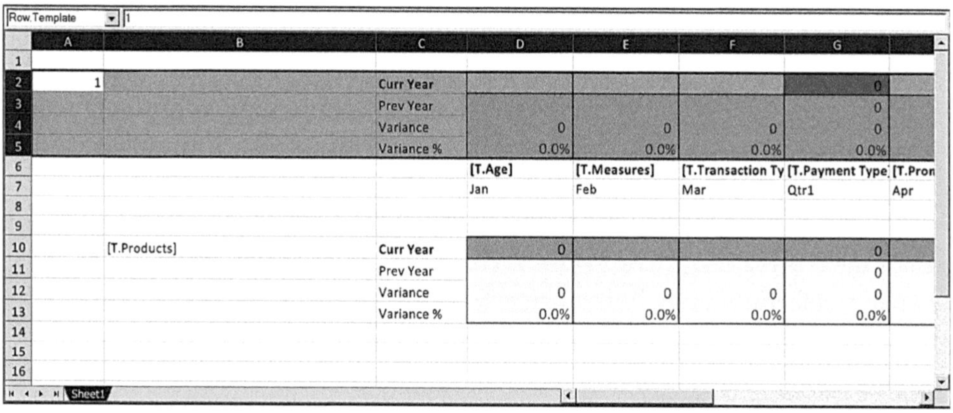

**Figure 7.37**   Row.Template.

7.6.4.3.2.4 Row.Template    The dynamically inserted level 0 Products use this range to define row and column contents, including formatting and cell formulas (see Figure 7.37). The role of the value "1" in cell A2 is described in the Insert.Marker section.

7.6.4.3.2.5 Insert.Marker    This is one row below the POV and column headers. This single cell range is the anchor for inserted rows (see Figure 7.38).

A. SUMIF, the Number 1, and Expanding a Range

Cell D10 (see Figure 7.39) has the following formula: =SUMIF ($A$8:$A$9,1,D$8:D$9) Why is this formula in that cell? How does the formula work? Why is its D10 location within the Row.Template range and how is its relation to the Insert.Marker range essential?

a. Importance

This View displays the level 0 descendants of an upper-level Product. Within that Dynamic Rowset, the Year dimension member Curr Year is

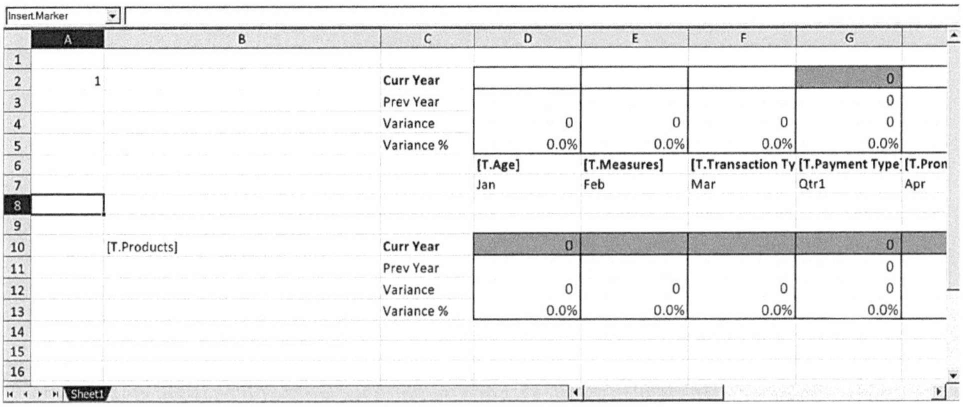

**Figure 7.38** Insert.Marker.

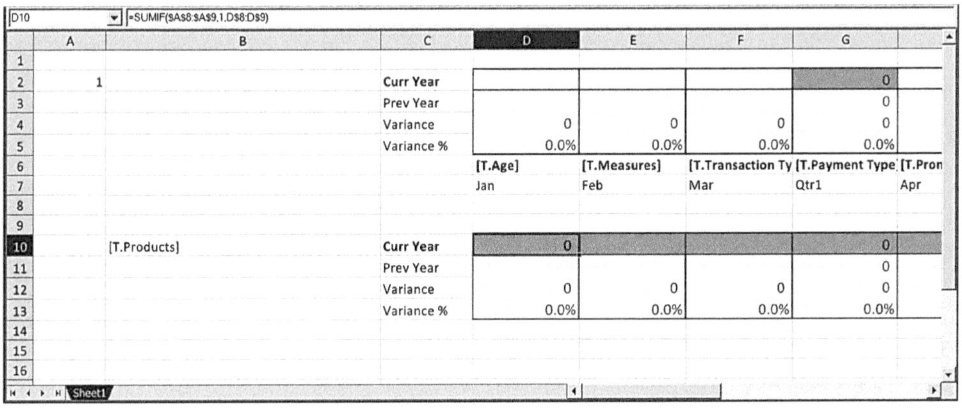

**Figure 7.39** Cell containing SUMIF formula.

retrieved. If this View were read-only, totals would be retrieved directly from Essbase. However, a read/write View that supports dynamic Product totals requires a sheet formula to sum the individual Product's Curr Year cells. The challenge with a cell formula that sums data is that it must have a static start and end range. If the sheet's contents are dynamic, there is no way to correctly capture subtotals with a SUM spreadsheet formula.

The SUMIF function solves the dynamic formula issue when combined with range inserts.

b. SUMIF

As shown in Table 7.3, a SUMIF cell formula is made up of three parts: range, criteria, and sum range in the form SUMIF(range, criteria, [sum_range]).

Using the formula in cell D10, SUMIF looks at cells $A$8 to $A$9 for the number 1. If that value exists, the cells $D$8 to $D$9 are summed.

**Table 7.3** SUMIF Cell Formula Parts

| COMPONENT | DESCRIPTION |
| --- | --- |
| Range | Cell range that is searched for the criteria value |
| Criteria | Search value |
| sum_range | Optional sum range based on criteria search success |

In the View template, D10 is valued to 0 because the value 1 is not found in cells A8 or A9. Moreover, cells D8 and D9 are blank. Why test for a value that does not exist and sums nulls? The answer is the impact of range expansion on cell formulas.

When a formula references a range of cells, copying and then inserting the copied cells back into that range expand the range and dynamically modify the formula to reflect the new larger range size. This is innate spreadsheet functionality and requires no explicit Workbook Script other than a range copy and insert.

- Formulas and Range Expansion

    The sample Excel spreadsheet in Figures 7.40 and 7.41 shows a SUMIF formula that interrogates cells A1 through A4 for the value of 1—if it finds that value in column A, column C's matching row values are summed. In the case of this example (Figure 7.41), the result is 4.

- Copying and Inserting

    If rows 3 and 4 are selected, copied, and then inserted back into the A1 to A4 range, the SUMIF member formula is moved to row 7 and dynamically reflects the new contents of rows 5 and 6 (see Figure 7.42).

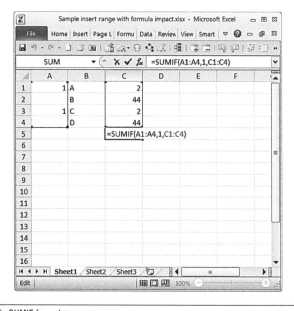

**Figure 7.40** Sample SUMIF formula.

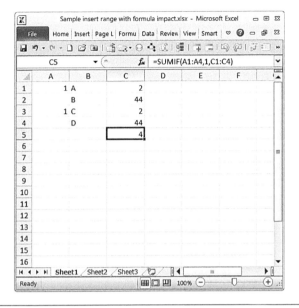

**Figure 7.41**  Sample SUMIF formula result.

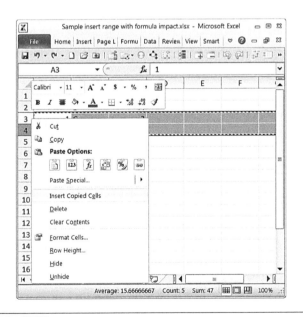

**Figure 7.42**  Expanding SUMIF range.

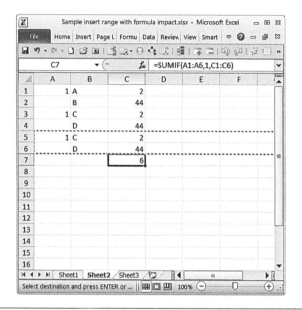

**Figure 7.43**   Result of expanded SUMIF range.

> – The New SUMIF
>    The SUMIF formula now tests rows A1 through A6 for the value 1,
>    when that is satisfied, it sums C1 through C6 (see Figure 7.43).
>  B. SUMIF and Insert Ranges in Dodeca
>    The same expansion of formula range occurs in the Dynamic Rowset
>    View. When the Row.Template range is iteratively inserted into Ess.Retrieve.
>    Range.1 at the Insert.Marker anchor range, the SUMIF formula in D10 (and
>    in all of the SUMIF formulas in row 10) is updated to reflect the new Ess.
>    Retrieve.Range.1 size. The 1 value in column A is also repeated from the Row.
>    Template range and is now in the correct location for the SUMIF to pick up
>    Curr Year rows.

Note the Digital Cameras, Camcorders, and Photo Printers ranges with their repeating values in column A. The SUMIF formula in rows 21 through 24 reflects the dynamically inserted rows and data. As shown in Figure 7.44, an example of this formula is in cell D21: =SUMIF($A$8:$A$20,1,D$8:D$20).

*7.6.4.4 Using Workbook Scripts to Dynamically Create Views*

*7.6.4.4.1 Events*   Again, in Figure 7.45, note the prefixed number 1 for the first Procedure. This View's AfterWorkbookOpen event was defined before AfterBuild so the Events' definition order coincidentally mimics their execution order. The definition order does not impact actual processing, but the practice of prefixing Procedure names with the event order, as in the case of 1-OnAfterWorkbookOpen, helps administrators quickly understand execution order.

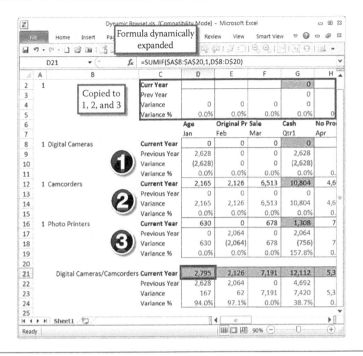

**Figure 7.44** SUMIF and insert ranges in Dodeca.

| On Event... | Active | Run Procedure | | Comment |
|---|---|---|---|---|
| ▶ AfterWorkbookOpen | ☑ | 1-OnAfterWorkbookOpen | ▾ | This Event runs first |
| AfterBuild | ☑ | OnAfterBuild | ▾ | This Event runs Second |

**Figure 7.45** Workbook Script events.

7.6.4.4.1.1 AfterWorkbookOpen Event    The procedure associated with this event has five Methods: SetCover, SetProtection, BuildRangeFromScript, SetHidden, and SetProtection (see Figure 7.46).

A. SetCover Method

The SetCover Method ensures that the workbook is visible by setting the Cover argument to FALSE (Figure 7.47).

B. SetProtection Method

The SetProtection Method unprotects the sheet by setting the Protected argument to FALSE (Figure 7.48).

C. BuildRangeFromScript Method

The BuildRangeFromScript Method is the core of this Workbook Script (see Figure 7.49). BuildRangeFromScript builds a range on a worksheet from the contents of a script. In the case of this Workbook Script, it

1. Uses the EssbaseReportScript Overload of the BuildRangeFromScript.
2. Uses an Essbase report script to query level 0 members from an upper-level parent.

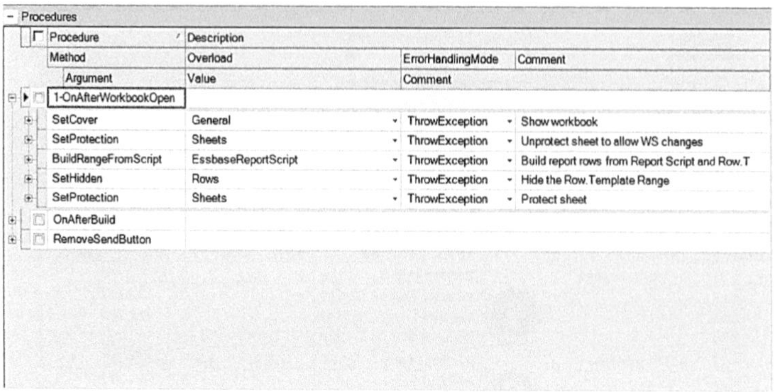

**Figure 7.46** Methods for AfterWorkbookOpen event.

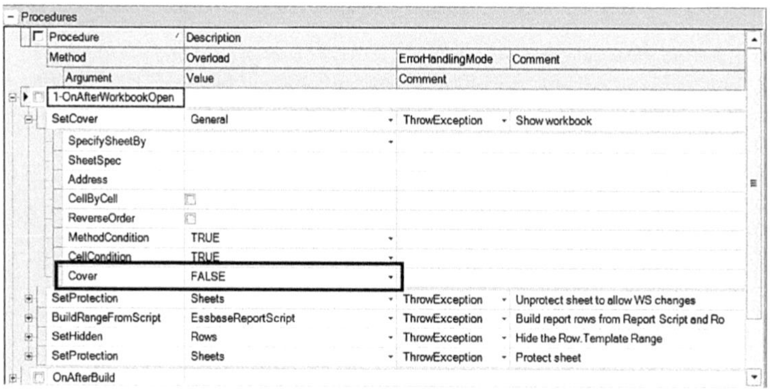

**Figure 7.47** SetCover Method.

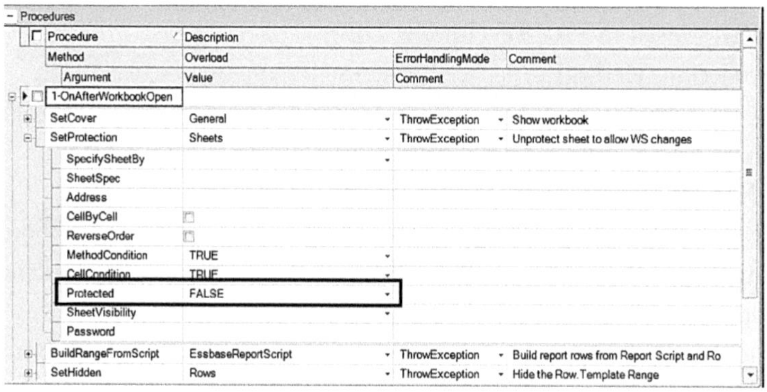

**Figure 7.48** SetProtection Method.

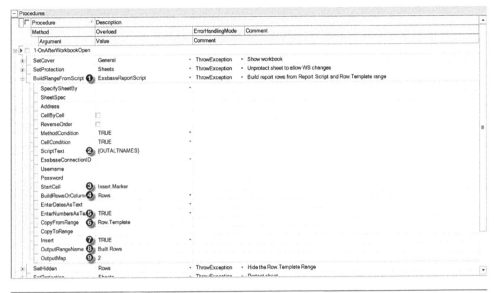

**Figure 7.49** BuildRangeFromScript Method.

3. Identifies the sheet range used to insert content.
4. Defines the insertion as row based.
5. Ensures that member names that are numeric are treated as text values.
6. Names the row template range from which to copy.
7. Sets the Insert argument to TRUE.
8. Identifies the output range.
9. Sets the column target for the inserted Products and row template.

a. BuildRangeFromScript Overloads
   The BuildRangeFromScript Method supports the data source Overloads listed in Table 7.4.

**Table 7.4** Supported Data Source Overloads

| OVERLOAD NAME | OVERLOAD DESCRIPTION |
|---|---|
| CartesianList | Build a range on the sheet based on the Cartesian product of values from two or more delimited string lists. |
| DataCache | Build a range on the sheet based on a DataCache created using the AddDataCache method. |
| DelimitedString | Loop a list of values specified by a delimited string. |
| EssbaseMdxQuery | Build a range on the sheet from the results of an Essbase MDX query. |
| EssbaseMemberQuery | Build a range on the sheet from an Essbase member query. |
| EssbaseReportScript | Build a range on the sheet from an Essbase report script. |
| SQLPassthroughDataSet | Build a range on the sheet based on a Dodeca SQLPassthroughDataSet. |
| SQLScript | Build a range on the sheet from the results of an SQL query. |
| URL | Loop values returned in XML format from a URL. Nodes named "value" will be used in the loop. |

In the case of this example, the EssbaseReportScript Overload is used to generate the member names for the insert range.

b. ScriptText Argument

The Essbase report script shown in Figure 7.50 uses the user-selected Product member to generate the level 0 descendants.

@TVal Function

@TVal, shown in Figure 7.51, is used to return a member name from a Selector token. [T.Products] is the automatically defined token for the Product dimension. That value is passed from the member Selector and evaluated via @TVal to return a string that is inserted into the report script at run time.

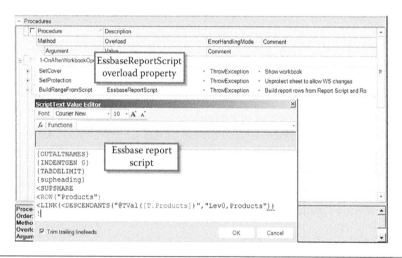

**Figure 7.50** ScriptText Argument.

**Figure 7.51** @TVal function.

Report Script in Essbase

Given the Product member Digital Cameras/Camcorders, the same Essbase report script returns both member names and data values. The same report, when executed in the Essbase Application Server console, returns both metadata and data (see Figure 7.52). The BuildRangeFromScript method knows to grab the member names from the first column in the tab-delimited output and ignores the data column.

c. StartCell Argument

StartCell defines the address of the first row of script output. A cell address in the form of $A$8 could be used, but a more flexible approach is to use the named range Insert.Marker.

d. BuildRowsOrColumns Argument

There are only two possible values for this Argument: Rows or Columns. This Workbook Script is inserting rows; therefore, the former value is used.

e. EnterNumbersAsText Argument

Setting this Argument to TRUE ensures that any member names that are numeric in nature, e.g., 100, are treated as text values. Without this setting, numeric member names would be treated as data and the Essbase retrieve would fail. This step is not strictly necessary in the case of this sample database's Product dimension, as it only uses alpha strings for member names.

f. CopyFromRange Argument

The Row.Template range is the source of cell formatting, protection, and formulas. The range contains four rows that correspond to the Year

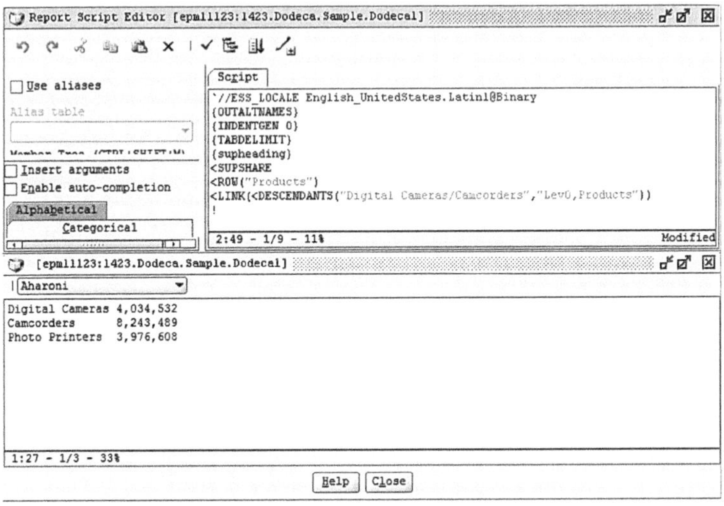

**Figure 7.52** Report Script in Essbase.

dimension level 0 members: Curr Year, Prev Year, Variance, and Variance %. This four-row block is inserted for each member in ScriptText's output.

g. Insert Argument

Setting this Argument to TRUE tells Dodeca to insert the iterated output of ReportFromScript and CopyFromRange at the StartCell range.

h. OutputRangeName Argument

ReportFromScript's output of Digital Cameras, Camcorders, and Photo Printers is written to the OutputRangeName Built.Rows as the outer nested dimension via multiple inserts of Row.Template. The Built. Rows range contains the inserted ranges (see Figure 7.53).

i. OutputMap Argument

This column receives the row output from ReportFromScript and CopyFromRange. As the BuildRangeFromScript Method is row based, the number 2 sets the output column to be column B.

D. SetHidden Method

Once the BuildRangeFromScript Method has completed, the Row.Template range is still visible in the sheet but is redundant as its role is only in building sheet content. The SetHidden Method's Hidden Argument is set to TRUE to hide that range (see Figure 7.54).

7.6.4.4.1.2 SetProtection Method Sheet processing is now complete. Just as SetProtection's Protected Argument was set to FALSE in the first step of this procedure, it must now be set to TRUE to lock all cells except month-level Curr Year cells, which have been formatted as unlocked (see Figure 7.55).

| Built.Rows | | | | | | | |
|---|---|---|---|---|---|---|---|
| | A | B | C | D | E | F | G |
| 1 | | | | | | | |
| 6 | | | | Age | Original Price | Sale | Cash | No Pro |
| 7 | | | | Jan | Feb | Mar | Qtr1 | Apr |
| 8 | 1 | Digital Cameras | Current Year | 0 | 0 | 0 | 0 | |
| 9 | | | Previous Year | 2,628 | 0 | 0 | 2,628 | |
| 10 | | | Variance | (2,628) | 0 | 0 | (2,628) | |
| 11 | | | Variance % | 0.0% | 0.0% | 0.0% | 0.0% | |
| 12 | 1 | Camcorders | Current Year | 2,165 | 2,126 | 6,513 | 10,804 | |
| 13 | | | Previous Year | 0 | 0 | 0 | 0 | |
| 14 | | | Variance | 2,165 | 2,126 | 6,513 | 10,804 | |
| 15 | | | Variance % | 0.0% | 0.0% | 0.0% | 0.0% | |
| 16 | 1 | Photo Printers | Current Year | 630 | 0 | 678 | 1,308 | |
| 17 | | | Previous Year | 0 | 2,064 | 0 | 2,064 | |
| 18 | | | Variance | 630 | (2,064) | 678 | (756) | |
| 19 | | | Variance % | 0.0% | 0.0% | 0.0% | 157.8% | |
| 20 | | | | | | | | |
| 21 | | Digital Cameras/Camcorders | Current Year | 2,795 | 2,126 | 7,191 | 12,112 | |
| 22 | | | Previous Year | 2,628 | 2,064 | 0 | 4,692 | |
| 23 | | | Variance | 167 | 62 | 7,191 | 7,420 | |

**Figure 7.53** Output RangeName Argument.

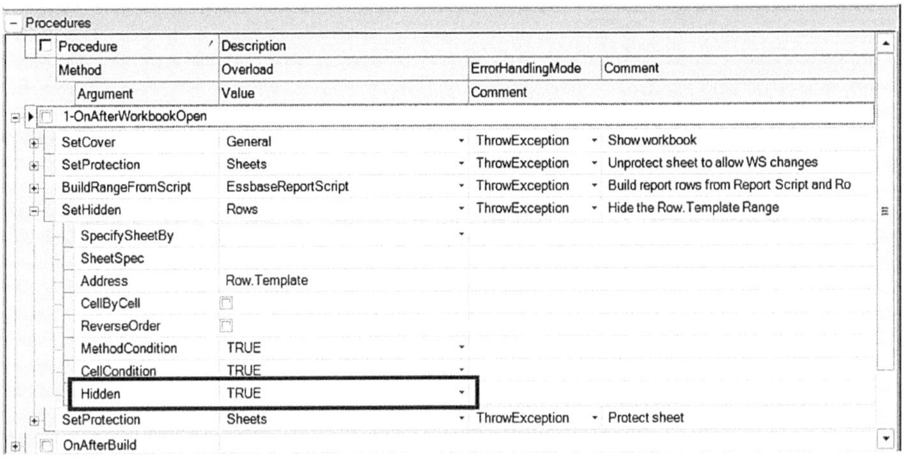

**Figure 7.54** SetHidden Method.

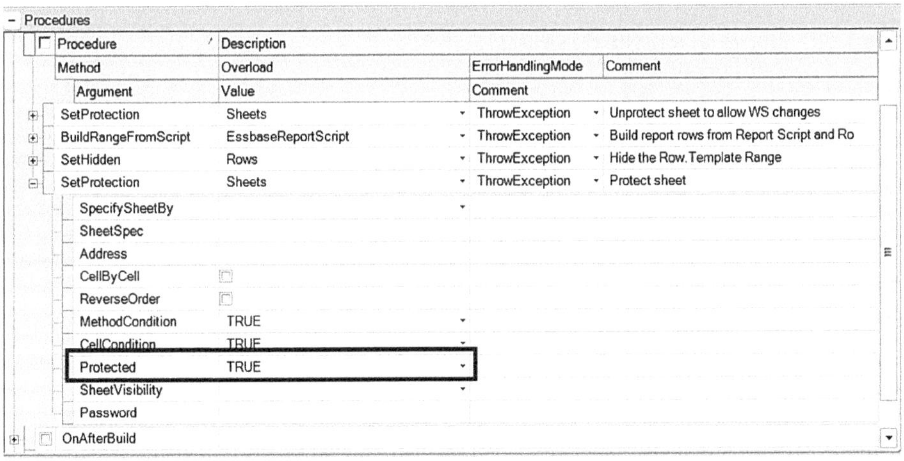

**Figure 7.55** SetProtection Method.

*7.6.4.4.2 OnAfterBuild and RemoveSendButton Procedures* The Send toolbar button should be visible only if all dimensions are set to level 0. See the Section 7.6.3.1.4.4 Procedures' Simple Write-back OnAfterBuild and RemoveSendButton for all settings and steps.

*7.6.4.5 Retrieval* Product dimension rows of this View are now fully dynamic. Figure 7.56 shows Product Handheld/PDAs. Figure 7.57 shows Product Other.

*7.6.4.6 Conclusion* Although the description of this View is involved, this is to show how each worksheet range and Workbook Script Procedure, Method, and Argument interact. From a development perspective, this View took approximately 15 minutes to build using the worksheet from the Simple Retrieve View as a base. The level of

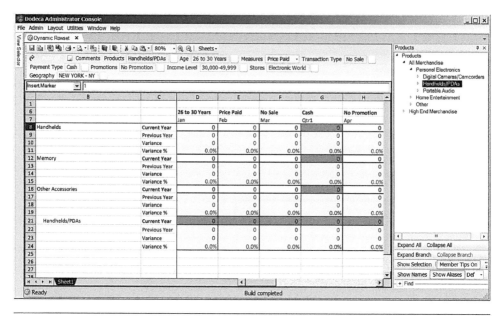

**Figure 7.56** Retrieval of Product Handheld/PDAs.

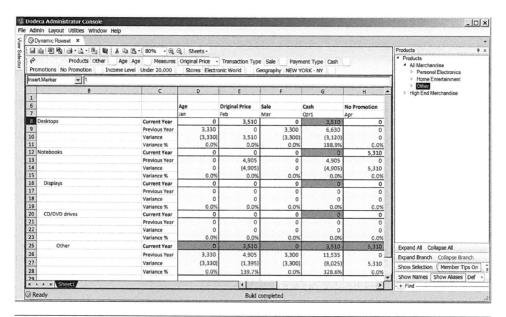

**Figure 7.57** Retrieval of Product Other.

customization in this View has increased compared with the Simple Retrieve View. The actual amount of code written is very small and consists mostly of tying together Workbook Script Methods and a single Essbase report script. The other advanced component of this View is difficult only if you are unfamiliar with spreadsheet inserts into a range with a dependent formula—there actually is no code involved in dynamically changing the SUMIF formula to support more or fewer rows.

This combination of Dodeca properties and extensibility with innate spreadsheet functionality is one of Dodeca's core features and advantages over other tools.

### 7.6.5 Products by City View

Thus far, the View use cases have only used Essbase as a data source. But Dodeca also supports relational data. Relational data sources can be used for drill-through to tables, SQL-only worksheets, or for reports that combine Essbase and relational data.

Many of the concepts that apply to Essbase Views such as Selectors, data connections, and worksheets apply to SQL Views, but given the different nature of a relational versus an Essbase data source, additional objects and settings exist that are unique to SQL Views.

#### 7.6.5.1 Logic
This SQL View uses a relational data source to query transaction-level sales data based on dimension selections that map to field values. This View uses Essbase Dimension Selectors to populate an SQL query that reads from the Dodeca_ Fact table.

Instead of using GROUP BY and SUM logic in the SQL query, Dodeca SQL grouping functionality drives spreadsheet grouping; SUBTOTAL cell formulas based on those grouping sections create dynamic totals.

#### 7.6.5.2 Before and After
The ranges used in an SQL View are conceptually the same as those in an Essbase View. As with the Dynamic Rowset Essbase View, the SQL View has a range that accepts SQL output, DataRange, and a range that acts as the anchor location for data inserts, StartCell. Figure 7.58 shows an SQL View template.

Relational database constructs such as connections, virtual return sets, and an SQL query are married to modified Dimension Selectors, data grouping, and spreadsheet subtotaling to return summarized and organized relational data in a spreadsheet container. No Workbook Scripts are required—the only code is the SQL query itself. Figure 7.59 shows an SQL View result.

#### 7.6.5.3 Rows, Columns, and Ranges
##### 7.6.5.3.1 Hidden Rows and Columns
In contrast to the Dynamic Rowset and even the Simple Retrieve templates, the SQL View has no hidden spreadsheet objects. Spreadsheet functionality is significantly simpler than Essbase View templates.

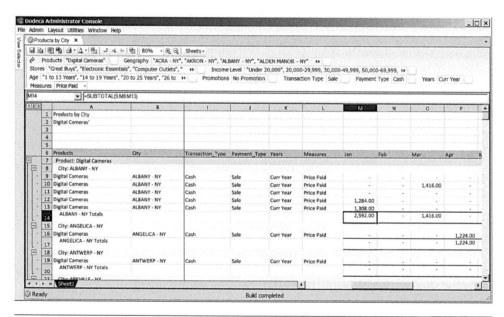

**Figure 7.58**    SQL View Template.

**Figure 7.59**    SQL View result.

The spreadsheet includes frozen panes to help manage row metadata and data, but this functionality is irrespective of the View type.

*7.6.5.3.2 The Role of Ranges*    This SQL View uses ranges (see Table 7.5) to identify the location of the range insertion, hold relational data passed as data ranges, and facilitate Product and Geography grouping.

7.6.5.3.2.1 DataRange    DataRange defines the target range of relational data. Each grouped Product and City is a separate data range that is created dynamically during the retrieval process (see Figure 7.60).

**Table 7.5**   Ranges in the SQL View

| RANGE NAME | RANGE ADDRESS |
|---|---|
| DataRange | Sheet1!$A$9:$X$10 |
| Group.Product | Sheet1!$A$7:$X$12 |
| Group.City | Sheet1!$A$8:$X$11 |
| StartCell | Sheet1!$A$13 |

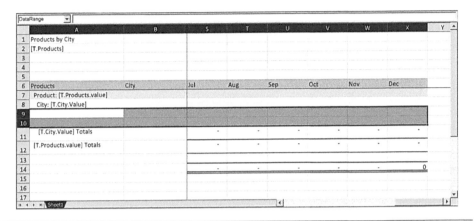

**Figure 7.60**   DataRange in SQL View.

**Table 7.6**   Range Naming Scheme in Sample SQL View

| PRODUCT | GEOGRAPHY | RANGE NAME |
|---|---|---|
| Memory | ALBANY–NY | DataRange_1.1 |
|  | ALDEN MANOR–NY | DataRange_1.2 |
|  | ANGELICA–NY | DataRange_1.3 |
| Other accessories | ALBANY–NY | DataRange_2.1 |
|  | ANGELICA–NY | DataRange_2.2 |
|  | ARKVILLE–NY | DataRange_2.3 |

The grouping process creates a two-part numbering scheme: DataRange_*Product Number.GeographyNumber.*

Using the example of two Products with each having three Geographies, the automatically created range naming scheme is shown in Table 7.6. The developer does not need to create these data ranges; I highlight them to illustrate how Dodeca programmatically generates the ranges. Figure 7.61 shows DataRange_1.1 selected.

7.6.5.3.2.2 Group.Product and Group.City   These ranges are used by Dodeca's grouping function and are removed from the retrieved spreadsheet.

The Geography (City) range is a subset of the Product range to support grouping order. Figure 7.62 shows the selected range Group.City; Group.Product starts at row 7 and ends at row 12.

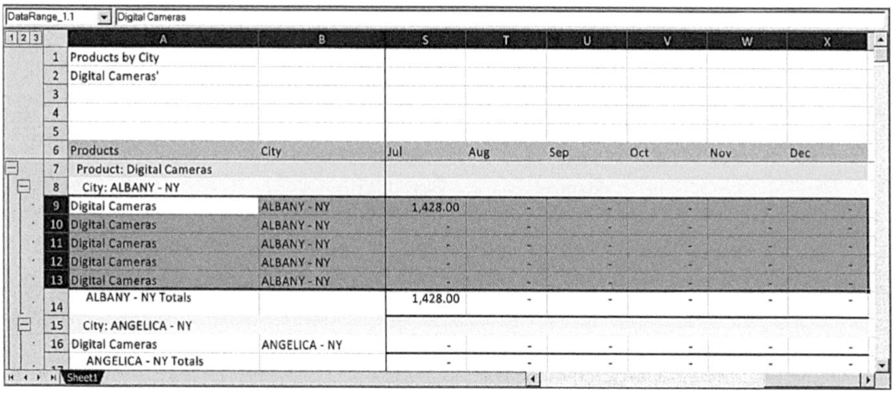

**Figure 7.61**   DataRange_1.1 selected.

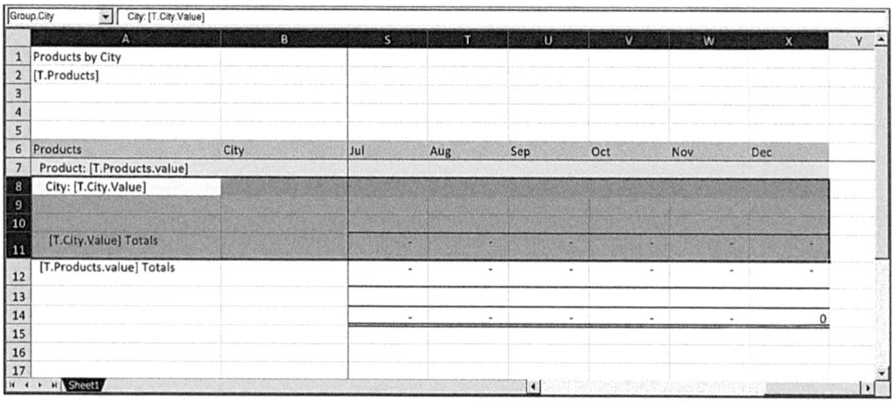

**Figure 7.62**   Group.Product and Group.City ranges.

The spreadsheet function SUBTOTAL is used to sum data within a spreadsheet group, be it Product, Geography, or the entire sheet. Dodeca's grouping function iteratively inserts Products and Geography into the target ranges. As illustrated in the Dynamic Rowset example, inserts into the ranges Group.Product and Group.City during data retrieval dynamically update the SUBTOTAL formula to reflect the correct row range.

In Figure 7.63, Rows 11, 12, and 14 show the Geography, Product, and total SUBTOTAL formulas in the template. In the retrieved View shown in Figure 7.64, rows 1290, 1291, and 1293 show the dynamically sized Geography (YULAN–NY), Product (Photo Printers), and total (Products Digital Cameras/Camcorders for all Cities in New York).

7.6.5.3.2.3 StartCell   This anchor range is the initial location of data insertion. As DataRanges are inserted above StartCell, the location for the next DataRange

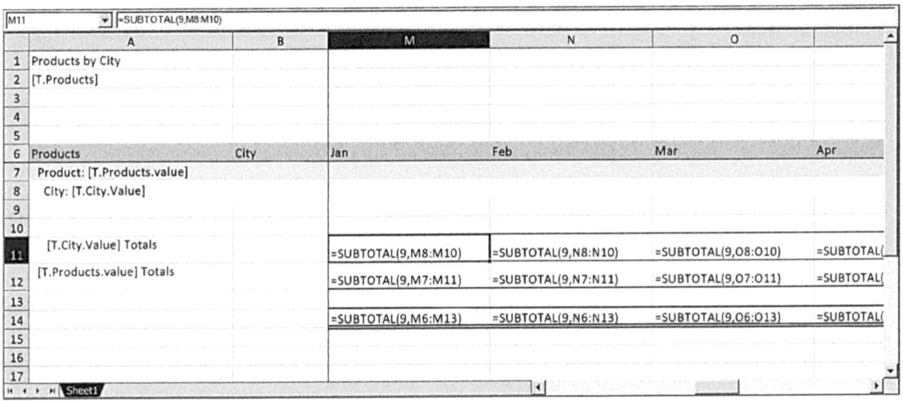

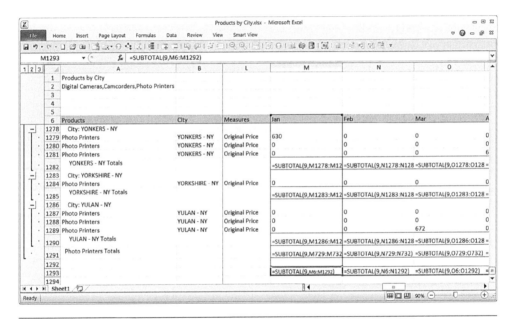

**Figure 7.63**  Use of SUBTOTAL.

**Figure 7.64**  Dynamic sizing in an SQL View.

insert is offset and the SUBTOTAL formula that sums all products and groups is dynamically expanded.

In contrast to DataRange*x_y*, StartCell is not replicated during data retrieval.

### 7.6.5.4 SQL View Terminology and Theory

*7.6.5.4.1 Terminology*   SQL Views utilize relational objects and constructs that do not apply to Essbase Views. Before discussing the theory behind SQL Views, Table 7.7 provides basic definitions of Dodeca SQL terminology.

**Table 7.7** Dodeca SQL Terminology Definitions

| TERM | DEFINITION |
|---|---|
| Query | At the core of every SQL View, an SQL query must exist. Essbase QBE queries are not possible with SQL Views. |
| SQL Connection | SQL schema/database connection information. An individual SQL connection is referred to by SQLConnectionID. |
| SQL Passthrough DataSet | Object that defines the SQL query. Each query contains both the actual SQL query and names the virtual table, known as a DataTable, that receives the results of that query. A single SQL Passthrough DataSet is referred to by SQLPassthroughDataSetID. |
| SQL Passthrough DataSet Ranges | A View property that names the target worksheet range or ranges, how the SQL data are written to the sheet, its initial start location, and whether worksheet grouping is to be used or not. A worksheet can support more than one range; each range is called a DataSet Range. |

*7.6.5.4.2 Theory*   SQL Views differ from Essbase Views in multiple ways. The following apply to SQL Views:

- At the core of the SQL View, it requires an SQL query to query, update, insert, and/or delete relational data. Again, Essbase's native QBE functionality is not available. This requirement to provide more of the logic and calculations increases the complexity of an SQL View.
- To define a relational data source, a connection to the SQL schema/database is defined via SQLConnectionID.
- The queries and virtual tables that receive the results of those queries are defined in the SQL Passthrough DataSets.
- As part of the SQL View configuration, administrators map DataTables to named ranges on the worksheet.
- SQL queries can be hardcoded or partially or fully driven by Dimension Selectors through tokenized code. SQL Views use Dimension Selectors to provide member names, be they hardcoded, sourced from Essbase Dimensions, or populated via other SQL queries to provide the values for tokenization. The administrator must code the SQL query to support Selectors that return more than one member.

SQL Passthrough DataSets contain SQL Connections. DataSet Ranges contain SQL Passthrough DataSets. The connection and data set are implicitly assigned through DataSet Ranges at the View level.

*7.6.5.4.3 Practical Application*   Using these definitions and general understanding of the way SQL Views work, the following sections show how to create an SQL-only View and how it performs. The following section on Essbase-to-SQL drill-through Views will leverage the Essbase Dynamic Rowset View and the SQL Products by City View.

| Data Warehouse | |
|---|---|
| ⊟ **Information** | |
| Description | |
| ID | Data Warehouse |
| Name | **Data Warehouse** |
| ⊟ **JDBC** | |
| ConnectionURL | jdbc:sqlserver://epm11123:DatabaseName=DEA_Dodeca:SelectMethod=cursor |
| DriverClass | com.microsoft.sqlserver.jdbc.SQLServerDriver |
| ⊟ **JNDI** | |
| DataSource | |
| ⊟ **Security** | |
| Password | •••••••• |
| UseAuthenticatedUsernameAndPassword | False |
| Username | **sa** |

**Figure 7.65**  SQL connections.

*7.6.5.5 SQL Connections*  Dodeca uses JDBC connections to connect to relational data sources. If a JDBC driver is installed and available for a given relational database, Dodeca supports the relational database.

After naming this connection "Data Warehouse," the user must name the schema or database in the ConnectionURL property. Finally, a username and password must be entered to allow seamless connections (see Figure 7.65). In contrast to Essbase data connections, SQL logins cannot be entered at runtime.

*7.6.5.6 SQL Passthrough DataSets*  The SQL Passthrough DataSet in this sample has a name and ID of Sales Details (see Figure 7.66). Somewhat confusingly, the query that is the core of this object is classified in the Misc category. It is not a miscellaneous property but instead the heart of the data set.

*7.6.5.6.1 Query*

7.6.5.6.1.1 Table Structure and Purpose  This query retrieves data from Dodeca_ Fact, a fact table that contains sales transaction history. All of the dimensions in the Dodeca.Sample Essbase database are represented.

Geography and Stores are parent/child tables that are joined against the Dodeca_ Fact table to match the data levels in Essbase.

7.6.5.6.1.2 Query Editor  Clicking on the Query definition button brings up the Query Editor dialog box (see Figure 7.67). As described in Table 7.8, this query uses three properties: SQLConnectionID, DataTableName, and SelectSQL.

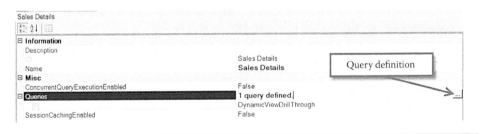

**Figure 7.66**  SQL Passthrough DataSets.

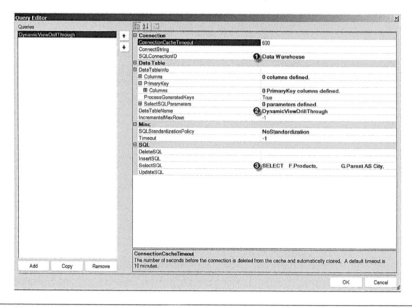

**Figure 7.67**   Query Editor.

**Table 7.8**   Query Editor Properties

| PROPERTY | VALUE | PURPOSE |
|---|---|---|
| SQLConnectionID | Data Warehouse | Database/schema SQL Connection |
| DataTableName | DynamicViewDrillThrough | Virtual table that receives query results |
| SelectSQL | See below section | Actual SQL query code. This View is read-only so only the SelectSQL property is defined |

SQL Views must have some kind of SQL query. Shown for this sample (Figure 7.68) is the Products by City View's query.

Tokens in the WHERE clause are passed from Selectors. The IN keyword allows Selector Lists that support multiple item selections to pass comma-delimited member lists; single members are also supported.

*7.6.5.7 View Definition*   Unlike the previous Essbase View examples, only two properties need to be explicitly set for this SQL View: SelectorsConfiguration and DataSetRanges (see Figure 7.69).

*7.6.5.7.1 Selectors*   The fields in the Dodeca_Fact table match the dimensions in the Dodeca.Sample Essbase database. This similarity allows existing Dimension Selectors to be used (see Figure 7.70), albeit with different Selector Lists that support multiple members per dimension, as compared with the WHERE clause that uses the IN keyword to support multiple member values.

```
SQL
Font  Courier New        ▼ 10 ▼ A⁺ A⁻

SELECT
      F.Products, G.Parent AS City, F.Geography,
      S.Parent AS Retailer , F.Stores, F.IncomeLevel,
      F.Age, F.Promotions, F.[Transaction Type] ,
      F.[Payment Type], F.Years, F.Measures,
      IsNull(F.Jan,0) AS Jan, IsNull(F.Feb,0) AS Feb, IsNull(F.Mar,0) AS Mar, IsNull(F.Apr,0)
AS Apr, IsNull(F.May,0) AS May, IsNull(F.Jun,0) AS Jun,
      IsNull(F.Jul,0) AS Jul, IsNull(F.Aug,0) AS Aug, IsNull(F.Sep,0) AS Sep, IsNull(F.Oct,0)
AS Oct, IsNull(F.Nov,0) AS Nov, IsNull(F.Dec,0) AS Dec
FROM Dodeca_Fact AS F
INNER JOIN Stores AS S
      ON S.Child = F.Stores
INNER JOIN Geography AS G
      ON G.Child = F.Geography
WHERE
      G.Parent IN ([T.Geography])
      AND S.Parent IN ([T.Stores])
      AND F.Products IN ([T.Products])
      AND F.IncomeLevel IN ([T.Income Level])
      AND F.Age IN ([T.Age])
      AND F.Promotions IN ([T.Promotions])
      AND F.[Transaction Type] IN ([T.Payment Type])
      AND F.[Payment Type] IN ([T.Transaction Type])
      AND F.Measures =  [T.Measures]
            AND F.Years = [T.Years]
ORDER BY F.Products, City, F.Geography


                                                    OK      Cancel
```

**Figure 7.68**  SQL Editor.

```
Products by City Settings
All  Required  Common | Expand All  Collapse All

⊞ Behavior
⊞ Cascade
⊞ Comments
⊞ Culture
⊞ Excel Template
⊞ Grid Properties
⊟ Selectors
  SelectorConfiguration                    10 selectors defined: Products, Geography, Stores, Income Lev
  SelectorControlDisplayMode               DockedControl
  SelectorDockedControlGroupStyle          Tabbed
  SelectorDockedControlLocation            Right
  SelectorLastUsedItemContext              BySelector
  SelectorLastUsedItemContextLabel
⊟ SQLPassthroughDataSet Ranges
  DataSetRanges                            1 DataSet range defined.
⊞ Status Information
```

**Figure 7.69**  Properties for SQL View.

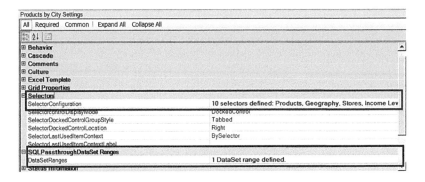

**Figure 7.70**  Using Dimension Selectors.

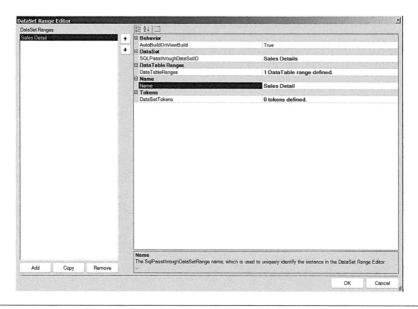

Geography_Tree_WhereInClause

| | |
|---|---|
| BaseMemberAsDescendantNode_RootNodeMemberValue | |
| BaseMemberNodePolicy | AddBaseMemberAsRootNode |
| MaxGenExpandable | 0 |
| MaxLevelSelectable | 0 |
| MemberDropContentOptions | Name, Alias, Generation, Level, IsShared |
| Prefill | False |
| RootNodeExpansionPolicy | ExpandSingleRootNode |
| | |
| DefaultSelectionString | |
| DelimitedString | Geography |
| DependentOnSelectorIDs | |
| NullLastUsedItemString | |
| NullSelectionText | Select a City |
| NullSelectionTokenValue | |
| BrowserCachingEnabled | True |
| TokenValueDelimiter | , |
| TokenValueFormat | |
| TokenValueItemEscapeSingleQuote | True |
| TokenValueItemFormat | '{0}' |
| ValidateDefaultSelection | False |

**Figure 7.71**   Geography_Tree_WhereInClause Selector List.

7.6.5.7.1.1 *Selector List*   The Dodeca_Fact table contains metadata fields that resolve to level 0 of Dodeca.Sample for all dimensions, except for Geography and Stores. In the case of those dimensions, the fact table is one level deeper than Essbase and joins to the Geography and Stores tables to select the appropriate transaction data (see Figure 7.71).

To enforce level 0 member selections, the MaxLevelSelectable property is set to 0.

Multiple selects are transformed into comma-delimited lists for the WHERE IN query clause by setting the TokenValueItemFormat string replacement token property to "{0}" and the TokenValueDelimiter property value to the comma symbol.

7.6.5.7.2 *DataSet Ranges*   Although only one DataSet Range is used in this View, multiple DataSet Ranges can be defined per View (see Figure 7.72).

**Figure 7.72**   DataSet Ranges.

**Table 7.9** DataTable Range Properties

| PROPERTY | VALUE | DESCRIPTION |
|---|---|---|
| DataSheetRangeName | DataRange | Target of DataTableName results. With grouping, the range name resolves to DataRange*x_y* on retrieval |
| DataTableName | DynamicViewDrillThrough | The DataTable Name from the Sales Details SQL Passthrough DataSet |
| SetDataFlags | InsertCells, NoColumnHeaders | Determines how data are copied to the sheet. The InsertCells setting copies the DataTableName into the DataSheetRangeName and expands the height of the data range on insert. This range expansion is how SUBTOTAL cell formulas are dynamically adjusted based on range height. NoColumnHeaders suppresses column headers from the relational retrieve |
| ExcelOutlineSummaryRowsLocation | AboveDetailRows | Locates the grouping +/– control relative to detail rows |
| GroupStartCell | StartCell | The range name that is used to anchor the outermost grouping |
| RowSortandGroupByInfoList | Defined in the next dialog box | Defines data sorting and grouping. In this sample, two levels of grouping and sorting—Product and Geography (City)—have been defined |

DataSet Ranges receive the contents of the SQL Passthrough DataSet's virtual DataTableName property and then write that information to the target sheet, sorting and grouping the data.

The SQLPassthroughDataSetID, "Sales Details," defines the DataTableName DynamicViewDrillThrough, which is visible in the DataTable Ranges property in the Query Editor screenshot (Figure 7.67).

Table 7.9 presents DataTable Range properties and Figure 7.73 shows the DataTable Range editor.

On Product and Geography (City) break, the RowSortAndGroupByInfo property sheet (see Figure 7.74) determines how the sorting and grouping are realized on the worksheet. Only the outer Product sort and group information is documented; the Geography properties are the same except for the dimension and range names. Table 7.10 presents the properties of RowSortAndGroupByInfo.

*7.6.5.7.3 Retrieval* This query returns Digital Cameras for all of the cities in New York, as shown in Figure 7.75.

Adding Camcorders and Photo Printers to the already selected Digital Cameras retrieves a larger data scope complete with individual product subtotals overall product totals (see Figure 7.76).

*7.6.5.8 Conclusion* Writing SQL Views is very much a case of defining spreadsheet ranges and then applying one SQL property after the other. The only code in this entire process is the simple SQL query.

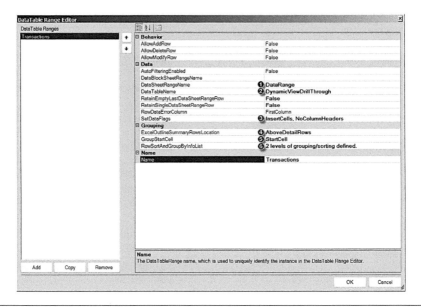

**Figure 7.73**   DataTable Range Editor.

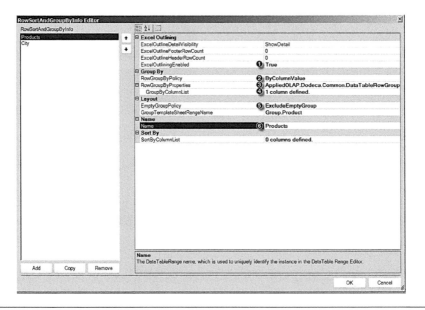

**Figure 7.74**   RowSortAndGroupByInfo Editor.

**Table 7.10** RowSortAndGroupByInfo Properties

| PROPERTY | VALUE | DESCRIPTION |
|---|---|---|
| ExcelOutliningEnabled | True | Spreadsheet outlining turned on for each group of rows |
| RowGroupByPolicy | ByColumnValue | Criteria to group data by column; column(s) defined in the GroupByColumnList |
| RowGroupByProperties | Automatically set by the RowGroupByPolicy value | Properties associated with the RowGroupByPolicy |
| GroupByColumnList | Products column with ascending sort | Row grouping and sort order. Column value combinations define group breaks on row change |
| EmptyGroupPolicy | ExcludeEmptyGroup | Exclude groups that have no data values |
| GroupTemplateSheetRangeName | Group.Product | Template range name that is copied for each group of rows |
| Name | Products | Virtual DataTable Range name for sort and group |

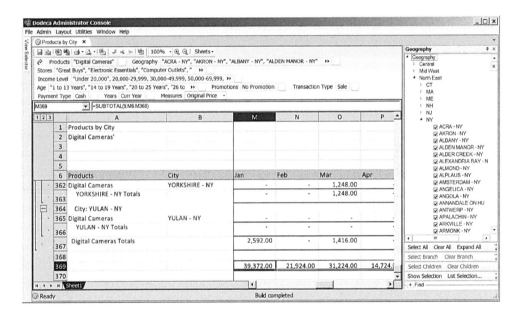

**Figure 7.75** Query retrieval in SQL View.

Is this involved process worthwhile? The answer must be yes for several reasons:

- Grouping, summing, and outlining are calculated on the client using native spreadsheet functionality.
- Dimension Selectors drive tokenized query code.
- Dimension Selectors can be populated from a variety of sources; when Essbase dimensions are used as a source of metadata, the next step of custom drill-through from Essbase to SQL is simple.
- Relational delete, insert, update, and select actions are fully supported.
- Administrator productivity is high using prebuilt Dodeca SQL functionality.
- Actual coding is quite small and is limited to the SQL query itself.

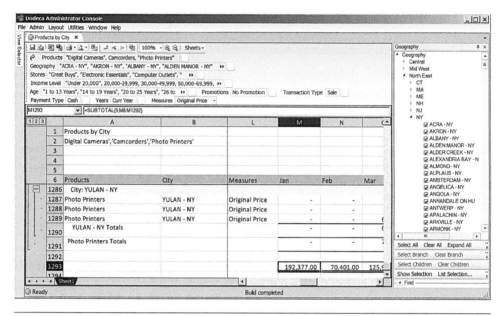

**Figure 7.76**   Query retrieval expanded.

If the proof of the pudding is in the eating, consider the amount of effort it would take to create a similar report in a tool like Excel. The beginning-to-end time of developing this in Dodeca is approximately 1 hour for a moderately skilled administrator.

### 7.6.6 Multilevel Drill-Through View

Dodeca natively supports data drill-through to SQL via Data Drillthrough View properties. Users can double-click on data cells, Dodeca will pass cell dimensional POV values to the query in the form of tokens, and the results are opened in a pre-defined SQL view like the Products by City View.

This built-in drill-through technique does not, by default, support multiple POV member selections, nor does it support upper-level member selections that dynamically select level 0 members. For example, the native functionality cannot perform a drill-through at the upper-level New York and Digital Cameras/Camcorders because it has no way of knowing that there are 385 level 0 cities and three level 0 cameras. If the SQL query can only work on level 0 members and upper-level members are passed to the query, the drill-through will fail. In common practice, users are prevented from selecting upper-level dimension members because of this inability to drill through.

The Products by City SQL View already supports multiple member selects. As explored below, Dodeca provides a way to select upper-level members and dynamically pass the level 0 descendants of those members to the tokenized SQL.

*7.6.6.1 Logic* A worksheet right-click data cell popup menu calls up the Open ViewForDataCellToolController custom tool to identify the cell dimensional context and use that tool's MemberToTokenConversionRules property to pass both level 0 and upper-level dimension member selects to the Sales Details SQL PassthroughDataSet's tokenized SQL query. That query will receive both single level 0 members and the level 0 descendants of upper-level members as tokenized metadata for WHERE IN clauses. As described in the previous use case examples, Dodeca requires little to no code to perform many advanced tasks, and this approach is no exception to that rule.

*7.6.6.2 Before and After* Figure 7.77 shows a right-click on the upper-level Product Digital Cameras/Camcorders. Note that the dimensions Age, Income Level, Stores, and Geography are also at upper levels.

*7.6.6.2.1 Template* This use case requires no new View template; it uses the existing Dynamic Rowset View as a source. SQL drill-through is that View with an additional feature: a data cell right-click menu that performs contextual drill-through to the relational source.

*7.6.6.2.2 Result* Dodeca determines and selects level 0 descendants from upper-level members (in this sample, Age, Income Level, and New York), combines them with explicitly set level 0 members (Digital Cameras, Price Paid, Sale, and No Promotion), and retrieves the combined level 0 metadata set by executing the Products by City SQL View (see Figure 7.78).

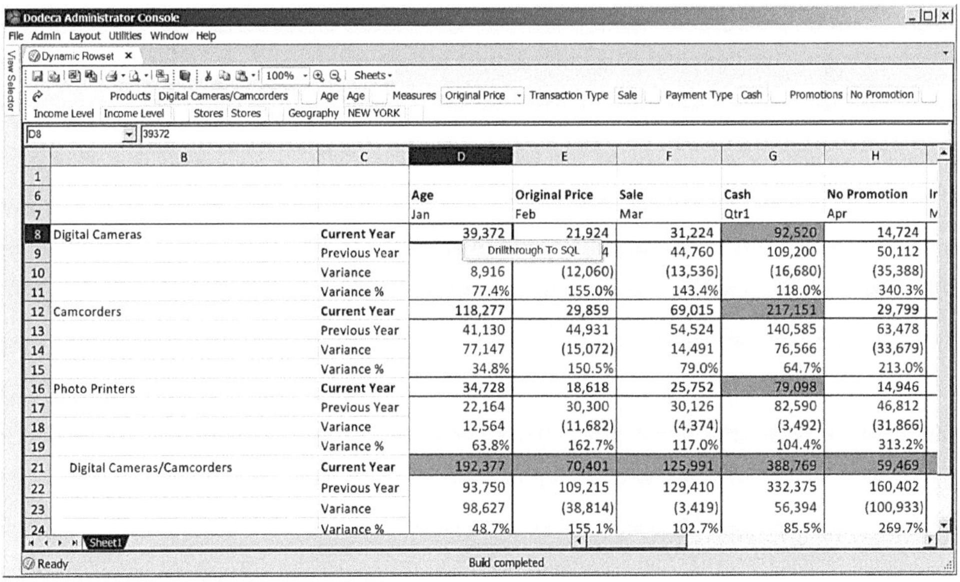

**Figure 7.77** SQL Drill-through right-click menu.

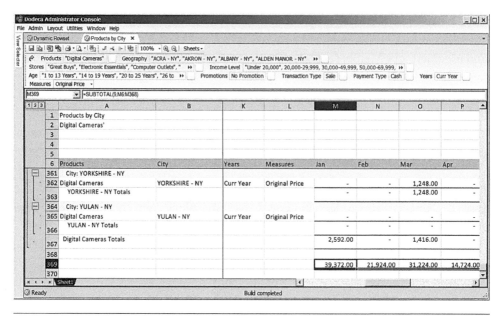

**Figure 7.78** Sample results of Mulitlevel Drill-Through View.

*7.6.6.3 When Is a Menu a Toolbar?* As you might imagine, the Dodeca developer needs to add a popup menu to the Dodeca application to perform this contextual drill-through. This is done via a Toolbar button, but that is not as crazy as it sounds. Think of Toolbar buttons as containers for actions that can be driven from a button or a menu bar element or a popup menu. For example, Microsoft Office uses buttons in place of traditional menus in its Ribbons. The button functionality in Excel's Insert Ribbon is also available via a right-click on a row or column header. The insert feature is defined once and is then accessible in multiple ways. Dodeca treats Toolbar buttons and menus the same way. See the steps for creating a popup menu in Figure 7.79.

*7.6.6.3.1 Toolbars Configuration* With the understanding that defining a menu occurs via Toolbar configuration, this example's predefined Toolbar definition is named Essbase View Standard Limited. Select it from the Toolbars Configurations Metadata Editor and click on the Toolbars Designer button.

7.6.6.3.1.1 Toolbar Designer   After clicking on the Tools tab, click on the New button and fill out the name of the popup menu. It is good practice to name the context menu with a clearly identifiable name for development; users do not see the menu name.

7.6.6.3.1.2 Popup Menu Designer   The DrillthroughToSQLContextMenu will be linked to a button that performs the drill-through. Although this example uses

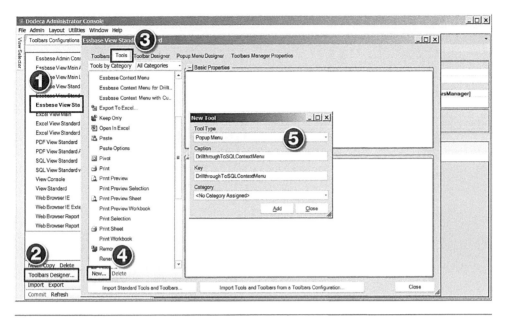

**Figure 7.79**    Steps for adding a popup menu.

a single menu button, more than one menu button could be added. The button (or menu item) will receive the logic—the menu itself has no function other than containing action buttons. So, create another new tool with the following caption and key: "Drillthrough to SQL" and "DrillthroughToSQLButton." Make sure that the Tool Type is tagged as "Button."

Switch over to the Popup Menu Designer and select the DrillthroughTo SQLContextMenu key (see Figure 7.80).

Once the popup menu is selected, drag the Drillthrough To SQL button (remember that this "button" acts as a menu item) to the DrillThroughToSQLContextMenu menu list area (Figure 7.81). At this point, close the Toolbars Designer.

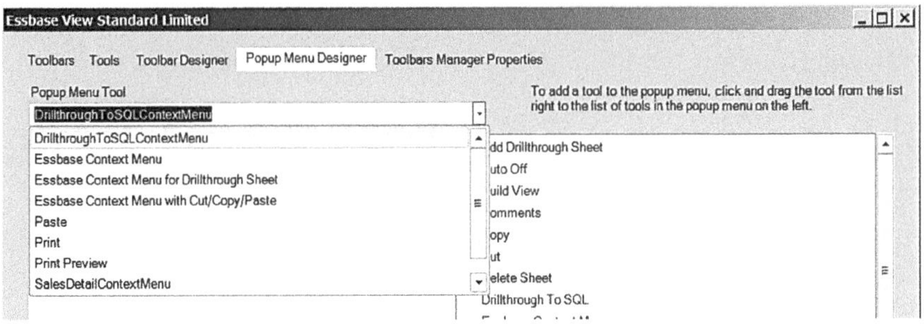

**Figure 7.80**    Popup menu designer

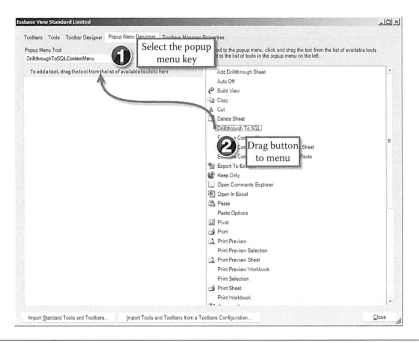

**Figure 7.81**   Moving new button to menu.

#### 7.6.6.3.2 *Configure Tools*

7.6.6.3.2.1 OpenViewForDataCellToolController   To assign actions to the button/ menu, open the Configure Tools editor, select the DrillthroughToSQLButton key, and last, select OpenViewForDataCellToolController in the Tool Controller drop-down control (see Figure 7.82).

7.6.6.3.2.2 MemberToTokenConversionRules   Click on the MemberToToken ConversionRules property, then select the Essbase Connection ID to import dimension members for token conversion (see Figure 7.83).

Add in dimensions and levels (for the purposes of this drill-through, pass level 0 or bottom-level members only) after making sure that all selections validate (see Figure 7.84).

The level 0 member set needs a target View to actually retrieve data. From the ViewID property, select the Products by City View (see Figure 7.85).

7.6.6.4 *Enabling in the View*   Once the DrillthroughToSQL button is configured, it must be enabled in the View's UI property group (Figure 7.86). The GridContextMenuID property passes cell dimension context to the DrillthroughToSQL popup menu. In turn, that menu's ViewID property opens the Products by City SQL View. Although it may seem reasonable to use the GridContextMenuIDForDrillthroughSheet property, remember that it is used for drill-through to Essbase, not SQL.

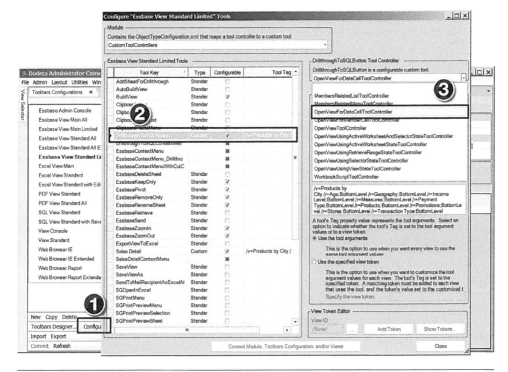

**Figure 7.82** Accessing tool controller.

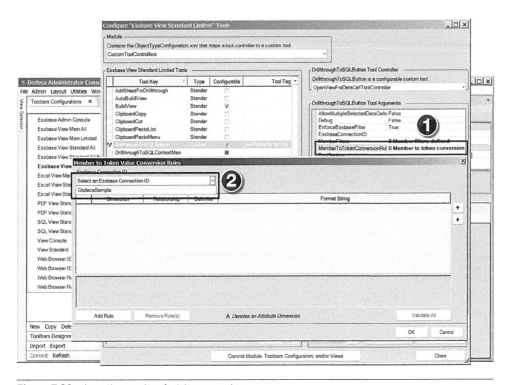

**Figure 7.83** Importing members for token conversion.

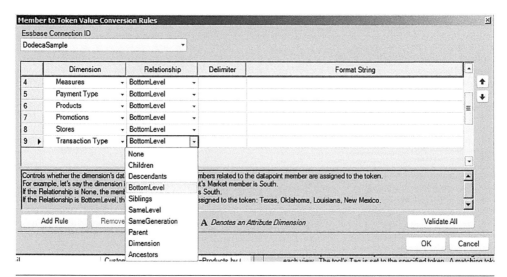

**Figure 7.84**   Adding dimensions and levels.

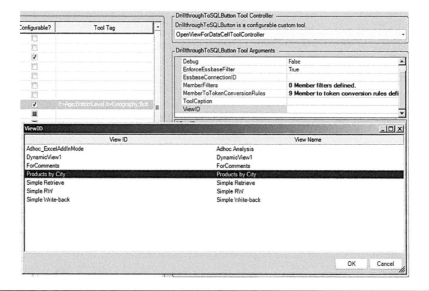

**Figure 7.85**   Setting up a target View.

*7.6.6.5 Retrieval*   Drill-through can occur at any dimension level (see Figure 7.87), whether in the POV or in the on-sheet Product dimension.

Products by City receives the dimensional context via the DrillthroughToSQL button and selects the correct level 0 members based on that selection to retrieve data below level 0 (see results in Figure 7.88).

*7.6.6.6 Conclusion*   Dodeca performs the complex process of linking Essbase and SQL Views with multilevel drill-through from Essbase to SQL in a code-free paradigm. This enhances developer productivity because the events and methods to

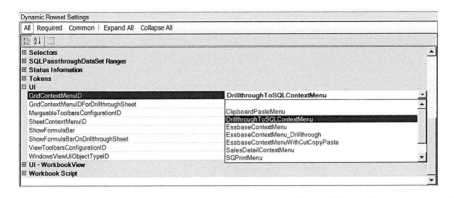

**Figure 7.86** Enabling in the View.

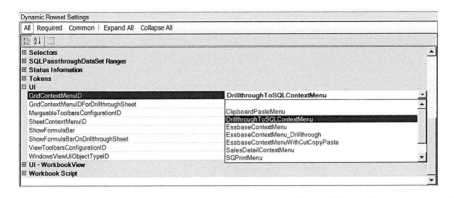

**Figure 7.87** Drill-though at another level.

perform the actions are all built in; developers join together pieces of functionality while Dodeca provides the architecture and infrastructure. The final result is sophisticated functionality.

### 7.6.7 Cell Comments

*7.6.7.1 Logic*   Essbase is a power tool for the analysis of numeric data. However, numbers alone do not fully describe data; without context, data can be difficult to understand. Text commentary can help explain data, but as noted, with the exception of text measures (which are simply popup lists), Essbase simply does not do textual data. This leaves the client layer as a place to enter commentary.

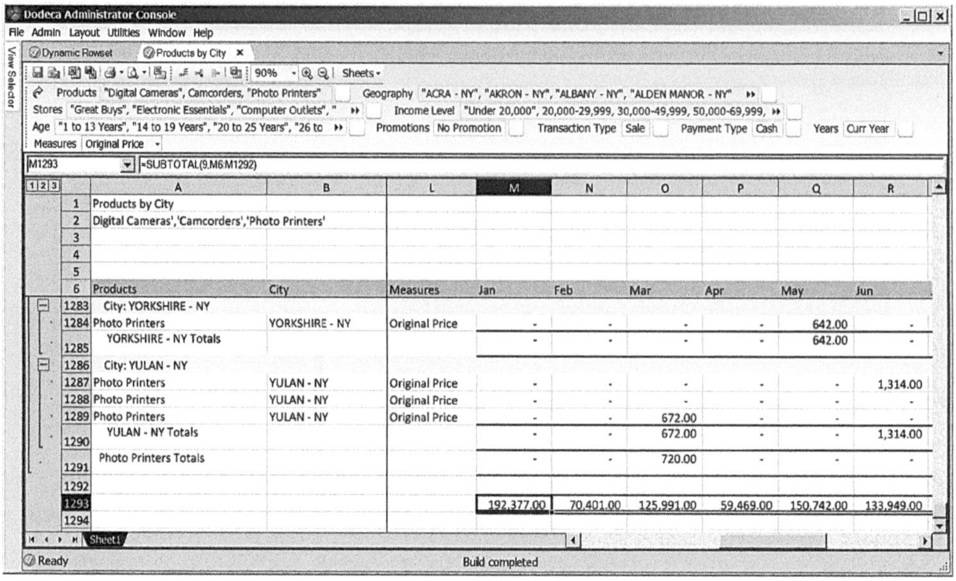

**Figure 7.88** Results of drill-through.

Excel supports text comments that are tied to individual cells. This absolute cell relationship loses relation to data through dimension pivots, member removes or adds, row and column inserts, or simple deletes. Furthermore, Excel cell comments do not show history. More than one person can modify a cell comment in a shared workbook, but there is no way to show comments in a threaded hierarchy or time/date stamp the comments.

Dodeca supports text commentary as part of its core functionality with relationally stored comments, a hierarchical comment thread interface, and user name and time/date stamping. Comments are tied to dimensional intersections, not cell addresses. In short, it is Essbase text commentary done right.

*7.6.7.2 Before and After* Text commentary requires no new ranges or additions to the sheet but instead displays comments in a hierarchical explorer pane. Figure 7.89 shows cell D8 selected after the Open Comments Explorer toolbar has been pressed.

In Figure 7.90 is cell D8's commentary with question and response.

*7.6.7.3 Enabling Comments*

*7.6.7.3.1 Adding the Button* Dodeca's Comment Explorer is a prebuilt Toolbar button. Enabling it in Dodeca requires import of a standard Tool.

As with the Multilevel Drillthrough example, this additional functionality is enabled in Dodeca by adding a new Toolbar button. Unlike the SQL drill-through example, this time, it really will be a button on a Toolbar. Keep in mind that commentary could be triggered by a popup menu if so desired.

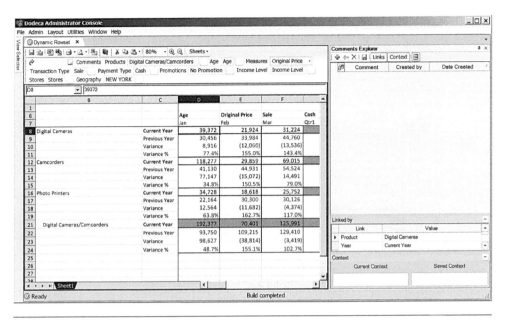

**Figure 7.89**   Cell selected for comments.

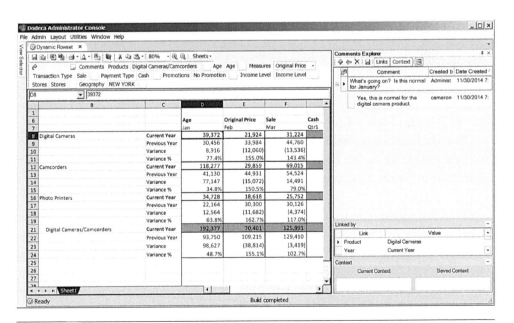

**Figure 7.90**   Cell comments.

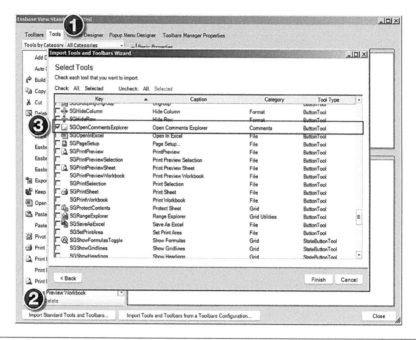

**Figure 7.91**    Bringing in Comment Explorer.

To bring the Comment Explorer into Dodeca, once in the Toolbars Designer, select the Tools menu, click on the Import Standard Tools and Toolbars button, and navigate to the Select Tools screen (you will page through Select Toolbars and Select Popup Menu Tools) to select the SGOpenCommentsExplorer Tool (see Figure 7.91).

Once the predefined button is imported, you will see the comment Tool in the Tools list. The default name is perfectly acceptable but will take up valuable toolbar real estate; rename it to "Comments" (Figure 7.92).

At this point, the button exists but needs to be added to a toolbar. Navigate to the Tools Designer menu, select the Toolbar (any Toolbar is valid, the Essbase Toolbar was selected for this example), and drag and drop the Comments button to that toolbar (see Figure 7.93).

Once the button is added to the Toolbar, the user can change the order of buttons and add groupings to the Toolbar. As shown by the list of the buttons in the right-hand pane in Figure 7.94, any number of default buttons could also be added.

*7.6.7.3.2 Enabling Comments in the View*   Using the existing Dynamic Rowset View, navigate to the Comments section of the View's properties, set the Allow CommentsExplorer to TRUE, and (optional) set the date/time and last username settings to FALSE. How much information the Comments Explorer displays is up to you, but keep in mind screen real estate.

The real heart of enabling Comments in a View is in the CommentRanges property, which brings up the Comment Range Configuration Ranges Editor (see Figure 7.95).

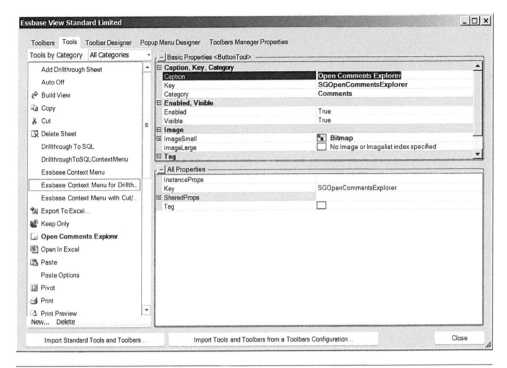

**Figure 7.92**    Creating Comments button.

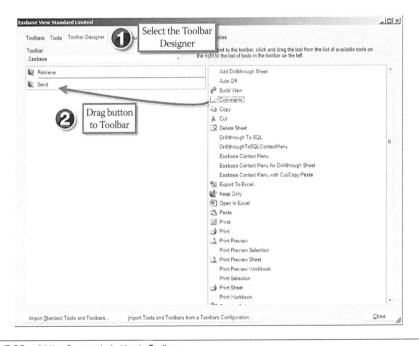

**Figure 7.93**    Adding Comments button to Toolbar.

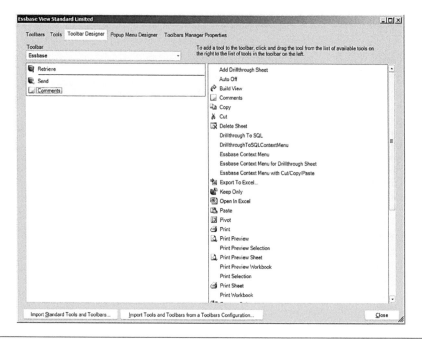

**Figure 7.94**   Toolbar button list.

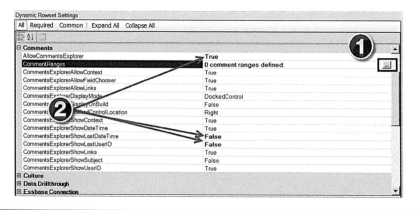

**Figure 7.95**   Enabling comments.

7.6.7.3.2.1 Linking Comments   In the Comment Range Configuration Ranges Editor, the Linking section's settings determine the comment ranges, the comment location rule, and comment dimensional intersection (see Figure 7.96).

A. Address comment range

The Address property defines allowed comments location. As documented in the Simple Retrieve View example, Dodeca automatically creates range names for internal processing on retrieval. Data comments make sense only when data exist. Although comments can go anywhere in Ess.DataRange.1, for the purposes of this example, comments are allowed only in editable data

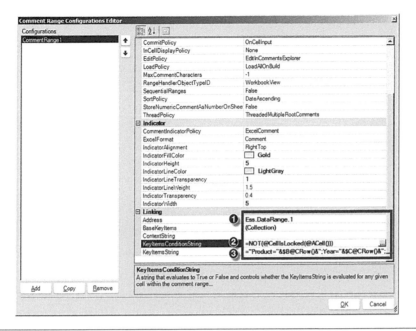

**Figure 7.96** Linking comments.

ranges. Referring again to the Simple Retrieve example, the spreadsheet template locks all cells but Current Year.

B. Restricting comments via KeyItemsConditionString

For the purposes of this use case, comments are restricted to Current Year cells. Testing for unlocked spreadsheets will identify allowed comment cells. Dodeca formulas are a combination of spreadsheet formula syntax and Dodeca functions, even when they are not directly on a spreadsheet template, e.g., the =NOT(*condition*) grammar. Note that Dodeca functions are resolved first, followed by the Excel formula.

**Locked Cell:** A TRUE or FALSE value determines if the KeyItemsCondition String allows commentary. The CellIsLocked function will return a TRUE if the cell is locked, so the NOT function is used to flip that to the required FALSE, and vice versa.

Formula:

```
=NOT(@CellIsLocked(@ACell()))
```

**Function name:** ActiveCell
**Usage:** @ACell()
**Description:** Returns the address of the active cell
**Function name:** CellIsLocked
**Usage:** @CellIsLocked([<Address>])

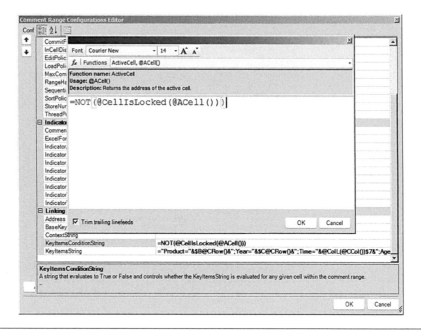

**Figure 7.97**　Locked cell formula in Dodeca.

**Description:** Returns TRUE or FALSE based on whether the cells in the specified range are locked.

**Parameters:** Address: Optional (defaults to the selected cell); the address of the cell to test.

Figure 7.97 shows the formula in Dodeca.

C. The KeyItemsString

To store comments, Dodeca needs to know the dimension intersection of the data comment. This is the same requirement Essbase has to serve up a data value, and it is described by the on-sheet dimensionality. If every dimension is represented on the sheet (and they must be), then a spreadsheet formula can read those members to define the data cell key. A combination of spreadsheet formula syntax and Dodeca functions generates a unique relational comment key on a cell-by-cell basis in a key–value pair. Dodeca stores the key–value pair as a semicolon-delimited list of dimensions and member names in the following format: DimensionName1=MemberName1;DimensionName2= MemberName2;DimensionName*X*=MemberName*X*;

The comment key definition for cell D8 is in three parts: POV, Column, and Row.

**POV:** The POV formula comes from row 6 columns D through T:

Formula:

```
="Age="&$D$6&";Price="&$E$6&";Sale="&$F$6&";Payment Type="&$G$6&";
Promotion="&$H$6&";Income Level="&$I$6&";Stores="&J6&";Geography="
&$K$6&";"
```

Result:

Age=Teens;Price=Price Paid;Sale=Sale;Payment Type=Cash;Promotion=Promo
  tions;Income Level=Income Level;Stores=Brick & Mortar;Geography=North
  East;

**Column:** The Time dimension is stored in row 7, columns D through T.

Formula:

```
="Time="&$D$7&";"
```

Result:

Time=Jan;

**Row:** The row dimensions are in row 8, columns B and C.

Formula:

```
="Product="&$B$8&";Year="&$C$8&";"
```

Result:

Product=Digital Cameras;Year=Current Year;

**Full Key**

Formula:

```
="Product="&$B$8&";Year="&$C$8&";"&"Time="&$D$7&";"&"Age="&$D$6&";
Price="&$E$6&";Sale="&$F$6&";Payment Type="&$G$6&";Promotion=
"&$H$6&";Income Level="&$I$6&";Stores="&J6&";Geography="&$K$6&";"
```

Result:

Product=Digital    Cameras;Year=Current    Year;Time=Jan;Age=Teens;Price=Price
  Paid;Sale=Sale;Payment    Type=Cash;Promotion=Promotions;Income    Level=
  Income Level;Stores=Brick & Mortar;Geography=North East;

a.  Dynamic Functions

  This result accurately defines the key for the cell D8 but cannot be used
  for any other cell. To make this cell formula dynamic, substitute hard-
  coded row and column references with Dodeca's formula functions to create this cell key formula:

```
="Product="&$B@CRow()&";Year="&$C@CRow()&";Time="&@ColL(@CCol())$7&
";Age="&$D$6&";Price="&$E$6&";Sale="&$F$6&";Payment Type="&$G$6&";
Promotion="&$H$6&";Income Level="&$I$6&";Stores="&J6&";Geography="
&$K$6&";"
```

  Three functions dynamically value POV, row, and column: CurrentRow,
  CurrentColumn, and ColumnLetter.

**Function name:** CurrentRow

**Usage:** @CRow()

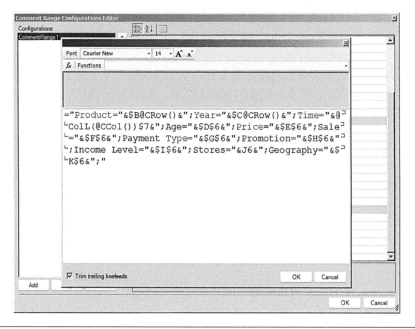

**Figure 7.98** Spreadsheet formula in Dodeca.

**Description:** Returns the number of the current row

**Function name:** CurrentColumn

**Usage:** @CCol()

**Description:** Returns the number of the current column

**Function name:** ColumnLetter

**Usage:** @ColL(<ColumnNumber>)

**Description:** Returns the Alphabetic representation of the specified column number

**Parameters:** ColumnNumber: The number of the column. 1=A, 2=B, 3=C, etc.

Note that ColumnLetter uses CurrentColumn to return an alpha value from a numeric column number for the purposes of creating a spreadsheet formula. Figure 7.98 shows the formula in Dodeca. Note the string and function keyword color coding.

*7.6.7.4 Result*   Once the View's Comments properties have been committed, the comments explorer is enabled by selecting a writable cell and clicking on the Comments toolbar button (see Figure 7.99).

*7.6.7.5 Conclusion*   Enabling commentary in Dodeca is as simple as importing a predefined button onto a toolbar and defining a comment range. View properties define how comments are displayed. Locating allowed comment ranges requires three properties, two of which are simple formulas. Configuration steps with no code, other

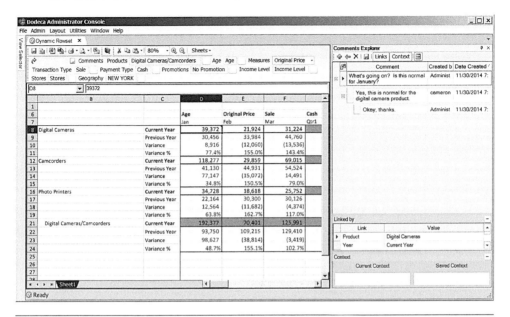

**Figure 7.99**   Enabling the Comments Explorer.

than formulas, enable relationally stored comments with usernames, date/time stamps, member combination links, and much more. Dodeca comments bring context to Essbase data and are another example of advanced functionality that is largely code free.

**Note:** The comments are not tied to the dimension intersections, the View or the sheet cell; other Views can display the comments.

## 7.7  Conclusion

This chapter is just barely an adequate introduction to Dodeca. If space and time allowed, all of this book could be about Dodeca, although the title would require a change. Essbase developers who have a chance to see Dodeca's power up close invariably become evangelists. As you might guess, I am one of those Essbase developers, and yes, I am a huge fan of the product. I was around at the very beginning of Essbase—in 1994, I had an Essbase 3.1 server under my desk—and I recall Essbase engendering the same kind of excitement and grassroots advocacy. That early passion was the foundation for Essbase's analytical database leadership today. I expect Dodeca to follow the same product trajectory.

Geeks are suspicious of product hyperbole and pressure that we hear and read in the computer press, from sales representatives, and from internal IT departments. Dodeca's managed spreadsheets cut through the noise by delivering on its promise of enhancing Essbase for both developers and the people who analyze Essbase data.

Dodeca's architecture is defined simply and logically on the server by web applications serving Essbase and relational data sources. The web application architecture and Java core mean that Dodeca runs on a wide variety of web application servers and ties to any relational database product that has a JDBC driver. The fat client, often viewed as a negative attribute, removes reliance on limited web technologies while enabling Dodeca's rich client feature set; Microsoft's ClickOnce distribution technology installs Dodeca on desktops automatically and without IT department resources.

The Dodeca rich client is simultaneously the user and administrator tool. A parameter in the web URL switches between user and administrator tool. All development work takes place in the administrator mode through special menus; the core interface to Views remains the same, ensuring consistency between developers and users.

Dodeca administration simplicity belies its sophistication. Migration and backup tools, full user provisioning and administration, centrally stored document repository, and integration with Essbase provisioning in Oracle Hyperion Shared Services are all part and parcel of the administration feature set. Dodeca is a mature product, ready for incorporation into corporate IT environments.

Developing in Dodeca has been the main focus of this chapter. The key to "writing" Dodeca code is the interplay between spreadsheets and Dodeca object properties. Dodeca property sheets, Excel formulas and worksheet concepts, SQL, and Workbook Scripts extend functionality beyond the core Essbase feature set. There really is nothing like this kind of development environment because it requires a conceptual leap on the part of the developer from standard procedural code, event driven or not, to Dodeca's paradigm. That change in mindset and approach grants the developer a high level of productivity because so much of what would normally require extensive procedural code is inherent in Dodeca's prebuilt objects.

Architecture, administration, and development elegance and simplicity are irrelevant to the user; their concern is their Essbase productivity. Dodeca delivers on this by combining the rich functionality of spreadsheets and the analytic and calculation power of Essbase.

Dodeca is an awesome Essbase tool because of its power: power that enables complex features and functionality, power that affords incredibly quick and simple development, power that leverages the familiar strengths of spreadsheets, power that manages those complex spreadsheets for data consistency, power that highlights the abilities of Essbase like no other tool. In my opinion, no other product combines these features in such a versatile and flexible way. Administrators, developers, and users love Dodeca because it lets them do their jobs better and faster.

## Copyright Notice Information

Dodeca is a registered trademark of Applied OLAP, Inc., and is used with permission.

## Acknowledgments

I am a huge fan of Applied OLAP's Dodeca; this chapter would not have been possible without my mentor (although he may not realize it) and friend Tim Tow's support, Billy Booth for his tireless editing to make sure I actually got the technical details and terminology right, Kevin deJesus for helping me build the examples you see in this chapter, and Derek Hill and Jay Zuercher for performing a rock-solid Dodeca install on this infrastructure-challenged author's VM. Lauren Prezby's fantastic artwork brings color and artistic flair to what otherwise would be a drab and colorless chapter.

# Smart View Your Way

## William Hodges

**Contents**

## 8.1 Introduction

An application is a new solution to a problem or requirement. But a feature that is already an integral part of a commercial software product is not an application. "Is that available out of the box?" is a common question heard during reviews of Hyperion Enterprise Performance Management (EPM) functionality, and a positive answer is welcomed. Implicit in this answer is the assertion that you will not need to think "out of the box" to derive the benefit of the feature. But the word *solution* implies a certain amount of "out-of-the-box" thinking. It is fair to ponder the possibility that the more out-of-the-box thinking is applied to a problem, the better the solution will be. Clearly, we are dealing here with two competing interpretations of the expression "out of the box."

This chapter is about Oracle Smart View, the default Essbase user interface, which can also interact with other software products. For many users, Essbase and Smart View are components of a larger solution combining a variety of technologies, in particular Hyperion Planning, Hyperion Financial Management (HFM), and Essbase. This chapter looks exclusively at the relationship between Smart View and Essbase, excluding from the discussion interactions between Smart View and other software products.

Even a brief observation of the Hyperion EPM solution development landscape will make evident the fact that entire careers can be built around perfecting the implementation of out-of-the-box functionality. Sooner than we might think, software will be 100 years old. The software of today is not what it was only a few years ago. Complexity has been reduced through componentization, allowing even more complexity, sophistication, and feature richness, and the Hyperion EPM software suite is a good example of this.

We value product expertise. Therefore, this chapter includes brief reviews of lesser-known and/or not completely intuitive features. We present these as part of a discussion of the development of features not available out of the box, the idea of which required a certain amount of out-of-the-box thinking, all in the hope of providing a foundation or a motivation for your own out-of-the-box exploration of new and original solutions.

### 8.1.1 What This Chapter Is Not

This chapter is not an exhaustive overview of all—or even some—of the out-of-the-box features available in Oracle Smart View. Rather, it is about thinking outside the box to improve the data gathering and analysis experience of everyday data analysts, by adding a few missing features and/or combining existing features in novel ways as effortlessly as possible, and to give you fodder for thought about design philosophy. Maybe someday, the features and approaches we propose will appear in the product as standard features, and the solutions presented here will no longer be necessary, but the experience initiated here will remain to guide and inform future solution explorations and designs. The chapter's first five sections are intended to build a context and a foundation for Section 8.6, MDX Editor SV 1.0.

Smart View is, as its name suggests, a better way to view data. It is also a means to input data into an information system and it can be used as an interface for the execution of data processing on a variety of external sources. But it is mostly and foremost a means to get data, do local manipulations, and present results in an interactive manner. The resulting data can be formatted in this medium. This chapter focuses exclusively on the data collection function and on improving the current standards regarding the utilization of this Oracle product to get and analyze data sourced from an Essbase cube.

This chapter is not primarily about Visual Basic for Applications (VBA) or even about the Microsoft Office ribbon, although necessarily much of the discussion involves these subjects. Given this approach, we have intentionally avoided certain details and concepts that would have to be included in a complete implementation of most of the ideas here discussed. The most obvious example of this is error handling.*

I regularly use the proposed solutions to complement what the product provides out of the box. I have found them helpful enough to merit spending time perfecting them. I hope they are helpful for you, at the very least as a foundation for further investigation and solution development.

### 8.1.2 What This Chapter Is

This chapter is a direct continuation of a theme launched by Robb Salzmann in Volume 1, Chapter 10 of this book series (Salzmann 2012). It is also a continuation of Gary Crisci's chapter in that it provides an approach for mastering multidimensional expression (MDX), from both a semantic and a syntactic perspective (Crisci 2012). The main objective of this chapter is to encourage you, the reader, to take advantage of opportunities to enhance the already excellent data gathering and data manipulation functionality of Smart View and to do it strategically for the sake of your own lasting productivity and a high rate of return on your investment. We hope that you will implement them and use this chapter's variety of sample solutions. But mostly, we hope they will trigger new ideas and opportunities that you will evolve into your own original solutions. Some of the simple but effective tools I have developed for my own use could not be discussed here because they address requirements too intrinsic to what I do. They have undoubtedly increased my productivity. I suspect the same could be said about tasks unique to your own situation. As the subject matter becomes daily routine, justifying investments of time and money toward higher levels of automation will be easier.

---

* There are multiple possible approaches for error handling. For example, Salzmann (2012, Section 10.4.13) proposes a treatment of error messages tailor-made for Smart View. Other more generic approaches can be found in VBA programming publications. Rather than prompt a discussion or questions about how to do error handling, this being a VBA topic rather than a Smart View topic, and because error handling takes up space and can be a distraction while reading code, we have intentionally excluded it. It remains essential to include some form of error handling in your implementations.

The specific code examples discussed (including Section 8.6) all belong to the category of personal tools, as opposed to the category of solutions for other users or clients. We believe that personal experience with code and productivity improvement will best prepare you to include similar ideas in applications written for others and that, in the end, what you develop for them will differ from what is illustrated here.

### 8.1.3 What We Must Assume You Already Know

Observing the evolution of a new Essbase and Smart View user is fascinating, from the blind stare at the beginning to the swift flying through all the menu options, zooming in and out, pivoting, etc., faster than anyone looking over their shoulder could begin to follow or comprehend. If the user was already an Excel power user, the contrast is accentuated by the combinations of Excel and Smart View actions they are able to perform. If you are reading this book, you are likely such a user and/or you manage or provide support to users who have reached this level of proficiency. So why continue to read? Simply (a) because there is still room for improvement, (b) because you may be working too hard, (c) because some of the advanced features we discuss you may not have considered, (d) because users need a clear idea of what functionality is already available in Smart View before undertaking any form of customization, and finally, (e) because some customization, if done right, can take any Smart View user to much higher levels of productivity without extensive effort.

### 8.1.4 Features to Consider and Compare

From the perspective of a user, Smart View is a WYSIWYG or a Query by Example data analysis and reporting environment. These designators are not as widely used today as they were in years past because they are so much an integral part of how we now interact with computers—in particular with Essbase through Smart View—that mentioning them would be redundant.

Under the surface and from a more technical point of view, Smart View can be considered to be an MDX query builder (Lackpour 2013).* Do you believe Smart View can build every possible MDX query you might ever need to get at the data you require? The most likely answer is no, but some readers might propose a yes answer

---

* Not everything Smart View does is query a database; therefore, it needs communication protocols that do more than asking for data. Notice, though, as Lackpour sufficiently clearly discovered, in those instances where the task at hand is strictly data collection, Smart View generates MDX code. What is important in this chapter is not whether Smart View uses MDX exclusively to communicate with Essbase (we know it does not) but whether MDX encapsulates better than other task definition languages the semantics needed to effectively communicate with an OLAP data provider for the purpose of asking for data (as opposed to, for example, launch a calculation or submit data). Since, from our perspective, it does, then we propose that, rather than trying to avoid at all costs to know anything about MDX, we try to find ways to as effortlessly as possible understand and utilize MDX.

and mention a new feature called Smart Queries. This chapter will show that even this very powerful Smart View tool has limitations. So, if the overall answer is no, we hope you will agree that data analysts (not computer programmers) should, at the very least, know something about borrowing, building, and/or executing MDX queries to be able to compensate for what Smart View, Query Designer, and Smart Query cannot do on their own, especially if tools exist that facilitate and guide the effort.

Section 8.6 of this chapter develops a methodology for building, executing, and saving MDX queries. All the other sections are a preparation and a context for what is discussed in Section 8.6. Ultimately, data analysts need to have at their disposal a sufficient inventory of easy and reliable paths to meaningful data. This chapter is an effort to cover as many angles as possible to make this possible. With this objective and as a preparation for Section 8.6 (which describes how easy it is to build an MDX editor), this chapter includes a quick review of Smart Slices, Smart Queries, Query Designer, cell functions, importing Workspace documents, drilling down by Formula, Dynamic Aggregation, and submitting MDX queries via the Smart View ribbon—all standard, out-of-the-box Smart View features.

### 8.1.5 Ways of Getting at the Data

Figure 8.1 is a graphical review of different ways an analyst may put together a data set for analysis in Excel. We will assume that you use most of the listed methods at least occasionally. Report scripts are less relevant today than when the Excel Add-in was still the preferred querying tool and report scripts could be executed directly in Excel (and because it was possible to build report scripts interactively using Essbase Query Designer). This no longer being the case, we only mention them as an option (which I still find more useful than the others sometimes).

Section 8.6 proposes the construction of a component-based MDX Editor to replace or supersede some of the options shown in Figure 8.2.

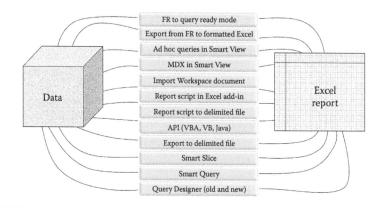

**Figure 8.1**   Ways to deposit Essbase data onto an Excel worksheet.

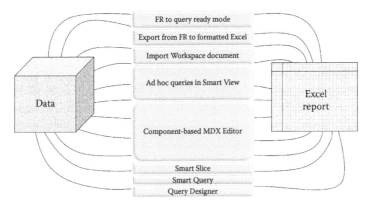

**Figure 8.2** The MDX Editor's role in your toolset.

### 8.1.6 Customization Is Risky Business

In the present context, customization means any form of scripting or coding beyond what is normally expected in any Hyperion EPM implementation, something that a new system administrator would not already expect to find and be ready to maintain. As discussed earlier, the Hyperion EPM suite has enough functionality to keep solution builders occupied for a long time and is equipped to satisfy most requirements presented to them. The risk we refer to here is the hidden cost or vulnerability that we do not consider when we focus exclusively on the intended short-term benefit. What, then, do you do when you know you can improve a solution but only through some form of customization? Our recommendation is to go for it but use caution when developing any type of customization. Build functionality that makes the solution much better while remaining as unessential and as simple as possible (unless customization is your specialty and stock in trade).* We believe Section 8.6 of this chapter complies with this requirement.

### 8.1.7 SmartView.bas

The solutions proposed in this chapter make use of a software component (formerly Spreadsheet Toolkit) that, for many years, required special licensing. Fortunately, this is no longer the case. The solutions in this chapter will require learning and using only about 5% of the functions available in SmartView.bas, meaning a user can accomplish a lot with a very small investment (see highlighted items in Figure 8.20).

---

* Building nonessential customization is a good thing and a best practice in the following sense: You do not want to be so dependent on custom code that an entire solution will be rendered useless if the code stops working for any reason and it is your sole responsibility to fix it. This is similar to saying that a surgeon who specializes in the use of computerized surgical tools should preferably also remain capable of operating without them. It would be very sad to lose a patient just because the tools are not functional or unavailable at a critical moment.

## 8.2 Background

You may by now be anxious to start coding. What follows in this section is theory, so if you skip it, please remember to come back to it later. It has been the guiding light for this entire chapter and I do not exaggerate in saying that without it, the chapter either would never have been written or would have been totally different.

### 8.2.1 History

The very first time I worked with Essbase, using the standard user environment available at the time (the Essbase Add-in), I quickly became disappointed and frustrated. I expected to find an appealing and self-explanatory interface, tightly integrated with the database, with direct access to a working environment where I could build calculation models—essentially an intuitive, monolithic product that would somehow guide me through the process of getting to the data and manipulating it so I could quickly find or produce the results I needed. Instead, all I found was the same, familiar worksheet program and nothing that would immediately suggest what I should do next. I felt cheated.

Today, I think the original developers were geniuses. I do not know if they were guided by academic research findings and recommendations, or if they knew such research had been in existence for more than 10 years. But the very same design principles I was teaching in a vacuum as a part of a university degree program are what allowed me to quickly understand how misplaced my expectations were. Today, I consider the progenitor of Essbase, Arbor Software, very wise in their decision not to build a user interface. It was, in fact, a direct application of sound design principles.

### 8.2.2 Design Principles

Doing Smart View "your way" does not mean doing it alone. Although most Essbase developers may intuitively apply good design principles, the EPM application development field has evolved in a pragmatic and opportunistic way. To justify this paragraph's first assertion, I will relate what EPM developers do to what theorists were recommending as far back as the 1970s. This will help explain what Essbase developers do and why, and we can proceed with the confidence that comes from knowing that we are following research-supported design principles.

Decision support and performance management are not transactional applications. They are not like payroll processing applications, for example. They must be in constant evolution and adaptation because decision environments are in constant evolution and adaptation. Technology is also in constant evolution and adaptation, so integrating these improvements as soon as they become available is vital for decision support and performance management. Solution development strategies must anticipate and prepare for change. One strategy to deal with change, first proposed in the late 1970s, was to recognize three levels of technology (tools, generators, applications) and five participant roles (tool smith, technical supporter, solution builder, designer, and manager/user) (Sprague and Carlson 1982). According to that research-supported proposal, rather than building applications from scratch, the community responsible for the implementation of decision support should push for the development of application development platforms consisting of a strategic combination of tools. This research characterized these platforms as "generators" and proposed an architecture consisting of three subsystems: a data management system, a model management system, and a dialog management system. Essbase can be considered a generator because it combines the management of data (with loading and unloading mechanisms), the management of models (combinations of calculations and formulas acting as a unified solution), and the management of user–computer interaction: an Excel add-in. Implicit in Arbor's decision not to build a custom interface was the integration into their own solution of the entire future evolution and feature richness of Excel.

The success of our applications, particularly our user interfaces built with Smart View, will correlate to our ability to build reusable and expandable modules.

### 8.2.3 A Guide to Oracle Smart View Documentation

Company websites change through time. Oracle has recently focused on facilitating access to information and software, and improvements such as the Oracle Help Center will surely continue.* Essbase (and Smart View) is listed under "Database." The links lead directly to the documentation on the latest release. Given the high degree of backward compatibility built into Smart View, getting the latest information (and the latest version of the software) will serve you well in most circumstances and will keep you informed of what is available if you cannot install the latest version right away. The documentation is a collection of documents for different audiences, and it typically includes a history of recent version changes, fixes, and known issues. Smart View version numbers run ahead of Essbase version numbers and are no longer tied to Essbase software version numbers because of its multiclient nature. The solutions discussed in this chapter were tested with the latest available version of Smart View at the time: Oracle Smart View for Office, Release 11.1.2.5.210.

### 8.3 Going Beyond the Everyday to Extract Value from Our Data

Section 8.1 was an invitation to explore solutions that extend the out-of-the-box capabilities of the Hyperion EPM suite. Section 8.2 gave reasons to believe that successful customization is possible. In this section, we explore opportunities within the data analysis area. We first look critically at some advanced data querying features to

---

* http://docs.oracle.com.

determine their usefulness and limitations, based on a collection of typical reporting requirements. Then, we consider ways to use the VBA SmartView.bas programming interface to extend the capabilities of the available features.*

### 8.3.1 Ad hoc Analysis Is Still the Overall Latest and Greatest Solution

Nothing proposed in this document can compete with out-of-the-box Smart View in overall value delivery. "Slicing-and-dicing" would be just a slogan if this were not true. Thinking with the data and having a dialog with the data imply a certain back and forth that is contrary to what tools like Smart View, Query Designer, Smart Query, or MDX Editor SV 1.0 (described in Section 8.6) have been built to do for you. That standard Smart View is superior to all is so obvious, I state it only because going beyond the everyday with Smart View implies bypassing or ignoring methods of inquiry available in ad hoc Smart View. Think of the product of this chapter not as a way of rejecting Smart View but as a complement to its native functionality.

We already have made the assumption that you are an accomplished Smart View user (see Section 8.1.3). You know how quickly slicing and dicing can get old once all the learning has taken place and you just want to get to the data. Consider the number of clicks it takes a super user to execute a complex ad hoc data drill in Smart View and compare that to a single click to run a well-designed predefined query.

### 8.3.2 MDX: The Litmus Test and the Judge

If MDX is the de facto standard for communicating with OLAP databases in general and Oracle Essbase in particular, then it is reasonable to use it as a litmus test for other ways of getting at data and to use its capabilities as our list of requirements for any point-and-click solution. Furthermore, anything we can do to make MDX more accessible to data analysts is an opportunity to enhance the capabilities of our existing environments. Table 8.1 shows a preview of features available in MDX but not in Smart View or any of its accessory tools such as Smart Slices, Smart Query, and Query Designer.

### 8.3.3 The Status Quo

So you and/or your users have reached the point of smart underutilization. Without guided research, users at this level of proficiency will begin to develop their own tricks and reinventing the wheel. This approach is redundant because many of the tricks they have developed exist already as built-in product features that users are not aware of; these features are easier to master than users typically think. In this section, we cover

---

* There could also be a separate discussion about the wisdom of building turnkey applications using this technology as opposed to technologies built specifically for that purpose. But since such solutions are possible and in fact exist in industry, we must include them as a category.

**Table 8.1** High-Level Tool Comparison

| | REQUIREMENT | MDX | SMART VIEW (Excel) | SMART SLICES | QUERY DESIGNER | SMART QUERY | HFR (ESSBASE CONNECTION) | THIS CHAPTER, SECTION 8.6 |
|---|---|---|---|---|---|---|---|---|
| 1 | Filtering | Yes | No (Excel) | Via Attributes In definition but not permanent | Via Attributes Filter() with limited options[a] | Yes, major selling point | Yes, but expensive | Yes |
| 2 | Count, Max, Min, Avg, Sum | Yes | Yes | Sum only (implicit) | Count(), Sum() | No | Yes | Yes |
| 3 | Persistence | EAS, Text file | As Excel file | Analytic Provider Services (APS) | Hidden sheet | Smart Query Repository | Workspace | Custom Repository |
| 4 | Sharing with other users | EAS, Text file | E-mail Excel file | APS (shared connections) | E-mail Excel file | E-mail Excel file | Workspace | Custom Repository |
| 5 | Parameters | In EAS StrToMbr() | SubVars | SubVars during definition only | SubVars StrToMbr() | No | SubVars, POV, Prompts | Yes |
| 6 | Parent before children | Yes (as default and as option) | No | Yes | Yes + ORDER() | Yes | With two separate queries | Yes |
| 7 | User-defined members | Yes | No | No | No | 1/2 (limited) | Yes | Yes |
| 8 | Modules | With Member With Set | No | No | No | Sets, Filters | Rows, columns | Yes |
| 9 | Is a query | Yes | Yes | No | Yes | Yes | Collection thereof | Yes |
| 10 | Column suppression | Yes | No | No | No | No | Yes | Yes |

[a] Limited enough to give the impression that it is not supported. But in some simple cases, it works.

the basics, building a foundation for further research into out-of-the-box and custom solutions that might fit your specific requirements.

### 8.3.4 Demystifying New/Advanced/Rarely Used Features

Smart View offers three similarly named tools (plus the Cell functions tool) to simplify accessing data in one form or another. Table 8.2 provides a quick overview, focusing on each tool's purpose and differentiating them from each other in more detail than in Table 8.1. This section provides an even more detailed discussion.

*8.3.4.1 Smart Slices, Smart Queries, Query Designer, and Cell Functions* Table 8.2 provides a detailed comparison of the features in these four tools. First, we compared the tools by requirements and test environments. Then we created a small collection of standard Smart View queries and attempted to replicate them using each of the tools or features discussed in Table 8.2. Table 8.3 summarizes the results of this exercise. This summary demonstrates that each of the tools was better or the only tool that could handle the listed requirement and that no one tool could do it all. This lack of an overall winner justifies our search for a better overall solution and an explicit understanding of how the tools need to be combined for the purpose of building Essbase client applications.

The Sample.Basic cube was slightly modified to include one additional measure named "Commissions." The measure was created as a dynamic calc member of the measures dimension. Its formula was defined as follows:

```
IF ( @IsLev("Year",0) and @IsLev("Market",0) and @IsLev("Product",0) )
      IF ( "Sales" <> #MISSING )
      IF ( "Marketing" / "Sales" < 0.05 )
      "Sales" * 0.03;
      ENDIF
      ENDIF
ENDIF
```

From a business point of view, this formula says that if no corporate-sponsored marketing was applied in the corresponding market, then the only explanation for the sales during the period must be an extraordinary effort by the local sales force and they should be compensated. Of course, this is a simplification of reality. Maybe, a very expensive campaign ran during all the previous months and the company is seeing the fruits of that effort during the current month. The point of the exercise is to mention a case where a calculation must happen at level 0 at query time and it must then be aggregated so that the result participates in upper-level summary calculations. In a block storage option (BSO) cube, this requires the inclusion of an attribute dimension, not as a filter, but as a real dimension.*

We also added a branch to the product dimension to complement the "Diet" branch (see Figure 8.3). Notice in particular the level 1 members 100R, 200R, 300R, and

---

* For further details about situations where this is an unavoidable business requirement, see Hodges (2014).

**Table 8.2** Detailed Tool Comparison

| NO. | CRITERION | SMART SLICES | QUERY DESIGNER | SMART QUERY | CELL FUNCTIONS |
|---|---|---|---|---|---|
| 1 | Core characteristic | Not a query, but rather a subset of the cube, that must be saved for later use as an alternate data source. All the user will be able to see is the data contained in the Smart Slice. Think of a donut | A wizard or template for building MDX queries. It does not do everything but it is very flexible and code can be modified. Once the query is built, Query Designer can be abandoned | Component based. Once built, it becomes a permanent entity that can be used and reused. Components saved individually. Can also be used as a starting point | Each cell is independent from every other cell; the end result may be exactly the same. Similar in concept to the relationship between a partition and the @XRef() function |
| 2 | Modular (made up of components that can be rearranged to build other queries) | Only in the sense that it is a segment of the cube it belongs to, it is navigable (i.e., drillable), so each new state is a new query. A regular user cannot replicate and modify Smart Slices | Clauses within cells have distinct identities. MDX set expressions cannot span multiple cells | Claim: Filters and Sets can be saved in a personal repository for future inclusion in other queries | Each cell is a separate entity, which can be very important and useful. |
| 3 | Can replicate | Partially, by creating a new one based on members on a sheet (which could be the contents of another Smart Slice) | Copying: the query sheet, the code, the workbook | Analyze Clone Repository | Copy and paste |
| 4 | Time tested (if it is still around, it must be useful) | Oldest tool with a shareable output | Very oldest. Time tested. Very flexible | Newest Needs to mature | Precursor: EssCell() in Arbor's Excel add-in[a] |
| 5 | Productivity-to-effort ratio— what you get for your effort and investment in time and money | Shareable | Highest (based on the fact that it helps but gives you freedom to expand) | Steeper learning curve Long-term investment | High (but low volume) |
| 6 | Modifiable: you can open the object and manually change the code (as opposed to clicking on options) | You can move the functions around, the tool will read your code and adjust the definition, but its vocabulary is limited, so if you go beyond what it understands, it will return an error | You can do almost anything to the code, and if your syntax is correct, it will understand it and include your updates into its resulting query | Designed to take full control of the query construction process. Therefore, very constraining. If the level of complexity happens to be what it knows how to do, you will be fine | Each cell is independent from the rest. Easier if built from scratch (as opposed to copied using the special purpose copy/paste commands) |

(Continued)

**Table 8.2 (Continued)**   Detailed Tool Comparison

| NO. | CRITERION | SMART SLICES | QUERY DESIGNER | SMART QUERY | CELL FUNCTIONS |
|---|---|---|---|---|---|
| 7 | Tool's "Language Skills" (expressiveness) | Limited vocabulary Limited syntax, e.g., ([Year]. CHILDREN), but not CHILDREN([Year]) Case sensitive | Can host very complex queries. It may not "speak" MDX very well, but it "understands" a whole lot. Therefore, you can code pieces it could not write itself, but it will read them and include them in the final (hidden) query. Examples, EXCEPT, INTERSECT | "Speaks" better than the others, but it has a "narrow view of the world" | HsGetValue() has multiple implementations. When generated by Copy and Paste, one of the arguments is a "SVLink" string. This POV reference is a performance improvement feature |
| 8 | Vocabulary highlights | | Filter() but limited, Intersect(), Substring(), Order(), StrToMbr(), almost any common MDX clause, but not WITH MEMBER, WITH SET | Filters, logical operators, graphical and/or logic, custom members | Multiple implementations |
| 9 | Usefulness | • Display parent above children in Essbase connections<br>• Limit access<br>• Get to relevant data faster<br>• Hide irrelevant data (i.e., technical support data) | • A grid to build and test complex MDX queries one clause at a time<br>• Parent above children, since it is MDX | Most advanced but complex and limited in key areas. Eliminates the need to know MDX but requires you to learn its own logic, protocols, and user interface. For someone who already knows MDX, this can be counterproductive | More for reporting than for data analysis |
| 10 | Attribute dimensions participating as dimensions | Yes. But case sensitive, and can still add and remove them manually after data from the slice are displayed. If they disappear, you bring them back by adding them to the grid. You can add any attribute, not only the ones that were included in the definition | Yes | No | Yes |

*(Continued)*

**Table 8.2 (Continued)**   Detailed Tool Comparison

| NO. | CRITERION | SMART SLICES | QUERY DESIGNER | SMART QUERY | CELL FUNCTIONS |
|---|---|---|---|---|---|
| 11 | Attribute dimension calculations | SUM() only, implicit, not selectable by user | Yes | No | SUM() only. Copy will create, for example, "Attribute Calculations#Count," but it will be interpreted as an error |
| 12 | Attribute dimensions as Filters | No. Can still see members with other attributes, but not other attributes from same attribute dimension. Attribute can be removed | No. Standard behavior | Yes. Attributes treated as UDAs | Yes, participating as a dimension, when combined with corresponding base member |
| 13 | Repository | APS (Analytic Provider Services) Private and shared slices | Hidden sheet | Personal repository, not shareable. Can also save reusable components (sets and filters). Can be converted to regular ad hoc SV query and shared via e-mail, for example | N/A |
| 14 | Report Designer | Close relationship between Smart Slices and Report Designer reports. Topic beyond the scope of this chapter | Unrelated | Unrelated | Unrelated |
| 15 | Control over life cycle (over presence in workbook) | Smart Slice lives in APS. Smart Slice is a provider and relationship between worksheet and provider remains until it is deleted or changed | Once created, a query remains as a hidden sheet. Special attention is needed to avoid deleting the query inadvertently | A "Smart Query Sheet" is created. The easiest way to remove it may be to simply delete the sheet | Simple delete |
| 16 | Filters | No | Via attribute dimensions and MDX functions. The FILTER() function is not always recognized or processed correctly, but sometimes a filter can be written as an INTERSECT() | Major feature | See no. 12 |

*(Continued)*

**Table 8.2 (Continued)**   Detailed Tool Comparison

| NO. | CRITERION | SMART SLICES | QUERY DESIGNER | SMART QUERY | CELL FUNCTIONS |
|---|---|---|---|---|---|
| 17 | Dynamic Aggregation | Yes<br>Attribute dimensions participate as dimensions (not as filters). Attribute dimensions are used as filters to select what to include in the definition, but not as filters in the definition itself | Yes | No<br>Similar situation to Planning Connections in Hyperion Financial Reports | Yes |
| 18 | Duplicates allowed | Since this is a data set definition (not a query or report), it does not make sense to request for a slice to contain duplicates. SV will complain if you include duplicates in your Smart Slice definition. It would be up to queries or reports referencing the smart slice to select a member twice | Yes | Yes. And this feature is explicitly emphasized in the definition options and, consequently, in discussions about Smart Queries | Yes |
| 19 | Pivoting | OK | After query is applied, you are back in SV and can do anything you normally do in SV. To start over, select Query Designer, then reapply the query | You can use Smart Query to get your data, then click "Analyze" to move to a purely ad hoc mode | N/A<br>But you can put the function anywhere and that is a major advantage |
| 20 | Asymmetrical Reports | No. But suppression helps sometimes. Pivoting after initial display may also help | No | No | Totally, since each cell is independent from the rest. Totally arbitrary layouts are possible |

*(Continued)*

**Table 8.2 (Continued)**  Detailed Tool Comparison

| NO. | CRITERION | SMART SLICES | QUERY DESIGNER | SMART QUERY | CELL FUNCTIONS |
|---|---|---|---|---|---|
| 21 | Shared members | Must add manually | Implicit | Implicit | N/A |
| 22 | Outline order/Accounting order | Set in Smart Slice preferences | Is MDX. Outline order is default (ancestors first). After ad hoc manipulation of the results, order reverts to accounting statement order (totals below detail). Order() also available | Outline order. Good reason to use Smart Query to build a grid then switch to ad hoc mode | N/A |
| 23 | Custom member expressions | No | No | Yes | N/A |
| 24 | Filtering based on calculated member | No | No | No | N/A |
| 25 | Substitution variables | Can use it to help build the slice, but it is immediately replaced by its value | Yes, but are lost as soon as they are validated (unless you use StrToMbr()) | No | No |
| 26 | HsGetVariable()[b] | No | No. Not an MDX function | No. Not an MDX function | No |
| 27 | Member name and alias | No | Yes | No | N/A |
| 28 | Member Search & Selection | Slow, in layers | Fast, any level | Yes | In Wizard: fast, any level |
| 29 | Row suppression | All or nothing | Like SV | All or nothing | N/A |
| 30 | Column suppression | No | No | No | N/A |
| 31 | Can change alias | No | Yes | Yes | N/A |
| 32 | Functions, i.e., INTERSECT() | No | Yes | No | N/A |

[a] Additional information about the performance: Computer scientists use the terms *polymorphism* and *function overloading* when referring to functions with varying signatures or interfaces with the calling entity, in this case, you and/or Smart View. Instead of someone having to write different versions of the functions to implement contingent behaviors, the functions themselves implement different behaviors depending on the types of values they receive. A more rudimentary but similar effect can be accomplished with optional parameters and argument arrays. We mention these features and behaviors to highlight the fact that there are multiple ways to define cell function intersections in Smart View, to accompany this with some mnemonic context, and because of the performance implications discussed by Milella (2010).

[b] HsGetVariable() is a cell function. It provides a mechanism for retaining substitution variables in Smart View templates. Query Designer solves the problem with an MDX function: StrToMbr().

**Table 8.3** Deal-Breaker Comparison[a]

| NO. | QUERY | SMART SLICE | QUERY DESIGNER | SMART QUERY | CELL FUNCTIONS |
|-----|-------|-------------|----------------|-------------|----------------|
| 1 | Commissions (dynamic agg) | No | Without a problem | Cannot perform Dynamic Aggregations | Attribute dimensions can participate in cell function parameter lists |
| 2 | Summary results for public viewing | Yes | No | No | No |
| 3 | Calculated members | No | No | Yes | No |

[a] The fact that neither of the four options can fulfill all the requirements set forth in Table 8.3 was one of the incentives to produce a solution that can. This is the purpose of this chapter and more specifically of Section 8.6 (MDX Editor SV 1.0).

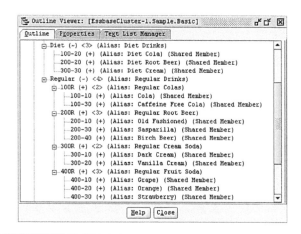

**Figure 8.3** Regular Drinks.

400R. This provided an opportunity to demonstrate using VBA code how to jump back and forth between related areas of the outline (e.g., from 100 to 100R then back to 100) and to practice building offline calculations to compare or combine the data from the two branches.

The conclusion was that none of the three tools (Smart Slices, Smart Queries, and Query Designer) nor cell functions can perform all three key functions I use in my daily work: Dynamic Aggregations, attribute dimensions as dimensions, and off-the-cube calculations (as Table 8.3's footnote indicates).

From my perspective, dynamic calculations is reason enough to rely more on Query Designer than on the other options to build complex queries. As a whole, the findings reinforced my motivation to build a tool to facilitate the execution of MDX queries. For sharing specific views on the data, I will continue to use Smart Slices. And I had better master Smart Query if I want to keep up with how most of the Smart View community will be building reusable complex queries. The next sections explore the main reasons each tool can be the best for a particular situation.

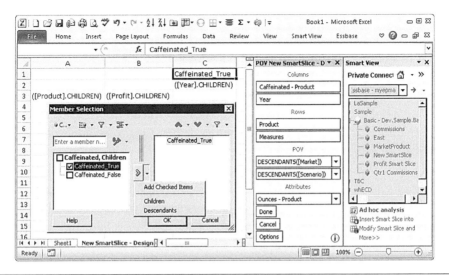

**Figure 8.4** Smart Slice definition.

*8.3.4.1.1 Smart Slices* Smart Slices are not queries, but virtual minicubes or subsets of the physical cube. Therefore, they must be built before executing an actual query. If you want to see exactly the default view on the Smart Slice, then you can think of your Smart Slice as an expandable query; you get your initial results and can then pivot and drill down and change POV settings to locate other data. I like to think of Smart Slices as collections of data donuts floating inside the cube. They are collections because changing POV settings amounts to selecting a different donut. I find this image fitting because it reminds me that a smart slice can exclude from view both ancestor data and descendant data; in other words, they make invisible or inaccessible both data further away from the center and data closer to the center. Continuing with the analogy, when you access a Smart Slice, you can see only what is inside the solid matter. Figure 8.4 illustrates the definition of one possible Smart Slice in Sample. Basic.*

As is true with any cube, the available data space is defined by all the possible combinations of members from participating dimensions. Consistent with this concept, you define your minicube by selecting members from each available dimension. You can select them one by one explicitly or dynamically by means of a member list expression. Only two of these are available: Children() and Descendants(). You get to use additional list expressions when looking for members to select. For example, you can request the list of all the Small markets. But all that does is list the markets in the selection box so you can then select them individually.

---

* In one of my test environments, I had to install web components owc11.exe. Why this was not already installed, I cannot explain. This Microsoft office extension was initially published as an extension for Office 2003. It works with Office 2007 and Office 2010 just as well. Without it, you cannot create Smart Slice Report Designer reports.

Returning to the notion of a donut, you will notice from the above definition that Year and Months are excluded. Also, only the children of Profit are included, so neither Profit will be available nor the components of Margin and Total Expenses.

Two features are worth noting. The first is the option to make parents appear above children when multiple levels are displayed, by clicking on Options. This alone makes slices worth building, in my opinion. If you need to run a query that requires ancestors to be displayed above their corresponding descendants, you simply query against a Smart Slice defined with enough scope to handle the same amount of data. The second is the option to include attribute dimensions as real dimensions.

You start a query against a Smart Slice the same way you start a query against a cube. Once a slice has been inserted into a sheet, it controls what you can see until you remove the relationship. You can do this by (a) inserting a different Smart Slice; (b) clicking on the Delete Smart View Info button in the Sheet Information dialog box available through the Smart View ribbon tab, the General group, and the Sheet Info button (Smart View > General > Sheet Info); or (c) resetting the connection by clicking Open then "Reset to default connection."* Of course, you can simply delete the sheet and start a new query on a different sheet. If you are not an administrator, you may need to get permission to be able to create Smart Slices. Smart Slices built on private connections are private; those built on shared connections are, by definition, shared and available to all users.

8.3.4.1.1.1 Annoyances and/or Limitations and/or Caveats   In regular Smart View Essbase ad hoc mode, attribute dimensions are optional, they can be brought into the query or taken away from the query at the user's discretion, and they implement a variety of aggregation functions (e.g., SUM and COUNT). Attribute dimensions in Smart Slice definitions are a convenience, not a permanent delimiter or filter. You can remove them at query time.† Dimension member names in Smart Slices are case sensitive. Unless you type them in exactly as they are defined in the outline or select them from one of the selection tools, Smart View will not recognize them. This warning is particularly applicable to attribute dimensions because any additional attribute dimension you might need (to narrow down your scope, break a set of numbers down into components, or add dimensionality) will have to be added to the query. You will not have a starting point from which to drill down. I typically type them in. The only dynamic calculation attribute dimensions provide in Smart Slices is SUM().

8.3.4.1.2 Query Designer   This is simply a tool to help you build a Smart View query as an MDX query. Its interface looks similar to the Smart Slice interface, but

---

* The Sheet Info button was introduced in Smart View version 11.1.2.2.
† To remove an attribute dimension included in the Smart Slice definition, make sure it is in the POV (not in the rows or columns); then, in the POV member selector, select the attribute dimension name; click Refresh. If you want to add the attribute dimension back, you can add only the member or members that were included in the Smart Slice definition.

its purpose is to help you locate and place dimension members and/or member list expressions on a blank sheet, with an important added feature: You have the choice of using the member selection tool or entering the text yourself, in which case, it often checks the validity of the expression as soon as you finish entering it. After selecting a connection, if you click on Query Designer (see Figure 8.5, bottom right-hand corner), Smart View creates a new sheet. The Query Designer link is also available on the Essbase tab, in the Analyze group under Query.

Query Designer retains expressions, not the result of executing the expression. So, it is an expression building tool, based on the MDX query language. Just as in ad hoc analysis you can either use wizards to generate lists of members or type in the member names one at a time, in Query Designer, you can use the tool to help you build the expressions, or you can type in the expressions, in which case the benefit you will derive will be Query Designer's immediate validation of your expression. Compared with the query definition capabilities of a Smart Slice, Query Designer is a much more sophisticated tool. Instead of having only two dynamic selection functions (Children() and Descendants()), it has several others, such as UDA() and Level(). In Figure 8.5, I checked three members, then clicked on Children. The selection tool inserted the three expressions in rows 2, 3, and 4 all at once. You can review the list of members that will be produced by an expression by clicking on the + next to its definition within the list of selected items in the Member Selection tool.

The sheet hosting these expressions was created by Query Designer. To give it a name, it took the name of the active sheet at the time the designer was launched and added "- Query" to it.

When you click on Apply Query, this sheet disappears and a new sheet appears; you might think the tab gets renamed, but it does not. The new sheet's name ends with "- Report" instead of "- Query." Pressing Alt-F11 brings up the VBA interface.

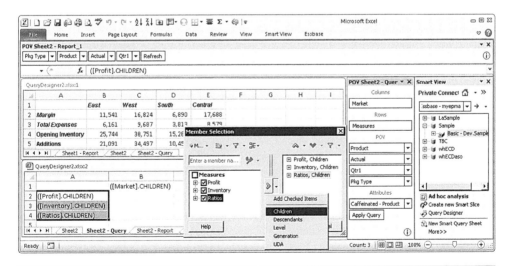

**Figure 8.5** Query Designer Query Definition.

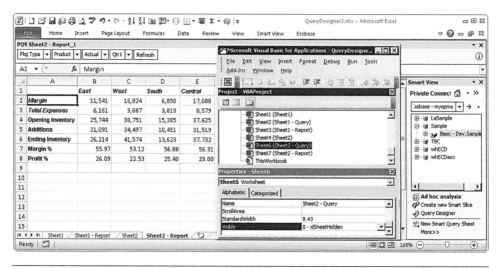

**Figure 8.6** Query Designer three sheets.

A quick review of the Workbook contents reveals that the workbook has the original sheet (whatever its name was) accompanied by two more sheets named the same but with the added suffixes mentioned above (see Figure 8.6). According to the "- Query" sheet's property list, it is hidden, which confirms that the sheet did not disappear, or was replaced, written over, destroyed. On an ongoing basis, Smart View will recognize a relationship between the latter two.* Clicking on Query Designer (bottom right-hand corner of the screen) while viewing a report will take you back to its definition.† In Designer, you may make adjustments and reapply the query, which will update the contents of the "- Report" sheet. The adjustments to the query can be entered manually. This flexibility allows you to gradually build complex queries (see Figure 8.7) that could not be defined interactively by clicking some button or launching some wizard.

You can build a query using the Member Selection tool and then expand it by adding MDX clauses as determined by your requirements. As an example, cell A6 of the "- Query" sheet in Figure 8.7 has a reference to a substitution variable, specified as required by MDX syntax. Notice also the presence of the functions ORDER(), ATTRIBUTE(), INTERSECT(), and SUBSTRING(). For all this

---

* I find seeing three sheets with similar default names very distracting. I have therefore developed the habit of first renaming the sheet from which I am going to launch Query Designer to something other than Sheet#. Then, immediately after I am in Query Designer, I delete the original sheet. This way, I am left with only two unequivocally named sheets, only one of which is always visible. You can delete the initial sheet, but you will discover that Smart View understandably complains when you delete either the dash query sheet or the dash report sheet. Smart View will complain yet still recreate the dash report sheet if you accidentally delete it but will not know what to do if you delete the dash query sheet. Once the initial pairwise relationship is established, you can rename the sheets any way you want to. You can change both their tab name and their object name (visible only in VBA design mode, i.e., when you press Alt-F11).

† Or Essbase Ribbon > Analysis Command Group > Query drop down menu > Query Designer.

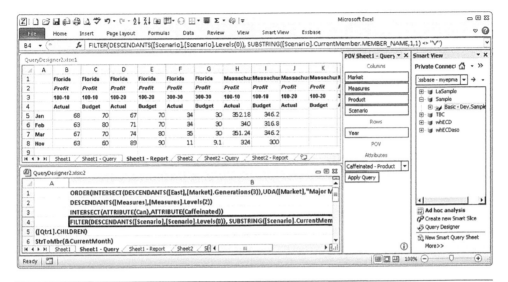

**Figure 8.7**    Modifying a Query Designer query.

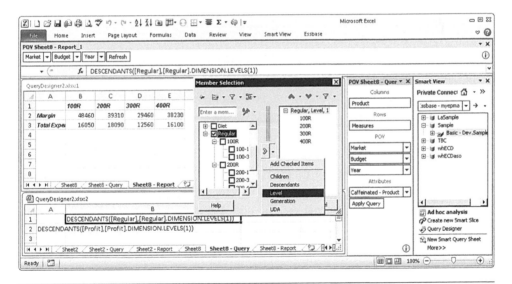

**Figure 8.8**    Level within Branch.

functionality, some tasks are still impossible, such as suppressing empty columns (see report columns J and K), which can be easily done in regular MDX statements (and in the MDX Editor described in Section 8.6). Figure 8.8 shows selection of a level within a branch.

8.3.4.1.2.1 Annoyances and/or Limitations and/or Caveats   It is not possible to save the query into a public or private repository for future use and/or to analyze the complete MDX from Query Designer (but you can save the Excel file, and this may be all you really need). Some common MDX clauses such as NON EMPTY cannot be included in Query Designer. The slicer is stored in the interface and cannot be handled as part of the code. Using substitution variables while defining a query is possible, but they are substituted immediately when entered, and so the original reference to the variable is also immediately lost (this can be solved by using StrToMbr()).* The very fact that queries can be modified and extended makes Query Designer a very solid option.

*8.3.4.1.3 Smart Query*    Smart Query is the most sophisticated and the most recently added query-building tool available in Smart View. It is an interactive tool for building complex MDX queries, one component or segment at a time. It has a sophisticated methodology for specifying filters. Each segment and filter can be saved separately, and therefore, new queries can be built by simply selecting and rearranging previously saved components. The MDX remains hidden within the tool and cannot be accessed for further tweaking or for analysis. For some users, eliminating the need to know that MDX is somewhere in the mix may be very beneficial; therefore, this can be seen as a major advantage. Smart Query has its own ribbon, a fact that I believe is indicative of its importance. Otherwise, the interface is similar to that of Query Designer. Smart Query output can be converted to a regular ad hoc analysis query using the Analyze button. Figure 8.9 shows the creation of a new Smart Query.

One very important feature distinguishing it from Smart Slices or Query Designer is the ability to create calculated members (the equivalent of WITH MEMBER dimension members in MDX). Figure 8.10 shows a simple query displaying three versions of COGS. COGSplus10pct and GOGSminus10pct are measures defined in Smart Query and do not exist in Essbase.

Filters added on to filters create the staircase arrangement you see in the lower right corner of Figure 8.10 and produce a series of AND conditions. Filters added to the set operate independently, that is, as OR conditions. In this example, New York, Massachusetts, and Florida are the only large markets in the Eastern region. Of these, only New York and Florida have actual costs of goods sold above 7000. Florida would have been eliminated if we had based the dollar value threshold on ([Budget],[COGS]) instead of ([Actual],[COGS]).

8.3.4.1.3.1 Annoyances and/or Limitations and/or Caveats    If Smart Query fits your requirements, you will appreciate its power and elegance. Learning to use the

---

* The StrToMbr() function keeps Query Designer from making the substitution when it evaluates the query, which it does as soon as you finish entering text into the cell. By doing this, you retain the substitution variable in the code. The function takes a string, so if the substitution variable's value includes double quotes, then StrToMbr(&SubVar) will work; otherwise, you will have to write StrToMbr("&SubVar"). If the substitution variable already has double quotes, the substitution variable, by itself, will not work in Query Designer anyway, because it will interpret the double quotes as part of the value. Using StrToMbr() in that case will accomplish two things: retain the variable between executions and convert the string to a dimension member.

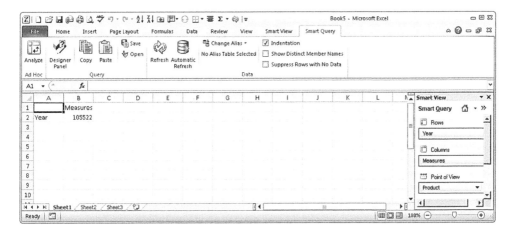

**Figure 8.9**   Creating a new Smart Query.

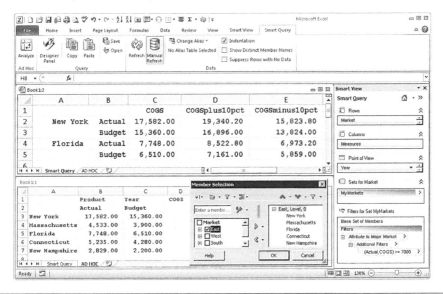

**Figure 8.10**   Calculated Members in Smart Query.

tool will require some effort to understand how to specify sets and selection conditions, but the effort will be worthwhile given the results. In my real-world work, I
must be able to use attribute dimensions as real dimensions, and for this reason, I cannot take advantage of Smart Query's features.* Using a tool to eliminate the need to
know MDX is in conflict with one of the primary motivations for writing this chapter:

---

\* If you are a Hyperion Planning and a Hyperion Reports developer, I think you will appreciate this
comparison: Hyperion Planning does not recognize attribute dimensions as dimensions, only as
attributes of dimension members. Reports using planning connections, for the same reason, cannot
include attribute dimensions operating as dimensions. But processing them just as attributes of the
members has powerful applications, for example, for the efficient display of attribute information using
<<MemberProperty()>> and for filtering. Similarly, Smart Query can use attribute dimensions for
filtering and during the member selection process.

to demystify and facilitate the learning of MDX and access its power. It is quite clear that a lot of effort was invested into Smart Query to replicate the power and expressiveness of MDX within a graphical interface mode of thinking. The specification of filters based on tuple values

```
e.g., ([Actual],[COGS]) > 7000
```

is quite elegant. But if you know some MDX, do not expect to find the same logic or semantics everywhere in Smart Query and be prepared for surprises.* If the chapter was about singing the glories of Smart Query, much more could be said and explained. Three things further justify Section 8.4.2.3 and Section 8.6: The MDX code is not visible; queries are saved to a personal repository, not to a shared repository; and attribute dimensions cannot participate as real dimensions. In spite of this, Smart Query remains a very powerful tool in its own right.

*8.3.4.2 Cell Functions*    Cell functions are an interesting feature in one special respect: With Smart View, a user can take any query and convert it to a collection of individual cell queries, then print the results. It would not be possible to tell from the printout whether the report was produced using a regular query or cell functions, but going through the motions can be very revealing.

The Edit command group on the Smart View tab has two buttons, Copy and Paste.† In the example in Figure 8.11, a query occupies cell range A1:I18. Can you affirm with certainty by looking at the contents of this range whether these numbers were actually obtained from an Essbase cube? From all appearances, they were, but determining the composition of the query is difficult. Select the range B2:I18 and then, on the Edit control group of the Smart View tab, click the Copy button. Then, select cell K2 and click the Paste button (see Figure 8.11).

Notice how this process did not copy data but instead copied multidimensional pointers to the database. The parameters look peculiar and will be discussed shortly. This demonstrates that column and row headings are not the only way to define what should be displayed in a cell.

In Figure 8.12, the user has copied not only the data cells but also the column headings. After refreshing the sheet, without actually consulting the contents of the cell, it is impossible to know whether the numbers were obtained in the usual manner or by means of a cell function.

This shows that one is not constrained by the grid model and that getting at data points in the cube directly is possible. But what about those strange-looking

---

* For example, in Smart Query, attribute dimensions and UDAs are used interchangeably. This is very consistent with what is explained in the footnote on p. 385 but can be very disconcerting when you know they are two very different programmatic constructs.
† "Copy Data Point" and "Paste Data Point" in previous versions.

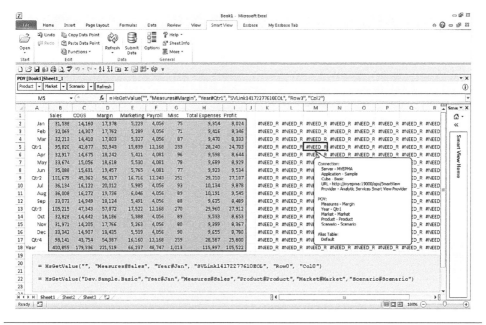

**Figure 8.11**   Creating cell functions using Copy.

parameters?* The bottom section of Figure 8.12 shows (a) the function created by the cell copying process just described and (b) the function as you would normally write it if you were creating it yourself. The first implementation of HsGetValue() shows two parameters we recognize as coming directly from the query. We know the cube has five dimensions. In the second implementation of HsGetValue(), the five parameters are specified. It is not possible to tell how exactly the other three parameters in the first implementation complete the dimensional specification. Even if you had all five dimensions included in the row and column headings, in which case all the dimensions will be explicitly listed, you still get an "SVlink" parameter followed by "Row0" and "Col0." And if you place the query and the cell functions further away from cell A1, you still get Row0 and Col0. What is important to understand in this situation is that when you create the function, all the base dimensions are mentioned in one form or another (see Matt Milella's [2010] post for additional information about performance).

You do not have to write the functions; you can use a wizard (see Figure 8.13).

---

* Computer scientists use the terms *polymorphism* and *function overloading* when referring to functions with varying signatures or interfaces with the calling entity, in this case, you and/or Smart View. Instead of someone having to write different versions of the functions to implement contingent behaviors, the functions themselves implement different behaviors depending on the types of values they receive. A more rudimentary but similar effect can be accomplished with optional parameters and argument arrays. We mention these features and behaviors to highlight the fact that there are multiple ways to define cell function intersections in Smart View, to accompany this with some mnemonic context, and because of the performance implications discussed by Milella (2010).

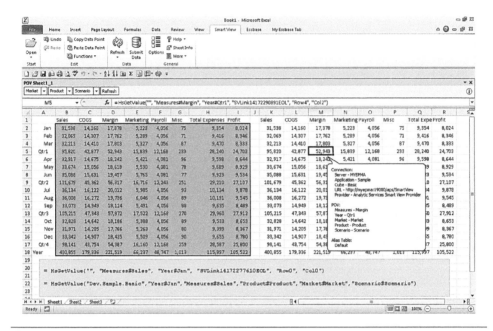

**Figure 8.12** Copy can copy headings.

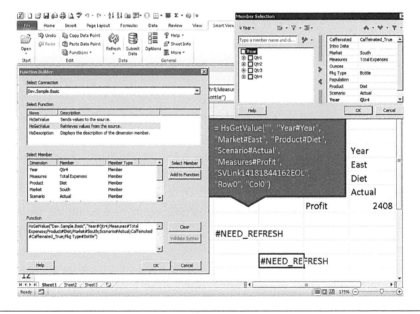

**Figure 8.13** Using the Function Builder wizard to build a cell function.

A very useful application of cell functions is the combination within a single grid of base data and attribute dimension data. Attribute dimensions have one disadvantage: Once they are introduced into a Smart View grid, they become applicable to all the cells. Since they are applicable to all the cells, they impose a dynamic calculation of all the cells on the report, which affects response time and may also affect what you

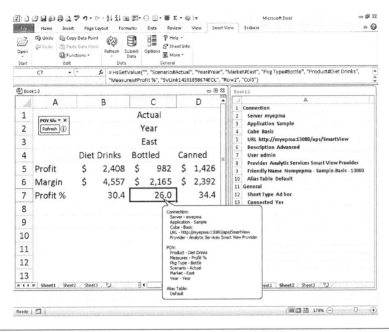

**Figure 8.14**   Finding practical uses for cell functions.

can get in terms of data. If one of the participating level 0 members (assuming the attribute dimension assignments are happening at level 0) has not been assigned an attribute value, its numbers will be excluded from the report. Consider the very simple report in Figure 8.14.

Column B displays profitability numbers for Diet Drinks in the eastern region. Report users would like to see these numbers broken down into two groups, bottled drinks and canned drinks. In Sample.Basic, the numbers can be obtained by adding the Pkg_Type attribute dimension to the report. The combination ([Diet Drinks],[Pkg_Type]) will display the same numbers shown by [Diet Drinks] alone before the attribute dimension was added; these numbers will be dynamically calculated. Instead of applying the attribute [Pkg_Type] to the base numbers, the implementation of the report in Figure 8.14 uses cell functions in columns C and D. The cell functions were actually generated by first applying the attribute dimension to the report, placing [Pkg_Type] somewhere in column B, [Bottle] somewhere in column C, and [Can] somewhere in column C. The report was refreshed. Then the numbers in columns C and D were copied to columns E and F using Copy and Paste from the Smart View tab.* As discussed earlier in this chapter, you can discover this by looking at the contents of the Formula Bar. Then, columns C and D were deleted and [Pkg_Type] was removed from the report. Finally, ranges B1:D1, B2:D2, and B3:D3 were merged to produce the formatted report you see in Figure 8.14. If we built the report, we know we built a guarantee that the numbers we see in column

---

* "Copy Data Point" and "Paste Data Point" in previous versions.

B come directly from stored, precalculated, upper-level members in the Product dimension. If adding the numbers in column C to the numbers in column D does not give us the exact same results as the numbers in column B, we will know that either (a) the database has not been aggregated or (b) one of our drinks is missing its [Pkg Type] designation.*

The built-in cell function descriptor that is displayed when the cursor is placed in a corresponding cell gives relevant details about the connection to the database and the application provider service responsible for handling the connection. The contents of the second sheet are the result of clicking Sheet Info on the same ribbon, copying the contents displayed by this button, and pasting them on this sheet.

*8.3.4.3 Drilling Down by Formula* Essbase outlines are collections of formulas as much as they are collections of hierarchical relationships. Technically, eliminating the hierarchies and replacing them with formulas are possible, but the reverse is not (unless the formulas are trivial and therefore redundant). Drilling down by formula is a new feature in Smart View. Although not as efficient and intuitively evident as hierarchical zoom-ins, formula-based outline navigation is still important and relevant. Also possible is building formulas merely to support outline navigation.

*8.3.4.4 Dynamic Aggregation* Attribute dimensions, by their very nature, implement dynamic binary allocations based on dimension member type (instead of some rate or percentage). Binary in this context means all or nothing, 100% or 0% of a given amount. Remove Population from the query in Figure 8.15 and the commission totals disappear. Why? Because the formula for Commissions requires that the calculation happen at level 0 and that it be subsequently dynamically aggregated.

Attribute dimensions are alternate hierarchies with two major characteristics differentiating them from regular alternate hierarchies: (a) They make intradimension cross-tabulation possible and (b) they implement "dumb" aggregation (they apply the same arithmetic operation to all the contributors to the total, ignoring unary operators). These differences may work for or against your purposes. In this example, Figure 8.15, Population plays the role of an aggregator and thus computes the upper-level values of Commissions.

*8.3.4.5 MDX* MDX is not as difficult to learn as some Hyperion EPM users might think. Gary Crisci's Chapter 6 of the first "Developing Essbase Applications" volume was a practical introduction to MDX for developers and for analysts wanting more control and power over data. Members of Oracle Developer Tools Users Group (ODTUG) have access to a KScope13 presentation titled "A Path to MDX Mastery"

---

* The purpose of the example was to construct a solution using a combination of regular intersections and cell functions. With the introduction of Multiple Grid Worksheets in version 11.1.2.1.102, we can produce the same effect using two grids, one including the attribute dimension and one excluding it.

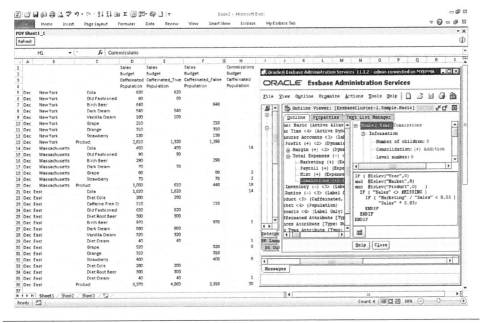

**Figure 8.15** Dynamic Aggregation.

that also attempts to demystify MDX but focuses on developing a learning strategy (Hodges 2013).*

MDX is not for everyone, which helps explain and justify the existence of the tools reviewed here, including Smart View itself. But MDX is the standard query language for OLAP and many OLAP querying tools have been specifically designed as a means to execute MDX without knowing MDX. In this section (and in Sections 8.4.2.3, 8.4.3, and 8.6), we explore a different approach: facilitating the use of the MDX language itself, rather than avoiding learning it or using it directly. Figure 8.16 shows a query built with Query Designer. Rows 6 to 15 show a reinterpretation of the query with extra code around it to turn it into a well-formed MDX query. The Notepad Window contains the same code after it was copied from Excel to Notepad.

In the interest of completeness, I compared the results obtained by applying the Query Designer query with the corresponding results obtained by executing the MDX code built by adding the missing components as previously shown, and the results were, as expected, identical. Figures 8.17 and 8.18 demonstrate a similar exercise with different circumstances and query components and, correspondingly, a different, even simpler, code completion approach. The notion of templates we could develop or memorize is beginning to evolve.

---

* ODTUG (http://www.odtug.com) is the user group for information about Oracle EPM solutions from a developer's perspective. The group has several membership levels; entry-level membership is free.

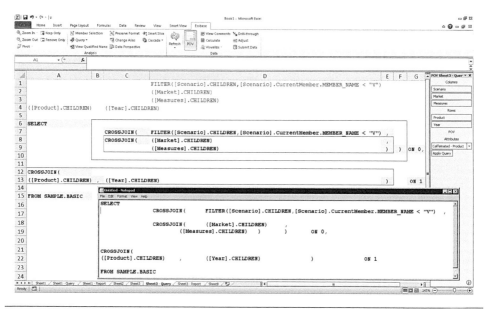

**Figure 8.16**   Easy steps to convert a Query Designer query to ready-to-run MDX: example 1.

**Figure 8.17**   Easy steps to convert a Query Designer query to ready-to-run MDX: example 2.

Figure 8.18 shows the results from the query. The grid on the top has the results produced by Query Designer; the grid on the bottom has the results produced by pasting the MDX into the Execute Free Form MDX Query Smart View tool and clicking on the Execute button.*

---

\* As you most likely know already, executing MDX queries this way does not provide any form of persistence; as soon as you click Execute, your code is lost. Building your queries elsewhere and then pasting them onto this tool is clearly the way to go. Sections 8.5 and 8.6.5 discuss solutions that provide persistence.

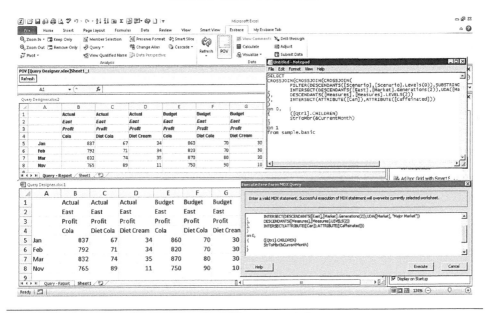

**Figure 8.18**    Query Designer Query run as free-form MDX query: example 2.

## 8.4 Your Own Features

We know that customization is risky business. As are other forms of cost of ownership, code maintenance costs are typically underestimated. Nevertheless, we have demonstrated that there are multiple opportunities to improve the data querying experience. In this section, we show that many of them require minimum effort and ongoing maintenance. If you apply some of the design principles discussed in Section 8.2 to the best of your ability, you should be able to develop more advanced functionality that will enhance, facilitate, and simplify the data querying process while remaining easy to maintain and easy to replace should you ever have to stop using it or get rid of it.

In this section, we propose a variety of components, progressing from simple to complex. We also present the entire code for the solution or instructions on where to find it. This section also acts as a quick preview of Sections 8.5 and 8.6, for which the topics are more involved.

All the product enhancements presented in this chapter are proposed as ideas for further study and personalization (see Table 8.4). They are solutions in their own right and have served this author well, but the intent is to elicit your own ideas of what would be useful to you and/or to the users you serve. Please remember the importance of using caution and keeping customization code simple. There are many hidden traps in customization. You do not want to attempt large customization projects until you know all of the traps and how to deal with them. This implies staying away from making a user interface experience as sophisticated as it could be—compromise will be necessary. This is better than trying to make the solution perfect then paying the prohibitive price of having to maintain the code. While reading this chapter, if you discover or suspect you have a better solution or think the solution could have been more complete, please remember this:

**Table 8.4**  Levels of Improvement

| LEVEL | IMPROVEMENT TYPE | DESCRIPTION | REMARKS |
|---|---|---|---|
| 1 | Configurations | Exploration of what can be accomplished by simply changing the product's configuration | Personalized ribbon tabs |
| 2 | Simple tools | Very simple macros, executable by means of keyboard shortcuts or the ribbon | |
| 3 | Templates | In this context, spreadsheet templates are meant to simplify or demystify certain querying tasks | Can be generated by code. This eliminates having to keep an inventory of templates |
| 4 | Modules/Components | Code to be utilized in various ways by different solutions | |
| 5 | Advanced tools | Similar to the tools discussed in no. 2, but more complex | The MDX editor discussed in Section 8.6 |
| 6 | Applications | Full-blown applications | Would be the subject of an entire book |

A primary goal in the development and presentation of these tools and solutions has been to discover and establish how much can be done with minimal effort and minimal initial knowledge. Once that is done, we all can pursue these ideas further on our own.

### 8.4.1 Configurations

This subsection explores the possibility of improving the Smart View data querying experience by simply changing the product's configuration. It is relatively easy to modify and extend an Excel ribbon and, therefore, the Smart View and Essbase ribbon tabs. The possibilities are endless; one book is considered the bible on the subject and a free tool exists to test ribbon definitions (Martin et al. 2008).* In my personalized ribbon (Figure 8.19), I combine Excel functionality, Smart View functionality, personal macros, hard-coded queries (i.e., simple reports), and access to the advanced tool discussed in Section 8.6. From a single place, I have access to all the enhancements discussed in this chapter and more.

Hiding the original tabs and adding a new one (a) eliminated the possibility of accidentally submitting data, (b) eliminated the need to switch tabs to complete any of my common daily tasks, and (c) placed the most often used buttons as close as possible to the tab itself for ease in clicking. The tab's location with respect to other tabs determines the best placement for the buttons themselves. My ribbon tab arrangements are still evolving; making adjustments and trying new ideas are easy. The ribbon displayed in Figure 8.19 is actually an early version. I chose to display screenshots of the ribbon at different stages of development precisely to highlight the fact that it has evolved.

When using my personalized Essbase tab, I have found that it is best to hide the Smart View and the Essbase tabs to keep Smart View from returning to a default ribbon tab where preprogrammed to do so.

---

* Free tool, originally from Microsoft; download from http://openxmldeveloper.org/blog.

**Figure 8.19**    Considering the construction of a personal Essbase ribbon.

One of the disadvantages or risks resulting from building a personal ribbon manually and hiding the original tabs is that the new components added to the product after the personal ribbon creation will likely not inherit the keytips.* So using, for example, the previously valid Alt-S-S keystroke to get the Options dialog box will no longer be available and you will have to press Alt-Y1-S instead. Other keystrokes will be even less accommodating. But most users rely on the ribbon tabs as a visual guide to buttons to click, so this limitation may remain unnoticed by many. Section 8.5 will show you how to create your own keytips. Another disadvantage is that, depending on the level of customization you implement, reactivating hidden components has the potential of permanently removing advanced customized components from the ribbon. Compensating for this is also discussed in Section 8.5.

### 8.4.2 Simple Tools

Most Excel users have had the opportunity or need to build a macro. Macros are the beginning of full-blown, professional, and even productionalized and commercialized Excel customization by means of the VBA programming language. Macros can be built from scratch or recorded. Recorded macros can be modified, simplified, optimized, and/or extended. Macros can then be executed by pressing Alt-F8 and selecting the appropriate one from a dialog box, or by pressing a preprogrammed keyboard shortcut, or by attaching the macro to a Ribbon command button. I hope you will find the following macros useful. They include calls to SmartView.bas functions; the code

---

* The keytips are the shortcuts the ribbon provides and displays as small rounded squares when the Alt or the / key are pressed.

is stored in the Personal Macros workbook. As a result of that storage location, they become permanently available. I have assigned a shortcut to most macros stored in my Personal Macros, and all use the control-key chord Shift-Ctl-Alt. This guarantees that the shortcut is not being used by any other Excel function or Add-in, although this may not be the case in your situation. My Personal Macros workbook contains a list of all my shortcuts so I can keep track of them. The assignments are refreshed every time I open Excel because they are executed by the Open_Workbook event in PERSONAL.XLSB, for example:

```
Application.OnKey "+^%N", XLSB_PATH & "NumberFormatNoDecimals"
```

Figure 8.20 highlights the fact that all the enhanced functionality described in this chapter was accomplished by accessing only about 10% (18 of 164 lines = 0.1098) of the SmartView.bas API (application programming interface).*

*8.4.2.1 Ancestor First*   Essbase Smart View drilldowns place ancestors below their respective descendants. Placing ancestors above descendants is displayed as a Smart View option (see Figure 8.21) but is available only when connecting to HFM. Selecting this is also possible when connecting to Smart Slices, and this may be a good reason to build a few of them. But another way to produce the same effect is a simple macro to sort based on hierarchical relationships between consecutive labels.†

*8.4.2.1.1 Code*

```
Public Sub AncestorFirst()
    MoveOrNot ActiveSheet, Selection(1).Column, Selection(1).Row _
                        , Selection(Selection.Cells.Count).Row
End Sub
Private Sub MoveOrNot(ByVal owks As Worksheet _
                    , ByVal iColumn As Integer _
                    , ByVal nFirstRow As Long _
                    , ByVal nLastRow As Long)
    Dim X, v, vtValues, vtPropertyValueString, t
    Dim sTemp As String
    Dim nRow As Long, nCandidateRow As Long, nComparisonCount As Long, nSwapCount As Long
    Dim bThereWasAChange As Boolean, bStoppedChanging As Boolean
```

---

* This metric is encouraging in at least three ways: It suggests a low-entry barrier, a high return on investment, and opportunities for even greater returns. The functions highlighted with a lighter background are functions we also could have used but didn't.

† This particular algorithm cannot handle multiple hierarchies at once. The purpose of this code is to demonstrate the use of SmartView.bas functions to accomplish a certain task. Taking care of every possible complexity (in this case the difference between shared members and stored members) and building an optimal algorithm are subjects beyond the scope of this chapter. Notice, nevertheless, the Boolean variable bStoppedChanging. When you start with a complete hierarchy in standard order, the moment an ancestor no longer has a descendant above it, you can confidently stop looking for other descendants. The algorithm will work if you sort each alternate hierarchy separately. Also, it does not recognize aliases, only member names (at least in my environments).

| MENU FUNCTIONS | GENERAL FUNCTIONS | CONNECTION FUNCTIONS | POV FUNCTIONS | OPTIONS FUNCTIONS |
|---|---|---|---|---|
| HypMenuVAbout | HypShowPanel | HypConnect | HypSetPOV | HypGetGlobalOption |
| HypMenuVAdjust | HypGetVersion | HypUIConnect | HypGetBackgroundPOV | HypSetGlobalOption |
| HypMenuVBusinessRules | HypGetLastError | HypConnected | HypSetBackgroundPOV | HypGetSheetOption |
| HypMenuVCalculation | HypShowPov | HypConnectionExists | HypGetPagePOVChoices | HypSetSheetOption |
| HypMenuVCascadeNewWorkbook | HypSetMenu | HypCreateConnection | HypSetPages | HypGetOption |
| HypMenuVCascadeSameWorkbook | HypCopyMetaData | HypCreateConnectionEx | HypGetMembers | HypSetOption |
| HypMenuVCellText | HypDeleteMetaData | HypDisconnect | HypSetMembers | HypDeleteAllMRUItems |
| HypMenuVCollapse | HypIsDataModified | HypDisconnectAll | HypGetActiveMember | |
| HypMenuVConnect | HypIsSmartViewContentPresent | HypDisconnectEx | HypSetActiveMember | |
| HypMenuVCopyDataPoints | HypIsFreeForm | HypGetSharedConnectionsURL | HypGetDimensions | DYNAMIC LINK FUNCTIONS |
| HypMenuVExpand | HypUndo | HypSetSharedConnectionsURL | HypSetDimensions | |
| HypMenuVFunctionBuilder | HypRedo | HypIsConnectedToSharedConnections | | HypUseLinkMacro |
| | | | | HypSetLinkMacro |
| HypMenuVInstruction | HypPreserveFormatting | HypRemoveConnection | | HypGetLinkMacro |
| HypMenuVKeepOnly | HypRemovePreservedFormats | HypInvalidateSSO | CALCULATION FUNCTIONS | HypGetSourceGrid |
| HypMenuVLRO | HypSetAliasTable | HypResetFriendlyName | HypListCalcScripts | HypDisplayToLinkView |
| HypMenuVMemberInformation | HypGetSubstitutionVariable | HypSetActiveConnection | HypExecuteCalcScript | HypGetConnectionInfo |
| HypMenuVMemberSelection | HypSetSubstitutionVariable | HypSetAsDefault | HypListCalcScriptsEx | HypSetConnectionInfo |
| HypMenuVMigrate | HypGetDatabaseNote | HypSetConnAliasTable | HypExecuteCalcScriptEx | HypGetRowCount |
| HypMenuVOptions | | | HypDeleteCalc | |
| HypMenuVPasteDataPoints | | | | |

**Figure 8.20** Inventory of SmartView.bas menu and API functions. Note: Skipped OBIEE, HFM, and HE functions. V 11.1.2.5 adds: HypHideRibbonMenu and HypHideRibbonMenuReset.

(*Continued*)

**MENU FUNCTIONS**

HypMenuVPivot
HypMenuVPOVManager
HypMenuVQueryDesigner
HypMenuVRedo
HypMenuVRefresh
HypMenuVRefreshAll
HypMenuVRefreshOfflineDefinition
HypMenuVRemoveOnly
HypMenuVRulesOnForm
HypMenuVRunReport
HypMenuVSelectForm
HypMenuVShowHelpHtml
HypMenuVSubmitData
HypMenuVSupportingDetails
HypMenuVSyncBack
HypMenuVTakeOffline
HypMenuVUndo
HypMenuVVisualizeinExcel
HypMenuVZoomIn
HypMenuVZoomOut
HypExecuteMenu

**AD HOC FUNCTIONS**

HypPerformAdhocOnForm
HypRetrieve
HypRetrieveRange
HypRetrieveNameRange
HypGetNameRangeList
HypRetrieveAllWorkbooks
HypExecuteQuery
HypSubmitData
HypPivot
HypPivotToGrid
HypPivotToPOV
HypKeepOnly
HypRemoveOnly
HypZoomIn
HypZoomOut

**CELL FUNCTIONS**

HypGetDimMbrsForDataCell
HypCell
HypFreeDataPoint
HypGetCellRangeForMbrCombination
HypGetDataPoint
HypIsCellWritable
HypSetCellsDirty
HypDeleteAllLROs
HypDeleteLROs
HypAddLRO
HypUpdateLRO
HypListLROs
HypRetrieveLRO
HypExecuteDrillThroughReport
HypGetDrillThroughReports

**MEMBER QUERY FUNCTIONS**

HypFindMember
HypFindMemberEx
HypGetAncestor
HypGetChildren
HypGetParent
HypIsAttribute
HypIsDescendant
HypIsAncestor
HypIsExpense
HypIsParent
HypIsChild
HypIsUDA
HypOtlGetMemberInfo
HypQueryMembers
HypGetMemberInformation
HypGetMemberInformationEx

**DYNAMIC LINK FUNCTIONS**

HypGetColCount
HypGetPOVCount
HypGetRowItems
HypSetRowItems
HypGetCollItems
HypSetCollItems
HypGetPOVItems
HypSetPOVItems

**MDX FUNCTIONS (*)**

HypExecuteMDXEx

**FORM FUNCTIONS**

HypOpenForm

**Figure 8.20** (Continued) Inventory of SmartView.bas menu and API functions. Note: Skipped OBIEE, HFM, and HE functions. V 11.1.2.5 adds: HypHideRibbonMenu and HypHideRibbonMenuReset.

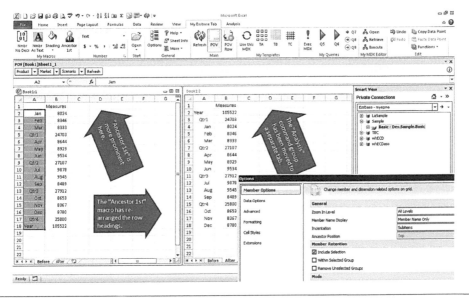

**Figure 8.21**   Ancestor First macro.

```
    If Len(Trim(owks.Cells(nLastRow - 1, iColumn).Value)) = 0 Then Exit Sub
    If nFirstRow >= nLastRow Then Exit Sub
    Application.ScreenUpdating = False
    nComparisonCount = 0: nSwapCount = 0
    nCandidateRow = nLastRow
    t = Now()
    Do
        nRow = nCandidateRow - 1
        bThereWasAChange = False
        Do
            X = HypIsDescendant(owks, Trim(owks.Cells(nCandidateRow, iColumn).Value) _
                          , Trim(owks.Cells(nRow, iColumn).Value))
            nComparisonCount = nComparisonCount + 1
            If X Then
                nSwapCount = nSwapCount + 1
                sTemp = Trim(owks.Cells(nCandidateRow, iColumn).Value)
                owks.Cells(nCandidateRow, iColumn).Value = Trim(owks.Cells(nRow, iColumn).Value)
                owks.Cells(nRow, iColumn).Value = sTemp
                bThereWasAChange = True
                nCandidateRow = nRow
                nRow = nCandidateRow - 1
            Else
                If bThereWasAChange Then bStoppedChanging = True
                nRow = nRow - 1
            End If
        Loop Until nRow < nFirstRow '' Or bStoppedChanging '' activating the second
          condition will speed up the algorithm
        bStoppedChanging = False
        If Not bThereWasAChange Then
            nLastRow = nLastRow - 1
        End If
        nCandidateRow = nLastRow
    Loop Until nFirstRow >= nLastRow
    X = HypRetrieve(owks)
    Debug.Print "Comparisons " & nComparisonCount, " Swaps : " & nSwapCount, Round((Now()
      - t) * 1000) & " milliseconds"
    Application.ScreenUpdating = True
End Sub
```

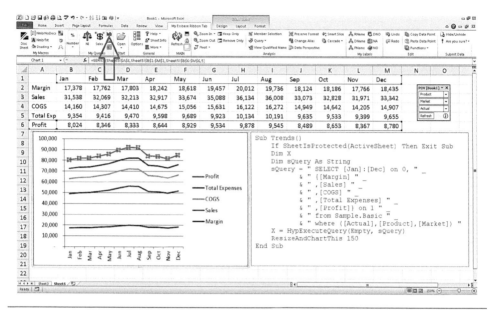

**Figure 8.22**  Simple Charting macro.

*8.4.2.2 Simple Charts*   With simple code, it is often possible to parse the results of a query and determine whether a chart can be produced, and then produce the chart. With this in mind, you can write generic macros and apply them to output you generate manually or by executing an MDX query. Figure 8.22 illustrates the automatic production of a multiline chart upon the execution of a macro called Trends. The user could have executed a regular ad hoc query or a free-form MDX query by placing it in the dialog box that appears when one selects Essbase > Analysis > Query > Execute MDX from the standard Essbase ribbon (as discussed in Section 8.3.4.5). In this example, the "Trends" macro executed an MDX query and then called a simple generic charting routine. The routine produced the multiline chart on the screenshot. All the code involved in this is shown in Figure 8.22 and in the code below. You can see how simple it is.*

*8.4.2.2.1 Code*

```
Sub ResizeAndChartThis(ByVal iZoomSize As Integer)
    Dim r As Range
    ActiveSheet.Range("A1").Select
    Set r = Selection.CurrentRegion
    r.Select
    Selection.NumberFormat = "_(* #,##0_);_(* (#,##0);_(* ""-""??_);_(@_)"
    ActiveSheet.Shapes.AddChart.Select
    ActiveChart.ChartType = xlLineStacked
    ActiveChart.SetSourceData Source:=r
    ActiveWindow.Zoom = iZoomSize
    ActiveWindow.ScrollRow = 1
```

---

* A similar tool is available as a "Super Pack" (see *, p. 399).

```
    ActiveWindow.ScrollColumn = 1
    ActiveSheet.Range("A1").Select
End Sub
```

*8.4.2.3 Executing Free-Form MDX from a Sheet Instead of from the Essbase Ribbon*    Of all the features discussed in this chapter, this is probably the most practical and the one with the most return on your investment.* In Section 8.5, we discuss the execution of this function from the ribbon and some of the details surrounding this capability. It is very easy to build a macro that will take an MDX statement written on one of the sheets in your workbook and execute it, depositing the results on a different sheet. It is also very easy to do simple validations to improve the probability that the script will run. This solution allows you to repeatedly modify your script and run it again, which you cannot do with the standard Smart View functionality. This essentially turns your Excel instance into a quick-and-dirty yet very effective MDX editor. Just being able to organize the query into components, placing each component in a separate cell, can be very helpful. This solution also allows you to save your queries for future use. Figure 8.23 looks similar to the ones in Section 8.3.4.5 but has one big difference: The results did not come from using the Analysis control group's Execute Free-Form MDX Query function, but rather from the Exec MDX button on my custom ribbon.

For the purposes of this discussion, we have isolated the Analysis control group by placing a copy of it on a special tab created for this purpose (see Figure 8.23). You would normally execute this from the Essbase Ribbon. The Essbase Ribbon's Analysis control group is available only while the active sheet is connected.

The macro's code is listed below (Sections 8.4.2.3.1 and 8.4.2.3.2). Notice in particular the use of the worksheet function Trim() instead of the VBA Trim() function. The worksheet function not only eliminates spaces around a string but also replaces sequences of spaces with a single space. When the user executes the ExecuteSimpleMDX public subroutine, it in turn calls the BuildMDXStatement() function, which concatenates all the cells in the A1:J40 range into a single string, trimming it so it is easier to parse and clean up. It then submits the resulting MDX for execution via the HypExecuteQuery() Smart View VBA function, depositing the results on the active sheet. By design, the macro executes the script written onto a sheet named MDX. The active sheet must be some other sheet. If you execute the macro while the script is displayed on the screen, you will be notified and directed to move to an empty sheet. You will also be notified if the active sheet is not yet connected or if the script contains obvious syntactical issues. You are responsible for (a) creating the MDX tab for the script and (b) connecting the active sheet. After execution, the

---

* Oracle publishes extensions to Smart View: http://www.oracle.com/technetwork/middleware/smart -view-for-office/downloads/index-088403.html. One in particular is most relevant to this chapter's discussion: Power Pack MDX Script Library Extension Version: 1.1.2.0. It has been designed to help you "Run MDX scripts and use them as a starting point for new queries. Compatible with Smart View 11.1.2.5.210 and above Updated 29-Apr-14."

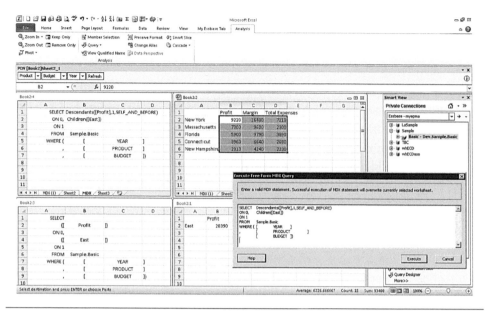

**Figure 8.23**  Execution of worksheet-resident MDX queries.

MDX worksheet can be copied or replicated so a different query may be written on the MDX worksheet. With this, you have the beginnings of an MDX query repository. An accompanying macro copies the contents of any sheet to the MDX sheet, so it is possible to both save many queries and execute any of them at any time. Figure 8.23 already shows evidence of this. The macro responsible for copying code from any sheet to the MDX sheet is the one labeled "Use this MDX," clearly displayed next to the Exec MDX button, in particular, in Figure 8.35.

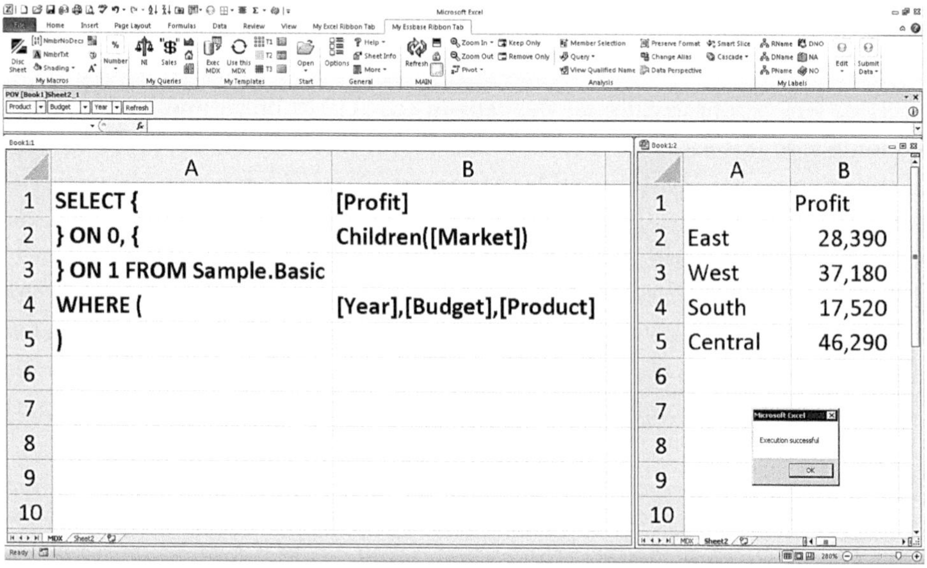

**Figure 8.24**  Simple MDX query validation.

Figure 8.24 demonstrates how, with minimal effort, you can leverage the Excel grid to separate fixed and variable query components. The very simple expression validation macro included here has identified common errors, and it is very easy to visually locate them (Figure 8.25). Section 8.5 refers back to this figure in discussing the ribbon and its self-adjusting behavior. After the syntactical errors are corrected, the query runs successfully and the results are displayed on the active sheet (see Figure 8.24).

In the example in Figure 8.25, I used one of the available templates. Templates will be discussed in Section 8.4.3. The code could have been entered by hand.

Figure 8.26 shows how VBA can also be used to add comments of any kind. The comment in cell A1 was copied from the template. The comment in cell B1 contains the text of the MDX query that produced the results displayed on the output sheet.

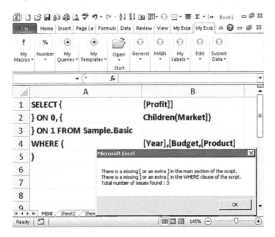

**Figure 8.25** A free-form MDX query and its results.

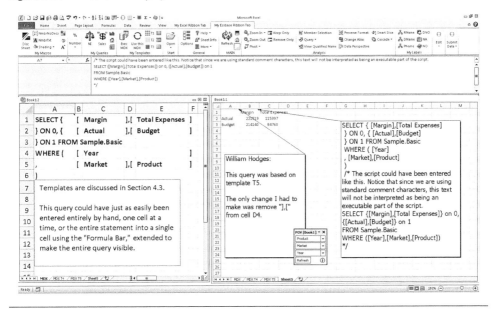

**Figure 8.26** Adding comments to queries, using commented templates.

*8.4.2.3.1 Code*

```
Public Sub ExecuteSimpleMDX()
    Dim sMDX As String
    Dim iAns As VbMsgBoxResult
    Dim X
    sMDX = BuildMDXStatement(ActiveWorkbook.Sheets("MDX"))
    If ThereAreSyntacticalIssues(sMDX) Then Exit Sub
    If WouldDestroyQuery(ActiveSheet) Then Exit Sub
    If Not IsSheetConnected(ActiveSheet) Then Exit Sub
    iAns = MsgBox(sMDX, vbOKCancel, "Does this look ok?")
    If iAns = vbOK Then
        X = HypExecuteQuery(Empty, sMDX)
        If X = 0 Then
            AddComments sMDX
            MsgBox "Execution successful"
        Else
            MsgBox "Error code: " & X
        End If
    End If
End Sub
```

*8.4.2.3.2 Supporting Functions*

```
Private Function BuildMDXStatement(ByRef oMDX As Worksheet) As String
    Dim n As Long, i As Integer
    Dim sMDX As String
    sMDX = ""
    For n = 1 To 40
        For i = 1 To 10
            sMDX = Replace(sMDX & " " _
                & Application.WorksheetFunction.Trim(oMDX.Cells(n, i).Value), vbTab, "")
        Next i
        sMDX = Replace(Replace(Application.WorksheetFunction.Trim(sMDX), vbTab, "") _
            , ",[ ]", "") & vbCrLf
    Next n
    sMDX = Replace(Replace(sMDX, "[ ", "["), " ]", "]")
    Debug.Print sMDX
    BuildMDXStatement = sMDX
End Function
Private Function WouldDestroyQuery(ByVal oWks As Worksheet) As Boolean
    If UCase(oWks.Name) = "MDX" Then
        MsgBox "Running the query on this worksheet would destroy the query." & vbCrLf & _
          "Please select a blank sheet."
        WouldDestroyQuery = True
    Else
        WouldDestroyQuery = False
    End If
End Function
Private Function IsSheetConnected(ByVal oWks As Worksheet) As Boolean
    If HypConnected(oWks) Then
        IsSheetConnected = True
    Else
        MsgBox "Please establish connection."
        IsSheetConnected = False
```

```
        End If
End Function
Private Function ThereAreSyntacticalIssues(ByVal sQuery As String) As Boolean
    Dim i As Integer, j As Integer, iLeftCount As Integer, iRightCount As Integer
    Dim q, vSection, vCharacterPairs
    Dim sMsg As String
    Dim iIssueCount As Integer
    vSection = Array("the main section", "the WHERE clause")
    vCharacterPairs = Array("()", "[]", "{}")
    q = Split(sQuery, "WHERE")
    ThereAreSyntacticalIssues = False: sMsg = "": iIssueCount = 0
    For i = 0 To UBound(q)
        For j = 0 To UBound(vCharacterPairs)
            iLeftCount = UBound(Split(q(i), Left(vCharacterPairs(j), 1)))
            iRightCount = UBound(Split(q(i), Right(vCharacterPairs(j), 1)))

            If iLeftCount <> iRightCount Then
                ThereAreSyntacticalIssues = True
                iIssueCount = iIssueCount + Abs(iLeftCount - iRightCount)
                ActiveWorkbook.Sheets("MDX").Activate
                If iLeftCount < iRightCount Then
                    sMsg = sMsg & "There is a missing " & Left(vCharacterPairs(j), 1) _
                                & " or an extra " & Right(vCharacterPairs(j), 1) _
                                & " in " & vSection(i) & " of the script." & vbCrLf
                ElseIf iLeftCount > iRightCount Then
                    sMsg = sMsg & "There is a missing " & Right(vCharacterPairs(j), 1) _
                                & " or an extra " & Left(vCharacterPairs(j), 1) _
                                & " in " & vSection(i) & " of the script." & vbCrLf
                End If
            End If
        Next j
    Next i
    If ThereAreSyntacticalIssues Then MsgBox sMsg & "Total number of issues found : " &
      iIssueCount
End Function

Private Sub AddComments(ByVal sMDX As String)
    If Not ActiveWorkbook.Sheets("MDX").Cells(1, 1).Comment Is Nothing Then
        With ActiveSheet.Cells(1, 1)
            .Clear
            .AddComment _
            Text:=ActiveWorkbook.Sheets("MDX").Cells(1, 1).Comment.Text
            With .Comment.Shape
                .Height = 250
                .Width = 200
                .Top = 110
                .Left = 10
                .Visible = True
                .TextFrame.Characters.Font.Size = 16
            End With
        End With
    End If
    With ActiveSheet.Cells(1, 2)
        If .Comment Is Nothing Then
            .AddComment Text:=sMDX
        Else
            .Comment.Text Text:=sMDX
        End If
        With .Comment.Shape
            .Height = 330
            .Width = 300
            .Top = 30
            .Left = 300
            .Visible = True
            .TextFrame.Characters.Font.Size = 16
```

```
      End With
   End With
End Sub
```

*8.4.2.4 POV Row*   Smart View 11.1.2.1.102 introduced the option to place the POV either on a POV toolbar or on the worksheet itself (the way page dimensions were displayed in the Excel Add-in). A drop-down menu (similar to cell validation in Excel) allows the selection of other dimension members from the same POV dimension. This new option has one complicating behavior: While the POV is being displayed in a POV toolbar, instead of removing the POV members from the spreadsheet, the first row is simply hidden. Repeated POV toggling actions can result in hiding more than one row, and users may prefer to still see the contents of the first row, even while the POV toolbar is displayed. The POV row macro was written to compensate by allowing the user to toggle the display of the first five rows of any worksheet. It is available through the command button next to the POV button in the Main command group of the My Essbase Ribbon Tab (discussed in Section 8.5). Below is the corresponding VBA code. This macro in particular illustrates how much a few lines of code can improve the experience of launching queries via Essbase Smart View.

### 8.4.2.4.1 Code

```
Sub UnhidePOVrow()
    Application.OnKey "+^%U", XLSB_PATH & "UnhidePOVrow"
    If ActiveSheet.Rows("1:1").Hidden = True Then
        ActiveSheet.Rows("1:5").Hidden = False
    Else
        ActiveSheet.Rows("1:1").Hidden = True
    End If
End Sub
```

*8.4.2.5 Standard Queries*   If you repeatedly execute certain Smart View queries, these are likely candidates for execution from your personal Smart View ribbon tab. It is possible to use VBA to place labels on an Excel worksheet, connect, and execute a refresh, but in this chapter, we focus on using MDX. So, whether you write the queries yourself or have someone write them for you, simply include them as macros in your PERSONAL.XLSB, as illustrated in Figure 8.27. With MDX, you can filter before getting the data and you can include user-defined dimension members, something you could not do in plain Smart View. The default listing of dimension members in MDX is in hierarchical order, but you can list ancestors after descendants the way Smart View displays its zoom-in results (look up 'Hierarchize' in the Essbase Technical Reference Manual). Again, this is not possible with plain Smart View. You can also sort by metadata as well as by data values using the ORDER() MDX function.

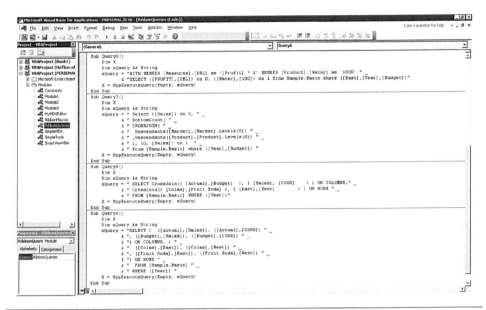

**Figure 8.27**   Running predefined queries from the ribbon.

Figure 8.27 shows how you can program standard queries you execute regularly so they can be executed like any other macro.

Figure 8.28 shows the results obtained from executing the queries in Figure 8.27 by clicking on buttons Q6, Q7, Q8, and Q9 in the My Queries command group of the corresponding My Essbase Ribbon Tab. For these macros to execute, the sheet must already be connected. Since the purpose is to keep the macros simple, the user is responsible for opening a connection before clicking on these buttons. Section 8.6 of

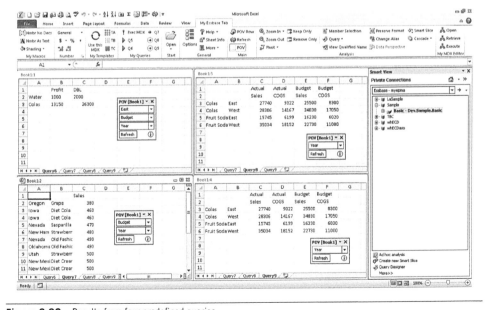

**Figure 8.28**   Results from four predefined queries.

this chapter is a more complete solution in this regard. At the discretion of the user, the mini-application described there can temporarily or permanently remember user credentials, eliminating the need to log in at every independent step.

Figure 8.29 shows a more recent version of my custom ribbon, with the standard queries better identified. The macros also perform additional tasks, such as formatting and building charts based on the data generated by the query.

If you compare the ribbon on the previous two screenshots with the ribbons in Section 8.5, you will notice several differences, which shows the evolutionary nature of tool development. The leftmost button on the custom ribbon was intended to be used to disconnect a sheet, which a user might want to do for a variety of reasons after the output has been generated, such as disconnecting or completely removing the connection information that remains after a sheet has been disconnected. In Figure 8.29, the Inventory tab was selected and then this button was pressed. This action disconnected the sheet and removed from the ribbon the Analysis control group, giving more room for all the other buttons to display their labels. The labels identifying the five reports can be clearly seen. The Trends report provides an example of the option to programmatically format the results of an MDX query. In this particular case, a graph has been created based on the results. The code responsible for the five queries is presented below. Charting is not done by the query itself; rather, the query calls a custom subroutine built as a general tool applicable to situations like this. The tool's code was presented in Section 8.4.2.2.

In Figure 8.30 (note the later version of the custom Essbase ribbon), I clicked on Qid and entered the name of a query saved as a text file (possibly in a shared network drive location). Qid accepts file names and query IDs. Query IDs identify predefined

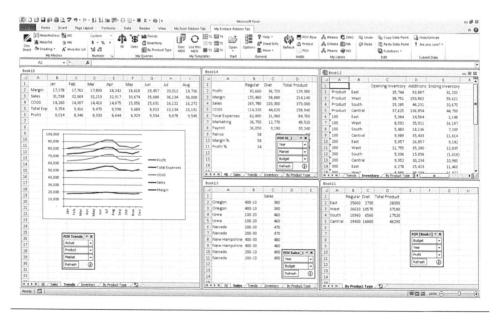

**Figure 8.29** Adding simple formatting to predefined queries.

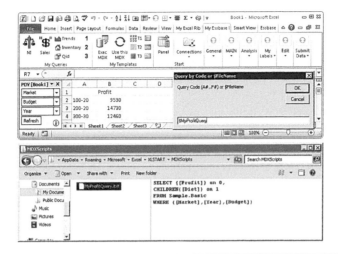

**Figure 8.30**    Executing MDX from a text file.

MDX queries stored as VBA subroutines. The code interprets anything following a "$" as indicating a file name. The file extension is optional. With this setup, the number of predefined queries a user would be able to run is practically limitless.

### 8.4.2.5.1 Code

```
Sub NI()
    If SheetIsProtected(ActiveSheet) Then Exit Sub
    Dim X: Dim sQuery As String
    sQuery = " WITH MEMBER [Product].[Total Product] as '[Product]' " _
        & " SELECT   " _
        & "   {[Regular],[Diet],[Total Product]} on 0 " _
        & " , NON EMPTY   " _
        & "   {Descendants([Profit]),Descendants([Ratios])} on 1 " _
        & " from [Sample.Basic] " _
        & " where ([Year],[Market],[Budget]) "
    If HypExecuteQuery(Empty, sQuery) <> 0 Then MsgBox X, vbCritical, "Error
detected"
End Sub
Sub Sales()
    If SheetIsProtected(ActiveSheet) Then Exit Sub
    Dim X
    Dim sQuery As String
    sQuery = " Select {[Sales]} on 0, " _
        & " BottomCount( " _
        & " CROSSJOIN( " _
        & "  Descendants([Market],[Market].Levels(0)) " _
        & " ,Descendants([Product],[Product].Levels(0)) " _
        & " ), 10, [Sales]) on 1  " _
        & " from [Sample.Basic] where ([Year],[Budget]) "
    If HypExecuteQuery(Empty, sQuery) <> 0 Then MsgBox X, vbCritical, "Error
        detected"
End Sub
Sub Trends()
    If SheetIsProtected(ActiveSheet) Then Exit Sub
```

```
    Dim X: Dim sQuery As String
    sQuery = " SELECT [Jan]:[Dec] on 0, " _
          & " {[Margin] " _
          & " ,[Sales] " _
          & " ,[COGS] " _
          & " ,[Total Expenses] " _
          & " ,[Profit]} on 1 " _
          & " from Sample.Basic " _
          & " where ([Actual],[Product],[Market]) "
    If HypExecuteQuery(Empty, sQuery) <> 0 Then MsgBox X, vbCritical, "Error
       detected"
    ResizeAndChartThis 150
End Sub
Sub Inventory()
    If SheetIsProtected(ActiveSheet) Then Exit Sub
    Dim X: Dim sQuery As String
    sQuery = " SELECT {[Opening Inventory],[Additions],[Ending Inventory]} on 0,
       " _
          & " CrossJoin(Descendants([Product],1,SELF_AND_
            BEFORE),Children([Market])) on 1 " _
          & " from Sample.Basic " _
          & " where ([Year],[Actual]) "
    If HypExecuteQuery(Empty, sQuery) <> 0 Then MsgBox X, vbCritical, "Error
       detected"
End Sub
Sub ByProductType()
    If SheetIsProtected(ActiveSheet) Then Exit Sub
    Dim X: Dim sQuery As String
    sQuery = " WITH MEMBER [Product].[Total Product] as '[Product]' " _
          & " SELECT {[Regular],[Diet],[Total Product]} on 0, " _
          & " Children([Market]) on 1 " _
          & " from [Sample.Basic] " _
          & " where ([Year],[Profit],[Budget]) "
    If HypExecuteQuery(Empty, sQuery) <> 0 Then MsgBox X, vbCritical, "Error
       detected"
End Sub
```

*8.4.2.6 Saved Queries* Since neither the macros nor the ribbon resides in the workbook being displayed (they are respectively in a hidden standard workbook called PERSONAL.XLSB and in an auxiliary file called Excel.officeUI), you are free to use the workbook as you wish, perhaps to save your queries and your results for future use or consultation (see Figure 8.31).

### 8.4.3 Templates

The term *template* is applicable to many situations. As one example, in this chapter, we focus on helping a user build an MDX query by providing most of the code and leaving only a few items open or unfinished for the user to complete. The approach or solution could be extended to other situations. This is just one example and one implementation of a much more encompassing mindset.

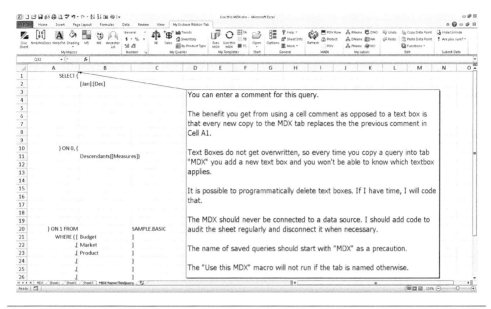

**Figure 8.31**   Saved Queries.

The example illustrated in Figure 8.32 is designed so that a user can click on one of the three template buttons (TA, TB, or TC). A template will be written to the MDX tab, which will be created if it does not exist. I copied the templates to the backup tabs labeled MDX (TA), MDX (TB), and MDX (TC) so you can see them. Typically, a user would first fill in the template and then copy it; it is always possible to get a blank copy by clicking on the corresponding button again.

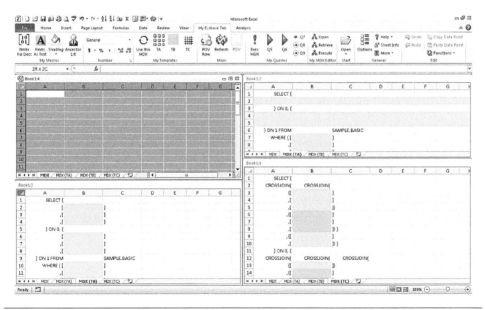

**Figure 8.32**   Building and leveraging an inventory of templates.

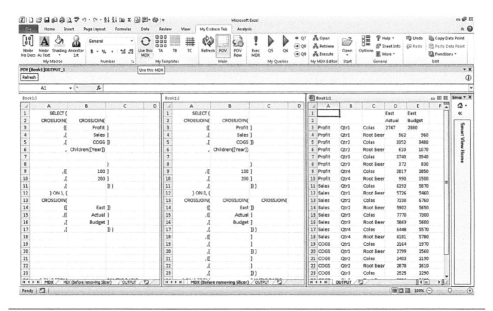

**Figure 8.33**   The code cleans up queries and removes unused template portions.

Figure 8.33 shows a filled-in template and the results obtained when the user clicked on the ! Exec MDX button. The user is not constrained by what the template presents. The user could just delete everything after reviewing the template and deciding it would be easier to build the query from scratch, or use the simplest available template and extend it, or remove sections of the template, or not use a template at all but start with a blank sheet and type in an MDX query from scratch (as we did in Section 8.4.2.3).

In Figure 8.33, the user started with template TC and filled it in with member names and a member set function. Then the user clicked on ! Exec MDX and got an error. The macro this button executes (see Section 8.4.2.3.1) is not smart enough to remove all unused portions of the template, only the most obvious ones. After removing all the superfluous template elements, the user clicked on the button again and got the results displayed in the third window.

*8.4.3.1 Parameterization*   Substitution variables are substituted when running a Smart View query or a Query Designer query. But when you execute an MDX query in the way described here, they are substituted on the fly at execution time so the variable name remains within the query definition itself. Aside from this, since you own the code that runs the query, you have many other options to implement dynamic executions. Some of these are listed in Section 8.6.4.

*8.4.4 Modules and Components*

The code in Section 8.4.2.1.1 consists of two modules, AncestorFirst() and MoveOrNot(). Although the same results could have been obtained using a single module, this design makes it possible to extend the functionality to more complex situations. MoveOrNot could be modified to work either horizontally or vertically. AncestorFirst() could be one instance of several callers or a more sophisticated caller applying the basic logic to, for example, hierarchize multidimensional row headings. More important than knowing how to use the SmartView.bas API (see Figure 8.20) is the ability to come up with simple, reliable algorithms. Any training in language-agnostic algorithm construction will be priceless in situations of this kind.

Sections 8.4.2.2.1 and 8.4.2.2.2 are additional examples of modularization. Ideally, any module should eventually become a tool (as defined in Section 8.4.2) and be made available to other situations.

### 8.4.5 Advanced Tools

The solutions proposed in Sections 8.4.2.2 and 8.4.3 should be helpful, but doing more is still possible to facilitate the execution of MDX queries and build a sophisticated collection of raw-data reports (as opposed to highly formatted reports) and empower data analysts to quickly and easily get to the answers they require. This is the focus of Section 8.6.

### 8.4.6 Applications

A short and simple definition of a turnkey Smart View application would be a software solution leveraging Smart View that does not look like Smart View. This is too restrictive to be 100% correct, but it emphasizes that the combination of data processing services we get from Smart View, Excel, and Essbase is sufficient to build packaged solutions, even commercial solutions. Guided by the principles presented in Section 8.2.2, in this chapter, we are more interested in understanding the building blocks and the process of developing the skills necessary to combine them into constantly evolving, one-of-a-kind applications, so we do no more than categorize them and acknowledge their potential existence.*

### 8.5 My Ribbon

Hierarchical menus, a revolutionary idea in the 1980s, had demonstrated their limitations by the mid-2000s. A new paradigm was needed, and after extensive research, Microsoft developed and introduced the "Ribbon," officially known as the "Fluent User Interface."[†,‡] Acceptance of this new paradigm by the user and the developer

---

* There could also be a separate discussion about the wisdom of building turnkey applications using this technology as opposed to technologies built specifically for that purpose. But since such solutions are possible and in fact exist in industry, we must include them as a category.
† See *, p. 412.
‡ http://en.wikipedia.org/wiki/Microsoft_Office_2007#Ribbon.

communities took some time, as did evolution of related customization tools (including the wizard now available within the Office suite itself). Both communities are now used to it and are actively exploring leveraging its capabilities. This section reviews opportunities to take advantage of this technology to improve the experience of interacting with Smart View and Essbase. This information should allow you to apply the chapter's ideas without requiring other sources of information, but the references throughout this chapter and the list at the end of the chapter provide additional tools and documentation. This section has two parallel objectives: (a) to provide opportunities to learn and use the technology and (b) to give specific examples of how this can be applied to the delivery of user-friendly, productivity-enhancing, Essbase data-querying solutions. As a first step toward both objectives, consider implementing and committing to regularly using a personal ribbon. Many options exist, and it is easy to get lost. Section 8.5.7 offers a strategy for navigating the process.

From a user's perspective, the Smart View Essbase add-in consists of one stationary ribbon (or ribbon tab, if you prefer to use the term to refer to the entire collection of ribbon tabs), hosting all the generic Smart View features, and one contingent ribbon tab, hosting all the features related exclusively to Essbase.* This design makes much sense in situations where multiple types of connections are possible (e.g., Essbase, HFM, Oracle Business Intelligence Enterprise Edition). Oracle's Smart View user manual (p. 18, V11.1.2.5) names 11 ribbons: Smart View, Essbase, Planning, Planning Ad Hoc, HFM, HFM Ad Hoc, Enterprise, Enterprise Ad Hoc, Oracle BI EE, Smart Query, and Oracle Hyperion Disclosure Management. There could be more.

Essbase Smart View users interact with only two Smart View ribbons or ribbon tabs on a regular basis and occasionally with a third one, Smart Query, available since version 11.1.2.2. Once the Smart View Add-in is installed, the Smart View ribbon tab appears as soon as you open Excel. The Essbase ribbon tab appears when you connect the active sheet to an Essbase cube and disappears when you completely disconnect the sheet or move to a disconnected sheet. You can verify this by connecting only some of your available sheets to Essbase. As you navigate through all the sheets (you might try [Ctrl]+[PgUp] and [Ctrl]+[PgDn] to do this), you will notice that the Essbase ribbon tab appears or disappears depending on whether the worksheet is associated with Essbase.

### 8.5.1 Modifying the Smart View and Essbase Ribbons

Excel ribbons are customizable. Since Office 2010, they can be customized interactively from within Excel (by right-clicking on the ribbon's background and then selecting Customize the Ribbon…). Simple changes are simple to make with the intuitive user interface. The options include, but are not limited to, adding custom tabs, adding components to existing tabs, and selecting to hide or display something. You can

---

* I use the terms *ribbon* and *ribbon tab* interchangeably depending on the context and the emphasis I believe it requires.

modify the Smart View and/or the Essbase ribbons, or you can build your own versions of them. Complex changes, on the other hand, can easily become unmanageable if customization is not your primary line of work. This section focuses on customizations that require manipulating the Excel.officeUI file. But why would you do any of this?

*8.5.1.1 Justification*   Reasons for modifying the ribbons include the following:

a. To keep the Submit button as far away as possible from the tabs or any other often-used button
b. To place the most-often-used buttons as close to the corresponding tab as possible
c. To use available space for often-used Excel commands, to stay within the Essbase and Smart View ribbons as long as possible
d. To put all the buttons you regularly use on a single tab
e. To organize the individual buttons differently and to change their accelerator keys (proper name: keytips)
f. To add functionality to Smart View (to execute macros by clicking buttons on the ribbon)

*8.5.1.2 Technical Details*

a. Buttons in the Essbase command groups cannot be removed individually, but new custom groups can be built to host custom buttons.
b. If you do not use all the commands in the Essbase and Smart View ribbon tabs, you might benefit from putting the commands you do use on a personal ribbon and hiding the original tabs. This is my preference and is demonstrated in this chapter.
c. Ribbon components adjust themselves to optimize the use of the available space. If a tab is already full and you add buttons to it, the icons and the text are rearranged and made smaller as needed to make room for the new buttons (see examples below).
d. If you leave the original ribbons intact, you will be able to easily move back and forth between a customized environment and a standard environment.

*8.5.2 Building Your Own Personal Ribbon*

If you rarely use Smart View to submit values to the database but your situation requires that you connect to Essbase in read/write mode, then you might agree that having a Submit button in two places, and in one case very close to the Refresh button, is asking for trouble.

Figure 8.34 shows two instantiations of my own personal Essbase ribbon, containing all the functionality I use often in my daily work. The Smart View and the Essbase

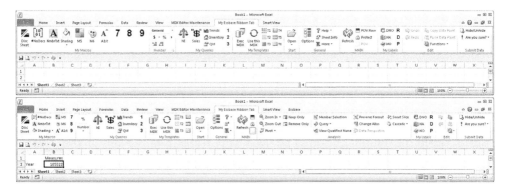

**Figure 8.34**   My personal ribbon in two states: disconnected and connected.

tabs are still available—later in the chapter, they no longer appear because I prefer to keep them hidden and make them visible only when necessary. Please note the Quick Access toolbar below the ribbon. It includes the Smart View Refresh button so that it is continuously available when moving between tabs. There is no Submit button. There is a control group labeled Submit Data, but this is just an access point to another location where it is possible to click to submit data.

On a printed page, it is difficult to see all the detail, but Figures 8.35 and 8.36 show the same ribbon with some of the button groups deactivated to leave more room for the other groups. Five versions are displayed, the first showing only 5 of the 10 button groups normally displayed on the ribbon (11 when connected); the second showing the same content but with the tab already selected, making the button keytips appear; the third with four of the previously hidden groups displayed; and the fourth with the not previously displayed Essbase Edit button group and with the custom Submit Data menu expanded. The fifth (Figure 8.36) focuses on demonstrating how the autoScale attribute can make the Analysis button group become much smaller than it normally is but still fully accessible. The fifth version is the only one that shows the ribbon in its connected state. The Notepad file behind the Excel Window shows the setting that determines how the Analysis group will behave if space on the ribbon is limited. We will discuss how to activate and deactivate groups further below. In the fourth example, owing to the extra amount of space available, the corresponding Number and General groups are wider than in the previous cases. These ribbon instances were set up only for readability on these pages; they defeat the purpose of having a single ribbon on the screen to access all the commonly used features.*

*8.5.2.1 Observations*   Figures 8.35 and 8.36 illustrate the following relevant facts:

   1. Button groups and buttons expand and contract based on the available space.

---

* These displays also required a smaller screen resolution so all the automatic adjustments would result in larger complete components.

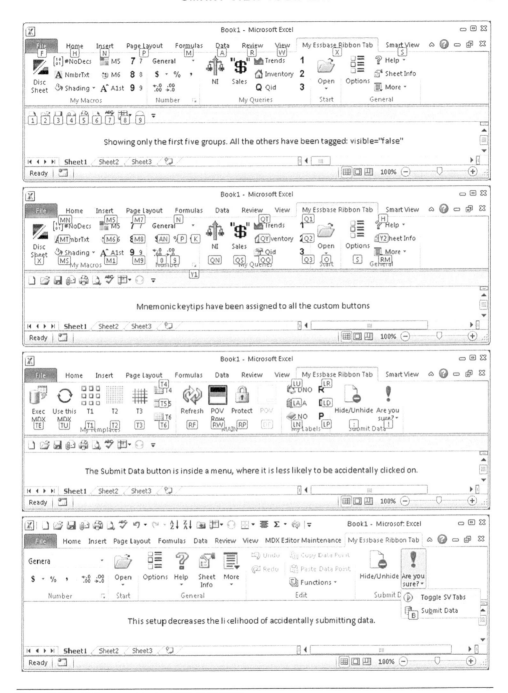

**Figure 8.35** Button groups, some visible, some hidden.

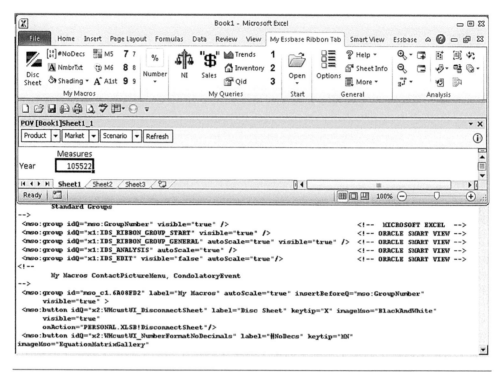

**Figure 8.36**  Autoscaled Analysis group—active sheet connected.

2. Excel's own View tab option to remove gridlines, headings, and the formula bar has been applied to have more space to display the items to be discussed.

3. The Essbase tab and the Analysis button group are not visible until the sheet is connected to Essbase. Adding the Analysis button group to the ribbon forces other button groups to contract, which can happen in two different ways. Your ribbon's overall behavior will ultimately depend on the specific combination of ribbon configuration settings you choose; they will determine which buttons have priority over the available space.

4. You are already familiar with the ribbon's keytips (even if you are not familiar with the term *keytip* itself). Smart View has been reserved the use of the letter S. The Essbase tab typically gets the generic keytip Y1. This personal ribbon's configuration file (Excel.officeUI; details discussed later) has reserved the use of the letter X for the My Essbase Ribbon Tab. The figures do not show this, but the configuration file has also reserved the use of the letter Z for the Essbase tab.

5. The Quick Access Toolbar automatically assigns numeric keytips to its buttons. Depending on your version of Excel, some assignments may be fixed and cannot be controlled. Adding more than nine buttons starts a two-digit sequence beginning with 09. The fourth instance in Figure 8.35 illustrates the addition of a few built-in buttons such as the button to insert a SUM()

worksheet function. The toolbar can be displayed above or below the ribbon (displaying it above the ribbon saves screen space).

6. Wherever possible, keytips have been assigned to all the custom buttons via the Excel.officeUI ribbon configuration file (see Figure 8.35). It is possible to use special characters as keytips (e.g., the buttons in the [Submit Data] button group). My selection of keyboard sequences for all the ribbon's controls was based on personal preferences. For example, to refresh a query, I can type Alt-XRF or /XRF; to protect a sheet, I can type Alt-XRP or /XRP.

7. The ribbon gives access to Excel tools (number formatting, shading), Essbase features, and custom programming code.

8. Buttons can be distinguished by their label, their keytip, and their icon. Excel provides the option to assign any available icon to any custom button. For example, the Exec MDX custom button has been assigned Microsoft's ImportMoreMenu icon. Steps to add icons to buttons are presented below. A button does not have to have a label, icon, or keytip, but the button's usefulness is reduced if it does not have at least one of them.

9. As suggested by its label, the My Macros button group executes macros. These reside in my PERSONAL.XLSB file. This is the file Excel uses for general purpose custom VBA code applicable to any open workbook. Since the personal ribbon is mostly a general purpose interface, not an interface for a specific Essbase application, and since placing the macros there requires minimal effort, PERSONAL.XLSB has been chosen to function as the host for all the personal Essbase ribbon macros. In this example, all except the A1st macro execute Excel macros. Programming macros for Smart View was discussed in Section 8.4.2. The ribbon provides a user interface for these macros, so you do not have to press Alt-F8 and scroll through a long list of available macros.

10. The buttons in the My Queries button group also execute macros, but these are all MDX queries, to be executed on a connected sheet using the HypExecuteQuery() SmartView.bas API function. This topic was discussed in Section 8.4.2.5.

11. Button Qid in the My Queries group opens a standard input box where you can enter a query identifier. This allows you to add queries to your existing inventory without having to change the ribbon itself. The queries can be hardcoded, as are the ones in Figure 8.25, or stored in text files, as demonstrated in Figure 8.30.*

12. The My Templates button group provides support for the features discussed in Section 8.4.3.

13. The MAIN control group has been designed to be the focus of all activity related to Smart View. The Analysis button group is displayed to its immediate

---

* Presently, these are stored in a personal folder, but they could also be stored on a network drive. Reading from a database is also a viable option.

right whenever the active sheet is connected. The POVrow icon, in particular, gives quick access to the functionality described in Section 8.4.2.4. The padlock icon executes Excel's ActiveSheet.Protect command.

14. The My Labels group was designed to give quick access to the Smart View option to display names or names and aliases and to manipulate dimension member names already being displayed in cells; this provides a way to jump from one area of the Essbase cube to another (see Section 8.3.4.1 and Figure 8.3). The first feature is particularly useful for quickly switching from uniquely identified shared members to their corresponding stored member. The second feature is very useful to me, given the legacy application designs I work with, but may not be applicable at all in your situation. Another use for this tool might be to switch a query to a related inventory part number.

15. The submit button is still available, but you have to go through some trouble to get to it, which is a good thing.

16. The MDX Editor Maintenance tab (the custom tab to the left of the My Essbase Ribbon Tab, see fourth Smart View instance in Figure 8.35) demonstrates the possibility of adding multiple custom tabs. Its purpose pertains to the subject matter in Section 8.6, but it also keeps the My Essbase Ribbon Tab and the Refresh button close to each other when the active sheet is connected to Essbase, making it very easy to quickly Refresh a sheet (almost as easy as clicking the My Essbase Ribbon Tab twice).

17. To get to the submit button, you need to click on the "Are you sure?" dropdown menu. Use the Hide/Unhide button to toggle the availability of the menu for additional protection. Use the Toggle SV tabs button to show or hide the standard Smart View tabs (in addition to the My Essbase Ribbon tab). This chapter does not discuss programmatic interactions with the ribbon using a feature known as callbacks. Therefore, these two toggle buttons are not meant to be considered operational but simply indicators of what is possible. By adding components to the ribbon, it is possible to force the last group to shrink into a single button, effectively changing the group into a menu. This may be all you need to hide the submit button. I was specifically interested in exploring advanced features. But if you need to stay with an implementation that can be maintained interactively, all you need to do is avoid features that the Customize the Ribbon... wizard cannot handle.

### 8.5.3 Configuring the Ribbon

Figure 8.37 provides a good starting point for this section's discussion and illustrates what happens when the control groups on a ribbon cannot all be displayed: Those that do not fit are shrunk into a single button. If an icon has been assigned to the group, then the group icon is displayed. In Figure 8.37, none of the groups have been assigned an icon, so all are displaying a default image. This is the same ribbon that displayed

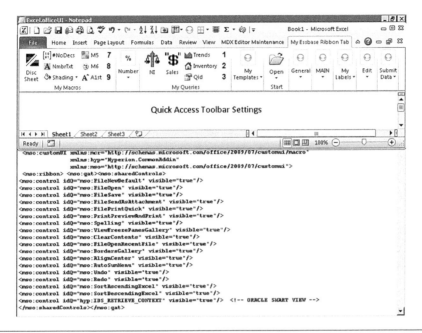

**Figure 8.37**  Quick Access Toolbar settings.

completely in earlier figures. In this case, it did not fit because the screen on which it is being displayed has a lower resolution. The Excel window is being displayed on top of an instance of Notepad. Both applications occupy the entire width of the screen, but the length of the vertical axis of Excel has been reduced to show the contents of the Notepad behind it. Notepad is displaying the contents of the Excel.officeUI file that defines Excel's ribbon. All you can see are the Quick Access Toolbar settings. To make a toolbar button appear or disappear, all you have to do is change the visible attribute. To permanently remove a button as a ready-to-use option, simply remove the corresponding row from the file. Practically any item that could appear on the ribbon can also be made to appear on the toolbar. All the buttons mentioned between the <mso:qat> and the </mso:qat> tags are Microsoft Excel options except the last one, which represents the Refresh button from Oracle Smart View. Excel interprets the list by referencing the namespaces mentioned at the beginning. The "<!--" and "-->" tags serve the purpose of delimiting a comment. All the comments were added manually.

Just as you can show or hide a Quick Access Toolbar button, you can also show or hide an entire tab, a button group on a tab, or a button within a custom button group. The entire contents of the Excel.officeUI are available in Section 8.4.6.3. Figure 8.38 shows the contents that define My Essbase Ribbon Tab up to the definition of the My Macros button group. The tab definition itself does not currently have but could have a visible="true" attribute. Every component on the tab, on the other hand, has a visible="something" attribute and, therefore, can be made to appear or remain hidden when Excel (and its ribbon) is loaded into memory. Several components have also been assigned an autoScale="something" attribute to control whether the group should stay

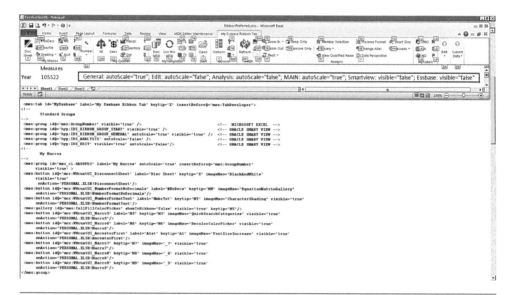

**Figure 8.38**   The My Macros section of the Excel.officeUI file.

**Figure 8.39**   Autoscaling the Analysis button group.

expanded as long as possible or quickly cede some of its display area to other buttons before deciding it must shrink down to a single icon, as did the My Templates, General, MAIN, My Labels, Edit, and Submit Data groups in the previous example (Figure 8.37).

Notice in particular the behavior of the Analysis button group when its autoScale attribute is set to "true" (see Figure 8.39). Although the Analysis group, when fully expanded, takes up too much space, I believe it is so important to the effective use of Smart View that I prefer to allow other groups to autoScale first, or even shrink down to a single icon, rather than foregoing the benefit of the Analysis group being fully displayed. You may have a different opinion in this regard.

### 8.5.4 Evolution and Comparisons

Comparing the screenshots in this section with similar screenshots in previous sections (in particular Figures 8.19, 8.21, 8.22, 8.28, 8.31, 8.32, and 8.33) highlights variations in ribbon content. These are simply because of evolution through time. Rather than synchronizing all the screenshots to show a single version, we emphasize the evolutionary nature of this type of project, especially if it is the development of a personal tool over which you have full control. As new opportunities arise or new ideas develop, you have the freedom to improve your solution.

### 8.5.5 Options and Approaches

Users can customize the ribbon gradually, in accordance with resources and level of expertise, while still keeping a long-term goal in mind. Table 8.5 identifies six levels of evolutionary involvement in this type of project. All the solutions in this chapter, even the most advanced, belong either to level 1 or 2.

Level 1 leverages two native features within Excel that allow you to build ribbon customizations in a manner of minutes.

a. Since Excel Version 2010, ribbons can be customized manually and interactively; Excel saves the configuration in a file called Excel.officeUI, typically in one of the folders under the AppData user folder.
b. A user can record general purpose macros and save them in a default location, a hidden macro-enabled binary file called PERSONAL.XLB, also in one of the folders under AppData user folder.

Thus, with minimal effort and avoiding having to figure out an overall design and organization of components, you can complete customization very quickly. But more is possible, and adding more functionality does not require starting over. Smart View, your PERSONAL.XLB file, and your Excel.officeUI file all work as interchangeable parts. You can have multiple copies of the Excel.officeUI file and load any one of them at any time.

The result when you let Excel manage the changes might be too convoluted and messy. Attempting some advanced features may destroy your work, so you always

**Table 8.5** Ribbon Customization Learning Curve

| LVL | DISTINGUISHING CHARACTERISTIC | APPEAL | REMARKS |
|---|---|---|---|
| 1 | Persistence managed by Excel | Simplest | Customize manually using interactive customization of the ribbon itself in Excel. Store macros in PERSONAL.XLSB |
| 2 | Modified Excel.office UI | Next step | With minor tweaks, your interactive customization can be made to resemble a programmed customization. You start using Custom UI Editor for Microsoft Office |
| 3 | Workbook component | Most popular | Macro enabled (FileName.xlsm) file includes customUI.xml file |
| 4 | Callbacks | VBA can talk to the ribbon | Without callbacks, the ribbon can launch VBA code, but VBA cannot interact with the ribbon, for example, to hide a button |
| 5 | Workbook template | Original is not changed | Template: FileName.xltm |
| 6 | Excel Add-in | Tighter integration with Excel | Add-in: FileName.xlam |

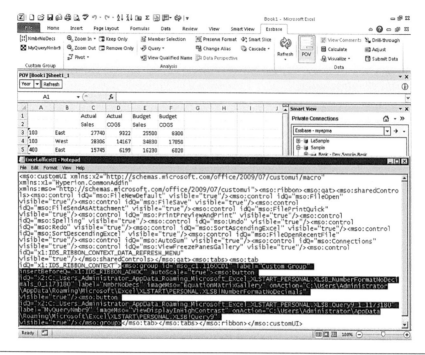

**Figure 8.40** Excel.officeUI hosts the configuration of the ribbon. See http://www.developingessbasebook.com for this code.

should keep a backup copy of your latest Excel.officeUI file. But as long as you keep your customizations simple, this will work fine. Section 8.5.6.1 and Figure 8.40 present the contents of an Excel.officeUI file generated automatically by Excel upon the addition to the Essbase tab of one custom group with two buttons on it. Section 8.5.6.2 shows code generated by Excel after completing a much more extensive customization, then simplified a little to make it more readable. Section 8.5.6.3 shows the complete contents of a very recent Excel.officeUI file in one of my environments. It still traces its origins back to the initial file generated by Excel, but it has been extensively edited with some sections added manually, and it has been processed by the CustomUI Editor multiple times.

Once level 1 customization (as defined here) is reached, you can extend it by adding minor tweaks to the .officeUI file, writing new UI files from scratch following the example of the one generated automatically by Excel, modifying recorded macros, and/or building new ones from scratch in the Visual Basic Editor (Alt-F11), etc. At some point in this stage, you will be able to let loose of all the interactive ribbon customization work you did during the first level and you will find yourself in full control of your ribbon customizations. At the beginning of level 2, you start using specialized programming tools such as the CustomUI Editor, developed by Microsoft and available for download for free.* Toward the end of level 2, Notepad will be all you need.

---

* CustomUIEditor, originally from Microsoft, downloadable from http://openxmldeveloper.org/blog/b /openxmldeveloper/archive/2006/05/25/customuieditor.aspx.

You might use the CustomUI Editor to find deeply hidden typographical errors, but Notepad will be sufficient and quicker to use. Discussing in this chapter the advanced methods in levels 3 through 6 would be contrary to our objectives and could even be discouraging, making the task look too complicated to even consider. Therefore, we will only discuss levels 1 and 2 in further detail.

### 8.5.6 Examples

Before any customization takes place, no Excel.officeUI file exists on the user's AppData folder group. But as soon as something is changed and the ribbon is no longer in its default state, the file is created and all details related to the customization are included in the file. This subsection shows three stages of development to try. Stage 1: You add to the Essbase ribbon one custom group containing two buttons; one button executes a predefined MDX query and the other one adds a number format to the currently selected range. Stage 2: You make many more changes; Excel produces a very difficult to read file; you manipulate the file a little to make it more readable. Stage 3: You begin to understand and manage and rearrange and augment all the sections within the Excel.officeUI file. There is no turning back at this point because it would open the possibility for destruction of complex customization features that the Customize the Ribbon… wizard cannot handle, even simple ones like comments enclosed in "<!-- -->" tags, and because you find that it is much easier to edit the Excel.officeUI file, which by now you know very well. Sections 8.5.6.1 through 8.5.6.3 provide additional details.

*8.5.6.1 Stage 1: One Group, Two Buttons* The highlighted section in Figure 8.40 represents the added group. Notice in particular the very long identifiers and the explicit paths to the PERSONAL.XLSB file. "x1:IDS_RIBBON_CONTEXT" is the Essbase ribbon tab. It is the only tab mentioned between the <mso:tabs> and </mso:tabs> markers because it is the only modification made to any of the ribbon tabs. When created by Excel, this file does not contain any end-of-line characters, another reason it is difficult to read. The custom group is automatically added at the beginning or at the end of the tab. Controlling its position requires making a manual change to the Excel.officeUI file to add insertBefore or insertAfter attributes. This file typically resides in the following folder:

```
C:\Users\<userId>\AppData\Local\Microsoft\Office
```

Section 8.5.6.3 delves further into the subject of editing the Excel.officeUI.

*8.5.6.2 Stage 2: More Extensive Manual Customization* The following code segment was extracted from the Excel.officeUI created by Excel after many of the additions discussed in this chapter had been implemented. Rearranging the contents was necessary just to be able to present them here. The rows containing a sequence of dots ("....") represent excluded chunks of code. I have respected the general structure, and what is being displayed is representative of what has been excluded. Each item is now described on a separate line, the identifiers are shorter, and a certain amount of hierarchical indentation facilitates understanding the hierarchical relationships implied by the ribbon's definition. Although it was sufficient up to this point to modify the file interactively within Excel by clicking on the Customize the Ribbon... option that opens when you right-click on the ribbon's background, making any kind of adjustment is quickly becoming a burden. The very fact that it was possible to make changes suggests that not every character generated by Excel is necessary and points us to a different approach for managing our ribbon.

```
<mso:customUI xmlns:x2="http://schemas.microsoft.com/office/2009/07/customui/
   macro"
              xmlns:x1="Hyperion.CommonAddin"
              xmlns:mso="http://schemas.microsoft.com/office/2009/07/customui">
<mso:ribbon>

<mso:qat>
 <mso:sharedControls>
  <mso:control idQ="mso:FileNewDefault" visible="true"/>
  <mso:control idQ="mso:FileOpen" visible="true"/>
  <mso:control idQ="mso:FileSave" visible="true"/>
....
....
  <mso:control idQ="mso:ViewFreezePanesGallery" visible="true"/>
  <mso:control idQ="x1:IDS_RIBBON_CONTEXT_DATA_REFRESH_MENU" visible="true"/>
 </mso:sharedControls>
</mso:qat>
<mso:tabs>
  <mso:tab idQ="x1:IDS_SMARTVIEW"  visible="false"/>
  <mso:tab idQ="x1:IDS_RIBBON_CONTEXT"  visible="false"/>
  <mso:tab id="mso_c1.F4FEBD"  label="My Essbase
    Tab"insertAfterQ="x1:IDS_RIBBON_CONTEXT">
  <mso:group id="mso_c1.7B5A51"  label="My Macros" autoScale="true">
  <mso:button
   idQ="x2:XLSTART_PERSONAL.XLSB_NumberFormatNoDecimals_0_8F36FA"
   label="Nmbr No Decs" imageMso="EquationMatrixGallery"
   onAction="C:\Users\wh\AppData\Roaming\Microsoft\Excel\XLSTART\PERSONAL.
     XLSB!NumberFormatNoDecimals"
   visible="true"/>
  <mso:button
   idQ="x2:XLSTART_PERSONAL.XLSB_NumberFormatText_1_8F36FA"
   label="Nmbr As Text" imageMso="CharacterShading"
   onAction="C:\Users\wh\AppData\Roaming\Microsoft\Excel\XLSTART\PERSONAL.
     XLSB!NumberFormatText"
   visible="true"/>
   <mso:gallery idQ="mso:CellFillColorPicker" showInRibbon="false"
     visible="true"/>
  <mso:button
   idQ="x2:XLSTART_PERSONAL.XLSB_AncestorFirst_0_3FF3631"
   label="Ancestor !st" imageMso="CondolatoryEvent"
   onAction="C:\Users\wh\AppData\Roaming\Microsoft\Excel\XLSTART\PERSONAL.
     XLSB!AncestorFirst"
```

```
    visible="true"/>
 </mso:group>
....
....
</mso:tab>
</mso:tabs>
</mso:ribbon>
</mso:customUI>
```

*8.5.6.3 Stage 3: A Cleaner, Extensively Reformatted, and Augmented Excel officeUI File*  A cleaner version of the Excel.officeUI was produced with the help of the CustomUI Editor, developed by Microsoft but available, as per instructions by Microsoft, from the following site:

```
http://openxmldeveloper.org/blog/b/openxmldeveloper
  /archive/2006/05/25/customuieditor.aspx
```

This tool was useful in determining what is essential and what is not. Making changes and seeing that this did not cause errors or changes in behavior helped identify what could be done to simplify the file and make it more readable and manageable. This tool, with an advanced text editor, allowed us to (a) add line breaks to the original xml to facilitate formatting, (b) validate the syntax, (c) create separations between sections, (d) change the order of presentation within the file and the position on the ribbon, and (e) add comments.

The code below displays the entire contents of a shortened but working version of my personal ribbon's Excel.officeUI at the time this chapter was finalized. The complete version is available at the website for this book, http://developingessbasebook .com. A few comments:

a. I standardized the definition of namespaces; all are identified by a three-letter code (mcr, hyp, and mso). Thanks to this, most of them can be referenced using idQ="something," eliminating the need to decide whether to use idQ or idMso. The only items still identified by an unqualified ID are the custom tabs and the menu in the [Submit Data] group.

b. You can add comments anywhere, including at the beginning of the file (mso:customUI does not have to be the first line in the file).

c. The file does not need to include the standard XML file type identifier on the first line.

d. The items that I added (not just modified) are the following:
   i. The insertBefore and insertAfter attributes
   ii. The autoScale attribute
   iii. The keytip attribute
   iv. Manual line breaks to separate lines as shown on the page.
   v. The comments (the text between the <!-- and --> tags, including the tags themselves).

Section 8.5.7 offers additional details and recommendations for making the ribbon-building experience as rapid and as stress-free as possible.

```
<mso:customUI
    xmlns:mcr="http://schemas.microsoft.com/office/2009/07/customui/macro"
    xmlns:hyp="Hyperion.CommonAddin"
    xmlns:mso="http://schemas.microsoft.com/office/2009/07/customui">
<mso:ribbon>
<mso:qat>
<mso:sharedControls>
<mso:control idQ="mso:FileOpenRecentFile" visible="true"/>
<mso:control idQ="mso:AutoSumMenu" visible="true"/>
<mso:control idQ="hyp:IDS_RETRIEVE_CONTEXT" visible="true"/>
<!-- ORACLE SMART VIEW -->
</mso:sharedControls>
</mso:qat>
<!-- ~~(note that a comment cannot contain dashes)~~ Custom Ribbon Tabs ~~~~~  -->
<mso:tabs>
<mso:tab id="MyEssbase" label="My Essbase Ribbon Tab" keytip="X" insertBeforeQ="mso:
  TabDeveloper" visible="true">
<!-- ~~~~~~~~~~~~~~~~~~~~~ Standard Groups ~~~~~~~~~~~~~~~~~~~~~~~~~~~  -->
<mso:group idQ="mso:GroupNumber" visible="true" />
  <!-- MICROSOFT EXCEL  -->
<mso:group idQ="hyp:IDS_RIBBON_GROUP_START" visible="true" autoScale="false"/>
  <!-- ORACLE SMART VIEW -->
<mso:group idQ="hyp:IDS_RIBBON_GROUP_GENERAL" autoScale="true" visible="true" />
  <!-- ORACLE SMART VIEW -->
<mso:group idQ="hyp:IDS_ANALYSIS" autoScale="false" />
  <!-- ORACLE SMART VIEW -->
<mso:group idQ="hyp:IDS_EDIT" visible="true" autoScale="true"/>
  <!-- ORACLE SMART VIEW -->
<!-- ~~~~~~~~~~~~~~~~~~~~~~~~ My Queries ~~~~~~~~~~~~~~~~~~~~~~~~~~~~~~  -->
<mso:group id="m6E8B3E7" label="My Queries" imageMso="ViewGoForward"
autoScale="true" insertBeforeQ="mso:GroupNumber" visible="true" >
<mso:button idQ="mcr:WHcustUI_NI" label="NI" keytip="QN" imageMso="SetPertWeights"
visible="true" onAction="PERSONAL.XLSB!NI"/>
<mso:button idQ="mcr:WHcustUI_Sales" label="Sales" keytip="QS"
  imageMso="DollarSign" visible="true" onAction="PERSONAL.XLSB!Sales"/>
</mso:group>
<!-- ~~~~~~~~~~~~~~~~~~~~~~~ My Templates ~~~~~~~~~~~~~~~~~~~~~~~~~~~~~  -->
<mso:group id="Templates" label="My Templates" autoScale="true"
  insertBeforeQ="mso:GroupNumber" visible="true" >
<mso:button idQ="mcr:WHcustUI_ExecMDX" label="Exec MDX" keytip="TE"
imageMso="ImportMoreMenu" visible="true"
onAction="PERSONAL.XLSB!ExecuteSimpleMDX"/>
<mso:button idQ="mcr:WHcustUI_UseThisMDX" label="Use this MDX" keytip="TU"
  imageMso="RecurrenceEdit" visible="true" onAction="PERSONAL.XLSB!UseThisMDX"/>
<mso:button idQ="mcr:WHcustUI_BuildMDXTemplate1" label="T1" keytip="T1"
imageMso="SlidesPerPage9Slides" visible="true"
onAction="PERSONAL.XLSB!BuildMDXTemplate1"/>
</mso:group>
<!-- ~~~~~~~~~~~~~~~~~~~~~~~~ MAIN ~~~~~~~~~~~~~~~~~~~~~~~~~~~~~~~~~~~~  -->
<mso:group id="m6670DD" label="MAIN" autoScale="true"
  insertAfterQ="hyp:IDS_RIBBON_GROUP_GENERAL" visible="true" >
<mso:button idQ="mcr:WHcustUI_UnhidePOVrow" label="POV Row" keytip="RW"
imageMso="BlackAndWhiteInverseGrayscale"
onAction="PERSONAL.XLSB!UnhidePOVrow"/>
<mso:button idQ="mcr:WHcustUI_ProtectSheet" keytip="RP" label="Protect"
imageMso="Lock" onAction="PERSONAL.XLSB!ProtectSheet"/>
<mso:control idQ="hyp:IDS_RIBBON_DATA_REFRESH_MENU" keytip="RF"
  insertBeforeQ="mcr:WHcustUI_UnhidePOVrow"/>
```

```
<mso:control idQ="hyp:IDS_POV" visible="true" insertAfterQ="msoProtect"/>
</mso:group>
<!-- ~~~~~~~~~~~~~~~~~~~~~~~ Submit Data ~~~~~~~~~~~~~~~~~~~~~~~~~~~~~~~~~~~~~ -->
<mso:group id="mso_c2.C71934A" label="Submit Data" insertAfterQ="hyp:IDS_EDIT"
  autoScale="true" visible="true" >
<mso:button idQ="mcr:WHcustUI_HideUnhide" keytip=":" label="Hide/Unhide"
  imageMso="FilePermissionRestrictMenu" visible="true"
onAction="PERSONAL.XLSB!UnhidePOVrow"/>
<mso:menu id="menuId1" label="Are you sure?" keytip="!" imageMso="HighImportance"
visible="true">
<mso:control idQ="hyp:IDS_WRITEBACK" visible="true"/>
<mso:button idQ="mcr:WHcustUI_ToggleSVTabs" label="Toggle SV Tabs"
  imageMso="AnimationPreview" onAction="PERSONAL.XLSB!ToggleSVTabs"/>
</mso:menu>
</mso:group>
</mso:tab>
</mso:tabs>
</mso:ribbon>
</mso:customUI>
```

*8.5.6.4 Validation with the Help of Custom UI Editor for Microsoft Office* Figure 8.41 demonstrates the detection of a duplicate attribute during a file update.

## 8.5.7 *Learning Curve and Maintenance Process*

As your understanding of the relationship between the Excel.officeUI file and Excel itself evolves, so will your approaches to creating and updating the file itself. One of the purposes of this chapter is to alleviate discomfort and accelerate the learning curve. If your situation and objectives are similar to mine, then the information presented here should get you to your destination quickly and efficiently.

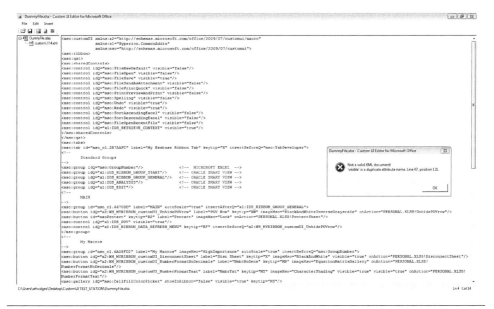

**Figure 8.41** Microsoft's Custom UI Editor in action.

The list below breaks out your best case scenario and is designed to help you save time and stay on track.

a. You have a standard ribbon; you have never added any customization; the possibility of destroying previous customizations is nonexistent.

b. You have Office 2010, so you can use the wizard within Excel to interactively make a few modifications to the ribbon.

c. You create a couple of simple macros and save them in your PERSONAL. XLSB. For guidance with this, open Excel, press F1, and enter "personal. xlsb" into the search box.

d. You right-click on the ribbon's background and select Customize the Ribbon… and follow your intuition. After, you make only a few modifications, locate your Excel.officeUI file, open it with Notepad, and try to interpret what you see. Understand that this file will exist only if modifications have been made. To remove all your modifications and return to a default state, simply delete this file.

e. You repeat steps a and b a few times. You try to understand the relationship between your choices of labels, visibility, and icons and what you see in your Excel.officeUI. You find the selection that allows you to assign macros to custom buttons and include buttons to execute the macros created earlier. You also try to understand the hierarchical relationships between a tab, a group, and a command.

f. You include in your modifications Smart View and Essbase components. These can be found by selecting All Tabs in the "Choose commands from:" drop-down menu. You may add components to the Smart View and Essbase tab to see what happens, but more important, you create a new tab and place a couple of your most often used Excel and Smart View commands on it.

g. You open the Excel.officeUI file using Notepad. You break up the contents into readable paragraphs, identify sections, and add indentations and comments (i.e., text between tags <!-- and -->). In other words, you simply make the file more readable. You will want to do this carefully to not introduce typographical errors that are later difficult to locate.

h. You study the relationship between the lines at the top of the file and the id attributes. The character string xmlns introduces an XML namespace; the characters following this string give the namespace an alias to be used within your Excel.officeUI file. The URL is just a label and does not trigger a connection to an external source. You can change these aliases. As shown in the contents of my Excel.officeUI (Section 8.5.6.3), I changed the alias for the Hyperion.Common.Addin namespace to "hyp:"

i. Reading through the file, you will come to understand that icons are identified by predefined names. The easiest way to add or change icons going forward will be to find a reference list on the Internet and add it to your list of favorite sites, but you can also use the Customize the Ribbon… wizard.* When you hover over an icon, a screentip appears. The last item, the character string between parentheses, is the icon's identifier. To add or change the icon on a button or a control group, add or modify the attribute "imageMso=" accordingly.

j. You remove unnecessary text. For example, since you are using your PERSONAL.XLSB file to store your macros, Excel does not need a full path to find the file. The identifiers (id="something") of custom components are arbitrary and can be shortened. The identifier "idQ=" is for "qualified" controls, meaning controls related to one of the namespaces mentioned at the top of the file. Just remember that "idQ=" goes with labels that start with an alias and a colon. "idMso=" is for built-in Microsoft Office controls.

k. You regularly make backup copies of your modified Excel.officeUI files to avoid destroying your changes by making an interactive modification within Excel. Excel will save the new ribbon specification immediately and will overwrite all the changes you made using Notepad.

l. You compare the contents of your Excel.officeUI file with the contents displayed in Section 8.5.6.3 and add any other modifications you might find useful. From this point on, you make all your changes using Notepad.

Building my personal Essbase ribbon was a trial-and-error, confusing, frustrating-at-times process because there are many options and ways to implement the technology. You can easily find yourself reading material that is not relevant to your objectives. The resources I relied on include Martin, Puls, and Hennig's book, Microsoft's CustomUI Editor, an advanced text editor capable of formatting xml files, and Excel custom ribbon export files generated after making manual modifications to the ribbon.[†] This was certainly much more material than was necessary to fulfill the requirements of this project.

There is a button in the customization wizard to export customizations to a file typically named Excel Customizations.exportedUI. You do not need to work with this file; the Excel.officeUI file is all you need to pay attention to. But if you try out this feature, then notice that it includes an extra item at the very top: `<mso:cmd app="Excel" dt="1" />`. This text should not be included in Excel.officeUI files.

### 8.5.7.1 Lessons Learned and Recommendations

1. Any experimentations that do not require access to Essbase may be better off prototyped on a separate machine that only has Excel. Your experiments will not interfere with ongoing requirements to work with Essbase.

---

\* Several other approaches are possible. Mentioning them all would not be practical and would be a distraction. Some may involve making additional commitments, for example, to download and install add-ins. With time, if this is a line of work you continue to pursue, you will inevitably discover other ways to obtain identifiers that you might prefer. Microsoft offers some options, for example, the 2007 Office System Add-In: Icons Gallery.

† Free tool, originally from Microsoft; download from http://openxmldeveloper.org/blog.

2. If you have customized your ribbon in any way, then you have an Excel.officeUI file in your AppData\Local\Microsoft\Office folder. You may start by checking to see whether this is the case. If you have such a file, make a backup of it or rename it.

3. Start developing the habit of making backup copies of this file. Excel overwrites the file whenever you make interactive changes to the ribbon. If you know you are going to be making changes that could delete earlier customizations, make a backup copy before you open Excel. I put my backup copies in a subfolder and add a timestamp to the name.

4. Review the Excel.officeUI at any time using a text editor, but be careful not to change it and save it unintentionally. Again, do not let Excel overwrite it, either.

5. You can maintain this file with a simple text editor such as Notepad, with a more advanced text editor capable of interpreting XML, with the CustomUI Editor from Microsoft, or with other more advanced tools.

6. Callbacks are not necessary unless you want your code to consult the ribbon or make changes to the ribbon. I have avoided this topic in this chapter; do not allow discussions about callbacks distract you from your initial goal. One of the nice features available in the CustomUI Editor is the automatic generation of callback signatures, but again you should not allow this information to distract you at this time.

7. Understand that maintaining an Excel.officeUI file and adding a customUI definition to an Excel file are two very different topics. Opening an Excel workbook using some file compression tool is not related to the subject of this chapter. But if you would like to use Microsoft's CustomUI Editor to validate a ribbon definition, take steps as if you want to add a customUI definition to an xlsx file (see Figure 8.41 and item 11, below).

8. If you have added advanced features to the ribbon by modifying the Excel.officeUI file (there is no other way to do this within Excel itself), these features will be destroyed if you make manual changes interactively because the Excel wizard that handles customizations will not know what to do with your changes and will exclude them from the new version of the file that it will write to disk immediately after the change is made. The only advanced feature in my ribbon is the menu in the Submit Data control group. I know how to add it back quickly if I accidentally cause it to be destroyed. I simply copy the corresponding xml from a previous backup into my current Excel.officeUI.

9. One possible way to protect the Excel.officeUI file from being modified is to make it read-only. But then you will no longer be able to perform any interactive customizations, not even to temporarily show or hide a component.

10. In one system I use, any change to the Excel.officeUI file is immediately picked up by an open instance of Excel. In the other, I have to close Excel then save the Excel.officeUI text file. While I am testing and making changes to the file, I keep

it continuously open in my text editor so any accidental changes made by closing Excel at an inopportune time will not make me lose all my customizations.

11. I have a folder on my desktop called "CustomUI Test_Station." In this folder, I keep a dummy xlsx file. An xlsx actually is a compressed xml archive. In it is the xml file that defines the ribbon of the xlsx file itself. My ribbon is not meant to be a ribbon within the file, but a ribbon for all interaction with Smart View. Therefore, as a rule, I do not add custom ribbons to Excel files. Other people may only talk about this type of ribbon development; you want to treat this as a different topic and perhaps totally avoid it. But this dummy file allows me to paste the contents of a new Excel.officeUI file to the customUI in the xlsx file and test it for syntax correctness (see also Section 8.5.6.4).

12. If an error exists in the Excel.officeUI file, Excel does not complain and you do not get error messages. Your custom ribbon is simply not loaded and you get the standard ribbon (with any ribbons defined in attached Add-ins). If, as in my case, your custom ribbon definition file assigns the visible="false" attribute to Smart View, the presence of the Smart View tab upon opening Excel indicates an error in the configuration file.

13. You will need a strategy for controlling the position of tabs and button groups. In my current Excel.officeUI specification of the My Essbase Ribbon Tab, I first listed the built-in components in left-to-right order, then all the custom components. I also added an insertBefore or an insertAfter attribute to every custom component and made it refer to a built-in component. All the custom components are listed in the order they should appear on the ribbon. In some cases, a reverse order may be necessary for some components. Before the development of this strategy, controls would not retain the position I originally selected for them, for reasons not worthy of attention here.

## 8.6 MDX Editor SV 1.0*

Two tendencies in information technology conflict with one another: (a) Users of friendly graphical interfaces would like to go "under the hood" and gain further control of their application by manipulating the code itself, and (b) technology users forced by any circumstance to interact with devices through programming code want to develop interfaces so they will not have to work so hard. One group seems to favor a middle man and the other seems to like to work harder.

This section turns upside down the question of whether Smart View, acting as a middle man (along with its accompanying tools Smart Slice, Query Designer, Smart Query, even Hyperion Financial Reports), actually uses MDX (eliminating for us the requirement to learn the language) or whether it is possible to obtain a copy of the MDX statement it generates (see Lackpour [2013]). Instead, it considers the possibility

---

* The solution described in this section is a packaged collection of features we expect will evolve. To help avoid ambiguous references to it, we have named it MDX Editor SV 1.0.

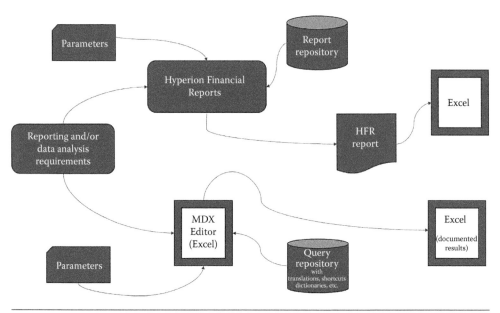

**Figure 8.42**  MDX results in an organizational context.

that fewer bells and whistles can, at times, improve the experience and the results. Section 8.4.2.3 demonstrated how much can be accomplished with a few lines of code.

This chapter provides instructions on how to build a solution to help you write, build, validate, execute, save, and manage MDX queries.* Upon execution, new tabs and, optionally, workbooks are created and a copy of the MDX query is displayed on an additional tab for documentation. The queries can be saved, shared, and catalogued for future use; they can include parameters; and they support shortcuts (devices to minimize the amount of work necessary to build new queries). As explained graphically by Figure 8.42, this provides an alternative to a typical situation in which an inventory of Hyperion Financial Reports is built and reports are executed just so the results can be exported to Excel to continue with interactive analysis. The benefit of this alternative is not only being able to get data more efficiently but also having more control over technical challenges in general.

The query repository is displayed as an external database. The proposed solution supports two options at the same time: (1) a repository within the Excel file as shown in the screenshots below and/or (2) an external database file (MS Access, Structured Query Language Server, a file system, or some open-source database). MDX Editor SV 1.0 implements the first option only.†

### 8.6.1 The Input Form

In contrast to Smart View (which allows you to build a query on the same sheet where the results will appear, using a query-by-example approach) or the EAS MDX

---

* See earlier note about Power Pack MDX Script Library Extension Version: 1.1.2.0.
† See *, p. 431.

editor (which lets you enter a query in free form, providing some IntelliSense-like support that sometimes can be a nuisance), MDX Editor SV 1.0 uses a requirements-gathering approach. The requirements input form is a meta-query that is organized to optimize the experience of defining the query rather than to prepare the space for the display of results. It is also designed to highlight, rather than hide, the semantics and the syntax of an MDX query. The standard form provides space for up to six slicer dimensions, six row dimensions, and six column dimensions. It also has space reserved for the definition of page dimensions, but this feature has not yet been implemented in MDX Editor SV 1.0. This implies support for up to 24 dimensions, but it is expected to be used for up to about 10 dimensions including attribute dimensions participating as real dimensions (not as filters). The design is a compromise between what is technically possible within the software, the efficient use of the space available on the screen, and the need to have a design that effectively supports a cognitive process.

Figure 8.43 shows the mini-form, which is a 3 × 3 × 3 × 3 version of the standard form. When a connection is established, the dimensions are loaded according to a convention similar to the one used by Smart View: The first dimension i n the outline goes to the row dimension (axis 1), the second dimension of the outline goes to the column dimension (axis 0), and the rest go to the slicer or POV. This results in a counterclockwise order starting from the lower right quadrant. The mini-form has enough space for Sample.Basic, a five-dimensional cube. With this form, you cannot assign four dimensions to one of the axes and one to the other. Doing that would require the standard version (illustrated on most other screenshots). But even in this mini-form, you can place all the dimensions on the axes and eliminate the need to specify a slicer. As soon as you load the MyMDXEditor.xlsm workbook and establish a connection, you can begin to define the sets that will participate in the query.

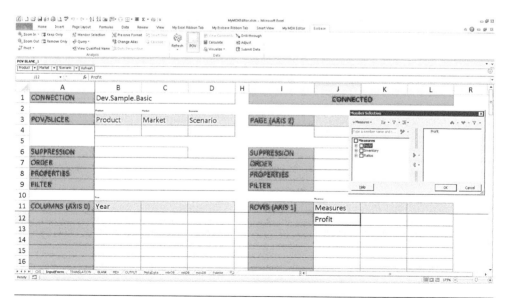

**Figure 8.43** MDX Editor SV 1.0.

Why "the sets"? Because MDX works with sets. Let us consider a two-dimensional data view:

```
SELECT {SET} on AXIS 0, {SET} on AXIS 1 FROM DATASOURCE WHERE (POV).
```

The result will be a cross-tabulation of all the elements in the first set with all the elements in the second set. A set can be one dimension member, several dimension members, one tuple, or several tuples.* A {SET} of {SET}s is a {SET} and a two-dimensional data view is something you can display on a screen or print on a sheet of paper.

Throughout the chapter, you have seen the use of templates to build MDX queries. This section shows how to build and use a template with more structure and more features. Templates are possible when a communication instrument has fixed/predictable components and variable/unpredictable components. Templates allow users to focus on the variable components. If they are well designed, they save time and effort while still giving users significant control of the overall content. Query Designer and Smart Query are templates. Smart Query, being more advanced and powerful, in the end limits what you can do compared with what you can do with Query Designer. Although the tool in this chapter faces similar challenges, it has one significant advantage: You do not have to adhere to a rigorous process. It helps you build the actual executable code, but you still control the code. If you decide not to use the template, you can still execute the code, store it, retrieve it, modify it, etc., in a manner reminiscent of what was illustrated in Section 8.4.2.3.

### 8.6.2 A Day in the Life of a Query

The screenshots below demonstrate the actual execution of the steps a user might follow to build a query, validate it, and execute it. Most screenshots in this section make use of windowing within Excel to obtain views of interrelated elements on a single screenshot. Normally, you would only see one Excel tab occupying the entire available screen space. This subsection (8.5.2) focuses on the user's experience. The VBA code that makes the experience possible is presented in Section 8.6.5.

*8.6.2.1 One, Two, Three, Done!*  MDX Editor SV 1.0 supports three types of activities. Executed in sequence, they constitute, in general, high-level terms, a three-step process: (1) define, (2) execute, (3) consume.

Figure 8.44 shows a ready-to-execute MDX query. (Also, refer back to Figure 8.43 for comparison, to better distinguish some of the components.) The placement of the input areas labeled COLUMNS (AXIS 0) and ROWS (AXIS 1) in spreadsheet row 11 bears no similarity or relationship to the location of the corresponding information

---

* A tuple is an intersection of two or more dimensions, for example, ([Jan],[Actual],[Profit]). For the purposes of generalizi ng the solution, (a) a tuple is just another element and (b) a dimension member is a one-dimensional tuple.

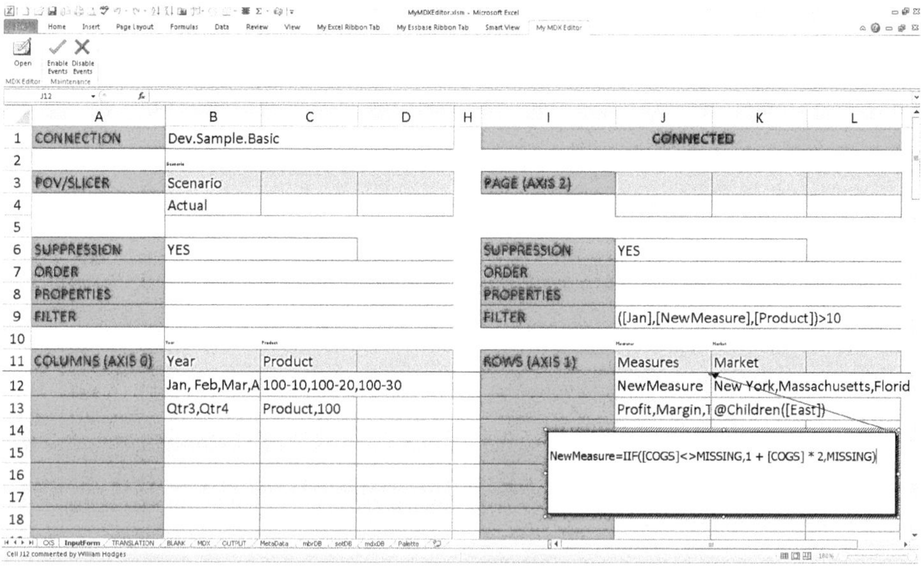

**Figure 8.44** Step 1 of 3: definition.

on a report. The form has five input areas: (1) CONNECTION, (2) POV/WHERE/ SLICER, (3) COLUMNS (AXIS 0), (4) ROWS (AXIS 1), and (5) PAGE (AXIS 2). The labels SUPPRESSION, ORDER, PROPERTIES, and FILTER do not identify an input item per se but reserve space for qualifying details applicable to the corresponding input area below them. A later section discusses the tools available to facilitate entering the data.

*8.6.2.1.1 Step 1 of 3: Define* The user can type in the query one character at a time, or select from menus and wizards. Once all the information is entered, the user can interpret the contents unequivocally and conclude, for example, that the query will need four CrossJoin clauses and one Filter clause. It will also have two NON EMPTY qualifiers. There will be a slicer and a WITH MEMBER clause. Step 1 is completed when the user has inserted all the applicable elements into cells.

The input form is the medium where you organize your thoughts about what is applicable and necessary (see Figure 8.44). But it also reinforces your understanding of MDX as a data set definition language, organizing into patterns any knowledge you have about what MDX is and what it does. The patterns you develop improve your understanding of what MDX is and why it works.

Upon translation to MDX, the resulting query will look like this, but we are getting ahead of ourselves.

```
WITH MEMBER [Measures].[NewMeasure] as 'IIF([COGS]<>MISSING,1 + [COGS] *
  2,MISSING)'
SELECT NON EMPTY {
CROSSJOIN({[Jan],[Feb],[Mar],[Apr],[May],[Jun],[Qtr3],[Qtr4]}
        ,{[100-10],[100-20],[100-30]})
```

```
, CROSSJOIN({[Qtr3],[Qtr4]},{[Product],[100]})
} ON COLUMNS, NON EMPTY {
FILTER (
{ CROSSJOIN(
  {[NewMeasure]}
  ,{[New York],[Massachusetts],[Florida],[Connecticut],[New Hampshire]})
, CROSSJOIN({[Profit],[Margin],[Total Expenses]},Children([East])) }
,
  ([Jan],[NewMeasure],[Product]) > 10
)
} ON ROWS
FROM [Sample.Basic]
WHERE ([Actual])
```

The code that interpreted the query leveraged the form's structural components to quickly determine what keywords to add. From that, we could begin to explain semantic and syntactic elements and why just placing the labels the way we did allowed the code to quickly understand what needed to be done.

*8.6.2.1.2 Step 2 of 3: Execute*　Step 2 consists of translating the information entered into the Input Form into a ready-to-run MDX query and running it (see Figure 8.45). This second step has three substeps: (1) perform clause translations as required in order to have a full set of reliably valid query elements, (2) interpret or compile the ensemble of translated and fully validated components to build the MDX query, and (3) execute the query. This process is completed by clicking on TRANSLATE,

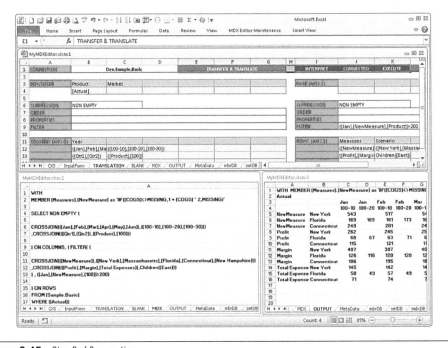

**Figure 8.45**　Step 2 of 3: execution.

INTERPRET, and EXECUTE in sequence (using the cells so labeled, in the top row of the TRANSLATION grid).

It may be that all of this could be completed within the Input Form. The intent of this tab is to have a work environment for the user and a work environment for the code. This sheet is protected and the user cannot make any modifications to its contents. The only thing the user can do here is click on the top cells, which operate as clickable buttons and perform the operations indicated by their text. During this step (step 2 of 3), the user can review the results of the interpretation/compilation process before executing the MDX. The code deposits the ready-to-run query on the tab named MDX.

*8.6.2.1.3 Step 3 of 3: Review Results, Publish Results, Save Query for Future Use* As shown in Figure 8.46, if the query runs successfully, the results will appear on tab OUTPUT. For documentation purposes, the query itself has been inserted into cell A1. This is an option; it would not prevent a user from subsequently applying standard Smart View commands to the grid to zoom in, rotate, keep-only, etc.

Cells L1 through M1 on the TRANSLATION tab serve as clickable buttons to perform additional actions related to data consumption: format, publish, save, and clear. These will be further illustrated later.

*8.6.2.2 Predefined Connections* The current design requires that connections be pre-defined (as opposed to defined at execution time) so the code can simply collect technical details from a connection definition table and proceed to connect and execute

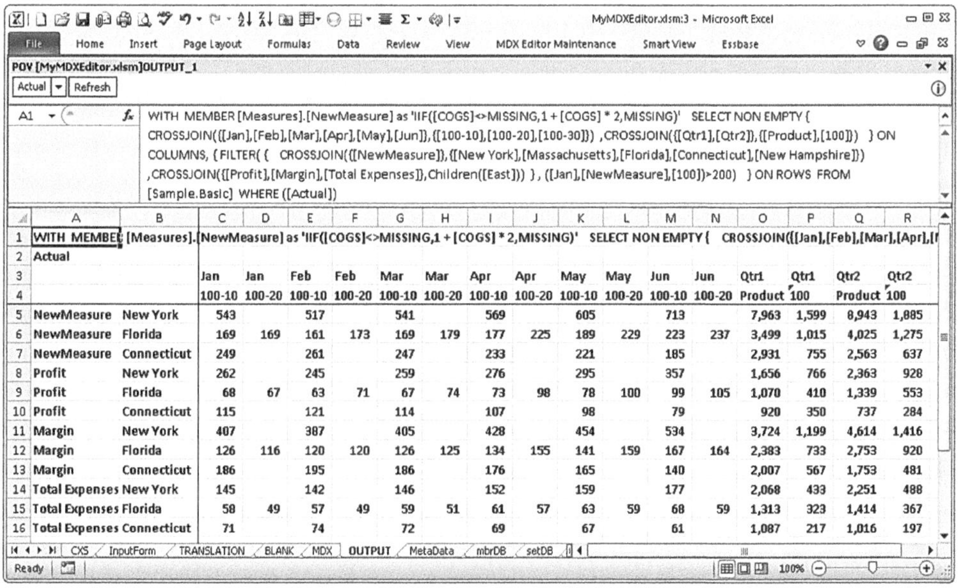

**Figure 8.46** Step 3 of 3: data consumption.

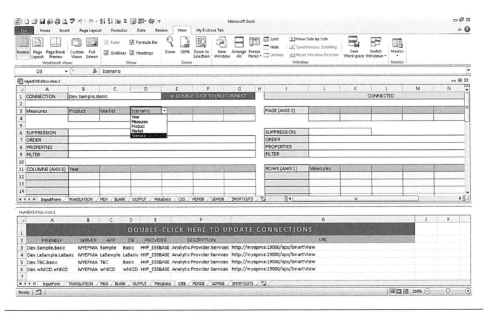

**Figure 8.47**  Inventory of predefined connections.

a query. Figure 8.47 concurrently displays two worksheets; normally, only one work-sheet is displayed at a time. Consistent with the principles discussed in Section 8.2.2, this display simply leverages the tools and features available in our dialog management system. In Figure 8.47, the top worksheet, named InputForm, contains the standard version of the input form where queries are defined, and the bottom one named CXS contains the current list of available data sources.*

The user would begin using MDX Editor SV 1.0 by listing connections on the CXS tab as shown and then double-clicking on its first row. This would update the user's Smart View private connections. One benefit of this approach is the establishment of a naming convention (e.g., environment or server dot application dot database, as illustrated by the CXS tab, column A).

*8.6.2.3 Interaction with the Input Form*   The top half of the screen (Figure 8.47) shows the main input form (which normally would occupy the entire screen). Upon accessing this form, the user begins by selecting a connection. The code behind the form then immediately connects to the corresponding database to obtain its list of dimensions and displays them as Smart View normally does: The outline's first dimension is the row

---

* You may notice that none of the screenshots in Section 8.6 display a custom ribbon. Most do not display a ribbon at all. The solutions in Sections 8.5 and 8.6 are completely independent of each other. My Essbase Ribbon Tab was purposely excluded from the Excel ribbon in Section 8.6 to emphasize that MDX Editor SV 1.0 does not require interaction with it or with any other ribbon tab. Figures 8.49 and 8.55 show a custom ribbon. This was built to facilitate interaction with the editor, but only during development and maintenance.

header, the second dimension is the column header, and all remaining dimensions are made a part of the POV (the slicer, in MDX terminology). Not only are the labels placed on the form, but drop-down selection boxes are also built in each cell so the user may easily make adjustments. At this point, it is possible to begin to rotate the report. One option is to simply exchange the labels COLUMNS (AXIS 0) and ROWS (AXIS 1) by clicking on either one. More important, this version of the tool (MDX Editor SV1.0) includes code responsible for reacting to interactive changes so that, for example, if a user adds a row dimension by selecting it from the drop-down box in an empty heading cell, the same label will automatically be removed from its previous location. Or, if a user changes a selection, the code behind the form will find the dimension's previous location and execute a swap. In either case, if members are selected by listing them below the heading, they will also move to their corresponding new location. Rather than a Smart View feature, this is an Excel VBA programming feature.

*8.6.2.3.1 MDX Query Segments* The XML of a Hyperion Planning form or of a Hyperion Financial Reports *.des file uses the notion of "segment" to identify a collection of intersections. While a tuple (MDX term) is the intersection of members of two or more dimensions, with one member per dimension participating in the definition, a segment combines lists of one or more members.

Any query axis may be defined very simply as a single dimension member, as a set of members from a single dimension, as a single tuple, as a list of explicitly listed tuples, or more generically a list of segments, some with lists defined explicitly, others by means of list expressions. Ultimately, within the context of our discussion, the definition of an axis has to be an MDX set. Table 8.6 presents a few examples.

The editor's input form makes the process of constructing segments rather intuitive. Each row is a segment. Lists of segments (i.e., items in consecutive rows) are easy to combine to form unions. The form's translation and validation code takes care

**Table 8.6** MDX Sets

| AXIS DEFINITION |
| --- |

```
1  { [East] }
2  { ( [Profit] , [East] ) }
3  { ( [Profit] , [West] ) , ( [Sales] , [East] ) }
4  CrossJoin ( Children ( [West] ) , Children ( [100] ) )
5  Union (
      Union (
        CrossJoin ( Children ( [West] ) , Children ( [100] ) )
        , { ( [New York] , [100-10] ) }
      )
      , { ( [Ohio] , [200] ) }
   )
6  { CrossJoin ( Children ( [West] ) , Children ( [100] ) ) , { ( [New York] , [100-
   10] ) } ,  { ( [Ohio] , [200] ) } }
```

of adding and validating all the MDX-specific syntactic components. All you have to do is list the components. For example, you would not have to type in expression number four in Table 8.6, only Children([West]) under Market and Children([100]) under Product. The code behind the form will build the CrossJoin Expression. Later in this section is a description of a simple wizard to build complex expressions before inputting them into a cell. The wizard allows the user to select templates or predefined expressions to eliminate the need to remember their exact syntax.

The input form is drawn by code, so many of its structural and cosmetic characteristics can be easily modified to fit the user's preferences. The form accomplishes the following.

a. As did the templates in Section 8.4, this form provides guidance in the process of building a query.
b. The code behind the form can validate each component, thus isolating syntactical issues and making it easier to understand and fix them.
c. The form's structure helps the user understand the structure of an MDX query and the rationale behind it.
d. The form provides guidance while still allowing the user some discretion, to the point of allowing 100% free form code in certain sections.
e. The user can bypass the form, go to a subsequent step where the ready-to-run query is deposited, and build a new one by hand.

*8.6.2.3.2 Member Selection*  Right-clicking on an input cell brings up Smart View's Member Selection wizard (see Figure 8.48).* The user can select one or several members. The same wizard is launched when selecting members for the slicer/POV, but in that case, the user can select only one member.

Double-clicking instead of right-clicking brings up a custom form called XEvaluator (for expression evaluator, see Figure 8.49). This form has several functions: (1) selecting from an inventory of saved shortcuts and/or their corresponding expressions, (2) selecting from an inventory of user-defined dimension members (expressions that will appear in WITH MEMBER clauses in the final MDX query), (3) creating new shortcuts or user-defined dimension members to use and/or save for future use, and (4) selecting an expression from the input form and modifying it and/or validating it. The user could also enter new shortcuts or user-defined dimension members directly into the corresponding repositories (tabs setDB and mbrDB) (Figure 8.55).

When the user selects a shortcut, the mnemonic is added to the cell as if it were a valid dimension member. The expression is added to the form as a cell comment. The translation process will use this setup to know what to do during the translation of the entire form. If the cell has a comment and the comment is a formula, then a

---

* This solution can be seen as a study on what can be accomplished by leveraging built-in mouse event detection functions instead of creating custom buttons, toolbars, or ribbon items.

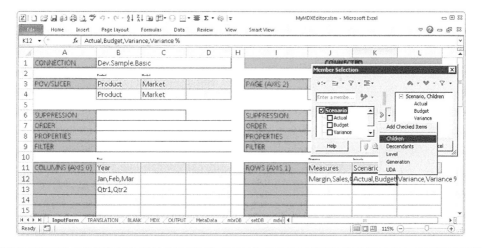

**Figure 8.48** Member Selection Wizard.

**Figure 8.49** Expression Evaluator.

corresponding WITH MEMBER clause will be added to the query. If the comment contains a valid MDX expression, then a corresponding WITH SET clause will be added to the query. WITH MEMBER clauses are required to support the inclusion of user-defined members. WITH SET clauses are a convenience, not a requirement; the expression could participate in the body of the query. But this approach simplifies the process of building the query because it turns every cell item into a syntactically valid query component. Typing in valid set expressions (as opposed to expression identifiers) is still possible, such as Children([Product]). The editor also accepts @ Children([Product]). Including the @ is preferable because it reminds the tool that it does not need to perform a translation of the expression (see Figure 8.44). When the final query is produced (see Section 8.6.2.3.4), the @ is automatically removed. The Translate and Evaluate buttons execute a local translation and/or validation to increase the likelihood that the script as a whole will also be valid (notice validation messages at the bottom of the VBA form).

*8.6.2.3.3 Translation*   Once collecting all of the query components has been completed, the user can move to the TRANSLATION tab, where all other activities take place. Normally, the first action there is to transfer/translate the query components to the TRANSLATION tab. All the components can be validated in isolation for syntactical and contextual validity. In other words, if the code segments pass all the tests and are fully processed and if they refer to existing elements from the corresponding data source, then they will successfully execute when used in a simple generic query (this is one possible way to test their validity).

*8.6.2.3.4 Interpretation*   The next action will normally be to INTERPRET or COMPILE the components to build a complete ready-to-run query. Figure 8.50 shows the output from one such interpretation.

*8.6.2.3.5 Execution*   Finally, clicking on EXECUTE will launch the execution of the MDX query, as shown in Figure 8.51.

As mentioned before, it remains possible to write free hand MDX on the tab labeled MDX and proceed as if the code had been built using the form. This action would be similar to the experience in Section 8.4.2.3, but the user could then apply other processing to it, as explained below.

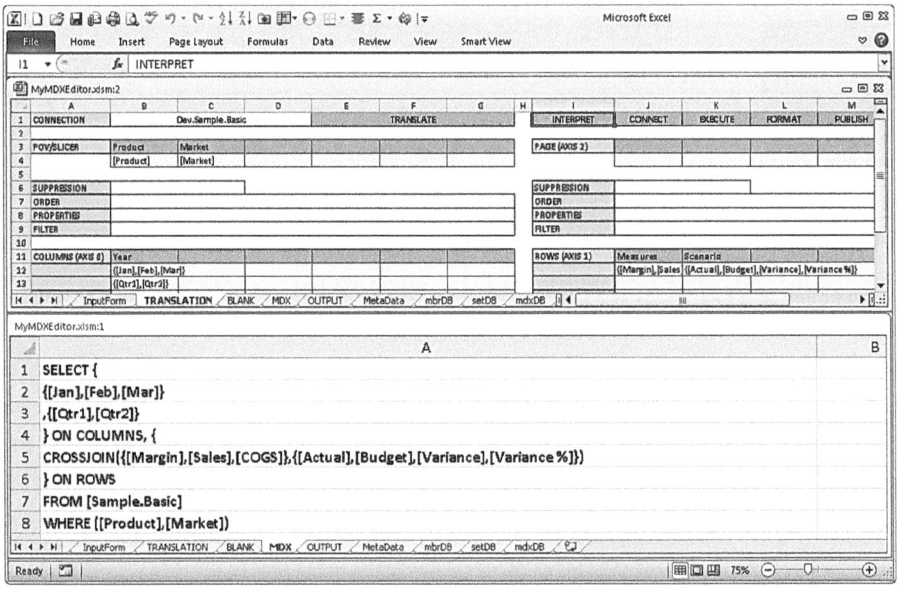

**Figure 8.50**   Interpretation.

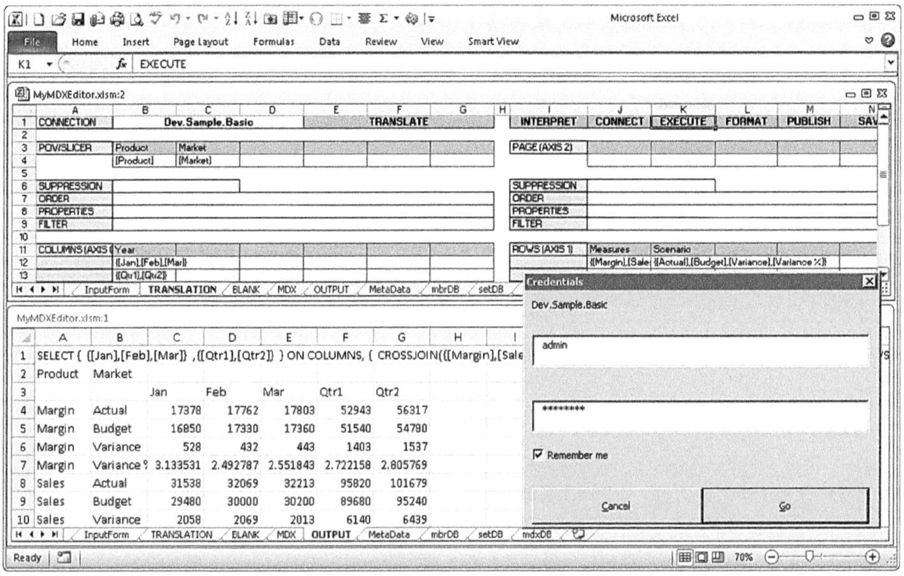

**Figure 8.51**   Execution.

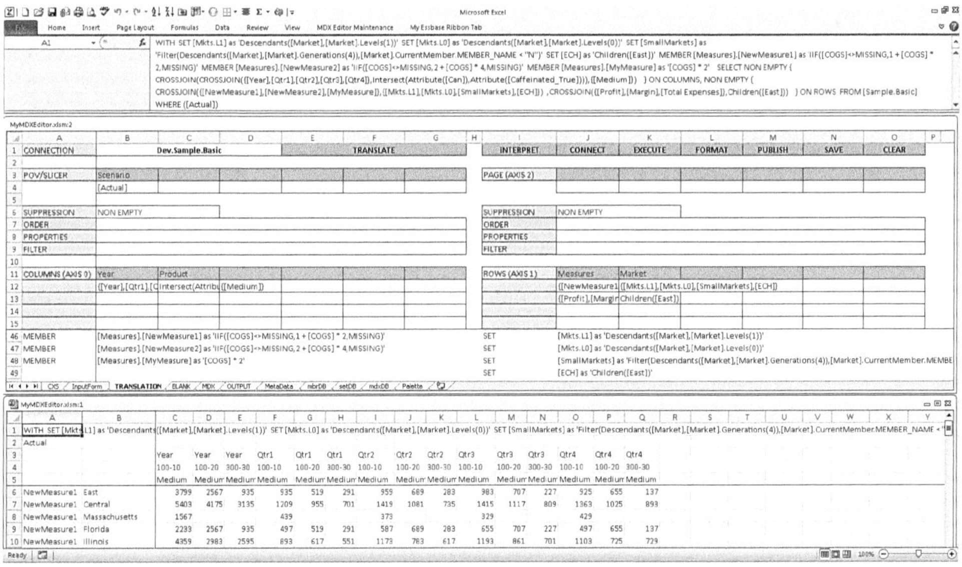

**Figure 8.52**   Execution with SETS, MEMBERS, and Attribute Dimensions.

Figure 8.52 demonstrates the translation and execution of a query that includes expressions built using the XEvaluator wizard. Cell A1 of the second sheet (the OUTPUT worksheet) contains, as a single string, the executable query.

*8.6.2.3.6 Publication*   The PUBLISH button (see Figure 8.53) allows the user to save the results in an external workbook.

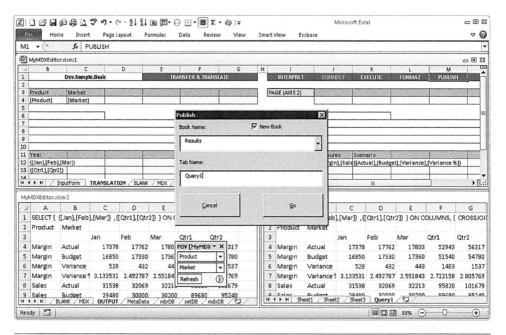

**Figure 8.53** Publication.

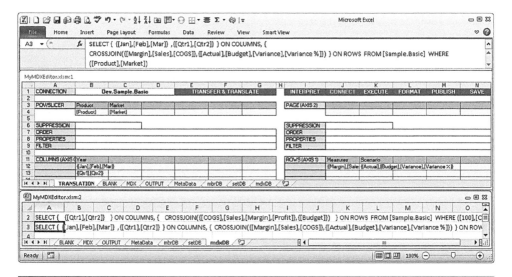

**Figure 8.54** Query archive.

*8.6.2.3.7 Saving the Query for Future Use* The user can also save the MDX query, as shown in Figure 8.54.

*8.6.2.3.8 The Repositories* MDX Editor SV 1.0 has three simple repositories or databases: mdxDB, mbrDB, and setDB. They are currently implemented as tabs in the MDXEditor.xlsm workbook. They could also be saved in an external database or as text files in a shared directory.

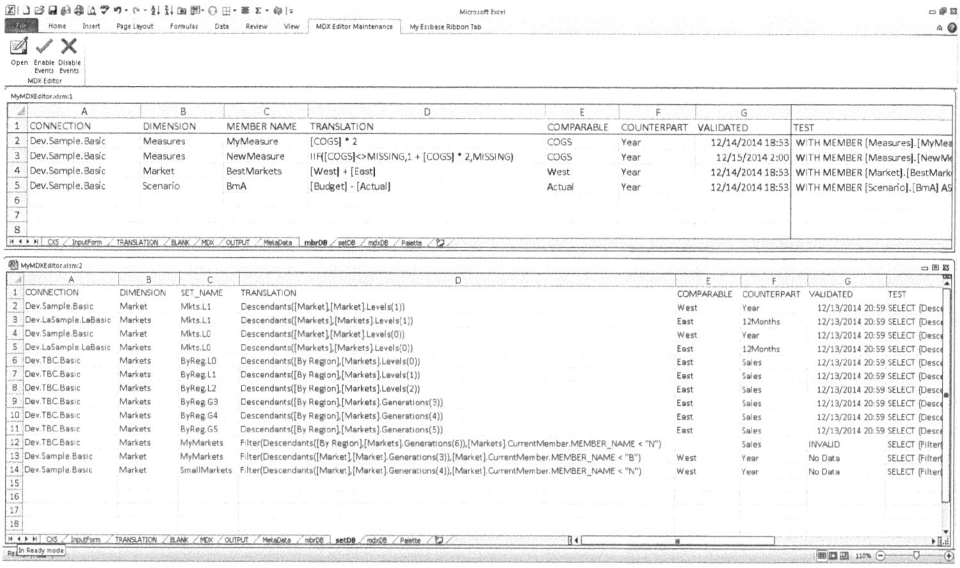

**Figure 8.55**   Member Expressions and Member Sets.

Expressions in the mbrDB and setDB repositories are supposed to be pretested so they can be expected not to cause any errors during the MDX query construction process or during the execution of the query. This is a good practice, not a requirement. The user can validate the expressions one at a time or all within one execution loop. Double-clicking on any row except the first row will validate the corresponding expression. Double-clicking on the first row will validate all the expressions on the sheet one by one. The date when the validation occurred is recorded. If an expression is found to be invalid, it is labeled accordingly. Validation is accomplished by programmatically building and executing simple queries using default members for all the dimensions except for the dimension to which the expression belongs. If the query succeeds, then the expression is determined to be valid. Figure 8.55 shows Member Expressions and Member Sets.

### 8.6.3  Simplicity and Modularity

To guard against complexity and ultimate obsolescence, MDX Editor SV 1.0 has been designed to have the fewest number of custom forms possible. There is a form to enter credentials, a form to enter or select cell expressions, and a form to publish query results. The primary data input form is not a form but, more simply, a properly formatted worksheet (see Figure 8.56).*

---

\* HypUIConnect() might be a better solution than frmCredentials. See the Oracle Smart View for Office Developer's Guide, https://docs.oracle.com/cd/E38438_01/epm.111223/sv_developer/frameset .htm?launch.htm.

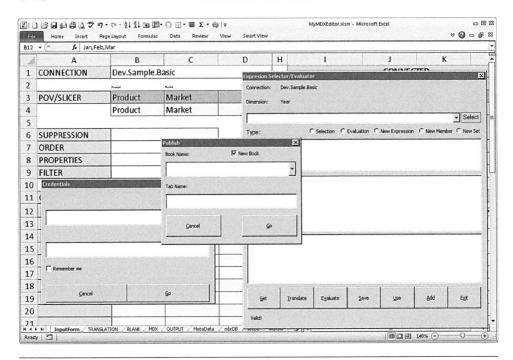

**Figure 8.56** Leveraging the Excel interface (keeping form development to a minimum).

Modularity and simplicity were also guiding principles for the construction of programming code provided in this chapter. This supported the construction and validation of general purpose components and made possible future building using existing components. It also allows for a return to the components to improve them without affecting the overall behavior of the tool.

MDX Editor SV 1.0, by default, has 10 worksheets or tabs (others can be added temporarily). Their purpose is explained in Table 8.7.

Each tab owns the code used to manipulate the data it contains. In programming terms, in this solution, the tabs are treated as objects with their own methods and properties encapsulated (i.e., hidden) where appropriate. The BLANK, the MetaData, and the OUTPUT tabs do not need any code. They are passive in that they receive the output generated by an MDX query. Since the OUTPUT tab can and most likely will be exported to an external workbook, it is important that it remain code-free throughout the process. BLANK, also being a sheet used to execute queries, is also code-free, even though it is reserved for internal use and is not supposed to be exported. MetaData is used to organize information obtained from the server. In MDX Editor SV 1.0, it is used exclusively to list the dimensions of the current data source. Since it may have to service requests from other editor components, it may eventually contain some VBA code, but it does not in the current design.

**Table 8.7** MDX Editor SV 1.0 Tabs

| NO. | TAB NAME | PURPOSE | HAS CODE |
|---|---|---|---|
| 1 | InputForm | This is the main user interface, where a user defines query requirements according to a specific methodology. The methodology implicitly enforces syntactic and semantic rules, facilitates leaning, and facilitates automated parsing, leading to the construction and successful execution of a corresponding MDX query. | Yes |
| 2 | TRANSLATION | A protected replica of the InputForm where all of the user's input has been converted, component by component, to a valid MDX expression | Yes |
| 3 | MDX | A blank sheet where the ready-to-execute MDX query is built before execution. This sheet can be accessed by the user and used to enter freeform MDX, bypassing the InputForm and the translation process altogether. | Yes |
| 4 | BLANK | Reserved for internal use, this is the sheet where the Editor displays the results of queries it executes while processing user input. For example, queries to obtain the dimensionality of a data source are executed here. | No |
| 5 | OUTPUT | This is also a blank tab. It is used to deposit the results of an MDX query and is the tab that is exported when results are published. | No |
| 6 | MetaData | This tab was included to have a place to keep any metadata information that might accelerate processing, eliminating the need to consult the database every time such information is required. | No |
| 7 | CXS | This tab has a listing of all the connections and their details (optionally including credentials in hidden cells, and only while the workbook is active). Notice the "remember me" check box in Figure 8.56.[a] | Yes |
| 8 | mdxDB | This tab provides storage for any query the user has built and would like to retain for repeated and/or future use. | Yes |
| 9 | mbrDB | This tab provides storage for user-defined dimension members. UDMs in this context are the equivalent of WITH MEMBER expressions in standard MDX and will be casted as such when included in an MDX query. | Yes |
| 10 | setDB | This tab provides storage for shortcut expressions designed to free the user from having to remember and/or type in long expressions. Since these expressions can be included in WITH SET clauses, and to establish an explicit correlation between the editor and MDX syntax, the tab has been named setDB. East.Lvl0 might be a good candidate. The user would enter this onto the input form. The input translation process would convert it to the expression Descendants([East],[Market].Levels(0)). | Yes |

[a] The HypUIConnect() function available in the most recent versions of Smart View was not used to allow for some backward compatibility. This function would have helped by eliminating the need to remember credentials under most circumstances. HypUIConnect() might be a better solution than frmCredentials. See the Oracle Smart View for Office Developer's Guide, https://docs.oracle.com/cd/E38438_01/epm.111223/sv_developer/frameset.htm?launch.htm.

### 8.6.4 Parameterization

Parameters are not needed when constructing and running queries because the user will define the focus and/or scope in the process of building the query. Parameterization may still be appropriate in the following cases:

a. Building a query that will be saved and reused; rather than editing the query at execution time, you would like it to prompt you
b. Making the query use Essbase substitution variables

c. Replicating Smart View's cascading feature, or expanding this feature to include multidimensional cascading

d. The amount of data to collect is too large for a single query, forcing the user to execute the query in segments (technically, a process similar to cascading)

Since the user controls the code that executes the MDX queries, you have a variety of options:

1. Allow and make the code recognize the presence of a string such as ${Product}, ${Market} in the MDX query, launching a VBA InputBox() for each unique instance, then using the Replace() VBA function to finalize the MDX query before submitting it to the HypExecuteQuery() SmartView.bas function.

2. Treat multiple entries in POV cells (row 4 of the InputForm) as a request to run a separate query for each entry and to create a separate OUTPUT tab for each; you could allow the use of functions (e.g., Children([Scenario])); you already have code to expand a function locally (the validation code in the frmXEvaluator form); you could place the resulting list in the corresponding cell or in the cell's comment box, or in some other more convenient location; this would be another way to do cascading, but since you own the code, this approach would allow you to cascade over multiple dimensions, not just one, using nested loops.

3. Include StrToMbr() functions in MDX queries to collect substitution variable values.

4. Use HypGetSubstitutionVariable() to separately download substitution variable values to Excel, then inject them into MDX queries where appropriate.

### 8.6.5 The Code

Including every single line of code supporting this application within the text of this chapter is not practical. The code has been made available separately. The chapter presents a full list of components and their purpose, followed by several subsections that present and briefly discuss key portions of the code. Table 8.8 lists functions and subroutines by tab and form. Sections 8.5.5.1, through 8.5.5.4 discuss four representative modules. To obtain a complete listing of all the code, please go to the website for this book.*

*8.6.5.1 Code behind the Input Form* `Worksheet _ BeforeDoubleClick()` is an example of using a built-in Excel VBA subroutine. This subroutine, along with `Worksheet _ BeforeRightClick()` and `Worksheet _ Change()`,

---

* http://developingessbasebook.com.

**Table 8.8** Inventory of Functions and Subroutines by Tab and Form

| NO. | TAB/FORM | FUNCTION (F)/SUB (S) NAME | F/S | TYPE/ PARAMETERS | REMARKS |
|---|---|---|---|---|---|
| 1.1 | InputForm | Worksheet_BeforeDoubleClick() | S | Native Excel Cell range Cancel option | Depending on the location of the click, it either starts a dialog to establish a connection or launches the expression evaluation form |
| 1.2 | | Worksheet_BeforeRightClick() | S | Native Excel Cell range Cancel option | Responsible for opening a member selection dialog box based on the name of the associated dimension. It responds only if the click happens on a valid cell |
| 1.3 | | Worksheet_Change() | S | Native Excel Cell range | Responds only to a change in the connection selection range. It is responsible for changing the contents of the dimension member headings to match the named connection |
| 1.4 | | Worksheet_SelectionChange() | S | Native Excel Cell range | Implemented to announce whether the BLANK worksheet (used during internal processing) is connected |
| 1.5 | | DrawForm() | S | None | Draws the form. Normally executed only once, during the construction of the workbook. It remains available in case the form needs to be rebuilt |
| 1.6 | | EstablishMetadataConnection() | S | Value of cell B1 | Launched by Worksheet_Change() when the user specifies a new connection. It connects BLANK to the source, executes a default retrieve, and calls UpdateMetadata() and InitializeHeadings() |
| 1.7 | | InitializeHeadings() | S | None | Populates the dimension headings, taking the labels in MetaData and distributing them according to a standard order |
| 1.8 | | UpdateColumnHeadingValidations() | S | None | Updates all the drop-down lists (implemented as validations) in the dimension heading cells |
| 1.9 | | UpdateMetadata() | S | Value of cell B1 | It accesses the BLANK tab and the MetaData tab. Copies labels from the results of a default connection in BLANK, listing them in column A of the MetaData tab. Based on the overall division-of-labor, modular design, it could be argued that it should have resided in the MetaData tab |
| 1.10 | | performMatrixRotation() | S | Target cell | Rearranges all the headings and the selections underneath the headings when the user adds or changes a heading |
| 1.11 | | AxisDimCount(), getLastPOVdimension(), isBLANKconnected() | F/S | Several | Utilities |

(Continued)

**Table 8.8 (Continued)**    Inventory of Functions and Subroutines by Tab and Form

| NO. | TAB/FORM | FUNCTION (F)/SUB (S) NAME | F/S | TYPE/ PARAMETERS | REMARKS |
|---|---|---|---|---|---|
| 2.1 | TRANSLATION | Worksheet_BeforeDoubleClick() | S | Native Excel Cell range Cancel option | Directs control to one of eight subroutines based on the location of the click. The options are Translate, Interpret, Connect, Execute, Format, Publish, Save, and Clear |
| 2.2 | | SimpleTranslate(), Translate(), CopyHeadings() | S | None | They copy the contents of InputForm, adding any missing syntactical elements |
| 2.3 | | Interpret() | S | None | Builds the corresponding MDX statement and places it on the MDX tab |
| 2.4 | | Execute() | S | None | Executes the MDX query deposited by the Interpret() routine on the MDX tab. This performs the same function as the MDX.ExecuteMDXQuery but in a simpler manner. It does not accept parameters |
| 2.5 | | Format() | S | None | Inactive. For future implementation |
| 2.6 | | Publish() | S | None | Displays the Publish form to request instructions to publish the contents of the OUTPUT tab |
| 2.7 | | Save() | S | None | Places a copy of the executed query in the next available row in the mdxDB table |
| 2.8 | | Clear() | S | None | Clears the contents of the TRANSLATION tab (and optionally the contents of the Input Form as well) |
| 2.9 | | DrawForm(), DecorateForm() | S | None | Normally executed only once, during the construction of the workbook. They remain available in case the form needs to be partially or completely rebuilt |
| 3.1 | MDX | ConnectWorksheet() | F | Sheet object Connection name | Connects the applicable sheet to the data source indicated by the connection name |
| 3.2 | | ExecuteMDXQuery() | F | Sheet object Connection name Query string bWithData bDisplayPOV bDisplayMDX bDisconnect | Executes the given query and deposits results on the indicated sheet. It starts by calling the ConnectWorksheet function to connect to the data source indicated by the connection name. The caller can request execution with or without data. The caller can also request that the POV be displayed on the sheet as well as the MDX query itself. Finally, the caller can elect to keep the connection open or to disconnect upon completion |
| 4 | BLANK | None | | | Hosts the results of the queries run privately by the editor |
| 5 | OUTPUT | None | | | Hosts the results of the queries run by the user |

(Continued)

**Table 8.8 (Continued)** Inventory of Functions and Subroutines by Tab and Form

| NO. | TAB/FORM | FUNCTION (F)/SUB (S) NAME | F/S | TYPE/ PARAMETERS | REMARKS |
|---|---|---|---|---|---|
| 6.1 | CXS | Worksheet_BeforeDoubleClick() | S | Native Excel Cell range Cancel option | Responds exclusively to a double click within the range "$A$1:$G$1" and is responsible for updating the connection definitions |
| 6.2 | | GetConnectionRow() | F | Connection name | Returns the row number of the named connection. The row number can then be used to locate other field contents, for example, the application name and the database name |
| 6.3 | | GetMDXsource() | F | Connection name | Returns the string used in the FROM clause of an MDX dimension, e.g., Simple.Basic, based on the given connection name |
| 6.4 | | getFriendlyNamesRange() | F | None | Returns as a string the range where all the FriendlyNames are located (useful in determining how many connections have been defined) |
| 6.5 | | DrawForm() | S | None | Normally executed only once, during the construction of the workbook |
| 7.1 | mdxDB | Worksheet_BeforeDoubleClick() | S | Native Excel Cancel option Active row | Selects the MDX query stored in this row and copies it to the MDX tab for execution |
| 8.1 | mbrDB (user-defined members) | Worksheet_BeforeDoubleClick() | S | Native Excel Cancel option Active row | Determines whether the requested action applies to all the expressions or to one |
| 8.2 | | BuildTestExpression() | S | Active row | Builds a simple generic MDX query using the given calculated member expression. If the query succeeds, then the expression and its interpretation are marked as valid |
| 8.3 | | TestExpression() | S | Active row | Launches the execution of the test expression |
| 8.4 | | ValidateAllExpressionss() | S | | Loops through all the expressions testing them one by one |
| 8.5 | | DrawForm() | S | | Draws the table where the expressions are stored |
| 9.1 | setDB (shortcuts) | Worksheet_BeforeDoubleClick() | S | Native Excel Cancel option Active row | Determines whether the requested action applies to all the expressions or to one |
| 9.2 | | BuildTestExpression() | S | Active row | Builds a simple generic MDX query using the given shortcut expression's interpretation. If the query succeeds, then the expression and its interpretation are marked as valid |
| 9.3 | | TestExpression() | S | Active row | Launches the execution of the test expression |

*(Continued)*

**Table 8.8 (Continued)**    Inventory of Functions and Subroutines by Tab and Form

| NO. | TAB/FORM | FUNCTION (F)/SUB (S) NAME | F/S | TYPE/ PARAMETERS | REMARKS |
|---|---|---|---|---|---|
| 9.4 | | ValidateAllExpressionss() | S | Active row | Loops through all the expressions testing them one by one |
| 9.5 | | DrawForm() | | | Draws the table where the expressions are stored |
| 10.1 | Credentials (Figure 8.51) | Initialize() | S | — | The three VBA forms were built manually but are redrawn every time they are loaded into memory for better control of their appearance and behavior |
| 10.2 | | Activate() | S | — | Prepares the form to anticipate user input. For as long as the form is in memory (it will remember the identity of the user). The form collects user credentials for the login process |
| 10.3 | | Cancel() | S | — | Hides the form |
| 10.4 | | Go() | S | — | Proceeds to the next step, usually connecting to a data source |
| 11.1 | Publish (Figure 8.53) | Initialize() | S | | The three VBA forms were built manually but are redrawn every time they are loaded into memory for better control of their appearance and behavior. This form collects information about the destination |
| 11.2 | | Cancel() | S | | Hides the form, cancels the action |
| 11.3 | | Go() | S | | Proceeds to create a copy of the output tab and to place it in a workbook according to instructions by the user |
| 12.1 | xEvaluator (Figure 8.49) | Initialize() | S | | The three VBA forms were built manually but are redrawn every time they are loaded into memory for better control of their appearance and behavior. |
| 12.2 | | Activate() | | | Refreshes the combo box with all the user-defined members and all the shortcuts applicable to the current connection |
| 12.3 | | Get() | S | — | Collects the contents of the active cell (including the comment, if there is one) and places them in the form's text boxes |
| 12.4 | | Translate() | S | — | Translates the contents of the input box, putting the translation in the second text box |
| 12.5 | | Evaluate() | S | — | Builds a generic query using the expression currently defined and executes it. If the query succeeds, then the expression is considered valid. If there are multiple expressions in the text boxes, it evaluates them individually in sequence |
| 12.6 | | Save() | S | — | Saves a newly defined calculated member or set in the corresponding table |
| 12.7 | | Use() | S | — | Places the contents of the input box in a cell and (if applicable) the contents of the translation box in a comment box |
| 12.8 | | Add() | S | — | Similar to "Use" but content added to current cell contents. Currently deactivated to keep the solution simple |
| 12.9 | | Exit() | S | — | Exit form |

allowed us to completely eliminate the need to use buttons or the ribbon to manipulate MDX Editor SV 1.0. The fields in the form act as buffers holding on to the user's credentials (applicable to a specific connection) for as long as the form remains in memory.

### 8.6.5.1.1 *InputForm.Worksheet_BeforeDoubleClick()*

```
Private Sub Worksheet_BeforeDoubleClick(ByVal Target As Range, Cancel As Boolean)
    Application.EnableEvents = False
    Cancel = True
    Dim x As Variant
    Dim nRow As Long
    '' LOCATION # 1: GCRS_CONNECTION_MESSAGE OR GCRS_CONNECTION_BANNER => CONNECT BLANK
        SHEET
    If Target.Address = GCRS_CONNECTION_MESSAGE Or Target.Address = GCRS_CONNECTION_BANNER
    Then
        Application.ScreenUpdating = False
        nRow = CXS.GetConnectionRow(UCase(Me.Cells(1, 2)))
        If IsEmpty(CXS.Cells(nRow, 8)) _
        Or IsEmpty(CXS.Cells(nRow, 9)) _
        Then
            frmCredentials.Show
            If frmCredentials.chkRememberMe Then
                CXS.Cells(nRow, 8) = frmCredentials.txtID.Text
                CXS.Cells(nRow, 9) = frmCredentials.txtWrd.Text
            End If
        Else
            frmCredentials.lblConnection = ActiveCell.Text
            frmCredentials.txtID = CXS.Cells(nRow, 8)
            frmCredentials.txtWrd = CXS.Cells(nRow, 9)
        End If
        BLANK.Activate
        x = HypConnect(BLANK, frmCredentials.txtID.Text _
                        , frmCredentials.txtWrd.Text _
                        , frmCredentials.lblConnection)
        Debug.Print x
        Me.Activate
        Me.Range("$I$1").Activate
        Application.ScreenUpdating = True
    ElseIf Not Intersect(Me.Range(GCRS_COLUMN_HEADINGS), Target) Is Nothing Then
        'DO NOTHING
    Else
    ''' LOCATION # 3: GCRS_AXIS_SELECTIONS => OPEN THE EVALUATION AND SHORTCUTS FORM
        Set x = Intersect(Me.Range(GCRS_AXIS_SELECTIONS), Target)
        If Not x Is Nothing Then
            If x = Target Then
                frmXEvaluator.Show
            End If
        End If
    End If
    Application.EnableEvents = True
End Sub
```

**8.6.5.2 *Code behind the XEvaluator Form*** The XEvaluator form gives the user the opportunity to validate each individual expression ahead of time (see Figure 8.49). If all the components are validated individually, the translation process only needs to copy the expressions to the TRANSLATION tab, build the MDX script, and execute it.

## 8.6.5.2.1  *frmXEvaluator.Evaluate_Click()*

```
Private Sub cmdEvaluate_Click()
    Dim sGenericMDX As String, sDisplayGenericMDX As String
    Dim sMember As String, sCounterPart As String, sDimension As String, sConnectionName As
        String
    Dim sWith As String, sExpression As String
    Dim retCode As Integer, nOutputRow As Long
    Dim v, vMembers, vExpressions
    Dim i As Integer, iMembers As Integer
    If Len(Me.txtTranslation.Value) > 0 Then
        If InStr(1, Me.txtTranslation.Text, "@", vbTextCompare) = 0 Then
            sDimension = ActiveSheet.Cells(11, ActiveCell.Column).Value
            If sDimension = MetaData.Cells(2, 1).Value Then
                sCounterPart = MetaData.Cells(3, 1).Value
            Else
                sCounterPart = MetaData.Cells(2, 1).Value
            End If
            Me.lblResult = ""
            sWith = ""
            vMembers = Split(Me.txtRaw.Text, ",")
            vExpressions = Split(Replace(Replace(Me.txtTranslation.Value, vbCr, ""), vbLf,
                ""), ";")
            If UBound(vMembers) = UBound(vExpressions) Then
                For i = 0 To UBound(vMembers)
                    Debug.Print vMembers(i), vExpressions(i)
                    Select Case UCase(Me.lblSelectionType)
                        Case "MEMBER":
                            sWith = "WITH MEMBER [" & sDimension & "].[" & vMembers(i) & "]
                                as '" & vExpressions(i) & "'"
                            sExpression = "[" & vMembers(i) & "]"
                        Case "SET":
                            sWith = "WITH SET [" & vMembers(i) & "] as '" & vExpressions(i)
                                & "'"
                            sExpression = "[" & vMembers(i) & "]"
                        Case Else:
                            sWith = ""
                            sExpression = Me.txtTranslation.Text
                    End Select
                    sGenericMDX = sWith & " SELECT {[" & sDimension & "], " & sExpression &
                        "}  ON ROWS, {[" _
                            & sCounterPart & "]} ON COLUMNS from " & 
                                AppDotDB(Trim(InputForm.Cells(1, 2)))
                    txtEvaluationQuery.Value = txtEvaluationQuery.Value & sGenericMDX &
                        vbCrLf
                    sConnectionName = InputForm.Range("B1").Value
                    BLANK.Activate
                    retCode = MDX.ConnectWorksheet(BLANK, sConnectionName)
                    If retCode = 0 Then
                        If Len(vExpressions(i)) > 50 Then
                            sDisplayGenericMDX = Left(vExpressions(i), 50) & "..."
                        Else
                            sDisplayGenericMDX = vExpressions(i)
                        End If
                        retCode = MDX.ExecuteMDXQuery(BLANK, sConnectionName, sGenericMDX,
                            True, True, True, False)
                        If retCode = 0 Then
                            nOutputRow = BLANK.Cells(65536, 1).End(xlUp).Row
                            If nOutputRow > 4 Then
                                lblResult = lblResult & " [VALID] "
                            Else
                                lblResult = lblResult & " [VALID, NO DATA] "
                            End If
                        Else
                            lblResult = lblResult & " [INVALID] "
                        End If
```

```
                        End If
                    Next i
                End If
                InputForm.Activate
            End If
        End If
    End If
End Sub
```

### 8.6.5.3 *Code behind the MDX Tab*  The MDX Tab has code to execute MDX queries in a variety of ways. The frmXEvaluator form calls this code when the user clicks on the Evaluate button.

#### 8.6.5.3.1 *MDX.ExecuteMDXQuery*

```
Public Function ExecuteMDXQuery(ByVal oSheet As Worksheet, ByVal sConnectionName As String,
ByVal sQuery As String, ByVal bWithData As Boolean, ByVal bDisplayPOV As Boolean, ByVal
bDisplayMDX As Boolean, ByVal bDisconnect As Boolean) As Long
    ' This function will attempt to execute a query. If it succeeds it will place the
        output on the target worksheet.
    ' Only two target worksheets are allowed at this time, BLANK & OUTPUT.
    ' The function will start by trying to make a connection. If it succeeds then it
        continues with the remaining tasks.
    Dim pos As Integer, nRow As Long, n As Long, sSlicer As String, retCode As Long
    Dim i As Integer, vArray, vType, X
    Dim infoTypes As Variant
    infoTypes = Array("ROW", "COLUMN", "POV")
    If Not oSheet Is BLANK And Not oSheet Is OUTPUT Then Exit Function
    If ConnectWorksheet(oSheet, sConnectionName) = 0 Then
        ' I.E., IF THE CONNECTION SUCCEEDS THEN...
        ' IF sQuery IS NULL THEN WE ARE SUPPOSED TO GET THE RECENTLY BUILT QUERY RESIDING
            ON THIS WORKSHEET
        If IsEmpty(sQuery) Or IsNull(sQuery) Or sQuery = "" Then
            nRow = Me.Cells(9999, 1).End(xlUp).Row
            sQuery = ""
            For n = 1 To nRow
                sQuery = sQuery & " " & Me.Cells(n, 1) & " "
            Next n
        End If
        ' THERE MAY BE SITUATIONS WHERE WE JUST WANT A DEFAULT STARTING QUERY.
        If sQuery <> REFRESH_WORKSHEET Then
            ' We want to know whether the query contains a slicer so we can properly
                display it on the output sheet
            pos = InStr(1, sQuery, "WHERE", vbTextCompare): Debug.Print pos
            If pos > 0 Then
                sSlicer = Replace(Replace(Replace(Replace(Mid(sQuery, pos + 6, _
                        Len(sQuery) - pos - 6), "(", ""), "[", ""), "]", ""), ")", "")
            Else
                sSlicer = ""
            End If
            ' As is possible elsewhere, we can run a query to get metadata only.
            ' We also provide the option to display other details such as the POV and the
                grid layout
            If bWithData Then HypSetGlobalOption 9, False Else HypSetGlobalOption 9, True
            oSheet.Activate
            retCode = HypExecuteQuery(Empty, sQuery): X = HypShowPov(False): DoEvents
            If bDisplayPOV Then
                oSheet.Range("A1").EntireRow.Insert
                If pos > 0 Then
                    vArray = Split(sSlicer & ",", ",")
                    If Not vArray Is Nothing Then
                        For i = 0 To UBound(vArray)
                            oSheet.Cells(1, i + 1).Value = vArray(i)
                        Next i
```

```
                         End If
                     End If
                     oSheet.Range("A1").EntireRow.Insert
                     retCode = HypGetDimensions(Empty, vArray, vType)
                     For i = 0 To UBound(vArray)
                         oSheet.Cells(1, i + 1).Value = CStr(infoTypes(vType(i))) & ":" &
                             vArray(i)
                     Next i
                 End If
                 If bDisplayMDX Then
                     oSheet.Range("A1").EntireRow.Insert
                     oSheet.Range("A1").Value = sQuery
                 End If
                 ExecuteMDXQuery = retCode
             Else
                 'IGNORE FOR NOW. THE INTENT IS TO PROVIDE THE OPTION TO CONNECT AND OBTAIN THE
                     DEFAULT QUERY
             End If
         End If
     End If
End Function
```

### 8.6.5.4 *Code behind the TRANSLATION Tab*    Since all the preparation work has been done, this routine only needs to convert the script on the MDX tab to a single string to pass it to the HypExecuteQuery() function for execution. The MDX tab has a more generic version that takes two parameters, sheet and connection, and is the version used to validate expressions.

#### 8.6.5.4.1 *TRANSLATION.Execute*

```
Public Sub Execute()
    Dim nRow As Long, n As Long
    Dim v
    Dim sQuery As String
    Dim sSlicer As String
    Dim retCode As Long
    MDX.Activate
    nRow = MDX.Cells(999, 1).End(xlUp).Row
    'nRow = BLANK.Cells(65536, 1).End(xlUp).Row
    sQuery = ""
    For n = 1 To nRow
        sQuery = sQuery & " " & MDX.Cells(n, 1) & " "
    Next n
    sSlicer = Replace( Replace( Replace( Replace( _
            Trim(MDX.Cells(n - 1, 1)), "WHERE (", ""), ")", ""), "]", ""), "[", "")
    sQuery = Trim(sQuery)
    OUTPUT.Activate: OUTPUT.Cells.Clear
    frmCredentials.lblConnection = TRANSLATION.Range("B1").Value
    frmCredentials.Show False
    retCode = HypConnect(Empty, frmCredentials.txtID _
                            , frmCredentials.txtWrd _
                            , TRANSLATION.Range("B1").Value)
    retCode = HypExecuteQuery(Empty, sQuery)
    retCode = HypDisconnect(Empty, True)
    OUTPUT.Range("A1:A2").EntireRow.Insert
    OUTPUT.Range("A1").Value = sQuery
    v = Split(sSlicer & ",", ",")
    For n = 0 To UBound(v) - 1
        OUTPUT.Cells(2, n + 1).Value = v(n)
    Next n
    OUTPUT.Range("A1").Activate
End Sub
```

## 8.7 And There You Have It

Although the path has been long and somewhat arduous, we have covered concepts that include customization, programming, and design philosophy; different ways of accessing data; the ins and outs of Smart View functionality; a dive into programming in Excel; incorporating Smart View into Excel; Excel ribbons; and, finally, the MDX Editor SV 1.0 as a capstone to both theory and practical application. I appreciate that this is a lot of information to read in a single chapter, and I encourage you to delve back into specific sections to really grasp the power of custom solutions in Excel and Smart View.

## 8.8 What Is Next

The product extensions discussed in this chapter are meant not only to implement and use but also to prompt new ideas and new enhancements. Keeping them simple and easy to maintain will continue to be an essential goal for making the investment worthwhile. Focusing on enhancements you can use in your daily work will keep them fresh and will provide a platform for continued skill improvement, empowering you to respond swiftly and effectively to similar requirements from clients. For more details, please visit the book's website, where code will be displayed.*

# Acknowledgments

My greatest gratitude goes to Cameron Lackpour for inviting me to participate in this project. Many people have influenced my professional and personal development, but here, I thank only those whose very specific actions have brought me to this very specific moment. Luc Landreville and his partners provided the opportunity to enter the world of consulting and introduced me to Arbor and to Rick Sawa, who introduced me to Essbase and to Bill Sterling, who introduced me to Gail Richards, who introduced me to Hackett. At Hackett, Kathy Horton insisted that I write, and Deanna Sunde introduced my work to ODTUG. At ODTUG, Tim German provided encouragement and advice and eventually introduced me to Cameron, who could have very easily chosen other authors but decided to extend the opportunity to me. Matt Milella of Oracle reviewed the chapter and proposed improvements while very graciously accepting my somewhat unorthodox presentation of technologies into which he has poured his very best efforts. After all is said and done, it is because Oracle Smart View is the enormously successful software product that it is that a beneficiary of it like myself can, with only a few tweaks, offer some additional value to readers and clients. Last but not least, Katy O'Grady made sure my text properly said what I thought it said properly. My family joins me in saying "Thank you very much to you all." The journey

---

* http://www.developingessbasebook.com.

has been long and at times very arduous, and my wife, children, and extended family have travelled it with me. I am and have done what they have helped me to become and to do. I dedicate all my work to them. The benefits shall all be theirs.

## References

Crisci, G. 2012. Practical MDX for Essbase developers. In *Developing Essbase Applications: Advanced Techniques for Finance and IT Professionals*, ed. C. Lackpour, 185–224. Boca Raton, FL: CRC Press.

Hodges, W. 2013. A path to MDX mastery. Kscope13 Presentation. Requires ODTUG membership. Available at http://www.odtug.com/tech-resources.

Hodges, W. 2014. Slow and fast-changing dimensions. *ODTUG Technical Journal*. Requires ODTUG membership. Available at http://www.odtug.com/technical-journal-corner, search archives.

Lackpour, C. 2013. Going under the covers with TRACE_MDX. Available at http://camerons-blog-for-essbase-hackers.blogspot.com/2013/04/going-under-covers-with-tracemdx.html.

Essbase Technical Reference Manual. Available at http://docs.oracle.com/cd/E57185_01/epm.1112/essbase_tech_ref/launch.html.

Martin, R., K. Puls and T. Hennig. 2008. *RibbonX: Customizing the Office 2007 Ribbon*. Indianapolis, IN: John Wiley & Sons.

Milella, M. 2010. Cell functions: Smart view 121.1.2 vs. classic add-in. Available at http://essbaselabs.blogspot.com/2010/05/cell-functions-smart-view-1112-vs.html.

Salzmann, R. 2012. Advanced smart view. In *Developing Essbase Applications: Advanced Techniques for Finance and IT Professionals*, ed. C. Lackpour, 351–371. Boca Raton, FL: CRC Press.

Sprague, Jr., R. H. and E. D. Carlson. 1982. *Building Effective Decision Support Systems*. Upper Saddle River, NJ: Prentice-Hall.

## Additional Resources

Microsoft Download Center. n.d. Office 2010 help files: Office fluent user interface control identifiers. Available at http://www.microsoft.com/en-us/download/details.aspx?id=6627 (accessed December 28, 2014).

Office Dev Center. 2011. Targeting user interface solutions to the 2007 and 2010 releases of Microsoft Office. Available at http://msdn.microsoft.com/en-us/library/office/ee704588 (v=office.14).aspx (accessed December 28, 2014).

Soltechs.net. 2014. Available button graphics for the Word custom UI ribbon control. Available at http://soltechs.net/CustomUI/imageMso01.asp (accessed December 28, 2014).

# Afterword

Ah, the Afterword…as the person who wrote the Foreword described it, the second place that anyone picking up the book will look.

For me—who understands about every fourth word of this book—the amount of effort put in by these authors is plain to see. The years of acquired skill and knowledge; the design, build, and testing of the numerous creative alternatives; the work on the bleeding edge of the software to ensure the latest, greatest information; and putting of fingers to keyboard time and again are positive proof that they have a passion for Essbase. This passion is now on display for all to read—or at least anyone willing to fork over the price of the book.

In all seriousness, this book that you are about to put down is an amalgam of stand-alone white papers, loosely coupled and lightly referenced across each other, that address how to effectively design and build an Essbase application. It tackles some seemingly simple challenges while causing you to lose sleep over how complex it can be made. At the same time, it treats a few extremely complex concepts and boils them down to utter simplicity while causing you to lose sleep over how ridiculously easy it really was. And it's all neatly wrapped up in a format that is certain to put you to sleep.

The nuances that go into load and performance testing alone take years of insightful inspection into the underpinnings of Essbase. Understanding how to translate the concurrency requirements, data distribution, and realistic test scenarios into viable test plans and the intricacies in executing them in conjunction with ongoing, and frequently delayed, development is an art form unto itself. In the pages of this book, it is presented more scientifically than I have seen previously.

In a similar vein, discussions about design alternatives and their impacts on the user and their query patterns, calculation requirements, and performance, among other variables, constitute another form of proverbial tribal knowledge that takes many projects to hone and a lifetime to master. It is that experience that continues to lead to consulting engagements for all of the authors and is described thoroughly within this book.

Having an in-depth description of a couple of the most common reporting environments and the design choices that can leverage them fully and easily is priceless. The efforts and hours that have been poured into the knowledge contained in those chapters are significant. As an aside, I can attest that sisters fight with brothers in a similar way that brothers fight among themselves, albeit usually in a more thought-out way. Which brings us to a chapter on Dodeca. On second thought, in the interest of self-preservation, I think I'll leave it there.

Although I could write paragraphs expounding well-deserved platitudes about each of the authors for the mind-blowing content, I do not want to make this book any heavier than I already have. Suffice to say, it has been my pleasure to know most of the authors for many years now and I find them to be some of the top talent and most passionate around the Essbase community. Although I might not always agree with them, delivering quality solutions is still an art and I never doubt that what they do or communicate is well thought out and will satisfy the needs of the task at hand with aplomb.

If you are reading this as a precursor to purchasing, bring the book to the counter or add it to your shopping cart and pay for it already. It will not disappoint. On the other hand, if this is the last you are reading before beginning the index, I trust that you have enjoyed the book and am confident you will return to it and the downloadable content as a reference tool going forward.

**Steve Liebermensch**
*Product Manager for Essbase, Oracle Corporation*

# Index

Page numbers followed by f and t indicate figures and tables, respectively.

## A

Account dimension, cube design, 84–85, 84f
case study, 96–98, 97f, 98f
Accounts dimension, flattening, 250–255
advantage, 254
dummy fact, 251f
flattened accounts, 255f
line-bar chart example using individual
metrics, 254f
logical grouping of accounts in
presentation layer, 251, 252f
multiple account hierarchies, 251f
physical cube columns, building, 252–255
converting to flattened columns, 252f
creating, 252–253, 253f
as single, accessible metrics, 254f
Action Framework, drill-through reports
with, 262–267
GO URL method, 262–264, 263f
drawbacks, 266
sample Essbase source report, 263, 263f
sample report from, 264, 264f
URL Action Link, creating, 264, 265f,
266f, 267f
limitations, 262

Action Link
executing, 272
process, 268, 270–271
creating, 270, 270f
rebuilding, 270, 270f
URL Action Link, creating, 264, 265f,
266f, 267f
ActiveSheet.Protect command, 418
Activities, MDX Editor SV 1.0, 434–437
data consumption, 437, 437f
defining, 434, 435–436, 435f
execution, 434, 436–437, 436f
Address comment range, 350, 351
Ad hoc Smart View, 368
Administration, Dodeca, 289–292
client, 289–292, 289f
interface, 289, 289f
menus, 290
administrator, 290–291, 290f
File menu, 290
user, 290, 290f
Utilities, 290
Window, 290
toolbars, 291, 291f
view template designer, 292